ALEKSANDR BLOK
BY KONSTANTIN MOCHULSKY

ALEKSANDR BLOK

BY KONSTANTIN MOCHULSKY

TRANSLATED BY DORIS V. JOHNSON

WAYNE STATE UNIVERSITY PRESS   DETROIT 1983

Originally published in Russian by YMCA-PRESS, Paris, in 1948. English translation © 1983 by Wayne State University Press, Detroit, Michigan. All rights are reserved. No part of this book may be reproduced without permission.

Library of Congress Cataloging in Publication Data

Mochul'skiĭ, K. (Konstantin), 1892–1948.
   Aleksandr Blok

   Translation of: Aleksandr Blok.
   Includes bibliographical references and indexes.
   1. Blok, Aleksandr Aleksandrovich, 1880–1921. 2. Poets, Russian—20th century—Biography. I. Title.
PG3453.B6Z6813   1983   891.71′3   82-20212
ISBN 0–8143–1726–X

Grateful acknowledgment is made to the National Endowment for the Humanities for financial assistance in publishing this volume.

CONTENTS

	Introduction	7
	Translator's Note	13
I.	Childhood and Youth, 1880–1900	17
II.	The Appearance of the "Beautiful Lady," 1901–1905	41
III.	War and Revolution, 1904–1903	91
IV.	*The Puppet Show,* 1906	118
V.	*The Snow Mask,* 1907	171
VI.	Public Activities, 1908–1909	209
VII.	*Retribution,* 1910–1911	256
VIII.	The Drama *The Rose and the Cross,* 1912–1913	293
IX.	Years of the World War, 1914–1917	348
X.	*The Twelve.* Last Years, 1918–1921	390
	Notes	435
	Index of Works by Blok	443
	Index of Names	448

INTRODUCTION

Aleksandr Blok, the greatest of the Russian symbolist poets, died at the age of forty. His brief life coincided with a period of unprecedented cultural and political turmoil in Russia's history. The assassination of Aleksandr II, the Russo-Japanese War of 1904–5, the "little revolution" of 1905, the First World War, and the revolutions of 1917 were merely the noisiest events in a turbulent period.

The cultural and literary scene reflected this turbulence. Russian symbolism represented, in part, a reaction to the political repressions following the tsar's assassination and to the materialism, positivism, and utilitarianism of both the political radicalism and of the developing industrialization and capitalism. Symbolism's battle for respectability was largely won by the time Blok appeared on the literary scene. But he was a participant, although often a reluctant one, in the literary polemics within the symbolist camp and, with less reluctance, in the later challenges to symbolism from the acmeists and futurists.

In view of the dreariness and the increasingly obvious deficiencies of Russian life even before the First World War, it is not surprising that Russian symbolism was oriented toward estheticism, toward the future, and, at least among its later representatives, toward mysticism, intuition, and eschatology. Since Blok's oeuvre best reflected those trends, he became a kind of cult figure for many intellectuals of his day. His status was strengthened both by the quality of his poetry and by a moral authority that acknowledged him as the "conscience" of Russian literature, at least until his acceptance of the October Revolution alienated many intellectuals.

Biographical information on Konstantin Vasilievich Mochulsky (1892–1948) is rather scanty; the following summary is based almost entirely on M. Kantor's Introduction to the original Russian edition of this book. Mochulsky was born in Odessa, the son of a professor of Russian literature at Novorossisk University. At St. Petersburg University he studied in the philology faculty, specializing in Romance and Germanic literature. After graduation he studied Romance literature there. In 1918 he was appointed to the faculty of Saratov University but because of the upheaval of the revolution could not take up his position. Instead, his first lectures were given at his father's university, Novorossisk.

Mochulsky left Russia in 1919. He first became a lecturer at the University of Sofia, and then at the Sorbonne, with which he was associated until 1941. In Paris he reviewed literary and theatrical works for a Russian-language émigré weekly, *The Link (Zveno)*, contributing feuilletons and some short stories under the name "Versilov."

During the late twenties or early thirties Mochulsky underwent a spiritual crisis, perhaps related to the deaths of two brothers and his mother a few years earlier. Once active in Russian literary circles in Montparnasse, he now began frequenting meetings of the Religious-Philosophical Academy, founded by Berdyaev, at which he gave a series of lectures on Western mystics and came under the influence of Father Sergey Bulgakov.

As a result of this crisis, Mochulsky turned to the Orthodox Church and apparently considered taking monastic vows. Mother Maria, who had founded and headed the society called Orthodox Action, with which Mochulsky was closely associated, dissuaded him, arguing that the whole world can be a monastic cell. Orthodox Action was devoted to religious work among the poor of Paris. Mochulsky also served on the faculty of St. Sergius Theological Academy until shortly before his death.

When Paris fell to the Germans in 1940, Mother Maria and several of her associates were arrested because of their efforts to help Jews. They were all deported, and most of them, including Mother Maria, died in Nazi concentration camps. Mochulsky escaped only because he was not with them at the time of the arrests. This blow and the physical deprivations of the Occupation probably undermined his health, and he died of tuberculosis in 1948.

Mochulsky is obviously sympathetic, at times perhaps too sympathetic, to the mystical and apocalyptic aspects (personal, spiritual, and political) of Blok's poetry. He was a later graduate of the same university as Blok and was from a similar cultural milieu. Mochulsky's own religious experiences also undoubtedly contributed to his understanding and acceptance of this aspect of Blok's poetry, which sometimes presents difficulties for critics.

Mochulsky's *Aleksandr Blok* was completed in 1945 and was published posthumously in Russian by YMCA-Press, Paris, in 1948. The book is generally regarded as an important contribution to literary scholarship and one of the best available studies on Blok. Slavic scholars acknowledge Mochulsky's value as a critic even when they do not share his perspective. His stature is indicated by the fact that his studies of Dostoevsky and Bely have recently been translated into English.

Mochulsky's approach in this book is threefold: the volume is a biography, a critical study, and a discussion of the Russian intellectual and cultural climate of the early twentieth century. Such an approach to Blok is a plausible one: Mochulsky emphasizes the links between Blok's poetry and his life (Blok himself said that his poems can be read as a diary), and Blok's frequent involvement in the polemics and the experiences of this rather noisy, violent period makes the historical dimension inevitable. The book, therefore, is more an account of Blok's emotional and spiritual life than of external facts. The facts are given, at least most of them, but in a rather bare-bones manner. Mochulsky sometimes presents details of the life only in relation to the poems or to the literary situation of the time. His focus is Blok, rather than the people around him. For example, though he is reticent about Lyubov Dmitrievna's extramarital affairs, he is much less so about Blok's.

Mochulsky had to rely for the most part on the sometimes inaccurate or biased accounts found in published reminiscences, letters, etc. Avril Pyman's excellent and much more complete two-volume biography in English, *The Life of Aleksandr Blok*, appeared in 1980, based on works published since Mochulsky's death and on unpublished Soviet sources. Nevertheless, in the main Mochulsky and Pyman are in agreement on biographical details. The biographical data are, in any case, subsidiary to the discussions of the poetry here. Mochulsky quotes Blok copiously, so that the book provides a useful introduction to Blok's poetry in and of itself.

Mochulsky's approach to the poetry is eclectic. He devotes considerable attention to poems which reflect Blok's relationships with his wife, Bely, Volokhova, and Delmas. He also finds Blok himself in the characters of his dramas, most notably *The Rose and the Cross*, where the three major male characters are seen as representing Blok at various stages of his life, and in *The Puppet Show*, which he believes foreshadows the complex relations among Blok, Bely, and Lyubov Dmitrievna.

But Mochulsky's study of the poetry is by no means limited to its relation to his life. The poetry is interpreted, or on occasion merely explained, a process which is particularly useful since Blok's poetry, especially the early poetry, is sometimes rather obscure. Stylistics are also treated in some detail, reflecting Mochulsky's earlier interest in formalist criticism. Particular emphasis is given to analyses of rhythm and of the sound system; rhyme, metaphor, parallelisms, and poetic lexicon receive sporadic, but pertinent, discussion.

Blok's prose also receives considerable attention: its lyrical and artistic qualities are examined, as is its function as a reflection of Blok's thought. The prose articles are the point of departure for the third major emphasis of Mochulsky's book—the cultural, philosophical, and artistic climate of the times. There are discussions of the thought of Vladimir Solovyov (about whom Mochulsky also published a book), of symbolism and its intramural quarrels (e.g., the polemic over mystical anarchism), and of the ongoing literary polemic, not always distinguished for its civility, between the symbolists and the acmeists.

Mochulsky makes the point, as does the poet, that Blok was not a philosopher, that he could only "argue musically." His thought does not run in a straight line, but in "ebbs and flows." Mochulsky stresses the split in Blok, the appearance of the "doubles," which produces apparent inconsistencies; he traces the evolution and interrelationships of themes and the occasional reappearance of earlier themes. A case in point is the sudden reappearance of the Eternal Feminine long after Blok had apparently abandoned her (or she him).

Blok read in nature signs of impending political events and drew philosophical conclusions from earthquakes, comets, and the first airplane flights. He both internalizes these events, making them part of his spiritual biography, and generalizes them, drawing from them conclusions about mankind's and Russia's future.

Blok's ability to "read" nature is but one aspect of what Mochulsky repeatedly refers to as Blok's "clairvoyance," which other critics have also noted. Instances of this prophetic gift are found in Blok's personal life, in the art of his time, and particularly in his predictions of the political developments (obviously in a very general way) of the first half of the twentieth century—the two revolutions in Russia and the world war.

One may disagree with some of Mochulsky's conclusions and opinions, for example, his low opinion of acmeism (although he recognizes and acknowledges its best poets), his generalizing statement about the "eternal religious foundation" of art (a view shared by many of the Russian symbolists), and his statement that Blok was "by nature Christian." On this latter point Mochulsky provides enough contrary evidence to make the reader aware that this is a personal judgment, a matter on which critical opinion can and does differ.

Nor is the organization of the book always polished. Mochulsky's discussion of the death of Lyubov's son, for example, is interrupted and taken up again later. The short section on poetic meter in general and on Russian prosody in particular, though not out of context, seems gratuitous for a Russian-speaking intellectual audience. The lack of careful organization is particularly evident in his discussion of *The Rose and the Cross*. Mochulsky discusses it three times: as the opera originally planned, the play itself, and the efforts made to stage it. At each point in the discussion Mochulsky offers new details of interpretation. Such lapses are, however, infrequent.

Although Mochulsky's scholarship and erudition are much in evidence here, and although his critical judgments are sound, one is very much aware that one is in the presence of an "involved" critic. The book tells us much about Mochulsky himself. His is the voice of an accomplished, if somewhat dated, stylist, lacking the dispassionate tone of later Western critics.

I would like to acknowledge my debt and express my gratitude for help with the difficult Russian to Mrs. Mira Wilson, Professor Assya Humesky, and Professor Vera Dunham. Special thanks are due Professor Tatjana Cizevska for her help with the Russian, for her efforts in tracking down obscure terms and references, and for her support and encouragement throughout this project. Wayne State University provided financial support for the typing, and the staff of the University Press has been supportive and cooperative throughout.

Doris Johnson

TRANSLATOR'S NOTE

My aim in this translation has been to provide a rendition which is accurate and accessible to readers with no knowledge of Russian. All translations of Blok's poetry and prose are my own. The translations are literal and, it is hoped, accurate; no attempt has been made to reproduce Blok's poetic style. Where questions of style are involved—the sound system, meter, rhyme scheme, etc.—the transliterated Russian is provided.

Two transliteration systems are utilized in the book. Proper names, journal titles, and Russian words occurring in the text are transliterated according to System I in J. Thomas Shaw's *The Transliteration of Modern Russian for English-Language Publications* in order to make such words at least theoretically pronounceable for the English reader. For the transliterations of Blok's poetry, System III from the same book has been adopted, except that the diacritical mark on *e* has been retained (ë). Mochulsky remarks in a footnote that *o* and *e* are phonetically equivalent. Since they do not *look* phonetically equivalent, the resultant ambiguity could be confusing to a reader not familiar with the system.

First names for which English equivalents exist are nevertheless given in their Russian spellings. Although "Alexander" would obviously be adequate for "Aleksandr," the inevitable and frequent combinations of the type "Alexander Alexanderovich" would offend the Russian eye and ear.

Mochulsky had a penchant for italics, which strikes us as rather dated; some of his italics have therefore been dropped, but Blok's have been retained throughout.

An attempt has been made to translate even essentially untranslatable Russian words, so as to burden the reader as little as possible. Where explanations are necessary, the Russian is given and explained in the notes. However, for one frequently used word, *poema*, this proved impractical. A *poema* is an epic or narrative poem of some length, with or without lyrical content. The common practice of translating the word as "poem" or "long poem" seemed to me inadequate; "longish lyrical-narrative poem" would be more descriptive for Blok, but is awkward for a term used so frequently by Mochulsky. The

Translator's Note difficulty is compounded by the fact that some of these works are actually rather short. Transliteration seemed the better part of valor here, and *poema* has been used throughout the text.

Mochulsky's references to his citations from secondary sources do not follow standard practice and are usually incomplete. In reference to books, for example, page numbers of quotations are never given. These notes have been left as Mochulsky presented them. However, I have added some substantive notes as an aid to those who are not Russian specialists. These addenda are indicated by [Tr.]; all other notes are Mochulsky's.

In a few instances in the translations of Blok's poetry and prose some words have been changed and a few passages rearranged to conform to the eight-volume Soviet edition of Blok's works published in 1960–63. In some cases Mochulsky's dates are in error, and the correct date has been supplied in brackets.

A further word should be added on footnoting of proper names by the translator. Footnoting of all the many names in the text was not practicable. Those omitted are names of persons identified clearly in the text itself, names which will be known to any educated reader, and names too obscure to require mention.

A NOTE ON TRANSLATIONS OF BLOK'S POETRY

All collections of modern Russian poetry contain some translations of Blok: *The Silver Age of Russian Poetry* (1971), an anthology edited by Carl and Ellendea Proffer, which has several of his poems and is excellent for the period as a whole; the dual-language *Modern Russian Poetry* (1966), edited by V. Markov and M. Sparks; and Sir Maurice Bowra's *A Book of Russian Verse* (1943). Jon Stallworthy and Peter France's *The Twelve and Other Poems* (1970) is devoted exclusively to translations of Blok. Lucy E. Vogel's *The Journey to Italy* (1973) gives the Italian poems in translation. Sir Cecil Kisch's study, *Alexander Blok, Prophet of Revolution* (1960) contains numerous translations.

CHAPTER I
CHILDHOOD AND YOUTH
1880–1900

Blok was of German descent on his father's side. Born in Mecklenburg, his great-great-grandfather, Johann von Blok, emigrated to Russia in 1755 and was a court physician during the reign of Empress Elizaveta Petrovna. His grandfather, a gentleman of the emperor's bed chamber and a marshal of nobility, married the daughter of Cherkasov, the governor of Pskov; the last two years of his life were spent in a psychiatric hospital. His son (the professor) and grandson (the poet) inherited his mental imbalance. Blok's father, Aleksandr Lvovich, finished the law faculty of Petersburg University brilliantly, was Professor A. D. Gradovsky's favorite pupil, and occupied the chair of public law at Warsaw University. His scholarly legacy is rather meager; two small books on public law and an unfinished work, "Politics in the Sphere of the Sciences," which he worked on for 21 years. In his first book, *State Power in European Society* (1880), Aleksandr Lvovich opposes the state and preaches revolutionary anarchism. "Wouldn't it be better," he writes, "for people to do away with a form of society (the state) which encumbers them and which they do not control?" Censorship originally condemned the book to be burnt. A. L. Blok's second book, *Political Literature in Russia and on Russia* (1884), is a curious mixture of scholarship and journalism, of pamphleteering and social utopia. The author sarcastically exposes bourgeois Europe and contrasts it with the Russian "realm of the peasant." His characterization of the Russian people is sharp and paradoxical; he eulogizes "the unscrupulousness, the caustic derision, the biting irony, the sincerity about our very evil which give us a proud consciousness of our barbaric advantages."[1]

Since the poet can hardly have known his father's writings, the similarity in their outlook is all the more striking. His father's idiosyncratic Slavophilism is reflected in Blok's articles on Russia and in his *poema*,[2] *The Scythians*.

In his youth Aleksandr Lvovich was very handsome; he had black hair and a long, pale face, was impetuous and affable, had gray-green eyes, fine features, thick eyebrows, bright red lips, and a grave look. He possessed great physical strength, laughed unexpectedly and loudly, and when excited stuttered a little. His son resembled his father in build and in general facial cast.

Aleksandr Lvovich had a split, discontented, tormentedly disharmonic nature. His scholarly career weighed heavily on his artistic temperament. At heart he was a poet; he could recite numerous poems, considered himself a stylist and a pupil of Flaubert, and finely polished his sentences. His books were written in a sharp, aphoristic language, with French *pointes* and literary venom. Blok says of his father: "His fate, rather unusual and gloomy, was full of complex contradictions. . . . He couldn't accommodate his constantly developing ideas in the concise forms which he sought; there was something convulsive and frightful in this search for concise forms, as there was in his entire mental and physical makeup."

An unsuccessful scholar and an unsuccessful poet, Aleksandr Lvovich found an outlet for his lyrical turmoil in music. E. Spektorsky, his pupil, recalls:

> Often when he would sit down at the piano in the middle of the night sounds would ring out which demonstrated that music was not merely technique for him, not merely an algebra of tones, but a living, almost mystical communion with the harmony (if not actual, at least possible) of the cosmos. [He loved Beethoven and Schumann and played with intensity, passion, inspiration.]

Blok inherited the element of music in his nature from his father. But the terrible malady from which the poet suffered—"the disease of irony"—is also a paternal legacy. In his book Aleksandr Lvovich wrote that "the harmonious combination of realism and idealism constitutes the loftiest meaning of Russian poetry, literature, and life." But he was torn between idealism and realism. A dreamer who had lost faith in dreams, a romantic poisoned by skepticism, a "Russian Byron," and a "demon"—he stamped the poet's imagination in a terrible and fateful way.

E. Spektorsky writes:

> Irony powerfully impelled his thought toward criticism of all illusion and also toward criticism which bears negative, more or less cheerless, fruit, fruit which scatters castles of air and gives nothing but reality in all its sad nakedness. But it was also accompanied by a kind of sadness, a nostalgia for illusion, a desire nevertheless not to part completely with the dream and to believe in it. . . . He possessed a firm, unbending, one may say an obstinate, will. What he began he finished. A mercilessly analytical mind seemed to amuse itself with the disharmony of actual, uniquely genuine reality and to shatter all dreams, all faith and hope. As a result—profound irony, disillusionment and resignation.

Thus stretched the threads from father to son: the same split in perception of the world, the same anxiety and dreaminess, the same musical-lyrical instinct, sense of doom, and poisoning with irony.

Blok's mother, Aleksandra Andreevna, was purely Russian. Her father was the famous professor of botany and rector of Petersburg University, Andrey Nikolaevich Beketov. In his youth an admirer of Fourier and Saint-Simon, he belonged to the noble generation of Russian romantic idealists. Loftiness of soul and childlike purity of heart, gentry liberalism, and unselfish service of the good, ideals of the epoch of the Great Reforms and of populism were combined in him with scholarly gifts, sensitivity, and virtuosity. Colleagues, students, and servants loved him. He defended the university's autonomy, was one of the founders of the Bestuzhev courses,[3] and was considered in government circles a revolutionary. For his favorite grandson, the future poet, the grandfather composed fairy tales and drew amusing pictures. In his *Autobiography* Blok calls Andrey Nikolaevich "a gentryman of the sixties," an "idealist of the first order." He writes:

> In his village of Shakhmatovo my grandfather would go out on the porch to talk with the peasants, waving his handkerchief; just as I. S. Turgenev when talking to his serfs would in embarrassment chip off bits of paint from the entrance, promising to give them whatever they asked for.... Meeting a peasant he knew, my grandfather would take him by the shoulder and begin his speech with the words: *"Eh bien, mon petit."* Sometimes the conversation ended there. His favorite interlocutors were inveterate swindlers and rogues, whom I will never forget.... Once my grandfather, seeing a peasant carrying on his shoulder a birch tree from the forest, said to him: "You're tired, let me help you." Moreover, the obvious circumstance that the birch tree had been cut down in our forest never even entered his head.

With affectionate humor the poet sketches a portrait of his grandfather in the *poema Retribution*:

> Family head, comrade-in-arms
> Of the forties: to this day
> One of the progressives,
> He preserves the civic sacred things.
> From Nicholas' time
> He has protected enlightenment,
> But he got somewhat lost
> In the humdrum of the new movement ...
> Turgenevian tranquility
> Is part of him; he is quite
> An excellent judge of wine,
> Can appreciate delicacy in food;
> The French language and Paris
> Are perhaps closer to him than his own.
>   . . . . .
> An ardent Westernizer in everything,
> At heart he is an old Russian *barin*.

Aleksandr Blok

Andrey Nikolaevich Beketov was married to Elizaveta Grigorievna Karelina, the daughter of a well-known scholar on Central Asia, G. S. Karelin. Blok's grandmother, raised on French culture, was very well read and knew five languages. She translated French and English; the list of her works is enormous. "Some of her translations are the best even to this day," Blok writes. She loved music and poetry, beautifully read aloud scenes from Ostrovsky[4] and Chekhov stories. She was a witty, bubbling woman with a clear mind and indestructible health. She combined "flaming romanticism" and "old-fashioned sentimentality." Elizaveta Grigorievna saw Gogol, the Dostoevsky brothers, L. Tolstoy, Maikov,[5] and A. Grigoriev[6] socially. F. M. Dostoevsky personally gave her an English novel which she translated for the journal *Time (Vremya)*. E. G. Karelina set the lofty literary tone of the family in which Blok grew up.

The Beketovs had four daughters: Ekaterina Andreevna Krasnova, the eldest, wrote stories and poems; Maria Andreevna was Blok's biographer; Sofia Andreevna married Kublitsky-Piottukh; and Aleksandra Andreevna, the youngest, was Blok's mother—she did verse and prose translations and wrote poems for children. In her childhood Aleksandra Andreevna—Asya—was a lively, impressionable, and capricious girl. Vivacity, sensitivity, and playfulness alternated with fits of groundless depression. There was hysteria in her sharp mood shifts, her stormy outbursts, and in her sudden enthusiasms. By the time she was sixteen she had become a lovely, slender young lady, flirtatious and dreamy. As she matured, a deep religiosity awoke in her. But this did not at all prevent her from being mad about the theater and falling in love with actors.

Aleksandra Andreevna met Aleksandr Lvovich Blok at a girl friend's dancing party. He began to visit the "rector's home" on the Neva embankment. On Saturdays the young people gathered on the upper floor, in a white hall with windows overlooking the Neva. They drank tea, ate sandwiches, played *petits jeux*, danced. On 7 January 1879 Aleksandra Andreevna married A. L. Blok. He was 27, she was 18. The newlyweds left for Warsaw and lived there for about two years. Blok's mother later recalled those years with horror. Aleksandr Lvovich's love expressed itself in insane jealousy, despotism, and cruelty. Aleksandra Andreevna was kept locked up, intimidated, and hungry. She later admitted to her sister: "In moments of anger Aleksandr Lvovich was so terrifying that my hair literally stood on end." The first child was born dead. These two terrible years decided the fate of Blok's mother: the predisposition to hysteria contributed to the onset of the nervous illness from which she suffered for the rest of her life. In 1880 Aleksandr Lvovich came to Petersburg to defend his master's dissertation; he brought his wife, who was eight months pregnant. Her family didn't recognize their beautiful Asya in this exhausted, sick, faded woman. After a brilliant public defense A. L. Blok returned to Warsaw alone:

her parents insisted that Asya remain in the rector's home until her delivery.

On 16 November 1880 Aleksandra Andreevna gave birth to a son, Aleksandr, the future poet. The father came for Christmas and stayed with the Beketovs. He quarreled with his wife and came to hate her whole family. Aleksandra Andreevna was ill after the delivery; she couldn't nurse the child herself. Grandfather Beketov insisted that his son-in-law leave his wife in Petersburg until spring, and then persuaded his daughter to part from her husband forever. Threatening letters and telegrams about "serious illness" flew from Warsaw. After a long struggle Aleksandr Lvovich resigned himself to it but he never forgave the offense. Thus the future poet was fated to grow up without a father, to write him formal letters from time to time, and in rare meetings to feel his alienation and "fearsomeness."[7]

After his divorce from the poet's mother, Aleksandr Lvovich got married again—to Maria Timofeevna Belyaeva. His second marriage was as unsuccessful as the first. Maria Timofeevna left him, taking their three-year-old daughter, Angelina. A. L. Blok remained in Warsaw alone, locked into embittered solitude, and lived out his life as an eccentric and misanthrope. The poet describes his father:

> His photograph in the album showed him as very handsome, in profile, still young. A cruel look, his face gloomily lowered, matched perfectly the terrible stories about Warsaw. . . . The first time I remember him appearing at our place, his exterior turned out to be not at all so majestically infernal as I had imagined. He wasn't very tall, narrow in the shoulders, hunched, with sparse hair and a sparse beard. He stammered, but the main thing, which I hadn't expected at all, he was shy. . . . He would sit in a dark corner, disliked meeting strangers, was more and more silent at the table, and if he did put in a word would immediately begin to laugh a shy, unnatural, dejected laugh.

Not long before his father's death the son visited him in Warsaw:

> He sat at a table on an oilcloth sofa. He advised me not to take my overcoat off, because it was cold; he never heated the stove. He didn't keep a full-time servant but sometimes hired a woman by the day, calling her a "maid-servant." He ate in wretched "greasy spoons." At home he only drank tea.

After his father's death in 1909 and the trip to his funeral in Warsaw, Blok wrote *Retribution*, a *poema* in which he tries to explain his mysterious resemblance to his father—to the flaring up and dimming "demon" whose image relentlessly pursued him.

In the *poema* a romantic aureole surrounds his father's image. The leitmotif of the hawk precedes the young scholar's appearance in the Beketov house:

> Get up, go to the meadow in the morning:
> A hawk circles in the pale sky,
> Tracing circle after smooth circle.
> . . . . .
>
> And again, waving its enormous wing,
> It took flight—to trace circle after circle,
> To survey the deserted meadow
> With an unsatisfied and homeless eye.

The "Russian Byron" appears in the salon of the well-known public figure Anna Pavlovna Filosofova (in the *poema* she is called Olga Vrevskaya):

> Dostoevsky noticed him.
> "Who's that handsome man?" he asked
> Quietly, turning to Vrevskaya,
> "Resembling Byron."

In her book on Blok, M. A. Beketova confirms the authenticity of this meeting. "As they said at that time," she adds, "Dostoevsky intended to portray him as a main character in one of his novels." Dostoevsky's well-chosen word caught on; women whispered rapturously: "He is a Byron, that is, a demon." The author continues:

> He indeed resembled a proud lord
> In his arrogant expression,
> And in something I would call
> The somber flame of sorrow.

But the latter-day descendant of Onegin and Pechorin,[8] the last Russian romantic, is a demon with broken wings: his will is poisoned, the flame of passion has died out:

> Late scion of generations
> In which dwelt the rebellious fervor
> Of inhuman aspirations,
> He did resemble Byron,
> As a sick brother sometimes
> Resembles a healthy one:
> The same ruddy sheen,
> The same look of power,
> And the same yearning for the abyss.
> But the spirit is mysteriously bewitched
> By the weary coldness of disease,
> And the active flame dies out,
> And the efforts of raging will
> Are burdened by consciousness.

The leitmotif of the hawk returns:

> So—
> The predator turns his dull gaze,
> Spreading his diseased wings.

The "latter-day Byron" lands amid a "gentry family," charms the old folks with his old-fashioned courtesy and decorum, with his "animated and ardent conversation." After bursts of inspiration, sudden gloominess follows; at such times he sits at the piano:

> And there—amid the musical storm—
> Would suddenly arise (just as before)
> Some kind of image—sad, distant,
> Always inscrutable.

Romanticizing his hero, the poet draws his romance with the youngest daughter of the "gentry family" in intensely dramatic lines. The young girl is charmed by the guest's good looks, by the "demonic gleam" in his eyes. Her own home becomes a prison; he is her hero, her life and happiness. But the "demon" procrastinates; his "flaming passions" cool; his ironic mind struggles against the attraction. The motif of the hawk becomes a symbol of passion and hatred, of "love in the Vampire age":

> (Look: thus the predator stores his strength;
> Now waves his diseased wing,
> Swoops noiselessly down on the meadow,
> And will drink the living blood
> Of a mindless victim already trembling
> From horror . . .).

The first chapter of the *poema* ends with the daughter's return to her father's house:

> Suddenly she returns . . .
> What happened to her? How thin her transparent figure!
> Gaunt, exhausted, pale,
> And a child lies in her arms.

His aunt Maria Andreevna Beketova speaks with love about Blok's childhood. The boy was born weak and sickly but soon became stronger. "Sasha was a lively, indefatigably playful, interesting, but very difficult child: capricious, self-willed, with violent desires and insuperable dislikes." His grandmother, mother, and aunt adored him: the family made a real cult of little Sasha. His gentle nurse, Sonya, who read him Pushkin's fairy tales and Zhukovsky's[9] poems, had a great influence on him. "In games Sasha displayed reckless intensity and great power of imagination." Most of all he loved to draw ships and he kept this love all his life. When he turned three they took him to Trieste for sea bathing; from there the family went to Florence and spent nine months abroad. In the winter of 1884 the boy successfully fought off his only serious illness—pleurisy. The Beketovs spent their summers on the small property of Shakhmatovo (Klin district, Moscow province). They took Sasha there for the first time when he was six months old. All his life he loved Shakhmatovo with a special, mystical love. This hilly and forested country, with marshes, paths made of logs, ravines, crushed stone on the hillsides, yellow layers of clay, endless blue distances, quiet sunrises, and clear sunsets, this middle strip of Russia, is the homeland of Blok's poetry. The melody of his poems pours out over its boundless spaces. For Blok Shakhmatovo, near Moscow, is a "landscape of the soul," a symbol of Russia with her songs ringing with "prison despair." Dying, he recalled:

> . . . Forests, clearings,
> Both country roads and highways,
> Our Russian road,
> Our Russian mists,
> Our rustling in the oats.

M. A. Beketova relates:

> The landowner's estate stood on a high hill. One approached the house by a wide yard with round beds of sweetbrier, mentioned in the *poema Retribution*. On the other side of the house, toward the southeast, was a shady garden with old lindens. Opening the glass door of the dining room, whose windows faced the garden, and stepping onto the terrace, everyone was struck by the breadth and variety of the view which opened to the left. In front of the house a sandy patch with flower gardens; beyond this, ancient, spreading lindens and two tall pines. Centuries-old fir trees, birches, lindens, silver poplars, alternating with maples and hazelnut trees, formed groups and avenues. The garden had a great number of lilacs, bird-cherry trees, white and pink roses, a dense bed of white narcissus and another of purple irises. One of the side paths, shaded by very old birches, led to a wicket gate into an avenue of firs descending steeply to a pond. The pond lay in a narrow valley with a stream running through it, shaded by enormous firs, birches, and young alder thickets.

In the unfinished second chapter of the *poema Retribution* Blok recalls with tenderness this "corner of paradise" where his childhood passed. The Shakhmatovo estate is drawn in pale lines: flowering quietness, the distant ringing of a bell, the radiance of spring:

> An enormous silver poplar
> Stretched its tent over the house,
> A fragrant wall of sweetbrier
> Greeted those who entered the yard.
>   . . . . . .
> . . . Here one could clearly hear
> How silence blossoms and sleeps . . .

> . . . . .
> The sun casts leafy shadows,
> And the wind outside the window bends
> The centuries-old lilac bushes
> Which drown the old house;
> And some muffled sound,
> The sound of that same silence,
> Or the distant pealing of church bells,
> Or the rumble . . . of spring.
> . . . . .
> And the ringing balcony door
> Opened onto lindens and lilacs,
> And onto the blue cupola of the horizon,
> And onto the indolence of neighboring villages.
> . . . . .
> The church is white above the river,
> Beyond it more forests, fields . . .
> And the Russian earth radiates
> All the beauty of spring.

This "radiance of the Russian earth" pierced the child's heart; for the youth it became a mystical vision. Here, to these illuminated spaces, the Beautiful Lady would descend to him in azure and roses. And the first love for her is inseparable from love for his native land:

> . . . Your wind songs are for me
> Like the first tears of love.

In this "corner of paradise," inundated with lilac and sweetbrier, the golden curled, innocent boy grew:

> He was protected from coarse life
> By the tender care of women.
> The years flew serenely,
> Like a blue spring dream.

In an 1885 photograph the five-year-old boy's face is striking in its sad gentleness and angelic purity. At this age he was so beautiful that passers-by stopped in front of him on the street. Golden curls, huge blue eyes, a slender neck in a white lace collar—the appearance of a fairy-tale prince. The little boy wandered the fields and forests of Shakhmatovo for days on end. He was surrounded by friends: he passionately loved dogs, cats, rabbits, hedgehogs, even worms. Grandfather Beketov took him along on his botanical walks. Blok recalls:

> We would wander for hours through the meadows, marshes, and thickets; sometimes we covered tens of versts, getting lost in the forest; we dug grasses and grains out by the roots for a botanical collection; in addition, he would name plants and, identifying them, taught me the rudiments of botany, so that even now I remember many botanical names.

The future poet's comrades were his cousins Ferol and Andryusha Kublitsky, the sons of his aunt Sofia Andreevna. Sasha made up games, instigated all the pranks. M. A. Beketova maintains that "childish games captivated him for a long time, and in everyday considerations he remained a child almost to age eighteen." In his autobiography the poet confesses: "For a long time I had no 'life experiences.' I vaguely remember large Petersburg apartments with lots of people, with a nurse, toys, and Christmas trees, and the fragrant remote corner of our small country estate." Lyrical excitement awoke in him early: he began to write poems at the age of five. Blok writes: "Zhukovsky was my first inspiration. From early childhood I remember lyrical waves constantly dashing upon me, vaguely connected with someone's name. I remember the name of Polonsky."[10]

In 1889 a great change in the boy's life took place. After her divorce from Aleksandr Lvovich the poet's mother got married again, to Franz Feliksovich Kublitsky-Piottukh, a lieutenant in a grenadier guard regiment. Life in the Beketov "rector's house" was over. Mother and son moved to the barracks of the life-grenadier regiment on the Petersburg Side, on the Bolshaya Nevka embankment. The "officers' annex" was located in an enormous government building. Outside the windows were a wide river, steamers, skiffs, barges, and on the other shore factories, smokestacks, foggy winter sunsets. This stark and mournful Petersburg landscape is inseparable from Blok's "city" poems. The two poles of his poetry are village Rus[11] —Moscow Province, Shakhmatovo—and "urban" Russia—Petersburg. In rough drafts of the *poema Retribution* Blok relates the birth of his "new Petersburg" to his gymnasium years. "A new Petersburg is born," he writes, "prophesied by the 'obscurantist' Dostoevsky." Dostoevsky's prophecy was fulfilled in Blok's Petersburg poems.

The poet's stepfather, Franz Feliksovich Kublitsky, a simple and modest man, an honest officer, and great worker, was distinguished neither in appearance nor in talents. He was a devoted, loving husband, but the "climate" of the Beketov family—romanticism, poetry, art—was completely alien to him. The spoiled and demanding Aleksandra Andreevna, with her nervous sensitivity and "defiance," soon realized her mistake. She rebelled against the banality of the military milieu and regretted depriving her son of the atmosphere of his grandfather's house. After the second marriage she became more serious and introspective: spiritual interests appeared. "Franzik," as the family called him, treated his stepson with polite indifference. The boy repaid him in kind: this wasn't his own family, and he shrank into himself. The children's games, pranks, and liveliness came to an end.

In August 1889 Blok entered the Vvedensky gymnasium. He discusses his first impressions in the story "Confession of a Pagan" (1918):

> Mama took me to the gymnasium. For the first time in my life, from a cozy and quiet family, I landed among a crowd of smoothly cropped and loudly shouting boys: it somehow frightened me unbearably. I would

gladly have run away or hidden somewhere, but the classroom doors, although they were open, seemed an impassable boundary.

They seated me at the first desk, right in front of the rostrum.... I felt like a rooster whose beak they had drawn to the floor with chalk, who simply remained bent over and motionless, not daring to raise its head....

Mainly I felt that I no longer belonged to myself, that I had been given over to someone and to some place, and that it would be so from then on. To display my despair and horror, to express them in any words or movements or simply in tears was unthinkable; a false shame prevented it.

Little Blok's sensitivity and shyness were painful, and the first collision with reality a real tragedy. His whole soul was shaken, and in this tension of new emotions rushing over him erotic agitation awoke for the first time. He writes:

[A little boy] stood facing the blackboard, erasing the words written on it.... Here I experienced a feeling which can't be compared with anything else. The boy was rather tall, lean, and well proportioned. He had a delicate and regular profile, and his hair was not completely cropped; one could see that it was curly—one curl fell onto his forehead. I felt a keen and ardent adoration for him, for his face, for his whole figure, for his whole being, flooding my whole heart, my whole body with a burning wave.

I had experienced something similar in childhood, by the Christmas tree, when I played with children of my own age. The oldest of them was a well proportioned little Polish girl.... At that time waves of adoration also scorched me, but that feeling was somewhat different, probably mixed with a weight of awakening childish sensuality. This feeling was new, it was light and completely transporting. But it also contained a special ancient terror.

This rapture and terror contain a vague premonition of fate. For a moment the erotic element of his spirit was revealed to the boy. He chastely concealed the feeling. He continues:

For a long time I barely knew that boy on whom my glance fell on the first day of gymnasium life. We sat at different desks, separated from one another; my adoration was not rekindled, and he showed no special feeling for me. So it continued until fate brought us together again, and in a new way, by placing us ... at neighboring desks.... Dmitri—that was my neighbor's name—was hardly outstanding in class.... Even in the upper classes he remained just as delicate and well proportioned. His delicate face, his delicate skin revealing a completely adolescent blush, sprouted a barely noticeable tuft of beard and mustache. In face and body, as it seems to me now, he resembled the Lydian Dionysus.

These last words reveal the nature of Blok's "adoration." Not youthful sensuality, not even love, but a holy trepidation—this is the soul's touching the Dionysian element. That is why it seems to Blok that

Dmitri resembles Dionysus. This element carries both the life and the creative work of the poet; his lyrical theme is born of its music.

The gymnasium frightened the boy with its coarseness and stagnation: the teachers and tutors were poor, worn out by lessons, humiliated by the authorities; the pupils were depraved and stupid. "Our class was wild," Blok recalls. "Among us were great profligates, old smokers, precocious woman-chasers, cynics, wrestlers, and athletes."

The little gymnasium student would return from his classes confused and gloomy. "He would come from the gymnasium," M. A. Beketova writes. "His mother would approach with questions. In reply either outright silence or niggardly, monosyllabic answers. A kind of reserve, a special type of chasteness prevented him from revealing his soul . . . he was a proud child."

Once a year Aleksandr Lvovich came to Petersburg, and the son feared his visits. Blok tells of the tormenting relations with his father in *Retribution*:

> He never knew his father,
> They met only occasionally.
> Living in different cities,
> So alien in all their paths
> (Except, perhaps, the most secret),
> The father visited him like a guest,
> Stooped, with red circles
> Around his eyes. Behind the listless words
> Malice often stirred.
> His cynical, distressing mind
> Inspired despair and malicious ideas,
> Soiling the cloud of the son's thoughts.
> . . . . .
> And only a kind, flattering look
> Would sometimes fall stealthily
> On the son, like a strange riddle
> Bursting into a boring conversation.

Blok remembers how he, "playing mad pranks," once stuck a pin in his father's hand: the man screamed wildly, turning pale from pain.

They were alien, even hostile, to one another, but on the "most secret" paths they were mysteriously close and alike.

At home, locking himself in his room, Sasha enthusiastically took up sawing and the bookbinding craft. In the gymnasium he studied with boredom, hated mathematics, and loved ancient languages. In a schoolmate's unpublished memoirs we read:

> Blok blossomed unpretentiously amid all this gymnasium hubbub. Exactly, he blossomed; I can't think of a more apt term. The young, disorderly conduct of the school crowd didn't seem to touch him. . . . I remember his classically regular, pale, calm face with the clear, pensive eyes.

Blok read little in these years: the usual reading of a youth of the nineties—Mayne-Reid, Fenimore Cooper, Jules Verne, Dickens. Of the Russian poets he loved Pushkin, Zhukovsky, Lermontov; Fet and Nekrasov he discovered later. In 1894 he began to publish a handwritten journal, *Herald (Vestnik)*—one copy a month. His mother, grandmother, and cousins collaborated. The journal was illustrated with pictures cut out of *Cornfield (Niva)* and with drawings by grandfather Beketov and by Blok himself. The editor wrote novels (*Around America* or *In Pursuit of the Monster*, an imitation of Jules Verne), crime stories ("Vengeance for Vengeance"), fairy tales ("In Summer. Adventures of Beetles"), and *poemas* ("Fate," an imitation of Zhukovsky's "Smalholm Castle"). Blok's first poem was written when he was five years old:

> In the world lived a dear kitten.
> He was constantly dejected,
> No one knew why,
> Kotya[12] didn't say.

The *Herald* existed for three years.

His love for the theater dates from 1894; the poet retained it all his life. His first visit was to the Aleksandrinsky Theater to see Tolstoy's *Fruits of Enlightenment*. It made an enormous impression. Soon amateur theatricals began in Shakhmatovo. Kozma Prutkov's[13] *Quarrel of the Ancient Greek Philosophers about the Elegant* was performed. M. A. Beketova recalls:

> The philosophers—Sasha Blok and Ferol Kublitsky, both in white togas made from bed sheets, with oak wreaths on their heads—leaned on white altars. The stage scenery depicted the Acropolis, painted by Sasha's hand on an enormous piece of white cardboard, which leaned against an old birch tree.

Shakespeare followed Prutkov. Sasha, greatly inspired, declaimed the monologues of Hamlet, Romeo, and Othello.

Blok's first meeting with his second cousin, Vladimir Solovyov's nephew, Sergey Mikhailovich Solovyov, belongs to this period. The eight-year-old Seryozha came to Shakhmatovo from the Podsolnechnaya Station with his father:

> The bell rang gaily. All around—steep ravines, hills with little green squares of young rye. We passed a dark fir forest; the smallish Shakhmatovo appeared rather unexpectedly on a knoll: a few houses, the village near it was not visible.... We entered the house. Two aunts, whom I didn't know, appeared—Aunt Alya and Aunt Manya Beketov. They affectionately took me in tow.... Sasha returned sooner than expected.... A tall, radiant schoolboy, somehow listless and phlegmatic, a nasal voice.... Even then I was struck and charmed by his love for the technique of things literary and by his special neatness.

A draft of *Retribution* contains two short notes devoted to the gymnasium years:

> Then the gymnasium; beginning with lamp-lit mornings, then Lenten twilight with cracking ice and wind.
>
> The family is beginning to be a burden. Now the new already oppresses him. When he fasts as a gymnasium student—dark blue spring, twilight, incense, and ice sparkling in the puddles.

The adolescent had entered the difficult stage of approaching manhood: the first dreams of love, the first despair. In his *Autobiography* Blok notes: "At about 15 the first definite dreams of love were born, and with them fits of despair and irony, which found an outlet many years later in my first attempt at drama (*The Puppet Show*)."

In Blok's gymnasium photo the radiance of angelic purity had dimmed. The golden curls are cut short. The eyes are intent, the expression gloomy. The handsome, youthful face is open and noble. But the former ardor, the former feminine delicateness are gone—on his lips something stubborn and secret.

But to outward view Blok the gymnasium student was "always an immaculately, and even elegantly, dressed boy, very well bred and neat" (V. N. Knyazhnin, *A. A. Blok*, St. Petersburg: 1922).

Aleksandra Andreevna suffered from heart disease. In 1896 this disease was complicated by a nervous disorder; strange attacks resembling epilepsy appeared. She lived in a melancholy bordering on suicidal mania. The doctors sent her to Germany for treatment. In the summer of 1897 she went with her sister Maria Andreevna and her son to Bad Nauheim, where she soon improved. But through the years the nervous anxiety and tendency to see life tragically grew stronger and stronger.

In Bad Nauheim Blok experienced his first rapturous love. He met Ksenia Mikhailovna Sadovskaya, a Ukrainian beauty, dark-haired and blue-eyed. She wanted to captivate the shy boy and initiated their conversations. M. A. Beketova relates:

> They saw each other every day. Rising early, Blok would run to buy her roses, to get her a ticket to the baths. They went for walks and boat rides. All this lasted no more than a month. She left for Petersburg, where they met again after a long interval.

This first love determined Blok's fate as a poet. Erotic agitation aroused the music sleeping in his soul. From January 1898 lyrical poems poured out in a torrent. By the end of December 1900, 290 poems were written. The youthful passion scorched his soul but didn't illuminate it. There was sensual agitation, jealousy, disenchantment. Sadovskaya, a woman of fashion and a coquette, played with his inexperienced heart; she would attract him, then push him away. In Petersburg other meetings, explanations, tears occurred; then her image disappeared into the misty distance. The first "false" love was extinguished now by a real love—for Lyubov Dmitrievna Mendeleeva.

The motif of "deception" predominates in these lines dedicated to KMS:

> The road seemed false—
> I didn't return.
> Our love was deceived,
> Or the path carried us away . . .
> . . . . .
> We went recklessly
> Along this false road.
>   (1899)

Two years later the image of his first love was already the distant past. It was a "pale phantom," an "unneeded phantom":

> You won't deceive, pale phantom,
> Long ago experienced passions.
> Your discordant look, your poor image,
> Doesn't strike my soul.
> I know the distant past,
> But in the near future I don't expect
> Storms of passion. The young
> Is past. I won't find
> A flame in your weary
> But beckoning unneeded phantom.
> Only as an oppressive idea
> Do you still torment me.
>   (1900)

In this youthful poem Blok is still Pushkin's timid pupil. Twelve years pass. The "pale phantom" is long forgotten. But fate again brings the poet to Bad Nauheim. The year 1909 is tragic for him. And suddenly the past is resurrected. Again he is in the mist of a damp park; there is an iron bridge over a stream, a gray fence entwined with roses, a narrow avenue along a pond, the first green of spring and the sweet fragrance of its perfume. The first love comes to life, indestructible, undying. Eight poems of 1909, dedicated to "K. M. S." and combined under the title *Twelve Years Later*, are filled with poignant sadness:

> Blue-eyed one, so God created you.
> The guiding spirit of first love is over me.
>
> It arose, quiet, rain-washed;
> Sings like a stinging wasp.
>
> It dispels the traces of the past,
> Has no easy name.
>
> I see again slender arms,
> Hear again throaty sounds,
>
> Awake, I again sink
> Into the deep blue of your eyes.

The same sense of the eternity of the "first passion" in another poem:

> Or is the young genius of first passion
> Still inseparable from the soul,
> And you are forever betrothed
> To that long ago, unforgettable shadow?
> Call. She will come:
> The proud profile flashes by as before
> And the insinuating, drawn-out voice
> Whispers the former words.

He is again the shy, enamored boy in the "blue, blue captivity" of her eyes; again he meets her in the park in the sunset's glow:

> Streams whispering something,
> Head whirling . . .
> Your kisses, Little Russian,
> Your throaty words.

This accidental love encounter is lit by the light of time. Only in the elemental musical force awakened by it is the mysterious meaning of the first unsuccessful "love experience" revealed. This story is written in fire on the heavens. This well-known poem is dedicated to K. M. S.:

> Everything memory tries to preserve for me
> Disappears in the mindless years,
> But in the night sky this story
> Rises in a flaming zigzag.
> Life was long ago burnt up and narrated,
> One dreams only of first love,
> Like a priceless chest, tied crosswise
> With a ribbon crimson as blood.

Returning from Bad Nauheim to Shakhmatovo at the end of July 1897, Blok got sad news: his grandfather Andrey Nikolaevich Beketov was paralyzed. A nurse took him around the garden in a wheelchair. He lived for five more years in this condition (and died on 1 July 1902).

In the winter of 1897–98 the poet took up recitation and melodeclamation[14] (the poems of Apukhtin, Fet, Aleksey Tolstoy). He learned the role of Romeo and at Shakhmatovo put on the balcony scene. At this time he was dreaming seriously of an acting career. In a family questionnaire he answered the question what he wanted to be, "an actor of the imperial theaters," and the question what death he wanted to die, "on the stage from a heart attack."

Blok graduated from the gymnasium in the spring of 1898. After the trip to Bad Nauheim he changed suddenly and abruptly: he became more sociable, more free and easy; he dressed like a dandy, courted the young ladies, and led a social life. His *Diary* of 1918 contains a note about this period: "I was a dandy, uttered my share of banalities." In his *Reminiscences* S. M. Solovyov supports this self-evaluation:

Childhood and Youth

In August 1898 I met Blok in a copse at the border of our Dedovo [the Solovyovs' estate]. A tarantass appeared. In it sat a young man, elegantly dressed, with a halo of golden curls, a rose in his buttonhole, and a cane, beside him a young lady. He had just graduated from the gymnasium and was enjoying himself. The theater, flirtation, poems. His poetic calling had already been fully revealed. He imitated Fet in everything; there were as yet no ideas, but he sang. He wrote stereotyped poems about roses, sang Ophelia's praises. But something powerful and enchanting already rose in his melodies.

On a high hill eight versts from Shakhmatovo was situated Boblovo, the estate of the famous chemist Dmitri Ivanovich Mendeleev: an old park with a huge three-hundred-year-old oak tree, an orchard, flower beds. On the hilltop was a new house with broad terraces. Mendeleev's oldest daughter from a second marriage was a year younger than Blok. They had taken walks as children, then his grandfather took Sasha to Boblovo when he was fourteen. But the first planned meeting was in summer of 1898. In the *Diary* of 1918 Blok notes: "I came there [to Boblovo] on my white horse, in a white tunic, and with a riding crop. The mademoiselle and Lyubov Dmitrievna entertained me in a birch grove. L. D. at once made a powerful impression on me." Beketova describes the poet's future bride: "Lyubov Dmitrievna wore pink dresses and plaited her magnificent golden hair in a braid. Delicate, pinkish-white facial coloring, black brows, childlike blue eyes, and a stern unapproachable look.... Tall, graceful, feminine charm."

In the second chapter of *Retribution* there are drafts for an unwritten story about his first meeting with L. D. Mendeleeva. Here is the landscape of *Verses on the Beautiful Lady*:

> For a long time he rode around the neighboring hills and fields, and long ago his attention had been attracted by a jagged strip of forest on the crest of a hill on the horizon. A village lay near this strip on the steep descent of the hill. He went there in the *springtime*, and the sun was already setting when he rode into an old birch grove at the foot of the hill. Slanting sunset rays, clouds turned purple, the vision of a medieval fortress. He passes a village and rides toward the forest, ... turns, forcing the horse to jump a ditch; beyond the dampness and gloom a new clearing is visible. He rides out onto the clearing; a new, vast, unfamiliar distance opens before him, and to the side an orchard. A rosy girl, apple blossoms—he stops being a little boy.

The long wanderings over hills and fields prepare the way for the vision of the "rosy girl." She lives on the hill, beyond the jagged strip of forest. She is a distant princess in a medieval castle; he is a wandering knight on a white horse. She appears in the rays of sunset, in purple clouds; immense distances surround her. The fairy-tale theme of *Verses on the Beautiful Lady* is supplied by reality itself. That's how it was, that's how he saw her: as a princess of medieval legends.

"The lyrical poems of 1897 can all be seen as a diary," Blok maintains in his *Autobiography*. The poet's notebooks and letters permit us to appreciate the unparalleled truth of his lyrical confession.

The summer of 1898 was the beginning of a new life. Till age eighteen, according to M. A. Beketova's testimony, Blok remained a child. Now he "stops being a little boy": as with Dante on meeting Beatrice, in him *incipit vita nuova*.

Lyubov Dmitrievna was studying in the Shaffe gymnasium and dreaming of the stage. An amateur theatrical was put on in Boblovo. The stage was set up in a barn. Blok, in a black cape and black beret, a sword at his side, played Hamlet. Lyubov Dmitrievna, with a sheaf of wild flowers in her hand and her golden hair flowing loose, portrayed the mad Ophelia. Then they staged excerpts from *Woe from Wit* and the fountain scene from *Boris Godunov*. In the *Diary* of 1918 he writes: "We acted . . . scenes from *Woe from Wit* and *Hamlet* in a barn. The recitation went on. I hammed it up terribly, but I was already in love. Sirius and Vega."

That fall Blok entered the law faculty of St. Petersburg University. We read in the *Diary*:

> In the fall I had a smart frock coat made. I entered the law faculty, understanding nothing of jurisprudence (I envied some windbag, Prince Tenishev), for some reason tried to read Thun (?), some railroad legislation in Germany (?!). . . .
>
> By fall, on returning to Petersburg, visits to Zabalkansky [where the Mendeleevs lived] became rather more infrequent. L. D. was completing her studies in Shaffe, I was carried away with recitation and the stage . . . and acted in a dramatic club. . . .
>
> I don't remember whether I repeated the second course (or spent two years in the first course).[15] In any case I remained just as alien to juridical and economic studies to the end.

In the summer of 1899 Blok's trips from Shakhmatovo to Boblovo were renewed. A new performance was staged: scenes from Pushkin's *The Covetous Knight* and *The Stone Guest*, Gnedich's[16] *Burning Letters* and Chekhov's *The Proposal*. But the theater somehow didn't go well, the former enthusiasm was gone. The poet recollects in his *Diary*: "Returning at night on foot, bushes strewn with fireflies, pitch darkness and Lyubov Dmitrievna's sternness."

Blok notes S. M. Solovyov's arrival among the summer's events. "Seryozha," he writes, "had a kind of adoration for me, because I represented for him (and for myself) a fascinating and experienced Don Juan."

Lyubov Dmitrievna was haughty and unapproachable: "By fall I had, apparently, stopped going to Boblovo (L. D.'s sternness) . . . and from the start of my Petersburg life I didn't visit the Mendeleevs, assuming that this acquaintanceship was over."

During the fall in Petersburg there was a fleeting passion for a distant relative, Katya Khrustaleva, the beginning of his long friendship with Aleksandr Vasilievich Gippius, a final talk with K. M. Sadovskaya.

"Though in thought I kept coming back to her, I continually missed L. D."

During these last years of the nineteenth century Blok still didn't know that he was a poet. He recited monologues, studied classical roles, and believed in his vocation as a tragic actor. S. M. Solovyov reminisces about his recitations:

> At this time I most often would see him reciting. I remember his execution of Apukhtin's "The Madman" and Hamlet's monologue "To Be or Not to Be." This wasn't reading but precisely recitation: in the traditional actor's style, with gestures and verbal bursts. He did "The Madman" sitting, Hamlet standing, invariably in doorways. The concluding words, "Ophelia, oh nymph," he uttered with his hand brought to his half-closed eyes. He was very handsome in those years. His grandfather's face, warmed and softened by extreme youth, was elegant to the highest degree under his ashen curly hair. Impeccably well proportioned, in a smart, deftly tailored student frock coat, even his every movement was handsome. I remember: he stands leaning against the piano, cigarette in hand, and my cousin points to him and says to me: "Look how picturesquely Sasha smokes."

The year 1900 is a transitional one in Blok's life. The old ends, the new hasn't yet arrived. Vague expectations, forebodings, predawn anxiety: the twilight hours of *Ante Lucem*. The poet convinces himself that his friendship with L. D. is over but thinks about her constantly. At the beginning of January he attends Salvini's performance on tour in the role of *King Lear* at the Maly Theater. "I happened to sit beside Lyubov Dmitrievna and her mother. L. D. was at that time completing her course at the gymnasium (Shaffe)." The memory of Ophelia with the wild flowers in her hands in the play at Boblovo, of Sirius and Vega, shining over them on that summer night, is reflected in these lines:

> My soul, as before, is all lit up
> With the undimming radiance of past days.
> But early autumn, pensively sad,
> Enveloped me with its grieving breath.
> Parting is near. The night is dark.
> And, as in those young days, there rings in the distance:
> "The fair Ophelia: Nymph in thy orisons
> Be all my sins remembered!"
> And the soul is filled, in futile anxiety,
> With a distant and beautiful memory.
>   (28 May 1900)

The agitation of love is futile—she doesn't share it:

> I sighed to you about happiness,
> But you were contemptuously silent.
>   (12 October 1900)

The dreams of the stage were also deceptive. In January Blok joins the Petersburg Dramatic Circle and is assigned the "big dramatic role of the first lover." The performance is set for 6 February in the Pavlov auditorium. He writes his father enthusiastically:

> The poems move rather slowly, because dramatic art is a more real area, especially when you become part of a troupe which, even though it has moral aims, inevitably echoes of backstage—to a small degree, however, and far from the whole troupe: there are almost no professional actors, barristers are directing it.... I hope to gain some stage experience, acting on a large stage.

But Blok didn't succeed in playing a "principal role," due to the intrigues of another *jeune premier*. M. A. Beketova informs us that one of the old members of the circle opened Blok's eyes to this: "After talking to him, Aleksandr Aleksandrovich left the circle. An acting career ceased to seem so alluring, and little by little he completely dropped the idea."

His studies at the college of law progressed apathetically. Blok remained a second year in the second course; jurisprudence evoked aversion in him. At the end of the year he frankly admits to his father: "I almost never go to the university any more, which seems right to me, since I am in the second course for the second year; anyway it is useless for me to listen to lectures, probably because of my bad memory for such things." It seems to the poet that his life has come to a standstill; everything is hopeless and irreparable. He is at a crossroad:

> The poet in exile and in doubt
> Is at the crossing of two roads.
> Night impressions are dying out,
> The sunrise is both pale and distant.
>
> But the past gives no pointers,
> What to desire, where to go?
> And in doubt and in exile
> He stopped on the path.
>   (31 March 1900)

A note in the *Diary* reads:

> The departure for Shakhmatovo was somehow sad. The first Shakhmatovo poem (*With the undimming radiance of past days*) shows how the sadness of the memories of 1898, of what seemed (and actually was) lost, poured out again.... The reading of books, the history of philosophy, begins.... Submission to God and to Plato begins.

Returning to Petersburg in the fall, he attends the university lectures of Professor A. Vvedensky on the history of philosophy and makes a "special" study of Plato, using the translations of V. S. and M. S.

Solovyov (letter to his father, 26 September 1900). The study of Plato left a light, superficial trace on some of the *Ante Lucem* poems. The poet talks about the struggle in his soul between paganism and Christianity, calls himself a "disciple of the Hellenes," speaks solemnly about the world of ideas:

> The sage's reason emerged from the gloom,
> And in the celestial heights—without fear or effort—
> The wings of shimmering ideas rose up to him.

But all these rhetorical exercises are clearly of bookish origin. Blok read only Plato's *Socratic Dialogues* and they bored him. He confesses to his father:

> My philosophical studies, primarily Plato, aren't progressing very fast. I am still reading and rereading the first volume of his works—the *Socratic Dialogues*—in the Solovyovs' translation. Moreover, I often get into a bad mood, because all this (and much else which touches upon life in all its manifestations) seems very cloudy and unclear.

Blok the romantic didn't become a "Hellene." Platonic ideas entered his consciousness later, through the prism of Vladimir Solovyov's mystical poetry. He writes in the *Diary*: "By the end of 1900 something new is growing. The strange poem of 29 December (*Born in the dead of night*), where I admit that She conquered with frost the Hellenic sun in me (which didn't exist)."

The poem is significant. "She" is linked with the moon, the north, midnight and frost. She is "silvery in the frosty dust," She "chills the soul." These motifs of *The Snow Mask* appear even before *Verses on the Beautiful Lady*:

> Born in the dead of night,
> Like a pale companion of earth,
> Clad in the fabric of earth,
> You were silvery in the distance.
>
> I went to the leafless north,
> I went in the frosty dust,
> Heard your mysterious voice;
> You were silvery in the distance.

Further on in the *Diary* he notes: "In the autumn L. D. enrolled in the courses. My first Petersburg poem—14 September.... The beginning of God-fighting. *She* continues slowly to assume unearthly features. My perception is influenced by philology and illness and fleeting passions followed by repentance."

The poems of the end of 1900 are a transition to a new epoch, to the reign of the Beautiful Lady. The well-known poem, *I seek salvation*, must be considered a link connecting these two periods. *She* finally appears:

> I seek salvation.
> My fires burn on the mountain tops—
> They lit up the whole region of night.
> But brighter than all is my spirit's gaze,
> And You[17] in the distance. But is it You?
> I seek salvation.
> . . . . .
> Tired of ringing, the starry chorus grows quiet.
> Night departs. Doubt flees.
> You descend from the distant bright mountains.
> I have waited for You. I stretched out my spirit to You.
> In You is salvation.
> (25 November 1900)

The capitalized "You," the prayerful tone, the solemn orchestration, the agitated rhythm—She descends to earth, the one he will soon call "the Mysterious Sunset Maiden."

Blok's first attempt to publish his poems dates to the fall of 1900. From his *Autobiography*:

> Once, on a rainy autumn day, . . . I set out with my poems to an old friend of our family, Viktor Petrovich Ostrogorsky, now deceased. At that time he edited *God's World* (*Mir Bozhy*). Without saying who had sent me to him, I agitatedly gave him two small poems inspired by V. Vasnetsov's pictures, Sirin, Alkonost, and Gamayun. Running through the poems, he said: "Aren't you ashamed, young man, to occupy yourself with *this*, when God knows what is happening in the university!" He saw me out with fierce good nature. This was offensive at the time, but now it is more pleasant to remember it than much of the later praise.

The year 1900 is a sad year of disappointments: in his studies, in the theater, in poetry, in love. Blok writes a mournful letter to his aunt, Sofia Andreevna Kublitsky (31 [23] November 1900):

> Mama and I often "find ourselves in a melancholy state about earthly things.". . . In general it's rather hard to enjoy oneself; winter has come, the sky is gray for the most part, and Petersburg is, as always, continually agitated, noisy, although rather far from us, . . . and Plato and Christ speak of the immortality of the soul, in the university they instill juridical and other sciences.

In the period 1898–1900 Blok wrote 290 poems; he later selected 70 of them and combined them in the section entitled *Ante Lucem*. The *Autobiography* explains the "old-fashionedness" of these youthful attempts:

> My childhood was spent in my mother's family. . . . Here in general old-fashioned ideas about literary values and ideals reigned. To speak

vulgarly, *à la* Verlaine, *éloquence* predominated here. Peculiar to my mother alone were constant revolt and unrest about what was new, and my aspirations toward *musique* found support in her. . . . I am indebted till the grave to this dear, old-fashioned *éloquence* for the fact that for me literature did not begin with Verlaine, nor with decadence in general. . . .

Serious writing began when I was about 18. For three or four years I showed my writing only to my mother and my aunt.

Family traditions and my secluded life were conducive to my not knowing a line of the so-called "new poetry" before my first university courses. . . . Until then, mysticism, which saturated the air of the last years of the old and the first years of the new century, was incomprehensible to me; I was troubled by signs which I saw in nature but I considered all this "subjective" and carefully guarded myself from all of it.

Blok's youthful poems (*Ante Lucem*) really do continue the tradition of the "old poetry." The poet studies poetic creativity in Pushkin and Lermontov (the poems *You won't deceive me, pale phantom, When the crowd applauds the idols*); he imitates Polonsky's and Maikov's lyric style, even rehashes Apukhtin's romances (*Let the moon shine—the night is dark*). But the main channel along which his poetry flows is the lyrics of Zhukovsky and Fet. The sentimental romanticism of the author of *Svetlana*, the muted harmony of his melodies, possess the young poet's soul. These lines of Blok echo Zhukovsky's voice:

I aspire to luxurious freedom,
Rush to the beautiful land,
Where in the broad clear field
It is good, as in a marvelous dream . . .
                    (7 August 1898)

Those signs in nature which trouble him he tries to unravel through Fet's nature lyrics. The melody of *Ante Lucem* is born of the music of *Evening Lights*—the same nature symbolism, the same mysterious correspondences between the life of the world and the life of the spirit, the same image of the Beloved in the brilliance of day and the stars of night. As in Fet's work, Blok's early poems are constructed on a parallelism between natural phenomena and the state of the soul. The love theme is introduced by "remarks" about the "landscape." Here are the first lines of several poems: *The full moon rose over the meadow; Horizon of the heavens—the star Omega; The haze descended, fraught with fog; The clouds float idly and gravely; The morning's eye gaped; The midnight star rolled down; Glow in the sky. Deep night is dead; The last purple burned low.* The moon, stars, morning mists, clouds, evening glow, storm clouds, and wind are cosmic signs of emotional impulses.

Fet was godfather to the young Blok's poetry. But the pupil, mastering the technique of poetic creation (primarily iambic tetrameter), assimilating verse forms and variations of rhythm, already sings in *his own* voice—a voice still unsure and soft, but we already recognize that absolutely unique, rather muffled and trembling sound.

Aleksandr Blok

One poem in Fet's collection *Evening Lights* begins with the verse:

> The fallen leaf trembles from our movement,
> But the shadow of green above us is still fresh,
> And amid the joy of intimacy something says
> That this yellow leaf is our tomorrow.

In Blok's *Ante Lucem* there are two piercing verses:

> The fall day descends in slow succession,
> The yellow leaf whirls slowly,
> And the day is transparently fresh, and the air wonderfully pure—
> The soul will not escape invisible decay.
>
> Thus every day it grows older,
> And every year, just as the yellow leaf whirls,
> It always appears, and is remembered, and seems
> That the autumn of past years was not so sad.

The dependence of Blok's poem on Fet's is obvious: the same image symbol (the yellow leaf is an omen of death), the same autumnal limpidity of tone, the same meter, the same slow melody. Nevertheless, given all the formal similarity, how different these verses are *emotionally*. In Fet the fleeting thought of death merely sharpens the "joy of intimacy," love conquers fear, and the poem ends in a major key, in a cheerful "moral":

> It is time not to prematurely fear the future,
> It is time to learn to remember happiness!

Not so in Blok: "The soul will not escape invisible decay." The second verse takes up this theme, developing it in parallel images, reinforcing it by repetitions ("every day," "every year," "it always appears, and is remembered, and seems"), underlining it by harmonies, and concluding with an elegiac ending: "That the autumn of past years was not so sad."

The title of Blok's youthful collection *Ante Lucem* (*Before the Dawn*) is not a poetic metaphor. These poems were written *before* the appearance of the Light, before the descent of the Beautiful Lady. They are full of predawn languor. It is still night, but morning is drawing near:

> I walked in the dark of a rainy night
> And, by the window of an old house,
> I recognized the pensive eyes
> Of my despair.
>   (16 March 1900)

CHAPTER II
THE APPEARANCE OF THE "BEAUTIFUL LADY"
1901–1903

A new day is born in the light of a mystical dawn. The dawn was rising; they saw it. It was a reality of spiritual consciousness, an event of enormous importance. Both Blok and Bely and the whole generation of early symbolists testify to this; their veracity cannot be doubted. At the turn of the new century they all lived through a mystical experience, unexpected and incomprehensible. From it a symbolic art developed: a tragic attempt to express in words the essentially inexpressible. It is easy to assume the pose of a "sober realist" and to reject the "delirium of a sick imagination." But the spiritual reality does not thereby stop being a reality: besides, neither Blok, a law student raised in the spirit of old-fashioned "*éloquence*," nor Bely, a scientist, experienced any pathological exaltation. Remembering that time, Blok writes in his *Autobiography*: "The sober and healthy people who surrounded me at that time protected me, it seems, from the infection of mystical charlatanism." And Bely emphasizes the "unexpectedness of the fact and the inability to substantiate it." But the fact existed: the atmosphere of consciousness had changed. To describe this "event" with the aid of logical concepts was as impossible as a blind man explaining color or a deaf man sound. It was left to be explained by hints, symbols, verbal gestures: "A new wind blew," "the dawn is rising," "light struggles with darkness," "something resounds," "and—dawns, dawns, dawns...."

The "radiance of the atmosphere" was first apprehended musically, and the *Verses on the Beautiful Lady* were born of music; attempts at philosophical grounding came later. Hypotheses were constructed; Bely and Vyacheslav Ivanov advanced very complex theories of symbolism. As in the Middle Ages, the lava of mysticism, on cooling, hardened into scholasticism.

In 1901 a new breed of people—the "seers"—appears among the "realists" and "naturalists." Mysterious threads tie them together, a brotherhood is founded, a special secret language is devised. These are the "initiates," safeguarding the new discovery, having a premonition that the "dawn" signifies the beginning of a new era in the life of humanity. So far it is only an "emotional event" for the few, but it is destined to blaze up on a historical and cosmic plane. The early symbolists are seers and prophets: they are gripped by alarm and by the expectation of a worldwide catastrophe.

In his *Reminiscences of Blok* Bely affirms: "The youth of that time heard something resembling noise and saw something resembling light. We all gave ourselves up to the *elemental force* of coming times; gave ourselves up to the steps of the new age, which could be distinctly heard in the air." The brotherhood of "seers" united Blok, Bely, the family of M. S. Solovyov, the Medtner brothers, Z. Gippius, G. A. Rachinsky, A. S. Petrovsky, and many others. Among them were believers, atheists, and theosophists. But they all lived in the romantic atmosphere of the "dawn," they were people of a new disposition. There was not yet a symbolic "school": the few "eccentrics" who saw "something" and expected "something" lived in Moscow and Petersburg.

Z. N. Gippius wrote about dawns; E. K. Medtner traced the theme of dawn in music from Beethoven to Schumann; his brother, the composer, expressed the same theme in his first C-moll sonata. Sergey Solovyov plunged into the "Apocalypse"; Bely worked on his first *Symphony*; Blok met the dawn among the fields and forests of Shakhmatovo:

> The whole horizon in flame—and unbearably clear—
> And I wait silently—*mourning* and *loving*.

The philosopher Vladimir Sergeevich Solovyov played a decisive role in the early symbolists' sense of "vague agitation."

"For me and Seryozha [V. Solovyov's nephew]," Bely writes, "1901 passed under the sign of Solovyov's poetry." Blok also notes the same year. (*Autobiography*: "Here, linked with acute mystical and romantic experiences, Vladimir Solovyov's poetry possessed my whole being.")

The spiritual meeting of the young Blok and Bely with the singer of the "Eternal Friend" was providential. The paths of Russian symbolism were already outlined in Solovyov's theosophy. The mystical basis of his whole philosophy is his teaching about Sophia the Divine Wisdom; it didn't come from the books of Boehme, Pordage, or Paracelsus but from real life experience. In the poem "Three Meetings" the philosopher tells of "the most significant thing that had happened in his life to date." He saw this mysterious Eternal Friend three times. She first appeared to him when he was nine, on the holy day of Ascension, in a temple during the liturgy, at the singing of the Cherubic Hymn. Through the azure, herself woven of azure, with a "flower from otherworldly lands" in her hand, she appeared for a moment and immediately disappeared in an azure fog. But he really does experience a transformation of the world during the prayer of the Church about this transformation. Long years of spiritual search and struggle go by. The youth passes through materialism, God-defiance, idealistic philosophy, Schopenhauerian pessimism, "rational faith," an ardent turning to God.

In 1875 Solovyov goes to London to write his doctoral dissertation. There, in the British Museum, studying the literature on Sophia the Divine Wisdom, he passionately awaits Her radiant advent. And again in golden azure Her face appears to him, and Her voice calls him to Egypt. He abandons everything, rushes south; in the Thebaid desert, at dawn, She descends to him for the third and last time:

> ... And in purple of heavenly brilliance,
> Eyes full of azure fire,
> You looked at me, like the first radiance
> Of the universal day of creation.
>
> What is, what has been, what will be in the ages—
> One motionless gaze embraced everything here.
> Sea and rivers beneath me are blue,
> And the distant forest, and the peaks of snowy mountains.
>
> I saw everything, and everything was
> But one image of feminine beauty ...
> The measureless entered its dimension,
> Before me, in me—only you!

The poem ends with solemn words about the divine basis of the world and the victory of life over death:

> Still a prisoner of the vain world,
> Under the coarse rind of matter,
> Thus I began to see the incorruptible purple,
> And felt the radiance of divinity.
>
> Triumphing over death by premonition,
> And in dream overcoming the chain of time,
> Eternal friend, I will not call you.
> Forgive my uncertain melody.

In the three visions Solovyov is given a revelation of the divine unity of the universe. Time, space, matter disappear like a phantom. The unity of the cosmos, the "World Soul," is a personal image—the Eternal Feminine. She is an Empress who "from the ages has perceived the power of Divinity and the incorruptible radiance of beauty"; she is Sophia the Divine Wisdom about whom Solomon speaks in Proverbs: "Wisdom hath builded her house, she hath hewn out her seven pillars."

Solovyov's further philosophical work amounts to an attempt to translate the mystical intuition into the language of metaphysical concepts ("positive all-embracing unity") and to reveal it in a system of historiosophy, ethics, and religious-social structure.

He sets forth his teaching on Sophia in "Readings on God-Mankind" in the book *Russia and the Universal Church* and in the article "The Concept of Humanity in Auguste Comte." He approaches his original insight from different sides, struggles with enormous difficulties, collides with antinomies, hesitates, changes expressions, searches for exact wording. He wasn't destined to finish his construction: his Sophiology is merely outlined. By greatly simplifying Solovyov's very complex metaphysical considerations, we can define Sophia as the *ideal humanity in God*. Man has a divine basis which has abided in God with the ages, that "image and likeness" of God in whose contemplation God creates man. Humanity in God is the eternal body of God, the "chasuble of Divinity." The created world lives and breathes by the rays and reflections falling on it from the uncreated world. And in this lies its truth, goodness, and beauty. The created world, immersed in the stream of time, is granted independent existence and the freedom of self-determination. The World Soul fell away from God, forfeited its sovereign position among creatures, and the unity of the universe disintegrated. All creation became subject to vanity and the bondage of decay, not voluntarily, but by the will of that which had subjected it, that is, the World Soul. But evil and death cannot touch the eternal prototype of the sinful world—Sophia the Divine Wisdom. She protects the universe and humanity from final disintegration; she is the world's guardian angel, covering all creation with her wings and battling the forces of hell for possession of the World Soul. In its final form the teaching is dualistic: the uncreated world, humanity in God, Sophia, are juxtaposed to the created world; the World Soul, which fell away from God, languishes in the captivity of corruptibility and hopes for liberation.

Solovyov maintains that the truth about Sophia the Divine Wisdom had already been revealed for the religious inspiration of the Russian people in the eleventh century. On the icon of Sophia in the Novgorod cathedral, a feminine figure in a royal vestment sits on a throne; on the right is the Virgin Mother, on the left Saint John the Baptist, in the center Christ rises with uplifted arms, and above Him the heavenly world is visible in the person of several angels surrounding the Word of God, represented by the Gospel. This icon is not borrowed from Greece; it expresses a purely Russian mystical outlook. The regal and feminine being, receiving reverence from the fulfiller of the Old Testament and from the progenitress of the New, is Sophia the Divine Wisdom or *God-mankind*.

Both Blok and Bely saw Solovyov's mystical teaching through the prism of his poetry; the poet was more significant than the philosopher for them. Fascinated by the new sound of his lyrics, unexpected and at the same time kindred, they didn't see his poetic shortcomings. The romanticism of the erotic philosophic poetry, with its high-principled passion and prophetic inspiration, excited them. The pale colors, the diffuse outlines, the poverty of the rhymes, and the monotony of the meters—all the "old-fashionedness" of this lyric poetry—seemed to them the mark of its originality. The juxtaposition of two worlds ("the coarse rind of matter" and "the incorruptible purple"); the play on antitheses; the image-symbols (mists, blizzards, dawns, sunsets, the dove and snake, the bush, the radiant temple, the empress' chamber); the color symbols (white, blue, azure, indigo, gold)—they accepted all these features of Solovyov's mystical lyric as holy canon. Solovyov suggested to them the words to express the "ineffable," which they were experiencing.

Blok didn't know Solovyov personally. He saw him only once in his life, in February 1900 at the funeral of a relative. In the *Autobiography* he notes: "Of the events, phenomena and trends which in one way or another influenced me particularly strongly, I should mention the meeting with V. Solovyov, whom I saw only from a distance." This memory was indelible. In a 1910 article, "The Knight-Monk," the poet writes:

> I accompanied the coffin of the deceased on a colorless Petersburg day. Ahead of me walked a tall, thin man in an old fur coat, his head uncovered.... Long locks of steel-gray hair lay on the brown collar of his fur coat. The figure was so terribly unlike its surroundings that it seemed like a silhouette.... After a few minutes I looked up: the man was no longer there; he had somehow disappeared unobtrusively.

It was Solovyov. And this strange phantom permeated everything that Blok later heard and read about him. Solovyov's eyes had a "bottomless depth" and "total aloofness." "That was a pure spirit, as if not a living person, but a picture." Behind the unknown coffin the "solitary wanderer stepped slowly into an unknown distance beyond space or time."

And Blok wanted to forget all the brilliant and many-sided activities of the philosopher, publicist, critic, poet, human being, in order to see his new, otherworldly image. "Here the armor, the circle of the shield, and the blade of the sword under the folds of the black cassock glimmer with a pale light.... This is the knight-monk." The earthly concern of this "poor knight" was to liberate the captive tsarevna—the World Soul, passionately grieving in the embrace of Chaos. Blok considers the *poema Three Meetings* indisputable testimony: only proceeding from it can one understand the essence of the philosopher's teaching and personality:

> V. Solovyov's *poema*, addressed directly to the One Whom he here calls the Eternal Friend, says: "I, Vladimir Solovyov, born in Moscow, summoned You and saw You three times: at a Sunday liturgy in Moscow in 1867 [1862], when I was nine; in the British Museum in London in the fall of 1875 as a Master of Philosophy and Assistant Professor of Moscow University; in the desert near Cairo at the beginning of 1876."

Such is the inscription we read over the portrayal of the knight-monk: it radiates immaterial gold light. The article ends with the solemnly prophetic words: "The new world already stands at the door: tomorrow we will remember the golden light sparkling on the border of two so dissimilar centuries. The nineteenth made us forget the very names of the saints; the twentieth will perhaps see them with its own eyes." And the author quotes Solovyov's lines:

> And at this moment of invisible meeting
> An unearthly light will again illuminate you,
> And, mourning and loving, you will shake off
> The deep sleep of worldly consciousness.

Only one for whom Solovyov's mystical experience is his own personal experience can speak with such calm assurance, with such force of conviction and inspiration. The "Eternal Friend" who descended to the philosopher in the Egyptian desert appeared to his pupil in the Russian expanses of Shakhmatovo in the image of the "Beautiful Lady." Solovyov's image rose up before Blok at the turn of the new century: he proclaimed those events which must unfold in the world. In a 1920 article, "Vladimir Solovyov and Our Day," the author indicates the prophetic nature of Solovyov's appearance in Russia: "He was gripped by terrible anxiety, by an unrest which could lead to madness. And the forebodings were not deceptive: the new century brought with it world upheavals whose dimensions we are not able to imagine."

Returning to 1901, a year so significant for him, the year of the new world's birth, Blok writes:

> Today I permit myself to point out, purely dogmatically, without any critical analysis, as a witness not completely deprived of hearing and sight and not completely tongue-tied, that January 1901 was already under a completely different sign than December 1900, that the very beginning of the century was full of essentially new signs and premonitions.

Andrey Bely got to know Solovyov in the family of his brother, Mikhail Sergeevich. The philosopher's appearance struck the young decadent. Tall, black, dry, stooped, with an emaciated face and weak arms, he tonelessly read his prophetic "Three Conversations." Bely recalled:

> ... the enormous, charmed, gray eyes, the stooped back, the long beautiful head with a fluffy gray mane, the large mouth as if lacerated.... Solovyov sat, tired, with that stamp of self-sacrifice and of terrible grandeur, which rested on him in the last months; as if he saw what no one else saw and couldn't find the words to communicate his knowledge. But reading "The Story of Antichrist" he caught fire. At the words, "John arose, like a white candle," he too rose slightly, as if stretching upright in the armchair. It seems that heat lightning flickered in the windows.... Solovyov's face flickered in the lightning of inspiration![1]

In that same spring of 1900 Bely had a "meaningful conversation" with Solovyov; the philosopher seems to have been interested in the young symbolist's writing. They arranged to meet when the summer was over. But Solovyov died in July. In *Arabesques* Bely writes: "And the word not spoken between us became a watchword for me, just as his grave, lit by a red icon-lamp, later became a watchword for me. ... Vladimir Sergeevich later was for me a forerunner of the fever of religious searching."

The "Solovyovians" met in the home of M. S. and O. M. Solovyov; there was a real cult of the late philosopher. At the tea table Mikhail Sergeevich set forth his plans to publish his brother's works; the article "On the Meaning of Love" was discussed; they argued about the Antichrist in "Three Conversations"; the experience of the dawn was connected with Solovyov's image of the Eternal Feminine. A new joyfully excited feeling of peace found expression in the "teacher's" lines:

> Know now, the Eternal Feminine
> Is coming to earth in an incorruptible body.
> In the new Goddess' unfading light
> Heaven has merged with the abyss of waters.

Bely and Seryozha Solovyov were enchanted with the philosopher's poetry, dreamed about the transformation of erotic love in the spirit of the article "On the Meaning of Love," raved about theocracy, met the deceased in dreams and talked with him. The friends often visited Solovyov's grave in the Novodevichy Monastery, recalling his lines:

> Along a mysterious path, sad and sweet,
> You drew near the soul. . . . And—thank you.
> It is sweet for me to approach with dejected memories
> The quiet shores curtained by death.

And it seemed to them that the deceased could hear them. During the snowy winter of 1901 they wandered at night along the lanes of the Arbat; they believed that Solovyov's shadow flashed before them among the snowdrifts. On Sergey Solovyov's early poems and on Bely's youthful *Dramatic Symphony* lay reflections of "Solovyovian" light.

But in Solovyov there was not only light, there was also darkness. In his mystical experience the heavenly was interwoven with the earthly, the religious with the occult. The "evil flame of earthly fire" smoldered under the knightly adoration of the Eternal Feminine. In one of his best poems the philosopher speaks frankly about the "dark root" of the mystical roses:

> Light out of darkness. Over the black clod
> The faces of your roses
> Could not have arisen,
> If their dark submerged root
> Had not pierced
> The gloomy lap.

No other mystic had such intimate, personal relations with the Eternal Feminine as Solovyov. When his brother, Mikhail Sergeevich, was preparing to publish the works of the deceased, he discovered many notes in the margins of his manuscripts. In them, in a different handwriting, letters were jotted down signed "S." or "Sophie." Solovyov had written them in a medium's trance; it was a lover's correspondence with Sophia. The "friend" set meetings, got angry at her "unfaithful friend," left him, and returned again. He not only respected her, he also loved her, and was sure that she loved him. In his passionate nature, worship was inseparably linked with eros. And it is impossible to understand who is the heroine of the "mystical romance"—a real woman or an otherworldly being? This fateful duality concealed a danger of derangement, counterfeits, and distortions. On the eve of his death the philosopher went through the final and most terrible ordeal: he was expecting the revelation of the World Soul, the Heavenly Aphrodite, but her sinister double appeared to him.

In March 1900 Solovyov received a letter from a teacher and journalist in Nizhny Novgorod whom he didn't know, Anna Nikolaevna Schmidt. In it he learns that his correspondent is writing a mystical treatise on the Church and the Third Testament, and that she firmly believes that she is the incarnation of Sophia and that he is the incarnation of Christ. Frightened by the spinster's "holy madness," the philosopher replies with a stern letter. Nevertheless, a few days later he goes to Vladimir to meet her and tries to persuade her not to trust "visions and suggestion." The personal meeting with Anna Schmidt bitterly disappointed Solovyov.

But the appearance of the woman, half-lunatic and half-genius, the "mystical beloved" springing suddenly out of nonbeing in the last days of Solovyov's life, was not accidental. Anna Schmidt was a living parody of the philosopher's strange romance with the Eternal Friend. A. Bely saw her in Mikhail Sergeevich's home in 1901: "Watching her, I was all eyes: yes, yes, something very unpleasant in the small forehead, in the dry, tiny lips, in the small gray eyes; she had gray hair and a dress full of holes; a totally Sologubian 'gray untouchable.' "[2] The Heavenly Aphrodite and the "gray untouchable"—by such satanic mockery did the dark forces behind the "romance" with the Eternal Friend avenge themselves on the mystic. But Solovyov needed this meeting. Before his death he passed through a fire of purification: his adoration of the Eternal Feminine had to free itself of the temptation of occultism and eroticism. In April 1900, in the month when his only meeting with Anna Schmidt took place in Vladimir, he wrote a preface to the third edition of his poems. Made wiser by experience, the teacher warns his pupils of the temptations and derangements threatening them:

> The closer and more complete is the revelation of real beauty clothing Divinity and leading us by Its power to liberation from suffering and death, the narrower is the boundary separating that beauty from its counterfeit, from that deceptive and impotent beauty which only perpetuates the realm of suffering and death.

There is genuine clairvoyance in these words, as if Solovyov had a premonition of Blok's tragic fate, of his struggle with doubles and "counterfeits," of the terrible substitutions for the image of the "Beautiful Lady," of the appearance of the "Stranger" and the "Snow Mask," of breaks in the scarlet purple worlds, and of the transformation of the "radiant temple" into a "Puppet Show."

The "Beautiful Lady"

Blok calls the year 1901 exceptionally important to him and decisive for his fate. This is the year of the Beautiful Lady's appearance. The 1918 *Diary* singles out 25 January 1901: "Strolling on Monetnaya in a completely *special* mood":

> At the end of January and the beginning of February (still blue snows around the regimental church—also toward evening), She clearly manifests herself. The living one turns out to be the World Soul (as was evident later), separated, captive, and pining . . . and She is already in daylight, that is after the night from which I have been looking at her. That is, She is committed to some aspiration and is "about to leave," I am allowed only to look and to bless her departure.

This first, still helpless record of "experience" is striking for the similarity of Blok's mysticism to Solovyov's, even *before he knew him*. Only in April was the world of the poetry of the author of "Three Meetings" revealed to Blok: "Mama gave me the book of V. Solovyov's poems for Easter this year" (note in the *Diary*). But the mysterious "She" has already appeared at the end of January. And, just as with Solovyov, "She" is not identified with the World Soul, but is contrasted to it. She is a divine being, the World Soul is created. And, also as with Solovyov, the World Soul is seen as pining in captivity to the fallen world and waiting for liberation. Love whispers: the World Soul is incarnated in the image of the beloved; its depression and "aspiration" shine in the living features of the face of the beloved. Blok, the youth, steps onto the mystical path with the fearlessness of a sleepwalker; he walks surely and easily along the brink of an abyss. From this time the smallest details of his meetings with the beloved take on the deepest significance for him:

> In this state I met Lyubov Dmitrievna on Vasilievsky Island (where I was going to buy a dachshund who was soon named Krabb). She got out of a sleigh on Andreevskaya Square, walked to her courses along the Sixth Line,[3] along Sredny Prospect, to the Tenth Line. I followed, unnoticed by Her (here is the shop window of the photographer's studio near Sredny Prospect). . . .
> Next morning I saw Her again from a distance when I went for Krabb (and brought him in a warm hood, in an exceptional state, which mama didn't know about).
> I resigned myself to the ignorance and pain (psychologically)—of L. D. M.'s continual sternness.

Spring comes, and the encounter with V. Solovyov's poetry, which "took possession of his whole being." We read in the *Diary*: "In the spring the walks near the islands and in the field behind Staraya Derevnya began, where there occurred what I defined as Visions (sunsets)."

This emotional state left its mark on a poem written on 17 May 1901. Its last verse:

> Filled with insight, I am here at last;
> I have crossed the boundary line;
> I only await the predictable vision
> Before flying off into another void.

This spring he reads the first collection of *Northern Flowers* from the Scorpion publishing house. "Briusov (especially) took on that same color for me, so that in the following '*mystical summer*' this book also played a special role."

In *Northern Flowers* Blok read excerpts from Briusov's *poema* "The Secluded Ones," in which he depicts the horror of the future city-house "with a glass skull covering the globe" and sings the rapture of death and destruction. It is possible that it was precisely Briusov's passion for the end of the world that struck Blok. Among the other contributors to the collection there stood out Ivan Konevskoy, a poet of rare and keen originality; the tongue-tied prophet Aleksandr Dobrolyubov; Sologub; Balmont;[4] Baltrushaitis. The sounds of their poems entered the general melody of Blok's "mystical summer." On 2 May, in a letter to his father, dry and reserved as usual, he hints at his exceptional emotional state: "Spring sensed its power and echoed in my mood to the utmost. It is time to settle city accounts and temporarily move toward *contemplation*." The hidden meaning of this "contemplation" is revealed in the *Diary* as intense work on himself, as its own kind of mystical discipline. "That same May," Blok writes, "I tried 'inner armor' for the first time, to protect myself from Her sternness with a 'secret knowledge.' "

This is expressed in the lines:

> I feel, I believe, I know,
> You won't entice me with a prophet's sympathy.
> I contain in myself more than enough
> Of those fires with which you burn.
> (17 May 1901)

The proud assurance of the "prophet"—"I contain the universe"—grew from a consciousness of his growing powers. Blok notes: "This, apparently, was the threshold of the coming 'sorcery,' as was the unusual merging with nature." The tonality of love changed. "Love," he continues, "began to become less a lofty calling, but the object of both was one and the same face." Then follow unusually important "fortune-telling" and "premonitions of a change of countenance."

The accumulation of strength and the "inner armor" are reflected in the plane of everyday relationships. The poet notes: "L. D. sometimes displayed a kind of attention to me. This was probably because I shone brightly." This surprising admission has the lofty simplicity of honesty. He shone with a light granted him, and he humbly testified to the light's existence.

In the summer, Sofia Andreevna Kublitskaya's family left for Barnaul and invited Blok to visit them. Lyubov Dmitrievna gave him to understand that his departure would be unpleasant for her. Using various pretexts, he politely declines the invitation in a letter to his aunt on 5 July, and adds: "I am content with the reality around me." And in the *Diary*: "I was so filled with the lofty, that I ceased to regret the past."

Blok leaves Shakhmatova for a few days to go to his grandmother Kovalenskaya's estate, Dedovo; there he meets M. S. Solovyov's family (Blok's great-aunt A. G. Kovalenskaya was Olga Mikhailovna Solovyova's mother).

In the *Diary* he notes briefly his meeting Vladimir Solovyov's brother, so significant for him: "Here I went to Dedovo, where . . . I had serious conversations with the Solovyovs. On parting, Uncle Misha [Mikhail Sergeevich] gave me a cigar and the just issued first volume of V. Solovyov."

We learn about Blok's "serious conversations" with the Solovyovs from Bely's *Reminiscences*. He had long known of "Sasha" Blok's existence. Back in 1897 the Solovyovs had told him about their relative, the gymnasium student who also wrote poems and was mad about the theater. After meeting his second cousin in Dedovo, Seryozha Solovyov writes Bely an ecstatic letter: he had wandered through the fields with Blok a great deal and had talked about V. Solovyov's poetry and philosophy. He adds joyfully that Blok also believes in the real existence of Sophia the Divine Wisdom and sees a revelation of Her countenance in Solovyov's lyrics. For him, too, the old world is collapsing, the dawn of the new era predicted by the philosopher is rising. "Solovyov's letter about Blok," Bely concludes, "is an event; I understood: we had met a brother on the way."

From August 1901, the Solovyovs and Bely immerse themselves in reading Blok's poems. They find in them the music which resounded in the air around them. "It seemed that Blok had written only what the air spoke to the consciousness," Bely writes. "He stormed the golden pink and tense atmosphere of the epoch with words. . . . They contained the sharpest, most intense expression of Solovyov's theosophy, tied to life."

Bely and Sergey Solovyov took in Blok's poetry ecstatically; the duality of certain lines alarmed Olga Mikhailovna ("But I am afraid: You will change Your countenance"); Mikhail Sergeevich feared the young mystic's "maximalism" and doubted the purity of his experience. Bely recopied Blok's poems and read them to his university friends. Soon a circle of admirers of the singer of the Beautiful Lady was formed in Moscow. On 3 September Olga Mikhailovna wrote to the poet's mother:

Dear Alya, I wanted to hurry and communicate something pleasant to you. Sasha's poems made an unusual, hard to describe, surprising, enormous impression on Borya Bugaev,[5] whose opinion we all value highly and whom we consider the most perceptive of all the people we know. Borya showed the poems to his friend Petrovsky, a very strange, mystical young man, and the impression on Petrovsky was the same.

Blok in 1901 should not be imagined as an ecstatic visionary, congealed in "secret knowledge" and "fortune-telling." According to M. A. Beketova's testimony, the summer in Shakhmatovo before the Kublitsky cousins' departure for Siberia passed "as usual, in lively tomfoolery. All three cousins rode horseback together, put on amusing performances, laughed a lot." After the Kublitskys' departure, Blok writes to Sofia Andreevna on 5 September: "The summer passed very well for me, I am awfully satisfied with it (in general). And the weather was somehow exceptionally radiant. . . . Toward the end I rode on horseback far around the vicinity, even into some places I didn't know well."

Visions of the Beautiful Lady and "lively tomfoolery"—such is Blok's innate duality, the two-sidedness of his life. The summer he called "mystical" could be filled with childish gaiety.

Autumn came. The *Diary* states: "Autumn was filled with intense expectation. . . . There were wanderings around Boblovo (with searching for a place of achievements). Ivlevo. A church forest. I remember a farewell. L. D. came out into the living room (cold bright autumn) with a powdered face." On the eve of his departure from Shakhmatovo he writes his aunt: "A wonderful autumn, completely crystal, fresh: in the last days everything turned very yellow and red, only the winter crops are pure green and everywhere vast. . . . So beautiful . . . that it's a pity to leave." The poet and his mother leave for Petersburg in the same train with S. M. Solovyov. Solovyov told him that Borya Bugaev lives in Moscow and loves the poems about the Beautiful Lady very much.

Returning to Petersburg, Blok decides to leave the legal faculty, which he hated, and to transfer to the philological. But he is afraid that his father will be dissatisfied and will stop sending money. Finally, after long hesitation, he tells Aleksandr Lvovich about this "important change in his life" and assures him that he is completely incapable of "practical studies"; only "laziness and unconsciousness" had prompted him to choose the legal faculty as the easiest. Now he feels "a very definite urge for philologic knowledge."

His father unexpectedly responds with consent and approval. Blok writes him a grateful letter with an openness unusual for him:

> My new work is not only reconciled with, but even merges completely with, the contemplation which is natural to me personally (because I hardly ever contemplate passively). More than that, I no longer see the former division, and this contributes even more to my "lucidity."

He "likes terribly" the philosophy professor A. I. Vvedensky; he attends Professor F. F. Zelinsky's lectures and those of Assistant Professor Ernshtedt, "who understand the whole essence of classical antiquity." The letter quotes the Bible, Thales, and V. Solovyov's poems. And a poem is added at the end:

> Early hour. In the path, unseen,
> A dream flares up.

The hints at "contemplation" and "lucidity" and the quotations from Solovyov are significant. The diligent philology student's "work" conceals his other "secret life."

In *Notebook* No. 1 we find the following remark:

> In Znamenie I had a prophetic dream. Something in time burst, and she appeared to me clearly, addressed me in a different way, and the mysterious was revealed. I saw my family going away, but I, passing through, suddenly stopped in front of her at the door. She was alone. She rose to meet me, suddenly stretched out her hand, and obscurely spoke strange words about how I love her. Holding Solovyov's poems in my hands, I gave them to her. And suddenly they were no longer poems, but a small German book, and I was mistaken. But she kept stretching out her arms—and my heart stopped. And that very second, on the brink of clairvoyance, I, of course, woke up. And it obviously had to be so, because otherwise I would have apprehended the unearthly and as if I were awake—the dream itself would have turned into a prophetic state.

Thus, in the lover's subconscious Her image is connected with Solovyov's poetry, in her sternness the "secret tenderness" is revealed, and, "on the brink of clairvoyance," the heavenly comes into contact with the earthly.

And Lyubov Dmitrievna was in reality distant and unapproachable as before. Blok notes: "September passed in a comparative inner slowdown. L. D. again did not seem to show anything. In October new fits of despair began. (She is leaving. Before me—the 'limit of knowledge of God')."

The poem *You are leaving the earthly vale*, dated 6 October, ends with the verse:

> Abandon the universe's impotence,
> Your peace is now inviolable.
> Before me the limit of knowledge of God,
> Inescapable twilight, black smoke.

"I experienced strong jealousy," he continues in the *Diary*, "(without apparent cause). The meeting of 17 October was portentous." Her image loses earthly outline—fleshless, transparent, radiant, she is a heavenly vision:

> Alone, in flowers, I wait for another spring.
> Go away—I sense the seraphim,

Your earthly dreams are alien to me here.
(17 October 1901)

> In November my manifest sorcery began, because I *called forth the doubles.* . . .
> L. D. went to M. M. Chitau for lessons. I would wait for her to come out, watched out for her, and sometimes accompanied her from Gagarinskaya-Liteinaya as far as Zabalkansky (end of November, beginning of December).

The lines of 27 November are about this waiting:

> I waited a long time—you came out late.
> But my spirit came alive in waiting.
> Twilight descended, but tearlessly
> I strained both sight and hearing.

And now she is no longer a fleshless angel in the roses of the autumnal sunset; she is an "enchantress . . . in a white snowstorm, in a snowy moan." The "Petersburg motifs" of cold, darkness, and snowstorm sound for the first time:

> You in a white snowstorm, in a snowy moan,
> Again surface like an enchantress,
> And the cupolas of the churches blend
> In the eternal light, in the eternal ringing.

That same day, in a letter to his aunt S. A. Kublitskaya, Blok announces that this year he is less dependent on the "weight of the weather" because he is "beginning to feel underfoot the real mystical soil," the "immovable source of life . . . always and in all circumstances immovable."

The diary ends on an uneasy note about the emergence of the "double," about the first still vague rustling of the "stirring chaos":

> The frost appeared—the "snowstorm," the "importunate one," and the *tsarina* clanging the door, two old men, the "poison" (of flowers not sent), the one who accomplishes and the one who utilizes the fruits of accomplishment ("the other I"), someone "laughing and tender."

Thus ended the year 1901.

Who is this double, this "other I," where is he from? Why is he betrothed to the tsarina by the "cold of winters"?

> The importunate one stands on the road,
> White—he peers into the frosty night.
> I go to meet him in profound alarm,
> He, reeling, steps aside.

The poet is gripped by depression, "worn out by immortality," but the double, white, lifeless, "celebrates the victory of the grave." In the frosty night, like a white phantom in a white snowstorm, death enters Blok's world. And he knows: this is his "other I."

Blok wrote several hundred poems in 1901. The poet later included only a small number of them in the cycle *Verses on the Beautiful Lady*.

In 1937 Blok's youthful diary of 1902 was published in the collection *Literary Legacy (Literaturnoe nasledstvo)*. This enormously important "human document" permits us for the first time to penetrate the poet's secret life and to understand the tragic history of his love for L. D. Mendeleeva. Before us opens a new, hitherto unknown image of the Beautiful Lady.

In January 1902 Blok notes down his thoughts on poetry, on the Eternal Feminine and symbolism:

> Poems are a prayer. At first the inspired poet-apostle composes it in divine ecstasy. And everything for which he composes it conceals his real God. . . . And if that is so, then God is in everything, all the more not just in infinite heaven, but also in the "spring song" and in a "woman's love" [Tyutchev].

Reflections on poetry and personal experiences are for him inseparable. He continues, but now about himself:

> January spring—more a hope and feeling of spring than spring itself—it trembled and disclosed what unclearly and weakly still rushed over the soul and over thought. . . .
> And I kept waiting for a vision, waiting for autumn. But it hadn't come yet. It began to ring differently and responded differently. Or did it only seem so? . . .
> Coming forward to defend myself, I mentally cross myself and summon the great Feminine shadow which passed before me "with the majesty of a tsarina" [Polonsky] and was embodied in the ringing abyss of the dark world.

And again on poetry he writes:

> Modern poets are often reproached for "incomprehensibility." But they cannot write differently. . . .
> Man, becoming refined, feels the need to conceal the secret of his existence, which he feels too vividly and nakedly. . . . He seeks night for his inspirations.

These words are striking. Blok was saying about himself that it was harder for him to "experience" than to "contemplate." Z. N. Gippius, on first meeting the poet, intuitively sensed his tragic defenselessness "before everything, before his own self, before other people, before life and before death." The secret of existence was completely exposed to him—he was mortally wounded by it, and as if ashamed of it, and he hid in mists.

Further on Blok speaks of the "giant" Solovyov, of the appearance of the first flowers of symbolism: "In hitherto unprecedented, blissful torments something new, as yet unknown, so far only dimly felt, begins to be born. All this is the work of the Eternal God. We still see only dimly, shuddering, and dimly await the end." Symbolic poetry is full of depression, discontent, aspirations for union with God. "One of the great paradoxes by which seekers live," Blok writes, "may be considered the fact that there is no greater closeness than the greatest remoteness, no greater sadness than the greatest joy." Here again the personal and the general are indissolubly merged. The author attempts to understand his living experience in the perspective of Russian poetry. He speaks of the Eternal Feminine in the poems of Tyutchev, Fet, Polonsky, and V. Solovyov, and concludes: "Contemporary poetry in general has departed into mysticism and, as one of the brightest mystical constellations, the Eternal Feminine has rolled into the blue depths of the sky of poetry."

Blok is not a theoretician, not a "thinker." Z. N. Gippius understood this at once. In an article "My Lunar Friend" she writes: "It cannot be said that he had no relation to reality, still less than he 'wasn't intelligent.' At the same time, everything that we call philosophy, logic, metaphysics bounced off him; it didn't apply to him." Blok didn't reason about the Eternal Feminine, he lived it. Fate faced him with a staggering reality. Reverence for the unearthly Beautiful Lady and love for a living woman, L. D. Mendeleeva, merged in his consciousness. The combination, unfathomable and fateful for his human lot, was an inalterable fact of experience. The worshipper of the Eternal Feminine burned with erotic fire for her earthly incarnation. One such burst of passion occurred during their 29 January meeting. Shaken by this event, he writes to Lyubov Dmitrievna that same day:

> What happened today should change, and has changed, a great deal which has been inertly awaiting its opportunity for three and a half years. Every theory went directly into practice—to my misfortune, tragic. Now the future holds before me only the pure you and—forgive the insanity of the term in relation to you—the motionless Sun of the Testament. My life, that is, my ability to live, is inconceivable without that certain Spirit, which comes to me from you, unknown and still only dimly felt.

But the "evil flame of earthly fire," to use Solovyov's words, blazing up, fanned into a conflagration. A week later Blok writes Lyubov Dmitrievna a frightful letter containing "invocations," utter despair, and a premonition of death:

> The time is already approaching when everything must move far ahead. Before, the discontent of aspirations poured out in poems—now not even poems can help, and my terrible desire assumed dimensions which threaten the spirit. Hope still resounds somewhere high up in the sky, inspiring the hearing. . . . I call you with every invocation. Answer, and understand that the silence cannot continue and will end one way or

another.... For there is no returning to the former paths. These paths have become useless for my life.

But Lyubov Dmitrievna's silence continued. Blok succeeded in mastering his agitation, in retiring into himself. Two days after the "imploring" letter, he writes again—with restraint, almost formally. But this calm is more terrible than the recent despair:

> 7 February. (1) First of all, permit me to ask your pardon for what happened on 29 January.
> (2) I must tell you that what you didn't hear to the end and what I didn't express completely must retain its force for the time being: at present it seems to me that you don't want to, and perhaps can't, hear this out. I am speaking this way because I foresee any other way out as worse....
> (3) Regarding the fact of my visits: Do you want them to continue?

But the next day (8 February) he writes his father a calm, reasoned letter in which he talks about university matters, examinations, and disturbances, and discusses "a certain remoteness from the external world, ... which finds a solution in a rather large number of poems." Outwardly nothing seems to have changed, life goes on as before, but the *Diary* entry for 9 March sets forth in detail a plan for suicide. This terrible entry is entitled "*In ecstasy—the end*":

> Decide deliberately in advance that you must die. Prepare a revolver or rope (!?). Set the day. In the interval before suicide, now be reconciled, now quarrel. Try to amuse yourself, and in the midst of the amusements let your heart be gripped suddenly by a vow, importunate and made before a cross, or STILL BETTER, before a woman you love, that on a definite date you will kill yourself.... On the day set, when you know that you can meet her without obstacles and can speak—from ecstasy your blood begins to pound in your veins. Then do what you have to do, either do it or speak. *We will not hinder you and will look after you.* If you make a mistake, we will be *very* amused, you will be *very* pitiful. Therefore it is better at once, don't beat around the bush....
> You will do everything if you wish (1) more quickly and (2) here, to experience something (1) new, (2) important, that is, if you have no patience and no faith in anything else.

Who are these "they," whispering insidious and mocking advice to Blok? From what dark worlds did the tempters spring, enticing the victim with the ecstasy of death, with the promise of a "new and important" experience? Something in their voices reminds one of Ivan Karamazov's devil-sponger. But this entry contains more than mystical haziness. There is also youthful intoxication with the dream of suicide and the unbearable pain of unhappy love. Let us not forget that Blok was twenty-two.

In another entry a few days later he tries to express his experience of the "change of countenance" in a poetic myth. (*But I am afraid: you will change your countenance.* Poems of 1901):

> The earth once had a nearly omniscient Being....
> And the Young Being opened into a flower of strange and terrible splendor, for it wafted ineffable holiness; but its face reflected the world's evil. And so the smile of God and the smile of the Devil did battle in it. And the Earth, all in trepidation, cherished the offspring and secretly expected the Devil's victory—and desired it.

This lofty gnostic revelation was given to the clairvoyant poet: in the fallen world the World Soul is split; it contains heavenly sanctity and worldly evil. God and the Devil do battle for it. It is not the Divine Sophia, but only her earthly reflection, the "child of earth," a two-faced and equivocal being. This explains the lines:

> But I am afraid: You will change your countenance,
> And arouse insolent suspicion.
> Changing your usual features in the end.

On 26 March Blok's meeting with D. S. and Z. N. Merezhkovsky takes place. In the *Autobiography* he numbers making this acquaintance among the events which "particularly strongly influenced him."

Z. N. Gippius had heard about Blok before she met him. Olga Mikhailovna Solovyova had written to her:

> And don't you know anything about your just discovered Petersburg poet? He is a young student, of course nowhere published. But maybe you are by chance acquainted with him? His name is Blok. Borya (Bugaev) is so enraptured with his poems that he literally rolls on the floor. I really don't know what to say. I am copying a little for you. Write me what you think.

Blok comes to the Merezhkovskys to buy a ticket for Dmitri Sergeevich's lecture. Zinaida Nikolaevna recognizes in him the "just discovered" poet and introduces him to Merezhkovsky. In the summer a "mystical" correspondence between him and Gippius begins. From Gippius he gets Bely's article on Merezhkovsky's book *Tolstoy and Dostoevsky*[6] and is struck by his spiritual affinity with its author. He notes in the *Diary* (2 April): "And won't it be a sign of a certain 'end' if I begin a correspondence with Bugaev? I must think about this."

Z. N. Gippius draws a portrait of the Blok of 1902:

> He doesn't strike me as handsome. Over a thin and high forehead (everything in his face and in him is thin and high, although he is of medium height)—a thick cap of brown hair. Regular features, motionless, as calm as if made of wood or stone. A very interesting face. Few movements, and a voice to match: it too seems to me "thin," but at the same time it is low and as hollow as though it comes from a deep well. Blok pronounces every word slowly and with effort, as if tearing it from some kind of meditation.... There is something sweet in this student's whole appearance.... Yes, sweet, childlike—"not terrifying."

That is how Z. N. Gippius saw Blok: he seemed to her thin, motionless, torpid. Georgy Chulkov meets him two years later. Here is his impression:

> In Blok, in his face, there was something melodious, harmonious, and well-proportioned. A kind of magic violin indeed sang in him. There was something Germanic in his beauty.... Blok's gestures, barely perceptible, restrained, stern, rhythmic, were especially captivating.... But in his eyes, so bright and seemingly beautiful, there was something lifeless.

Both Gippius and Chulkov sensed the split in Blok. For Gippius, the "sweet and childlike" is united with the "wooden and stony"; for Chulkov, beauty and harmony are united with "lifeless" eyes. *New Path*'s (Novy Put') secretary, P. P. Pertsov, made Blok's acquaintance in the journal's editorial office:

> A tall, stately youth with wavy blond hair, with prominent, firm facial features and a strange touch of old age on his nonetheless handsome face. There was something remotely Byronic in him, although he struck no poses.... Bright, prominent eyes looked with assurance and wisdom.

Here too there is something "strange" on his "nonetheless" handsome face: Byronism and an appearance of old age. All three observers note the disharmony of Blok's face.

The Merezhkovskys introduce Blok to the circle of their searchings. A flood of new ideas bursts into his closed-in, "half asleep" life. The *Diary* reflects a certain confusion in the dreamer, faced with his new friends' "theories" and "syntheses":

> Am I really approaching the negation of art's purity, its inexorable transition into religion? I sensed this bent (only I couldn't formulate it, but Bugaev, D. Merezhkovsky, and Z. Gippius found it) long ago. *Excelsior!* (Merezhkovsky's apt word). God grant to contain it all....
>
> It will be very important for me to read Merezhkovsky on Tolstoy and Dostoevsky.

And, in a rough draft of a letter to Gippius, he objects politely to the Merezhkovskys' militant slogan: the synthesis of esthetics and ethics, of eros and love, of paganism and "old Christianity." He prefers another "synthesis"—apocalyptic—and gives a curious reason for his preference: this synthesis comes "against one's will" and perhaps means to do nothing. The Merezhkovskys' ideological fever and stormy religious community both attract and frighten his passive, contemplative nature—frighten more than attract.

In June the condition of his paralyzed grandfather, A. N. Beketov, took a sharp turn for the worse. His death was expected any day. This approach of death arouses a severe mystical alarm in the grandson. He notes in the *Diary*:

> 26 June, before night. It drizzled almost all day today. Horribly dark night. Already in the evening, at tea, horror nudged me—I remembered a Boblovo superstition. . . .
>
> Dida [grandfather] is very bad. I seem to sense his rapid end, especially today.
>
> The rustle of rain isn't always ordinary. There was a strange creaking under the floor. The dog is uneasy. There is something, there is something. Nothing is yet visible in the mirror, however, but someone was walking around the house.

He relates the content of the "Boblovo superstition" in a letter to Gippius:

> In one of the neighboring villages here there's a strange . . . superstition: "It [death] is rushing along the rye" (literally, and nothing more). It seems that this "it" has now disappeared for the time being. Here's a coincidence, some elusive dream, but one perceptibly linked with that Petersburg which "rises with the fog" (in Dostoevsky) and with your "invisible city, Kitezh":[7] they will all return *different* "on the last day."

And the poet is prepared to reconcile himself to his "personal end," since he believes that the transformation of the world will come, that the "dream of resurrection" will conquer death. "Then in mortal sleep," he continues, "this dream of resurrection must appear—'it, rushing along the rye,' just as the 'new city of Petersburg, descending from the sky' appears to Dostoevsky. . . . What is stamped on someone will be dreamed 'then.' "

On 1 July, in the seventy-seventh year of his life, Andrey Nikolaevich Beketov died in Shakhmatovo. He had been paralyzed for five years, and his death was not unexpected for the family. M. A. Beketova writes:

> Aleksandr Aleksandrovich placed him in the coffin with his own hands. His attitude toward death was always radiant. During the funeral rites he lit the candles by the coffin himself. His white shirt, embroidered in red along the lapel, his curly head, the concentrated expression of the large, reverential eyes in these days of the service for the deceased remained ineradicable in my memory.

In the poem *On Grandfather's Death* the poet relates that the family, gathered by the grandfather's bed at his death hour, saw out the window an old man, "with a brisk gait," "with vivacious eyes," walking away from them along the road. The last verse is full of joy:

> But it was sweet to watch the soul,
> And to see gaiety in its departure.
> Our hour came. To remember and to love,
> And to celebrate another home.

Lyubov Dmitrievna visited her Mendeleev relatives for a whole month. She returned to Boblovo on 21 July. We read in the *Diary*: "She looked good: as almost always—sullen; she barely speaks to me. What I should undertake now I don't yet know. It is quite possible that there will again be an outburst."

But he doesn't want this. He knows that this was a fall. He tries to convince himself that he doesn't need earthly love. He yearns for another love—selfless and submissive:

> I *don't* want embraces. Because embraces (sudden consent) are merely a momentary jolt. "*Habit*"—a fetid monster—follows.
>
> I *don't* want words. There have been and *will be* words; words are infinitely changeable, and one foresees no end to them. . . . There will be no more *fear*.
>
> There will be no more DISDAIN (in many forms). Is it true that I have given up EVERYTHING (that is, life's mysticism and contemplation) for one thing? *It is true*.
>
> I want super-words and super-embraces. I WANT WHAT WILL BE. . . . If someone wants something, it will happen. So it will be. What I want will be, but I don't know what it is, because I don't know what I want. And how could I know this *for the present*. . . .
>
> *What* I want will come true.

This is also an incantation, a struggle against the dark agitation of the blood, using the magic of suggestion. The dream of an unprecedented, impossible love evoked by the paradoxes of Solovyov's "The Meaning of Love." Ascetic eroticism called up to transform human relations and to bring the approach of the reign of the Spirit closer. In another *Diary* note the poet speaks of sex as an "overturned, disfigured heaven." Sex is a diabolical perversion of love. "Earth," he notes, "in the image of a universal prostitute, laughs at the gullible paganism which burns incense to her." Blok inherited the Platonic eros and ascetic disgust toward sex from Solovyov. For him, sensuality and passion are always demonic, beginning with the Stranger and ending with the prostitute Katya in *The Twelve*.

Blok sends Z. N. Gippius his poems. She praises them, but warns the young poet against excessive obscurity, and demands of him a "third, judicious stage"—"intelligibility in the name of the Unintelligible." Under the Merezhkovskys' influence, Blok looks back at the path he has traversed; he wants to "leave the purely mystical path and to view it calmly from above." He writes to his father (5 August) about this turning point in his spiritual life: "Abandoning the excessive fantasy of my recent mysticism, I keep dreaming about the sharp (but is it sudden?) turn in the road which must lead out of the 'darkness' . . . into 'God's light.' But, on second view, this light can turn out to be an even more metaphysical, an even 'more terrible,' darkness." Important admissions about himself follow: his realism always borders on the fantastic; it is always harder and more painful for him to "experience" than to contemplate. At the end of the letter he boldly calls himself an "apocalyptic," sometimes "hoping for the resurrection of the dead and the life of the world to come." This premonition of a "turning point" didn't deceive the poet: the period of the poems on the Beautiful Lady was coming to an end. The "mystical path," fantastic and obscure, was traversed. Gippius was not mistaken: it is impossible to abide forever in the enchanted world of dreams, visions, sorcery. More life, more air are needed. But where to go? And is he capable of leaving? In a state of depression he writes (16 August) to Zinaida Nikolaevna:

> I didn't answer you immediately because for several days in a row I felt horribly despondent.... All of life is slow, there is little of it, little counterweight to extreme mysticism. And it draws after it an "invincible inner shallowing." I very much appreciated these words of yours.

But Gippius would have been surprised had she known that her "lunar friend" (as she called Blok) responded to her calls to life with a passionate will for death. He wants to die, not out of weariness or despair, but because the burden of his "impossible" love for Her is simply beyond his strength. This isn't weakness at all; on the contrary, it has the greatest exertion of energy, striving to be resolved in a "higher action," in an ecstasy of self-destruction. "Man can destroy himself," Blok notes in the *Diary*. "This is his highest possibility (power).... Consequently, the *summus passus* will be from this state, that is, from life. And there is no way out but death." Mocking imps had enticed the poet to suicide before; now another, more terrible, phantom convinces him of this—the shadow of Kirilov in *The Possessed*. Suicide as the highest affirmation of personality and its will to life— Blok undergoes the same temptation as Dostoevsky's hero.

And suddenly, after these gloomy reflections, two rough drafts of letters to Lyubov Dmitrievna, probably not sent. The sudden change is striking; we seem to descend from the icy ether to the warm earth. We see not a mystic, not an esoteric, but again a youth in love, an open human heart. Blok remembers the past winter, when he would wait for Lyubov Dmitrievna on Gagarinskaya, near the house where the dramatic classes of Chitau were located, and accompany her along the Petersburg streets. These letters are equal in worth to the poet's poems:

> Do you remember those days, those twilights? I would wait for an hour, two, three. Sometimes you weren't there at all. But, my God, if you were! Then this wretched, vulgar, stingy entrance door, so dear to me, would suddenly clang and bang, slamming. Light ran down from the dim yellow lamp. Your figure, your lines, so long familiar in every detail, studied, observed with love, would appear. You were probably wearing a not quite fashionable coat of black fur, not very new; a little cap; under it a huge, heavy, golden bundle of hair lay on the collar, sinking into the fur. Pink, flushed cheeks were set off by the same black fur. You held your dress with long, curved fingers in a black glove—woolen or kid. You held a muff in the other hand, and it swung as you moved. You walked fast, swaying a little, bending a little to the right and to the left, looking ahead,

sometimes smiling. . . . (All this is dear to me.) So tall and "stately," frosty. Now and then, in severe frost, your hair was hidden in a white woolen kerchief. When I would catch up with you, you would turn around with an unusually familiar movement of your shoulders and neck, would always look unfriendly, reticent, sober at first. Your hand would barely touch mine (and in general your hand always hurried to tear itself away). When I walked up to you, you would approach slowly. Sometimes you didn't move at all. I would get confused, speak horrible stupidities (perhaps banalities), be despondent. Suddenly my heart would be overrun by a kind of suffocating wave, . . . and suddenly, awfully rarely—but it did happen!—a subtle word, a slight whisper, a tiny movement, perhaps a fleeting tremor—or it's better to think that all this was only my imagination. After this again even more vague, even more motionless.

You always said good-bye very coldly, as you had greeted me . . . . I wrote down, as something so important, the like of which had happened rarely in the past, I can even say simply, in my whole life nothing of the kind had happened—and will it happen? Always questions, anxious and half-malicious questions. When will this end, Lord?

At the beginning of September Blok returns to Petersburg and in the train records in his *Notebook*: "The summer just ended was nearly fruitless. Hopes remained vague, small, meager. The opposite of hope is also implied. It is taken into consideration."

From 2 September there is a short note "for memory": "A large military revolver costs twenty-six rubles. Buy a small pocket gun (how much?). Lock it up with these notebooks, and the rough drafts of poems, and her letters and portraits, etc."

In Petersburg a fit of disorderly conduct comes upon him: he roams the streets and tears off notices from the walls. He notes:

> Today, Friday, 13 September, I behaved very badly (as if I will soon really be *kaput*—mental derangement: *quem Deus vult perdere prius dementat*). But I was under the windows. . . . I tore off a notice about a fire at house No. 32 and about the actress Mde. Chitau on the Gagarinskaya Embankment. Had already torn one almost off at No. 19, but a policeman, cabman, yardman were standing there. People were walking. And the doorman wasn't dozing either. He was probably suspicious of me. Another time.

This state of quiet mental derangement really bordered on insanity. And he makes a decision—to commit suicide. He writes to Z. N. Gippius (14 September) that his soul is again on fire, that this time he—even he—will achieve something. "It is time to arouse the new and ineffable, which I have been trying to achieve for a long time and unsuccessfully." Such a vague cover conceals the thought of suicide. And, hinting at his street exploits (tearing off the placards), he adds: "In the meantime, I am thinning out my condensed, lightning-filled atmosphere with a cruel harlequinade."

The decision taken greatly intensifies his spiritual power, gives him inhuman courage: to reveal the whole truth to Lyubov Dmitrievna, to explain to her the "complex state of their relationship." Only on the point of death can such confessions be made. Here is that improbable letter:

> I am getting right down to business. I met you four years ago in circumstances which usually make one fall in love. This latter fact happened quickly then. I will pass over that time in silence, because it is too distant. . . . Now the state of affairs has changed to such an extent that I must disturb you with this document, not simply due to love, which one can always keep to oneself, but due to extreme necessity. The thing is, I am firmly convinced that a mysterious and almost incomprehensible bond exists between you and me. . . . By way of explanation I will note at the outset that so-called life (among people) has interest for me only where it touches you. . . . From this it quite definitely follows that I have been trying to approach you somehow for a long time (even to be your slave, perhaps; forgive the banalities which not unintentionally dot this letter). It goes without saying that this is impertinent and in essence even unattainable. But my long and deep faith in you (as in the earthly incarnation of the notorious Immaculate Virgin or the Eternal Feminine, if you like) excuses me. Another excuse (if an excuse is needed) is nonetheless a certain reserve (but you know that it was sometimes broken by trifles). Thus, having faith, I want intimacy—on whatever basis you like. But, on closer examination, the intimacy proves unattainable, first, for the simple reason that you are too opposed to it (of course I don't murmur and don't dare to murmur), and, further, because it is impossible to invent a form appropriate for this very, I announce to you, complex relationship. . . . Thus, more and more losing hope, I am *at present* arriving at a decision.

There is no symbolic vagueness or ambiguity. It is said simply, with intentional "banality": for him she is the incarnation of the Eternal Feminine, and the forms for such a love relationship do not yet exist on earth. The rough draft remained unfinished, but we understand *what* decision he is arriving at. And yet, despite the finality of this decision, despite the impossibility of such a love and the beloved's sternness, a hope still flickers; the words "at present" give the poet away: "I am *at present* arriving at a decision."

But the letter is not sent, and the decision is set aside. A degree of soberness and calm sets in. At the end of September Blok spends two days at the Merezhkovskys' dacha near Luga. In a letter to his father he talks of walks in the forest, boat rides around the lake in the company of Zinaida Vengerova and A. V. Kartashev, a professor of the Theological Academy. The conversations—about the Antichrist and the "common cause"—were rather abstract. For the first time a critical note is heard in relation to the Merezhkovskys: "Zinaida Nikolaevna . . . plays with questions with a complexity peculiar to her "rebelliousness". . . . My impression of Merezhkovsky's doctrines themselves became even more clouded, and I am already completely unable to either affirm or deny anything." In conclusion he announces the forthcoming appearance in print of the journal *New Path*, the impending staging of Euripides' *The Hippolytus* in Merezhkovsky's translation, and the imminent beginning of the activity of the religious-philosophical society.

Blok feels himself an alien in the Merezhkovsky circle. This "inner absence" did not escape the perspicacious Zinaida Nikolaevna. She notes in her reminiscences: "It is impossible to communicate any of my conversations with Blok. To understand this, one must know Blok. While with you, he was always somewhere else." And, knowing nothing of the tragedy which her "lunar friend" was experiencing at this time, she guesses the main thing: "As time progressed, a twofold characteristic of Blok appeared clearer and clearer to me: his tragic nature first of all, and, secondly, a kind of vulnerability."

Blok's poems begin to attract attention: the assistant professor B. Nikolsky takes three poems for a student collection, the editors of *New Path* promise to publish a whole cycle of his poems, Briusov proposes publishing his poems in the miscellany *Northern Flowers*.

But both the literary successes and the friendship with the Merezhkovskys are an "illusory world" for the poet. The period of calm soon ends. In the *Diary* we find an entry for 12 October: "After I'm gone look over my books too. They are interesting; some have inscriptions. And there are good books. I will also request that a few be distributed, I will designate later to whom—and I will inscribe them. I will mark the list in these same pages." And on the same page:

> Filled with pure love,
> Faithful to the sweet dream,
> He inscribed LDM[8] on his shield
> In his own blood.

Finally, we find the last conversation with her written in the pages of the *Diary*. With all his being Blok has a premonition of an approaching "crisis." It actually comes a week later:

> It would terrify me to remain with you. Even more so for my whole life. As it is I sometimes am afraid and tremble in your invisible presence. I could be deprived of reason, or of life itself. This occurs more in the evenings and at night. Don't you really sense this somehow? I don't believe it, rather I think the opposite. Sometimes I feel the nearness of a complete and dizzying flight. This happens in the evening and at night—on the street. At such times my outward calm and valor have no limits, my persistence and obstinacy likewise. It has already been like this for a long time. And I tremble, tremble, more and more. Where is the crisis—near at hand or is there still a long way to go? But to remain with you, with you, with you.

The "crisis" comes on 7 November. Blok goes to a party at the Assembly of the Nobility, where he is supposed to meet Lyubov Dmitrievna. Before this he writes the following note:

My address: Petersburg Side, barracks of the Grenadier Guard regiment, apartment of Colonel Kublitsky, No. 13. 7 November 1902. City of Petersburg.

I ask that no one be blamed for my death. Its causes are entirely abstract and have nothing to do with "human" relationships. I believe in one holy catholic and apostolic church. I hope for the resurrection of the dead and the life of the world to come. Amen.

The poet Aleksandr Blok.

A decisive talk with Lyubov Dmitrievna took place at the party. In the middle of the next page of the diary, in short lines in the form of a column, he writes:

7 November 1902, city of Petersburg. Student party at the Assembly of the Nobility. Those of little faith will see God. Mother of Light! I glorify You!

The poet Aleksandr Blok.

Today, 7 November 1902 that occurred which has never yet happened, for which I have waited four years. Just as I am finishing this notebook, so too the notebook of my poems on this 7 November (the night of the 7th to the 8th).

I am enclosing the ticket and the letter[9] written before the party and I am finishing tonight both notebooks. Today is Thursday. Saturday at two o'clock in the afternoon. Kazan Cathedral. I first, in an amusing Russian style, proclaimed the virtues of Felitsa.

A. Blok.
City of Petersburg, 7–8 November 1902

The entries are completely insane. Triumph and rapture and mystical ecstasy and childish mischief, but chiefly happiness, flooding the soul, almost unbearable. With the event of 7 November an epoch in Blok's life ends, the epoch of *Verses on the Beautiful Lady*. The last poem of this cycle is dated 5 November. Two months later he proposed formally to Lyubov Dmitrievna.

The last months of 1902 pass in great excitement, in a "rapid succession of things," as Blok expresses it. The friendship with the Merezhkovskys continues; Dmitri Sergeevich reads him a chapter from his new novel *Peter and Alexis*. On the reception day of World of Art he meets "celebrities among the artists and men of letters"; in Moscow he is quoted with V. Solovyov. On reading Bely's *Symphony*, he senses in him a friend and writes to M. S. Solovyov: "Andrey Bely's heart blossoms in a really strange, almost creepy way. Strange that I have never met and never exchanged a word with this person so close and dear to me." A few weeks later a correspondence between the two poets begins. He finds another person close in spirit in the editor of *New Path*, Pyotr Petrovich Pertsov. Responding to the latter's enthusiastic praise of his poems, Blok writes:

What is especially and unutterably dear to me is the fact that I see with my own eyes a new votary of Her! And it is no longer so terrifying to stand at the altar, on the threshold of a menacing revelation, when you and Vladimir Solovyov stand in front. I can only speak (and even shriek) in someone else's great words, infinitely precious to me:

> I had long waited for the friends of these songs . . .
> Oh, how wonderful is my today.
>
> [Fet]

Her signs and promises were not false: She didn't deceive him. He writes with pride to his father that his "mysticism" had been justified: "I sense a need and I anticipate soon an inspired poem or even a prosaic excursus into the realm of mysticism which, in justifying itself by the course of my everyday 'exploits and deeds,' thereby justifies my 'vagabond dreams.'"

The *Verses on the Beautiful Lady* are Blok's poetic diary. Of the poems written in 1901 and 1902 he selected about half, arranged them in strictly chronological order, and divided them into six sections (I. Saint Petersburg. Spring, 1901; II. Shakhmatovo. Summer and fall, 1901; III. St. Petersburg. Fall and winter, 1901; etc.). The poet admitted that "technically the book is very weak" and called it the "poor child of my youth." But he loved his imperfect youthful poems and returned to them continually in his last years: he reworked them, corrected them, printed them in journals, put together new collections, one of which, *Beyond the Border of Past Days*, appeared the year before his death (in 1920). According to V. Pyast's testimony, the dying Blok told his mother: "You know what? I wrote only *a first volume*. All the rest is trivia."

In notes to *Verses on the Beautiful Lady* the poet wrote in 1911:

> This book . . . was written in solitude; here the rural predominates over the urban. All the attention is directed to the signs which nature gave generously to those who listened to her in faith. . . .
> The fourth chapter (1901) is most important: . . . it illuminates for the first time the vague searching of the three introductory chapters; it is that "magic prism" through which I made out for the first time, even though "unclearly," the entire "free distance of the novel."

M. A. Beketova informs us that in the last years of his life Blok intended to publish a book, *Verses on the Beautiful Lady*, on the model of Dante's *Vita Nuova*. Each poem was to be preceded by commentaries of the type: "Today I met my donna and wrote this poem." We find traces of such a project in a draft of the foreword to an intended new edition of the first book in 1918. The poet writes that, reworking his youthful poems again and again, he got lost in the forest of his own past. Then it occurred to him to make use of the device which Dante chose when writing *The New Life*. The rough draft ends with the solemn words: "Asking the help and quiet counsel of the One about Whom this book is written, I want to succeed in writing it in words so simple that they would help others to understand its singularly necessary content. 1918.

Day of the Assumption of the Virgin Mother." That same August, in 1918, Blok begins his "Dantesque" commentaries in the *Diary*. They consist of biographical notes (from spring 1897 to winter 1901) and annotations to thirty-nine poems of 1901. The plan of a detailed mystical interpretation turned out to be too complicated, and the author didn't return to it again. Nevertheless, these extremely involved esoterica contain valuable confessions and mystical flights which allow us to penetrate the poet's secret life.

Blok writes about January 1901 that it

> began with self-absorbed solitude, with sorrow for the past, in which there were certain "testaments." (Till the end of January SHE isn't mentioned in the poems, there is only Her music.) . . .
> On 29 January, *in a song of the spring wind and the living past of better days, Her sonorous songs* were heard. . . .
> In this way everything is already blended in this spring (unusually early, evident in January: the *past* with the future, which is in the wind).

Her approach is in music, in the song's sounds, in the spring wind.

February is marked by the beginning of a battle "with hell" ("passionate haze"). In the poems of this month the poet sees "almost a portent of that hellish provocation with inner doubles which will later destroy me." She is revealed to the contemplator—and the most secret thing in Her is sadness. In this connection he notes: "In this idea, as I learned later, there proved to be a kinship with the idea of the captive World Soul, which V. Solovyov last cherished. I didn't know all this yet, but I sensed Plato. At the same time I myself was merely dumbfounded."

This admission throws light on the spiritual connection between V. Solovyov and Blok. The pupil was indebted to the teacher for the philosophical formulation of his experience, but not for the experience itself. The mystical life can't be studied, it contains the deepest and the unique essence of personality. But the philosopher's terminology is reflected in the poet's verse. He notes: "Daydreaming—V. Solovyov's term—is dual; dreams, also V. Solovyov's term, are also dual."

In March the meeting with Her finally takes place. "I met her here," he writes, "and her earthly image, in no way out of harmony with the unearthly, called out a *storm of exultation* in me." He writes further on, with greater exactness:

> Her image, appearing before me in those surroundings which I recognized as having a *not accidental* significance, probably called out in me not only prophetic exultation but also human love, which I perhaps displayed in every word or glance, evidently calling up a new manifestation of her severity.

In these surprising words Blok perhaps comes closest of all to Dante: the same blending of the heavenly with the earthly, the same completeness of the incarnation of the divine image in the earthly beloved, and the same simplicity in the unheard-of statement that "the earthly image is in no way out of harmony with the unearthly." The combination of religious worship with human love, the *mystical realism*, is in equal measure characteristic of both the singer of Beatrice and the knight of the Beautiful Lady.

Meeting a nine-year-old girl on the street in Florence, Dante, in the sonnets of *Vita Nuova*, spoke of the "storm of exultation" and of human love just as simply as did the Russian poet of the twentieth century.

In April troubled sounds burst into the music of exultation:

> The sunset shimmers with phantoms, forcing *tears and fire and song*, but someone whispers that I, changed, will someday return to the same field—*lifeless, altered by the evil laws of time, with a random song* (that is, as a poet and a man, but not as a prophet and possessor of a mystery).

The Blok of 1918, author of the commentaries, sees a prophecy of his terrible coming fate in the hints of the youthful poems: he is fated to be changed from a prophet into an artist, to exchange the radiant visage for a "work of art."

May begins with "gloomy forebodings." The poet departs into "cold lands," his wandering is endless; but the *sound* from the other shore of the darkening river seems to him to be her answer. "Thus, unprepared, split, I end the first period of my *earthly* life—Peterburgian. (Here there is not yet a capital Y, i.e., You)."

The commentary breaks off here. Blok didn't manage to finish his *Vita Nuova*.

The lexical fabric of *Verses on the Beautiful Lady* is not rich. The young poet doesn't depart from the circle of images and rhythms of Fet, Polonsky, and V. Solovyov. His nature lyrics continue the tradition of Platonizing poetry, searching for the infinite in the finite and looking behind the transparent reality of the "charmed there" (Zhukovsky's words). This dualism is reflected in all the features of his poetic form: the division of verses into two halves, the parallelism of images, the sound repetitions, the antitheses of word combinations. The poet separates sharply the "coarse rind of matter" from the "radiance of Divinity" (V. Solovyov's expression) concealed beneath it, contrasting them to one another, like light and darkness, warmth and cold, quietness and storm. His favorite words are night, shadows, darkness, frost. The sad earth is drowning in fog and haze, storm clouds move along the dark sky, a cold wind drives the clouds. These word symbols are repeated with cheerless monotony. But two words are the real leitmotifs in the music of fogs and snows: "twilight" and "shadows." The first occurs thirty-one times, the second, twenty-three times, and their persistent repetition acquires hypnotic power: reality is disembodied, colors fade, objects are changed into shadows, light and darkness merge into twilight. Thus the "rind of matter" thins completely so that rays of otherworldly light can spurt out from beneath it.

In contrast to apparent reality, genuine reality—mystical—is presented, using all the epithets for light. When She appears *streams of light* flood the sky; fiery *dawn* strews the earth with *roses;* the *clear day* rises; *morning* flames up in the blue; *dawn* glows above the forest; "the whole horizon is *aflame* and unbearably *clear*." Instead of a winter night, the radiance of spring; instead of misty haze, gold in the azure; instead of snowy blizzards, "ringing quiet." There are three colors for the "world's vanity": black, white, and gray—the black of night, the white of snow, and the gray of twilight. There are mystical colors for the "genuine" world: gold, blue, azure. The first "signs" the poet reads in nature relate to the symbolism of light: its struggle with darkness, its life in colors, shadings, and halftones. Blok's gaze is fixed on the sky, from which he awaits Her arrival. Glowing skies, daybreaks, sunsets, stars, and clouds speak to him of Her. He barely sees the earth on which he stands. When She is absent, the earth is lost in twilights. When She approaches, the fields, forest, and mountains are enveloped in rosy mist. In *Verses on the Beautiful Lady* we would look in vain for "pictures of nature" or "artistic descriptions." The poet doesn't describe, he merely outlines the contours in a pale, almost a dotted, line. But this landscape, so meager, so sparingly outlined, has a magical effect. It too is split, as is everything in these poems. The wilderness expanse of Shakhmatovo is contrasted to the peopled streets of Petersburg. But in both places the same phantomlike quality. Here are Shakhmatovo's surroundings, the place of the first "visions": forest, damp fields, wandering lights across the river—"above Your high mountain the jagged forest stretched." Beyond, there are mountains, a deserted valley, damp grain fields: "the water roars, the forest is black, the fields are silent"; "a distant plain all around, and crowds of charred stumps"; "sandy hillocks in the fields"; "stones over a grave"; "swamp fire"; "tangled grass"; "a cold wind batters the naked twigs."

These are all the "pictures of nature." These are all the gifts which the beggarly earth prepares for Her, its empress. An enigmatic poem of 1901 begins with the verse:

> Winter will pass—you will see
> My plains and marshes
> And you will say: "How much beauty!
> What lifeless somnolence!"

And the poet answers: I waited for You among these plains and marshes, "waited endlessly":

> And in my soul remained a gloomy trace
> Of this lifeless beauty.

The "gloomy trace" remained throughout his life. And in *Unexpected Joy* and *The Snow Mask* love for the "lifeless beauty" already overflows in a lyrical torrent.

Blok buried the "picturesquely beautiful" romantic landscape amid the plains and marshes of Shakhmatovo.

His "urban landscape" is no less phantomlike and fantastic. Petersburg is a pale apparition, a varicolored mirage; it is woven of mists and light and can disperse like smoke at any moment. "Sleepy, dim" streets, "yellow lights," the banks of the Neva, the distant rumble of the crowd, and the pealing of the bells—this is not a real city, merely its shining and ringing aura:

> The sleepy sketch of dim streets,
> The city, dimly lit,
> Looks into the rosy distance.

or:

> The door creaked. The hand began to tremble.
> I went out into the sleepy streets.
> There, in the sky, clouds wander,
> Lit up through the fog.

And through the fog—streaky spots of light:

> A row of lanterns running away . . .
> Yellow lights gleamed
> And electric candles.

But there were only premonitions and visions on the plains of Shakhmatovo: in Petersburg real meetings with the poet's future bride took place. He waited for her by the house on the Gagarinskaya Embankment and accompanied her along the evening streets. Amid the phantoms and shadows this house was the only living thing in the lifeless city. All its peculiarities were engraved on his memory like mysterious signs of fate:

> The door awning whitened in the twilight
> Under the sign "Flowers," bolted down.
> There the rumble of footsteps disappeared and was lost
> On the staircase in the yellow lamp light.

Further are noted: a window curtained with an immovable blind, a cornice like a frowning forehead, a staircase over the gloomy yard, a door opening, its glass ringing.

All these "realistic" details are extremely important to him, since they are part of Her earthly incarnation.

At the center of *Verses on the Beautiful Lady* stands the image of a mysterious Virgin descending to earth and revealing herself to the faith and love of the poet-prophet. In creating this mystery play Blok uses the symbolic images and philosophical terminology of V. Solov-

The "Beautiful Lady"

yov. Sometimes he practically repeats his teacher's words. For example, we read in Solovyov:

> And the former world in unfading radiance
> Arises again before the sensitive soul.

and in Blok:

> The soul, as before, is all illuminated
> With the unfading radiance of past days.

But Solovyov is more a philosopher than a poet: his Eternal Friend is more Wisdom than Love; his poems are chilled by theosophical meditation and inseparably connected with the schema of a philosophical system. Not so in Blok: he brings to his reverence for the Eternal Feminine the youthful passion, daring, impatience, depression, and the demands of one in love. The *Verses on the Beautiful Lady* are full of such agitation, such agonizing tension that one becomes frightened for the author. This is no longer love, but a "holy frenzy," almost a flagellant rite. All emotions fuse into one desire: "I am waiting for you," "I sense your coming," "Come!" Everything is blended here: an appeal, command, inquiry, incantation, the trembling of faith, rapture, and despair, prayer and fortune-telling. This imperious "I am waiting!" rings throughout the poem: "I am waiting for the beautiful Angel." "Should I wait for the sudden meeting or not?" "I am only waiting for a prearranged vision." "I am awaiting a call, I seek an answer." "I wait in enthralling agitation." "I am illuminated and await your footsteps." "I wait there, in the flicker of a red icon-lamp, for the Beautiful Lady." She is inscrutable, inaccessible; She calls from the fog, beckons from the other shore, diffuses into the azure. And he struggles with loneliness and despair, does battle with doubles, and invokes, invokes: She must come! She is already coming! She is here! "I know you are here, you are near." "You will come to my cell." "I know you will come again in the evening." "Longed-for friend, will you ascend to my porch?" "She will surely come." "You will respond to my love." "I will overtake you in the tower chamber." Sometimes—so rarely!—she responds with words of love: "I have descended; I will be with you till morning." "Come, I will calm you." But is this her voice? Isn't it an echo of his frenzied appeals?

The unique lyrical melody which we link with Blok's name is born out of the agitation of love: a broad and melancholy melody, "piercing sounds," uneven breathing. The emotional power of *Verses on the Beautiful Lady* is enhanced by their concealed dialogue form. She is always with him; he is always turned to her. "Thou" resounds in more than half the poems. The second person pronoun, capitalized, combines reverence (we address God as Thou) and the intimacy of love (Thou is a friend, relative, beloved). Direct, personal address is Blok's constant poetic device. He doesn't speak, he converses: he asks questions, exclaims, seeks sympathy, asks advice.

The paradoxicality of the structure of *Verses on the Beautiful Lady* lies in the fact that the *mystery of the Epiphany* stands at the center of this "novel in verse" (Blok's expression). As does V. Solovyov, Blok believes that history is ended, that the Kingdom of the Spirit and the transformation of the world is imminent. He solemnly professes his faith in a poem with an epigraph from the Apocalypse, "And the spirit and the Bride say: Come":

The "Beautiful Lady"

> I believe in the Sun of the Testament,
> I see dawns in the distance.
> I await the universal light.
> From the spring earth . . .
> . . . . .
> I pass forests
> Of sacred lilies.
> The heavens above me
> Are filled with angels' wings.

But Blok is a maximalist. The premonitions of the Russian apocalyptics of the beginning of the century become reality for him. The transformation has *already* come, heaven has *already* bent down to earth, the Eternal Divine Wisdom is *already* descending to the world. The inspired words of V. Solovyov can serve as an epigraph to his poems of this period:

> Know, the Eternal Feminine now
> Is coming to earth in an incorruptible body.

For Blok this is not prophecy about the future but a statement about the present, not "will come" but "is coming"—now, this minute.

In these verses the poet testifies to the *theophany* occurring in the world. At first he only sees signs of her approach: her "ringing songs" are heard in the distance, "her swan song." Then her features are barely visible in the "scarlet twilight." In lights and dawns she "closes the last circles." But the fog disperses, the bottomless azure opens, the sun rises, and:

> Imperturbable, You trod
> The dark steps and, Quiet, You surfaced . . .
> . . . . .
> And, Serene, You flowed with the sun.

She is "strong in azure," herself a goddess, "is proud of her beauty equal to the gods," and "flourished in the azure." The whole universe is reflected in her, the divine prototype of the world:

> Seas, fields, and mountains, and forest
> Are limitlessly blue before You;
> Birds call to one another in the free height.
> The fog rises, the heavens redden.

Aleksandr Blok   Everything earthly is subject to Her, the empress:

> I and the world—snows, streams,
> Sun, songs, stars, birds,
> Rows of vague thoughts—
> All are subject, all are Yours.

She sparkles in the blue like an "unattainable star," shines like a diamond over the high mountain; like a fairy-tale princess she has "the sun, moon, and stars in her hair." What earthly names can one call Her, the Unearthly? The poet at first timidly unites lyrical epithets with the indefinite sign "She": Imperturbable, Quiet, Serene, Melodious, Distant, Bright, Tender, Holy. Then, in a barely audible whisper, he surrounds Her inexpressible essence with words. "Daughter of the blissful land," "spirit filled with immortality," "your mysterious genius"—how indecisive and shy are these pale appellations! Finally, the Name appears for the first time:

> Appear to me without anger
> Mysterious Sunset Virgin,
> And unite with fire tomorrow and yesterday.

And only in February 1902 is Her real face revealed: She is the *Sovereign of the universe*. This month marks the height of the poet's mystical ascent: he is already in Favor, in the light of the Transfiguration. His words ring with unprecedented daring:

> All visions are so momentary—
> Will I believe them?
> But I, accidental, poor, temporal,
> Am perhaps loved
> By the Sovereign of the universe,
> By inexpressible beauty.

Fateful words, they contain the tragedy of Blok's life. To fathom the depth of his terrible fall "afterwards," one must remember the radiant heights to which he rose "at first." Otherwise the fate of the "fallen angel" would remain incomprehensible to us.

The name is uttered, and Her Mystery is revealed in a rainbow of holy appellations: "Virgin, Dawn, Bush," "You, eternal love," "You are crowned," "Virgin-Protectress," "Majestic Eternal Spouse"—only once in the book is She called the Beautiful Lady:

> I enter dark temples,
> Perform a humble rite.
> There I wait for the Beautiful Lady
> In the glimmer of red icon-lamps.

Thus the poet relates the greatest event of his life in lyrical poems.

The genuineness of this testimony is indisputable: his whole life and art prove it. Blok's "experience" should be appreciated in all its significance. It places him in a line with Jacob Boehme, Swedenborg, Saint-Martin, Vladimir Solovyov. He is a seer by the Spirit.

But not disembodied spirit. This event of his spiritual life is reflected in its whole spiritual-corporeal nature. And if spirituality is not purified and is not brightened by religious feats and by ascesis, the premature illumination by the Spirit can call forth terrible outbursts, can beget destructive storms. The depths of the unconscious will reflect in its bosom a light like the fire of passions; the lower instincts will gush to the surface; the soul's dark forces will send out their doubles. It was as if Blok were foreordained to this split: he is not only a prophet, but also a man in love, and his reverence for the "Majestic Eternal Spouse" on the spiritual plane intersected his love for his fiancee on the emotional plane. A clash of these two enormous forces was inevitable. Such shocks cleave man's integral being.

Olga Mikhailovna Solovyova, Bely relates, was quite alarmed by the 1901 poem *I sense Your coming*. It contains the line: "But I am afraid: You will change your countenance."

She could have found still more alarming confessions in Blok's first book. A 1902 poem, *I am a trembling creature*, ends with the following lines:

> You don't know what goals
> You conceal in the depths of Your Roses,
> What angels have flown down,
> Who has become calm at the threshold . . .
> In You hide in expectation
> Great light and evil darkness—
> The clue to all knowledge
> And the delirium of a great mind.

In whom is this "evil darkness?" Is it in the Divine Wisdom, in the Sovereign of the Universe? How could such blasphemy burst into hymns and prayers? Or has his premonition already come true—has She "changed her countenance"? No, the poet is not talking about *change*, but about *substitution*: another is growing up before her, is overshadowing her, taking on her features. And he knows this. In the poem *The day will come—and the great will be accomplished* we read:

> You are another, mute, faceless,
> You have hidden, you do witchcraft in silence.

The "faceless phantom" is contrasted to the "radiant visage." The Sovereign of the universe is a sorceress, an enchantress. The first shines in the azure, the second whirls in the snowstorm. He speaks of her again:

> You in a white blizzard, in a snowy moan,
> Again surface like an enchantress.

He calls her "an evil virgin," exclaims about her: "How deceitful you are and how white!" She whispers to him: "Not a friend, but an enemy." Under her inimical power his soul is exhausted. In the poem *I keep telling your fortune* the poet confesses:

> At times I look into your eyes
> And see a fateful flame.

The "transformation" of the image of the Beautiful Lady into the Stranger, the Snow Mask, Faina, etc., has become a banality in the literature on Blok. In 1918, in an unpublished preface to the first book, the poet protests against such a "false interpretation":

> To this day I sometimes encounter discussions about the "transformation" of the image of the Beautiful Lady into the images of my later books: the Stranger, the Snow Mask, Russia, etc. As if the transformation of one image into another is a simple and natural matter! And the chief thing: as if an essence possessing independent existence can be transformed into a phantom, an image, an idea, a dream!

The Beautiful Lady is the only genuine reality; all the rest—the sorceress, evil virgins, mute and faceless—are phantoms of the astral world. A ray of light, falling from the sky onto the surface of the "abyss," breaks up into innumerable reflections; phantoms, doubles, imposters rise to meet him from the dark bosom of chaos. The radiant visage is distorted in the mirror of passions and carnal desires. Love is soiled by lust, knowledge of God by demonism. The poet sees Her as two-faced because he himself is split. On the spiritual plane he is a devout and pure monk, living in a monastery, working in his cell and praying in the temple. An atmosphere of church rites surrounds him: "lofty cathedrals," "gloomy choirs," "the flicker of candles," "praying people," "the pealing of bells," "in the icon's light," "the pale wax of the candles." He awaits Her advent into the temple, and his soul is filled with visions of paradise: "the wings of the seraphim," "the white, white Angel of God," "the Angel with the sword of the Annunciation." On this plane the poet's language sounds stern and solemn, loaded with Church Slavonic words. But this plane is intersected by another—the emotional—and darkness rises against the appeal for light. The monk proves to be an imposter; in the blinding light from above he sees his own depth for the first time—and shudders. In his poem, *I love to visit lofty cathedrals, humbling my soul*, we read terrible confessions:

> I fear my two-faced soul
> And I carefully bury
> My wild and demonic image
> In this holy armor.

> In my superstitious prayer
> I seek protection in Christ,
> But under the hypocritical mask
> Lying lips laugh.

He saw *this too*—not only the light of transfiguration, but also the demonic power. And he spoke of this with the same pitiless honesty.

The personality split, when the highest truth becomes a lie and prayer is broken by Satanic laughter, engenders the "white rows" of doubles:

> On a wild and gloomy night
> The son of the bottomless depth—
> The pale-faced phantom roams
> The fields of my land.

The poet addresses him in another poem:

> I know you, my two-faced confidant,
> My dear friend, inimical to the end.

The most terrible thing in the double is the *absence of a face*: it contains a threat of the disintegration of personality, of complete non-being. The poet talks about this last secret in a terrifying poem of 1902:

> But on the last day, in an unfathomable hour,
> Breaking every law,
> He will get up, the lawless phantom,
> Reflected in the mirror's smooth surface.
>
> And in that hour the likeness of a face
> Will enter the empty passageway,
> And the shadowless mirror
> Will reflect the Newcomer's image.

The theme of death already sounds in these lines: *The Steps of the Commander*, and the theme of *The Puppet Show* is already presented in *Verses on the Beautiful Lady*. In the poem *He appeared at the stately ball* the last two verses are a harlequinade:

> He rose and lifted his owlish gaze
> And looks—fixedly—alone,
> Where, behind pale Columbine,
> The ringing Harlequin was running.
>
> And there—in the corner—under the icons,
> In a motley rumpled crowd,
> Rolling his childlike eyes,
> The deceived Pierrot trembles.

Aleksandr Blok

In *Verses on the Beautiful Lady* all the paths of Blok's later poetic wanderings begin, the seeds of his whole future flowering are sown. In this book the "great light and evil darkness" are the apex of mystical ascent and dizziness above the abyss. In this tragic split is found the inexhaustible lyrical theme of the Eternal Feminine and the *Terrible World*.

In the first days of January 1903 the correspondence between Blok and Bely begins. Bely writes Blok a flowery "philosophical" letter. It crosses Blok's letter in the mail. Thus their letters and their life paths symbolically intersect. Blok criticizes Bely's article "The Form of Art." He finds duality in it: the word "music" is used by the author both in its ordinary meaning and in the meaning of "music of the spheres," a symbol of the One of whom V. Solovyov sang.

The letter struck Bely: it had mystical depth, a brilliant dialectic, polemical ardor, humor. He had to defend and justify himself in his reply. But sad events broke off the correspondence.

Mikhail Sergeevich Solovyov suffered from an enlarged heart; in January he fell ill with pneumonia. On the night of his death, suffering a nervous disorder, Olga Mikhailovna shot herself. Bely spent this tragic night in their apartment, made the funeral arrangements, and sent the orphaned Seryozha off to Kiev, where the family of Prince E. N. Trubetskoy took him in hand. The Solovyov circle collapsed. This was a terrible blow to the many friends of the deceased. Blok learned of Solovyov's death from Z. N. Gippius' letter: he went to his mother, knelt before her, and silently embraced her.

Bely received some sympathetic, tender lines from him, and the correspondence between them was resumed. Its theme was the new revelation of Sophia the Divine Wisdom in our recent times. Bely asks: how is one to understand Her? Blok answers: abstract speculation doesn't interest him; he knows one path—the mystical; one must receive Her into one's heart by faith. She reveals herself only to the individual, not to the masses; the radiance of Her face transforms all objects. He sees Her as the World Soul, the Soul of humanity, but feels powerless to communicate this revelation to people. He therefore doesn't preach, but finds expression in intimate lyrical poems. For poets She is the Muse: Dante, Goethe, Baudelaire, Fet knew Her.

But in our eschatological time a revolution of the spirit is approaching. In earlier times the Divine Wisdom was beyond our consciousness, now She is entering it, is becoming immanent. She is uniting with man, is making a New Covenant with him, is introducing him to the Kingdom of the Spirit.

Bely asks: what do Her changes of countenance mean? How can there be in Her a "great light and evil darkness"? Blok indignantly rejects any "transformation" of Her visage. She is unchanging and motionless, She is at peace. Where movement and change begin, substitution occurs. Another, dark, earthly (Blok calls her Astarte), is trying to replace Her. Lunar mists, in which Her face is broken up and distorted, rise to meet Her from earth.

Retelling the content of Blok's letters from memory, Bely announces:

> I emphasize Blok's face at that time, concealed from everyone—the face of a profound mystic. *This* Blok is not known; while so much in Blok's muse sounds different without a knowledge of Blok . . . Blok's letters are a manifestation of rare culture, and someday these letters will be the fourth book of his poems . . . Blok is a completely concrete philosopher, groping for a musical theme for culture.

Blok's poems were printed for the first time in the March edition of *New Path*. The author gave the title *From the Dedications* to this cycle of ten poems. The poems were sent to the censor without capital letters ("You"), but the *"majuscules"* were later restored. That same spring Blok's poems appeared in the *Literary Artistic Collection* of the students of Petersburg University and in the anthology *Northern Flowers*. Here they are called *Verses on the Beautiful Lady* for the first time. The poet notes in his *Autobiography*: "I consider this the year of my literary baptism." The newspaper *Banner (Znamya)* responded to Blok's first appearance with the following note: "Poems of the poet A. Blok, exhumed from somewhere (it's at least good that it isn't Heinrich Blok[10]), mere verbiage, offensive both to common sense and to the printed word . . . *New Path* should be sent to an old lunatic asylum."

Spring passes in serene concentration and joyful intensity. Blok is preparing for his examinations. "I'm writing few poems," he informs his father, "and not very good ones, somehow transitional. I am probably sensing a transition from mystical confusion to mystical clarity." This thirst for clarity, for life, for simple human joy explains his cooling toward the Petersburg and Moscow "mystics." In the summer his mother's heart disease becomes acute, and Blok accompanies her to Bad Nauheim for treatment. His marriage to Lyubov Dmitrievna is set for 17 August; he parts with his fiancée for six weeks. Before going abroad he sends Sergey Solovyov and Andrey Bely invitations to be best men[11] of the bride.

Blok's letters of this time speak of an important work occurring within him; he seems to be looking back at his past, reevaluating, "defining himself." And this new "maturity" is expressed first of all in his cooling toward the Merezhkovskys. His gradual departure from them had already begun at the end of the preceding year. In the *Diary* entry for 13 December 1902 we find an unusually penetrating and merciless evaluation of Merezhkovsky. Blok notes:

> The life drama of man (angels who haven't forgotten their leader, but have left their abode) and of the public figure (the half-awakened universal consciousness). Failure in life (one must stand in a draft), in art

(late, and not enough), in religion ("sooner, sooner, Zina, soon?" "In a few years." "A long time yet. I have an eternal split in my new novel. . . . If only someone would spit in my direction. . . . I have a great sadness. . . . Priests, the *Hippolytus*,[12] the journal[13] . . . it doesn't matter: Zina, you shout so, one can hear it through all the doors!"). There is not, and will not be, a last scream; all the screams are the penultimate ones. I have said everything, the time to shout came, I got a cold, lost my voice. I went to Simanovsky for treatment—returned, afraid of the frost. . . .

Knowing this, he gives a *rational* way out. He says: "Come to her, Lord!" as if saying: "Zina, isn't there any milk?" The lantern blinked and went out—till the next blinking. The mouth laughs, the eyes are silent (it is always thus). Boredom of blinking. It blinked at us constantly. We "are used to it": the certain, unbearable word, terrible for him. . . . The marsh is passable and safer than our quagmires.

Cruel and unjust words, but that is exactly how the rational, split Merezhkovsky must have seemed to the mystic Blok. He derisively tells Sergey Solovyov how Merezhkovsky, setting out for the Aleksandr Nevsky Monastery, fell into a hitherto unfamiliar hatchway, broke the glass, and hurt himself quite seriously. Z. N. Gippius sees symbolism in this and reproaches the professors of the Ecclesiastical Academy. Blok concludes:

Merezhkovsky's significance is quickly exhausted—at precisely the moment when many of us will clearly see that it is time to "be lost in contemplation" of something else. . . . One cannot howl so about things which demand that the voice be lowered. . . . Again I find it difficult to decide if there is love in him: he is often "nice." For now he is generally so complicated that in the future he will prove simple.

Blok believed that mystical experiences are very intimate and personal, that it is impossible to convey them to the collective, that they can only be hinted about in lyrical poems. Therefore "religious community" and "the mysticism of the circles" were profoundly inimical to him. From Bad Nauheim he writes his father that he had grown cold to *New Path*; that Z. N. Gippius and her friends were not sympathetic to his marriage and find in it a "disharmony" with the poems:

I find this rather strange, since it is difficult to catch the completely abstract theories which the Merezhkovskys introduce absolutely into life, even to the point of denying the reality of two inalterable facts: the wedding and the poems (as if either of them were not real!). The chief reproach expressed to me is that I do not seem "to sense the end" that clearly ensues (in their opinion) from my life circumstances. In simplified form the Merezhkovskys' reproach comes down to the following exclamation: "How can you marry, when tomorrow the world ends?"

In the middle of July Blok and his mother return to Shakhmatovo from abroad. He writes his father about the troubles connected with the wedding: about difficulties with the priest, with the birth certificate, with the university authorities. At the end of the letter he reports: "Now I go often (almost every day) to Boblovo on horseback. I feel cheerful and strong. I am reading and writing very little."

The *Notebook* has two summer entries. The first is: "I degenerated from the Blok family. Delicate. A romantic. But such a clown." And the second is: " 'Prohibition' should remain even in marriage. 'The Young Girl of the Pink Wicket-gate' . . . . The untouched eternal Virgin of the Rainbow Gate." This gnostic name for the Eternal Feminine speaks not about a bridegroom's love, but about a knight's service.

Blok's spiritual maturity is expressed with special clarity in his correspondence with Sergey Solovyov. After the tragic death of his parents, the sixteen-year-old Seryozha went through an acute mystical period. His second cousin's "clarity" and "sobriety" seemed to him a cooling toward Solovyov's legacy. Blok writes him often, solicitously and tenderly, but insists on his own retreat from battle positions; he is faithful to the past, but is no longer a warrior, only a silent spectator:

> Early morning has passed. The day is approaching, my eyes have widened, the same *daimonion* keeps singing inwardly, and I have a need, of long standing and deeply rooted, *to be silent for a time*. It will hardly ever be given to me to have my say. And I look on and stubbornly want (not by my own, but by a higher, will) to look on from the side. I am not fully armed. And I am condemned to examine the "bluish haze," not daring to throw down the gauntlet, like Andrey Bely. But I won't forget anything and will not be tempted by anything and would like, when he and later you are wounded by an enemy, for both of you to come and drink tea with me.

For Seryozha, dreaming of the creation of a "Solovyov sect," such evasiveness and flippancy on Blok's part were incomprehensible and offensive.

M. A. Beketova recalls the wedding of Aleksandr Aleksandrovich and Lyubov Dmitrievna with unflagging tenderness. Sergey Solovyov was the bride's best man; the second best man, Andrey Bely, was unable to attend because of his father's death. The marriage ceremony took place in an old church of Catherine's time in the village of Tarakanovo. The bride arrived on a troika with her father and sister. Dmitri Ivanovich Mendeleev led her solemnly into the church. On the heads of the newlyweds were placed crowns not of gold but of antique silver, in accord with the ancient custom. After the wedding everyone went to Boblovo. The peasants brought bread and salt, the old nurse showered them with hops. The newlyweds didn't stay till the end of the wedding feast; they hurried to the train and left for Petersburg.

In the fall Sergey Solovyov tells Bely that Blok's wedding was a *mystery play*. There was a special atmosphere, prayerful and mysterious, and a radiance in the air that day. And all the participants felt this. Soon after the wedding the bride's best man, the Polish Catholic Count Rozvadovsky left for Poland and took monastic vows; he had made a knightly, mystical cult of Blok's bride. And Solovyov repeats ecstatically that both the bride and groom understood their responsibility: they were entering new paths, were dedicating themselves to the service of the One who had united them:

> But in me is a secret knowledge
> Of endless love for You.

And both knew: for such a feat "unearthly powers are needed."

In the Petersburg apartment of Blok's stepfather two rooms, completely separate with windows on the embankment, had been prepared for the young couple with the Beketovs' old furniture, the grandfather's sofa, a bookcase, and an Oriental rug on the floor. Blok writes his mother short, practical letters about the layout of the apartment, about purchases, a servant, financial difficulties, gifts, visits. Happiness shines through all these domestic trifles: "The apartment is amazingly nice. L. [Lyuba] likes it all very much." "Everything is fine (knock wood)." "Today we celebrated Lyuba's birthday in a field outside Petersburg (in Novaya Derevnya); we ate rolls, sweet pies, and apples under a haystack in the field." "We were in the botanical garden at a sale and bought lots of flowers exceptionally cheaply." "Our rooms are also very beautiful in the evenings from the window. Each room has two large icons and also small ones. We bought icon-lamps and light them."

In September Lyubov Dmitrievna again takes up her studies in the drama courses. Aleksandr Aleksandrovich attends lectures at the university: he specializes in Russian literature with Professor Shlyapkin, writes papers and "ponders" his candidate's essay. *New Path* finds scant room for his short reviews. He writes his father: "*New Path* is not too gracious to me, nor I to it." He is more frank with his mother: "I feel utterly and finally that *New Path* is rubbish. Bugaev agrees completely."

After Blok's wedding Sergey Solovyov becomes a friend of Count Rozvadovsky; Aleksandr Aleksandrovich is very pleased. He writes his mother:

> I am terribly glad about Seryozha's friendship with Rozvadovsky.
> ... He is to the highest degree encouragingly practical. ... He *will bring* to the blood of our priestly Germanic mysticism a *large measure* of Polish political-religious stock and a measure of religious liberalism. That is important for synthesis(!!!).

The ironic tone and the "synthesis" with three exclamation marks speak of the poet's unswerving departure from the recent past.

In November, for the first time after the wedding, Blok sets out for the Merezhkovskys. "I was at the Merezhkovskys," he writes Sergey Solovyov. "He was nice and gentle. She was unusually dry. In her view I do nothing but decline. First of all, I married, and, what is more, I am now participating in *Griffin (Grif)*.[14] Z. N. Gippius recalls this visit of Blok's:

> Yes, he was there, for the first time after his wedding. He seemed to me absolutely the same, not changed one iota. A bit gentler, but perhaps we were simply overjoyed to see one another.
> "Isn't it true that, speaking of Her, you never think, *cannot* think, about any real woman?"
> He even lowered his eyes, as if ashamed that I could ask such questions. "Well, of course, no, never." On parting: "You don't want to introduce me to your wife?" "No, I don't. It's not at all necessary."

It isn't difficult to imagine how Blok must have inwardly shrunk from such intimate questions!

Gippius and Blok—what dissimilar, what antithetical souls they were! His inarticulateness annoyed her; she complains about his "stingy, heavy, hollow words"; her "verbal frivolity" horrifies him. "Maturity didn't come to Blok," she writes, "he remained, despite rare depth, beyond the pale of 'responsibility.' Nonetheless, he felt the weight of each human word, trembled when holy names were taken in vain in his presence, and bent beneath the weight of the responsibility he had taken on himself." He bore his "secret knowledge" under the visor of a "poor knight"; she discussed the "sacred" with the lack of constraint of a woman of the world. The sense of "obligation" is the theme of Blok's correspondence with Sergey Solovyov. In a November letter:

> All the changes of life, mine personally, yours, ours, both those and others, etc., etc., have all bound me in a white shroud, *have obligated me to something*. Everything that has happened cut off my path of retreat to life's childhood.... And this is fine, and for the best.

But Gippius reiterated: "Blok is a pensive child; he will never attain maturity."

The appearance of Briusov's book of poems *Urbi et Orbi* was a major event in Blok's literary life. Its daring struck him, as did the virtuosity of its poetic technique; it opened new countries hitherto unconquered by poetry. For a long time he could not free himself from the fascination, almost hypnosis, of this influential and weighty book. He writes to Solovyov:

> I am barely extricating myself from the weight of his poems. Briusov has been tormenting me roughly from the time you left.... Recently, reading his poems aloud is extremely difficult for me, due to throat spasms. About like reading Pushkin's "Arion" or "The Stormy Day Is Spent."...
> However, it must be assumed that I myself will soon write poems which will prove to be duplicates of Briusov.

It is difficult for us now to understand the enigma of Briusov's powerful, almost magical, impact on his contemporaries. A comparison of his poems with Pushkin's "Arion" sounds almost like blasphemy to us. But in the perspective of the time Briusov really was a "great magician" of verse who revolutionized Russian poetics, enriched it by introducing new meters and rhythms, and expanded its boundaries almost infinitely. Blok writes a rapturous letter to the author of *Urbi et Orbi*:

> Deeply respected Valery Yakovlevich!
> I read *Urbi et Orbi* every evening. Since this moment is one such evening, I, despite all my *reserve*, simply cannot be silent.
> What more will you do after this? Nothing? I have a heap of poems in my head, but *yours I never imagined possible*. I don't know whether anyone understands what is known *to you*, or whether it will *soon* be understood. Despite all the excesses of this letter, I can only now be silent!

In *Urbi et Orbi* the poet found a poem dedicated to the "juniors" with the epigraph: "I wait there for A. Blok's Beautiful Lady." In the poem Briusov confesses with touching frankness that he would very much like to penetrate the chamber where the "juniors" are feasting with the Beautiful Lady, but he is powerless to do so. Here is the first verse:

> They see Her. They hear Her.
> The bride and bridegroom in a lit-up palace!
> The lamps sway the quiet flame,
> And the reflections flash joyfully in the crown.

And the last verse:

> There, there, behind the doors—wedding rejoicing.
> In the lit-up palace the groom is with his bride!
> I would smash iron bolts, I would tear them off,
> But my fingers are helpless, and my voice is silent.

The "great magician" was jealous and quick to take offense. The luxuriant, triumphant, shameless carnality of *Urbi et Orbi* must have struck the incorporeal singer of the Beautiful Lady. Blok heard the sounds of the world, the melody of the World Soul; Briusov saw the flesh of the earth, its plastic movement, form, color. Blok was a musician, Briusov a painter and sculptor. Briusov's inability to "soar" into the azure angered him. Blok, worn out by varicolored fogs, craved to be "incarnated." But most importantly, Briusov revealed to Blok the dark poetry of the modern city. And this theme entered Blok's lyric forever.

By the end of 1903 it had become clear to Blok that an unprecedented flourishing of Russian poetry was approaching. The publishing houses Scorpion and Griffin put out book after book. The poems of Sologub, Briusov, Z. Gippius appear. Blok writes his father:

> During that period my chief "impressions" were concentrated on literature's present, and I personally, without reservations, can discern in it

the threads of a real Renaissance. . . . The Petersburg positivists have now had willy-nilly to take this into account. The new art grows in breadth. Burenin[15] will apparently have to end his earthly career with foam in his mouth.

Blok's charming poetic letter to Solovyov is imbued with this mood of an approaching Russian Renaissance: poetry will return to the romance of the Middle Ages; poets will again become knights and troubadors; instead of "sighing weariness," real life will come:

> Soon the Middle Ages for poetry will come. Poets will be beautiful and proud, they will return to the most fascinating source of pure poetry, they will string all the pearls of the sea bottom and the city into necklaces for the young girls of every country. Such a rebirth of poetry seems to me possible that all the old genres, from folk to court, from factory song to serenade, will be resurrected. But at the same time there will be repeated a nomadic life, with arms in hand and ready to hand, stilettos under velvet cloaks, the whole life of the page or troubador or crusader or duenna or "lady of the heart," of everyone together and in complete individuality— *for their whole life.* This as a reaction to the position of theology on the one hand and of sighing weariness on the other. . . . What about us, desiring life? I personally want, descending from the astrological tower, then to leave the pink bush and to descend into a ditch, without fail into moonlit blue grass. . . . It will be difficult with my "waxen demons," but I will try nevertheless.

His dreamy, mystical youth is over: that is now merely an "astrological tower" and "theology." It is time to descend to the ditch, to the grass, it is time to begin life!

We recognize something familiar in this letter: is this not the voice of the knight Bertran by the tower in the drama *The Rose and the Cross*?

Blok frequented Assistant Professor B. Nikolsky's literary circle, which met in a large auditorium—the *jeu de paume* of Petersburg University. They met at a long table lit by several green lamps. The poets Blok, Kondratiev, Leonid Semyonov, and others recited. Blok had enemies and admirers. One student proposed reading an essay "On Music in the Poetry of Blok and Balmont"; another was preparing a report against the "decadents." One of the circle's participants recalls: "I heard Blok and understood nothing, but was immediately and forever, like everyone else, captivated by the inner music of Blok's reading. . . . Whoever heard Blok could not possibly listen to someone else reading his poems." The poet Sergey Gorodetsky writes of his meetings with Blok at the university: "He wore a neat student's frock coat, always buttoned. The collar was bright blue (the fashion was for dark). His hair curled like a nimbus around his Appollonian forehead, and he was all clean, bright, I would say solitary."

The cycle *Verses on the Beautiful Lady* ends on the significant date 7

Aleksandr Blok

November 1902: on this day Lyubov Dmitrievna Mendeleeva became Blok's bride. The poems of the end of 1902 and of 1903 are perhaps the brightest and most joyful of all the poet's lyrics.[16]

A poem of 8 November is imbued with religious ecstasy. At last She came to the faithful sentry, and his prayer to Her rings with a triumphant Hosanna:

> I guarded them in John's temple,
> An unmoving sentry—I guarded the icon-lights.
>
> And here She is, and to Her my Hosanna—
> The crown of my labors—beyond all reward.
>
> I hid my face, and years passed.
> I spent many years in Her service.
>
> And the evening ray lit the firmament;
> She gave me a Regal Reply.

A poem preserved in the poet's rough-draft notebooks (7–8 November 1902) is even more ecstatic. It begins with exclamations:

> Hosanna! You enter the tower chamber!
> You are a voice, you are the Glory of the Empress!
> We sing, we wail and believe,
> But the purple robes weigh us down.

This is that state of bliss where words lose their meaning, where man's whole being is shaken, where he "sings and wails," rejoicing, blessing, and praying. Another poem expresses a superstitious fear of the unexpected realization of hopes, of the infinite:

> What I will tell you, I don't know.
> Maybe I will die of happiness.
> But, burning with evening fire,
> I will draw you to the bonfire too.

Infinite love tears the human heart asunder; there is no room for it in this world; joy itself becomes pain and, confronted by beauty, tenderness is consumed by tears:

> What I loved in your swanlike beauty
> Is eternally beautiful, but the heart is unhappy.
>
> I do not conceal that I cry, worshipping.

And the last verse:

> Again the sky frowned, and the weather will be bad;
> There is no place for the loving heart to escape pain.
> Just as the end of happiness is terrible to the happy,
> So the free fear captivity.

Divine Love descends to the world; and he—"the ruler of earthly beauty," in whose heart the mystery is accomplished—knows that "life has no solution," that the union of heaven and earth is a task beyond the power of human wisdom:

> And, powerful, I count as before,
> I practice witchcraft and tell fortunes again;
> How with passionate life will I, a wise tsar,
> Unite You, Love?

The well-known poem on the tsarina and the tsarevna is constructed on this comparison of human wisdom with the grace of the Spirit. The tsarina "searches for meaning," reads the Book of the Dove, which contains the "blue riddles," the "gold and red headpieces." But white birds, cooing doves, fly to the tsarevna. And the wise tsarina bows before the tsarevna's "dovelike meekness":

> You are strong, tsarina, in depth,
> In your book the pages are gilded.
> But the Bride, with innocence alone,
> Will pray, tsarina, away your numbers.

The poet renounces his "spiritual authority," sorcery, fortune-telling, he believes that the Bride, by her meekness and wisdom, will solve all of life's riddles.

The parable of the tsarina and tsarevna is characteristic of the serene emotional state of the poet during this happy period. The past seems "arrogance" to him—he wants purity and humility:

> An end to all-knowing pride.
> Falling out of love with the past twilight,
> Forever devoted to the Sacred,
> I will obey You in everything.
>
> Winter will pass—in the singing blizzard
> It already rings from afar.
> The regal arcs closed up,
> The soul is blissful, You are near.

Several days before the wedding the poet talks about knightly fidelity and the vow of service. He knows that not happiness, but a difficult feat, lies before him:

> We stand on the right path,
> Not for the first time have we avoided captivity.
> Lead me. To pass through everything
> We need unearthly powers.
>   (11 August 1903)

But humbly entrusting his life to her, he doesn't absolve himself of the terrible responsibility for her fate. He is a knight and a bridegroom, mystically betrothed to her. He speaks of his duty in the solemn language of the Apocalypse:

> I am a sword honed on both edges;
> I rule, Archangel, Her Fate.
> A green stone burns in my shield,
> Lit not by me, by the Lord's hand.

They are united in a secret love. Let silence guard this secret from people:

> I won't go out to meet people,
> I fear abuse and praise.
> To You Alone will I answer
> For being silent all my life.

And the last verse:

> I will come out to a holiday of silence,
> They won't notice my face.
> But in me is the hidden knowledge
> Of endless love for You.

In the poem *She was fifteen* the poet tells the "tale of his love in few and simple words: the first childhood meeting, the talk at the ball, the meeting in church. And the infrequent conversations, and the long separations, and the years of silence—everything had a secret meaning: "what happened, happened in the heights." And the poet ends:

> With this tale of long, blissful searching
> My sultry, singing breast is full.
> I constructed a building of these songs,
> But other songs—I will sing someday.

The childlike purity and frenzied chastity of the poems of this time, addressed to the Bride, are striking. Earthly love and passion never burst into the prayerful contemplation of the Beloved. Blok's notebooks preserve a poem, *My enchanted evening is long*, containing the verse:

> Someone's eyes look at me
> Motionlessly and long through the trees.
> Everything in the heart is childishly innocent
> And doesn't need passionate rewards.

But there was passion—the *Diary* testifies to this. The "childlike innocence" was attained through struggles, through the victory of spirit over flesh. The poet didn't include one of the 1903 poems in the section *Crossroads*: it appeared only in the 1920 collection *Beyond the Border of Past Days*. It casts unexpected light into the depths of his "Platonic" generation. Here are a few lines from it:

> Dead of night places a slow cover,
> Winter puts out the lamps with raging snow.
>   . . . . .
> Alone I wait, I wait, I wait for you, for you.
> Your profile, figure, and laughter by the black walls.
>
> And I live, live, live on my doubt about you.
> Come, come, come—my soul is weary.
>   . . . . .
> Alone I wait, I wait for you, for you alone.
>   (18 April 1903)

The poems of the end of 1902 and of 1903, dedicated to his fiancée and then to his young wife, are a solemn epilogue to the cycle *Verses on the Beautiful Lady*. That is why, publishing the first volume of a collection of his poems in 1911, the author placed them directly after this cycle, collecting them in the section entitled *Crossroads*. If the line "I sense Your coming. The years pass" can be taken as an epigraph to *Verses on the Beautiful Lady*, then the line "And here She is, and to Her my Hosanna" fits the section *Crossroads*. But in *Crossroads*, alongside the poems, symbolic in the highest sense, to his bride, there are also others which bear the stamp of affected decadence. They are connected with the theme of "doubles," which invaded the melody of *Verses on the Beautiful Lady* with a disturbing whisper. In *Crossroads* this theme is developed in short lyric tales, darkly allegorical and deliberately obscure. They remind one of a record of delirium, of nightmares. Their alogical structure and disconnected images are enveloped in horror. A. Bely would have said that "little horrors" are concealed in them.

Here a black person runs around the city, extinguishing lanterns, clambering on ladders, and then weeping in the dawn. Here some people shout and screech at round tables. Suddenly someone enters and says: "Here is my bride." And then one who "staggered and roared with laughter" presses himself to the table and weeps. Here an old woman tells fortunes by the entrance—and suddenly fire envelops the house:

> On the abandoned place of the fortune-telling
> Someone got up and unfurled a flag.

Here doubles in Harlequin costume hang about the bazaar: one a youth, the other an old man, but they "plodded along, embraced"—and Columbine from her blue window never recognizes the beloved.

In these "decadent" poems sound the first notes of that romantic irony with which Blok was afflicted at the time of writing *The Puppet Show*.

Aleksandr Blok

At the end of 1903 new poetic forms appear in Blok's lyric. The paths of *Verses on the Beautiful Lady* were traversed to the end. The poet felt himself at a "Crossroads": he was trying to break the magic circle of his youthful poetry. Enthralled by Briusov's book *Urbi et Orbi*, he imitates his images and rhythms. A new theme arises in his poems: the city, the factory, workers, urban poverty, gypsies, the puppetshow booth.

Here is *The Factory*:

> In the neighboring house the windows are yellow.
> In the evenings—in the evenings
> The pensive bolts creak,
> People come up to the gates.

Here is an urban event: a woman makes the sign of the cross over her children, leaves the house, and lies down under a train:

> Mama is not in pain, rosy children,
> Mama lay on the rails herself.
> To the good person, the fat neighbor lady,
> Thank you, thank you. Mama couldn't . . .
>
> Mama is fine. Mama died.

And, finally, the gypsies:

> They brought the show-booth to the smoking city,
> Pretty gypsy girls and drunken gypsy men.
>
> And they strewed jokes, screeched from the carts,
> And beside them someone dragged along with a bag.

However timid Blok's first steps in the direction of "artistic realism," he is nonetheless in Briusov's debt for broadening his poetic world. His transition from *Verses on the Beautiful Lady* to the collection *Unexpected Joy* is achieved under the sign of the author of *Urbi et Orbi*.

CHAPTER III
WAR AND REVOLUTION
1904–1905

On 10 January 1904 Blok and his wife went to Moscow. They took up residence on Spiridonovka, in a small empty apartment with faded brown wallpaper and old furniture belonging to a distant relative, A. M. Markonet. Vladimir Fyodorovich Markonet, history teacher, longtime resident of Moscow, habitué of the Club of the Nobility, a good-natured eccentric amused by the decadents, lived in the same house. But he took a sudden liking to "Sasha" Blok; he would come to visit every morning and would even praise his poems. He later spoke with tenderness about him to Bely:[1]

> And Sasha Blok is a genuine, an excellent poet. . . . We would go out in the street, he would come to a point, like a dog. He would remark on the weather and at once raise his head and notice everything: what color the sky was, what the dawn was like, and what tints the clouds had. And he would notice shadows—spring or winter shadows. . . . One doesn't have to read him, it's at once obvious that he is a poet.

Blok's letters and diaries are filled with meteorological notes. He was acutely sensitive to the weather. Even in the dry summary of events which he sent to his mother during his stay in Moscow, one finds entries about the color of the sky, about sunrises and sunsets, and about the wind. For example: "We're sitting with Bugaev and Petrovsky beneath the whistling of the wind." "I leave Bugaev's house. Behind my back a red dawn reflected on the cupolas. It flows joyfully from the roofs." "The cupolas of the central cathedral (in Novodevichy Monastery), gold in the deep blue azure through the poplar branches." "Strange half-sky—lilac. Green star, horned moon."

Azure, dawns, green stars, lilac sunsets, wind—this is not at all the "poetic setting" of Blok's lyric, not even a "spiritual landscape": this flows through his veins with his blood, is inhaled into his lungs with the air, is a part of his physiology.

On the day of their arrival Blok and Lyubov Dmitrievna set out to make Bely's acquaintance. The friends' meeting, four years in preparation, finally took place. Bely was struck by Blok's appearance, which was not at all as he had imagined the author of *Verses on the Beautiful Lady*. In his imagination dwelt an image of a visionary with a pale, sickly face, thin clenched lips, a phosphorescent gaze continually fixed on the distance, hair thrown back. The "real" Blok was different: a tall stately youth resembling the "fine young stalwart" of a fairy tale. His face had a healthy, evenly weathered, pinkish color; his movements were restrained; he had correctness, even "good breeding." Blok was dressed in an excellently tailored student frock coat with a drawn-in waist and a high collar. Bely was confused and a bit disappointed. Is this young man, a Peterburger and a member of the gentry of *quite good* tone, really the author of mystical letters, the singer of the Eternal Feminine? Embarrassed, the host hastened to fuss over his guests. Blok noticed and also became confused. Both dawdled in embarrassment in the entrance hall. Then Bely introduced the Bloks to his mother, Aleksandra Dmitrievna. The four sat together in the living room and were awkwardly silent. Bely recalled the clear frosty day, the sun's pink rays and Blok's curly head, bent to the side, the bewildered blue eyes, and the forced frozen smile. Lyubov Dmitrievna, calm and at ease, was also silent. Finally they began to talk about Moscow, about Scorpion, about Briusov, about the weather. They smiled at the "formal" tone of the conversation—and Bely at once launched into a very complicated analysis of this "tone." Blok listened with a kind, shy smile; his large, fine blue eyes looked attentive; they displayed keen observation, trust, and severity. Even on this first contact the friends sensed how close they were to one another, and how far apart. Blok was restrained, reserved, taciturn; Bely was expansive, bustling, a fidget and chatterbox—he gushed torrents of words, brilliant improvisations, arguments, theories. In him dwelt not only a Moscow Hegelian of the forties, but also a Repetilov.[2] Blok was prepared to answer "final questions" decisively and boldly, but he had an aversion to "prefaces." Irresponsible verbiage, roundabout approaches, abstract methods frightened him, causing almost physical pain. Bely sums up: "I appeared more intelligent, more nervous, weaker, more democratic, more absent minded; A. A. appeared more intellectual, healthier, more attentive."[3]

But the main difference did not lie in the fact that Bely was sanguine and Blok melancholic; it was in the very depths of their personalities. Blok defined it in one insightful phrase. "Do you know, Borya," he once said to Bely, "you are a prodigal, and I am a carouser." This meant that Bely squanders his spiritual wealth in words; Blok is capable of surrendering himself completely. Bely notes: "In Blok was concealed an unknown Lermontov, a Pestel,[4] ready for anything. My ideas, extreme, probably concealed a careful minimalist and gradualist, groping for the road. . . . I didn't proceed to a firm yes or no. A. A. did."

For Blok too the meeting with Bely was a surprise, almost a disappointment. For a moment he doubted him, feared that the spiritual, the sacred, which he valued in him, would drown in his chaotic emotional state. He says in a short note in a letter to his mother: "Bugaev (not at all as he had seemed)."

But the mutual attraction overcame the force of repulsion. From the first meeting they came to love one another, and this love became fate for both. Their paths drew together, parted, crossed again. They caused each other much suffering, but in the main this love-hate determined their lives—both personal and literary.

In Moscow the style of relationship which was maintained until the final break was already created. Bely felt Blok to be *older*, he impressed him with his *quiet strength*: "It radiated in the silence of a healthy, outwardly beautiful, appearance. Of course A. A. was handsome (very, very) at that time; I would say he was radiant." This was not the mystical radiance of the knight of the Beautiful Lady, but "a kind of light and rosy warmth, physiological and vital." Bely insightfully compares Blok to a quiet pond whose bottom conceals a large, rarely-surfacing fish. The surface is smooth, without ripples or sheen—but the world is reflected in its mirror, and now and then heavy waves of its depths rise from the bottom.

Bely concludes his surprising analysis of his first impression of Blok with an important admission: "Blok is the crucial hour of my life, a variation on the theme of fate. He is both unexpected joy and—sorrow. All this sounded in the first meeting; it arose between us."

For the outside observer the hidden likeness of the two friends was overshadowed by their sharp external difference. Z. N. Gippius, insightful and acute, sees only the *contrast* between Blok and Bely. Let us compare her deposition with the testimony of the author of *Reminiscences of Blok*:

> It is difficult to imagine two beings more opposite than Borya Bugaev and Blok. If it was difficult to call Borya anything but Borya, it wouldn't enter your head to call Blok Sasha. The serious, particularly motionless Blok and the always twisting, always dancing Borya. Blok's meager, weighty words and Borya's ceaselessly flowing, cascading speeches, with gestures, with eternally changing face, almost to the point of a grimace; now he smiles, now very amusingly and very nicely frowns and squints. . . . Blok is all firm, as if made of wood or stone. Borya is all soft, sweet, affectionate. Blok's hair is dark, luxuriant, but lies heavily. Borya's is lighter than down and yellowish as a barely hatched chick. . . . Blok—both friend and foe felt this—was unusually, exceptionally truthful. . . . Borya Bugaev was faithlessness personified. Such is his nature. . . . Both had purely childish sides, but different: from Blok a child, stubborn, frightened, alone in an unfamiliar place, looked out; in Borya dwelt a pet, a visionary, capricious, lawless, now naive, now affecting naiveté.

The portraits of the poets are brilliantly drawn; the likeness is caught. It is true that Z. N. Gippius somewhat exaggerated Blok's "stoniness" and Bely's "fluffiness" for the effect of contrast. The look of a "frightened child" is not characteristic of Blok, though he probably looked that way amid the God-seekers of the Merezhkovskys' salon.

The Bloks spent two whirlwind weeks in Moscow, visiting friends, dining with relatives, becoming acquainted with the Scorpion and Griffin writers, attending literary meetings, and viewing Moscow antiquities. At the center of this literary-social life stood everyday contact with "Borya" Bugaev and "Seryozha" Solovyov. Seryozha, Blok's relative and Bely's very close friend, set the tone of the relationship, united the friends in a kind of "mystical brotherhood." At the same time the seventeen-year-old theologian burned with the ideas of Solovyovian "Theocracy" and strove to realize them immediately in life. He had a project ready for the future theocratic organization of Russia, which he divided into communes run by councils of the initiated. At their head stood three spiritual leaders, corresponding to the Solovyovian triad—high priest, tsar and prophet. In himself Seryozha saw the high priest, the Petrine base; in Bely, the tsar, the Pauline base; and in Blok, the prophet, the Johannine base. Peter, Paul, and John made up the mystical brotherhood, united by the cult of Sophia, who would appear to the world. But the heavenly Wisdom must have its earthly embodiment, its living icon in the world, so to speak. Solovyov summoned Lyubov Dmitrievna to this high calling. If such a brotherhood is formed, a future revolution of the spirit will be prepared in it; tsarist power will collapse; Orthodoxy, Autocracy and Nationalism will be replaced by Theocracy, Sophia and the People. This utopia was an extreme inference from Solovyov's teaching. The philosopher's nephew invested it with youthful inspiration and sectarian dogmatism. And at the same time he protected it from criticism, surrounding it with comic jokes and parodies. In Seryozha the precociously developed theologian was very peacefully reconciled with the wit, the gymnasium student. His grotesques, monstrous caricatures, and loud improvisations amused the "initiates." He was much given to laughter, loud and expansive. In letters to his mother from Moscow Blok continually notes this duality of Seryozha, inherited from his uncle Vladimir Sergeevich:

> Seryozha retires, shouting, to a German exam.... Seryozha put on a Chekhov play on the Stanislavsky stage. (10 January).
> Seryozha's shouts woke me at noon. (11 January).
> Seryozha comes in the morning. The three of us go to the Novodevichy Monastery by horse-car. Seryozha shouts to the whole car, makes a row, talking about the recent resurrection of several dead people, about the fact that the Antichrist is advancing troops from Belgium. He spoke in Greek. Everyone looked at him in amazement.... We return, not without the previous scandals, to the city. (12 January).
> The four of us go to Sokolniky at the other end of Moscow, accompanied by Seryozha's gaiety and scandals in the horse-car.

Seryozha's disorderly conduct must have embarrassed the quiet Blok, but it didn't prevent him from seeing his "serious" and "sincere" side. Among the friends—Blok, Lyubov Dmitrievna, Bely and Seryozha—mysterious and important conversations take place. On 12 January Blok tells his mother about an evening spent at Solovyov's. After dinner with the family, the friends retreat to Seryozha's room. "The four of us lock ourselves in," Blok writes. "We drink altar wine, clink glasses. A meaningful conversation—weightily important and excellent. . . . We return home . . . we read poems. Night." The following entry is from 14 January: "I have just returned from Seryozha. Our conversation, the two of us, was unusually important, gratifying, bright and joyous. We talked a lot about Lyuba."

The conversations of the four together took place in a strange, tense atmosphere. Seryozha and Bely felt that this is "not accidental," that there is a "mystery" in the union of the four. And they tried to unravel the mystery, dreamed about the mystery play of human relationships. There was exaltation, but also inspiration. Bely recalls how, during one such "rite," he agitatedly suggested that they all "leave"—leave this dying world and go into the forests, into isolated monasteries. "Ah, how good it would be for all of us to go there together!" he exclaimed. And it seemed that a secret circle was developing, united by reverence for Her, who is already coming into the world.

How did Blok react to this incipient brotherhood? Did he believe in it? He both did and didn't believe. He tempered his friends' childish exaltation with good-natured humor. When Seryozha got entangled in the systems of his theocratic community, Blok would slowly turn to his wife and express his impression aloud: "You know, Lyuba, I think that Seryozha. . . . " And there was so much irresistable, gentle humor in these serious remarks that it was impossible not to laugh. When Bely, dancing around the room, would begin to "orate," Blok disarmed him with a simple inclination of his head and by opening wide his arms; he brilliantly parodied his way of singing poems. Thus the "elder" restrained the enthusiasm of the juniors. But he did believe in the "mystery," and he rejoiced that his reverence for the Beautiful Lady, whose "living icon" he found in the image of his beloved wife, was so ardently shared by the "brothers."

It is most difficult of all to discover the mental state of the woman who became the mystical symbol of this union. Did Lyubov Dmitrievna believe in her lofty calling? Did she feel rays of imperishable light on herself? Did she accept the reverence? She was silent. "No, I can't speak," she announced, "I listen." Bely writes about her:

> Lyubov Dmitrievna listened, cozily curled (feet and all) into a little ball in the corner of the sofa, in a bright purple housecoat, with a shawl over her shoulders, her golden head lying on her arm. She listened and her eyes shone. . . . Outside the window the snow looked pink. A ray of sunset lit her face, young, blooming. A pink sunbeam settled on her head. She smiled at us.

They saw in her an elder sister, and all three felt like knights of the fair-haired Lady.

This cult was a prologue to the drama of Blok's and Bely's life.

Of the new people whom they met in Moscow, Blok especially valued Grigory Alekseevich Rachinsky, a friend of the Solovyovs. A well-known collector and connoisseur of art, Rachinsky was distinguished for his enormous erudition, passionate love of poetry, knowledge of philosophy, inexhaustible curiosity and kindness. He presided at religious-philosophical meetings and argued, arms waving and spectacles gleaming, in the literary circles. He was a walking encyclopedia on the history of Christianity and a patron of the young symbolists. In his concise letters to his mother Blok remarks: "We enter the Rachinskys' apartment. Both the hosts and the apartment are striking. Grigory Alekseevich speaks to me about Balmont and Voloshin.[5] His wife's name day, Lopatin, guests, small artistically cozy rooms (by Iverskaya). . . . Rachinsky kisses Lyuba's hand (always)." (12 January). The second visit charmed the poet even more:

> We went to the Rachinskys for dinner. Everything was unusual. Grigory Alekseevich makes an exceptional impression, as does the whole setting of their home, the dinner, etc. After dinner I read them a mass of poems. Rachinsky said ecstatically that he hadn't expected that I am better than Briusov (but he can't endure Balmont). We left at twelve, after much conversation.

Another "big person" whose acquaintance Blok made in Moscow was Bishop Anthony, who was living in retirement at the Donskoy Monastery. A stern ascetic with a long white beard, having the gift of insight, he was greatly respected in intellectual circles. The Merezhkovskys went to see him, Bely and A. S. Petrovsky visited him; they brought the Bloks. The poet writes his mother:

> The fourteenth, Wednesday. Morning. Bugaev, Petrovsky, Sokolova and I go to the Donskoy Monastery to see Anthony. We sit with him, speak much and well. Lyuba finds it good, and I also, much of it. About Merezhkovsky and *New Path*. He promised to visit us in Petersburg. Handsome, sometimes formidable, thin, with burning eyes, but without "penetrating insight," with a tinge of irony. About the schema,[6] about marriage.

Blok and his wife went twice to the Novodevichy Monastery to pay their respects to the graves of relatives: the Solovyovs, Markonets, and Kovalenskys. On 16 January, after requiems, Sergey Solovyov, Bely and Blok had memorial services at the graves of Vladimir Sergeevich, Mikhail Sergeevich and Olga Mikhailovna Solovyov.

But the visits to Rachinsky, the trip to Bishop Anthony, the visits to Novodevichy Monastery, and the inspection of the Kremlin cathedrals were only episodes in the poet's Moscow life. Almost all of his time was devoted to getting to know the literary circles, joining with poets and symbolist writers. The day after his arrival he found himself at Bely's at a "Sunday" of the Argonaut circle. About twenty-five people assembled; admirers crowded around Bely. It was noisy, disorderly; chairs clattered, some people left, others arrived, there was a rumble of voices. Blok listened to the questions with ceremonial politeness and had no chance to answer them; a perplexed smile wandered on his face. Balmont read his poems in a haughty voice, defiantly and contemptuously. Thin, with a pale face, small ginger beard, and squinting, browless eyes behind a gold pince-nez, with a small, reddish nose, he read his lines nasally, breaking them off sharply with exclamatory intonations. Then Briusov read in a guttural voice, switching now to an eagle's scream, now to a dove's cooing. Bely wittily characterizes his manner: "V. Briusov in his reading serves well-baked lines on the table, like a dish in a magnificent setting: 'Help yourself!'" Blok writes his mother: "Briusov, in the ladies' absence, read two poems—"The White Horseman" and "Come by the familiar path." Even more important than *Urbi et Orbi*!" Blok read the poems *The Factory* and *Three Little Rays*. His reading at first disappointed Bely: "Blok read in a businesslike, subdued voice, a bit twangy, and he swallowed the word-endings. No raising or lowering of the voice, no differences at the pauses were felt: he stepped along the metric feet as if shackled in armor, heavy." Blok informs his mother:

> After Balmont, Briusov and Sokolova left, Andrey Bely and I read a mass of poems (after the second supper). Night. Andrey Bely is inimitable(!). I read *She rose in radiance*. A small group of people in black frock-coats exclaims, jumps up from the chairs, shouts that I am the foremost poet in Russia. We leave at three in the morning. Everyone thanks me, shakes my hand.

The Argonauts had loved Blok's verse for a long time. Now he became for them an Orpheus. Enthusiastic admirers of both sexes surrounded him; Moscow called the young poet its own. The attitude of the "maîtres" was more restrained. Briusov analyzed Blok's poems sternly and explained in detail to the author why one line was good, but another was no good at all. Balmont took an instant dislike to Blok. On 13 January A. A. went to the Scorpion publishing house. At that time the first volume of the new journal *Scales* (*Vesy*) had just appeared—Briusov, the editor, invited him to collaborate. In the editorial office decorated with a portrait of Nietzsche, Blok met the editor of Scorpion, Sergey Aleksandrovich Polyakov. Small, stooped, with a pale, old-appearing face, shy and bashful, he was extremely well educated, a polyglot and a mathematician, and unselfishly devoted to art. Beside Polyakov stood his inseparable friend, the gloomy Lithuanian poet, Yurgis Kazimirovich Baltrushaitis. A stern face, hewn from stone, gray eyes, and light hair—there was something of the northern Viking in him. His poems were about mountain heights, cliffs, Lithuanian fields and sky.

That same evening Blok is present at a reception in Griffin, another publishing house. The muddled, preposterous meeting of poets, mystics, theosophists, and decadent barristers makes a painful impression on him. He writes his mother:

> I read my poems—some people are ecstatic. Supper. Bell. The drunken Balmont enters. Sad, childish, red eyed. He talks to Lyuba and to me. Kobylinsky (Ellis) quarrels with him and leaves (very unpleasant scene). Balmont asks me to read. I read. Balmont is ecstatic, says "he no longer likes his own poems" . . . "You grew up in the country" and much more. He reads his poems, half-drunkenly but well.

Bely in his *Reminiscences* adds rather oppressive details to this account:

> At the meeting at Sokolov's M. Ertel was present—historian appointed to the university on graduation, occultist, Sanskritologist; the theosophists later considered him a "secret teacher"; he combined deep erudition and charlatanism. At some point, approaching a state of ecstasy, Ertel began to yell that all Moscow is enveloped in theurgy. Some theosophist proclaimed that the Initiated are already marching, and a mystically disposed barrister whispered: "Gentlemen, the table is shaking."

Bely adds: "Blok turned gray from suffering." Out of this pain the theme of *The Puppet Show* subsequently grew.

Bely is in despair. He is ashamed for the Muscovites, for himself. His dream of a new harmony of the collective, of the mystery play of human relationships, is overturned by banality and farce. And he undergoes a shameful defeat in his personal life. Blok guessed his distress. They left Sokolov's. A soft snow was falling. Blok took him by the arm, said tenderly: "I understand: all this is coarse; neither this nor that, what surrounds you." And it helped Bely, with his flayed skin. He felt that Blok was a "quiet, all-understanding brother." Later he received from him from Petersburg verses with the lines:

> I will embrace firmly the neck
> Of one who is silent from pain.

On 15 January Bely dragged Blok to a religious meeting of a university circle, where he read a paper, "Symbolism as *Weltanschauung*." Among the students interested in the "religious problem" he saw three young men whose names were later inscribed in the history of Russian religious thought. Vladimir Frantsevich Ern, in whose small room in the Church of the Savior the meetings took place, was retained in the philosophy department after graduation by Professor S. N. Trubetskoy. Tall and thin, with a mustacheless, effeminate face, he had a warrior's temperament and fought the western "philosophy of nonbeing" for the genuine reality of the spirit. In 1911 he published his well-known collection of articles, *The Battle for Logos*. V. A. [V. P.] Sventsitsky, with a red face, red beard and burning eyes, a mystic and revolutionary, tried to combine "the faith of the early Christian fathers with the protesting radicalism of Herzen." The most outstanding of the three was P. A. Florensky, then a student in the mathematics faculty, later a priest-professor and author of the famous book *The Pillar and Foundation of Truth*. Pale, emaciated, with a quiet, tired voice, he seemed fragile, limpid, sickly. But one sensed enormous spiritual strength, flashes of genius.

Bely's paper "Symbolism as *Weltanschauung*" evoked sharp arguments. Blok sat silent, awkward, lifeless—he felt himself a stranger. After the meeting he told Bely: "No, that's not the thing: there's something painful among all these people."

The poet had a premonition of the painful dramas which would subsequently be played out in the circle. From it was formed a strange religious-revolutionary "Brotherhood of Struggle," which distributed to the clergy and the military proclamations stamped with a black cross.

Finally, just before his departure, Blok was present at a meeting at Sergey Solovyov's, where the theosophist Pavel Nikolaevich Batyushkov read a paper.

A. A. and L. D. intended to leave on 22 January, but postponed their departure for two days in order to attend a performance of Chekhov's *Cherry Orchard* at the Art Theater. Blok writes his mother: "In general, we are tired." He thinks about the quiet Petersburg apartment with joy: "I want the holy, the quiet, and the white. I want books; I don't expect anything from the people in Petersburg but 'literary conversations' in the best case, and banal mockery or 'winking at something else' in the worst." His impression of Moscow is ambivalent. He valued and came to love much in it; much he rejected:

> There will be so much of the good in my memories of Moscow that I'll live on it for a long time. I know for sure that we are a thousand times right not seeing people in Petersburg; they are in Moscow. One can never lose sight of the existence of Moscow, of everything here that is the best and the purest.

But along with this is an aversion for the "mystical mob": he no longer wants to see the Petersburg student-mystics and adds that Lyubov Dmitrievna shares this. He was also not very fond of the Moscow "maîtres." He writes: "The drunken Balmont repelled me. Briusov's *personality* [underlined] I don't find very desirable either."

But in general the Moscow trip revitalized and heartened him. He made new friends and was acknowledged as one of the foremost poets of Russia.

Returning to Petersburg, the Bloks began to live an isolated, measured life. Aleksandr Aleksandrovich attended lectures at the university and was busy with the "Slavic essay" and the "Russian paper." Lyubov Dmitrievna attended the Bestuzhev courses. The poet didn't visit literary circles and made friends only with Evgeny Pavlovich

Ivanov, a beginning writer and critic, and with Z. N. Gippius' sister, the artist Tatyana Nikolaevna, who was doing the poet's portrait. The correspondence with Bely and Solovyov was practically broken off. In early spring (at the end of April) Blok and his wife moved to Shakhmatovo. His letters to his mother from the country are matter-of-fact, cheerful, buoyant. From a refined Petersburg poet-symbolist, he ecstatically transforms himself into a practical landowner, a thrifty proprietor. He writes in detail about clearing the garden, tree felling, sinking a well, the kitchen garden, and the cattleyard. He reports that a sow gave birth to sixteen rosy piglets; another sow and a hog "with intelligent and calm facial expression are in a separate dormitory." This "naturalism" calms him very much after his transcendental wanderings. He returned to earth with tenderness, mowed grass, felled trees, dug ditches. Blok loved physical work—he had strong muscles and a true eye. "Work is the same everywhere," he announced, "whether setting up a stove or writing poems." Before his examinations in April, S. Solovyov came to Shakhmatovo. He exposed the Merezhkovskys' religious heresy with fury and trampled Gippius' portrait in the first volume of *Scales*. "Several times," Blok writes, "we tried to persuade him to list the definitive arguments against the Merezhkovskys, but he spit in disgust just for the time being." A slight rift in the relations of the "brothers" was felt; the conversations were "rather confused, nothing unified." Seryozha's fanatical storms evidently tired Blok. He adds: "Besides that, I wanted to rest here and to become healthy, since my nerves were severely unsettled." In May Seryozha came for twenty-four hours, was gay and as usual roared with laughter. Blok sought his advice on a very embarrassing matter: in the middle of May Anna Nikolaevna Schmidt was to visit Shakhmatovo. She had long and persistently tried to obtain a meeting with the poet. Blok begs Seryozha to come with her; he refuses. He asks his mother to move up her arrival:

> Anna Nikolaevna considers herself the incarnation of the World Soul, longing for God. Fortunately, she already knows from Seryozha that my poems are not addressed to her. In any case, the situation is embarrassing, and I will have to have a conversation with her in private, and then together.... Better come on the tenth. She is a very talkative woman.

Blok's meeting with the "World Soul" did occur. Lyubov Dmitrievna was present. Aleksandr Aleksandrovich maintained an embarrassed silence. A. Schmidt understood that he didn't acknowledge her as Sophia and didn't appear again.

In Shakhmatovo the Bloks settled down in a separate annex consisting of four small rooms with a covered balcony. After his mother's arrival (in the middle of May) they began to arrange their new quarters. M. A. Beketova sensitively describes their gay fussing about. Blok's mother gave Lyubov Dmitrievna the grandfather's trunk, which contained varicolored scraps of material, paper fans, and many other treasures. The Bloks furnished their little house cozily. They had a tiny living room with a green sofa, book shelves, and a large table. Fans, red paper fish, and little pictures hung on the walls. Then they began setting up the garden. They decorated the lawn with rosebushes; along the fence they dug out a ditch for trees, built a seat of turf, and along its sides planted two elms brought from Boblovo. M. A. Beketova delighted in the young couple; their life reminded her of a Russian fairy tale:

> The golden-curled fairy-tale tsarevich demolished trees, planted sacred flowers in the tower-chamber garden. And the tsarevna came out of the tower-chamber and sat in the sun to dry her hair: not exactly Melisanda, not exactly a beauty from the fairy tales of Perrault.... Here she sorts over beads and strings them—so tall, stately, in a sarafan or a pink dress, with a white kerchief over her black brows.

The touching "Aunt Manya" would have so liked for her pet "Sashura"'s life to become an enchanted fairy-tale. But the spring and summer of 1904 were not at all an idyll for Blok. He saw that the spiritual atmosphere of the world was darkening: the "radiance" was departing, and the dawns being extinguished. In the spring the war with Japan began—the first thunderclap of impending catastrophe. The world was entering a new, *tragic* epoch. The poet perceives the change visually: before it was azure, rose, gold; now purple and violet gush out. He wrote:

The purple west oppresses,
Like a leaden handshake . . .
   . . . . .
No one knows the end,
And confusion replaces gaiety.

And a poem dedicated to Bely has the line: "I understood that it will be dark."

Something new was growing in him, and he wanted to believe it was for the better, that it should be so. In the spring he writes to S. Solovyov:

> I feel that something important to me is occurring here, and right after our mystical meetings in Moscow. In any case I can word it (as carefully as possible) this way: something in me is breaking off, and something new, in the positive sense, is coming, and this is *desirable* to me as never before.

The change in "lighting" is reflected in the poems. Themes and rhythms change; instead of the former harmony, dissonances grind. He continues in a letter to Seryozha:

> I am writing long poems, . . . indecent, which, however, I like more

than the previous ones and which seem stronger. Don't abuse me for the indecencies. Through them everything in me has *the same* "diffuseness" as before, but in the form of shouts, madness, and often wracking dissonances.

The confessions in the *Notebook* are franker: *the Beautiful Lady has deserted him*. He doesn't hear or see Her anymore. He has practically stopped writing poems. Is it really necessary to forget everything that has been and to become a sober positivist? Here are these mournful entries:

> End of April 1904. We live much faster than those around us. We plunge into the violet cold of the day before them. *To sense* Her—only in early youth and just before death (Seryozha says just as it was with V. Solovyov). Now a bit more sense. To reject some things. Meanwhile during the summer to lose some memories, to become stronger, to sober up, to compare a great deal, to read, and to do much thinking. *Truce with the positivists*? All things are possible.
>
> 1 May. I am weak, untalented, infirm. None of this matters. SHE may always appear over the jagged mountains. . . .
>
> Again uneasiness at nightfall. And often. And as if I will know everything. But somnolence during the day. To work as best one can. To write poems—it is time, it is time! I want to. I love her.
>
> 7 May, *ante noctem*. Lord! No poems for a long time! How will this end? What blackness in the soul. How exhausting!

Bely goes to Shakhmatovo at the beginning of July. Quite unexpectedly, A. S. Petrovsky, whom Blok hadn't invited, joins him. Aleksandra Andreevna and Maria Andreevna, the poet's mother and aunt, met them. The one-story house with an addition had cozy, bright rooms. Everything was simple, clean, dignified—the style of a modest gentry estate. The poet's mother—slender, nervous, modestly dressed—impressed Bely by her youthful appearance, animation, and acute observation. She led the guests into the garden and from there into the field. They saw Aleksandr Aleksandrovich and Lyubov Dmitrievna from a distance, returning from a walk. She walked slowly, in a pink dress with a white parasol, young, strong, fair haired; she reminded one of Flora. Blok wore a white Russian shirt embroidered with red swans, was hatless, sunburned, and broad shouldered. They met joyfully. Even the uninvited Petrovsky cheered up. Blok knew how to be a cordial and affectionate host. He loved to show guests his Shakhmatovo. Bely remembered the purple color of the sweetbrier, the spicy odors, the screech of the martins, the sun, and the warm wind; but he couldn't remember the conversations with Blok: "In general there were no conversations between me and Aleksandr Aleksandrovich. There was a cozy, warm, laconic friendship and the host's hospitality and kindness. It was sensed in the atmosphere established in Blok's house (completely, entirely). He is ready to share his soul." And for Bely, worn down by his involved, complicated life with his eternal crises and conflicts, the bright days in Shakhmatovo remained in his memory as "days of a real mystery play." Their echo is preserved in the lyrical article "Green Meadow,"[7] where Russia is depicted as a large green meadow strewn with flowers and lit up by dawns.

At sunset they went walking. They cut across a clearing, walked through a grove and came out into a field. A hill came into view in the distance. Lyubov Dmitrievna pointed and said: "I lived there," and Bely recalled Blok's poem: *You lived on a high hill.*

"The first day of our life at Blok's" he recalls, "passed like a Blok poem. And the row of later days are cycles of poems."

Blok didn't like to talk about himself and didn't know how, but he was too honest to lend support to illusions. He knew that the spiritual dawn was over, that night was approaching, that before him is not a path, but bad roads. He felt that the "mystical brotherhood" had failed and that the "rite" of souls to which they had so irresponsibly given themselves was temptation and anguish. And when Bely spoke rapturously about theurgy, meditated at the tea table among people, and stood stock still in silent ecstasy, Blok experienced physical suffering. Once he led Bely into the field and began to explain that he and Seryozha wrongly consider him somehow especially radiant: he is dark. And he repeated: "You think so wrongly. I am not a mystic at all. I don't understand mysticism." He talked about his lethargy, about the yoke of ancestry, about his bad heredity. In these confessions the theme of the *poema Retribution* sounded for the first time.

Bely and Solovyov lived on self-delusion; Blok wanted truth. They stubbornly rejected the "dark" Blok. They were children; he was an adult.

Finally, after several days' delay, Seryozha came, having passed his last examinations and already wearing a student's jacket. The Shakhmatovo idyll ended in gay buffoonery. Seryozha portrayed a parody on the opera *Queen of Spades*, singing the arias out of tune in all the voices, and composed a witty legend about a sect of "Blokites." In the twenty-second century a professor of culture, the academician Lapan, comes to the conclusion that V. Solovyov's friend Sofia Petrovna Khitrovo had never existed. "S. P. Kh." is a symbol, a cryptogram, and stands for Sophia the Wisdom of Christ. And Lapan's pupil, the very erudite Pampan, developing his method further, proves that the poet Blok was never married, that Lyubov Dmitrievna is also a symbol. In Blok's poetry Sophia becomes Lyubov and is called Dmitrievna in connection with the Eleusinian mysteries in honor of Demeter. In these caricatures S. Solovyov parodied that half-mystical, half-enamored cult of the poet's wife to which the "Blokites" had surrendered themselves. M. A. Beketova writes:

> In their ecstasies there was a considerable measure of affectation. They gave Lyubov Dmitrievna absolutely no peace, drawing mystical conclusions and generalizations from her gestures, movements, hairdos. She

had only to put on a bright ribbon, sometimes simply to wave her hand, when already the "Blokites" would exchange significant glances and pronounce their conclusions aloud.... There remained a kind of unpleasant aftertaste. Aleksandr Aleksandrovich himself never joked about such things.

Perhaps during this "playing at mystery," so painful for him, he was already conceiving his *Puppet Show*.

This summer the "fits of despair and irony" to which he refers in his *Autobiography* began. From the "bad roads" of the sect of "Blokites" he seeks a way out in friendship with E. P. Ivanov, who sharply rejected the muddled mysticism of Bely and Solovyov. He writes Blok that there is only one path—Christ. In two remarkable letters to his new friend the poet makes a tragic confession: he doesn't know Christ and is afraid to know Him. On 15 June 1904 he writes to Ivanov:

> We both complain about the impoverishment of the soul. But not for anything—I tell you now once and for all—will I go to Christ for healing. *I don't know Him and have never known Him.* There is no fire in this renunciation, only sheer negation, at times bitter, at times indifferent. An empty word for me, a term falling away "like funeral ashes."

In another letter (28 June 1904) there sounds no longer indifference, but despair and a premonition of impending reckoning:

> I am blind, drunk, perceiving only the sharp corners of madness.... My thread spins, rocking everything measuredly, sometimes growing taut. A mad, entrancing gallop—on a tether! But the tether is long; we will see. I just want to take the bit between the teeth and drink hard. You say that the Galilean may appear to me at any turning—so be it. But for God's sake, not now....
>
> You are *not* the cause of my flight from Him. *The times* are such. You *know* Him, I believe this. A. Bely assures me that I am with Him....
>
> Only in the quiet will we see the Dawn. We are in revolt, we are much stained in blood. I am stained with blood. A *split*, especially. I am "*sometimes*" also tormented by Christ. But all this tomorrow.

Startling words! In them there is no longer "sheer indifferent negation," but *a revolt against Christ*. And not only faith in Him, but the certainty that a meeting with Him is inevitable. Blok fears this meeting, wants to postpone it at all costs, to take the bit, to drink hard, if only to avoid the "Galilean." How strong is his feeling of general guilt for the blood shed on the fields of Manchuria: "I am stained with blood."

The Bloks return to Petersburg in August. The university studies are resumed; A. A. is finishing his long candidate's work, "Bolotov and Novikov." In October his first book, *Verses on the Beautiful Lady*, comes out in the Griffin publishing house. The poet sends his father a copy and writes him that he is much indebted to V. Solovyov's poems.

"Someday," he adds, "we will meet V. Solovyov personally, but in the spacious and bright showcase of heaven rather than in the showcases of bookstores lit by universal 'gases.' " Aleksandr Lvovich responds to the sending of the collection with a malicious letter, declaring his son's poems incomprehensible and reproaching him for self-promotion and eroticism. Blok is stung and justifies himself. He knows that his poems were understood "to the minutest detail and sometimes even to the point of tears" by quite simple people. He is sure he had written—whether badly or well—"about what is eternal and completely beyond doubt, which must sooner or later be grasped by everyone." But Aleksandr Lvovich was not the only one to react negatively to *Verses on the Beautiful Lady*. They were received no less severely in the Merezhkovskys' circle. In the December issue of *New Path*, Z. Gippius wrote that the young poet is still too obscure, that his mystical poems are not artistic, that "they smell of death." The poems devoted to the Beautiful Lady are written under the powerful influence of V. Solovyov; those without the Lady "are often a weak, mild delirium, like a limpid nightmare, not terrifying nor even very unpleasant, but simply barely existing: that incomprehensibility which one doesn't want to understand."

The newspapers unanimously reviled the young decadent, and sales of the collection were "slow."

In 1904 Briusov's star rises high and quickly sets over Blok's poetic horizon. Although he writes to his mother from Moscow that Briusov's personality is for him "not too desirable," he nonetheless continues to believe in his significance as a man and a poet, and to consider *Urbi et Orbi* a great event in his life. Under the influence of the recent Moscow meetings he writes to Sergey Solovyov:

> Briusov now frightens and alarms me. I see in him, however, immeasurably more light than in the Merezhkovskys. I recall that Briusov's apocalypticism (that is, his drawing poetically close to revelation) is not lit exclusively by crimson or exclusively by rational whiteness as is the Merezhkovskys'. That he is *more perturbed* than they (a *real* madman), that there is something *childish* in his facial expressions, in something indefinable. That he may be *positively good*. Finally, that he no doubt bears within him many *possibilities* which Merezhkovsky doesn't bear at all, because he won't say *more*. Moreover, it now seems to me that Briusov is more important than anyone else, even Merezhkovsky. Oh, yes! Briusov's attitude toward V. Solovyov is *positive*, but Merezhkovsky's is completely negative. One day Merezhkovsky said: "We have read much Solovyov. So what, an *intelligent* man(!?!)."...
>
> Besides, I cannot at all hope to reach Briusov's level, even the present-day Briusov.

In such a mood Blok writes a review of *Urbi et Orbi* for *New Path*. It extolled the perfection of form and the finished composition of the book. "Briusov," he writes, "has transmitted the subtlest and most agonizing inspirations and ideas in simple and honed words." The author notes with joy the "contiguity of Briusov's ideas with the central idea of V. Solovyov's poems—reverence for the Mother Earth."

Not satisfied with this laudatory response, Blok reviews the same book again for *Scales*. It was so complimentary to the author that Briusov, an unofficial editor of the journal, decided not to print it. The reviewer speaks of the "striking lyre" and the "stringed scourge," of the "one in many," of the "buried treasure." "Someone in white and gold, someone strong, strikes with a melodious sword." Thus, by piling up symbols, the author attempts to transmit his impression of the poetic magic of Briusov's poems. He ends his review with a quotation from Andrey Bely:

> The stupefied magician, idle,
> Prophet of premature spring.

By the end of the year Briusov's hypnotic effect is dissipated. Blok begins to understand that a void gapes behind the luxurious marble facade of the "maître's" poems, that his magic is half-baked, and that there is no mystery beneath his mysteriousness. Bely recalls how, in the summer of 1904 in Shakhmatovo, Blok told him that Briusov is not a poet but a *mathematician*. This definition pierces the very depth of Briusov's formal, measured and dissected craftsmanship.

In a 21 October 1904 letter to S. Solovyov, the recent devotee dethrones the "great magician":

> Why do you attribute such significance to Briusov? . . . A year has passed since *Urbi et Orbi* began to tear us all in two. But the halves have little by little re-attached, the wounds are healing, one wants something else. The "magician" doesn't eternally horrify, but only when his outline suddenly appears in a "break in the clouds." The next time you notice details in the outline ("pointed beard") and then too the buttons of the frock coat, and then, finally, you begin to say: "Why does this blackish gentleman keep standing there?"

The final formula on Briusov is given in a letter to Solovyov of January 1905. "I understand nothing," Blok announces, "about Briusov, except that he is a brilliant poet of the Alexandrine period of Russian literature."

The formula is quite exact: we would merely soften the epithet "brilliant."

Nonetheless, despite the brief intoxication with the poison of Briusov's poetry, Blok couldn't laugh off the "magician with the pointed beard." He is indebted to him not only for his "urban themes"—factories, restaurants, taverns, streets flooded with electricity, cellars of poverty, and dens of debauchery—he overheard in his poetry the light steps of his own mysterious Stranger.

Here is how Briusov describes a meeting with an unknown woman on the streets of the nocturnal city:

> She passed by and intoxicated
> With the wearying twilight of perfume

> And set off with a rapid glance
> The possibility of impossible dreams.
> Through the iron street noise
> I am drunk with blue fire.
> I suddenly heard avid laughter,
> And snakes wound round me . . .
> . . . And in the horror of stubborn struggle
> Amid vows, supplications, and threats,
> I was enmeshed in the black moisture
> Of her loose-flowing hair.

Of course Briusov's demonic-erotic poems are not artistically commensurable with the quiet music of *The Stranger*. But they helped Blok to embody his vision of unearthly beauty ("And they, blue, fathomless, flower on the distant shore") in images of the fatefully everyday.

Andrey Bely came to Petersburg on the historic day of 9 January 1905—the day the workers were shot down on Palace Square. He set out for the barracks of the grenadier guard regiment where Blok lived, passed through the broad corridor with the doors to the officers' apartments, rang at a door bound with thick felt bearing a brass plate, "Franz Feliksovich Kublitsky-Piottukh." In a white living room with windows on the frozen Neva, a yellow parquet floor gleamed; there was old furniture, a large piano. In a dining room with orange wallpaper the family was having breakfast. Blok was wearing a black wool shirt without a belt. A wide white collar revealed his strong "Byronic" neck. Everyone was upset. Aleksandra Andreevna was worried about her husband, who had been sent to put down the rebels. Blok's agitation struck Bely: A. A. kept jumping up, pacing around the room, going up to the windows, smoking cigarette after cigarette. He already knew that the troops had fired on the crowd, that there were fatalities.

Bely takes up residence at the Merezhkovskys and joins their "circle." He meets Filosofov, Minsky, Kartashev, Rozanov, Sologub. In order to rest from the stormy "religious society" of the Merezhkovskys he escapes to Blok. Aleksandr Aleksandrovich stood apart from the problems agitating the "God seekers." Historical Christianity was alien to him; the Church and Church history left him indifferent. He lived outside history and "historicism"; he had his own direct experience, on which he lived and about which he was chastely silent. All the rest seemed unnecessary to him. But, despite the gulf separating him from the Merezhkovskys, he loved them dearly as exceptional people. He understood Zinaida Nikolaevna completely, in all her refined and capricious singularity, and valued her poetic gift highly. When Bely, weary and rumpled, would enter his quiet room, Blok would seat him in a soft armchair, unhurriedly extend his enormous wooden cigarette case, and—ask him no questions. He would smoke, smile, be silent, repeating slowly: "You don't have to tell me. . . . I know, I know everything." Bely recalls:

There was something so charming and comfortable in Aleksandr Aleksandrovich that one wanted to sit with him for hours. The arch smile, the weary eyes (I first noticed weariness in his eyes in Petersburg), the mute conversation, interrupted by drawing on a cigarette, seemed to me an invitation to rest.

Sometimes Blok took his friend to walk along the lanes of the Petersburg Side. Bely recognized them later in the poems of *Unexpected Joy*: fences, the Neva Embankment, the red streak of sunset, black daws, workers returning from the factory. Blok said: "You know, here somehow . . . it's very sad. An utterly shabby life." The events of 1904–5 awoke in him acute attentiveness to reality, bitter sympathy for the mistreated common people. A whole cycle of poems in the collection *Unexpected Joy* is devoted to the theme of the "city."

In January 1905 the monthly journal *Questions of Life (Voprosy Zhizni)* began to appear under Bulgakov's and Berdyaev's editorship. Blok collaborated on it. He informs his father: "Now I have the opportunity to work a lot with them—to write reviews, sometimes articles on poets, and to place poems. I am writing very many reviews on the most varied books, primarily fiction and literary-historical." But Blok's collaboration on *Questions of Life* didn't last long; it had already stopped in August. The journal continued its existence, with difficulty, until the end of 1905.

Blok's first literary-critical notes had appeared in 1903 in *New Path*. These were timid student notes, vague impressions, lyricism. In 1905 the style of his critical prose becomes simpler and stronger: this is the year of his birth as a prose writer. Of eighteen reviews and articles written for *Questions of Life*, for *Art (Iskusstvo)*, and for *Golden Fleece (Zolotoe Runo)*, two articles on Balmont and a long article on Vyacheslav Ivanov are noteworthy. Blok had a faultless sense of poetic authenticity, an aversion to pretentious "prettiness," and contempt for any kind of "decadent charlatanism." His style is not yet completely free of lyrical impressionism, but his evaluations are always correct.

In 1905 Blok finished his candidate's essay, "Bolotov and Novikov," which earned Professor Shlyapkin's laudatory comment. The author declines his teacher's suggestion to prepare this work for publication, considering it derivative. "Bolotov and Novikov" was first published in a posthumous collection of Blok's work in 1932, based on a rough manuscript. I. A. Shlyapkin had lost the finished copy. Blok's graduation essay, based on authentic and little-known memoirs illuminating the history of Russian Masonry, hasn't lost its interest even now.

On 28 March Blok writes to his father about his literary life:

> Meetings with diverse people are becoming more frequent. The Merezhkovsky circle has become less self-contained. Many have recently also

come from Russia (as opposed to Petersburg). But nonetheless Sergey Solovyov, Boris Nikolaevich Bugaev (Andrey Bely) and Evgeny Pavlovich Ivanov (from *New Path*) remain the closest. Until now the Merezhkovskys, maliciously hated by almost everyone for one thing or another, to a great extent have played the role of "background" for the association. It is true that they are often to blame for this themselves (especially Z. N. Gippius). But I don't foresee their replacement, and one won't find others for a long while who will roar as they do (in their own sphere of magnificent theories, often verging on the absurd, always talented, always an eyesore to worldly and spiritual people).

Further on he declares that there is no longer any decadence in Russia, that its remnants are taking shelter somewhere in Moscow—these are the untalented "Griffinettes"[8] and gymnasium students who talk much and boringly at meetings about black lilies. Blok ends the letter: "Going out into the 'field beyond Petersburg' onto the highway, I feel completely real. My 'well-being' is not upset by anything except religious impressions in the very broad sense."

There were disorders at the university, state commissions were widespread, lectures were discontinued, examinations were postponed indefinitely. Blok and his wife therefore go to Shakhmatovo in early spring. With what joy he returns to his native soil, to his beloved fields and forests. Blok writes to E. P. Ivanov: "Full spring. Everything flows and sings. The sort of dawn from which my soul takes its lineage. Thawed patches and a sky so transparent that it is clear Who is beyond it. It smells of manure and last year's grass is green." And he writes in another letter (23 May):

> When we arrived the orgy of the trees was frightening—juices simply hummed in the forests and fields. After a few days the forests had already stopped being pervaded with quiet and became full of noise. Now they are all obviously enjoying themselves. . . . During one of the many thunderstorms there appeared a crown of slanting rays—from the eyes of the Father. The sun is raging in the wind. This is clear at sunset through the blue and sultry curtain.

It is impossible to read these lines without agitation. This is not a "description of spring," but spring itself, with its brilliance, smell, quivering: "the forests are enjoying themselves," "the sun is raging in the wind."

In one of his letters E. P. Ivanov tells Blok with restrained irony about the project of a certain "mystical rite" at the poet N. M. Minsky's:

> At Minsky's, in accord with the suggestion of V. Ivanov and of Minsky himself, it was decided to hold a meeting where they would celebrate God, carry out rites, each according to his own understanding, but "together." They hope to obtain in a joint meeting that sought-for religious quality which they cannot obtain remaining alone. They decided to assemble by midnight and to carry out rhythmical movements, dances,

whirling, and, finally, a special kind of "rhythmical symbolic body positions."

Blok answers contemptuously:

> I don't accept the "sacrifice" at Minsky's, I don't want to.... His presence alone can spoil everything. I have a big question mark about V. Ivanov (as a person of *action* and will). He "strives" somewhere, perhaps obliquely, rapaciously, and to the point. In his eyes the old bird of romanticism: "thinking about himself."

What a "puppet show booth" such flagellant rites with "symbolic body positions" must have seemed to the mystic Blok! Later he will attack with indignation this "contagion of mystical charlatanism."

In June, Bely and S. Solovyov come to Shakhmatovo. How unlike was this meeting of the three knights of the Lady to the mystical meeting of the previous year! Bely at once sensed that something had happened. Both Aleksandr Aleksandrovich and Lyubov Dmitrievna had changed. The former unity was gone. Blok went alone to the forest; he would sit there for hours on marshy hummocks; he wrote almost no poems. Lyubov Dmitrievna would shut herself alone in her room. One sensed a hidden battle between her and Aleksandra Andreevna. The "triangle" was coming apart. It was difficult and uncomfortable for everyone. S. Solovyov didn't see this change because he, obstinately, fanatically, didn't want to see it. He demanded fidelity to the covenant, insisted on the "mystical community" and on theocratic ideals, thrust "Solovyovism" despotically on his friends, though he himself had somewhat departed from it. With malicious obstinacy he tried to bring back the past; Lyubov Dmitrievna would turn pale and walk away; in the period of gloom which had descended on their life they now seemed to her a mockery.

But the author of *Verses on the Beautiful Lady* read his new poem to his erstwhile "brothers":

> And we sit, little fools,
> Weakness, water spirits.
> The caps are green,
> And on backwards.

Blok felt that *She had left irrevocably*; everything is irreparable, everything is in darkness. Sergey Solovyov was indignant: Blok is an apostate, he is leaving John's temple. And sitting at the dinner table became lacerating. Solovyov spoke ironically about the "inarticulateness" of Blok's poems. Aleksandra Andreevna would get offended and reproach him for "Dostoevskianism." Blok would sit alien, "widening his eyes perplexedly, with a half-opened sorrowful mouth distorted by a smile." Once Bely couldn't endure it: at the table, in everyone's presence, he suddenly tore off his cross and threw it in the grass. By this completely "symbolic" gesture he showed that the mystical union of the three knights at the feet of the Beautiful Lady was broken forever. He writes:

> The soul's drama was accomplished. The huge "blue bird" was perishing; the Beautiful Lady was being reborn as Columbine, and the knights as "mystics"; the rosy atmosphere was proving to be the flimsiest paper, which someone had pierced; there was nothing behind the paper.... *The Puppet Show*, written half a year later, portrayed all this.

The friends' meeting in Shakhmatovo ended dramatically. One evening Bely was reading the Bloks his poem "Child of the Sun." Sergey Solovyov went for a walk and was gone all night. An alarm was raised; there were many "swamp windows" in the neighboring forests into which it was easy to fall at night. The inhabitants of the Shakhmatovo estate spent a sleepless night; they sent out horses, dispatched messengers. In the morning Bely set out for the market at the village of Tarakanovo and came across Seryozha's tracks. At about three o'clock he himself drove gaily up in a troika. Aleksandra Andreevna, agitated, spoke many sharp words. Seryozha answered that he could not have behaved differently because of a "mystical necessity" and that for a "personal obligation" he was even ready to step over a man's life. Blok's mother called him an egoist. Bely became offended for his friend and left Shakhmatovo the next day. Solovyov was too insulted to show the Bloks his hurt; he stayed with them two more days. The second cousins played cards in silent rage and parted enemies.

Later, in Dedovo, Solovyov tried to explain his strange behavior to Blok. He had mechanically set out for the forest and had suddenly caught sight of the sunset and of a star over it. He had suddenly decided that for the salvation of the "mystical brotherhood" he had to follow the star through the forest and the swamp, always straight ahead, without wavering, not turning back. And he had set out straight ahead. Night caught him in the forest. He had made his way with difficulty to Boblovo, where a dog began to bark and he saw a girl in a pink dress. It was Lyubov Dmitrievna's sister, Maria Dmitrievna Mendeleeva. They received him cordially in Boblovo and kept him for the night. Solovyov's outrageous behavior was to him a feat of sacrificial love: he had followed the star as Vladimir Solovyov had rushed from London to the Egyptian desert in pursuit of the Eternal Friend.

Seryozha's "heroic lyric" was the last flaring of the fire with which the "foursome" had once burned. What had so recently seemed to be prophetic inspiration was now childishness.

Solovyov, Bely, and Blok exchanged a few cold letters. Then Lyubov Dmitrievna announced to Bely that the correspondence between them was ending. He replied that he was breaking off relations with her and with Aleksandr Aleksandrovich.

Soon after Blok wrote the lines:

> For what is more pleasant
> Than the loss of one's best friends.

In book 4–5 of *Questions of Life*, G. Chulkov's article "The Poetry of V. Solovyov" appeared. In it the author, with exaggerated sharpness, emphasizes the split in Solovyov's *Weltanschauung*. The philosopher strove to unite the world and Christ, the religion of Christ with the religion of earth. But in his poetry he could not hide his contempt for this life and this world. "The poetry of death and chaos celebrates its dark victory in his poems." Chulkov explains this discord by the irreconcilability of historical Christianity with love of life. S. N. Bulgakov, in the sixth issue of *Questions of Life* brilliantly showed the complete groundlessness of Chulkov's thesis. Blok also commented on it. In a 23 June letter to Chulkov he maintains that there was no discord in Solovyov, that he was not at all an ascetic. Speaking about his teacher, Blok is actually speaking about himself—about the "tragic gaiety" which gripped him in those revolutionary years:

> There was absolutely no odor of "black death." Rather, in my opinion, it smelled of the active gaiety of a spirit finally liberating itself. . . . In the period of his major perceptions and major inexpressible gaiety, Solovyov understood the secret of *playing* with mortal despair. . . .
> The *knowledge* filled Solovyov with ineffable sweetness and gaiety, . . . and when he was dying his rich cup overflowed, not from diminution, but from excess (and a drop of it fell on me).

Under the sign of "playing" Blok enters a new epoch in his life: the epoch of *Unexpected Joy*, *The Night Violet*, and *The Puppet Show*. The "mystery play of the transformation of the world" is turned into an artistic game, into a *commedia dell'arte*, prophecy is vanquished by artistry. But let us not forget: this "gaiety of the liberated spirit" is a "playing with mortal despair."

Blok feels with all his being that something new is imminent, that only ashes from the past remained. And he goes gaily to meet fate. His letters to E. P. Ivanov are filled with passionate expectation. On 25 June he writes him:

> Do you know that WE are among those from whom at least once in life a whirlwind must arise? *We expect whirlwinds from ourselves.* . . . I want action, I feel that the fire is again drawing near, that life does not wait (it has no time to wait—the fire will come). I want to hate much, I want to be harsher. . . . The fire is again near—what kind I don't know. The old is collapsing. I will never accept Christ. . . . Perhaps, perhaps it will be fine, much harmony all around. . . .
> What an important time! A great time! Joyous.

And on 5 August he again writes about joy: "But it is strange, strange, I want to rejoice, for my past (both recent and distant) and *perhaps* for the future. For days now I have felt that I am growing younger. For days I become a frivolous little boy...." And he writes at the end of the letter: "I will speak *approximately*: I am further than ever from *religion*.... For the time being our paths will not coincide. But you are among those dearest to me in the world. Something will happen between us in the future." The following lines speak about acceptance of life, about a gay love for God:

> I recognize you, life, I accept you,
> And I greet you with ringing shield.

His favorite writer—Dostoevsky—leads Blok from depression and despair to a new tragic acceptance of the world. He spends the summer of 1905 under his sign. Blok is immersed in the world of the creator of *Crime and Punishment*. He writes of his passion to E. P. Ivanov and adds: "The soul does not lie compactly and passionately on his pages, as always happens, but rather seems to *dance* on them." Petersburg—the city loved and hated, transformed by Dostoevsky into a poetic theme of genius—enters Blok's art forever. We find the first ominous reflection of Petersburg in Blok's soul in a 26 [25] June letter to E. P. Ivanov. It, this reflection, is an image of a dark, obsessed, terrible Russia.

Blok writes his friend in passion and despair:

> A terrible malice toward Petersburg is seething in me, *because I know* that this foul, rotten nucleus where our daring languishes and withers is surrounded by such abysses, such bottomless swamps as the human eye has not seen nor the ear heard. I got to the outskirts of our city; I know, I know that there the wind still has a long time to whine, the devils to be there, imposters to whistle into their fists. For a long time yet there will be a revelation near Lakhta, heavenly dawns will agitate the breast, sprinkle it with the salt of tears, and draw World Ineffability out of the cesspool. But we live, we live *every day* in horror, stench and despair, in factory smoke, in the crackle of debauched smiles, in the glow of loathsome automobiles, howling at the Dawn, daring to conjecture about the Dawn. Petersburg, I feel, is a gigantic brothel. In it one *cannot rest, cannot learn everything*. Rest is brief there only when the masts creak, barges rock, in the *outlying districts*, on the islands, right by the bay, in the twilight.... As a matter of fact I write so much and so clamorously because I want to express my hatred for my beloved city, to express it namely to you, because you will understand especially, loving it as I do.

This letter gives the lyrical theme of the "urban poems" of *Unexpected Joy*.

On 27 August Blok and his wife returned to Petersburg and learned that, despite the strike, the state examinations would be held in October. Aleksandr Aleksandrovich and Lyubov Dmitrievna began to prepare. In September it turned out that there would be no examinations that year. Blok becomes acquainted with Professor S. A. Vengerov, who suggests a literary project to him: to put together a compilative "Survey of the Literature on Griboedov" and to translate several of Byron's youthful poems for an edition of Brockhaus and Efron. The revolution agitated Blok. He roamed the streets a great deal, mixed with the crowd, listened to orators at meetings. At one time it even seemed to him that he sympathized with the Social Democrats. On the eve of the October manifesto (16 October) he wrote to E. P. Ivanov:

> I have raised a revolution against myself. I prayed to three Virgins in Kazan and St. Isaac's Cathedrals. Neither happiness nor joy is necessary. On the roof of the Winter Palace one can now observe a sad cuirassier with lowered sword. His sharp profile looks sad against the gray sky. Petersburg is more entrancing than any other city in the world, I think, in these October days. When I was at St. Isaac's Cathedral, the doors to Peter[9] suddenly opened (workers carrying boards), and I had to go out to Peter from the darkest and once coziest corner—from the Mother of God.

The poet who had so recently written to E. P. Ivanov, "I am further than ever from religion," prays to the Virgin in a dark corner of the cathedral and asks for nothing—neither happiness, nor joy. When we read in the literature on Blok about his hostility to Christianity, let us not forget that there was in his soul "a cozy corner near the Mother of God." The poet recalls the cuirassier on the Winter Palace in the poem *The gray sky is still beautiful*:

> And cold lights in the gray sky
> Clothed the tsar's Winter Palace.
> And the armored warrior in black won't answer
> Until dawn overtakes him.
>
> Then, reddening above the watery abyss,
> Let him lower his sword more gloomily,
> To lie dead in a useless struggle
> With the savage mob for an ancient fairy tale.

In another poem, *The Meeting*, a street orator is depicted who "intelligently and sharply" utters "dusty words":

> And gray, like the arches of night,
> He knew the limits of everything.
> He clanked confidently
> The chains of onerous freedom.

Suddenly a stone flies out of the crowd, broken glass rings, police whistles are heard. The orator lies with a pierced head, calm and stern, as if he:

Had confidently breathed
The night breath of freedom.

And all the same, despite his aversion for the "savage mob," Blok was with the crowd on 17 October, on the day of general rejoicing. "He even took part," writes M. A. Beketova, "in one of the street processions and carried a red flag at its head." S. Gorodetsky confirms this:

> I remember that Lyubov Dmitrievna said to me with pride: "Sasha carried a red flag in one of the first workers' demonstrations." . . . Vast projects fermented within him. He said that he was writing a *poema*, had finished only the fragment about ships which was included in *Unexpected Joy*.

The fragment about the ships to which Gorodetsky refers was printed under the title *Her Coming* and is divided into seven songs: *Workers on the Dock, So It Was, Song of the Sailors, Voice in the Clouds, The Ships Are Coming, The Ships Have Arrived*, and *Dawn*.

At the year's end (30 December) the poet speaks frankly to his father about his attitude toward the revolution:

> My attitude toward the "liberation movement" was, alas, expressed almost exclusively in liberal conversations and once even in sympathy toward the Social Democrats. Now I am departing more and more, having absorbed everything I can from the "general public," having discarded what my soul doesn't accept. And it accepts almost nothing *of that*—so let what it strives for replace it. I will never become either a revolutionary or a "builder of life," and not because I see no sense in the one or the other, but simply due to the nature, quality, and *theme* of my emotional experiences.

These words are exceptionally important for understanding the Blok of 1917, the author of the *poema The Twelve*.

In 1905, after the breakup of the "mystical triangle," new people enter Blok's life. He becomes friends with student writers: V. A. Pestovsky, who wrote symbolic poems under the pen name "Pyast," the poet S. I. Gorodetsky, and Leonid Semyonov. In his memoirs Pyast tells about the circle of "young art" which they created. Blok, Pyast, Gorodetsky, Kondratiev, V. A. Yunger, N. V. Nedobrovo, P. P. Potyomkin, Yakov Godin, P. S. Mosolov and E. P. Ivanov took part in it. They met at Blok's, at Gorodetsky's, read poems and listened to music. Meyerhold talked about the Kommissarzhevskaya Theater. Gorodetsky—large nosed, long haired, sly eyed—enlivened the meeting with his indefatigability and gaiety. He wrote poems in the Russian folk style ("Vital Sap"), assembled collections of handicraft, took up painting, got excited over politics. He behaved with the sweep and manner of a fairy-tale stalwart. The circle existed till the spring of 1906. Pyast recalled one of his meetings with Blok on the street:

> *Blok:* How strange all this is.
> *Pyast:* What?
> *Blok:* Our meeting.
> *Pyast:* When I was on the way to see you I had a lot to say to you, but now I don't know if it will work out.
> *Blok:* How well I know it. I know it from experience. It hardly ever works out. Therefore recently I speak conventionally. And how! Blasphemously conventionally about what is most important, about the most inward things.... But do you know? Sometimes it does work out. Suddenly, on the street, just as now, in the dark, in a fine rain, it happens that one will say much....
> ... Have you experienced ecstasies?
> *Pyast:* If you take the most general, the going forth from the sensual world, then, certainly, yes.
> *Blok:* But it seems to me there is always something in them besides going forth. In the end there has to be a merging with the world. As in V. Solovyov's poems. In the beginning I was depressed and then joyful. It is born of depression and ends with enlightenment.

And suddenly he adds: "But I have never known Christ." "This was said," Pyast writes, "without any preliminaries; in all that preceded not a word about Christ was uttered." Pyast replies that he had sensed Christ only once in his life. Blok says: "Well, and I too, perhaps, only once. And also, it seems, very superficially.... Barely.... Neither Christ nor Antichrist."

This conversation of the poets on a Petersburg street on a rainy October evening is right out of Dostoevsky. And Blok's mention of Christ, so unexpected and sad, forces one involuntarily to recall the atheist Kirilov in *The Possessed*, whom "God had tormented" all of his life.

The break with Blok depressed Bely unbearably. Finally he couldn't stand it and rushed to Petersburg without waiting for the end of the strike. He stayed in furnished rooms on Karavannaya and sent Blok a letter: they must meet, must have it out; either break for good or end the quarrel. And he set a meeting with Aleksandr Aleksandrovich and Lyubov Dmitrievna in the Palkin restaurant.

In the packed room, to the singing of red-suited Neapolitans, Bely made an examination of conscience. The quarrel due to S. Solovyov, the break, the discontinuance of the correspondence were all on the surface. Now he sees that deep down he loves Lyubov Dmitrievna with an insane love and believes that she loves him too. He had rushed to Petersburg to deliver ultimatums, to her and to Blok: "Who does she choose, him or Blok?" "You can destroy me, you can ask me to get out of your way. If you don't do this, the moment will come (and it is near) when I will demand of you that you don't hinder me."

In the restaurant hall, to the offensive singing of the Neapolitans, three people—Bely, Blok, and his wife—entered a terrible world of passion and suffering in which their souls were to burn to ashes.[10]

Finally the Bloks arrived. "I distinctly remember," Bely writes, "the student's well-proportioned figure, with head tilted high and eyes opened before him, quietly making his way between the tables. Lyubov Dmitrievna walked in front, thinner, in a black dress, with a kind of nervous gait, head lowered." They smiled at each other and at once the whole past, the good, returned. They gaily drank tea. Aleksandr Aleksandrovich depicted humorously how they had "played robbers." Bely shifted from despair to rowdy ecstasy—he wanted to burst into song, to start dancing. He interpreted Lyubov Dmitrievna's tenderness as permission to love her; he read Blok's brotherly smile thus: "Borya, I have removed myself." And he decided that his friend was sacrificing himself, giving his Beautiful Lady up to him. He bowed to his magnanimity, was ready to weep, but accepted the sacrifice. Here was displayed the elemental quality of Bely's nature, his real element "beyond good and evil," his complete moral irresponsibility. The "ultimatum" wasn't presented—it seemed to Bely that they understood each other without words.

Bely spent two happy months in Saint Petersburg and left for Moscow convinced that L. D. loved him.

CHAPTER IV
THE PUPPET SHOW
1906

In January 1906 G. S. Chulkov, preparing the anthology *Torches* for the press, suggested that Blok write a play. He advised him to redo the 1905 poem *The Puppet Show* in dramatic form. The idea for the drama attracted Blok, and the play was written in a few days. On 21 January he informs Chulkov: "I hope I'll succeed in writing the puppet show booth perhaps earlier than you write. Yesterday I conceived and wrote a lot." Two days later he writes: "*The Puppet Show* is finished, but not completely polished; I am still working on it now. I hoped to see you at Sologub's yesterday to tell you. I have many doubts. When can you read it?"

The play's connection with the poem of the same name is purely external—in the style of puppet theater and the sounds of "infernal music." The dramatic action—the story of Pierrot's unhappy love—developed unexpectedly in the process of reworking.

The poem *The Puppet Show* begins with a "preamble":

Here the puppet show is open
For merry and nice children;
A little girl and boy watch
Ladies, kings, and demons.
And this infernal music sounds,
A doleful violin bow howls.
A terrible demon seized a chubby little boy
And cranberry juice trickles down.

The dramatic form is barely outlined in the poem's division into the monologues of the "little boy" and the "little girl." The little boy says that the clown will be rescued, that a procession with torches is already approaching; this is probably the queen herself coming? The little girl replies sadly that the queen doesn't come at night and that the procession is a "retinue of hell."

The poem ends with the clown's melodramatic death:

> Suddenly the clown bent over the footlights
> And shouts: "Help!
> I am bleeding cranberry juice!
> Bandaged with a rag.
> On my head—a cardboard helmet!
> And in my hand—a wooden sword!"
>
> The little girls and boys began to cry,
> And the gay puppetshow disappeared.

Thus the theme of death is refracted in a prism of "romantic irony." Everything on earth is make believe, the world is a puppet theater, people are clowns; their sufferings, passions, death itself, are stage properties. These aren't knights, but marionettes in cardboard helmets, with cranberry juice in their veins. Only children can take the puppetshow representation of life seriously and mourn the clown's death.

In such a mood the play *The Puppet Show* was written. The motifs of the torch procession, the wooden sword, the cranberry juice—derisive symbols of the theater of life—entered the play from the poem.

The Puppet Show was born of despair and irony. The poet notes in his *Autobiography*: "At about fifteen the first definite dreams of love were born, and with them, fits of despair and irony, which found a resolution many years later in my first dramatic attempt (*The Puppet Show*, lyrical scenes)."

In calling his first dramatic attempt "lyrical scenes," the poet indicates the peculiar features of the dramatic genre he created. A lyrical wave, seething and flying upward, breaks into a mist of spray. And in this mist a rainbow of transparent images plays, round dances of masks flash, the action springs up. But the wave will recede, the rainbow will fade, and the "characters" will topple into emptiness. These are merely bubbles engendered by the lyrical stream, by the "music of the soul" of the poet Pierrot. An irresistable magical melody inundates us from his very first words:

> Unfaithful one! Where are you? Through the sleepy streets
> A long chain of lanterns stretches out,
> And couple after couple the lovers come,
> Warmed by the light of their love.
> Where are you? Why after the last couple
> Couldn't we too join the appointed circle?
> I will go to strum a sad guitar
> Under the window where you are dancing in a chorus of friends!

Such breadth of melody, such rhythms and harmonies we have not heard in Blok before. Pierrot, "in loose white overalls, pensive, downcast, pale, browless, and without mustache," resignedly plays his pitiful role in the show-booth of life, but is nonetheless a real tragic hero. He fights for his love and perishes. His tragedy is symbolically concentrated in two scenes; their enigmatic language is obscure to the uninitiated. But, knowing the poet's secret life, we read his confession with agitation. He speaks honestly and simply about his fate. The first scene is a gathering of "mystics." "Mystics of both sexes in frock coats and fashionable dresses sit with rapt expressions at a lighted table." Blok remembers the meeting of the Moscow Argonauts, the Petersburg symbolists, the rites at Minsky's with the "special kind of rhythmical-symbolic body positions." In a note to *The Puppet Show* he gives a malicious characterization of the "mystics":

> We can recognize these people sitting under an electric light around a table in a room with unlit corners. Their faces are all meaningful. None of them bears the stamp of simple-heartedness. They converse animatedly and nervously, as if every moment drawing near to something distant, having a premonition of the quiet flight of something they cannot yet express in words. . . . In a word, these people are maniacs, people with "upset equilibrium." Whether they gather together or each sits in his corner, they think one thought: about the approach, and about what is approaching.

In *The Puppet Show* the mystics' rite is parodied. Here is their dialogue:

> "Do you hear?"
> "Yes."
> "An event approaches."
>   . . . . .
> "Are you waiting?"
> "I am waiting."
> "Its arrival is already near."
>   . . . . .
> "A maiden from a distant land is approaching. Oh—a void in her eyes!"
>   . . . . .
> "She is drawing near—and in a moment the voices will die away."
> "Yes, silence will descend."
> "For a long time?"
> "Yes."

And suddenly, "completely unexpectedly and with no one knowing from where, there appears at the table an extraordinarily beautiful girl with a simple and calm face."

The mystics are shaken. She has come! She is white, a scythe[1] behind her shoulders—this is Death. Pierrot kneels prayerfully before the girl. Tears choke him. But, having heard the whispering of the mystics, he "goes up to the girl, takes her by the hand, and leads her to the middle of the stage. He speaks in a ringing and joyful voice, like the first peal of a bell: 'Gentlemen! You are mistaken! This is Columbine! This is my bride.' "

The mystics are horrified. The chairman admonishes Pierrot:

> Gentlemen, our poor friend has lost his mind through fear.... He hasn't plumbed the depths and wasn't prepared to meet the Pale Friend humbly in the final hour. We will magnanimously forgive the simpleton. ... But, I ask you, look at her features once more. You see how white her clothing is and how pale her features.... Do you really not see the scythe behind her shoulders? Don't you recognize death?

Pierrot answers with a confused smile: "I am leaving! Either you are right and I am an unfortunate lunatic, or you have lost your minds and I am a lonely, misunderstood worshipper. Carry me, snow storm, through the streets!"

But, at the moment he is preparing to leave, Columbine comes up to him and says: "I will not leave you."

On this the first act of Pierrot's tragedy ends. He had won his living bride from the mystics threatening to transform her into a dead symbol, into an image of death. And she followed him.

Let us remember the tragic summer of 1905 in Shakhmatovo, when a battle over "Solovyovian testaments" was being waged between the silent and gloomy Blok and the frenzied and indignant Sergey Solovyov. One thing was concealed beneath the conversations about the "mystical triangle" and about the "theocratic brotherhood": Blok's stubborn striving to put an end to the collective cult of the Eternal Feminine in the person of his young wife. The significant exchange of whispers and winks of the "knights" took on deformed and comic forms. This humiliated Blok and offended Lyubov Dmitrievna. And the poet broke harshly with S. Solovyov and left Bely. The epoch of "dawns" had passed for him. He wanted to see his wife not as a symbol and prototype, but as a living woman, "with a simple and calm face." Composing the chairman's speech, he remembered Solovyov's pathetic exhortations and answered them with irony.

But the "mystics' scene" is not only the end of the tragedy's first act, it is also the beginning of the second. "A well-proportioned youth in Harlequin costume appears. On it sing bells with silvery voices." He goes up to Columbine and says:

> I wait for you at the crossroads, friend,
> In the gray twilight of the winter day!
> My blizzard sings above you,
> Ringing the bells for you!

"He puts his hand on Pierrot's shoulder. Pierrot falls prone and lies motionless in the loose white overalls. Harlequin leads Columbine away by the hand. She smiled at him."

The girl, only just won by Pierrot from the mystics, is again lost to him. Her words haven't yet stopped ringing: "I will not leave you," and she is already leaving with Harlequin: "She smiled at him."

The lyrical theme of the second scene is Columbine's transformation into a "cardboard bride." The theme is given in Pierrot's monologue, on a background of whirling masks, to the quiet sounds of music. The forsaken Pierrot tells of the love of Columbine and Harlequin:

> I stood between two lanterns
> And listened to their voices;
> As they whispered, covering themselves with cloaks,
> Night kissed their eyes
>
> And the silvery blizzard twined
> A wedding ring for them.
> And through the night I saw—the friend
> Smiled in his face.

And the unexpected end of romantic love is absurd and ludicrous. When Harlequin seated his friend in the sleigh, she suddenly fell face down in the snow:

> She couldn't keep her place, sitting! . . .
> And I couldn't suppress my laughter!

The friend turned out to be cardboard. The ludicrous misfortune unites the rivals; they roam the snowy streets together. Harlequin, cuddling Pierrot tenderly, whispers to him:

> . . . "My brother, we together,
> Inseparable for many days . . .
> Will mourn the bride,
> Your cardboard bride!"

Short dialogues of three couples in love, the episode with the clown bleeding cranberry juice, and the torch procession follow. Harlequin steps out of the chorus like a coryphaeus and introduces a new lyrical theme—acceptance of the world as a gay spring holiday. His song rings with rejoicing:

> Here no one dares to understand
> That spring is floating in the heights!
> Here no one knows how to love,
> Here they live in mournful sleep!
> Hail, world! You are with me again!
> Your soul has long been close to me!
> I go to breathe your spring
> Through your golden window.

But the Harlequin's "spring feast," like his love, ends in ludicrous failure: "He leaps out the window. The distance, visible through the window, proves to be painted on paper. . . . Harlequin flew head over heels into a void." Pierrot's downfall directly follows Harlequin's downfall.

On the background of the dawn death stands in white shrouds.

Everyone scatters in horror, only Pierrot goes to meet her: "And, as he approached, Her features begin to come alive. Color begins to play on Her dull cheeks. . . . On the background of the dawn, in a window recess, stands a beautiful girl—Columbine—with a quiet smile on Her calm face." But Pierrot's love is powerless to effect a miracle. At the moment when the author of the play, appearing on the stage, wants to join the lovers' hands, the scenery is raised, it flies upward. Pierrot remains alone, lying helplessly on the stage.

The theme of the cardboard bride dies away in the pensive Pierrot's half-sad, half-funny complaint:

> She lay face down and white.
> Oh, our dance was gay!
> But she couldn't get up at all.
> She was a cardboard bride.
>
> And now I stand, pale of face,
> But it's wrong for you to laugh at me.
> What can be done? She fell prone. . . .
> I am very sad. And are you amused?

In *The Puppet Show* the lyrical theme of Pierrot's and Columbine's love is illuminated by the footlights of the marionette theater. And this theatrical illumination reveals love's duality. The lovers are actors, the characters are masks, the bride is cardboard. To the audience the human tragedy may seem like gay buffoonery. To emphasize the nature of the "performance," the poet allows the author to burst into his own play and to protest against the actors' wilfulness. By these devices the "divine lightness" of playing with reality is created, the combination of truth and fiction, of dream and irony—all the characteristic features of the romantic theater from Shakespeare to Tieck and Hoffmann.

But no literary analysis explains the basic enigma of *The Puppet Show*: the *future* is reflected in the magic mirror of the "lyrical scenes," events which in reality have not yet occurred. In the scene of the masks the central theme of Pierrot's love for Columbine is reinforced by three variations, by the dialogues of the three couples in love. The first couple ("he in blue, she in pink") "imagines itself to be in church and looks upward into the cupola." This is an image of mystical love with its ecstasies and dark doubles ("someone dark stands by the column"). The third couple is an image of knightly love. "He is all in severe straight lines, tall and pensive, in a cardboard helmet; he draws a circle with a huge wooden sword on the floor in front of her." The knight speaks to his Lady about the miraculousness of their meeting, about eternal happiness, about the nearness of the Day. She repeats his last words like an echo. This is all that remained of the *Verses on the Beautiful Lady*—a cardboard helmet, a wooden sword and, instead of Her voice, the hollow echo of the poet's own words. And between these two variations on the love theme—love as prayer and love as service—is placed a third—love as passion. "She is in front, in a black mask and swirling red cloak. He is behind, all in black, lithe, in a red mask and a black cape. Their movements are rapid. He pursues her, now overtaking her, now outstripping her."

She:

> Follow me! Overtake me!
> I am more passionate and sadder than your bride!
> Embrace me with your lithe arm.
> Drain my dark goblet to the bottom.

He:

> I vowed passionate love—to another.
> You flashed a fiery gaze at me,
> You led me to a remote lane,
> You poisoned me with a deadly poison.

He calls her a sorceress, knows that she will destroy him, but, submissive to fate, "follows her along a sinister road."

The first and third variations depict Blok's past symbolically. The mysticism of the epoch of *Ante Lucem* and the knightly service of the time of *Verses on the Beautiful Lady* are reflected in them in an ironic perspective. The second variation reflects *what hasn't yet come*—the period of *The Snow Mask* and *Faina*, the fiery circle of passion of 1907–8, at whose center stands the actress N. N. Volokhova. The snowy whirlwinds, flying up around the "sorceress" in the black mask, are already revealed to the poet's clairvoyance. But this is not all. The mystery of foresight can be extended to the whole play. If Pierrot is "pensive, downcast, and pale"—an ironic reflection of the poet himself —then the headlong, dancing Harlequin, on whom "the bells sing with silvery voices," who summons him to the spring feast of life, leaps out the window, and falls into the void, is a derisive sketch of Andrey Bely. And again the enigma of the vision of the future confronts us. When *The Puppet Show* was written, Blok still didn't know that his best friend was his rival, that he intended to take his "bride" away from him. The tragedy involving him, Lyubov Dmitrievna, and Bely was played out several months later, and the reconciliation of the former enemies, united by the mutual loss of the "cardboard friend," occurred many years later. Really, don't Harlequin's words ring with prophecy:

> . . . "My brother, we together,
> Inseparable for many days. . . .
> Will mourn the bride,
> Your cardboard bride!"

Finally, the transformation of the "beautiful girl with the simple and calm face" into a "cardboard friend," into a theatrical personage, anticipates Lyubov Dmitrievna's acting career.

In the January days of 1906, through the "magic crystal" of poetry, Blok saw his own, his wife's, and his friend's future fate. Did he suspect the prophetic significance of his "dramatic experiment"?

But the artistic value of *The Puppet Show* doesn't depend on its turning to the future. The play's first listeners, and later spectators, were enchanted by the incomparable charm of this *Commedia dell'Arte*. Russian neo-romanticism of the twentieth century produced no more poetic, musical, and light-winged work than this sadly derisive harlequinade.[2]

Blok's inspirer, Chulkov, liked *The Puppet Show* very much: he wrote an enthusiastic article[3] about it. The winter of 1906 was the time of greatest closeness between them. Blok writes to his new friend: "Dear Georgy Ivanovich, I love you very tenderly and you love me too. But understand me just as you understood me in what you wrote about *The Puppet Show*. . . . Please know that I really love you very much. I kiss you firmly."

Blok sensed spring extraordinarily early, rather, he had a premonition of it. In his diary we meet the expression "January spring." A letter to P. P. Pertsov of 31 January already describes the approach of spring:

> The quiet spring thaw is beginning. You raise your eyes to the window and it is already twilight. And you know that it is spring, and in the sky a gray puff of cloud floats onto another and floats past, and the delicate azure will be revealed, and the melting snow breaks into bloom.

Further on he speaks of Pushkin and Lermontov. These thoughts will later enter his first lyrical article, "Troubled Times."

Having dethroned the "mystics" in *The Puppet Show*, the poet thinks agonizingly about his "mystical" past. Where was his mistake? Why did the path of ecstasies and visions prove to be a false path, and the "radiant temple" a puppetshow booth? After all, he hadn't pretended, had deceived neither himself nor others, had actually seen Her only in the fields of Shakhmatovo. The fruit of these reflections is an entry in the *Notebook*, "Religion and Mysticism" (January 1906). In its depth and the keenness of its thought this comparative characterization of religion and mysticism belongs to the most significant of Blok's writings. Mysticism and religion, the author boldly declares, have nothing in common. "Mysticism is the soul's Bohemia, religion is a standing on guard." Art is by nature mystical, but not religious. It is a monastery with its own rule and there is no place for religion in it: "*Mysticism in the everyday* is a wonderful and rich theme, *historical-literary*, subtle. It came to us from the West. Meanwhile, they are often inclined to take this theme, so akin to the soul of 'decadence,' for a *religious* one. What falsehood in this.

Further on, the "void" of mysticism is contrasted to the "fullness" of religion:

> Mysticism appears most . . . in ecstasy (which we will define as the conclusion of a union with the world against people). Religion is alien to

ecstasy (we should sleep and eat and read and walk religiously): it is union with people against the world as INERTNESS. . . .

The extreme inference of religion is *fullness*, of mysticism *inertness* and *emptiness*. Hysteria, depravity, estheticism flow from mysticism. *But religion can also sanctify mysticism.* . . . The cornerstone of religion is God, that of mysticism is mystery. . . .

Mysticism requires ecstasy. Ecstasy is solitude. Ecstasy is not religious. Mystics love to be poets, artists. Religious people *don't*; they separate themselves and their trade (art).

Mystics are very demanding. Religious people are unassuming.

Mystics are egotistical, religious people are self-respecting.

There is much truth in these glittering aphorisms. Blok has in mind natural, innate mysticism and completely ignores Christian mysticism. For him ecstasy is only a merging with nature, and not an ascent to God. He cannot imagine religious art, although it has and does exist. His tragedy lies in the fact that Deity was revealed to him as the cosmic principle of the Eternal Feminine, and not as the God-man face of Christ. He believed in Sophia without believing in Christ. In his note there is a yearning for religious life, a striving to break away from the inertness of mysticism toward the fullness of religion, and a resigned hopelessness. He knows that he is foredoomed to languish in the "monastery of art," where "there is no place for religion."

The Bloks called Bely to Petersburg, advised him to leave Moscow once and for all. Aleksandr Aleksandrovich saw all his growing attachment to Lyubov Dmitrievna, but believed that their three-sided union would become still stronger for this. He loved "Borya" and knew that the latter loved him too. On 13 January he dedicates a poem to him, beginning with the verse:

Dear brother! Night is falling.
The bells are barely audible.
It was white over the plain—
The sleepy-eyed girl has passed by.

The poet recalls the wanderings on the islands with his friend, when the sunsets died out behind a bank of reeds, the light of a semaphore showed green beyond the forest, and the smooth surface of the Gulf of Finland opened out before them. And the poem ends:

Returning, we will lie down cozily
On a rug in front of the stove,
And will quietly retell
Our sister everything we saw. . . .

We will finish. She will get up quietly from the armchair,
Silent and stern,
Will say to each of us: "Be cheerful.
Snows lie beyond the window."

Thus Blok dreamed of friendship *à trois*—the two brothers and the "silent sister." The arrival of the "brother" turned the idyll into a tragedy. The passion of one obsessed burst into the quiet affection. Bely came in February. In the book *Between Two Revolutions* there is a dim reflection of the four insane months spent in Petersburg. Bely writes:

> February–May. Life's outward events are entangled.... Now I rush to Moscow like a shot from a gun muzzle; now I speed like a bomb away from Moscow—to explode at Shch's[4] locked doors, to force them open for myself, and to debate: whom does Shch love? Which of the two?...
> February–March. The Peter of this time is alive in me, like rough copies in a notebook difficult to make out.

He stayed in furnished rooms on Karavannaya and sent Lyubov Dmitrievna an enormous bush of blue hydrangeas. It seemed to him that the Bloks considered this gift tasteless and he, offended, at once shrank into himself. His pathological suspiciousness grew. Everything was wrong; it was cold in the Bloks' white rooms. The hosts were friendly, but reserved. Bely notes:

> So it was that evening. I came, moved, perhaps forever. Lyubov Dmitrievna and Aleksandr Aleksandrovich sent for me, but I came and saw that there was no need to come. Their life is here in Petersburg; I am a Muscovite. It turns out that I am a kind of adjutant here.

This first impression was enough to instill in him first ill will and, soon, even animosity toward Blok. He portrays him as gloomy, a "deaf-mute," surrounded by a "gray-lilac, gray-green atmosphere": "Blok often sat in deep shadows, from which his long nose would protrude. The yellowish stale tint of his face grown thin, the bags under his eyes, the circles—all this said without words: 'I don't understand.'"

Bely reads Blok his article on Merezhkovsky's *Trilogy*, written in an "archaic-rhetorical" style, where "Gogol and Karamzin[5] were interwoven with the style of Bishop Hilarion."[6] He was writing it to propitiate Dmitri Sergeevich, who had been angered by his recent attacks on Dostoevsky. The article was unsuccessful, and Blok didn't like it. He tried in jocular fashion to portray the dressing down the author would receive from "Zina" (Zinaida Nikolaevna), "Dima" (Filosofov), "Tata," and "Nata" (Gippius' sisters). But Blok's jests irritated Bely. He says in *Reminiscences* that the poet's "unresponsiveness" "irritated" him, and his "idiotic look" provoked fury. He tried by involved arguments to justify his growing hatred for his friend, ashamed to admit that it was based on the most primitive jealousy. Reading *The Puppet Show* dealt the last blow to his love for Blok, a "blow to the heart by the heaviest hammer," as he expressed it. He had been expecting a mystery play for the Intimate Theater, about which the Bloks, V. Ivanov and he dreamt, but heard the "profanation of sacred things." Gorodetsky, Pyast, E. P. Ivanov, and Bely assembled in the green living room. Everyone sprawled in soft armchairs. Blok began to read in a monotone. The mystics, the "cardboard bride," Harlequin tearing the sky asunder—everything sounded to Bely like a mockery and a challenge, and he picked up the gauntlet. He couldn't help recognizing that he was confronted with a "very magnificent work of art," but he was convinced that it was bought at the price of the soul's destruction. V. Pyast writes in his *Reminiscences*: "Blok reads his fresh first experiment at creating drama, *The Puppet Show*. The breath of new trepidation passes through the living room."

The poet finally sensed Bely's animosity and began to avoid him. During his visits, under the pretext of the forthcoming examinations, he would go into the next room and sit there with a book. Bely spent the evenings in long conversations with Lyubov Dmitrievna. A. A. would appear for a moment with a "strained, puzzled smile" and go out for a walk to refresh himself after his studies. The stay-at-home Blok gradually gets used to tramping the streets and suburbs of Petersburg.

In his conversations with Lyubov Dmitrievna, her living face is revealed to Bely for the first time. Until now she had been for him a symbol, a sign, the incarnation of the Eternal Feminine. Now there is before him a real woman, who understands that the past is ended, that the brotherhood united around her had collapsed, and that she is no longer the "Beautiful Lady." Protest and rebellion sound in her words: why was this role assigned to her? She is not a doll, but a person, with her own personal destiny. She is bored with being the "bright daughter of dark chaos," she wants to be a woman and an actress.

"The dimensions of the break in Aleksandr Aleksandrovich's soul," Bely writes, "became apparent from Lyubov Dmitrievna's stories—another Blok! But she said that one had to take care of him, that much in him is sick and childish." Perhaps in the depths of her soul she sensed dimly her responsibility for the crisis the poet was experiencing.

Bely and Lyubov Dmitrievna would go to exhibits at the Hermitage and return for dinner. The taciturn Blok would come out. Being together in a threesome became more and more difficult for them; the alienation increased.

Bely finally decided to acknowledge his fault to the Merezhkovskys. They reproached him, shamed him—and forgave him. He again settled down in the house of Muruzi. Zinaida Nikolaevna, having taken upon herself the responsibilities of a confidante, wanted to meet Lyubov Dmitrievna. Bely brought the Bloks to the Merezhkovskys'. The women's meeting was friendly; joining hands, they sat side by side on the sofa and began to talk animatedly. Blok sat aloof and kept silent. No one addressed him; it was clear that no one needed him.

The tension of Bely's relations with Blok was becoming unbearable. Finally it was necessary to have it out. But Blok stubbornly avoided the decisive conversation. Bely read in his childishly perplexed eyes: "Borya, no! We had better remain silent. Let's wait." And he began to talk about trifles, tried to joke. But Bely couldn't wait. With a desperate effort of will and passion he succeeded in breaking down Lyubov

Dmitrievna's resistance: she agreed to join her life with his. This drama is described briefly in the book *Between Two Revolutions*:

> Shch [Lyubov Dmitrievna] confessed that she loves me—and Blok. But a day later she doesn't love me or Blok. Still another day later she loves him like a sister, but me in an "earthy way." But a day later everything is reversed.... Finally, Shch loves only me; if she later says the opposite, I must struggle with her at the cost of life (hers and mine). I vowed to her that I would smash all the impediments between us or would destroy myself....
>
> I face Blok with this: "I must talk to you." His eyes ask: "Please don't." But he understood that it was an ultimatum and, tearing himself from his reading, he looked at me very, very openly and, stretching a smile over his pain, said: "Why not, I am glad."

The three go into the study and lock themselves in. Lyubov Dmitrievna curls into a ball in the corner of the sofa, ready to jump up at any moment and rush between them.

"I stood before him," Bely writes, "breast to breast, at the moment still fraternally, prepared if need be even to take a blow directed straight at the heart, but not to renounce the vow just given to Shch." Bely says that Lyubov Dmitrievna loves him and that they have decided to go abroad together: "I told him everything and waited. I won't forget: his face seemed to open up. Open, it stretched its blue eyes, also opened, toward me. On his pale face (he was pale in those days) the lips trembled—the lips opened childishly."

Bely expected a duel, the crossing of foils. By his tone and gestures he was telling his rival: "Attack!" But his foil met an unprotected breast. Blok said quietly: "I am glad.... Here.... Why not." "And the Marquis Posa, so demonstratively brandishing his sword, was forced to lower it. Silence fell. Suddenly from the corner of the sofa Lyubov Dmitrievna's voice was heard: 'Sasha, really?' And again everyone fell silent."

Bely felt his friend's "hidden courage" and greatness:

> He was beautiful at that moment: in the lifeless face and ashen-reddish hair and in the gesture of his bent neck, proudly thrown back, open, and expressing courage.... He rose over the table against the background of a window which revealed an expanse of icy water. Crows flew by and blue-black, gray-black clouds, merging with smoke, hung lazily. And one sensed the footsteps of fate.

Bely rushes to Moscow for talks with his mother and to get money for the trip abroad with Lyubov Dmitrievna. He is in a state bordering on madness—unsure of her, unsure of himself. Her letters only increase his confusion. He recalls:

> A deluge of letters from Shch. On such and such a date she loves me. On such and such a date she loves Blok. On such and such a date not Blok,

but me. She calls to me and asks me not to forget my vow. And again, she doesn't love me.

Before Easter Lyubov Dmitrievna falls ill with influenza, is in a high fever. Blok writes Bely a polite letter advising him to postpone his arrival in Petersburg: Lyubov Dmitrievna is ill, and he is busy preparing for the state examinations. Aleksandra Andreevna makes the same request in her letter. Bely suspects a conspiracy and goes to Petersburg at once. Aleksandra Andreevna doesn't receive him. Blok meets him amiably and introduces him to the German translator Hans Günther.

He finally succeeds in talking things out with Lyubov Dmitrievna. She can't understand herself, hesitates, torments herself. Why, she loves Sasha and knows that he loves her—how can she leave him? Bely launches into eloquence, charm, entreaties, threats. "Finally," he writes, "my position is taken for the umpteenth time. Convinced that I am ready for anything for her sake, she admits that she loves me. True love triumphs. We are going to Italy."

The decision is made: they will part for two months, meet in August, and go abroad. "What are two months," Bely consoles himself, "a life together is ahead!" Blok knows about this plan. What does he think about parting from his wife? Bely enters his study. Blok meets him with the words: "Hello, Borya! Let's go, mama wants to see you."

Bely asks Lyubov Dmitrievna how Sasha is taking their decision. She answers: "He sat on the rug, squatting and saying: 'So this is how it will be with me.'"

The day of Bely's departure arrives: "Breakfast, the last at the Bloks. Played 'You fell victim' on farewell. Played it and left for Moscow. A. A. was at an examination. I didn't bid him farewell. L. D., I remember, waved her white handkerchief at me from the window."

Blok opposed Bely's hysterical torment with self-control and inner discipline. He protected himself, as with armor, by preparing for the examinations: he led a regular life, sat at his books in the afternoon, went walking in the evening. V. Pyast is delighted with the methodical tenor of his life:

> From the beginning of Lent Blok in the most thorough way switches his whole custom to that required for the examination vigil. The ordeal itself won't be soon, but Blok is already "invisible" to everyone except those directly related to the matter on his mind.... Besides that, he very regularly gets up at the same time, eats, drinks, goes out (far, on foot) at definite times, then studies almost the same number of hours every day and goes to bed at the same time. On finishing each exam he allows himself a longer walk and, it seems, drops into a restaurant and drinks red wine.... Insofar as I remember, he taught G. I. Chulkov "to drink red wine," having himself become accustomed to do just this between examinations.

Blok's favorite places were the wretched lanes of the Petersburg

Side, the island expanses, the uninhabited highway beyond Novaya Derevnya, the fields beyond the Narsky gates. For longer walks he would set out for Ozerki, Shuvalovsky Park, Lesnoy. The suburbs of Petersburg are the landscape of his poems of this epoch—he gave them poetic immortality.

G. I. Chulkov was often his companion on these wanderings: "I remember well the sleepless Petersburg white nights, my nocturnal wandering with Blok, and the long conversations somewhere on the islands, on a bench, or over a glass of wine in the corner of a questionable drinking-house. What forebodings there were! And how horribly they have come true." Chulkov guessed Blok's trouble, but explained it by the "contagion of mystical irony." "That 'mystical irony,'" he continues, "which the romantics loved to talk about, poisoned the soul of the lyricists at that time. And this was, perhaps, the onset of a fatal illness." Chulkov enthusiastically developed the ideas of "mystical anarchism." Blok would listen silently, thinking his own thoughts. Observing him, Chulkov reached a terrible conclusion: "At this time Blok was the personification of catastrophe. Only no. He was at that time already a madman and had already burnt his ships."

The poet's companion showed insight: he saw "madness" beneath the armor of the orderly and industrious student.

Bely recalls one of the poet's tragic returns to his home:

> Once, at midnight, he entered, in a crumpled frock coat, strangely gray, sat down, and turned to stone near the wall. Lyubov Dmitrievna: "Sasha, are you drunk?" Aleksandr Aleksandrovich agreed: "Yes, Lyuba, drunk." He had returned that day from the islands. In a restaurant he had written the poem *The Stranger*.

Who of our generation doesn't remember it by heart:

Po večeram nad restoranami
Gorjačij vozdux dik i glux
I pravit okrikami p'janymi
Vesennij i tletvornyj dux.

In the evenings over the restaurants
The burning air is wild and still,
And the noxious spring spirit
Rules the drunken shouts.

The sound of the first verse alone, with its open A's and its repetition of the liquids R and N (*večerami-restoranami*) already carries one away with enchanting music. The solemn A echoes it in the verse:

I každyj večer, v čas naznačennyj
(Il' èto tol'ko snitsja mne?)
Devičij stan, šelkami sxvačennyj
V tumannom dvižetsja okne.

And every evening, at a set time
(Or am I only dreaming this?),
A girl's figure, clothed in silk,
Moves in the foggy window.

But here the A sound is orchestrated with the sibilants Ž, Č, Š (*každyj večer, čas, naznačennyj, devičij, šelkami, sxvačennyj, dvižetsja*), and these overtones accompany the melody with the rustle and swish of transparent silks. The most magical verse is:

I vejut drevnimi pover'jami
Eë uprugie šelka,
I šljapa s traurnymi per'jami,
I v kol'cax uzkaja ruka.

And her resilient silks,
And the hat with mourning feathers,
And the slender hand in rings,
Smell of ancient superstitions.

Here again the trumpet of R's rumbles (*drevnimi, pover'jami, uprugie, per'jami, ruka*) and the high A falls steeply into the muted U (*uprugie šelka, uzkaja ruka*).

The mysterious vision is contained in the banal frame of the Sestroretsk landscape: the dust of the lanes, bakery biscuits, wits in derbies, sleepy footmen, drunks with rabbit eyes. And in the noxious spring spirit, amid childlike weeping and feminine screeching, she alone lives, she alone triumphs:

And I see an enchanted shore
And an enchanted distance.

The drunken poet, on returning home, took from his pocket a crumpled piece of paper with the hastily jotted down lines. They brought him fame. They were bought dearly.

On 25 April Blok informs his father that he has his last examinations in twenty days, that he is tired and in a "pessimistic mood," and adds: "Recently I am writing almost nothing, and am paying no visits. Ivanov's literary Sundays and famous Wednesdays have for a long time not attracted me much. I am completely forgetting how to talk and am absorbed in myself."

Nevertheless, in order to make money, Blok has to write reviews almost every week for the literary sheet *Monday*, which is connected with the newspaper *The Word (Slovo)*. An old acquaintance, P. P. Pertsov, former secretary of *New Path*, drew him to this work.[7] He writes on the most varied authors: Balmont, Briusov, Gornfeld, Annensky, Verhaeren, Schnitzler, Edgar Poe, Leconte. The reviews are written conscientiously, with noble simplicity, but somehow indifferently. One feels that this is work done "to order." Finally, on 5 May, Blok finishes the state examinations "with distinction." "I sometimes loved the university," he writes his father, "and am sorry to leave it, but perhaps out of habit, like the regret of the prisoner of Chillon." But in his *Autobiography* he notes:

> The university didn't play a particularly important role in my life, but in any case higher education gave a certain intellectual discipline and certain habits which help me a lot in historical-literary work and especially in my attempts at criticism and even in artistic work (materials for the drama *The Rose and the Cross*). With the years I value more and more what the university gave me in the person of my respected professors A. I. Sobolevsky, I. A. Shlyapkin, S. F. Platonov, A. I. Vvedensky, and F. F. Zelinsky.

Two days after finishing the exams Blok writes to Pyast:

> There is no more bourgeois being in the world than a young person who has finished his exams! But I have finished compiling a collection of poems and have finished a *poema* I have been thinking about for half a year. I will rest in the country and write—and hear little about "religion and mysticism," which rejoices me. . . .
> I only superficially regret that we didn't say goodbye. On that day, as on many others, it seems I went "to drink red wine." (I put it in quotation marks because this process has already become a strict formula for me, from which many theoretical conclusions follow.)

The collection mentioned by the poet came out at the end of the year under the title *Unexpected Joy*; the *poema* is *Night Violet*. It has a curious history. At the beginning of December 1905 Blok wrote to E. P. Ivanov: "On 16 October I dreamed something I have been living on till now. Such amazing dreams occur once a year, or every two years." From this dream arose the *poema* which entered the collection *Unexpected Joy*. It was provided with the following note by the author: "*Night Violet*. This *poema* is an almost exact description of a dream I had."

It is a strange dream and a strange *poema*. It is written in free verse, borrowed from Verhaeren by way of Briusov, and whimsically combines a description of the Petersburg marshes with a legend of Scandinavian kings, knights, and singers sitting in a hut by an enormous beer barrel and sunk in age-long sleep. The king and queen, their crowned hair turned green, doze on a rickety bench. The princess—a "homely girl with an imperceptible face"—indifferently spins yarn, and a knight who is in love with her

> sits doomed
> At one and the same thought
> And at the same beer mug,
> Standing beside him on the bench.

The princess turns out to be the Night Violet, stupefied by the "marsh somnolence." The doleful *poema* ends unexpectedly with a joyful premonition:

> Thus the fatal spinning wheel spins
> A living and fleeting dream,
> That Joy will come unexpectedly
> And that it will be perfect.
>
> And the Night Violet blooms.

This is probably an exact description of the dream. But a dream is not yet a work of art, and the hut in the marsh with the Scandinavian kings and beer mugs arouses serious bewilderment.

The atmosphere which immerses the *poema* is characteristic for the author of *Unexpected Joy*. It is saturated with the poisonous exhalations of the marshes:

> Above the moist plain stuck out
> Cabbage stumps, birch trees, and pussywillows,
> And it smelled of the marsh.

And further:

> Foot bridges were thrown
> Over the stagnant and brackish water,
> And the path meandered
> Through the lilac-green twilight.

The ominous lilac-green air and the "red band of sunset"—such is the poet's world. Azure, whiteness, gold sink into marsh mist. Not the lilies of angels, not the roses of the Beautiful Lady, but the thorn-apple of the Night Violet.

Blok's *poema* is wrenchingly discordant; it contains dregs and bitterness, confusion and malice. The reader doesn't believe in the arrival of unexpected joy; he feels one thing—the poet is infinitely unhappy.

Blok's note to Chulkov (10 May) can serve as a real commentary to *Night Violet*: "Yesterday Evgeny Pavlovich Ivanov and I were coming to see you in the evening, but suddenly turned and went to the islands and then to Ozerki—to get drunk. We saw the red Sunset." The red sunset is the same as in the *poema*:

> And above the sickly hummock,
> And above the red strip of sunset—
> The air bated its expectation.

In May the Bloks went to Shakhmatovo. They were estranged from one another; it was difficult for them to be together. Aleksandr Aleksandrovich, after a terrible winter, sinks into exhaustion. One can judge his state by a letter-confession to E. P. Ivanov:

Horrible desolation. I no longer see or hear anything. I can't write poems. It's ridiculous even to think about them. I hate my own decadence and lash out at it in those around me, who are less guilty of it than I. The end of decadence has come.... Everyone has overstrained themselves and prematurely considered their own sick and refined spirits to be sacred, and now they are paying for this.... Quiet has come—the most diabolical, despite the revolution....

... What you write is dearest of all to me, because there are no quotations from the Holy Scriptures. I have abandoned nihilism once and for all; I speak calmly and grieve little over this, because I mostly am sad, about what I don't know.... There is no reason, nor beginning, nor end to this for those who are sad.... The moment I note down decadent poems (I cannot write others) I simply tell lies. There is much stupidity and filth in my head.

For the whole summer Blok entered only one phrase in his notebook: "Green boredom, and the city is gray boredom."

Blok's *The Puppet Show* appeared in the spring in the collection *Torches*. The book opened with a pretentious article by the editor, G. I. Chulkov, on "mystical anarchism":

> A hundred-voiced howl—one can't live *so*—finds response in the hearts of poets, and this revolt is refracted distinctively in the individual soul. According to our plan, *Torches* should reveal that desired inner alarm which is so characteristic for modernity. We don't aim for unanimity. Only one thing draws us together—an uncompromising attitude toward the power of external compulsory norms on man. We understand the meaning of life to be in humanity's search for ultimate freedom. We lift our torch in the name of the affirmation of personality and in the name of a free union of people based on love for the future transformed world.

A sonnet by V. Ivanov was printed in the collection; one line reads: "I—the will struggles—will not accept the world."

In *Scales* (May 1906) Briusov berated the "new current" with great malice:

> Thus, before us is a new current in literature, to a certain degree a new "literary school." Its first manifesto in the form of a modest note on the Theater-Studio can already be found in last year's September issue of *Questions of Life*. Mr. Georgy Chulkov, the present editor of *Torches*, informs us that "we are experiencing a cultural crisis," that it is therefore necessary to "find new mystical experience," and he cautions artists against "symbolism, bred in the hothouses of bourgeois culture," and against "pitiful decadence." In the note the new direction bears the name "mystical anarchism," and this oxymoronic name has since then acquired a certain fame. The collection *Torches* is disappointing.... "Really," one thinks, "will this I. Bunin or Mme. Allegro or Mr. Rafalovich reveal to us an unknown 'inner alarm'?..." To collect in an anthology poems and stories of authors "who don't accept the world" is just like asking collaboration only from authors with yellow eyes or with last names in vowels and sibilants.

In conclusion, Briusov gives a short review of *The Puppet Show*:

> The dramatic sketch *The Puppet Show* is written in the conventional manner of the theater of marionettes or pantomime. The heroes have wooden gestures, like dolls', and their speech is like a falsetto on the Petrushka shows. But this renunciation of our artistic complexity, this new form of simplification, reveals a kind of unexpected depth.

In the same volume of *Scales*, in a review on Leonid Andreev, Andrey Bely touches, in passing, on "mystical anarchism":

> Mystical anarchism is the only answer of living personality to all the unsatisfactory theories about the meaning of life, an organic antidote of our personality against all the toxins which poison it. But mystical anarchism, advanced as a theory, as an understood and accepted method of life, withstands no criticism. Religious experiences, predetermining anarchic revolt, once they are realized, change into theories of religions and cultures which impose burdens and bonds on us. That is why . . . we will rise up against any theorizing of anarchistic experiences.

In the next issue of *Scales*, Vyacheslav Ivanov came forward in Chulkov's defense ("On the 'Torchbearers' and Other Collective Names"). Very rhetorically he explains that mystical anarchism is the same thing as "superindividualism" or "mystical energetics," while under anarchism one should understand the "synthesis of individualism and collectivity," and under mysticism, "freedom and holy madness." "Why," the author concludes, "anarchistic mysticism is already anarchy, and true anarchy is already mysticism." V. Ivanov's profundity convinced no one and introduced even greater confusion. When, in the summer of 1906, G. Chulkov's book *On Mystical Anarchism* came out, with an introductory article by V. Ivanov, "On Nonacceptance of the World," a real literary scandal erupted. Chulkov was preaching not only a political, but also a spiritual, revolution. The leap from the realm of necessity to the realm of freedom will only be possible when history ends. The approach to the desired end of history is revolution. The whole historical edifice must be burnt down. This will not only be the material flame of struggle, it will also be a spiritual flame, that is, a complete renunciation of false bourgeois values. Chulkov declares:

> Perhaps the socialists, of all those who haven't stepped over the boundary of mysticism, are the people closest to us, insofar as they sincerely hate property. . . . The old bourgeois order must be destroyed, so as to clear the field for the final battle. There, in a free socialist society, the mutinous spirit of the great man-Messiah will arise to lead humanity from mechanical organization to the wonderful incarnation of Eternal Wisdom.

This preposterous jumble of Marxism, anarchism, mysticism, and eschatology, tasteless but completely inoffensive, called forth a protracted and stormy polemic which revealed the deep crisis of the symbolist school, the beginning of its collapse. And in the history of the disintegration of symbolism "Vyacheslav the Magnificent"[8] was destined to play a fateful role.

Chulkov sends his book, *On Mystical Anarchism*, to Blok with a friendly inscription. The latter thanks him and calls Chulkov's short articles "arrows which wound, landing straight in the heart." But at once he makes a reservation:

> I accept separately almost everything that you write, but not as a whole. The whole (mystical anarchism) seems to me not to withstand criticism, in contrast to its particulars. It doesn't seem to exist yet, and it seems that what will be can be born in another area. In my opinion, you didn't guess the "name," and is it yet possible to guess it while the edifice is shaking? And will that yet be? Everything is tormenting and open to question.

And the more Blok meditated on "mystical anarchism," the more decisive was his denial. It is hardly possible to believe Chulkov's self-satisfied declaration:[9] "It seems to me that it has fallen just to my lot to teach Blok 'to listen to the music of revolution.' Blok sensed the truth of mystical anarchism. But he got confused and retreated." This was not a very plausible assertion.

Bely spent the summer of 1906 in Dedovo with S. Solovyov. His correspondence with Lyubov Dmitrievna took on a dramatic character. She wrote that she had changed during this time, had done much thinking, and understood that it was all delirium and that she had never really loved him. He bombarded her with very long letters in which he tried to prove that cowardice and hypocrisy were speaking in her, that she was a bourgeois, clinging to Philistine well-being. The letters contained references to Kant, Cohen, Rickert, the apostle Paul, and John the Theologian. In reply she accused him of abstractness and *mania grandiosa* and begged him not to come to Petersburg in the fall.

"I gloomily thought out the form of violence," Bely writes. "It was clearly evident that some kind of bomb would be thrown. Why, she is betraying her own 'I.' And how many times, falling on the table, did I beg her in letters: spare yourself, yourself!"

He felt himself to be a terrorist. All Russia was living on this: expropriation, attempted murders, murders. He approved of this and, wandering along the dusty roads, would sing: "We will renounce the old world!"

By chance Bely finds himself in Moscow and receives a note from Blok. Aleksandr Aleksandrovich is in Moscow. He has come for negotiations with the editors of *Golden Fleece* and arranges a meeting with Bely in the Prague restaurant in the Arbat.

This is how the scene is described in the book *Between Two Revolutions*:[10]

> Emptying room. Snow white tables and at one sits a shaven "Arab," but not Blok. He, seeing me, got up awkwardly. He extended his hand indecisively, flinging at the waiter: "Tokay."

And we sat down to deliver an ultimatum. He delivers it, flustered and nasal. It would be better for me not to go. In reply I threaten war on such and such a date. This date is at hand; there's nothing more to talk about. I jump up, waving my napkin, which falls at the feet of the waiter, who is hurrying up with a fat bottle in his hand. He uncorks it, fills the glasses while Blok is getting up, strangely blinking his expressive eyes. Without turning around he goes to the exit, throwing a ten-ruble note to the waiter, who is cowering in amazement. I go after him. The two glasses on the tray foam, and we descend the stairs, he in front, I after him.

Two hours later Bely rushes to Dedovo, collapses into S. Solovyov's arms. He decides to starve himself, but the watchful Seryozha forestalls this intention. They return to Moscow together. Bely locks himself in the empty apartment (his mother was spending the summer in Marienbad) and lives through the act of murder in the most minute detail. He admits: "Yes, I was abnormal in those days. Among my old things I found a black masquerade mask, put it on, and sat for a week from morning till night in the mask. . . . I wanted to dress as a blood-stained domino and run through the streets that way."

Hence the theme of the red domino in the novel *Petersburg* and the motif of the mask in the poems of this time:

And they hammered a half-mask
To the lid of the coffin.

The violent Ellis calls on him, carried away with the idea of terrorism, and on friendly terms with the expropriator-maximalists. Unknown "comrades," suspicious subjects with dark eyes, girl students, and agitators spend day and night in his room on Sennaya Square. He tells Bely: "I enter my room, want to lie down—there's a comrade on the bed. I stumble—there's a comrade on the floor across the door. That's the way it is every night."

Ellis isn't at all surprised that Bely sits in a mask: this is quite natural. He recommends radical measures, aggravates his mood. And a decision is made: Ellis will go at once to Blok in Shakhmatovo with a challenge to a duel; he will be Bely's second.

Ellis returns the next day. He has had very long talks with Aleksandr Aleksandrovich. And the latter told him: "Why a duel, Lev Lvovich? On what grounds? There are no grounds. Borya is just terribly tired."

Ellis came back enchanted by the Bloks: they had inquired about Borya so solicitously and are of course expecting him in Petersburg in the fall.

Returning from Shakhmatovo in the fall, the Bloks moved from his mother's house to their own apartment. M. A. Beketova explains this departure "from under the mother's wing" by the "destructive spirit of revolution." "At this time all the new literature was calling for a rejection of conformity, for a renunciation of family and comfort. And Blok too was gripped by this mood." This is hardly true. The poet wasn't destroying his family, but leaving the family of his stepfather, who was alien to him, and relatives whom he hated. He and his wife wanted their own corner, inaccessible to people hostile to him.

The Bloks settled into a small "democratic" fourth-floor apartment on Lakhtinskaya Street. They had little money and the most modest furniture. The poet writes about his "garret" on the Petersburg Side:

> What in the world is higher
> Than bright garrets?
> I see chimneys, the roofs
> Of distant taverns.
> *(In the Garret)*

In another poem:

> One hope remained to me:
> To look at myself in the well of the yard.
> Day is breaking. Clothing shows white
> In the diffused light of morning.
> *(Windows Overlooking the Yard)*

And the same motif again:

> I walk, I roam downcast,
> Alone in my burrow.
> A sullen organ-grinder will come,
> Will weep in the yard.

This "urban landscape," revealed from the attic window, grows into the theme of man's fate (*In October*):

> I opened the window. How gloomy
>   The capital in October.
> An abused brown horse
>   Walks in the yard.
>   . . . . .
> Yes, and they drove me
>   Into the garret without any reason.[11]
> No one listened to my arguments
>   And my tobacco ran out.

Life passed, the star set. For the last time his wings unfold, and he throws himself down:

> I fly, I fly to a little boy
>   Amid the whirlwind and flame. . . .
> Everything, everything as of old, as it used to be,
>   Only—without me.

In September Bely is in Petersburg again. Lyubov Dmitrievna writes him that they haven't yet settled into the new apartment, and asks him to wait a bit before calling on them. For ten days he sits in a half-dark room on Karavannaya and waits. With despair in his soul he wanders the gloomy streets. Finally an invitation from Lyubov Dmitrievna arrives. Their conversation lasts five minutes. We don't know its content. Bely writes about it this way:

> Only five minutes! Each one like a fall from a cliff, with a loss of consciousness. Then a new fall. Five minutes, five falls, taking away faith in oneself, in man. In the fifth minute I catch myself in the same pose as in the Prague in front of Blok.

He rushes downstairs, runs out into the fog onto the street, wants to throw himself into the Neva. But beneath him he sees barges and fishing preserves and decides to wait until daybreak. In the room on Karavannaya he writes a farewell letter to his mother and spends a sleepless night. At nine in the morning a messenger brings a note from Lyubov Dmitrievna: she asks him to come at once. A conciliatory conversation takes place. Bely says: "I won't describe how we decided to part, not to see each other for a year, to examine *all this* in ourselves, to postpone a decision, to meet anew."

That same day he leaves for Moscow and two and one-half weeks later goes abroad.

Why did Lyubov Dmitrievna so pitilessly "destroy" Bely, with whom she had recently wanted to unite her fate? Why in five minutes did she kill his "faith in himself," his "faith in man," and nearly drive him to suicide? Of course she was exasperated by his "insanities," by his stubborn importunities, by his threats and quotations from Cohen and Rickert. Of course she understood her mistake and knew that she didn't love him. But nonetheless it is impossible to explain her cruelty by all these reasons.

V. F. Khodasevich,[12] a completely reliable witness and Bely's close friend, suggests to us a solution. In 1922 in Berlin, the author of *Symphony* was on the brink of mental illness. He uttered to Khodasevich endless monologue-confessions, which brought his confidant to the point of complete exhaustion. After one of these hours-long sessions, Khodasevich fainted. In his reminiscences of Bely he depicts his friend's romance with Lyubov Dmitrievna thus:

> Apparently the Lady at first received the brotherly feelings offered by Bely favorably. When Bely shifted from brotherly feelings to feelings of a different shade, his problem was greatly complicated. But at the moment when his importunings were close to being crowned with success, his duality burst out. He had the insanity to assure himself that he was incorrectly and "badly" understood, and declared this to a lady who probably suffered a great deal before responding with agreement. Anger and contempt took possession of her. And she repaid him a hundred times more offensively and painfully than Nina Petrovskaya. From that moment Bely came to love her for real, and forever. The pain dulled with the years, but seared for a long time.

The first edition of Blok's lyrical drama *The King on the Square* is provided in the manuscript with a note: "Finished in prose and rough draft on 3 August 1906." He wrote E. P. Ivanov about it on 6 August:

> After your departure I began to write a play, wrote it all in prose, quite a lot. While I was writing it, I was gay and cheerful. When I read it aloud everyone (including me) saw that it was no good at all—just a rough sketch. So I will now be bored again and will probably loaf until I take up the play again. I have to rework it and put it into verse.

The manuscript of the second edition bears the note: "Second variant finished on 10 October." On 13 October he reads the play in a small circle of friends (Chulkov, Sologub, Syunnerberg, Kondratiev, the Ivanov brothers).

The lyrical drama *The King on the Square* is connected with the poetic themes of the collection *Unexpected Joy*. In its preface the poet outlines the basic leitmotif of the play: "One can hear how the sea boils and the ships' sirens howl. We will all flow to the pier, where signal lights have been lit. The hearts of the peoples will ignite with new Joy when the great ships appear beyond the narrow cape." This dependence of the drama on the lyrical system of *Unexpected Joy* is defined still more precisely by the author in a note to the *poema Her Coming* (in the second edition of *Unexpected Joy*). He announces: "I have decided to place this weak and unfinished *poema* here because it is characteristic for that book and that time, as devoted to various 'unrealized hopes' (according to my plans of that time). . . . The same theme is developed in the lyrical drama *The King on the Square*."

It is very significant that the cycle of these poems is entitled in the manuscript "From the *poema The Coming of the Beautiful Lady*." The poetic connection of the heroine of the play—the daughter of the Builder—with the inspiration for *Verses on the Beautiful Lady* is thereby established. The *poema Her Coming*, consisting of seven poems (*Workers on the Dock, So It Was, Song of the Sailors, Voice in the Clouds, The Ships Are Coming, The Ships Have Arrived,* and *Dawn*), is filled with intense, joyful expectation: they are coming!

> The lighthouses search keenly
> For the ships beyond the breakers.

The sailors sing about their betrothal to the sea depth:

Blue sea!
Red dawns!
You, wind, drunk,
Tousle the hair!
Salt wind,
Carry the voices!
You, free wind,
Furl the sails!

Verses are preserved in the manuscript in which the figure of the stone king appears:

> He was a giant. On a precipitous slope
> His solemn profile rose and died out.

His voice, "simple and gay," resembles thunder:

> The gay one prophesied golden freedom,
> And the night was lit up by the prophet's words . . .

And here the ships arrived—the image of the Daughter of the Builder arises:

> And already there—behind that braid[13]—
> Unexpectedly bright,
> With clouded beauty,
> The beautiful one waited for them.

All the details of the ships' arrival enter the drama from the *poema*: rockets scatter in the sky, the west grows dim, and twilight descends:

> Turbulent crowds in a premonition of happiness
> Came out onto the shore to meet the ships.

The hopes are fulfilled—the ships bring people happiness and freedom. The *poema* was written in December 1904. At that time the poet believed that the dawn of freedom was breaking over Russia. *The King on the Square* ends in destruction and death; in 1906 Blok scoffs at "unrealized hopes." His letter to Briusov about *The King on the Square* testifies to his disillusionment with the revolution of 1905:

> I myself am not completely satisfied with it, either from the formal or the external side. . . . I still have little mastery of technique. I am somewhat afraid of its variation in style; perhaps symbol alternates with allegory, perhaps in places it borders on the old "realism." But in essence that's what I wanted, and in the summer when I was working out the plan, I experienced a strong inner "excitement." Probably the revolution breathed on me and shattered something within my soul, so that jagged splinters scattered all around, sometimes perhaps accidentally.

Reading the drama now, we don't sense any "excitement": time has carried away the thin coating of topicality; a poetic fairy tale, strange and sad, has remained.

The King on the Square, a lyrical drama in three acts with a prologue, is the same recording of a dream as the *poema Night Violet*.

In the *poema* the queen, sitting at a spinning wheel, casts a spell on the poet, plunging him into a magic sleep. In the play the Daughter of the Builder, "a tall beauty in clinging black silk," leads him after her. His soul is handed over to her "dark melodies," and he recognizes in her his own youth, his first love, his bright queen:

> For the last time—in the savage gloom—
> I see: a queen's crown sparkles
> In your dark hair!
> Or did the lightning glide?
> How your face lit up!

In the sorrowful music accompanying the appearance of the Daughter of the Builder, the image of the Night Violet, breathing narcotic marsh fumes, begins to gleam with the rays of another vision—*The Stranger*. The "beauty in clinging black silk" blends with the "lady in resilient silk" in a "hat with mourning feathers."

The poet pines in the world, gripped by madness, perishing in hunger and poverty. In the first act, in the conversation of the three strangers, motifs of despair and death sound. "What happiness to die," says one. "Let's go alone—to burn and destroy," takes up another. "People no longer believe in anything. The world has forgotten about prophets and poets; it must be committed to flames." The second says: "Tell me one final thing: do you believe that destruction is liberating?" The first replies: "I don't believe it." The second adds: "Thank you. I don't believe it either." They fall silent.

But in this darkness of despair only "mindless fantasy" shines, "what was once called a lofty dream." People believe that some sort of ships will come from the sea and everything will be saved. In its hour of death, humanity is gripped by an "insane dream" of beauty which transforms the world. It is incarnated symbolically in the Daughter of the Builder, who wants to return youth to the old king. She says to the poet:

> I know a great book about a bright country,
> Where a beautiful maiden ascended
> To the death bed of the tsar
> And breathed youth into his senile heart.

The first meeting of the Poet with the Daughter of the Builder takes place in the second act. Just as the Stranger, she comes "breathing perfume and mists." "For some time the distant music of the sea is audible. While the Daughter of the Builder is slowly descending, the stage is shrouded in fog." The motif of the "enchanted shore" in *The Stranger* is expressed by a broad melody in *The King on the Square*:

> *Poet:*
> I see the shore of a new earth.
> . . . . .
> Sprays of sea foam blinded me.
> You move over the sea,
> And the shadow of ships rises behind you.
> . . . . .

Daughter of the Builder:
All life for you is a fairy tale.
Listen with your sleepy soul
To a fairy tale about evening life,
You, whom I have enchanted.

In the third act the expectation of the ships grips the city with joyful madness. Everyone bangs the axes more loudly: these are workers on the embankment building a tower to shoot off a rocket when the first ship appears on the sea. People fall dead from alarm and excitement; others die of hunger. A jester, the representative of common sense, mocks the dreamers. His fool's cap swings above the crowd gone mad. Twilight descends. The Daughter of the Builder appears to the Poet for the last time. "The wind plays in her black hair; in it her bright face is like the day." The lyrical theme of "recognition," the transformation of the Stranger into the Beautiful Lady of his youthful years, spills out in a ringing, triumphant song. These strange, jerky exchanges of dialogue, the exchange of calls of agitated voices in the darkness pierce the heart:

Poet:
This night I recognize you for the first time,
Daughter of the Builder:
You are seeing me for the last time.
Poet:
Why did youth flare up so brightly?
Will life really soon burn low?
Daughter of the Builder:
I have the mastery of your life.
Who is with me will be free.
. . . . . .
Poet:
You descended to me from lofty chambers,
You looked at the dawn as you are looking now.
Daughter of the Builder:
The past is gone.
Poet:
But the wind played in sleepy outlines,
And in your presence I was a bright poet,
Fanned by your wind.
And in your lowered eyes
I read that I am loved by you.
Daughter of the Builder:
Forget about the past. The past is gone.
(In the pale light of the lightning her dark silk seems to shine. A crown lit up in her dark hair. She suddenly embraces him.)

The Daughter of the Builder goes up onto the terrace and sits at the King's feet, embracing his gigantic knees. In the distance rockets fly up and shouts are heard: "The ships have arrived." The Poet climbs the steps to her. The infuriated crowd rushes after him, wailing and shouting, and shakes the columns. The terrace collapses, burying the Poet, the King, and the Daughter of the Builder.

Blok didn't succeed in transforming the lyrical theme into dramatic action. The play, without inner movement, without living characters, built on vague associations of lyrical motifs, seems formless—

> I can only speak vague things.
> The soul's legends are ineffable

—the Poet confesses, and this vagueness shrouds the play in dense fog. But a few quiet, lyrical stars shine in it, and it is impossible to tear oneself from them.[14]

From the rough-draft prose edition of *The King on the Square*, Blok singled out the Poet's conversation with the jester and the courtier and printed it separately in the journal *The Pass (Pereval)* (No. 6, 1907) under the title "On Love, Poetry, and State Service. A Dialogue."

Artistically insignificant, this work reflects the terrible crisis he experienced in 1906. The break with Bely and the separation from his wife shook his whole being to its depths: the very wellsprings of life were poisoned. Before him arose the question of the meaning of existence, the value of his poetic work. In the summer he was in "horrible desolation," couldn't write poems, hated his decadence, and was mortally depressed (letter to E. P. Ivanov). He speaks of this depression, of the poet's isolation amid a hostile world in the "Dialogue." Developing the old romantic theme of the "poet and the mob," Blok fills it with his own personal pain. The jester, "a man of common sense, of unknown rank," embodies the self-satisfied banality of the crowd. His words summarize the newspaper and magazine criticism, the gossip of men of letters and acquaintances who heard the "poet-decadent" every day. The jester holds forth:

> You are a poet, pining in the banality surrounding you. You pour out your complaints in poems, beautiful but incomprehensible. . . . In general I don't advise you to rush into accusatory literature. This is not your field. You are a pure artist. Your vague images will always find dozens of sensitive appreciators.

Then he gives a string of practical advice to help attain the favor of the beautiful lady "as soon as possible" and ends his announcement: "literature is positively harmful." "But the main thing is, don't speak so slowly and pensively; better be silent for the time being." The courtier replaces the jester; he himself once wrote poems and considered himself a "real judge of subjective lyricism." He asks the poet:

> If I am not mistaken, you, like Petrarch formerly, created in your mystical searching an intimate cult of woman and of feminine love? . . . Subjective lyricism is a great thing, young man. It gives the elect hours of esthetic rest and permits them, if only for the moment, to forget the voice

of the capricious mob.... Such poetry does not corrupt manners and morals.

The poet complains of depression, of his unfitness for life. The courtier suggests that he think about a diplomatic career.

Either the obtuse lack of understanding of the crowd or the insulting approval and patronage of the "connoisseurs of art"—such is the pitiful fate of the poet, this "senseless singing being" (words of the Builder in *The King on the Square*). And Blok asks derisively what he is to do: either write civic poems or enter state service.

Having finished *The King on the Square*, Blok started an article, "The Poetry of Spells and Incantations," which was ordered by Professor E. V. Anichkov for the *History of Russian Literature*, edited by E. Anichkov and D. Ovsyaniko-Kulikovsky.[15] He worked conscientiously on the major collections of texts and studied the literature on the question. The article reconstructs the emotional atmosphere in which the people live, amid vital and mysterious nature populated by "fantastic and strange beings": "They stretch out to us from behind every bush, from each twig, and from the bottom of the forest stream." The author speaks of folk magic, magicians, sorcerers, wizards, witches, folk superstitions and legends, and incantations and rites in which "gleams the gold of genuine poetry."

The study of folk superstitions is reflected in Blok's poems about his native land. The image of dark demonic Russia grew out of the work on spells and incantations. The article already gives rough drafts of the poems. Here is one example:

> In whirlwind columns witches and devils arrange vile dances and weddings; they can be driven away by throwing a knife into the middle of the whirlwind. It sticks in the earth, and whoever lifts it will see that the knife is bloody. Such a knife, "bloodied by the whirlwind," is indispensable for the witchcraft and incantations of love.... In the bewitched ring of Life plague, death, love—diabolical forces—stand exceptionally close to the folk soul.

And in the poem *Rus* we read:

> Where wizards and fortune-tellers
> Bewitch the standing grain.
> And witches revel with devils
> In the snowy road pillars.
>
> Where the blizzard sweeps wildly
> To the roof—a fragile dwelling—
> And a young girl sharpens a blade
> Against her evil lover under the snow.

"Dark, diabolical forces" "lead nocturnal round dances" on the roads and crossroads of Russia:

And the whirlwind, whistling in the naked twigs,
Sings legends of olden times. . . .

The face of Blok's *Rus* is not born of Russian *byliny*,[16] songs and fairy tales, but of the folk magic of spells and incantations. And this magic casts on it the dark light of demonism.

On 11 November 1906 Blok finished his third lyrical drama, *The Stranger*. It was originally entitled *Three Visions*. The poet read it to a few friends. On 19 November he informs his mother: "The day before yesterday Tanya [Tatyana Nikolaevna Gippius], Zhenya [E. P. Ivanov], Kuznetsov, and Chulkov liked *The Stranger*."

In the second edition of *Unexpected Joy* the following note was appended to the poem *The Stranger*: "Development of the theme of this and contiguous poems in the lyrical drama of the same name." Originally the following four-line verse stood as an epigraph to the drama:

And her resilient silks
Waft ancient superstitions,
And the hat with mourning feathers,
And a slender hand in rings.

In the collection *Unexpected Joy*, one can separate out a cycle of five poems devoted to the theme *The Stranger*. They are built on laying bare the metaphor of the stranger as a falling star. The famous stanza "In the evenings above the restaurants" prepares for this mysterious event. Meeting the unknown woman in a restaurant, the poet is agitated by the enigmatic quality and the familiarity of her strange image ("And shackled by strange closeness"). He vaguely, as in a dream ("or am I only dreaming this?"), remembers another reality, another charmed world. "Someone's sun" is entrusted to him; "obscure secrets" are assigned him; space is torn asunder. The walls of the restaurant have already disappeared, and her dark blue eyes blossom on the distant shore. In the next poem the theme of the restaurant meeting is varied, the image of the Stranger becomes more distinct:

She is shamelessly entrancing
And humiliatingly proud.

Amid the bustle, amid fat beer mugs:

Through a veil covered with beauty-patches,
Eyes and fine features.

Her resemblance to a star is introduced for the first time:

What am I waiting for, bewitched
By my lucky star,
Both stunned and agitated
By wine, sunset, and you?

Aleksandr Blok

In the unearthly music carrying it on its wave, the surrounding banality takes on mysterious depth. Shaken, torn between two worlds, the poet questions the Stranger:

> Amid this mysterious banality
> Tell me, what am I to do with you—
> Unattainable and unique,
> Like the smoky-blue evening?

In three adjacent poems the metaphor woman-star leaves the fog of comparisons, resemblance, likenesses, and rises to triumphal identity. The Stranger is not a woman *resembling* a star: she *is* a star. This is her past: she sparkled in the sky and fell to earth like a fiery comet. And this is her "obscure secret" guessed by the poet-clairvoyant.

In the poem *There in the night's howling cold* he sees her face "in the field of stars." In the blizzard's trills, to the tambourines of the snow-storms, she flies like a comet, "dragging bright stars in her train." The poem ends:

> And twining shrouds over the moment,
> All cloaked by the blizzards' stars,
> You float away into the snowy twilight,
> My friend predestined from the ages.

Her empirical image (the woman in the restaurant) drowned in the opening starry abyss. The long train of the black dress is the tail of a comet cloaked in stars.

Her celestial origin is revealed still more triumphantly, still more magnificently, in the next poem:

> The train, sprayed with stars,
> Blue, blue, blue gaze.
> Between earth and the heavens
> The bonfire is raised like a whirlwind.
>
> Life and death in eternal whirling;
> You—open to Milky Ways—
> Are hidden in thunder clouds.

With her hand, "slender, white, strange" (compare: "And the slender hand in rings") she gives him a torch-goblet. It will be poured out through the sky along the Milky Way—and She will then rise above the wasteland "to unfold the train of a comet." The realization of the metaphor (woman-star) is not the absorption of one element by another. The Stranger is *simultaneously and equally* really both a woman on earth and a star in the sky. In this identity of contradictions is the miracle of poetry, the height of romantic art. The comet floating through the Milky Way, hidden in storm clouds, shines with a "blue, blue, blue gaze," stretches out her slender white hand, draws a train splashed with stars.

In the last poem of the cycle the Stranger's cosmic nature is shown in the myth of the fall of a beautiful star. The cycle of poetic art is closed. The transformation of the world progresses through three holy stages: comparison, metaphor, and myth.

The poet addresses a woman met by chance on the street:

> Believe me, we both knew heaven;
> You flowed like a blood-stained star.
> I measured your path in sorrow,
> When you began to fall.
>
> We knew with ineffable knowledge
> One and the same height
> And together fell behind the fog,
> Tracing an oblique line.

But even now, "in the unlit gates," her gaze is just as bright as it once was in the "misty heights"; and it also passes along the dark street:

> And the same sky behind you,
> And you drag your train like that star!

Her silvery, slender waist is the Milky Way of her celestial homeland.

Blok intended to develop the myth of *The Stranger* in dramatic form. The inner nature of the myth, steadily striving toward drama, impelled him to this. He wrote the play about the star's fall, about the appearance of the Stranger amid the "mysterious banality" of modern life. The lyrical drama consists of three pictures—"visions." The first "vision" is the "street tavern." The setting is described in detail:

> The dull white light of the acetylene lantern quavers in the crumpled lamp shade. On the wallpaper completely identical ships with enormous flags are depicted. Their prows cut the blue water. Beyond the door . . . passers-by in fur coats and girls in kerchiefs walk—beneath the blue evening snow.

On the counter, a beer barrel; two waiters with forelocks, in green aprons. "At the table sits a drunken old man—the very image of Verlaine. At another, a pale man the very image of Hauptmann." The solitary visitor goes up to the counter with an unsure gait and rummages in the tub of boiled crabs. A girl in a kerchief enters and excitedly tells her companion how a guest of the night wanted to rob her and how they dragged him to the police station. A man in a yellow coat is selling a cameo depicting "a pleasant woman in a tunic," sitting on a globe. A drunken seminarian speaks tearfully about some dancer. And his drinking companion answers: "Dreamer. You drink because of that. And we are all dreamers. Kiss me, friend." The drunken Verlaine mutters: "And everything passes away. And to each his own trouble." The picture of "mysterious banality" prepares the transition into the world of "visions." Written according to all the rules of "realism," it is no more "real" than the fantastic quality of the next scene. Blok studied Dostoevsky—not for nothing did he take two excerpts from *The Idiot* as epigraphs to his drama.

In M. A. Beketova's book we find an important note regarding the scene in the tavern. She writes:

> *The Stranger* is inspired by wanderings through out-of-the-way corners of the Petersburg Side. The bar of the "First Vision" is located at the corner of Geslerovsky Lane and Zeleninaya Street. The whole setting, beginning with the ships on the wallpaper and ending with the characters, is drawn from life. The "very images" of Verlaine and Hauptmann, the man fingering the crabs, the girl in the kerchief, the curio seller—all these are faces which the poet saw during his visits to the tavern with the ships.

Describing "from life" the bar on Zeleninaya Street, the poet also depicted himself in it with no less realism. Here he sits at a table with a notebook in front of him and exchanges confidences with the waiters. His intimate confessions sound sad, almost ironical. This is the image of Blok the vagrant, the visitor of night restaurants, drinking red wine, a homeless and orphaned solitary.

"Just listen," he says to the dumbfounded waiter. "To wander the streets, to catch fragments of unfamiliar words, then to come here and confide my soul to straw men."

> The waiter: Incomprehensible, but very refined. The poet (drinks): To see many women's faces. Hundreds of eyes, large and deep, blue, dark, light.... To love them. To want them.... And amid this fire of gazes, amid the whirlwind of gazes, one face arises suddenly, as if blooming under the blue snow: the uniquely beautiful face of the Stranger, under a heavy dark veil.... The feathers on her hat shake.... The narrow hand, constricted by a glove, holds the rustling dress.... She approaches slowly. ... She approaches ... (Drinks greedily).

Thus the poem *The Stranger* is made into drama. And here is the transformation of the Stranger into the Ruler of the World. The poet buys the cameo and looks at the goddess depicted on it:

> Again she surrounds the globe. And again we are in the power of Her spell. Here She twirls her flowering wand. Here She twirls me.... And I twirl with Her. Under the blue ... under the evening snow.
> (And slowly the tavern walls begin to twirl. The ceiling stretches out into infinity. The ships on the wallpaper sail, foaming the blue waters. The sky opens—wintry, blue, cold—and in it, "The Second Vision.")

A dark bridge across a large river; beyond it an endless straight avenue with chains of lanterns and trees white with hoar-frost. It is snowing. Furious yardmen drag the drunken poet. On the bridge an astrologer observes the fall of a blinding star:

> After a moment a beautiful woman in black walks along the bridge.... Everything becomes like a fairy tale—the dark bridge and the slumbering

blue ships. The Stranger freezes by the bridge railing, still preserving her pale falling luster.... One just as blue as she mounts onto the bridge from the dark avenue. Also in snow. Also beautiful. He wavers like a quiet blue flame.

The lyrical dialogue between the Stranger, still preserving her starry luster, and the poet's soul, still trembling like a blue flame, is real verbal magic. The first two verses, written in trochaic tetrameter with hyperdactyllic endings and incomplete rhymes, are inexplicably beautiful:

Goluboj:
V bleske zimnej noči tajuščaja,
Obrati ko mne svoj lik.
Ty snegami tixo vejuščaja,
Podari mne lëgkij *sneg.*
Neznakomka:
Oči—zvëzdy umirajuščie,
Uklonivšis' ot puti.
O tebe, moj legkovejuščij,
Ja grustila v vysote.

The Blue One:
Hiding in the brilliance of the winter night,
Turn your face to me.
You, quietly wafting snow,
Give me light snow.
The Stranger:
Eyes are dying stars.
Deviating from the path,
I grieved in the heights,
About you, my lightly fluttering one.

These "rhythmoids," introducing dissonance into harmony (*tajuščaja:vejuščaja, lik:sneg, umirajuščij:legkovejuščij, puti:vysote*) are like muffled echoes of a celestial song. The change of accented vowel gives the melody a strident, wracking, cracked quality.

The Blue One says he has been waiting for her for centuries, says he always sang only of her, saw only her star in the sky. The Stranger answers:

The falling maiden-star
Wants earthly words.

Earthly passion awakes in her voice; she asks for embraces. The Blue One says quietly: "I don't dare to touch you."

The bluish snow pillar rises rapidly and disappears. In its place appears a man in a derby, who "doesn't at all mind embracing the beauty" and gallantly leads her away by the arm.

The astrologer bemoans the fall of the shining star and notes in his scrolls: "Maria—the star—fell." The poet appears, already sober. He is looking for the "tall woman in black." Too late. "The snow covered up her delicate tracks. Both weep under the blue snow."

The "Third Vision" moderates after the high tension of the second picture. We again find ourselves in the world of banality, but now this isn't the vulgar banality of the tavern, but the refined banality of the society drawing room. The author plays with the device of enigmatic correspondences, rather arbitrary and artificial. Thus the young man Misha, in an immaculate dinner jacket, in the drawing room, carried away with the barefoot Serpentina, corresponds to the seminarian in the tavern telling about the dancer; a deaf old man chewing biscuits, to the drunken Verlaine; a gallant cavalier, leading the Stranger away, to Hauptmann, etc. The mistress of the house declares: "Our excellent poet will read us his excellent poem, again, I hope, about the beautiful lady?" The Stranger, now named Maria, appears. The poet looks at her pensively, takes a few steps around the room:

> One could see by his face that he was remembering something with an agonizing effort. . . . For a moment it seemed that he had remembered everything. . . . The Stranger tarries in the depths by a dark half-opened window curtain. . . . The poet reels from terrible tension. But he forgot everything. [The Stranger disappears.] Beyond the window burns a brilliant star. Blue snow is falling.

Thus the drama ends. Only to ecstasy and to love is it given to transform the world, to "recognize" in someone met by chance a "star of the first magnitude." But ecstasy passes; the poet forgot everything, "in his eyes are emptiness and gloom." He looks at Maria and doesn't recognize her.

The lyrical drama *The Stranger* is not only one of Blok's most perfect works, but also a masterpiece of romantic theater.

In it the fate of the author is inscribed in symbolic letters. The one who appeared to him in the years of his youth in the image of the Beautiful Lady, the one who lit up his life like a beautiful blue star, was torn from her orbit and fell to earth. And the "falling maiden-star" wanted earthly words, earthly embraces. The knight's chaste adoration no longer satisfies her. And here "another" appears and leads "the beauty" away. The poet transformed his personal tragedy into a work of art. But he experienced the artist's victory as the man's downfall. Didn't he really carry onto the stage his own bleeding heart, didn't he really play out his own drama before the public? This is what he writes to E. P. Ivanov on 15 November 1906:

> I know that I am ceasing to be a person of the abyss and am rapidly changing into a writer. I know that I am breaking every day. I know what is made of cardboard.
>
> But first, I don't know how to repent of this and I think that it is late to repent, that *that* youth has passed, and I am determined to kill this youth by more and more writing. Anichkov once told me how my double will

make faces over my grave, and I approved and believed this, insofar as my present soul can believe anything at all. . . .

I know that I don't feel like myself. But with me is my doom, and I am rather proud of it and flirt with it.

You are a *man*, but I am ceasing to be a man and am becoming more and more a clown. Let it be so. . . .

I haven't lost the abyss forever. I always hear it out of the corner of my ear; even when I am completely broken and completely dead . . . I can't and don't want to hate myself. You know, I love my face.

I renounced you when the man in me was still being broken. Now I am broken, and I *deeply respect and love you* (as the dead love the living).

This is the background on which Blok's "lightnings of art" flash. The black void of death is curtained by the theatrical decoration with silver stars, fiery comets, blue light, and painted ships. The writer-buffoon is breaking in public view and flirts with his own doom. The man in him had long since died.

In 1906 Blok became good friends with Vyacheslav Ivanov, the author of very subtle poems ("Pilot Stars," "Transparence") and a scholarly researcher of the religion of Dionysus. His brilliant study "The Hellenic Religion of the Suffering God" was printed on the pages of *New Path* (1904) and *Questions of Life* (1905). Ivanov was attempting to prove the origin of religion from orgies, from ecstatic states of the soul; in the illumination of Dionysian religion the whole world assumes the aspect of a suffering god. "Dionysian ecstasy," he wrote, "is the only force resolving pessimistic despair." Through suffering and sacrifice man comes to resurrection into a new life. Blok was entranced by Ivanov's passionate preaching. Beginning in October 1906, he unfailingly visited his "Wednesdays" in the Tower. In November they went together to Moscow at the invitation of the editors of the journal *Golden Fleece*. Blok wrote E. P. Ivanov: "Moscow treated me rather well. I became quite friendly with Vyacheslav [Ivanov], and we understood much in each other." The influence of Ivanov's "Dionysianism" was reflected in the poet's October–December 1906 entries in the *Notebook*:

Often, more and more often, physical weariness comes upon me. It is probably the same with pregnant women—a curse for bearing flesh. For me, a curse for rebirth. It is impossible to summon Dionysus cheaply—this contains all the summoning of Bacchus, according to V. Ivanov's own words. If I am not transformed, I will die thus, in weariness.

And the second entry reads:

I have been dissatisfied with my poems since spring. The last were *The Stranger* and *Night Violet*. Then began the summer depression, then active Petersburg and two dramas, in which I said what was necessary and was already writing poems so-so, half-needed. I stretched, rushed into rhymes. But perhaps my new fresh cycle will come soon. And Aleksandr Blok—to Dionysus.

There is something childishly touching in the poet's hope of escaping despair through "Dionysian transformation," in his simple faith in his teacher's ideas. But even Dionysus doesn't save him. On 21 December Blok notes: "My barrenness (no poems, nothing, for a month and a half now) and my weariness. To go to Finland for the holidays, for example." And a few days later he outlines a plan for a drama, *Dionysus the Hyperborean*. The leader leads "the people into the distant mountains in search of Dionysus the Hyperborean." They reach the summit of World Beauty, but he leads them still higher, endlessly—"unless they grow wings." One weak "youth *remains alone in the icy mountains.* . . . He is prepared to die. But in him SINGS A MEASURE OF THE PATH he has traversed. . . . And, running up the cliffs, he calls loudly and furiously. . . . And here her low voice ANSWERS the last dying cry."

Dionysus the Hyperborean remained unwritten. V. Ivanov's influence proved to be short lived; Blok soon departed from him with hostility and irritation.

The end of the year was noteworthy for the poet for his entry into the world of the theater. A new period in his life had begun.

In 1904 Vera Fyodorovna Kommissarzhevskaya, leaving the public stage, founded her own theater. She had been seeking "new paths" for two seasons, without, however, making up her mind to break with the old traditions. In the spring of 1906 the actress ventured on a radical reform of both repertory and production. She dreamed of creating "a theater of the free actor, a theater of the spirit, in which everything external depends on the internal." The young and talented innovator Vsevolod Emilievich Meyerhold was invited to the post of managing director. A. Bely sketched his profile:

> Vsevolod Emilievich begins to live in me concretely in the sparsely furnished room: a table, a few chairs along the smooth, bluish gray wall. Meyerhold comes toward me from this background with elbows bent, in the same gray lounge suit. . . . He is too dry, too thin, unusually tall, angular. In the yellow-gray skin of the face with sunken cheeks is stuck a nose like a finger in a tightly stretched glove. The forehead slopes, the lips are thin and drily concealed by the nose, whose purpose resembles the scent of a borzoi—to smell out what is most essential.

With ardent enthusiasm he sets about building the New Theater. On his initiative a circle of "The Young" was formed, "Saturdays" where actors met with writers and artists of the "new direction." G. I. Chulkov, having become friends with Meyerhold, introduced him to Blok, and the poet began to visit the club on Officers' Street. There he met the young artists S. Yu. Sudeikin and N. N. Sapunov and the actresses Verigina, Mundt, Glebovaya-Sudeikina, and Volokhova. On one of the Saturdays G. I. Chulkov read his article on *The Puppet Show* for the theater troupe; on another Blok read *The King on the Square* with great success. Meyerhold was enthralled by both dramas, and they were accepted for production. Rehearsals of *The Puppet Show* began. Sapunov designed the decorations and costumes, Kuzmin composed the music for the play. The author gave directions and followed the director's work with excitement. After a "rehearsal without decorations" he wrote to V. E. Meyerhold:

> Dear Vsevolod Emilievich!
> I am writing to you hastily about what I noticed yesterday. As I already told you, I liked that general tone so much that new perspectives on *The Puppet Show* were opened to me. It seems to me that this is no longer just lyricism, but that it already contains the framework of a play.... But believe me, I must be around your theater, *The Puppet Show* must go on there. For me there is in this a *purifying* moment, a way out of lyrical solitude. And beside that, I am profoundly calm about the foundation of my *lyrical* soul, because I know and see what a true sense of measure just your theater preserves.

The first performance of *The Puppet Show* took place on 30 December. Blok's play ran with Maeterlinck's drama *The Miracle of Saint Anthony*. Meyerhold played Pierrot. This is how he describes his production:

> The sides and back of the whole stage are covered with canvas of a dark blue color. This blue space serves as a background and sets off the colors of the decorations of the little "mini-theater" built on the stage.... In front of the "mini-theater" on the stage, along the whole row of footlights, an empty area will be left. Here the author appears, as if serving as an intermediary between the audience and what takes place on the small stage. The action begins on a signal from a large drum. At first music plays, and one can see the prompter climbing into the box and lighting the candles. On the stage of the "mini-theater," parallel with the footlights, is a long table covered to the floor with a black cloth. The "mystics" sit at the table in such a way that the audience sees only the upper part of their figures. Frightened by a bit of dialogue, the mystics so lower their heads that headless and armless busts suddenly are left at the table. It turns out that the figures' contours were cut *out of cardboard*, and frock coats, shirt-fronts, collars, and cuffs were daubed on them with charcoal and chalk. The actors' arms were pushed into round openings cut in the cardboard busts, and the heads merely rested on the cardboard collars. Harlequin appears for the first time from under the mystics' table. When the author runs out onto the proscenium they don't let him finish the tirade he had begun.... Someone unseen pulls him back on a string by the tails of his frock coat ... so that he wouldn't dare to interrupt the solemn course of the action on the stage.... When Pierrot finishes his long monologue, the bench and the pedestal with the Cupid, together with the decorations, rise before the audience's eyes and a traditional columned hall descends.

Such a "modernistic" production produced a storm in the theater. Part of the audience whistled furiously, another part applauded frenziedly.

M. A. Beketova writes:

The Puppet Show ran many times, with variable success. This was Meyerhold's best production. At the last performance of this season the young people arranged an ovation for the author. . . . Endless gossip and ohing and ahing surrounded the play. The lyricism conquered everyone, but the meaning was hopelessly incomprehensible and obscure.

The production of *The Puppet Show* is etched into Blok's biography in a deep line. This line separates the past from the future—the diffident knight of the Beautiful Lady from the lover drunk with passion of *The Snow Mask* and *Faina*.

After the first performance, at a "paper ball" at Vera Ivanovna's, an actress from the Suvorinsky theater, a woman with black "winged" eyes entered the poet's life—Natalya Nikolaevna Volokhova:

> Here she appeared. She eclipsed
> All the well dressed, all the friends,
> And my soul stepped into
> The circle destined for it.

In 1906 Blok wrote his first lyrical article, "Troubled Times," which can be viewed as a psychological commentary on the collection *Unexpected Joy*. It is inspired by alarm at the impending end, by a feeling of inexorable destruction. At one time in Russia there was the pure and bright holiday of Christmas, a holiday of the hearth, reminiscences of a golden age. Now a "large, gray animal" has crept into our life—a fat female spider which has woven around our houses, streets, cities "a gray web of boredom." A terrible quiet had settled in. Only the "decadents" were shouting about destruction, but no one listened to them, and even they themselves were poisoned by the spider venom. People "became fidgety and pale faced"; first they lost God, then the world, finally themselves. "What's to be done? What's to be done?" the author exclaims. "There is no more hearth and home. . . . Joy has turned cold, the hearths have gone out. Time is no longer. The doors are opened to the blizzardy square. But even on the square the spiderweb triumphs." Blok paints the ominous face of the modern city: "the lanterns barely glimmer, . . . on the crossroads . . . drunken gaiety, laughter, red skirts." People whirl in frenzied hysteria, like unhappy masks. In the drafts of the unpeopled streets tramps appear; the voice of the blizzard had led them out of warm dwellings, had deprived them of their hearths, and calls them to an endless road. They wander into intense heat and cold along the macadam roads, orphaned, doomed, banished:

> This is a holy procession, a stately dance of idle thousand-eyed Russia, which no longer has anything to lose. . . . Russia dances to the sound of a long and doleful song about the rejection of conformity. . . . Somewhere in the distance a voice or a bell pours out, and still further away rowan trees seem to wave a sleeve, all strewn with red berries.

For Blok the tireless striving of poverty-ridden, vagrant Russia is like the whirling of a horseman lost at night amid a swamp. The images of the *poema Night Violet* surround us again. The imaginary flower—the night violet—looks into the horseman's eyes with the gaze of a bride. And the lyrical wave boils up. "The beauty in this gaze," the poet writes, "and the despair and happiness which no one on earth has known. Because he who has recognized this happiness will whirl and whirl eternally along the marshes, from hummock to hummock in the violet fog under a large green star."

The third part of the article is devoted to Russian literature. Over it, the author asserts, waterspouts have always soared and are soaring; perhaps no other literature has experienced so many insights and so many weaknesses as has Russian. It had three demons: Lermontov, Gogol, and Dostoevsky. The first climbed a mountain ridge, and in the ravines the world rushed past at his feet, a world possessed, insane, incarnated for suffering. But he, standing above the abyss, never incarnated anything, but looked with prophetic boredom at the images wandering below. Nor did Gogol incarnate anything. Like the sorcerer in "A Terrible Vengeance," he buried himself in the boundless feather-grass of the Ukrainian steppes and thought one protracted thought. "And his fleeting visions, disembodied phantoms, wandered uneasily through the wide world." The third—Dostoevsky—dreamed about God, about Russia, about the defense of the humiliated and insulted, about the incarnation of his dream. But before his eyes only a terrible face was incarnated, the face of Parfen Rogozhin,[17] a fiend of chaos and emptiness. Modern literature learned wisdom from Lermontov's and Gogol's sorcery, from Dostoevsky's falls. Blok speaks of the poems of Z. N. Gippius and F. Sologub. In the former, quiet sings and blooms: "the pale sunset and the slender greenish sickle of the moon is the music of its light touch." In Sologub: "Death is the radiance of the star Mair, the bliss of one betrothed to the quiet country of Oile. Death is the joy of calming, the Bride is Silence."

The article breaks off with a disturbed and terrible question: "And what if all earthly and Russian silence, all our aimless freedom and joy, are woven from a spider web? If the fat female spider weaves and weaves the web of our happiness, our life, our reality—who will tear the web?"

Blok was right in calling his article lyrical. He was creating a new form of prose where ideas and images are subordinated to the musical system and settle into a distinctive rhythmic order. Reasoning becomes "emotional melody," logical consistency is replaced by poetic correspondences. Blok's prose is not addressed to the mind, but to the heart and the imagination. From it we won't learn how his epoch thought and created, but we will hear *how* its air rang.

In December 1906 Blok's second collection of poems, *Unexpected Joy*, came out in the Scorpion publishing house.[18] Republishing his poems in the Musaget publishing house in 1916, the author radically revised this collection, did away with the title, supplemented it with poems of 1907 and 1908 and divided it into four sections: *Earth's Bubbles, Night Violet, Miscellaneous Poems,* and *The City.* In this form the collection made up a part of the second book of poems. This text must be considered definitive and canonical. In August 1906 Blok wrote an introduction to *Unexpected Joy* ("Instead of a Preface"). In it he tries to lay open in lyrical images the "soul of my book." He writes:

> *Unexpected Joy* is my image of the coming world. The awakening earth leads small shaggy creatures into the forest borders. They only know how to shout "farewell" to winter, to turn somersaults, and to tease passers-by. I attached myself to them, only because they are good-natured and mute creatures, with the affection of a silent soul withdrawn into itself, for which the world is a show-booth, a spectacle.
>
> ... Such the soul would have remained, if human abodes—the cities—hadn't disturbed it. There, in magical whirlwind and light, are terrible and wonderful visions of life. Nights—snow queens—drag their trains in sprays of stars. The dead fall on the turbulent streets, and a wonder-working astringent drink—red wine—deafens so that ears don't hear murder, blinds so that eyes don't see death. And the silent girl at the narrow table spins for me my Ring of Suffering all night. Her work gives birth in me to quiet songs of despair, songs of Resignation.
>
> ... Above the world, where the wind always blows, where one can't distinguish anything through the tears with which the wind clouds the eyes. Autumn rises, tall and broad. It comes to light above the damp of the swamps and rests the golden crown of its forests on the blue sky. Then one can understand how high the sky is, how wide the earth, how deep the seas, and how free the soul. Unexpected Joy is near at hand.

And the poet ends the introduction with the buoyant theme of the "ships": "One can hear how the sea boils up and the ship sirens howl. We will all flow to the pier, where the signal lights have been lit. The hearts of the peoples will ignite with new Joy when the great ships appear beyond the narrow cape." This "poem in prose" gives a counterpoint to the motifs of the book. Republishing the collection in 1912, Blok wrote:

> *Unexpected Joy* is a transitional book. The *Verses on the Beautiful Lady* have not yet died down, but already the basic section is linked to *Snowy Night.* Anyone who has looked at the dates of the book will understand why all the characteristics of a time of transition mark it.

In the first poem of the collection the poet already bids farewell to his departed youth, to the Beautiful Lady who has abandoned him forever:

> You left forever into the fields.
> Hallowed be Thy Name!
> Again the red lances of sunset
> Stretched their points toward me.

He is alone in the "sleepy world," he "sleeps in the fields," and his sleep resembles death:

> Oh, wrench out the rusty soul!
> Give me eternal rest with the saints,
> You, Who hold the sea and dry land
> Motionless in your delicate Hand!

Thus he sees off his prayerful and dreaming youth with the solemn words of church services, with the mournful hymns of the memorial service for the dead.

The first section, *Earth's Bubbles*, bears an epigraph from *Macbeth*: "The earth hath bubbles, as the water has, And these are of them." The abandoned knight's magic dream is interrupted; his eyes are opened, and he sees a deserted land all around; in the lace of the birch trees, far away, the lilac slopes of a ravine; spring is coming, the first grass breaks through the ground, which is still hard. Gradually the eyes become accustomed to the marsh mist. He makes out its teeming, scurrying, and rustling "inhabitants." Here are the "marsh imps":

> And we sit, little fools,
> Weakness, water spirits.
> The caps are green,
> And on backwards.
>
> The plague-infected sleep of the water,
> The rust of the wave . . .
> We are the forgotten traces
> Of someone's depth . . .

Here are the "springtime creatures":

> You will languish, repent,
> And bite and bark,
> You, green, strong, small,
> Dear, imaginary creatures.

Here the imps and dwarfs surround the old woman-wanderer and touchingly ask her not to take them with her to the holy places:

> And the shaggy small ones repent,
> Look, touched, at the crutches,
> Humbly turn somersaults in the grass,
> Raise dust with their hooves.

And here too the "little swamp priest" is a charming creation of Blokian fantasy:

> He prays quietly,
> Smiles, bows,
> Raising his hat.

And he bandages the wounded paw
Of a lame, hobbling frog
With healing grass.
He crosses it and lets it go:
"Step onto your native path.
  "My soul is glad
"For every reptile
"And every animal,
"And for every creed."

And he prays quietly,
Raising his hat,
For the stalk which bends,
For the wounded animal paw,
  And for the Roman Pope.

Tatyana Nikolaevna Gippius had an album with the German inscription: "*Kindisch.*" In it she drew fantastic figures of imps, swamp priests, droll gnomes, and monsters. Blok loved to scrutinize these drawings, and they influenced his poems. He put much tenderness and humor in his swamp dwellers. But the awakening knight does not just see the water spirits poking about near him: the whole wide wonderful world opens before him. Blok conveys the feeling of late autumn amazingly: purity, transparence, cold, open sky, forests penetrated with silence, the green sickle of the moon in the blue, the lace of the delicate birch tree, the narrow strip of sunset, and—silence. The radiant sadness and tenderness of the autumn light are new in Russian poetry, a purely Blokian landscape. In the poem *Autumn Dances* misty female figures do round dances in the green clearing; their arms are stretched toward the sky, their hair flows loosely. Autumn smiles at them through tears:

With us, to us—light-winged youth—
An airy fate is given us . . .
And where does our Joy come from,
And from where does Quietness float?

So the dead knight comes to life. He can't fly; his wings are broken. Around him are the mosses, hummocks, and hollows of the swamp. But this poor land is illuminated by her, below as well as above. His sorrow is replaced by Joy. Not long ago he had parted from her: "You left forever into the fields."

And here she is with him again, on earth as in heaven—the eternal Sovereign of days:

I am with you forever, I'll never leave,
And will give up autumn freedom.
In these hollows the quiet water dozes,
Locking the gates to the insane springs.

> Oh, Sovereign of days! With Your scarlet ribbon
> You have enclosed the pale azure firmament.
> I know, I know the caress of my Friend—
> The olden days of the illuminated swamps.

The *poema Night Violet,* already familiar to us, occupies the second section. The third, *Miscellaneous Poems,* unites the poems of 1904–8. In October 1906 Blok entered in his *Notebook*: "Every poem is a veil stretched on the spikes of a few words. These words shine like stars. Because of them the poem exists." The poems of this section are supported on such word-stars. The words, ringing for the poet with a mysterious, obscure music, are saturated with lyrical energy of such tension that the poem's fabric comes to life and rings through their touch. These words are few, and they are simple: night, silence, road, Russia, death. But before Blok we didn't know their unfathomable meaning, their innumerable echoes.

The subdued music of the lyrical theme of *death* meets us in the very first poems, not as image, but as sound and rhyme:

> I kratok put' sred' dolgoj noči,
> Druz'ja, blizka nočnaja tverd'!
> I daže rifmy net koroče
> Gluxoj, krylatoj rifmy: *smert'*.

> And short is the path amid the long night,
> Friends, the night arch is near!
> And there is even no rhyme shorter
> Than the muffled, winged rhyme—*death*.

Oh no, neither youth, nor spring, nor life, nor love know such magical songs as does death:

> Ona zovët. Ona manit,
> V snegax zemlja i tverd'.
> Čto mne poët? Čto mne zvenit?
> Inaja žizn'? Gluxaja smert'?

> She[19] calls. She beckons,
> The earth and sky are in snows.
> What sings to me? What rings to me?
> Another life? Lonely death?

Again the "muffled rhyme," *tverd'*:*smert'*. This long poem (*Conceived at night, I am born at night*) is written with a regular alternation of four-foot and three-foot iambics. Then the last line is suddenly lengthened (four feet instead of three). The word "death" hangs on it like a heavy weight.

How quiet is her approach. She touches the dead one with a mother's hands. He says to her:

Aleksandr Blok

> You will dress me in silver,
>   And when I die
> The moon will come out—a celestial Pierrot,
>   The red jester will rise in the open heights.

Death is the beautiful goddess of the night:

> In long black attire,
> In a crowd of black chariots,
> In pale phosphorescent radiance.

And her music is the music of the spheres. And how she resembles the One who descended to him in azure in the years of his youth:

> Who are You, getting me drunk
> On night potions?
> Who are You, Feminine Name,
> In a nimbus of red light?

Then the pipe sang of love in the spring fields; now death sings "in the voice of piercing storms." But in the mortal delirium these songs merge, grow, overflow with solemn, funereal melody:

> I sought the White Maiden.
> Do you hear? Do you believe? Do you sleep?
> I sought the Ancient Maiden
> And my bugle pealed.

Now she sleeps amidst eagles "on the dark summit of a cliff," but he is with her; for a long time he has been in the embrace of white death:

> We were—and we departed,
> And I remember the funeral sound:
> How they carried my heavy coffin,
> How the clumps of earth fell.

The "word-stars" love-death weave their rays in Blok. Two torrents of sound and rhythm, two parallel rows of images, and the transformation is accomplished: love is as strong as death. It is sweet to kiss dead lips:

> I will be dead—with face raised.
> She will come who loves more in the world,
> Will kiss my dead lips,
> Will cover me with a fragrant shawl.

Another lyrical theme is connected with the *poema Her Coming*. "Ships" is a magic word for Blok: light-winged birds with slender masts and filled sails rock on its open, airy sound. While still a child, he drew ships. For him they were the image of happiness, of hope, of liberation.

When ships pass through Blok's poems a lighthouse lamp burns in the darkness, the voices of the ships' sirens set the tune, and the heart is wrung with childlike joy:

The Puppet Show

> There the last lantern lit up,
> Illuminating the mysterious pier.
> There a ship ascended, like a tsar,
> And yesterday put out to sea.
>
> Its sails showed faintly gray,
> Carrying triumph out to sea.

The ship is a tsar, it carries triumph, waves of poetic sound images radiate from it. Let us recall the famous poem:

> The young girl sang in the church choir
> Of all the weary in a foreign land,
> Of all the ships put out to sea,
> Of all who have forgotten their joy.

Her voice promised joy to everyone, but in Blok joy is mysteriously connected with ships:

> And it seemed to everyone there would be joy,
> That all the ships are in a quiet bay,
> That in the strange land the weary people
> Had found a radiant life.

For that reason the finale rings so tragically. Joy deceived them. The *ships won't return*:

> A child, taking communion, wept
> That none of them would return.

The poet's imagination is captivated by images of ships. In his annex at Shakhmatovo, cutting out a dormer window, he looks at the evening sky, and the rosy clouds form for him the light outlines of ships:

> The whole sunset sky is in somnolence,
> The dale's shadows lengthen,
> And on the rosy stern dies out
> The spring helmsman sailing away . . .
>
> Here we sail away with him into the dark,
> And the flying ship disappears . . .
> Here the helmsman—like a falling star—
> Farewell! . . . flies to the stern . . . .

In the poem *Leave me in my far-off place* the poet speaks to his beloved of his constancy and innocence. The shore is dark and the distance deserted, but he is true to his dream and as before awaits a miracle. He clothes this confession in the allegory of a ship. For him the ship is not a metaphor, but an emotional reality and a mystical experience:

> The approaching sail is near at times
> And dream catches fire.
> And here, above the endless expanse
> The soul is occupied with the miraculous.
> . . . . .
> But the distance is deserted and calm,
> And I always the same—by the rudder.
> And I sing always just as harmoniously,
> The dream of my native ship.

The poem-dialogue *The Poet* was written under Maeterlinck's influence. The motif of the ship passes in a tone of irony. The poet and his daughter look at the sea. He tells her that he wants to go beyond the sea, "where the Beautiful Lady lives." The daughter asks:

> "And this Lady—is she good?"
>   "Yes."
> "Then why doesn't she come?"
>   "She will never come.
> "She doesn't travel on a steamship."
> Night approached.
> Papa's talk with his daughter ended.

The ship was changed into a "steamship." Andrey Bely stormed. "The Beautiful Lady doesn't travel on a steamship." What blasphemy!

In the symphonic whole of Blok's lyric the central theme grows slowly over the years. In *Verses on the Beautiful Lady* it is barely audible; in a dull rumble it accompanies the motifs of prayers and visions. In *Unexpected Joy* it is interwoven with melodies of joy-sadness, silence, white death, and blue ships. At first it is formless and diffuse, then gradually the fog disperses and its image-symbols are revealed: paths, roads, boundless spaces, deserted distances, wind, clouds running across the sky—eternal motion, eternal striving. How unsure are the poet's first attempts to catch the incomprehensible voice sounding to him in the distance! In the poem *Son and Mother* the motif of "wandering" is furnished with the knightly setting already familiar to us from the first collection:

> The son is covered by the shadow of the cross.
> The son abandons his paternal home.

But this "departure from home" is not yet "vagabondage." The knight sets out to struggle with dark forces. He is in "dazzling armor," in a "helmet of dawn," a sword in his hand. He drives away the night darkness with his arrows. And, having accomplished a purifying feat, he returns home wounded:

> The son didn't forget his own mother:
> The son returned to die.

The image of the "path" is also motivated by the knightly feat in another poem, *So inspiredly, so melodiously*. The tsarevna sees the knight off on the campaign. She believes in his return:

> Go, go, you will return young,
> And faithful to your duty.

He will wander for long years in a foreign land, but she "will watch over him on the way." And his farewell words ring with joyful faith:

> Farewell, tsarevna. My path is long—
> I go beyond the fiery springtime.

These lines are like a dream of the past, of the tsarevna-Beautiful Lady who "left forever into the fields." The echo of the songs dying away is barely audible. And suddenly everything changes: castles, towers, helmets, armor disappear like a rising curtain. After impotent groping, there is a sudden miraculous discovery. The "path" is not a knightly campaign, not a departure for war, but the wandering of a homeless poor man, of a beggar "singing psalms." Blok finds the theme of his life and his lyrics: he discovers vagrant, dark Rus, its rending, violent, wild, and tender music, and becomes a great Russian poet. The poem *Do not lure me, freedom* ushers us into this new world. The poet addresses Mother Earth. He isn't destined to be a guest at the green feast of spring; his fate is to wander the roads:

> And I will go along the road,
>   Along the painful path—
> To live with my wretched soul
>   As a beggarly poor man.

As soon as the poet touched the lyrical theme of Russian wandering, his verse changed wonderfully. These are new rhythms—headlong, breathtaking; new sounds—of melancholy folk tunes; and new perfection—of verbal form.

Blok is already singing *Verses on Russia* in *Unexpected Joy*:

> I go out onto a path open to the gaze,
> The wind bends the supple bushes,
> Crushed stone lay along the slopes,
> Meager layers of yellow clay.

Who doesn't remember this "sobbing" landscape—autumn in damp dales, the red color of the rowans, a girl's figured sleeve, the beggar singing psalms? In whose memory do these drawn-out trochaics with transitions from deep U to open A not ring?

> Net, idu ja v put' nikem ne zvanyj.
> I zemlja da budet mne legka!
> Budu slušat' golos Rusi p'janoj,
> Otdyxat' pod kryšej kabaka.

> No, I go onto the path uninvited,
> And may the earth be light for me!
> I will listen to the voice of drunken Rus,
> Will rest under the tavern roof.

The path as a symbol of Russia, of its expanses, of its "vast distances," of its depression and its frenzied striving, and the *tramp-beggar* born of this path are here new "word-stars" of Blok's lyric.

The astonishing poem *Rus* is lit up by them:

> You are unusual even in sleep.
> I won't touch your clothing.
> I doze—and behind the dozing a mystery.
> And in the mystery you will sleep, Rus!

The image of demonic, witchcraft Rus is constructed from the material of the work on Russian spells and incantations: dense forests, swamps, the glow of fires, pillars of snow where witches whirl, nocturnal round dances of dissimilar peoples, paths and crossroads, wind and blizzard, terrible poverty-ridden Russia. And it is all in motion, in flight, tossed upward and rising in whirlwinds. Its soul is in this whirlwind. The dark face is merely a cover concealing a mystery. The poem ends with the solemn mystical verses:

> Živuju dušu ukačala,
> Rus', na svoix prostorax, ty,
> I vot—ona ne zapjatnala
> Pervonačal'noj čistoty.

> Dremlju—i za dremotoj tajna,
> I v tajne počivaet Rus',
> Ona i v snax neobyčajna,
> Eë odeždy ne kosnus'.

> You rocked the living soul to sleep,
> Rus, on your expanses,
> And here it didn't soil
> Its pristine purity.

> I doze—and behind the dozing a mystery—
> And Rus sleeps in the mystery.
> She is unusual even in sleep,
> I won't touch her clothing.

Let us note the incomparable mastery of the "sound chiaroscuro," of the contrast of the dark U's with the light A's. After the muffled melody on U (*živuju dušu, Rus'*), with what triumphant trumpets sound the assonances on A:

The Puppet Show

I vot—ona ne zapjatnala
Pervonacal'noj čistoty.

The "living soul" of Russia, her "beggarly" nature, are illuminated by supernatural light. Her mystery is somewhat revealed in the poem *Here He is, Christ, in chains and roses*, evoked by Nesterov's landscapes. The blue sky, the fields, forests, ravines merge into the features of an icon Image:

In the simple framework of the blue sky
His icon looks out the window,
A beggarly artist created the sky,
But the image and the blue sky are one.

The Image of Christ is stamped on the Russian land, humble and poor. And to understand Him, one must become a rover, a wanderer, a "beggar singing psalms":

And you won't understand the blue eye,
Until you yourself become like a path.

The "path," "striving," "wandering," "Russia," "Christ"—such is the line of growth of the lyrical wave in Blok's verse.

The last section of the book, entitled *The City*, is distinguished for its very great integrity of structure. The apocalyptic vision of the modern city growing out of Blok's dark music goes back to Gogol's romantic grotesque ("Nevsky Prospect") and to Dostoevsky's "fantastic realism" (*Crime and Punishment*).

Blok has only one predecessor in Russian poetry—Briusov. His "urban verse," inspired by Verhaeren, helped the poet to understand the city as humanity's terrible fate, as a portent of the destruction of our world. In Blok's verse the city is a living being, hungry, merciless, shameless, and stinking. Like a fat female spider (the article "Troubled Times"), it enmeshed the life of people in a web. The poet seizes on the vile and banal features of urban life, because for him these are signs of a great human tragedy. And each detail he touches on—gas lantern, crooked lanes, factory smokestack, tavern—is suddenly removed, like painted theater scenery, revealing behind it "bottomless gaps into eternity." Intentionally coarse realism borders on the most unrestrained fantasy. The massiveness of the house-tombs, the weight of the roadway stones are illusory. Blok's city, like Dostoevsky's Petersburg, can vanish like smoke at any moment. It is not reality, but a death image of doomed humanity. Describing a square, streets, dives, and factories, the poet is telling the story of the destruction of his own soul. The "substantiality" and "materiality" of his descriptions are completely emotionalized and spiritualized. The city is transformed into a lyrical theme, its evil weight into a flight of heavenly bodies.

Let us observe carefully the terrible features of its face. An empty lane, the sun setting behind a smokestack; a solitary lantern blinks in the distance; clouds, smoke, overturned tubs, a damp fence, factory soot (the poem *Deception*). The well of the yard: forgotten yellow candles burn in someone's window; a hungry cat presses herself against the gutter of a roof (*Windows Overlooking the Yard*). Here is the curse of labor:

> We have passed all the gates,
> And have seen in every window,
> How heavily the work lies
> On each bent back.
>   (*Cold Day*)

The workers emerge from the basements, from the darkness of the cellars, dragging picks and shovels. The gray crowd pours out into the city like the sea and crawls along the stones of the roadway. ("They rose from the darkness of the cellars"). Here is the curse of debauchery:

> A man and a whore woke up in a room,
> Slowly came to amid the charcoal gloom.

The woman throws herself out the window onto the stones of the roadway:

> Little boys, women, yardmen noticed something,
> Waved their arms, tracing an unfamiliar pattern.
>   (*The Last Day*)

When darkness descends on the city, and lights are lit in the windows, when the lanes smell of the sea, and the factory whistles sing, women in red cloaks pass along the street, and their voices ring like strings:

> Whom did you notice in the slippery darkness?
> Whose windows shine through the fog?
> Here a restaurant's as bright as a temple,
> And a temple is open like a restaurant.

The city's nights are poisoned with sensuality. All the faces are marked with the sign of death:

> The moon floated in the pale azure
> Like a bent finger.

> Everyone to whom I came
> Had a mouth scarlet as a cross.
> . . . . .
> The women's gaze was dull and vacant,
> And their gaze was terrible.
> I knew that their lips' convulsions
> Revealed their shame.

In the poem *The Invisible One* the city-beast's insatiable lust is laid bare in apocalyptic profundity. The soil departs from beneath our feet; we glance into an abyss. There is gaiety in the night tavern; a crowd of drunks bursts into the dive to the rouged prostitutes:

> Who soiled the sky with blood?
> Who hung out the bloody lantern?

The poem ends with a prophetic image of the Whore astride the Beast:

> The evening inscription is drunk
> Above the door open to the shop. . . .
> On a Crimson Beast, the Woman
> Mixed in the mad crush
> With a splashing cup of wine.

But after the songs about the curse of labor, poverty, hard drinking, and debauchery, lacerating and raucous like the sounds of a street organ, there is the blinding contrast of ball music with the glitter and splendor of the night city. "In the electric waking dream," how beautiful are the women, how proud the men's gazes. Varicolored shadows, strewn with pearls, lit by shafts of light, whirl in the flying rhythm of the waltz:

> In the taverns, in the lanes, in the windings,
> In an electric waking dream,
> I endlessly sought the beautiful ones
> And those undyingly in love with fame.

And from the "music of the glitter" angelic visions arise:

> And couple after couple flashed by . . .
> I awaited the bright angel's coming to us,
> So that here, in the rejoicing of the sidewalk,
> He would bring one woman within reach of the heavens.

By interweaving the lyrical motifs of the city, by the play on contrasts of darkness and light, the introduction of the central theme—the Stranger—is slowly and solemnly prepared:

> In the evenings over the restaurants. . . .

She stands in the center of the section *The City* like a resolution of all the dissonances, like the end of all paths. She is a magical fusion of diabolic and angelic features, in which "the daughter of nocturnal gaiety" drags "a train sprayed with stars." She passes through the circles of hell, along the streets, taverns, restaurants, but:

> This gaze is no less bright
> Than it was in the foggy heights.

Blok's "city" poems are love poems. The city is his fate, his death, his hatred and love. How often, speaking about it, he is unable to master his agitation and explodes a verse with exclamations. In the poem *Deception* the narration is suddenly interrupted by a cry: How terrible! How homeless!

In *The Ditty*:

> Spring, spring! How empty is the air!
> How exorbitantly meager the evening!

The Legend begins with an address:

> Lord, do you hear? Lord, will you forgive?
> Spring floated high in the blue.

In the poem *Drowsiness lay down on the gray stones* the last three lines ring like a frenzied shout:

> Oh, city! Oh, wind! Oh, snowstorms!
> Oh, abyss of azure torn to shreds!
> I am here! I am innocent! I am with you! I am with you!

Blok's city is the "scenery of the soul," but not a landscape of Petersburg. It has neither the Neva, nor the embankments, nor the prospects, nor the palaces. But nonetheless every Peterburger will at once recognize in his verse the inexplicable, ineffable "air" of the northern capital. And the distancing of Blok the romantic from the classic Pushkin will strike him involuntarily. The majestic Petersburg of *The Bronze Horseman* is simply beyond Blok's field of vision. But he has his own *Bronze Horseman*—the poem *Peter*, which one may guess to be a deliberate challenge to Pushkin. The bronze Peter guards his city; in his outstretched hand the flame of a torch dances. A sea of lust, debauchery, and sin pours out at the foot of Peter's statue:

> There, on a rock, the gay tsar
> Waved a fetid censer,
> And the urban soot, like a chasuble,
> Clothed the beckoning lantern!

The "gay tsar" ruling over the devil's sabbath is Blok's sneer at Pushkin's "powerful ruler of fate."

CHAPTER V

THE SNOW MASK
1907

On 28 December 1906 Blok outlines in the *Notebook* the plan of a drama, *Dionysus the Hyperborean*. "A weak youth," left in solitude in the icy mountains, calls "loudly and insistently." "Her low voice ANSWERS the last dying cry." The outline breaks off here. But he writes in a later entry: "Who is She? A god or a demon? Tomorrow I will look again. *More calmly. Less anxiously.* Not tastelessly, so as to disturb nothing. It is a question of something much more important. Here a quotation for memory." Under the word "quotation" the following rough draft of a letter is given: "28 December. Today I am committed to you. I ask you to approach me. I must speak a few words to you alone. I ask you to accept this as simply as I write it. I respect you deeply."

The first poem of the collection *The Snow Mask* is dated 29 December. It is called *Snow Wine*:

> And again, flashing from the wine cup,
> You inspired fear in the heart
> With your innocent smile.
> In your heavy serpentine hair.

And further:

> And you laugh wonderful laughter,
> You coil in the golden chalice,
> And over your sable fur
> The blue wind plays.

These lines on the woman-wine, on the woman-serpent, are dedicated to the actress Natalya Nikolaevna Volokhova. There is no doubt that the entry in the notebook ("Who is She? A god or a demon?") and the rough draft of the letter also relate to her. The poet is persuading himself to examine the image arising before him in the snowstorm more calmly, less agitatedly. The face of the "dark-eyed maiden" is enigmatic and threatening. A year later he wrote:

> And I spent a mad year
> By the black train....

In M. A. Beketova's book we read:

> I'll say one thing: the poet didn't embellish his "snow maiden." Whoever saw her then, at the time of his passion, knows how wonderfully charming she was. Tall, slender figure, pale face, fine features, black hair, and eyes exactly "winged," black, wide open, "poppies of malicious eyes." The smile was even more striking, teeth of sparkling whiteness, a kind of exultant, victorious smile. Someone said at that time that her eyes and smile, blazing up, slashed the darkness. Others said: "An Old-Believer Madonna."

Bely's impression was different. He didn't like Volokhova; he saw her "lilac, dark aura":

> Very thin, pale and tall, with black, wild and tormenting eyes with blue under them, with skinny and narrow hands, lips dry and very pursed, with a wasp waist, black-haired and dressed all in black—she seemed *réservée*. Aleksandr Aleksandrovich was obviously afraid of her; he was very deferential to her. I remember how, getting up and waving her gloves, she said something to him imperiously. He stood up, bent his head low, listened to her—and quailed. "Well, let's go!" And rustling her black, silk, it seems, skirt she went toward the exit. And A. A. followed her, deferentially handing her her coat. There was obviously something violet in her.

The word "dark" suited her very well; there was something "dark" in her. Just before his death Blok remembered this mad winter of 1907, when he "blindly surrendered himself to the elemental force" (note on *The Twelve*). For the first time passion intoxicated him with the wine of the snowstorm, sent him whirling, stunned him. The "snow maiden" sang him a song of love and destruction:

> With the sleeve of my snowstorms
>   I will smother,
> With the silver of my gaieties
>   I will deafen.

The transition from *Unexpected Joy* to *The Snow Mask* is striking. In the former, there is motionlessness, quiet, mist on the swamp, the stupefying odor of the Night Violet, in the latter, whirlwind, blizzard, a flight over the abyss, the singing bugle of snowstorms, the bottomless blue of the winter sky, the sparkle of falling stars:

> The snowstorm soared,
> A star fell,

> After it—another . . .
> And star after star
> > Rushed off,
> > Revealing
> New abysses
> In a starry whirlwind.

Everything had changed—both rhythms and sounds and the whole world.

Blok didn't live, he flew, rejoicing and choking from the flight. Thirty poems of the cycle *The Snow Mask*, in the manuscript called *Lyrical Poema*, were written in a couple of weeks (from 23 December 1906 to 13 January 1907). Never before had he experienced such intensity and inspiration. The rapture didn't cool, and its triumphal music deadened both the feeling of guilt and the premonition of death. "When I live at such an accelerated tempo as this winter," he wrote his mother, "I am 'satisfied.' But I readily admit that I can feel despair should this tempo slacken. ('I fell so low that even the Angels can't hold me up with their large wings,' says Beatrice)."[1] Blok even changed physically. Seeing him after a long separation, Bely was struck by his appearance: "nothing remained of the lifeless, gray Blok of 1906, who resembled a waning moon, a distorted mouth." He again let his hair grow (in 1906 it was short). In his whole figure one sensed temperedness and calm courage. He had become simpler, more pensive. His former soulfulness had burned through, and behind it a blue starry sky was revealed. Bely writes:

> Stars out of the night, out of the night of tragedy. Out of the night of tragedy I sensed Blok that night, and I understood that the period of shadows or evil spirits of *Unexpected Joy* had ended for him. Of course on a dark night there are no shadows, there is peaceful, even darkness lit up by stars. Blok sat before me, having crossed the boundary of *The Snow Mask*.

This winter the poet was particularly handsome. P. N. [V. N.] Knyazhnin describes him:

> His face is usually stern, but the smile transforms it completely. I can't now remember another such smile, a smile tender and offering up its whole self. . . . But the face changes. Sometimes it is a beautiful mold from an ancient god, sometimes there is something birdlike in it. . . . But this is rare. Almost always it is an expression of concentrated strength, the impression of a foreign sailor born in Dunkirk or in Helgoland. Measured step, muscular torso, nothing flabby. Behind the external severity, an abyss of goodness, but not of sentimentality. Only once did I see him violently angry, but even this violence boiled somewhere inside, and externally was almost impassive: without shouting, without gestures, but the more terrible for that.

With great mastery Bely painted "Blok in love, in the foyer of the Kommissarzhevskaya Theater." The premiere of Maeterlinck's *Pelléas et Mélisande* was playing. The poet stood by a wall, talking with a lady:

> He stood, head raised and revealing his beautiful neck, with the haughty half-smile he displayed at that time. It was very becoming to him. A cap of bright and, as if smoking, curly hair harmonized with the pinkened face. Through the haughty expression of the lips I noticed anxiety in his gaze. Waving a white rose, he paid no attention to a pushy lady. His eyes roamed the auditorium as if looking for someone. Suddenly his look changed; it became alert. He fixed his eyes on one point and slowly turned his head, again reminding me of a portrait of Oscar Wilde. . . . Then he very absentmindedly took his leave and with rapid, light, young footsteps almost ran through the crowd, cleaving the space of the foyer. The tails of his unbuttoned frock coat flowed from his waist.

Blok was running to meet the one to whom he had dedicated *The Snow Mask*: "I dedicate these poems to You, tall woman in black, with eyes winged and in love with the light and darkness of my snow city." S. Gorodetsky recalled a night in Vyacheslav Ivanov's tower when Blok read poems from *The Snow Mask*:

> A large garret with a narrow window straight to the stars. Candles in candelabra. L. D. Zinovieva-Annibal in a tunic. . . . We assembled late. After twelve, Vyacheslav and Anichkov or someone else gave reports on the themes of mystical anarchism, collective individualism, the suffering god of Hellenic religion, the collective theater, Christ and Antichrist, etc. We argued violently and at length. Toward morning, after the debate, the reading of poems began. . . . In his long frock coat, with the soft necktie tied with elegant casualness, in a nimbus of ashen-gold hair, Blok was at that time romantically handsome. . . . He would go slowly to the table with the candles, look around at everyone with his stony eyes and would himself turn to stone until the silence became complete. And he began to speak, holding the verse steady agonizingly well and slowing the tempo slightly on the rhymes. . . . Everyone was in love with him.

Natalya Nikolaevna Volokhova was an actress of the Kommissarzhevskaya Theater. She was lit by the magical luster of the footlights and surrounded by the romantic aureole of the theater. Her face was concealed under an actress' mask. Her slender figure moved on a background of stylized scenery; in front of her the dark abyss of the auditorium, the enamoured crowd. Blok's love was flooded with the electric light of the theater footlights; in his love reality was interwoven with stage illusion, the truth of life with the "splendid lie" of art. His beloved—the "Snow Mask"—is half-reality, half-dream, both a real woman and a poet's vision. The curtain parts, the music sounds, the footlights glare. She appears on the stage:

> I was confused and gay.
> Your dark silk teased me;
> When *your* heavy curtain
> Parted, the theater became silent.

> The bright ring of footlights
> Separated us like living flame,
> And the music transformed
> And burnt your face.
>
> And here again the candles shine,
> The soul is alone, the soul is blind . . .
> Your splendid shoulders,
> The crowd drunk on you . . .
>
> A star, departed from the world,
> You are far away above the plain . . .
> The silver lyre trembles
> In your outstretched hand. . . .

There was "virtuosity" in the poet's appearance in the era of *The Snow Mask*, the finished beauty of a work of art. As if he too were standing on the stage, talentedly playing the role of a handsome poet in love. Blok, with a haughty smile and a white rose in his hand, seeking for her with his eyes in the foyer of the theater, Blok, reading poems "in the tower" by candelabra light on the background of a window looking out into the starry night, seems to be the hero of a romantic *poema*. B. Eichenbaum perceptively transmits the impression of "life being created" in his article "Blok's Fate":[2]

> Blok became for us a tragic actor playing himself. . . . His young countenance merged with his poetry, like the makeup of a tragic actor with his monologue. When Blok would make his appearance, it became almost terrifying: he so resembled himself. Some ship's boy from a northern ship—a youth lithe and at the same time a bit clumsy, a bit angular in his movements, impetuous and strangely calm, with a smile almost childish and at the same time enigmatic, with a voice deep, but hollow and monotonous, with eyes too transparent, in which pale waves of the northern seas seemed to shine, with a youthfully delicate face, but as if "scorched by the rays of the polar lights."

The conversion of life into art, the transformation of the living face into the mask of a tragic actor, is Blok's terrible "fate." He knew the inevitability of this path. "I don't have real life," he wrote his mother. "I want it to at least be sold for real gold (as with Alberich),[3] but not for hearth and home or for fears (as with Zhenya).[4] The worse life is, the better one can create, but life and profession are incompatible." The knight of the Beautiful Lady becomes reconciled to the fate of a professional man of letters.

At the end of January 1907 Lyubov Dmitrievna's father, Dmitri Ivanovich Mendeleev, died. All of Petersburg attended the famous scientist's funeral. The father left his daughter a small inheritance. She began to take lessons in elocution and plastic movements, preparing for her entry onto the stage.

The Bloks' life continued at an "accelerated tempo." The poet performs in the Petersburg University Circle of Youth, reads *The Stranger* there, attends religious-philosophical meetings, takes a great interest in Wagner's operas and the new productions of the Art Theater (*Woe from Wit* and *Brandt*). He accompanies N. N. Volokhova to performances of Kommissarzhevskaya's theater. Actors, poets, artists often gather at the Bloks' in the evenings. There, at the end of January, A. A. reads the play *The Stranger* and poems from *The Snow Mask* to Sologub, V. Ivanov, Chulkov, Pyast, Hoffman, Kondratiev, and Gorodetsky. In February, K. A. Somov paints his portrait, ordered by *Golden Fleece*; M. A. Kuzmin and other poets come during the sittings. Blok doesn't like the portrait: the artist made his face heavier, accentuated the sensual swelling of his lips, the feminine roundness of his chin, and the lusterless immobility of his gaze.

But the "gaiety of death" was concealed under the young poet's social life:

> There is no end to the blizzard,
> And for me it is gay to perish;
> It led me into a charmed circle,
> Curtained with the silver of its blizzards....

In a letter to E. P. Ivanov he asked: "Dear one, believe me, right now I have a right to ask this of you. Mainly believe that it is *now terrifying* and there is no more level ground."

Instead of level ground, a starry abyss is revealed beyond the whirlwinds and snowstorms:

> There will be no spring, and it isn't necessary;
> The third christening will be—Death.

But spring came, and with it came separation from Volokhova. On 20 April Blok enters in his *Notebook*: "Only Natalya Nikolaevna is Russian, with her Russian 'accidentalness': not knowing where she is from, proud, beautiful, and free. With petty slavish habits and vast freedom.... Will we meet somehow in August? We are weary, monstrously weary." And he writes in another entry: "The radiant one is always with me. She will yet return to me. I am no longer young; there is much of the 'cold broad daylight' in my soul. But the beautiful evening is near."

In the spring the Bloks gave up their apartment on Lakhtinskaya Street. Lyubov Dmitrievna left for Shakhmatovo alone. Aleksandr Aleksandrovich moved into the grenadiers' barracks with his mother. He would go to Shakhmatovo for a short time and again return to Petersburg. Lyubov Dmitrievna was diligently preparing for the stage, studying roles, taking up elocution. Blok pined in the city and roamed the neighborhoods. In the evening he would often set out with Chulkov for Ozerki, Sestroretsk. They drank red wine. G. I. Chulkov recalls:

> My relations with Blok were always uneven. At one time we would see each other very often (it once happened that we didn't part for three days, roaming, and spending the night in the neighborhood of Petersburg), at another time we didn't want to look at each other. . . . *There were reasons for this.*

We have a basis for assuming that one of these reasons was Chulkov's complicated relations with Lyubov Dmitrievna. By autumn a divergence between the friends had already begun, which led to a complete break a year later. On 28 September Blok wrote his mother: "I see Chulkov now and then; it is always unpleasant both for him and for me."

Out of the impressions of the roaming outside the city and of the trips to Sestroretsk, Shuvalovo, and the Dunes grew the small descriptive-narrative *poema Free Thoughts*, which the poet dedicated to his constant companion—Chulkov.

The group of the journal *Scales* boycotted N. P. Ryabushinsky's publishing house, Golden Fleece. In the summer he suggested that Blok head the literary section of his journal. Bely, having fired on the "*Scales* Peterburgers" and having savagely attacked Blok, became completely furious. The tone of his improprieties against the author of *The Puppet Show* became almost indecent. Briusov writes his father (21 June 1907) about the literary manners and morals of the epoch:

> There are all kinds of discord among the decadents, as you partly see by *Scales*. All four factions of decadents—"Scorpions," "Golden Fleecers," "Passists," and "Horaeists"—are at odds with one another and caustically abuse one another in their own organs, otherwise one can't survive. You have read how we attacked the "Petersburg litterateurs" ("The Stamped Galosh," Bely's article). This is an attack against *Horae* and in particular against A. Blok. Blok answers this for us in *Golden Fleece*, which is glad to repay us abuse for abuse. Of course *The Pass* also doesn't hold its tongue! . . . In a word, full-scale battle.

In July 1907 Blok's literary surveys began to appear in *Golden Fleece*. In the first of these ("On the Realists") we confront a new face of the poet, a face turned to the people, to the earth, to Russia. This is no longer a youthful dreamer and mystic, this is a mature, sad, concentratedly serious Blok. He writes about social writers, chroniclers of daily life, and revolutionaries united around the collections of *Znanie*.[5] In modernistic circles it was considered good form to hold that "gray" literature in contempt. Blok didn't share this prejudice. He defends Gorky from the "refined" criticism of Filosofov and from Merezhkovsky's tendency to see in the author of *Foma Gordeev* only an "inner vagabond" and "future cad." The author is sure that behind all of Gorky's banalities there is concealed "that vast depression which has no name and no measure." "I further contend," he writes, "that, if there is a real concept 'Russia,' or, better 'Rus,' . . . if there exists that great, boundless, broad, melancholy, and promised land that we are used to unite under the name Rus—then one must to a vast degree consider Gorky its spokesman." These words contain a bold challenge to the theoreticians of symbolism, Bely and Merezhkovsky. We already hear the voice of the future author of *Verses on Russia*. Blok's attitude toward Leonid Andreev is no less sympathetic. Carefully analyzing his story "Judas Iscariot and Others," he concludes:

> One can say that Andreev is on the brink of the tragedy which we all expect and for which we all long. He is one of the few on whom we can place our hope that this magical and lyrical, beautiful, but terrible, sleep in which our literature is stagnating, will be dispelled.

This is a personal confession: the poet wants to wake up from his beautiful, but terrible, lyrical sleep and to see real life. Even second-rate revolutionary fiction writers don't repel the critic:

> This is "conventional" literature, in which the mutiny of revolution sometimes completely overshadows the mutiny of the soul, and the voice of the crowd overshadows the voice of the individual. The masses need this literature, but something in it is also indispensable to the intelligentsia. It is useful when the wind of events and the world music stifle the music of alienated souls and their innermost little drafts.

This is already close to the "music of revolution," which Blok heard when he was writing *The Twelve*. The article ends with a high evaluation of Sologub's novel *The Petty Demon* and with a new and terrible "personal confession":

> And it happens that everyone becomes a Peredonov [hero of *The Petty Demon*]. And it happens that the lantern of the bright heart of such a seeking man will go out, and the "Eternal Feminine" he sought will turn into a smoky bluish Untouchable One. So it is, and it is useless to hide this. . . . And the position of people such as Peredonov is, I think, really tormenting: the earth, and not the idea, punishes them.

The head spins from such gaps into the abyss. The knight of the Beautiful Lady bore within him a vile Peredonov and expected punishment from the outraged Mother-Earth. The whole tragedy is simple: "so it is, and it is useless to hide this."

Blok's second literary survey, "On Lyric Poetry," appeared in *Golden Fleece* on 3 July. Amid the mountain heights, in the lilac twilight, a man lay down, possessor of all the world's riches, but a beggar not knowing where to lay his head. "This man—a fallen Angel-Demon—is the *first lyricist*." Lermontov and Vrubel created a cursed song and colored legend about him. The lyricist gives people nothing, but people come and take. The lyricist is "poor and radiant," but people create incalculable wealth from his "radiant generosity." Thus lyric poetry unites both poison and constructive force. The lyric poet says: *"That's how I want it."* This catchword contains his curse and blessing, his slavery and freedom. He is locked in the "deep prison" of his own world, in the vicious circle of his own "I." He is buried alive, he is solitary. From these assertions the author pulls out "two general passages . . . for the edification of certain critics." The first general passage: *"Lyric poetry is lyric poetry, and the poet is a poet"*:

> D. V. Filosofov and Andrey Bely are beginning to reproach lyric poetry for philistinism, blasphemy, hooliganism, etc. It remains to ask, why don't they reproach it for immorality? . . . The poet is completely free in his creativity, and no one has a right to demand of him that he like green meadows more than houses of prostitution.

The second general passage: *"Poets are interesting for what distinguishes them from one another, and not for how they resemble one another"*:

> It follows from this that grouping poets by schools, by "relation to the world," by "manner of perception," is a useless and a thankless labor. . . . No tendencies have power over poets. Poets can be neither "esthetic individualists," nor "pure symbolists," nor "mystical realists," nor "mystical anarchists," nor "collective individualists."

In such a restrained and noble tone Blok answered the "brigand" attacks of the "Muscovites."

But Bely's improprieties and insinuations finally wearied Blok. In August he writes him a formally polite letter in which he asserts that he has nothing in common with any mystical realisms and anarchisms, that all his works written so far seem to him symbolic and romantic, that he sees in them an organic continuation of *Verses on the Beautiful Lady*. "In conclusion," he writes, "I ask you, even if briefly, *to show me the basic point of your disagreement with me*. I don't catch this point because, I repeat, I react to the latest narrow theories just as you do."

Before receiving this letter Bely had sent Blok an offensive message. As at the beginning of their correspondence, the letters crossed in the mail. Bely's letter:

> Dear Sir, Aleksandr Aleksandrovich: I hasten to inform you of news pleasant to both of us. Our relations are broken off forever. It was hard for me to cross out your inner cast of mind, since I have the habit of taking seriously the inner connection with one or another person, once this person calls himself my friend. I therefore was very tormented, wanted to take you to task for your many acts (which would have been unpleasant both for me and for you). From a distance I continued to keep an eye on you. Finally, when your petition, *pardon*, the article on the realists, appeared in *Fleece*, where you shamelessly wrote what you don't believe, it all became clear to me. A talk with you became superfluous. Now I am at ease and calm. I hasten to notify you that, if we ever chance to meet (may God prevent it), and you first give me your hand, I will greet you. If you try to

pretend we are not acquainted or avoid meeting me, that will be more pleasant for me.

Blok answered this letter with a challenge to a duel:

> 8 August 1907. Dear Sir, Boris Nikolaevich: Your behavior with regard to me, your gossipy hints in print about my personal life, your last letter, in which you laughably slander me and announce that you "kept an eye on me from a distance" all the time, and, finally, your boastful printed and written declarations that you alone in all the world "suffer" and that no one but you knows how to suffer—all this has bored me enough.
>
> It didn't enter my head to take offense at all this, since I don't consider it possible to be offended either by a spy shadowing me or by a lackey suspecting me of dishonesty. Not wishing, Dear Sir, to accuse you of servility and spying, I am inclined to impute your behavior either to some great misunderstanding and complete ignorance of me on your part, . . . or to a peculiar kind of mental illness.
>
> Whatever the reasons which called forth your attacks on me, I give you *ten days from the date of this letter* to either retract your words, which you don't believe, or to send me your second. If you don't do one or the other *by 18 August*, I will myself be compelled to take appropriate measures.

The next day Blok sends an agitated letter to E. P. Ivanov, asking him to be his second. Ivanov dodges being a second, and begs him to calm down and abandon the duel. Blok shouldn't forget that Bely's unhappy love for Lyubov Dmitrievna was at the bottom of the whole drama. "Obviously," writes E. Ivanov, "the man has been embittered in love, and of course sheer offended self-esteem plays an enormous role here, but also love, of course, and that demands sympathy."

In the meantime Bely received Blok's letter of 6 August, and answered him on the tenth. On 11 August he received the challenge to the duel and that same day wrote a second letter.

In the first letter (10 August), Bely summarizes his accusations: a group of "mystical hooligans" had formed around Blok in Petersburg—all kinds of myth makers, anarchists, and individualists who paint his name on their banners. Chulkov in *Torches* does nothing but shout "we, we" and quote Blok and Ivanov. Gorodetsky in his article "On the Bright Path" uttered the famous aphorism: "Every poet must be an anarchist. For how can it be otherwise?" Finally, E. Semyonov in *Mercure de France*, assigning poets to "tendencies," placed V. Ivanov, Chulkov, S. Gorodetsky, and Blok in the group of "mystical anarchists." All these new "isms" loudly proclaim a "victory over symbolism." In the article "Young Poetry" Chulkov wrote about a *new* literary current which arose after *Scales* and, moreover, named V. Ivanov and Blok! Why is Blok silent? Why doesn't he announce in print that he doesn't sympathize with all these "isms" which so strenuously adhere to him? And Bely continues heatedly:

> For a year and a half I have been shouting at you, sometimes in letters,

sometimes simply in an inward appeal: "Understand, understand." You see, not only personal relations are at the basis of my distrust, my failure to understand you. If the goal of everything is *The Puppet Show*, then the apparent agreements about the main thing are a deception. But even if I was injured through a series of mistakes, I will not betray the *last thing: I know, I believe*. And you are silent.

In response to the challenge to the duel, he writes Blok (11 August) an inspired and sincere letter. The literary misunderstandings collapse like a cardboard house; behind them the real reason for the "discord" is revealed—the tragedy of the relations among Blok, his wife, and Bely. He begins:

What you write ("great misunderstanding") is obviously completely just. It is already a year and a half since you did everything to prevent this misunderstanding from blowing over, but would, on the contrary, make it stronger. After our misunderstandings of last year (in August), I told myself frankly: "I must be wrong; it must be cleared up." I turned to you in complete readiness to accept your explanations about the nature of our relations. Rather *insultingly* for me, you said nothing. . . . And I so needed this, because I really had such a liking for you in the depths of my soul as I have rarely had for anyone. I went abroad only because I had such a liking for you (for you and your wife). I thought that external distance would clear up the muddle of our relations (in which I was perhaps just as wrong as you, but I wanted *truth*, wanted words spoken honestly and not indefinite, unfathomable silences). I was wrong. . . . I continued to love you terribly and to believe in you. . . . I wanted to prepare the soil by our correspondence, so that the *silence* oppressing me would be dispersed and so that at last, on meeting personally, we would see each other's real faces. You replied again with a letter whose general tone seemed offensive to me. . . . Here I simply stopped writing to you. . . . I then began to read your lines carefully, to reread your letters and verse, to catch avidly your every printed line. . . . This interest in your person even prompted me to tell you that I had been keeping an eye on you for a long time. You took it in the literal and exact sense ("spying"). This is when I saw that the gulf between us had grown to the final limit.

The letter ends with a refusal to duel and with a request for a personal meeting. "As soon as you sincerely agree," Bely writes, "to such a conversation, I will willingly do everything possible to understand, not only with my mind, but also with my heart, *just what is happening between us*."

Before us is an unusual human document. Bely takes from his friend his beloved wife, smashes his life; Blok silently gets out of his way. But Bely's love ends in a tragic rupture; he is unhappy and needs the sympathy of the friend he had nearly destroyed. Blok's "unfathomable silence" torments and exasperates him. And he takes revenge for it by a malicious and mean literary polemic. We are ready to say that Blok couldn't have had a greater enemy than Bely. And actually no one in his life had caused him so much harm, so much suffering. But this is only half of the truth; the other half is the fact that no one had ever loved him as Bely did. The letter we have just read is the letter of a *man in love*. It was Bely's tragedy that he was in love not only with Lyubov Dmitrievna, but also with Aleksandr Aleksandrovich, and that both these insane loves were deeply unhappy. Everything proceeds from this: the hatred and the jealousy and the suspiciousness and the rage. He defamed, insulted, ridiculed Blok, and: "I continued to love you terribly."

Blok answers Bely's letter with a surprising message (15–17 August) in which, with a kind of inhuman insight and honesty, he relates the story of their *fateful friendship*:

> Our acquaintanceship by mail began when you informed me through Olga Mikhailovna Solovyova that you wanted to write to me. I wrote you at once, and our first letters crossed in the mail. The very first letters, as I think now, told the difference in our *temperaments* and the strange incompatibility between us—*fateful*, I would say. This is how I would express it: I in advance deeply loved and respected you and your verse. Your ideas were unusually important to me, and most of all (this is the main thing) I felt a *mysterious affinity* between us, whose name I never knew and never sought. At that time I was living very unstably, so that one of two things predominated in my life: either a terrible intensity of mystical experiences (*always lofty*) or a terrible mental laziness, weariness, forgetfulness of everything. By the way, I think that everything in my life simply went, and will go for a long time, along the same path. *Now* the whole difference is only that "cold broad daylight" is upon me, and at that time I was "in the morning fog.". . . *As before*, so during our acquaintanceship by letter, when you loved me and believed me, I *always* had *the same* fiery experiences . . . alternating with mental laziness, plus the sobriety of broad daylight. . . . And so I insist that I haven't changed *essentially*. Now—to proceed. At the time in my life when we met I recognized that both the *Dramatic Symphony* (I don't remember, before or after the acquaintanceship) and all our correspondence, interwoven with my life, formed for me a symphony of unusual and fateful complexity. *I didn't understand that complexity.* I know one thing: *it was difficult for me to understand you and difficult to write to you.* I explained this by my *laziness*. Just a year later we met. *It was difficult for me to talk to you,* and I again explained this by my laziness. But that wasn't the only reason. *Probably the main reason* is expressed in the following circumstances. You remember that that same summer you came to Shakhmatovo with Petrovsky. I remember sharply and clearly how the first night . . . we walked in the moonlight, and you talked a lot and, as usual, I was silent. When we said goodbye and went to our rooms I felt a *mystical fear* of you. As far as I remember, I never told you about this fact of our acquaintanceship, which was very real to me. In that, perhaps, lies my great mystical guilt. That night I felt and experienced intensely that we are of a "*different spirit*," that we are spiritual enemies. But I—*very much the skeptic*—was at that time agonizingly the skeptic. And the next morning drove away my fear. For me, as before, it was only difficult with you. I think that you sensed what was taking place within me, as in general you sensed a great deal, that was *inscrutable* (for me, even till now), subtly. . . . Then again our letters and our meetings,

which in recent years became more frequent, thanks to that which you know.... You and I both in letters and verbally declared ourselves in love with one another, but did this in different ways. And even in this we didn't understand one another. You, in my opinion, didn't approach me as I acknowledged myself, and to this day don't approach me so. You wanted, and want, to know my moral, philosophical, religious physiognomy. I *don't know how to*, in fact I can't, reveal it to you without connecting it with the events of my life, with my experiences. Some of these events and experiences *no one in the world* knows, and I didn't, and don't, want to communicate them even to you.... I don't have a philosophical *credo* because I am not educated philosophically. I don't believe in God and don't dare to believe, because doesn't believing in God mean to have painful, lyrical, meager ideas about him? ... I am prepared to say rather, so that you will know me, that I *very much* believe in myself, that I feel in myself a kind of *healthy wholeness* and the capacity to be a *human being*— free, independent, and honest.... *All this I have experienced and bear within myself*—I bear my psychological characteristics like a cross, my aspirations to the beautiful I bear like my noble soul.

And here is one of my psychological characteristics: *I prefer people to ideas.* ... My fear of "offending" a person flows from this preference....

How soporific, wearisome, and terrible all this is, Boris Nikolaevich. I am not undertaking to bind up and settle things. Yesterday, under the impression of your letters, I went to Moscow and from the Prague restaurant wrote you a letter about what I would have liked to say to you sincerely and seriously. I tore this letter in two; it seemed that one can't say everything in writing. Now I continue, and here is why: when the servant returned with the reply that you were not at home (this after ten o'clock in the evening), it seemed to me that it had to be so, that nevertheless we won't settle things verbally. But I decided to continue writing, returned from Moscow at once, and here I am writing. I talked the whole way with a young coachman. Now I have very major complications in my personal life.... But I am healthy and simple, I am becoming *simpler and simpler*, as much as I can....

The drama of my *Weltanschauung* (I'm not old enough for tragedy) consists in the fact that I am a *lyric poet*. To be a lyric poet is terrifying and gay. The terror and gaiety conceal an abyss to which one can fly, and nothing will remain. Gaiety and terror is a soporific blanket. *If I hadn't worn this soporific blanket over my eyes*, if I weren't guided by the Unknown Terror from which *only my soul* protects me, *I wouldn't have written* a single one of the poems to which you attribute importance.

Now, about something else....

My heart, *as before*, lies closer to you than to the "torchbearers." ... Among the "torchbearers" ... V. Ivanov, a person of profound mind and soul, stands alone for me....

If I blaspheme, my blasphemies are *abundantly* covered by my *standing on guard*. So it was, so it is, and so it will be. My soul is an unchanging sentry, it keeps watch over its own and won't abandon its post. At night doubts and fears beset even the sentry....

"We are alien to one another," you say. Pose the question differently: will you make up your mind *to believe a lyric poet* such as I, that is, in the worst case a blind man with an unsettled *Weltanschauung*, a person who says *no* more often than *yes*? Keep in mind that it is a question *of me, who has never changed essentially.* . . . If all this is so, then admit that you are *fed up* with reckoning with such a wavering, lyrical soul as mine. . . .

But here I ask you, "as at confession," in your words: are you sure you are more *faithful* than I? I maintain that, through all my unfaithfulness, betrayal, falls, doubts, mistakes—I am *faithful.* . . . At the bottom of my soul lies no *Puppet Show, I swear.*

At the end of the letter Blok says he agrees with all of Bely's reproaches concerning "mystical anarchism," and promises to announce in print his nonparticipation in this "trend." The letter ends with the words:

I am ready to talk to you. I have no unfathomable silences. I want it simpler, simpler, simpler. Perhaps if we had spoken to each other, we would have succeeded in clearing up all the details of our relationship, of our offenses to one another in the most intimate areas. It's impossible to write about this.

Blok's letter is not only a lofty artistic work, it is also the only lyrical confession in our literature. This is a clairvoyant's introspection. The image of the blind poet with the blanket of "terror and gaiety" over his eyes, the one knowing the Unknown Terror, the unchanging sentry guarding the sacred, the guard, faithful despite all the changes and falls, the free and whole person bearing his humanity like a cross, the mystic with "fiery experiences" and the "cold of broad daylight in his soul"—this image is unforgettable.

The understanding of the fateful meaning of the friendship with Bely, based on the feeling of mysterious affinity and mystical fear, raises the relations of the two friend-enemies to the height of tragedy. Bely was staggered by this letter. He answers Blok:

Your letter made a deep and powerful impression on me. I understood much about you *for certain*. All the tragedy of the growing failure to understand you on my part perhaps stems from the fact that this letter wasn't written a year and a half ago. You probably didn't suspect how very much I suffered from doubts about you in the last year and a half. . . . Your letter is a fact of enormous importance for me, because I really always considered our relationship *fateful* (independent of the difference or similarity, independent of the position of things established between us). . . . I think it is important, necessary, for us to see each other. . . . I am very much expecting either you or a letter indicating your address. Believe me, I took your letter with the same depth of sincerity in which you wrote it. Thank you! I press your hand firmly. Respectfully, Boris Bugaev.

On 24 August Blok came to Moscow. "I remember," Bely writes, "that on the day of Aleksandr Aleksandrovich's arrival I was terribly excited." At seven o'clock a ring was heard. On the threshold stood Blok, in a dark overcoat and dark hat, tanned and smiling. The conversation between the friends lasted twelve hours. They were both joyful; the past seemed to have returned; they had found one another again.

Blok considered S. Solovyov mainly responsible for muddling their relationship. Bely blamed Lyubov Dmitrievna: it was she who had poisoned their friendship. It was finally decided that in the future they would believe one another, whatever happened, and would "detach personal relations from polemics, from literature, from their relationship to Lyubov Dmitrievna, to Sergey Mikhailovich [Solovyov], and to Aleksandra Andreevna." They talked about *Golden Fleece*, about Briusov's quarrel with Ryabushinsky, about Chulkov and mystical anarchism. Bely writes:

> I disagreed with Aleksandr Aleksandrovich on many questions of literary polemics. But now there was no longer passion in this disagreement. We decided that we would henceforth be in different groups, and would even fight ideologically. But let this fight not overshadow our trust and respect for each other.

At eleven at night Bely's mother called them to tea. She loved Blok tenderly and rejoiced in the reconciliation. Everyone was relaxed and comfortable. Aleksandr Aleksandrovich said absurd things with a serious face. After tea the friends' conversation lasted until four in the morning. The train to Petersburg left at seven. Bely accompanied Blok through the Moscow dawn. They sat in a tearoom near Nikolaevsky Station with the coachmen. Blok said on farewell: "So we will believe. And we won't let people, whoever they may be, come between us." Bely ends his story: "So our twelve-hour conversation (from seven to seven) ended warmly. I crossed out the past. In so doing, Shch (that is, Lyubov Dmitrievna) was crossed out for me as a matter of principle."

Having learned from Bely about Semyonov's article in *Mercure de France*, Blok at once (17 August) wrote to Chulkov:

> *Scales* considers me a mystical anarchist because of *Mercure de France*. I haven't read what Semyonov writes there, but A. Bely, with whom my relations are now very complicated, told me about it. This is what I think: I have no relationship at all to mystical anarchism in essence. He stresses not what makes up the essence of my soul; he stresses my *instability, my faithlessness*. I
>> Will not disturb immobility
>> And won't descend from the heights,
>> Preserving my unwavering soul
>> In my unprecedented hell.
>
> That's the first thing. The second is that I never regarded mystical anarchism as a theory, but interpreted it lyrically. With all this I not only do not consider myself a mystical anarchist, but recognize the necessity of repudiating it in print, for example, in a letter to the editors of *Scales*.

On 26 August he sent to Chulkov the text of his letter to the editors of *Scales*, and adds:

> I will do this in *Scales* because I deeply respect *Scales* (although I disagree with it in much) and I feel just as solidly tied to it as to *New Path*.

Scales both was and is an event for me and, in my opinion, also an event in general, and the most integrated and militant journal now. . . .
   I *now* consider it my *mystical duty* to emphasize my lack of solidarity with mystical anarchism in such a decisive form. I never attributed significance to mystical anarchism and, in my opinion, it would have been forgotten, had they not now blown it up.

The complete capitulation of "mystical anarchism" took place on 23 September. On that day Chulkov, V. Ivanov, and Blok publicly repudiated this ill-starred "trend." In a letter to the editors of the newspaper *Comrade* (*Tovarishch*), Chulkov protested against the classification of writers and asserted that mystical anarchism is not a literary school, but a new relation to the world. In the same issue of *Comrade*, V. Ivanov solemnly repudiated this "relation to the world." On the same day, in a letter to the editors of *Scales*, Blok wrote:

Dear Editor:
   I ask you to place the following in your esteemed journal: In the 16 July issue of *Mercure de France* Mr. Semyonov gives some tendentious schema in which modern Russian symbolist poets are placed in cages of "decadence," "neo-Christian mysticism," and "mystical anarchism." Not to mention that the author of the schema manifested violent hatred for the poets, separating those who are close and uniting those who are far apart, not to mention that the whole schema is, in my opinion, completely arbitrary, and that Filosofov and Berdyaev are numbered among the poets, I consider it my duty to announce: highly regarding the art of Vyacheslav Ivanov and Sergey Gorodetsky, with whom I landed in the same cage, I never had, and do not have, anything in common with "mystical anarchism," to which my verse and prose bear witness.

The twelve-hour conversation with Bely opened Blok's eyes to the ambiguity of his position in the group of Petersburg litterateurs. He moves away not only from Chulkov and Gorodetsky, but also from the "Dionysian" V. Ivanov. We read in the *Notebook*: "My difference of opinion with V. Ivanov in terminology and *pathos* (especially the latter). His terms can offend me: *myth, individual collectivity, barbarity*. Why not speak more simply? There is nothing essentially new in this."
   And he adds: "My difference of opinion with V. Ivanov (barbarity). . . . My agreement with Andrey Bely. I don't consider it a disgrace, either for myself or for anyone, to learn from A. Bely. I raise objections to him now not in essence, but only at his method of criticizing."
   And he says in a third note on V. Ivanov: "His stifling eroticism and rather repulsive frivolity are unpleasant to me."
   Blok frees himself from the constraint of his literary friends. He wants to be "his own man" and "to keep his soul unwavering."

In the fall the Bloks rented an apartment on Galernaya Street: four small rooms along a corridor. The apartment was in a courtyard, on the second floor, and was rather gloomy. Lyubov Dmitrievna, having received an inheritance from her father, bought mahogany chairs and a book shelf with a bronze Cupid. This Cupid is familiar to us from Blok's verse. In *The Snow Mask*, the poem *Behind Masks* ends with the verse:

> And books dozed in the cupboard.
> There—a naked little boy
> Stuck to the carved, antique door
> By one wing.

The poem *Pale Legends* has a similar ending:

> And lost, in love,
> Not able to stick,
> Flown away from the bookcase door,
>   A Cupid.

In the middle of September Aleksandra Andreevna moved to Revel, where Franz Feliksovich was assigned a regiment. Parting from her son depressed her, and the duties of a commander's wife in a strange city instilled real horror.

Blok's September letters to his mother are filled with sadness:

> I have seen lots of people, and it was all sad. Everyone somehow concealed, reticent, guarding themselves from the intrusions of others. It seems I am the same. (20 September).
> ... Mama, I haven't written for a long time, and I write little due to a great number of cares—serious and petty. The serious ones concern life—Lyuba, Natalya Nikolaevna, and Borya. Borya is coming to see me soon. He is closer and closer to me and is horribly unhappy.

The petty cares are literary: he has to write many articles and reviews; he wants to study the history of the theater and the Russian schism. The drama *The Song of Fate* is progressing slowly. He had met L. Andreev and was present at his first "Wednesday." Yushkevich, Chirikov, Sergey Uspensky, Volynsky, and Tan were present. Andreev had a toothache and, at his request, Blok read his new story, "Darkness." "Andreev," he writes, "is simple, nice, serious, and pensive." Poets come to Blok for advice, as do editors and guests. The theater life had ended. "I don't see Natalya Nikolaevna often," he adds.

In September Blok's third extensive literary survey, "On Drama," appears in *Golden Fleece*. Drama in Russia, the author maintains, was always accidental: it lacked not only technique, language, and inspiration—it even lacked action. Innumerable dramas of writers of the *Znanie* group are strikingly insignificant. Symbolic dramas like Briusov's *The Earth* and V. Ivanov's *Tantalus* are accidental and not national. The author singles out Andreev's *Life of a Man*, on which he lavishes exaggerated praise, and M. Kuzmin's *Comedy on Evdokia from Heliopolis*. How can one explain the poverty of contemporary Russian theater?

Blok thinks that "supple, cunning, perfidious lyricism" is at fault in this. Our era has been poisoned by it:

> It seems the very air is suffused with lyricism because free movements have disappeared, just as have strong passions, and the loud voice has been replaced by a whisper. The most subtle lyrical poisons have corroded the simple columns and strong chains supporting and binding together the drama.

Blok had written about the "curse" of lyric poetry in the article "On Lyric Poetry" and about the "instability" and "faithlessness" of the lyricist's soul in a letter to Bely. More and more he perceived his great gift of song as a terrible and destructive fate.[6]

On 4 October the Kiev journal *In the World of Art (V mire iskusstva)* set up an "evening of art," to which Bely, Blok, S. A. Sokolov-Krechetov, and Nina Petrovskaya were invited. Kiev was plastered with placards depicting a kind of shaggy faun. Bely and Blok stayed at the same hotel. Both were embarrassed by the provincial advertising and lack of taste. They were to appear in an opera theater seating 3,500 people; the tickets were sold out. Bely recalls how Blok, washing up from the road, washed his hands and smiled archly:

> "And you know—it somehow isn't right; even very wrong: won't they beat us!" And a chuckle escaped, that special deep chuckle, which made things inexpressibly agreeable. This chuckle was rare for Blok, and few knew it; it contained childlike trustfulness and a good-natured laugh at the world and at himself and his interlocutor. Everything was peculiarly lit up by the chuckle and slightly Dickensian, slightly fantastic; one imagined Pickwicks.

Evening came. From a magnificent dais above the orchestra, Bely, in a hoarse voice, explained briefly to the Kievans what symbolic art is. Then N. Petrovskaya, Blok, Professor De la Bart and S. Sokolov read. "The evening was filled with 'scandal,'" Bely writes. "And the representatives of the new direction, who had been called from Petersburg and Moscow with such pomp, would have triumphantly failed in Kiev, had S. A. Sokolov not rescued them." With his inherent nervousness, Bely exaggerates the "scandal." Blok informs his mother: "The evening came off very well. Its success wasn't bad." After the evening a reception was held in a restaurant, with speeches and toasts. The next day students, journalists, writers, and tenors came. They took the poets around the city and entertained them in restaurants. Kiev seemed to Blok "boring and flat." But he was struck by the gloomy romanticism of a view of the city from a distance. He writes his mother:

> One can stand on a high hill in the twilight. On one side a prison outside the city, surrounded by a ditch. A red moon is rising, and sentries are walking. And in front tall weeds (corpses of those who have been killed are sometimes found in them). Beyond the weeds lies all of Kiev, like an

amphitheater, white and gold from the churches, until twilight gushed over it. And later, Kiev all in lights, and far beyond it seas of railroad electricity and blue haze.

On 6 October Bely was to give a lecture, and Blok stayed with him in Kiev another day. "We got practically no sleep," he tells his mother. "During the day people didn't leave us alone, and at night I talked with Borya—it was very nice." At night on the eve of the lecture Bely had a severe attack of nerves. There was a cholera epidemic in Kiev at this time, and the overanxious poet imagined that he was infected. Half-dressed, he ran to Blok, woke him, and announced that he had come down with cholera. Blok spent the whole night with him, calmed him, massaged his arms. "I won't forget the attention with which he surrounded me," Bely recalls. Calming down, he began to complain to his friend about his loneliness, his unhappy life. Suddenly Blok said: "You know what; it isn't good for you to return to Moscow alone. Here's what I suggest: we'll go to Petersburg." Bely began to talk about his quarrel with Lyubov Dmitrievna. Blok retorted that the reasons for the quarrel no longer existed, that it was long since time to make up. "But what will Lyubov Dmitrievna say at my unexpected appearance?" Bely asked. Blok replied: "Why she already knows, I've talked to her." How much generosity, human kindness, and pity for the "unhappy Borya" there was in this action of Blok's!

By morning Bely's attack has passed. But he was still hoarse, and Blok offered to read the lecture for him from the manuscript. He studied it carefully. But by evening Bely's voice had returned, and he delivered the lecture with great success. "That evening," he writes, "Aleksandr Aleksandrovich, with the most tender solicitude, didn't leave me alone for a step. He sat beside me on the lecturer's platform, brought me hot tea. . . . After the lecture he wrapped my throat so I wouldn't catch cold." They arrived in Petersburg on 8 October, a rainy, cold morning. Blok took Bely to the Hotel d'Angleterre and said on leaving: "I'll go now. I have to let Lyuba know. Come have breakfast with us, and don't be afraid!"

Bely awaited his "explanation" with Lyubov Dmitrievna agitatedly. But there was no explanation. She met him simply, but he understood at once that she didn't want to return to the past. The change in her struck him; she seemed to him to have grown and gotten thinner. Before she was quiet, taciturn, absorbed. Now she talked a lot, rapidly and ecstatically. Lyubov Dmitrievna was preparing for the stage. She led a stormy social life and was full of all sorts of cares and bustling about. A tone of light, playful causerie was established between her and Bely. Bely noticed that the Bloks' whole lifestyle had changed sharply:

> Aleksandr Aleksandrovich and Lyubov Dmitrievna seemed to surround themselves with a whirlwind of gaiety, but this whirlwind didn't bring them together. Lyubov Dmitrievna flies off from life with Aleksandr Aleksandrovich on the whirlwind of gaiety, and Aleksandr Alek-

sandrovich flies away from her. I noticed that they are flying apart, meeting at the tea table, at dinner, and flying apart again. I saw that this gaiety is the gaiety of tragedy and of flight over an abyss.

All the couple's interests were centered around the theater, and their life was theatrical; it was not the mystery play they had dreamed about in their youth, but a *commedia dell'arte*.

In the evenings they often sat in a fivesome: Lyubov Dmitrievna, her friend, the gay blond actress Verigina, N. N. Volokhova, Blok, and Bely. Meyerhold, Kuzmin, Gorodetsky, and the artist Somov were invariably present. Blok complains to his mother: "Every day people, and into society. Even Lyuba is getting terribly tired and is left alone for scarcely a minute." And in another letter he wrote: "I am constantly busy—this saves me." And he wrote again a few days later: "I send out poems, make plans, and the whole time passes at all this, except when I roam the streets—in the movie houses and beerhalls."

Journal matters called Bely to Moscow. On saying goodbye, Lyubov Dmitrievna told him: "Move to us, to Petersburg. I guarantee you—it will be gay." And Bely adds sadly: "The words 'gay,' 'to have a good time,' seemed to me to be the most frequent in Lyubov Dmitrievna's vocabulary." Literary life in Moscow seethed. The Society of Free Esthetics was formed; its meetings took place in the Literary-Artistic Circle. Briusov, Ellis, Baltrushaitis, Sadovskoy, the artist Serov, and the collector Girshman took part in it. The Moscow Religious-Philosophical Society came to life with S. N. Bulgakov's move to Moscow. P. E. d'Alheim set up a House of Song and commissioned Bely to organize a literary section in it. Finally, at M. K. Morozova's on Smolensky Boulevard a "philosophical circle" of young people gathered, where I. L. Ilyin, B. A. Fokht, G. G. Schpett, B. P. Vysheslavtsev, Prince E. N. Trubetskoy, and A. K. Toporkov read reports. But Bely abandoned all this and at the beginning of November moved to Petersburg with the intention of settling there permanently. He decided to get a decisive answer from Lyubov Dmitrievna. The talk finally took place:

> I, like Foma, put my finger on the wound of our tormenting relations and became convinced that the essence of what I don't understand about Shch lies for me in the fact that Shch doesn't need understanding. Everything is too simple, one sees in her that which is most offensively simple. . . . My last word about Shch: A doll!

This means that he understands that Lyubov Dmitrievna doesn't love him. How outraged he had been not so long ago that the Beautiful Lady in *The Puppet Show* turned out to be a "cardboard bride." And now he himself speaks the "last word" on her—a "doll." Bely didn't live in Petersburg long; he practically didn't visit the Bloks. Aleksandr Aleksandrovich tells his mother briefly: "Borya came the other day. He has been here twice. He won't come to see us very often." Bely soon returned to Moscow. A dead period had fallen on his relations with Blok. It lasted three years.

But Blok continued to live a complicated, involved, tormented life. He performed often at concerts whose proceeds went for the benefit of "political criminals." He set up conspiratorial relations with a certain Comrade Andrey and with the young revolutionary Zvereva. Lyubov Dmitrievna studied diction with the actress D. M. Musina and dance with the ballet master Presnyakov. The poet tells his mother about his life in a letter of 27 November:

> Mama, it is now night here, and I came home early, sober for a change, because Natalya Nikolaevna wouldn't let me in to the theater club to play lotto and drink. I'm sitting and waiting for Lyuba, who has gone somewhere.... We have just been to Olenina's concert together. On the thirtieth N. N. and I are reading at a concert. On the first she is playing Fra Solness,[7] on the fifth the three of us are going to Duncan,[8] on the sixth we are reading *The Stranger* in the New Theater, by parts (N. N. the Stranger,... I the Blue One, Meyerhold, Davidovsky, et al.). On the tenth Duncan again. During the day I am now writing a large critique for *Fleece*, and N. N. is studying a role. In the evenings we see each other at her place, in restaurants, on the islands, etc. It snows now and then, and a biting wind....
>
> Do you know that Lyuba is going with Meyerhold for Lent and for the summer on a trip (with the troupe) to western cities, then to the Caucasus, then perhaps to the Crimea with N. N. (during the summer).... N. N. will remain here for the first month of Lent and will later join the troupe (in the Caucasus). Maybe I will go too?

Such is the outward story of his life. But here is the inner story (in a letter of 9 December 1907 to his mother):

> It's getting harder and harder to live—it's very cold. Senseless squandering of lots of money and a complete void all around: as if everyone had stopped loving and deserted me, but they probably never did love me. I found myself on a kind of island in an empty and cold sea.... Only we three on the whole island, treating one another somehow strangely—everything is very cramped.... We all long for different things. I know that I must, and have a possibility to, find a profession and hope in art.... But I don't have the strength—it is so cold. For these two women with seeking souls, very different, but in some way incredibly alike, it is also terrible and cold.... My depression is not unfocused—I see too much clearly and soberly and am too bound to much in life. Right now I'm sitting alone. It is evening: in an hour Lyuba and probably N. N. will return from the Ancient Theater.... I have just come from the bath, so that I am indulging in sad thoughts in comfort. I feel no guilt.

The island in the cold sea and the three people on it, "treating one another somehow strangely" and longing for "different things"—and no one is to blame—are all equally unhappy. The snowstorms of *The Snow Mask* and *The Earth in Snow* sing of this cold loneliness *à trois*. The poet tells enigmatically and vaguely of the "mad year" spent by the "black train" in the "fairy tale about one who won't understand it." This is the most affected, the most "decadent," of all his works. But under the mannered allegories are the "golden serpents in a dark goblet of wine," the "hideous dwarfs flying after their lady's train," the "gold and delicate stiletto which catches her black hair." Behind all the suffocating demonism and estheticism of this rough sketch one can surmise something deeply hidden in the poet's soul:

> The subtle sorcery of the dark woman no longer let him close his eyes at night. Already his face flamed with growing passion and his eyelids grew heavy as lead from sleepless thought. And in his imagination she took on a terrible and attractive form. Now she seemed to him a serpent, and her silken dresses were then like a snake whistling among the grasses; now she appeared to him in a crown of stars and in a heavy costume strewn with stars. And he no longer knew dream from waking, spending slow hours over the back of an armchair in which she was silent and dozed like a lazy lioness, lit by the dying coals of the fireplace. And, kissing her hand strewn with rings, he scorched his lips on the touch of the stones, cold and precious. She loved to pass through the hall with him and in the throng to drop her handkerchief, so that he would be the first to pick it up, and to look into his eyes with eyes full of promise, so that he would be confused and become still thinner, taller, and more supple, so that he would abruptly push away the youth enraptured by her, opening a path in the crowd for her.

Once she came to him at night and was herself "like a troubled night full of evil visions and dark designs." In a voice "more passionate and tender than ever" she asked him to commit a great treachery, "extracted from him a mournful vow" and betrayed him first. But he didn't keep his vow, and the betrayal didn't touch his heart:

> Forever irrevocable, she left, indignant and bearing within her outrage for the vow he broke. He went out onto the street. Above him stretched the deep autumn sky. Great Passion and Great Quiet struggled in his soul. And the Quiet triumphed. And there a threatening comet rose above the earth, scattering its violent train over the Quiet.

In this strange fairy tale there is a lyrical commentary on the verses of *The Snow Mask*. The "dark woman," the "serpent," and the "comet" are three images of the one who:

> Led, chained with her gaze,
> And embraced with her arm,
> And with cold supervisions
> Handed over to white death. . . .

She tempted the poet's heart with the seduction of a "great treachery" and left him forever, flying into the sky like a violent comet.

The years 1906 and 1907 were the most tragic and most creatively intense of Blok's life. His whole being was shaken. He "gave himself blindly to the elemental force," and creates "works of art" out of despair, passion, and death. He realizes that life is played out but wants at least to sell it dearly, "for the pure gold" of poetry.

In 1907, in addition to a series of long critical surveys and reviews, he writes a second "lyrical article," "The Maiden of the Pink Gate and the Ant Tsar." The poet reminisces about his life in southern Germany at the Bad Nauheim resort: the old romantic town with the tall Gothic cathedral and the mysterious garden laid out on the castle's ramparts; the country of Germanic legend; the arcade running steeply upward buried in roses and dahlias. It seems that medieval pages, lithe and laughing boys, flash in the rose bushes. They are searching for the Lady and don't find her. It is impossible to find her. The Lady "with deep blue eyes" is only an apparition. Distant, she never draws near, but instead of her comes the porter's pretty daughter with flaxen braids. One can kiss her, one can marry her, and then open a bakery on Bürgerstrasse. And the dreamy pages as before will call her "The Maiden of the Pink Gate." The author continues: "This contains all of romanticism. From time immemorial in the West they have sought Helen, the unattainable perfect beauty.... The motionless knight—the West—forgot everything, staring at the heavenly roses from under his visor.... And his dreams end in nothing. They will not be realized." Blok seeks a homeland for his romantic soul and finds it in the West, in the land of Germanic legend, "where there are tender tones, languorous roses, airiness, a dream of that which is beyond the limits, a search for the impossible." He also dreamt of "*das Ewig-Weibliche*" and married the porter's pretty daughter. But he also has a second homeland—Russia. From his work, "Poetry of Spells and Incantations," the author introduces into the article the legend about an ant tsar, sitting deep in the earth on a crimson stone. "And in all there were visible only forest paths and a tumbledown anthill and a peasant with a shovel—and the gold sings." This gold is the heart of the Russian people, creating a living legend. "They take nothing with them. Neither money, nor historical reminiscences, these Russian people ... these quiet swamp "seers.' " The article ends with a description of the Siberian taiga, where northern "seers" live in the very center of shamanism. The author recalls his friend Georgy Chulkov's stories and poems about this mysterious country.

Thus romanticism of the Germanic West and "shamanist," singing Russia collide in Blok's soul. The split and the union of opposites is the source of his lyric poetry.

Blok translates *Le Miracle de Théophile* of the twelfth-century *trouvère* Rutebeuf for the Ancient Theater set up by the well-known theatrical figure, Baron N. V. Drizen. This ancient legend about a man who sold his soul to the devil and was saved through the intercession of the Mother of God lies at the basis of the medieval legend of Doctor Faustus. Blok translated the "miracle play" in simple folk language, in light and amusing verse (iambic tetrameter with adjacent masculine rhymes). He succeeded in preserving the artlessness and charming freshness of the original. *The Miracle Play of Theophile* was staged in the

Ancient Theater in December 1907, ran many times, and had great success.

That same year Blok was recruited by S. A. Vengerov for editorial work on the publication of the first volume of Pushkin's works [*Pushkin*. Vol. 1. Library of Great Writers, ed. by S. A. Vengerov. (Brockhaus-Efron, publisher)]. The notes for twenty-eight of Pushkin's lyceum poems belong to him. The poet did enormous work studying the manuscripts, comparing the printed editions, and elucidating the sources and literary influences. His commentaries are worthy of a Pushkin scholar. They are distinguished for their accuracy and deep insight into the poetic style of the young Pushkin.

In the collection *The Earth in Snow* Blok's introduction is entitled "Instead of a Preface." Two epigraphs precede it. The first consists of one line: "Why, comet, did you burst into our harmonious circle?" and is signed with the initials L. B. The second is Apollon Grigoriev's poem *The Comet*, which contains the lines:

> Incomplete, all full of discord,
> Of the unbridled elements of furious argument,
> Still burning itself, and on its path
> Threatening other stars with striving and fire. . . .
> What does it need the general confusion for?
> For the destruction of harmony? . . .

The poet's wife is the author of the first epigraph. Blok answers her question with A. Grigoriev's lines:

> Sent by struggle to the harmonious circle of creation,
> May it fulfill by the path of struggle and trial
> The aim of purification and the aim of self-creation.

Thus, with the aid of another poet close to him in spirit, Blok attempts to justify and explain the incursion into his life of an "incomplete," a burning comet, an unbridled elemental force destroying the harmony of his "harmonious circle." The fateful woman is a comet sent to him for "struggle and trial." He believed he would come out of the fire of passions purified. The epigraph to the first of the three poems, which is dedicated to Volokhova, and which is a prologue to *The Snow Mask*, is also taken from Grigoriev. Blok's acquaintance with Apollon Grigoriev's poetry in 1907 was ordained by fate. It took place at a crisis in his life. Hitherto the philosopher-mystic V. Solovyov was the poet's companion, his "*duca, signor e maestro*."[9] Now the singer of the Eternal Feminine departs, and the dissolute, wild, inspired, and drunken Apollon Grigoriev takes his place. He has a surplus of a bubbling, spontaneously violent life, unrestrained passions, the despair of the folk song, an impetuous gypsy quality, vagabondage, and destruction. Blok took into his soul, read in Grigoriev's bitter fate signs of his own.

In the poems of the "populist and man of the soil",[10] who had squandered his talent in drink, he found the sounds of a "cracked human violin," which transfixed him forever. The lyrical themes of *The Earth in Snow* are interwoven with Grigoriev's favorite images. The homeless vagabond in a terrible and phantasmal city; Petersburg, the taverns, restaurants, gypsies, guitar, the "seven-stringed friend," the destructive passion, and the astringent wine; the beloved, in whose eyes "an unstarry light shines, the bright light of a comet," who attracts and bites "like a snake"; and in the distance dark, nomadic "gypsy" Rus, in its boundless flood of song—in this world Blok recognized his soul's homeland. He passionately absorbed the gypsy tradition of Russian poetry from Pushkin and Baratynsky, through Fet and Polonsky, to Grigoriev, and in the chain of his image-symbols (the comet, the Snow Maiden, the Stranger, Faina), a new link appeared—the Gypsy. Grigoriev's poem *The Hungarian Gypsy Girl* captivated him, and he told E. F. Knipovich: "*The Hungarian Gypsy Girl* is as close to me as if I had written it myself." In the gypsy girl's look—wilfull and insolent—there appeared to him the elemental force of Russian folk wandering. A merging of these two images occurred in the drama *The Song of Fate*, in which a Russian country girl, a schismatic with the monastic name Faina, leaving for the city, becomes a gypsy.

Grigoriev's poetry, seething and consumed by a fury of passion, is in harmony with the dramatic themes of *Verses on Russia* and *The Rose and the Cross*. The motif "joy-suffering" of Blok's Gaetan has something in common with Grigoriev's usual refrains: "bliss and suffering," "happiness-torment," "pleasure in torment."

Blok didn't "borrow from" and didn't "imitate" Grigoriev; he recognized himself in the forgotten failed poet of the forties, the lyrical reflection of his own face.[11]

In 1914 and 1915, preparing an edition of Grigoriev's poems for the press, Blok wrote an introductory article, "The Fate of Apollon Grigoriev." Grigoriev, the ideologue of "rootedness in the soil,"[12] collaborator of *Moskvityanin*, friend of Dostoevsky, theater critic, translator, and poet, is somewhat "stylized" in Blok's portrayal. But precisely this subjectivity of perception, this inclusion of Grigoriev in the poet's personal world, is unusually indicative. Looking closely into the life of the author of *The Comet*, Blok discusses the fate of the lyric poet in general and his own fate:

> The stronger the lyric poet, the more completely is his fate reflected in his verse. . . . A person's childhood and youth show us that divine plan by which he was created; they show how a person was "conceived of." Grigoriev's fate did not turn out as it could have turned out; this often happens. But his not very ordinary life and perhaps still more than his life, his verse, testify to the fact that Grigoriev was conceived of loftily. . . .

[The following paragraphs are quoted out of sequence to make Mochulsky's point.]

... In Grigoriev's fate, however "human" (in the bad sense of the word), reflections of the World Soul nevertheless quiver. Grigoriev's soul is linked to "depths."...

A man who through his love heard, even if dimly, a *distant call*; who was *really* overcome by demons; who talked about certain *miracles*, even if they had "fallen silent"; whose depression and raptures were not linked *solely* with his small drunken human soul—this man could have possessed a different power....

... [Grigoriev's poetry] contains a definite assertion of a link with the beloved in eternity (alas, for the last time!), a feeling of extreme tension in the world strings resulting from the approach of chaos, a pouring through the veins of those demonic forces which watch over the poet and soon rush upon him ... the sounds of a cracked human violin.

Grigoriev's face draws closer and closer to Blok's face, and the two faces merge. Whose fate "reflects the World Soul"? Who heard the "distant call"? Who spoke of miracles? Was it really Grigoriev?

The cycle of thirty poems *The Snow Mask* comes out as a separate book in April 1907 (Horae publishing house). It is later included with other poems of this year in the collection *The Earth in Snow*, which appeared in print in September 1908 (Golden Fleece publishing house). In the canonical text of the *Collected Poems*, the poems of 1907 lose the title *The Earth in Snow* and are distributed among three sections: *The Snow Mask*, *Faina*, and *Free Thoughts*. The foreword written by the poet for *The Earth in Snow* did not appear in the *Collected Works* and remained unknown to the majority of Blok's readers. Nevertheless this is a real lyrical *poema*, shedding light on the tragic meaning of the lines about passion and death. The poet tries to explain the "inexorable logic" of his three books:

> *Verses on the Beautiful Lady* is early morning dawn; ... *Unexpected Joy* is the first burning and mournful ecstasies, the first pages of the book of life. ... And now *The Earth in Snow*. The fruit of mournful raptures, a cup of bitter wine. When a madman loses his way will you not show him the path? I don't accept it—follow your own path. I myself know the countries of the world, the heart's sounds, the forest paths, the overgrown ravines, the lights in the huts of my native land, my companion's dark eyes.
>
> What of it if Fate, like a circus rider, has burst from the dim flickering of the wings, and her dashing steed, blinded by the streams of light, by the roar of human voices, by the cracking of the whips, has dashed around the arena, knocking the parapet with its hooves? And now Fate—an easy rider in a translucent tunic, all pink, tremblingly shy in the arena, brazenly shameless in passion, with a sinuous whip accidentally lashed the pitiful clown, who grimaces before the eyes of the amphitheater—lashed right on the white pancake of his face. The clown's soul blazes with laughter, despair, and passion. Blood streams from beneath the red triangular brows—because of it he can't see the road. He walks, staggering and jesting. But don't stretch out your hand and don't rescue him.
>
> Far away in the darkness shines the huge torch of a soul in love. If I get lost with him, there is no one to rescue me, because Fate itself has

transformed this splendor, this inescapable rapture, this clear conscience, this joyful depression—into nothing. And I will stretch out my hand to her, and will kneel at her feet—even if she is in the image of a circus rider in net stockings with blue clocks, with a slender and insulting whip, with the eyes of a captivating Philistine, shining only out of the habit of always shining, shining to the grave.

Thus the image of Fate is revealed: the Beloved is a circus rider with a whip, a Philistine with eyes shining out of habit. And here is her other aspect—the Gypsy:

So life unfolds. So, amazed at everything, regretting nothing, the soul passes along the road of suffering. You will part. This is where you live, here in these dusty little houses you rock children and you toil. . . . But from a distance a free, insolent, brazen gypsy girl with a saffron face, with depthless passion in her black eyes, comes to you. She comes slowly, strolling, resting between nights of passion. Yellow coins jingle in her black hair, her red-yellow kerchief is covered with dust. You must get up and give her the road and bow silently. . . .

But not even Fate will be victorious. Because at the end of the path full of falls, contradictions, mournful raptures, and unneeded depression stretches one eternal and boundless plain—the primordial homeland, perhaps Russia itself. . . . And the snows carpeting the earth, before spring. For the time being the snow blinds the eyes, and the cold, chaining the soul, blocks the paths. From a distance the lonely Peddler's song is heard—a triumphantly sad, inviting melody carried by the blizzard: "Oh, full, full is the box!"[13]

Blok draws the ascending melodic line of his poems with a lyricism of images and rhythms: the Rider, the Gypsy, Russia—the three images of the poet's fate, the three voices leading the song.

The poems of *The Snow Mask* are a record of motion in sound. The meaning of the words is subordinated to the element of song, broad, headlong, soaring. This is the blizzard singing in a human voice, the wind whistling, the snowstorm trumpeting. The world rose like a whirlwind and tore off in a breathtaking flight. Snow whirls, stars fall, ships sink in the blizzardy sea, the heart slips over the abyss. The verb "to fly" is endlessly repeated:

And, dragging snow sprays behind us,
We fly into millions of abysses . . .

or:

Above the boundless snows
  We will fly up!
Beyond the foggy seas
  We will burn out.
        . . . . .

To fly like a ringing arrow
Into an abyss of black stars!

In the poem *Voices* "two will rush off in the sphere of snowstorms." *She* lures him into an abyss. His death hurries, in a voice breathless from the flight:

Oh, overtake! Oh, catch up!
. . . . .
Listen! Listen! I am a head wind!
We are in the moon's circle!
We are in a starry abyss!

His heart "slides" with her "into abysses" like a mountain avalanche. And everything rushes with them. He says in the poem *Caught by a Blizzard*:

And the ravaging,
    Exorbitant years rushed;
Like a heart grown cold,
    They rolled away forever.

In the poem *At the Call of the Blizzard* he writes:

You lowered your eyes,
And we rushed off.
And new sounds rose to meet us,
Snow flew,
The horns of night,
Flying down, rang out.

The movement, flight, whirling are intensified by the abundance of imperative intonations:

Blow, sparkling filaments,
Float, starry pieces of ice,
Valley blizzards, catch your breath!
                    (*Wings*)

"Awaken! . . . Submit! . . . Return!" "Away! Fly away! . . . " "Fly away, holy flock!" "Glitter, last needle. . . . " "Get up! . . . Sweep! . . . Kill me! . . . Burn me! . . . " "Pierce me, winged gaze!" And, finally:

Secretly the heart asks for death.
Light heart, glide . . .
                    (*Doomed*)

The "airy merry-go-round" whirls, the "quiet dance" of the blizzard continues. And these snowstorms, the falling stars, and flights into the abyss are only symbols of emotional events. The poet conjectures:

And does my passion and tenderness
Want to spend itself in the snowstorm?
           (*Confusion*)

All the "blizzard" themes of *The Snow Mask* are a successive unfolding of one metaphor. The usual—and hackneyed from overuse—expression "whirlwind of passion" is developed in the dramatic *poema* about the Snow Maiden who leads one to death. If all romantic poetry is poetry of metaphor, then Blok's lyric is indeed the summit of this poetry.

But the inspired words and sounds of these verses only accompany their flight. Their inner movement is created by *rhythm*. Before *The Snow Mask*, iambics predominated in Blok's poetry. Now he shifts to a second schema: of the thirty poems in the collection, only six are written in iambic. The light and rapid trochaic, the basic style of the folk song, takes first place. It seems that the "triumphantly sad, inviting melody" of Nekrasov's *Peddler*, his bold, dancing trochaics, ring in the poet's memory: "Oj, polna, polna korobuska."

The variety of Blok's trochaic rhythms is striking. Here is regular trochaic tetrameter:

    I tvoi mne svetjat oči
    Najavu ili vo sne?
    Daže v poldne, daže v dne
    Razmetalis' kosmy noči . . .

    And your eyes shine at me;
    Awake or in a dream?
    Even at noon, even in day time,
    The mane of night tossed. . . .
           (*Confusion*)

But this meter is comparatively rare. The poet prefers complex combinations of two-, three-, and four-foot trochaics. These breaking, hurried rhythms carry the poem *Alarm*:

    Serdce, slyšiš'
    Lëgkij šag
    Za soboj?

    Serdce, vidiš':
    Kto-to podal znak,
    Tajnyj znak rukoj?

    Ty li? Ty li?
    V'jugi plyli,
    Lunnyj serp zastyl . . .

    Heart, do you hear
    The light step
    Behind you?

Aleksandr Blok

> Heart, do you see,
> Someone gave a sign,
> A secret hand sign?
>
> Is it you? Is it you?
> Blizzards floated,
> The moon's sickle froze. . . .

And the end:

> Čtob letet' streloj zvenjaščej
> V propast' čërnyx zvëzd!
>
> To fly like a ringing arrow
> Into an abyss of black stars!

In the poem *Away!* trochaic tetrameter alternates with dimeter:

> I struit moë vesel'e
>   Dva luča.
>
> To gorjat i dremljut maki
>   Zlyx očej.
>
> And my gaiety streams
>   Two rays.
>
> Now the poppies of evil eyes
>   Burn and doze.

The sharp breaks are softened in the poem *And Again Snows*, where tetrameter ends in a trimeter line:

> I vdali, vdali, vdali,
> Meždu nebom i zemlëj
>   Veselitsja smert'.
>
> And in the distance, the distance, the distance,
> Between sky and earth,
>   Death enjoyed itself.

Still greater swiftness is achieved by combining trochaic with anapest. In the amazing poem *Her Songs* passionate, menacing words ring with magical incantations:

> Rukavom moix metelej
>   Zadušu.
> Serebrom moix veselij
>   Oglušu.
> Na vozdušnoj karuseli
>   Zakružu.
> Prjažej sputannoj kudeli
>   Obov'ju.

Lëgkoj bragoj snežnyx xmelej
   Napoju.

With the sleeve of my snowstorms
   I will smother.
With the silver of my gaieties
   I will deafen.
On an airy merry-go-round
   I will whirl.
With yarn of tangled tow
   I will entwine.
With the light home brew of snow hops
   I will intoxicate.

But the poem *Caught by a Blizzard* is a real miracle of rhythm. Its first part is written in tonic verse, intense, uneven, trembling with emotion:

V nebe vspyxnuli tëmnye oči
Tak jasno!
I ja pozabyl primety
Strany prekrasnoj—
V bleske tvoëm, kometa!
V bleske tvoëm, srebrosnežnaja noč'!

Dark eyes flared up in the sky
So clearly!
And I forgot the signs
Of the beautiful country—
In your radiance, comet!
In your radiance, snowy silver night!

And suddenly the rhythm is broken and song trochaics burst in:

I neslis' opustošajuščie
Nepomernye goda,
Slovno serdce zastyvajuščee
Zakatilos' navsegda.

And the ravaging,
Exorbitant years rushed;
Like a heart grown cold,
They rolled away forever.

These hyperdactyllic rhymes (*opustošajuščie, zastyvajuščee*) halt the verse's momentum; they seem to be suspended in a void.

The rhythmics of *The Snow Mask* are a pattern of unusual complexity and subtlety, still awaiting its investigator.

In the cycle *Faina* the whirling of the blizzard slackens. The dancing trochaics are replaced by heavy iambics, by pathetic anapests, by balanced amphibrachs. The rhythmic fabric changes so markedly that we at once sense a move into another world. The flight "in the sphere of snowstorms" ends in a descent to earth. The shadows, sweeping past in the starry abyss, are transformed into human images: the poet and his beloved are before us:

> And I spent a mad year
> By the black train. For the torments,
> For the days of agony and adversity,
> Hands touched my hair,
> Dark eyes looked,
> The blue storm panted. . . .

His "joyless passion" passed beyond the third guard. He lies at her feet in a dark hall. The fire has burned down in the fireplace; she is leaving. In the distance a slammed door clatters. He can't endure it; he runs after her, and catches up to her in the unsteady light of a lane:

> And, as into an abyss, we enter
> The lap of night. Our climb is steep . . .
> And delirium. And darkness. Eyes shine.
> Hair flows on her shoulders.
> . . . . .
> Yes! Night is with us! And with new power
> The daytime night surrounds us,
> So that, with tormenting passion,
> The enfeebled day would die out. . . .

But she is "faithless," "perfidious." He meets her by the entrance, speaks disconnected words to her. But she tears herself away from him and flies "like an escaping bird" into the foul weather and the darkness. His whole life is a torment of passion and despair:

> I move from torture to torture
> Along a wide band of flame.
> You only tease me with the impossible,
> Torment me with the unthinkable.

He follows her "like a timid shadow," hides "like a mindless and obedient slave." He doesn't fear her insulting contempt, her whip:

> Why be impassive? Why—winged?
> Scourge and reproach a hundred times,
> Just to be damned for a moment
> With you—in the light of the night glow.

The slavery of passion, the humiliation of the conquered. And, like Zemfira in *The Gypsies*,[14] Faina sings to him mockingly and brazenly:

> Hey, take care! I am all serpent!
> Look: I was yours for a moment,
> And abandoned you!

> You repel me! Go away!
> I'll be with someone else tonight!
> Look for your own wife!
>
> Go, she will drive away sorrow,
> Let her caress you, let her kiss you,
> Go—I'll lash with the whip!

Not so long ago he had called her "a star of tender dreams" and had seen in her a wonderful image of his Muse. It seemed to him that she incarnated his vision of the Snow Maiden, of the mysterious Stranger. Her silks also sang, her hand strewn with rings was also slender; and the same distances were revealed behind her veil (*Here she appeared. Overshadowed*). But here in the rustle of her silks he heard a serpent's hissing, and in the "ginger twilight" the eye furtively watched the "serpentine faithlessness." His love turned into passion after touching the slimy and cold scales; the beloved brought him the bliss of death:

> Crawl to me like a creeping snake,
> Stun me in the dead of night.
> Torment me with languorous lips,
> Suffocate me with black tresses.

The snake becomes an image-symbol of this incinerating passion:

> You are above me in your shawl,
> A snake—with healing sting.

The Snow Maiden came to love the "inscrutable" city, Petersburg; she whirled like a snowstorm in the Russian expanses, poured herself out in the despair of a folk song. Who is she? Whose songs are these? Whose dance is this?

> By what light
>   Do you tease and entice?
> In this whirling
>   When will you tire?
> Whose songs? And sounds?
> What do I fear?
> The plaintive sounds
> And—free Rus?

And the end:

> And the features shine with strange radiance . . .
>   Bold dance!
> Oh, song! Oh, boldness! Oh, death! Oh, mask!
>   Accordion—is it you?

Thus the transition to the blending of the image of the "perfidious, faithless beloved" with the wild, intoxicating gypsy Russia is prepared.

Aleksandr Blok One of Blok's most perfect creations is the violent, frenzied, bold, dancing *Accordion, accordion*:

> Accordion, accordion!
> Hey, sing, squeal, and burn!
> Hey, yellow buttercups,
> Spring flowers!
> . . . . .
> Faithless, sly,
> Perfidious—dance!
> And be forever poison
> To the squandered soul!
>
> I'll lose my mind, lose my mind,
> I love, raving,
> That you are all night and all darkness,
> And all—intoxicating.
>
> That you took away my soul,
> Exhausted it with poison,
> That I sing of you, of you,
> And there is no end to the songs!

The magic of this breaking-loose, breathless, carrying-away melody "carried by the blizzard" has no equal.

The serpent, rustling black silks, and the rider "with a slender and insulting whip," "faithless, sly, perfidious," disappear in the whirlwind which caught up the free and insolent gypsy. And she dances and screeches and drives one mad. But what expanses all around, what distances are revealed beyond the circle she outlines:

> The plaintive sounds
> And—free Rus.

And there is no longer the slave's humiliation by "the black train," no prison of endless passion. The face of the homeland is revealed in evil beauty and cruel tenderness, and the poet will also speak of it:

> That you are all night and all darkness,
> And all—intoxicating.

And he also "loves her, raving."

The elevation of unhappy passion for a woman to the level of mystical love for his homeland is Blok's great spiritual victory. The Snow Maiden lured him, led him away to death:

> She leads, and I see: a depth
> Compressed by dark granite.
> She flows, she sings,
> She, the accursed one, calls.

From the temptation of suicide the poet runs into the fields, to Russian roads, along which roam wanderers as homeless and unhappy as he. The heart burns with new light; the snows melt, and the snowstorms depart; the earth before him is in the radiance of spring. In triumphant lines he celebrates his return to life:

The Snow Mask

> Oh, spring without end and without limit—
> Dream without end and without limit!
> I recognize you, life! I accept!
> And I greet you with ringing shield!
> . . . . .
> I accept the remote villages
> And the wells of the earthly cities!
> The lit-up expanse of the sky
> And the exhaustion of slave labors!

And the ending:

> And I look and measure the enmity,
> Hating, cursing, and loving.
> For torment, for death—I know—
> All the same, I accept you!

This poem was written on 24 October 1907. This is an important date in Blok's life, the beginning of his leaving "lyrical solitude" for the expanse of "nationality" and "civic-mindedness." The poet later included a few 1908 poems in the cycle *Faina*, including an epilogue to the romance with the Snow Maiden. The last lines are cold and pitiless:

> Now passes before me
> Your *dethroned shadow*. . . .
>
> With kindness? Or with reproach?
> Or hating, avenging, grieving?
> Or do you want to be a verdict to me?
> I don't know: *I have forgotten you.*
>   (20 November 1908)

Four small *poemas*, written in calm, slow, unrhymed iambic pentameter, enter the third section of *Free Thoughts*. After the lyrical whirlwinds of *The Snow Mask* and *Faina* come the lofty harmony of the epic tale, unhurried observations, quiet thoughts, long descriptions. This is the calm after the storm, leaving the circle of soulfulness for the clear, cool world of lakes, pines, dunes. The romantic studies Pushkin's simplicity, measure, calm wisdom. He is transformed into a sailor of the northern seas, with a tanned and weather-beaten face:

> My soul is simple. The salt wind
> Of the seas and the resinous breath of pine
> Nourished it. And in it all the same signs

> As on my weather-beaten face.
> And I am handsome, with the indigent beauty
> Of shifting dunes and northern seas.

This isn't invented. The salt of the northern seas really was in Blok's blood: it is the ancient legacy of his Germanic ancestors. Not without reason did V. N. Knyazhnin notice in the poet's appearance a resemblance to a "foreign sailor, born in Dunkirk or in Helgoland."

To become a simple, healthy person, to accept life thoughtlessly, joyfully, is the romantic's eternal dream. The poet passes by a hippodrome: before his eyes the yellow jockey is mortally wounded. He lies, arms outstretched, with his face turned to the sky: "It is so good and free to die."

On another evening he walks along an embankment. Workers are hauling firewood from the barges. Shouts are heard: "He fell! He fell!" They drag a drowned man from the water. How simple death is. The poet exclaims:

> Heart!
> Be my guide. And death,
> Observe me with a smile. . . .
> . . . . .
> I want
> Always to look into human eyes,
> And to drink wine, and to kiss women. . . .
> . . . . .
> And to sing songs! And to listen to the wind in the world!
> *(On Death)*

The dreamer longs for "realism." He, like Ivan Karamazov's devil, wanted to be incarnated into a "250-pound merchant woman." And he wanted to live like everyone else, without complex emotions and poetic illusions. On a bench in Shuvalovsky park he sees a "melancholy girl"; the lyrical theme of a sad and proud beauty already rings in his soul. But an officer in a tight tunic, "with a flabby rump," approaches the "stranger" and gives her a long, smacking kiss. Life teaches irony:

> I roar with laughter. I run upwards. I throw
> Pinecones, sand at them; I screech, I dance
> Among the graves, invisible and tall. . . .

He wants to observe death with a smile; to meet human love with loud laughter; to cure passion with irony. And, coming home, he finds on the table a "tragic actress's letter":

> "I am all tired out. I am all ill.
> Flowers don't rejoice me. Write . . .
> Forgive, and burn this raving . . . "
>
> And languorous words. . . . And lengthy handwriting.
> Weary as her weary train. . . .

What was so recently still experienced tragically has now become ludicrous. She is not a Snow Maiden at all, but just a broken, decadent actress (*Above the Lake*).

He wants to forget the black Petersburg nights, to become a sailor on a northern sea, to go out on a motorboat into the "vast, caressing salt," and to see a beauty in the blue fog—a sea yacht under full sail with the precious gem of a lantern on the slender mast (*In the Northern Sea*). Returning to shore, he wants to meet on its slope a woman with eyes red from sun and sand:

> She came. Her beastlike glance crossed
> My beastlike glance. She burst out laughing.
>
> . . . . .
>
> I pursued her a long way. Scratched
> My face on pine needles, bloodied my hands,
> And tore my clothes to tatters. Shouted and pursued
> Her like a wild beast; again shouted and called.

Then, out of breath, he fell on the sand and thought:

> "Today is night
> And tomorrow is night. I won't leave here
> Until I hunt her down, like a wild animal. . . ."
>   (*In the Dunes*)

The buoyant tone of these "free thoughts" of simplification and the "natural life" are not infectious. One doesn't believe in this "naturalness."

At the end of November Blok prepares a long critical survey, "Literary Review of 1907," for *Golden Fleece*. He writes to his mother that, studying contemporary literature, he has drawn "very definite conclusions":

> (1) Translated literature predominates over original; (2) criticism and commentary over creativity. So it will be for another 50 to 100 years, and then a great writer will appear from the "abyss of the people" and will destroy the very memory of us all. It's amusing to look at the tiny group of the Russian intelligentsia, which in *ten* years has exchanged a heap of *Weltanschauungen* and split into fifty enemy camps, and at the many-millioned people who *since the fifteenth century* have carried the same unchanging idea of God. . . . Klyuev's letter opened my eyes once and for all. So we correctly burn life down, because "playful chance" will preserve nothing of us, except this great beauty which is perhaps now shimmering before us in the morning after.

Nikolai Klyuev, "a young peasant from a far-northern province, a beginning poet," started to correspond with Blok. He showered praise on the "heavenly images" of his verse and simultaneously exposed the intelligentsia. Blok answered him, as he said, "in the spirit of a repentant nobleman." In an arrogant epistle, Klyuev prophesied the appearance of a great writer from the common people and talked about the impassable gulf separating "gentry" writers from peasant Rus. Here is an example of his "pure folk style": "One wants to get high above the world, to sob out the taste for darkness in fiery, starry tears, and, raising the aspergillum of purification, to sprinkle the bloody earth." This typical semi-intellectual, an imitator of Nekrasov and Koltsov, prophesies in the name of the whole Russian people with brazen overfamiliarity. And this letter made a very strong impression on Blok. And he repents to this "real stalwart"![15]

Of course it wasn't Klyuev's hysterics which determined the poet's revolt against the Russian intelligentsia; they weren't the cause, but the emotional ground for his transition to the position of populism.

In the introductory part of the survey "Literary Review for 1907" Blok attacks the intelligentsia, calling it a "universal misunderstanding" and predicting its imminent destruction. He demands of writer-esthetes that their life be complete martyrdom, of lyric poets that they realize their responsibility to the workers and peasants, of "representatives of the religious-philosophical persuasion" that they cease their blasphemous chatter. Never before had the poet spoken in such a tone—accusatory, indignant, embittered. The nihilist was awakening in the romantic, ready to acknowledge the whole esthetic and spiritual culture of the Russian renaissance of the twentieth century as a "worthless fact of the life of the intelligentsia." He speaks with special hatred about the religious-philosophical meetings:

> Educated and venomous intellectuals, grown gray in arguments about Christ and Antichrist, ladies, wives, daughters, sisters-in-law in respectable blouses, meditative philosophers, priests glossy from self-satisfied fat—all this inconceivable and hideous jumble, the idiotic flash of words. . . . And all this becomes fashionably accessible to the assistant professors' wives and to philanthropic ladies. But on the street—wind; prostitutes freeze; . . . people are hung. And in the country—reaction. And it is difficult, cold, loathsome to live in Russia.

This is a characteristically Russian revolt, a typical Russian search for the "truth of life," moral maximalism, and elemental nihilism. The populists of the seventies donned peasant shirts and bast shoes; Gogol tortured himself with starvation; Tolstoy renounced *War and Peace* and *Anna Karenina*; the symbolist Aleksandr Dobrolyubov retreated to a monastery; Blok repented to the "peasant" poet Klyuev. In the age-old feeling of the "injustice" of the culture there is the Russian barbarism and the great Russian strength.

CHAPTER VI
PUBLIC ACTIVITIES
1908–1909

In January 1908 Blok wrote Briusov: "All my other literary work has for the time being been overshadowed by a long play I have been tormenting myself over for a year." From these words one might conclude that the conception of the drama *Song of Fate* dates back to the beginning of 1907. But the rough drafts preserve no trace of work relating to this time. It is possible that the poet destroyed the original sketches before he died. In a notebook we find a note by the author, dated 1921, where he states that he had "destroyed the sketch of a *talented* scene between Helen, the Friend, Faina, and Herman in a gambling house," and also "all other sketches." At the beginning of 1908 Blok is working intensely on *Song of Fate*. On 8 January he writes his mother:

> I have already sketched three acts, that is, I have already reached a turning point. The most difficult is done and there now remains only the last exertion of all my powers and much hard and stubborn labor. Here I am not lazy (for example, I am discarding entirely the well-written, but conceptually unsatisfactory, fifth act).

And two days later he informs E. P. Ivanov: "I don't go anywhere, because the drama is progressing (although slowly and painfully)." In the middle of January the fourth act is being written:

> The drama is progressing; I am now writing the fourth act. This is a whole area of life which I build, break up, and arrange in my own way. I meet long familiar faces and put them in various situations according to my own will. They have capricious dispositions and reveal a lot to me on meeting. (Letter to his mother, 17 January.)

By the end of January the "general framework" of the play is ready. Blok informs his mother: "It is essential to finish soon. It is called *Song of Fate*, a drama in four acts and seven scenes. Many scenes are ready, as well as the general framework." He reads the play to his aunt Maria Andreevna Beketova, and she makes "some real observations." He writes his mother with annoyance:

> The damned abstractness haunts me in this play too, although perhaps less than in the rest. For this I am angry at my father (!). . . . He is a decadent to the marrow of his bones, because the poison of decadence consists simply in the fact that richness, vividness, vitality, expressiveness, not only typical but distinctive, are lost. . . . But there is still very much richness in life, which the artist must bring to realization.

In April he is "greatly reworking and polishing" the play. Finally, on 1 May, it is finished. He informs his mother:

> Today at my place I read *Song of Fate* to about fifteen people, and at Chulkov's on Sunday to about twenty-five people. Many changes. The epigraph to the whole drama: there is no fear in love, but perfect love casts out fear, because there is suffering in fear. He who fears is not perfected in love (in Greek). *Song of Fate* is very important to me, I am afraid for it. This is my favorite child; it is already a year old (from April to April).

Blok remained very satisfied with the impression his play made on the listeners. He writes his mother:

> I am collecting, listening attentively to all the opinions, both of writers and nonwriters. This time how they react is very important to me. This is the first piece in which I am groping . . . and not just for lyrical ground, as I define for myself the significance of *Song of Fate*, and therefore I love it more than all I have written.

On 4 May he reads the play at Chulkov's in the presence of Leonid Andreev and his wife, Sologub, Volynsky, V. Ivanov, Syunnerberg, Lansere and his wife, Voloshin, Kuzmin, the actress Shchegoleva, the publishers of *Torches* (*Fakely*) and *Sweetbrier* (*Shipovnik*), and the Polish writer Nalepinsky.

In May, during the Art Theater's tour in Petersburg, Blok reads his drama to a "committee" consisting of Stanislavsky, Nemirovich-Danchenko, and Burdzhalov. M. A. Beketova relates:

> During the reading V. I. Nemirovich-Danchenko exclaimed: "God, God, what a talented lad!" K. S. Stanislavsky became especially animated after the reading of the second act (Hall of the Exhibition). Right then he began to outline a plan for staging it and made several observations about details. The matter was considered practically settled: the theater is taking the drama. But they promised to send a final answer from Moscow.

On Stanislavsky's advice Blok reworked the fourth and fifth scenes of the original edition into one, called "In the Wasteland." He reads the play in this changed form to Meyerhold in July. The latter "criticizes it severely." Blok admits to his mother: "I again have doubts about the play. Let it again lie for the time being. Zhenya [E. P. Ivanov], as before, regards it negatively." Nevertheless he sends *Song of Fate* to Stanislavsky in August, and only in November gets a telegram from him: "We won't succeed in staging the play this season. Details by letter in a week. I must advise you to publish the play." However, the letter with details doesn't arrive in a week, but in a month. This is how Blok sets forth its content to his mother:

> In essence, he came to love me and *Song of Fate*, but not a single character in it. He reread the play four times, writes a mass of observations, very modestly, very well. I answered him in a very long letter, mainly about *what* Russia is for me, which puzzles him. Both Lyuba and I have the impression that he won't put the play on, and I'm not grieving over this, because I believe in Stanislavsky.

In his *Diary* the poet later wrote: "I believed this, in other words I was done with it, because I myself, stepping aside from the play, was disappointed in it."

Merezhkovsky and Meyerhold offered to intercede to have *Song of Fate* staged in the Aleksandrinsky Theater; V. F. Kommissarzhevskaya wanted to stage it in her theater; Leonid Andreev advised him to give it to the New Theater. But Blok declined all these suggestions. The play was printed in April 1909 in Sweetbrier's ninth anthology and passed unnoticed. In the author's words, it was "buried."

The seven scenes of the "dramatic *poema*" *Song of Fate* dramatize the lyrical theme of the verses *The Earth in Snow*. The first scene, written in pale Maeterlinckian tones, leads us to Herman's white "bright" house. A tall monk appears, resembling an angel with broken wings. Through the window he shows Herman "a vast world, blue, unknown, enticing," and Herman goes away "to the people." Abandoning his own home, his beloved wife, and his old mother, he prays: "Lord! I can't go on this way any more. It is too good for me in my quiet white house. Give me the strength to part from it and to see what life in the world is. Keep for me only the ardor of my young soul and my living conscience, Lord!" Helen, Herman's wife, sobbing, blesses him: "Go, my dear, go, my regal one! Go where the song of fate resounds." In the second scene, the monk tells Helen about the schismatic Faina: over the steep slope of a wide river "Faina stood all night long and looked into distant Rus as if waiting for someone." From the other shore, from behind the monastery fence, the monk saw Faina. And when she ran away from her native village, he left the cloister and wandered after her into the "dark night." But he didn't find her.

In this way the poem *The Monk* from the cycle *Faina* becomes drama. The monk bows and prays, and neither the abbot nor the brothers suspect

> That the blissful soul's wax is melting
> In the bright flame of the candle....

> That no prayers are necessary,
> When you walk along the river
> Beyond the monastery fence
> In your monastic cowl.
>
> That here—you madly lashed me
> With flowering hops,
> And I lost count of the weeks
> Of my criminal beauty.

In the play the monk tells Helen how "in the evening in the village I lashed Faina's soul with hops, and all the grandfathers on the sleeping planks knew that she had broken into a dance." We recall the verse:

> I look—she threw up her arms,
> Broke into a sweeping dance,
> Strewed everyone with flowers
> And poured herself out in song.
>   (*Accordion, accordion*)

Even the description of Faina's appearance—"like a nun, she wore a black dress, and only her eyes shone from beneath the shawl"—goes back to the rough draft of the poem *The Snow Maiden*:

> And she speaks in a simple and clear
> But unfamiliar language,
> Her eyes shine beneath the shawl
> With madly impassive radiance.

The third scene is in the gigantic hall of a world industrial exhibition, with machines, locomotives, automobiles, motorboats, and airplanes. Herman appears with his friend. He is drunk with the wind, the music, the movement; he is in love with the "living world's diversity." An old professor extols science and progress; the crowd roars with laughter. The famous music hall singer Faina mounts the stage. We recognize the woman-serpent of *The Snow Mask*, we hear *Faina's Song*, which is renamed *Song of Fate* in the drama:

> She wears a simple black dress which hugs her slender figure like a snake skin. A precious gem shines in her dark hair, setting off still more the fire of her enormous eyes. A long whip in her hand. Not bowing, unsmiling, Faina looks round at the crowd and makes a faint signal with the whip. The crowd is silent.

Faina, eyes narrowed, sings the *Song of Fate*—popular couplets in a serious, high-pitched, and inviting voice:

> When I look into your eyes
> With the narrow eyes of a snake,
> And press your hand, loving,
> Hey, take care! I am all serpent!

Herman is perturbed. So this is the feast of culture! The seeking spirit has been replaced by the machine, the lofty dream has become a gypsy girl! He addresses Faina:

> You have poisoned the heart with sweet venom,
> . . . . .
> You have swept the soul with a black train!
> Accursed! You have jeered enough!
> Away with the mask! A human being is before you!

Faina strikes Herman on the face with the whip; a red welt remains on his face. He falls to his knees, his gaze riveted on her. She says sadly: "Poor thing!" In the foreword to the collection *The Earth in Snow* Blok evoked two images of Fate with great lyrical power: the circus rider with the whip, and the free and brazen gypsy girl. In the drama the action arises from the lap of music: the rider is transformed into a music hall singer, the clown into the dreamer Herman. The snake, come to life in the whistling, sinuous whip, stings the hero mortally.

In the fourth scene, after a satirical depiction of Faina's devotees—writers, artists, symbolist poets—Herman's meeting with Faina takes place. He tells her: "I understood a lot. Here everything is just beginning. Since you struck me with the whip . . . You are eternal. Like a star." "Faina turns Herman by the shoulders and looks into his eyes with laughing, narrowed eyes. He shuts his eyes. Then she throws her arms around his neck and kisses him on the lips with avid curiosity."

The viewer had to exert his imagination to believe in the transformation of the schismatic nun into a famous music hall singer; the metamorphosis of the music hall singer into the bride of Russian songs, calling her predestined one in the open field, demands an even greater effort. The move from Faina's dressing room to the world of half-fairy tale folklore is striking in its unexpectedness.

In the fifth scene:

> A vast wasteland, lit by the autumn moon. . . . An endless plain. . . . The autumn ponds show silver through the pale gold of the maples, and a drowsy white swan rocks in the background, half hidden in the reeds. . . . Faina appears on the background of the boundless distance and glowing sky. . . . She sits on the edge of the precipice, embracing her knees, and looks into the distance, conjuring with her eyes.

Not only does the stage setting change—the very style and rhythm of the play changes. From the blizzards of *The Snow Mask* we are transported into the world of folk poetry. Here are the invocations with which Faina bewitches the predestined one:

> My betrothed! Come, look. I have been waiting for you for a long time, have looked into all eyes, have all spread myself in the dawn, have all poured myself out in songs, have arrayed myself all in blue mists, like a bride in a bridal veil. . . . Listen to my voice, my voice winds like a silvery

river! Shake off my white hands, take the heavy cross from my maiden's breast.... Autumn wind, carry my voice! Overflowing river, carry news of me to my dear one!

Faina tears the scarlet ribbon from her waist and throws it down the precipice.

This wave of Russian folk melody burst into Blok's drama wilfully and spontaneously; in July 1908, at the very peak of work on redoing the play for Stanislavsky, inspiration gripped him. The first three poems of the cycle *On the Field of Kulikovo* were written in a few days: *The river spread. It flows, mourns lazily* (7 June); *We halted above the steppe at midnight* (8 June); and *At night when Mamai lay in hiding with the horde* (14 June). And this lyrical excitement, begetting Blok's most brilliant poems, is woven into the play. Faina took on the features of a mysterious Maiden descending to the warrior "over the sleeping Nepryadva"; her voice also calls beyond the foggy river. Night birds trace circles over her, the wind dashes against the thorny weeds (feather-grass in the poem), and swans cry in the distance:

> Before the dark and ominous Don,
> Amid the night fields,
> With a prophetic heart I heard Your voice
> In the cries of the swans.
> . . . . .
> The eagle's screech above the Tatar camp
> Threatened misfortune
> And the Nepryadva was adorned in fog,
> Like a princess in a bridal veil.

Let us remember Faina's incantation: "all arrayed in blue mists, like a bride in a bridal veil."

The dreamer Herman, leaving the white Maeterlinckian house, is suddenly lit with a mystical light. For a moment it seems that a "holy banner" flashed above him, that his heart was pierced "by the arrow of ancient Tatar ferocity," that his friend is saying to him:

> "Hone your sword,
> Not to fight the Tatars in vain,
> To fall dead for the holy cause."

The themes of a warrior's feat and a holy death for the fatherland are introduced into Herman's dialogue with his friend. Herman talks about his love: "Then I heard stirring music—it pursues me to this day, louder and louder with each sunrise, more and more triumphant.... I didn't leave in my own name. The wind called me, it sang me a song. I am in terrible uneasiness, as before a feat." And here, "with growing passion," in a frenzy of love, Herman relates his lyrical motifs of the poems of *On the Field of Kulikovo*. The ecstatic, half-mad eloquence of the monologue takes one's breath away:

Take me for a madman, if you like. Yes, perhaps I am on the threshold of insanity or . . . insight! Everything that has been, everything that will be, has beset me, as if in these days I am living the life of all ages, living the torments of my native land. I remember the terrible day of the battle of Kulikovo. The prince climbed the hill with his troops, the earth shook with the creaking of Tatar carts, the eagle's scream threatened adversity. Then ominous night crept down, and the Nepryadva was adorned in fog, like a bride in a bridal veil. The prince and the commander stood at the foot of the hill and listened to the earth. The swans and geese splashed restlessly, the widow sobbed, the mother clung to her son's stirrup. Only over the Russian camp stood quietness, and the distant summer lightning blazed. But the wind drove the fog away, just such an autumn morning descended and, I remember, also smelled of burning. And the shining banner of the prince moved from the hill. When a monk and a Tatar first fell dead, the hosts collided and fought all day, hacked, battled. . . . And the fresh troops had to lie in ambush all day, only to watch and to weep and to long for battle. . . . And the commander repeated, warning: "It is still too early, our time hasn't come." Lord, I know, like every warrior in this ambush force, how the heart begs for work, and how early it still is, early! . . . That's why I don't sleep at night. I'm waiting with all my heart for the one who will come and say: "Your hour has struck! It is time!"

But Herman's illumination, flaring up suddenly, dies out just as suddenly. The motif of the homeland is muffled by the triumphant music of Passion-Fate. The finale of this scene is the drama's highest lyrical ascent. Faina appears. In a trumpeting voice the swan cries out to meet the rising sun. "Filling the air with her passionately ringing voice, Faina echoes him. Faina: 'Come to me! I am tired of living! Free me! . . . Prince! Friend! Bridegroom!' The whole world orchestra takes up Faina's passionate appeal. . . . Smashing all fetters, breaking all dams, the whole sea of world violins celebrates the victory of passion." Faina recognizes her predestined one in Herman. They fly away on a troika. "The voice of the bells on the collar, conquering those on the harness, joins the world orchestra, takes precedence in it, and then gets lost, disappears, dying away somewhere in the distance on the radiant plain."

This "world orchestra" plunges the drama into a vibrating, fiery, elemental force. The specific gravity of the words is increased by the whole force of cosmic resonance.

In the sixth scene the monk sends Helen to meet Herman. In the seventh, and last, Faina and Herman are on a deserted, snow-covered plain. The snowstorm sets the tune. The blizzard melodies of *The Snow Mask* return again. Herman takes up the motif of the poem *Second Christening*:

In my soul a new kind of coldness,
Bracing and healthy, like winter.
. . . . .
Burning, like Faina's dark gaze,

Aleksandr Blok

> As if I am christened with a second christening
> In another, a cold, snow font.

Now it is all the same to him—to live or to die. The blow of the whip killed all the past. "There is nothing to lose, there is nothing sacred. . . . The soul is like the *earth in snow*." He lies down in the snow. The snowstorm gathers momentum. His whole life passes before him as in a dream: a vast city, white house, mother, wife, the hero in a winged helmet with a sword on his shoulder. Everything is over. Now, there is only Fate. Faina abandons him. Herman remains alone in the darkness, in the snowstorm. He says: "What am I, a beggar, to do? Where am I to go?" The song of the peddler is heard: "Oh, full, full is the box."

The peddler rescues the freezing Herman, leads him to the light. The finale with the peddler is a dramatization of the last words of the preface to the collection *The Earth in Snow*:

> Not even Fate will be victorious, because at the end of the path . . . one eternal and boundless plain stretches out—the primordial homeland, perhaps Russia herself. . . . For the time being the snow blinds the eyes. . . . From a distance the lonely peddler's song is heard: "Oh, full, full is the box."

Nekrasov's peddler is a symbol of folk, peasant Russia. The motif of the homeland, ringing so triumphantly in the fifth scene, returns in the finale as a distant and muffled echo. Herman won't freeze in the snowstorm of passion: the peddler will lead him out—*to the homeland*.

Blok dreamed of a way out of his "lyrical isolation," hoped "to find firm and not only lyrical soil," wanted to write a real drama with living people, with action and conflict, with human passions. But he didn't succeed. *Song of Fate*, his "favorite child," despite the lofty lyrical flights, is not a "real drama." Musical waves pour out and sing in it, but no human voices speak. Stanislavsky didn't take to a single character in the play, and indeed it would be hard to take to these misty phantoms begotten by the sounds of the "world orchestra." The element of lyric poetry is just the opposite of the element of drama. The lyric poet dreams only about himself, the shadows of his own songs flash before him. To make "characters" of them, to put them on the stage, to light them with footlights means to kill them. Blok soon understood this and came to hate the play. In 1910 he wrote: "Already I definitely consider *Song of Fate* an idiotic play." In 1912 Meyerhold again proposes to the poet staging *Song of Fate* in the Aleksandrinsky Theater. He prepares to redo it. "I will try," he notes in his diary, "to discard from it everything banal, everything stupid, and everything of Leonid Andreev which protrudes from it. We'll see what then remains of this rather stupid Herman." But he didn't undertake to redo it. Only in 1918, preparing a new edition of his *Theater*, did the poet substantially rework his unsuccessful drama. He shortened the lyrical monologues and eliminated the traces of "conventional and mystical style." The play appeared in a separate volume in the publishing house Alkonost in 1919.

Simultaneously with the work on *Song of Fate* Blok translates Grillparzer's *The Ancestress (Die Ahnfrau)*. He writes his mother (8 January): "The other day Kommissarzhevskaya sent for me. For about an hour and a half we talked everything over very nicely. . . . She asked for a translation of some German play for next season. I suggested Grillparzer's drama to her." At the end of May the translation is finished. A. N. Benois is painting the stage settings. "Benois and I," Blok informs his mother, "sat for about six hours, because I had made mistakes in the translation, and he was kind enough and patient enough to discuss my idiocies with me. Yesterday I measured the stage in the theater with him and Dobuzhinsky." The translator wrote a short article about Grillparzer's play and read it to the actors of the Kommissarzhevskaya troupe ("On an Old Play"). In it, relating the content of the romantic tragedy of Fate, in which the ghost of the criminal Ancestress wanders through the gloomy halls of the castle and destroys the family she had conceived in sin and damnation, the author tries to "superimpose" the drama of the Austrian writer on the Russian present and to see in it a symbolic picture of the destruction of the Russian nobility. The publicist in him defeats the literary critic. Grillparzer's *The Ancestress*, in Blok's translation, came out as a separate booklet by the Pantheon publishing house in November 1908. In January 1909 it was staged in the Kommissarzhevskaya Theater.

The real dimensions of the tragedy that Blok, the author of an unsuccessful drama, endured become understandable only against the background of his reflections on the theater. In March 1908, in the Theatrical Club on Liteinaya, he gave his first public lecture; the long article "On the Theater," which appeared in three issues of *Golden Fleece*, later grew out of it. The first and larger part of it is directed at the contemporary theater and is full of shattering criticism; the second part focuses on the future and is inspired by faith in the birth of a new folk theater. Why, the author asks, "has hostility existed" since olden times "between literature and the theater, between the writer and the actor?" And he answers: the writer is first of all a human being, "he is placed in the world to bare his soul to those who are spiritually hungry." He should give up his whole soul to people; he bears a great responsibility. The actor is irresponsible. He is a sham. A talented Lear or Romeo often turns out to be in life an ignorant and coarse ruffian who has long since lost his human dignity. The writer turns away from the stage in distaste. The director appears and becomes an autocrat of the theater. He takes the play away from the author and interprets it to the actors according to his own understanding. This elevation of the director at the expense of the playwright and the actor is a symptom of the theater's disease. Finally there is the audience. In Andreev's *The*

Life of a Man, "someone in gray" addresses the audience: "Look and listen, you who came here for entertainment and laughter, you are doomed to death!" The intellectual theater audience of our day, the bored, indifferent and surfeited crowd, is doomed to death. Our time is transitional; despair lies in wait for us at every crossroad. Each of us needs to "remain alone, like a post in a snowy field, to squander his soul, to grieve and not know where to go, to become 'poor in spirit.' " And then the only road will open—"the road to action." "Perhaps," he exclaims, "our entire struggle is a *struggle for wholeness of life against the duality of esthetics.*" Contemptuously discarding the "esthetic" formula, "art for art's sake," the author poses a *utilitarian* question: is the theater necessary or unnecessary? And he answers it with an inspired eulogy to the theater: "The theater is the very flesh of art, that lofty region where 'the word becomes flesh.'. . . Precisely in the theater must art collide with life itself, invariably melodious, rich, varied." Contemporary, doomed society doesn't need the theater. But a storm is coming, swallows are already rushing through the air, the renewal of art is imminent: the *folk theater* is being born. It will be a theater of great passions and staggering happenings. "Sooner or later there will knock on the doors of our theaters not this surfeited crowd of the contemporary intelligentsia, but a new, living, demanding, insolent crowd. Let us be ready to meet this *youth*." The article ends on this lofty, ecstatic note. Blok destroys esthetics in the name of a new "beautiful usefulness." The peddler—the people—leads the lost Herman onto the road. Believing passionately that the theater is an area where "the word becomes flesh," the poet works intensely on his own "drama of great passions." But the discovered path to life ends in tragic failure.

The year 1908 is one of the most heroic in Blok's life. The dreamer wanted to wake up. Like Herman in *Song of Fate* he nearly perished in the snowstorms, but heard the "triumphant invocatory" melody of the peddler and frenziedly desired life, action. He quickly puts into practice his new thoughts about duty, usefulness, service to the people. He has so many "lofty plans and intentions" that he "sometimes loses heart." He has to overcome his reserve, his aristocratic fastidiousness, to throw himself headlong into a world strange and inimical to him, to write articles, to preach, to give lectures, to perform at public meetings, *to act*. Enough of being a decadent and a lyric poet—it is time to become a man and a citizen. He writes his mother: "I must write lectures and articles and in general prove myself often, eloquently, and with doubtful results." All of 1908 passes in intense activity; verse takes second place; publicistics and social preaching are in first place. In the article "Three Questions" (*Golden Fleece*, No. 2), Blok notes three periods in the history of the new art. In the first period, the question "how?" was posed—the question of the forms of art. By the persistent labors of the masters (for example, Briusov), enormous results were achieved. In the second period, one of general recognition and vulgarization, the question "what?" arose—the question of the artist's spiritual content. This question exposed many counterfeits who had mastered the new forms with suspicious ease. Now, in the third period, the most dangerous, but also the most Russian, question is posed: "what for?"—the question of the necessity and usefulness of artistic works: "To the artist's eternal concern about form and content is joined a new concern about *obligation*.... In the awareness of obligation, of great responsibility, and of links to the people and society, the artist finds the strength to travel rhythmically the only necessary path." Thus Blok summarizes his new credo—that of a populist and public-spirited man.

In "Letters on Poetry" (*Golden Fleece*, Nos. 7, 9, and 10), analyzing in detail the verse of Minsky, Sologub, Kuzmin, Bunin and S. Solovyov, the poet gives a striking definition of the artistic value of a literary work:

> Only what is the writer's confession, only that work in which he *burnt himself to ashes* . . . only that can be great. If this burnt soul, presented on a platter in the form of a beautiful work of art to the surfeited and arrogant crowd—to Herodias—if this soul is enormous, it does not merely agitate one generation, one people, or one century. Even if that soul isn't great, it must sooner or later agitate at least its own contemporaries, not with its art, not even with its novelty, but only by the *sincerity of self-sacrifice*.

And Blok was such a tragic poet. By the "pale glow of art" we read about the "consuming fire" of his soul:

Life has long since been burnt up and narrated.

The article "Questions, Questions, and Questions" (*Golden Fleece*, Nos. 11–12), later included by the author in the section "Lyrical Articles," is devoted to the "renewal of the religious-philosophical meetings" in Petersburg and to the "differentiation" of the new art: "My aim is to put a distorting mirror up to the most benevolent, most idealistic, intellectual of our day, filled with the most noble intentions. Perhaps he will see in it a scrap of his weary soul." People of the "new religious consciousness" want to "start a 'mission' among the intelligentsia." The first upsetting question: "is it true that our intelligentsia 'bears the living God in its heart'?" Other questions stem from it, persistent, adhesive, ironic. Who knows, perhaps literature in all Europe and Russia has ended? Perhaps the Russian nobility has become extinct once and for all, and instead of Pushkin, Tolstoy, Turgenev, a new ruling class has appeared, not even the "*raznochinets*,"[1] but simply the "apothecary." Gripped by a passion for destruction, Blok comes out sharply against the "theoretician of symbolism," Bely, and asserts that the symbolic school "*was only a dream, a fantasy, an invention, or the hope of a few representatives of 'the new art,'* but never existed in Russian reality." This paradoxical declaration was a deliberate challenge to his former friends. The author is ready to deny the most obvious facts if only he can be done with his hated decadent past. It is better to be a Pisarev, a nihilist of the sixties, than a symbolist or "mystical anarchist." To burn down everything that was valued, to smash the old idols, to destroy the very memory of the "tender morning dreams," to remain alone "like a post in a snowy field"—this is what the poet wants. Entries in the *Notebooks* testify even more eloquently to this. On 25 September Blok notes:

> I can't accept either the two abysses (God and the devil),[2] the two paths of good,[3] the "two threads woven together"[4] (mysticism, scholasticism, dialectics, metaphysics, theology, philology), or the theory of knowledge (Bely), or irony (the intelligentsia's mystical anarchism), or "all the harbors" (decadence).

He writes in another entry: "Praise to the Creator! I have inwardly forever settled accounts with my best friends and 'patrons' (A. Bely foremost). Finally! (I mean the half-mad ones—A. Bely—and the windbags—Merezhkovsky.)" And he notes in another place: "Alone—*tabula rasa*. To search for people. To write a lecture on the only possible overcoming of isolation—joining the folk soul and taking up public service." In a feuilleton, "Evenings of Art" (the newspaper *Speech* [*Rech*], 22 October), Blok addresses writers, artists, and organizers of evenings of art with a pathetic challenge not to take part in action harmful to society. Fashionable "evenings of art" beget an atmosphere of banality and vulgarity, spawn a breed of people of the "modern style," and thereby become *cells of social reaction*. The poet himself had performed at such evenings many times, seduced by their "philanthropic aim." But he understands that his *civic duty* doesn't permit him to take part in a harmful action.

The poet's speech in the role of accuser and preacher met with dead silence. Blok was declaiming in a wilderness.

In that same newspaper, *Speech* (7 December), Blok published one of his most brilliant and terrible articles, "Irony." Analyzing the fatal disease of irony, with which contemporary society is stricken, the author sees in it "the disease of personality, the disease of individuality," the fatal heritage of the "horrifying nineteenth century, . . . which threw over the living face of man a cheap brocade cover of mechanics, of positivism and economic materialism, which buried the human voice in the roar of machines." Diagnosing this disease, linking Dostoevsky's irony with Heine's "provocateur's mockery," with Andreev's "red laughter" and with the sad humor of the "Russian Verlaine, Sologub," Blok confesses and repents. He admits his own "two-facedness." Behind the face of the socially active man, preaching morality and "civic duty," another grimaces and makes faces, "twitching convulsively from inner laughter"; a man stricken with irony begins with a "provocateur's diabolically mocking smile" and ends "with violence and blasphemy." The poet makes terrible admissions:

> Everything is equal for them before the face of accursed irony: good and evil, the clear sky and the cesspool, Dante's Beatrice and Sologub's Untouchable. Everything is mixed up, as in a tavern and in darkness. The

winy truth *in vino veritas*[5] is shown to the world, everything is one, the world is one. I am drunk; ergo—if I want to "I will accept" the world as a whole, will fall on my knees before the Untouchable, will seduce Beatrice; wallowing in a ditch, I will believe I'm soaring in the heavens. If I want, "I will not accept" the world; I will prove that Beatrice and the Untouchable are one and the same. It suits me so, for I am drunk. And what is asked of a drunken man? Drunk on irony and laughter, as on vodka; in the same way everything is depersonalized, everything is "dishonored," nothing matters.

The "exhausting laughter" of irony is Blok's dark double. Fits of "despair and irony" had begun to visit him from his youthful years. The young singer of the Beautiful Lady already knew this split:

In my superstitious prayer
I seek Christ's protection,
But behind a hypocritical mask
Deceitful lips laugh.

The double, roaring with laughter, mocked that which was sacred in the "lyrical dramas," led the poet into taverns, and taught him to drink "red wine":

I am nailed to the tavern bar.
I've long been drunk. So what!

An heir of the "transcendental irony" of the German romantics, Blok is a living fusion of two worlds, a man of catastrophic consciousness.

On 2 and 21 November, before performances of Ibsen's *The Master Builder*, Blok twice reads a paper on Ibsen to the actors of V. F. Kommissarzhevskaya's troupe. He says that the great Norwegian dramatist, with "unflinching consistency," broke connections with his parental home, then with society, and, finally, with his homeland. In this moment he is the author of Brandt. Alone in his world fame, he stands on a mountain top face to face with God. And then he takes the last, decisive step: he returns to people, treats society's ulcers, becomes a publicist and reformer. Performances of Ibsen's dramas are a long-desired holiday at which votaries of usefulness and votaries of beauty can stretch out their hands to one another. In his great works esthetics and ethics are reconciled in a sense of something higher. "This higher," the author concludes, "I will call a sense of the beautiful."

In Ibsen's art, "the great book of life," Blok saw the realization of his own dream: the synthesis of usefulness and beauty in a new "sense of the beautiful." On 30 November Blok reads his paper for the third time in the Psychoneurological Institute. He writes about it to his mother: "Today I read a paper on Ibsen in some pseudoinstitution of higher learning, for whose benefit I don't know, among some. . . . This made me terribly angry. But a coed I knew came, and we had a very good talk on every topic."

Blok's publicistic activity achieves its highest point in his two sensation-provoking appearances at the Petersburg Religious-Philosophical Society. He read two papers there: "Russia and the Intelligentsia" and "Elemental Force and Culture." In them he put all his effort, all his will for the revolution of the spirit.

The main thesis of the paper "Russia and the Intelligentsia" is already familiar to us: "There are really not only two concepts, but two realities: the people and the intelligentsia; 150 million on the one hand, and a few hundred thousand on the other; people who fail mutually to understand one another in the most fundamental things." Between the people and the intelligentsia there is an "inaccessible barrier" which determines the tragedy of Russia. "For the time being such a gate stands; the intelligentsia is condemned to wander, to move, and to revolve in a vicious circle." Without a higher principle "all kinds of mutiny and violence" are inevitable, "beginning with the vulgar 'God-defiance' of the decadents and ending with open self-destruction—with depravity, drunkenness, suicides of all types." The intelligentsia, possessed more and more by a "will to death," rushes, out of a sense of self-preservation, to the people, who have from time immemorial carried within them a "will to life," and dashes against ironical smiles and silence and "perhaps against something even more terrible and unexpected." Blok ends the article with a reference to Gogol's famous troika. "What," he asks, "if the troika, around which 'the torn-asunder air thunders and becomes wind,' *flies directly at us*? Rushing to the people, we are rushing straight under the feet of the mad troika, to certain destruction." Such a tragic premonition concludes the poet's call to a new life. A return to the homeland, a turning to the people—is this not a sign of the intelligentsia's "will to death"? Love for the people, is it not the deathbed delirium of the doomed? "One may even imagine," the author writes, "as happens in terrible dreams and nightmares, that the darkness originates from the fact that the shaggy breast of a shaft-horse hung over us, and the heavy hooves are about to descend."

The passionate, lyrical eloquence of this communication upset its listeners. Two days before the session of the Religious-Philosophical Society Blok read his paper at the Merezhkovskys'. "It made a powerful impression on everyone; there will be very many objections. And there will be a large audience" (letter to his mother, 12 November). At the meeting of the society on 13 November, after Blok's lecture, an "incident" occurred: the police prohibited discussion. But the lecturer was left satisfied with his audience. He writes his mother: "They listened to me very well. After the meeting the sectarians, about five people, surrounded me and invited me to their place. I will go.... I have the very best impression from my paper. I saw that there were people who need me and who listen to me." Blok was preparing to publish his lecture in *Russian Thought* (*Russkaya Mysl*), but the editor of the journal, the well-known social and political figure Pyotr Berngardovich Struve, was indignant at the "naive article of a just-awakened person" and refused to place it in *Russian Thought*. The Merezhkovskys defended Blok and, out of solidarity with him, left Struve's journal. Of course the editor of *Russian Thought* was right: Blok's article is naive in the "political sense." But it was impossible to evaluate it in a "political sense."

Whether the poet's inspired performance was useful to Russian society we don't know. One thing is beyond doubt: the poet saved one human soul from death. This is what he writes his mother:

> After the religious-philosophical meeting Zhenya [E. P. Ivanov] and I went to our place to drink tea, and a half hour later a very nice girl rang—from the audience, a Russian, the daughter of a priest. Very profound and gloomy, eighteen years old. She sat with me till after two in the morning.... Most important of all is the fact that, judging by everything, she had come to ask (not directly, but obliquely, rather not me, but the "power" which she sees in me) whether or not she should commit suicide. She left, it seems, more cheerful than she had come.

The Russian girl, "profound and gloomy," coming at night to a poet she didn't know to ask whether she had to commit suicide—this one episode contains not only the whole "style of the epoch" but perhaps also the "style" of Russia.

G. I. Chulkov was depressed by Blok's essay. "On 10 December," the poet informs his mother, "I quarreled with Chulkov, a life or death argument about 'Russia and the Intelligentsia.'" In his memoirs Chulkov writes: "Unpleasant for me in his lecture was that unbearable, suffocating pessimism of which all this lyrical inarticulateness smelled. ... At that time I published an article, 'Face to Face,' in which I declared: 'We all have a premonition of catastrophe. These premonitions, however, shouldn't extinguish our reason.'"

On 12 December the poet repeats his lecture at the Literary Society. He depicts this meeting to his mother expressively:

> The animation was extraordinary. Nicest of all for me were: Korolenko's speech, Stolpner's fiery abuse, Merezhkovsky's defense, and the charming attitude toward me of the old men from *Russian Wealth* (*Russkoe Bogatstvo*)—P. F. [I. F.] Annensky, G. K. Gradovsky, Vengerov, et al. They fed me candies, applauded, and treated me like a favorite grandson, with a kind of crystal purity, trust, and kindness. The hall was full.... I was terribly excited, with a good inward excitement, concerning the theme and not the audience. I am used to the audience once and for all.[6]

At the next meeting of the Religious-Philosophical Society, after a short lecture by Rozanov,[7] the discussion of Blok's paper finally took place. It was not only animated, but even violent. The lecturer answered his opponents with a second paper, "Elemental Force and Culture." He read it at the 30 December session of the Religious-Philosophical Society.

Blok is surprised at the unusual optimism of the majority of the objections. To his words about the "inaccessible barrier" between the intelligentsia and the people, they answered that no split existed, that the disease was curable, that the district doctors and doctors' assistants live with the people soul to soul. This optimism is the "Apollonian dream" of culture. Humanity is ceaselessly and persistently building its ant hill. And suddenly the forest beast's foot steps into the very middle of it; the needle of the seismograph deflects and in forty seconds Calabria and Messina perish. The elemental force countervails culture:

> The vengeance of Culture, which has reared up with the "steel bristle" of bayonets and machines, was ignited. This is only a sign that another vengeance was also ignited—an elemental and earthly vengeance. We live between the two bonfires of ignited vengeance, between the two camps. [A relentless sense of catastrophe has settled in the hearts of people of the last generations.] We are living through a terrible crisis. We still don't know exactly what events we are to expect, but *the needle of the seismograph has already deflected in our hearts*. We already see ourselves as if on the background of the glow, on a light lacy airplane high above the earth. And under our feet is a rumbling and fire-spitting mountain, along which, freeing themselves, crawl streams of red-hot lava beyond the fogs of ash.[8]

In essence Blok isn't opposing anything of his opponents'. He only knows how to argue *musically*, and here a new wave of music swept over him: the distant rumble of collapsing Messina. The question of the people and the intelligentsia grows to a pathetic opposition of culture and elemental force. The intelligentsia builds its culture on the "unhardened crust," beneath which the "terrible elemental force of earth—the elemental folk force"—rages. This premonition of impending catastrophes—the world wars and social revolutions of the twentieth century—places the clairvoyant Blok in a line with Russian writers and thinkers of the prophetic type: Gogol, Dostoevsky, V. Solovyov, Fyodorov and Berdyaev.

Blok's "civic activity" ends in eschatology, calls to "vital action" in howls about destruction. And these are not contradictions, but simply the ebb and flow of lyrical waves. The poet's thought isn't subject to the rules of logical consistency; it is governed by the law of musical rhythm.

Blok's vast, intense activity of 1908, his social service and heroic self-education, proceed on the background of an "unsuccessful personal life" and spiritual isolation. In January 1908 the break between Kommissarzhevskaya and Meyerhold occurs. The young producer gives up her theater and collects her own troupe, which L. D. Blok and N. N. Volokhova join. In February they go on tour to the provinces. Lyubov Dmitrievna comes for a few days now and then and leaves again. Until August, Blok lives alone in the apartment, which seems to him enormous, empty, and cold. He imposes strict discipline on himself: work, articles, literary surveys, a play, translations, lectures, and papers. He trains himself in clarity and simplicity. "I somehow rejoice at my isolated and free life. I walk a lot, see people . . . I feel spring very much" (letter to his mother, 12 March). On 10 April, informing his mother of Lyubov Dmitrievna's arrival, he adds: "We are both cheerful and gay. My work is progressing, and also clarity of emotions and thoughts and readiness to work. I hadn't lived so clearly and simply as this month for a long time." On 3 May: "And I am alone here—I am forging my own fate and in the former atmosphere of love am strengthening my spiritual and bodily muscles." On 7 August: "A brisk and fresh autumn has arrived, mama." On 16 November: "I am again in a mood for action." And, finally, on 24 November: "And I continue to live very actively and am satisfied with this for the most part."

What a terrible struggle this energy and cheerfulness cost Blok! What mortal depression underlay this "activity"! One can find horrible admissions in the letters to his mother:

> It is unbearably hard for me to live. . . . Such cold isolation—one gads about the taverns and drinks. (8 January)
> You are right, mama, of course it's better not to drink. But sometimes such depression comes, that one drinks because of it. (30 January)
> We drank champagne under dull blue and rainy dawns. For some reason I ate my fill of oysters. . . . But "everything is innocent." The main thing is that this doesn't overtax me. My life rolls on its normal course, past depraved and amusing dreams, in massive waves. I work, I wander, I think. I am fed up with living alone. (28 April)
> Mama, in the last days I go to bed every other night and waste a lot of energy on wine, boating, roaming the fields and forests, and on women. (18 May)

At the beginning of June he goes to his mother in Shakhmatovo for a month, and writes to G. I. Chulkov from there: "It is very luxuriant, damp, hot here. My house is buried in flowering lilacs. . . . Regarding alcoholic beverages, I feel as if I had 'taken the pledge.' But I only endure the fixed time in order not to break the vow" (14 June).

Returning from Shakhmatovo, the poet takes up "house building": he breaks down the partition between two small rooms, makes a large, bright dining room. He writes in an 18 June [July] *Notebook* entry: "I drink at Ozerki. I wrote Lyuba a letter today. The day was tormenting and hot—I am getting drunk. 'Be the mistress of my house.' And the house is rebuilt. What was horrible this winter is eliminated. I don't know, I don't know. Today it's quiet." That same day he admits to his mother: "Everything has grown hateful, mortal depression. . . . Horrible loneliness and hopelessness. This period will probably pass too, like everything else."

In this moment of mortal depression, having removed from the house everything that reminded him of the "mad year spent by the black train," he writes to Lyubov Dmitrievna. The quotation from

Nekrasov, "be the mistress of my house," may be interpreted as a hand outstretched, as an attempt at reconciliation. But he doesn't much believe in it. Again depression sets in, and again wandering and drunkenness. To his mother on 24 July he writes: "Yesterday and today I'm not leaving the house. I have a slight fever, apparently from too much to drink. I drank alone and also with Chulkov and Zaitsev—I drank a lot." B. K. Zaitsev remembers these meetings:

> Blok already looked different. His features were more sharply marked, his weight had increased, the color of his face had coarsened. Youth had departed, a "complete adult" appeared. Something fermented in this adult. Some kind of wind swayed all of him, he even seemed to walk unsteadily. And not gay at heart—that was the impression he made. We would go in a landau to the islands, to night restaurants, around night places with blue electric globes, with a soft damp wind. We drank a lot and rather stupidly, we, of course, had very lofty discussions. . . . Blok was rather gloomy, one sensed something weary, stale in him. . . . His face took on a copper tint from the wine, his neck was nicely white in the turned-down collar, his eyes reddened, dulled. But the glassiness of their gaze even increased. In general he had strange eyes.

Thus the summer passes. The poet writes to Pyast that he had wanted to visit him many times, but didn't make up his mind, "because I continued to lead my idiotic wandering life," and in parentheses: "for some reason dear to me." Finally a telegram arrives from Lyubov Dmitrievna: she will come soon. On 4 August Blok writes his mother; this seems to be the only joyful letter of the whole year:

> Mama, I just received your letter and a telegram from Lyuba. She will probably come on the *ninth*, she has already left, and rejoices in this. Now—basta! I am no longer a drunken debauchee as I still was yesterday and the day before! . . . I feel healthy and cheerful again. But the depression and weariness were, in Sologub's expression, "higher than the mountains."

At the end of August Blok and his wife go to Shakhmatovo and live there till late autumn.

How did Aleksandr Aleksandrovich and Lyubov Dmitrievna meet? Did a reconciliation take place? Perhaps one can look for the answer to this question in the sketch of the first act of a new drama conceived by the poet (*Notebook* 19–20, November 1908):

First Act.
　Writer. A study with heavy drapes at the windows. Books. Flowers. Perfume. A woman. . . .
　　　　　　　　　. . . . .
　His wife returns. A child. He understands. She cries.

In February 1909 Lyubov Dmitrievna gave birth to a boy, Mitya. Blok loved him like a son. The child died eight days later.

Let us return to the sketch of the drama:

> But he was not only seen at parties, in the study, amid the crowd or books, proud and imperious. Not only rushing past with this woman. Not only the secret glory of female love surrounds him.
> He was seen at night in the wet snow, plodding helplessly along under the moon, homeless, hunched over, weary, despairing of everything. He himself knows the disease of depression consuming him and secretly loves it—and is tormented by it. He sometimes thinks of suicide. He, to whom they listen and whom they believe, knows nothing the greater part of his life. He only hopes for some kind of Russia, some universal rhythms of passions, and every day himself betrays both Russia and the passions. And he *doesn't understand* the formula of Ibsen and Gogol, haunting and tormenting to him. Or, rather: understanding (as everything), he doesn't accept, he is tainted (an intellectual).
> But *the child grows*.

The last phrase in italics is a new, blazing hope for salvation, for resurrection to a new life. Blok gives his whole heart to this as yet unborn child, someone else's. And the last entry on New Year's Eve records: "31 December 1908–1 January 1909. Lyubov Dmitrievna and I saw in the New Year together, quietly, serenely, sadly."

The poems of 1908—less numerous than the lyrical cycles of 1907—belong to the poet's most perfect creations. Blok enters the period of his poetic maturity; the technical mastery of his poems grows with each year. The last traces of decadent refinement disappear; a new "beautiful clarity," a new smoothness of form appear. The lack of measure and irregularity of the romantic gravitate more and more toward classical measure and stern simplicity.

The verses on contemporary poets are imbued with the accusatory passion of the articles "Russia and the Intelligentsia," "Elemental Force and Culture," and "Irony." In the poem *To My Friends* the motifs of the destruction of culture, familiar to us, are repeated: writers are hostile and alien to one another; their houses are poisoned; they are traitors in life and friendship; their souls are stricken with the disease of irony:

> What to do! Losing faith in happiness,
> We go mad from laughter.
> And, drunk, we see from the street
> How our houses are collapsing.

A sad lot to live so complexly, with such difficulty, and so festively in order to become after death the prey of late historians and critics. The poem ends with a cry of despair:

> To bury oneself in fresh weeds,
> To lose consciousness forever in sleep.
> Be silent, cursed books!
> I never wrote you!

The poem *Poets* is written in an even more biting satirical tone. In a deserted quarter on a marsh poets lived, worked, and got drunk. Getting drunk, they chattered cynically and headily. Then, like dogs, they crawled out of their kennels, dreamed of a golden age, cried about a pearly cloudlet and "with knowledge of the matter" were carried away with every passing woman. There is a sudden break in style in the finale. The poet addresses the reader and announces disdainfully that even such a life is inaccessible to him. The satire breaks off with a lyrical flight:

> You'll be satisfied with yourself and your wife,
> With your meager constitution,
> And here at the poet's—a world bout of hard drinking,
> And constitutions mean little to him.
>
> Let me die under a fence, like a dog,
> Let life trample me in the earth.
> I believe: now God covered me with snow,
> Now the blizzard kissed me!

The poet speaks with the ecstasy of despair about "the world bout of hard drinking," about life burnt up in passions and debauchery. In the poem *And I loved. And I came to know* he recalls the names of his mistresses:

> They were many. But I united them
> By one feature,
> By one insane beauty,
> Whose name is passion and my life.

There is a "fateful pleasure" in destruction. Hating, he loves his downfall; bleeding profusely, he experiences shameful pleasure. In the poem *The clock hand approaches midnight* the poet shyly confesses:

> ... I love you secretly,
> Solitary evenings, mute streets.
> I love you secretly, dark friend
> Of my depraved youth, of my burnt out life.

This tenderness, this velvety softness of sounds is more convincing than any self-accusation.

Debauchery and depression, intoxicating passion and the guttural, cracked sounds of the gypsy song are the poet's lyrical world. In *The Earth in Snow* we already hear inviting gypsy dance melodies (*Accordion, accordion!*). They spill out more and more unrestrainedly and violently. The rhythms of the poem *Come down, faded curtain* are amazing. These words aren't spoken, but sung drawlingly and frenziedly:

> Kak cyganka, platkami uzornymi
> Rasstilalacja ty predo mnoj,

Oj-li kosami issinja-černymi,
Oj-li burej strastej ognevoj!

Čto rydalos' mne v šopote, v zabyt'i,
Nezemnye l' kakie slova?
Sam ne svoj tol'ko byl ja, bez pamjati,
I xodila krugom golova. . . .

Like a gypsy girl figured kerchiefs,
You spread before me,
Oh, blue-black tresses,
Oh, a fiery storm of passions!

What sobbed to me in a whisper, in oblivion,
Unearthly words?
Only I was not myself, unconscious,
And my head whirled. . . .

The combination of dactyllic and masculine rhymes (*zabyt'i:pamjati, slova:golova*), the parallelism and repetition (*oj-li, kosami:oj-li burej*) intensifies even more these breath-catching verses.

The following poem moves with the same intensity of passion, the same breadth of "dissipated gaiety":

Vsë b tebe želat' vesel'ja,
Serdce, zoloto moë!
Ot poxmel'ja do poxmel'ja,
Ot privol'ja vnov' k privol'ju—
Bespečal'noe zit'ë.

Always to wish you gaiety,
My heart, my gold!
From hangover to hangover,
From freedom again to freedom—
Life alien to sadness.

The extra line bursts into the verse, destroying the symmetry: "from freedom again to freedom." This dissonance finds its authorization in the next verse, where the asymmetrical line, "Suddenly, with passionate pain," rhymes with the line "from freedom again to freedom":

No nizka zemnaja kel'ja,
Bledno zoloto tvoë!
V čas razgul'nogo vesel'ja,
Vdrug namašet strastnoj bol'ju
Čërnym kryl'em voron'ë.

But the earthly cell is low.
Pale is your gold!
In the hour of dissipated gaiety
Suddenly, with passionate pain,
The carrion crows flap their black wings.

Thus the two "extra" lines echo one another from a distance. This unexpected retardation of the dance rhythm, the destruction of the usual two-beat song style and its delayed restoration is the height of craftsmanship.

Of dissipated gypsiness is born Blok's famous masterpiece:

> Ja prigvoždën k traktirnoj stojke.
> Ja p'jan davno. Mne vsë—ravno.
> Von sčastie moë na trojke
> V srebristyj dym uneseno. . . .

> I am nailed to the tavern bar
> I've long been drunk. So what!
> Gone my happiness on a troika,
> Carried away in silvery smoke. . . .

In the muted melody both words and rhythms are intoxicated. We sense the severe hangover, the thick tongue, the halts, the repetitions, and the obtrusive images. Everything is in fog ("silvery smoke," "silvery haze," "dense darkness"). The troika speeds along, the bell rings, everything is like a dream: sparks in the darkness, the golden harness. Vague images, distant sounds—what are they speaking of? Of this: happiness flew away on a troika, sunk in snow. And this: happiness "scatters sparks" and the bell babbles about happiness:

> The bell on the shaft-bow babbles
> That happiness is gone. . . .

The last verse, with the lines cut in two by a complete pause, with the meaningless repetitions and low howling of Y and A (*ty:duša, p'janym:p'jana*), is simply terrifying:

> I tol'ko sbruja zolotaja
> Vsju noč' vidna . . . vsju noč' slyšna . . .
> A ty, duša . . . duša gluxaja . . .
> P'janym-p'jana . . . p'janym-p'jana. . . .

> And only the golden harness
> Is visible all night . . . Audible all night . . .
> And you, soul . . . deaf soul . . .
> Dead drunk . . . dead drunk. . . .

From the fumes of gypsy passion we are transported into the clear and cool world of the verses about Meri. The tender and sad songs are captivating in their simplicity:

> Sing quietly by the old door,
> We will trust the tender song,
> We will mourn with you, Meri.

In the poem *Night is already falling over the sea* the breath of the sea, the noise of the wind are heard. Ships with lights on their masts emerge from the haze of the evening bay, and in the light mist—She again:

> The promise is true:
> You are again before me.
> For a soul in love it's impossible
> Not to dream about sweet death.

"For a soul in love it's impossible"—the sounds dash like waves on wet sand.

There is unusual verbal magic in the poem *I didn't call you*: a night garden smelling of mint, a slender moon above it, a winged shadow in the lifeless world of night, and a mysterious melody breaking off. Here is the first verse:

> Ja ne zval tebja—sama ty
>   Podošla.
> Každyj večer—zapax mjaty,
> Mesjac uzkij i ščerbatyj,
>   Tiš' i mgla.

> I didn't call you—you came
>   Yourself.
> Every evening—the smell of mint,
> The slender and chipped moon,
>   Silence, and haze.

The third verse takes up the melody:

> Na trave, edva primjatoj,
>   Lëgkij sled.
> Svežij zapax dikoj mjaty,
> Neživoj, golubovatyj
>   Noči svet.

> On the grass, barely crumpled,
>   A light trace.
> The fresh odor of wild mint,
> The lifeless, bluish
>   World of night.

The poem *Grieving and crying and laughing* consists of two six-line verses, the first of them a complex pattern of sounds, rhythms and rhymes:

> Grustja i plača i smejas',
> Zvenjat ruč'i moix stixov
>   U nog tvoix,
>   I každyj stix

Aleksandr Blok

> Bežit, pletët živuju vjaz',
> Tvoix ne znaja beregov.

> Grieving and crying and laughing,
> The streams of my verse ring
>   At your feet,
>   And each line
> Runs, weaves a living bond,
> Not knowing your shores.

The first line rhymes with the fifth, the second with the sixth, the third with the fourth. The verse seems to be broken off in the middle by two colliding rhymes (*tvoix:stix*), and this meter is reinforced by the fact that the third and fourth rhyming lines are iambic dimeter amid the other lines of iambic tetrameter. The stream flows in an even spurt: "Grieving and crying and laughing / The streams of my verse ring." And suddenly the stream quivers and stops: "At your feet / And each line." And again the peaceful murmur of the water: "Runs, weaves a living bond."

Of the 1908 verses, poems inspired by the one who was once for the poet the Beautiful Lady stand out in their lofty lyrical style:

> When despair and malice die down,
> Sleep descends. And we both sleep soundly
>   On different strips of earth.

Even in dreams he sees her beautiful image:

> *You are always the same*, just as you once bloomed
> There, above the misty and jagged hill
>   In the meadows of unfading dawn.

We remember this jagged Boblovo hill from *Verses on the Beautiful Lady*. The poem is addressed to her—loved and irretrievably lost:

> You are as radiant as virgin snow,
> You are as white as a distant temple.
> I don't believe this long night
> And the endless evenings.

He awaits her return with anxiety, wants to believe that all is not lost. The last verse reads:

> For these ruinous torments
> Forgive the unfaithful one.
> You will extend your hand to the traitor,
> Will reward him with distant spring.

These are vain hopes. Everything is finished and everything is irreparable:

> She, as before, wanted
> To breathe her breath
> Into my exhausted body,
> Into my cold dwelling.

It is late; he is mortally ill. It is difficult for him to stretch out his hand to meet her, and between them are no longer "either words, or happiness, or offenses." And he says at the end:

> Eternity peered into my eyes,
> Brought down peace to my heart,
> With the cool moisture of the blue night
> Flooded the bonfire of agitation.

The theme of death is expressed with tragic simplicity in the remarkable poem *A night like any other night, and the street's deserted*. The long lines (5-foot trochaics), monotonous as rain drops, alternate with short lines (2-foot trochaics), where sounds are arranged in a descending scale (the first and second stanza—A; the third—E; the fourth—U). The impression of a funeral dirge, interrupted by blows of a grave shovel, is produced:

> A night like any other night, and the street's deserted,
>   So it always is!
> For whom were you innocent
>   And proud?
>   . . . . .
> Everyone in the world, everyone in the world knows:
>   There is no happiness.
> And how many times do they clench in their hands
>   A pistol!
>
> And how many times, laughing and crying,
>   Do they live again!
> A day like any other day; why, the problem is solved:
>   *Everyone will die.*

The cycle ends with one of his best-known poems, *About courage, about feats, about glory*. The personal pain (the break with his wife) is eased and brightened by the lyrical romanticism of the form. The poet utilizes the devices of the old-fashioned sentimental love song: parallelism, tailpiece, repetitions, variations of the same theme, play on the same intonations. Thus lines echo from one verse to another: from the first verse, "your face in a simple frame," to the last, "your face in its simple frame"; from the second verse, "you left the house," to the fourth, "On a damp night you left the house." Finally, in the fourth verse, "You wrapped yourself sadly in a blue cloak"; in the fifth, "I dreamed of your blue cloak." Words and sounds interweave, and one link draws another after it. An impression of continuity of melody, of deep breathing rhythm is produced.

Aleksandr Blok

This is how the "sentimental love song" sounds in Blok:

> About courage, about feats, about glory,
> I forgot on the sorrowful earth,
> When your face in a simple frame
> Shone before me on the table.

The melodic wave grows. The fourth verse reads:

> I called you, but you didn't look back.
> I shed tears, but you didn't descend.
> You wrapped yourself sadly in a blue cloak,
> On a damp night you left the house.

The love song is constructed in the form of a "ring"; the last verse repeats the theme of the first:

> No longer to dream of tenderness, of glory,
> Everything has passed, youth is gone!
> Your face in its simple frame
> I removed from the table with my own hand.

Blok's greatest poetic work is a cycle of five poems entitled *On the Field of Kulikovo*. Russian poetry after Tyutchev has created nothing more perfect. It is the crown not only of the symbolic art of the new age, but also of the whole Russian renaissance of the twentieth century. In this *poema* on Russia Blok rises above all schools and trends, becomes a Russian national poet, takes his place beside Pushkin, Lermontov and Tyutchev.

We can judge the process of creation of this cycle by the drama *Song of Fate*. There, in Herman's monologue, the raw historical material is already being reworked into a lyrical theme. The battle of Kulikovo had a mystical and prophetic meaning for Blok. In a note to the *poema* in the third volume of his *Collected Poems* he writes: "The battle of Kulikovo belongs, in the author's conviction, to the symbolic events of Russian history. Such events are destined to return. Their solution is still in the future." In the article "The People and the Intelligentsia" the poet contrasts the "roar of urban culture" to the "deep quiet" hanging over folk Russia. But this is the quiet before the battle: in it ripens the great and terrible fate of the Russian people, "the start of exalted and turbulent days." The author continues:

> Over the cities hangs a roar which even the experienced ear can't interpret; such a roar as hung over the Tatar camp on the eve of the battle of Kulikovo, as the legend states. Countless carts creak beyond the Nepryadva, a human howling persists, and on the foggy river geese and swans splash and cry uneasily. Sleep and silence seem to reign among ten million. But silence also hung over the camp of Dmitri Donskoy. But the commander Bobrok began to weep, pressing his ear to the ground: he

heard how the widow weeps inconsolably, how the mother clings to her son's stirrup. The distant and ominous summer lightning blazed over the Russian camp.

In the days of creating *On the Field of Kulikovo* the future was revealed to the clairvoyant Blok. In the "deep quiet" of the reaction of 1908 he discerned the roar of events: he knew that fiery ordeals, a sea of blood, and unparalleled glory await Russia. He heard the solemn and terrible music of the incinerating years: 1914, 1917, 1941–45.

The first poem of the cycle, *The river spread. It flows, mourns lazily*, at once envelops us in the scorching steppe wind. Russia is a whirlwind, an endless, eternal battle; her breast is pierced "by the arrow of ancient Tatar ferocity"; in the night haze, under frightened clouds, she rushes through blood and dust, gripped by "boundless despair," bleeding profusely, gone mad from horror and pain. The motion quickens with each verse. The lines are broken by exclamations, appeals, interruptions of breath:

And there is no end! Versts, precipices flash . . .
  Stop!
The frightened clouds are moving, moving,
  The sunset in blood!

The steppe and the haze, the khan's saber and the steppe mare, all this is the soul of Russia, her despair, her fate:

. . . Our path—in boundless despair,
In your despair, oh Rus!

The blood of the sunset is the blood of Russia's heart:

Sunset in blood! Blood streams from the heart!
  Cry, heart, cry . . .
There is no peace! The steppe mare
  Rushes at a gallop!

One can speak about this poem in Gogol's words: "The torn-asunder air thunders and becomes wind."

After the whirlwind introduction, a solemnly quiet poem, *We halted above the steppe at midnight*, follows. Swans cry out beyond the Nepryadva; the friend says to the warrior:

"Hone your sword,
Not to fight the Tatars in vain,
To fall dead for the holy cause!"

In the third poem, *At night when Mamai lay in hiding with the horde*, in the dark field facing the Don, under quiet summer lightning, in the cries of the swans, the warrior hears Her voice. She descends to him, and he says:

Aleksandr Blok

> And with the fog, above the sleeping Nepryadva,
> > Straight to me,
> You descended in clothing streaming light,
> > Not frightening off the horse.

And in the morning, when the horde advanced, he says:

> Your face, not of human making, on my shield
> > Shone forever.

This vision is the consummation of the mystical hopes of the singer of the Eternal Feminine. The pink fogs surrounding the Beautiful Lady dispersed. The Russian poet read Her name in the soul of the people: the name of the Immaculate Intercessor, the Mother of God. The fourth poem, *Again with age-old despair*, develops the lyrical theme of alarm and despair:

> I hear the rumble of battle
> And the Tatars' trumpet sounds,
> I see in the distance, over Rus,
> A broad and quiet conflagration.

He roams the dark field on a white horse:

> Wild passions are unleashed
> Under the yoke of the waning moon.

And again She calls him beyond the misty river, and again he implores:

> "Appear, my marvelous marvel!
> Teach me to be radiant!"

The fifth—and concluding—poem of the cycle bears as an epigraph lines from V. Solovyov: "And the coming day was clouded / By a haze of inescapable disasters."

The term is drawing near: again haze over the Kulikovo field, again deep quiet, but the heart recognizes "the beginning of exalted and turbulent days." It is ready:

> The heart can't live on peace,
> Not for nothing did the clouds gather.
> Heavy armor, as before a battle.
> Now your hour has struck—Pray!

The last, the final, word: "pray."

In the second poem the warrior, preparing to die "for the holy cause," says:

Pray for me at early matins,
Dear friend, radiant wife!

The "radiant wife" is Russia:

Oh, my Rus! My wife! To the point of pain
The long path is open before us!

Blok's *Verses on Russia* were variously assessed. Much was said about his Slavophilism, populism, and mystical patriotism. All these abstract words bounce off his poetry. Blok loves his native land not with a philosophical, but with a *personal*, erotic love. The "face not of human making" is revealed to this love, and love becomes a prayer.

The famous poem *Russia* serves as an epilogue to the *poema On the Field of Kulikovo*—a passionate declaration of love for his beggared, dark and beautiful native land:

Russia, beggared Russia,
To me your gray huts,
To me your wind songs,
Are like the first tears of love!

This is a different lyrical tone: Russia is no longer a "radiant wife," but a beloved "first love." The solemnly prayerful style is replaced by agitated, ardent declarations: not love, but in love. Russia is "a forest, and a field, and a patterned shawl to the brows"; she has a "brigand's beauty." The last, sixth stanza, falling outside the general style of the poem, is unusual: after five four-line verses, suddenly a six-line verse which retards, lengthens the melody, giving it unexpected resonance:

And the impossible is possible,
The long road is easy,
When flashes in the road's distance
A fleeting glance from under a scarf,
When rings with prison despair
The muted song of the coachman! . . .

Blok included the verses of 1908 in the third volume of his *Collected Poems*; depending on the lyrical themes, they were placed in the sections *Retribution, Miscellaneous Poems, Harps and Violins,* and *Native Land*.

In January 1909, never before had Z. N. Gippius seen her "lunar friend" so joyful:

And this is the period when I remember Blok simple, humane, with an unprecedentedly radiant face. In general, I don't remember his smile; if it existed it was fleeting, imperceptible. But during this period it is precisely the smile that I remember, preoccupied and gentle. And as if a different voice, warmer. This was when he was expecting his child, and most of all in the first days after its birth . . .

At tea in our dining room Blok is silent, doesn't look himself, radiant and absent-minded. "What are you thinking about?" "Here is what . . . how now . . . to bring him up . . . Mitka." This poor Mitka died on the eighth or tenth day. . . . In the child Blok sensed the chance to touch life with a quiet caress; the chance that life wouldn't answer him with a grimace, as always.

In February there are two short notes to E. P. Ivanov. On 2 February he writes: "Dear Zhenya. This morning Lyuba gave birth to a little boy." On 10 February he writes: "Mitya died today. Lyuba's fever is down." V. Zorgenfrei recalls (*Dreamers' Notes*, No. 6, 1922):

> In the early spring of 1909 Blok met me on Nevsky Prospect with a darkened look, with an elusive twitch in the features of his handsome, proud face, and in a brief conversation informed me of the birth and death of his son; a barely noticeable froth kept appearing and disappearing in the corner of his lips.

Lyubov Dmitrievna's return, the reconciliation with her, the birth of the child whom Blok had come to love even before his appearance in the world—all this he took as the promise of a new life. And he prepared for it joyfully. Mitya's death was fate's final blow, from which Blok never recovered. In the rough drafts to the autobiographical story "Neither Sleeping nor Waking," there is a note of 16 February 1909:

> We waited our whole lives for happiness as people wait for a train on an open, snow-covered platform—for long hours. They go blind from the snow and still they wait, for three lights to appear.
> Finally the . . . locomotive is here, but not for joy: everyone is so weary; it is so cold that one cannot even warm oneself in the heated coach.

Another rough draft is dated 3 March:

> She concealed herself, departed altogether into her own abdomen. Then came something completely different: she gave birth, screamed, got sick, slowly recovered. And then again something unlike her: she suddenly became a woman and beautiful.
> Exactly so. At first we waited for something, not calling it a child at all. Then the child was born; we loved him immediately, unexpectedly. Then again—the child died, weeks passed; as before there is nothing.
> Actually this together was all so short. But there was nothing at all in common between that, and the second, and the third. Only increasing malice and boredom link all this. But they are the only all-linking, all-embracing principles.

Finally, on 3 November, Blok sketches the plan for a story:

> A weary soul sits down by the threshold of a grave. Again spring, again the almond blooms on the slopes. The Magdalene walks past with a vessel,

Peter with the keys, Salome carries the head on a tray.... "Where is your body?" "My body is still wandering the earth and trying not to lose its soul, having lost it long ago. It tries to convince itself that it isn't lost."

The senior devil, completely infuriated: "Do you know what? I will send you to live in Russia!" The soul submissively agrees to this. The younger devils applaud the senior for his appalling ingenuity. The soul trudges around Russia in the twentieth century.

The poet places Pushkin's famous exclamation at the basis of the projected story: "The devil had me born in Russia with a mind and talent!" The story remained unwritten.

One of Blok's most tragic poems, *On the Death of an Infant*, is dedicated to Mitya's memory:

When under the cold spade
The sand and bright snow creaked,
In me, sad and free,
The man resigned himself.

Let this death be comprehensible—
In the soul, to the songs of the requiem,
Evil spots showed through
Of unforgettable injuries.

Already the hitherto kind hand
Contracted with menace.
Already despair rose and rushed about
In the poisoned soul.

I will stifle dull malice,
I will commit despair to oblivion.
To the holy little coffin
I will pray at night.

But—to kneel,
To thank You, grieving?
No. Over the infant, over the *blessed one*,
I will mourn without You.

This revolt against God, born of despair, opens a new period in the poet's life. In the third book of poems he gives it the title *The Terrible World*.

And first of all the "social service" stops abruptly: the societies, circles, salons, lectures, reports, debates become unbearable. "I am thinking," he writes his mother on 23 February, "of stopping all articles, lectures and papers, so as not to waste myself on trifles, but to return to art." A period of impenetrable gloom sets in. Blok confesses to his mother: "I have never before, mama, been in such a depressed state as in these days.... Everything I see is equally repellent to me and all people are oppressive." He complains to Chulkov:

> Never yet have I lived through such a period as the past month, of appalling emptiness. Now it seems to have eased up a bit.... And I am

terribly sick of people. I drank alone gloomily, but not so much as to reach the point of extreme swinishness—I drank boringly.

The "literary life" continues by force of inertia. In January Grillparzer's *The Ancestress*, translated by Blok, is staged in the Kommissarzhevskaya Theater. Despite Kuzmin's lovely music and A. N. Benois' excellent scenery, this drama of "fear and horror" was unsuccessful. On 19 March, the day of the hundredth anniversary of Gogol's birthday, Blok gives a speech, "A Child of Gogol,"[9] at a memorial gathering in the auditorium of the Assembly of the Nobility.

Gogol's whole life, the lecturer says, was a creative torment; like a woman, he carried a fetus beneath his heart and shuddered at the inevitability of childbirth, at the appearance of a new being. Gogol's child is Russia:

> She flashed before him, like a blinding vision. . . . She yielded herself to him in beauty and music, in the whistling of the wind, and in the flight of the headlong troika. . . . Following Gogol, we also dream of her. He, raising the curtain, for his daring insight, was the first to experience all the abasement of despair. . . . Not enduring the "grave everywhere unresponsive," he was broken.

Gogol's child—Russia—"looks at us from the dark blue abyss of the future and calls us there. What she will grow into, we don't know; we don't know what to call her."

This short speech is a polished lyrical "prose poem." The image of Russia as a child is suggested to the poet by the memory of little Mitya's birth and death.

In February Blok's article "The Poet's Soul" appears in the newspaper *Word*. In it he makes an important statement about the musical element supporting his lyricism:

> The writer's fate is a difficult, terrible, insidious fate. Especially in the Russia of our time. The only real justification for a writer is as the voice of the public, . . . not even the voice but as if the breath of the people's soul. [But contemporary writers don't hear this breath and are] probably unworthy of hearing it. . . . Behind the critical whooping and whistling, the menacing "silence of the people" is heard.

The chief indication that a given writer is not an accidental quantity is the sense of a *path*: it determines the writer's inner *rhythm*. "The loss of this rhythm is the most dangerous of all." And the author asserts:

> A tireless straining of the inner hearing, the attention as if to distant music, is the indispensable condition of the writer's way of life. Only by hearing the music of the distant "orchestra" (which is also the "world orchestra" of the people's soul) can one permit oneself a light "game."

Blok ends with a prediction: "In contemporary artists, who merely listen to the music, hope for the blessing of the people's soul is timid only because they are infinitely remote from it. But those who are filled with music will hear the sigh of the common soul, if not today, then tomorrow."

This article concludes the cycle of Blok's "populist" writings. In their rhythmical movement, his ideas on art form an original musical attitude to the world. The soul of the world is music, the "world orchestra," the elemental force of life, of movement, and of love. The people's soul is immersed in it, the collective consciousness, not yet torn from the lap of mother earth. Through inner rhythm a direct link to the "world orchestra" is given the poet: he *hears* the music and finds the people in it. In his assertion of the elemental basis of the world, Blok is true to the spirit of German romanticism: Novalis and Schelling, Wagner and Nietzsche join their voices to his. Blok's "populism" is not from his forefathers in spirit—the Slavophiles and Dostoevsky—but from his forefathers in blood—the Teutons from Mecklenburg.

That same winter of 1909 the poet translates thirteen of Heine's poems, which later enter the fourth collection of poems, *Night Hours* (1911), and places two literary articles, "Merezhkovsky" and "Balmont," in the newspaper *Speech*. On 14 April Blok and his wife leave for Italy. On the eve of departure he sees Chekhov's *Three Sisters* at the Art Theater and returns home "completely shaken." With deep emotion he writes his mother about Chekhov and Russia:

> *Three Sisters* is a corner of great Russian art, one of those preserved accidentally, by some miracle; not the bespattered corners of my mean, dirty, stupid, and bloody homeland, which tomorrow, thank the Lord, I am leaving. . . . I accepted Chekhov whole, as he is, into the pantheon of my soul and shared his tears, sorrow and humiliation. . . . We are all unhappy that our native land has prepared such soil for us—for malice and for quarreling with one another. We all live behind Chinese walls, half despising one another, and our only common enemy—the Russian state, organized religion, taverns, the treasury, and bureaucrats—doesn't show its face, but sets us against one another.

The "political" and "public" period of the poet's life is over. He goes to Italy to forget the past and to become "a human being." The letter ends with these words: "One must either not live in Russia at all, spit on her drunken snout, or isolate oneself from *humiliation*—from politics and also from 'community.' "

The Bloks spend ten days in Venice, "quietly, lazily, and restfully." They visit art galleries, are captivated by Bellini's painting, and, on the Lido, play with crabs and collect shells. "Every Russian artist," Blok writes his mother, "has the right, at least for a few years, to shut his ears from everything Russian and to see his other homeland—Europe, and especially Italy!"

Dead Ravenna struck the poet: Dante's grave, the ancient sarcophagi, the mosaics, the palace of Theodoric. He hated Florence. "I curse

Florence," he writes, "not only for the heat and mosquitos, but because it has given itself up to the European decay, has become a pompous city, and has mutilated nearly all its houses and streets." After Florence the Bloks visited Perugia, Assisi, Siena, and Pisa. On 19 June the poet writes his mother from Milan:

> I must confess that this trip hasn't turned out to be at all restful. On the contrary, we are both terribly tired and overstrung to the last degree. Milan is already the thirteenth city, and everywhere we look at almost everything. Really I can now take in nothing but art, the sky, and sometimes the sea. People are loathsome to me, all of life is horrible. European life is just as vile as Russian—in general, the whole life of people in the whole world is, in my opinion, a kind of monstrous, dirty puddle. . . . I would like to live very quietly for a while and to think—away from cities, movie theaters, restaurants, Italians, and Germans. All this is nothing but a rubbish pit. . . . More than ever I see that I will never accept anything of modern life and won't resign myself to anything. Its shameful order inspires only disgust in me. It is already impossible to change anything; no revolution will change it. All people are rotting, *a few* human beings will remain. I love only art, children, and death. Russia is for me still the same lyrical quantity. As a matter of fact, she is not, was not, and will not be.

This tragic letter introduces us to the black night of the poems *The Terrible World*. In the terrible force of negation, in the revolt against the whole universe, breathes the Luciferian spirit of Ivan Karamazov. The phrase "I love only art, *children* and death" is striking. Ivan Karamazov also loved children; his whole "revolt" grew out of his torment over the sufferings of children.

During the Italian trip Blok now and then made entries in his *Notebook*, some worth quoting. On 11 May: "Everyone says that she [Lyuba] is *bella*. They call her Miss. Only I . . . am a mystery." On 14 May: "Lyuba has again become prettier. She runs about. They call her *signorina* and say 'che bella.' " In Florence he notes:

> Sunday morning. . . . Tonight the devil overtook me and tore me to pieces again. I sit in an armchair—oh, if only one could always sleep. I see the Florentine tiles and the sky. Here they are—black spots. I still haven't completely sobered up, and therefore the truth about the black air hits me in the eye. It can't be hidden.

On the night of 11–12 June, in Marina di Pisa he writes:

> Waking up in the middle of the night to the noise of the wind and the sea, to the influence of the death of Mitya brought back to mind from Tolstoy,[10] and of some old, returned quietness, I think about the fact that for three or four years already I have been, imperceptibly to myself, drawn into an atmosphere of people completely alien to me. . . .
> One must turn sharply while consciousness is not yet lost, while it is not too late. The means—to give up literary income and find another. One must live somehow. . . . I am indebted to Italy at least for forgetting how

to laugh. God grant that it remain.... I would like to think much and quietly, to live quietly, to see a few people, to work, and to study. Is this really unrealizable?... How Lyuba could help me in this.

The last "Italian" entry on the night of 14–15 June reads:

> The sea is noisy. I wake up at night, uneasiness returns. At first about what I will do, how I will meet _____, how winter will come, to serve or not (apparently there's no point in writing for a long time, it's impossible —nothing important). Then—general anxiety, depression—for mama, for everything there.... During the day overstrung, tired, almost ill, vicious. All this may foreshadow either an onslaught of new misfortunes, events, losses, destructions, or a passing crisis, the beginning of something new again (?), the renewal of life, the return of inspiration.

During these sleepless nights, to the noise of the sea, Blok thought about renouncing art. He had never yet felt so acutely that life had fractured, that he is at a crossing. And his forebodings didn't deceive him: new "misfortunes and losses" did await him (his father's death in December of that year) and the "return of inspiration" (a torrent of lyrical poems in 1909).

From Italy Blok and his wife go to Bad Nauheim, and there he plunges into the romantic atmosphere, full of memories of youthful love, which is native to him. He writes his mother rapturously about the "beauty and kindredness" of Germany, about its "lofty lyricism." He rests from clamorous and unpleasant Italy, the "most unlyrical country" in the world. Germany is the homeland of the Gothic and only there is there a "real religion of life, Gothic life." Blok writes with tenderness about his beloved Bad Nauheim, where "as before the bubbling springs mysteriously whiten and smoke in the evenings, where there are the same mists over the lake and the same moist coolness in the park."

In the resort assembly hall the poet listened to much Wagner, and his "romantic philosophy," which found expression in the article "The Writer's Soul," becomes even stronger. In the *Notebook* we read:

> Wagner in Nauheim is something completely inexpressible, it recalls "*anamnesis.*"
> Music is the most perfect of the arts because it expresses and reflects more the designs of the Architect....
> Music creates the world, it is the world's spiritual body, the *idea* (fluid) of the world....
> Reaching its own limit, poetry would probably drown in music.
> The more my tools are perfected, the more discriminating I am, and must finally *grow altogether deaf* to everything that is not accompanied by music (such is *modern* life, politics, and the like).

Blok gives himself up to the elemental force, craves oblivion and merging with the World Soul. A new Dionysus, he dooms himself to being tormented by music. His fate is decided.

On 21 June the Bloks return to Russia. Crossing the border, the poet notes:

> Here is Russia.
> Light rain, fields, stunted bushes. A solitary guard with a rifle on his shoulder rides along the field. He whirls around....
> And this is Russian broad daylight after the vile Italian day (everything is rotting), after the morning translucence and Gothicism of the Teutonic cities.... Cosy, quiet, slow mire. But one wants terribly to live (*Three Sisters*) and therefore toward evenings waits with impatience—for Petersburg. And what is in this Petersburg? Always the same large, damp, cosy Reghitza.
> And Lyuba is asleep facing me, covered by my overcoat. Above her hangs her shabby child's hat.

After spending nine days in Petersburg, the Bloks move to Shakhmatovo. There Aleksandra Andreevna, having arrived from Revel, meets them. Her health alarms her son: her nervous disorder is so serious that the doctors insist on placing the patient in a sanatorium.

In Shakhmatovo Blok enters in his *Notebook*: "I am indebted to the West for stirring in me the spirit of searching and the spirit of unpretentiousness. I fear losing both again.... Demon of laughter, depart from me and from my thought. I also want to drive away other demons. 8 July, late evening, in the annex." Mystical agitation, which had visited him in his youth in the same Shakhmatovo house, returns to the poet. Again he feels Her elusive breeze and again, as ten years before, he prays to Her. The entry begins: "The Russian revolution has ended. All the charred logs have burned to ashes.... All nature was again bewitched, soon after people were bewitched. The World Soul pines, again, again." And directly after this:

> Lyuba has returned from Boblovo, as in the past alien, her good looks gone....
> There will be much more. But You—return, return, return—at the end of the ordeals appointed to us. We will pray to You amid the future fear and passion allotted us. Again I will wait—always Your slave, unfaithful to You, but returning again, again.
> Leave to me memory keen as now. Don't lull my keen anxiety to sleep. Don't interrupt my torments. Let me see Your dawn. Return.

And this after all the fits of demonic irony, the scoffing at the "mystics," the renunciations of the Beautiful Lady, and the blasphemies of *The Puppet Show* and *The Stranger*! Blok's musical soul, like the ocean, is exposed to storms, to ebbs and flows. But its depth is immovable and transparent. He is loyal, despite all the faithlessness, innocent in all his falls:

> Leave me in my far-off place.
> I am faithful. I am innocent.

After long wanderings, the knight returns to the Beautiful Lady. He has never stopped loving her and with her also the one whose earthly image revealed the World Soul to him. On 22–23 September he notes:

> Night. The night feeling of the irreparableness of everything creeps in even during the day. Everyone will turn away and spit—and let them. I had my youth. I fear death and I fear life. The past is dearest of all; Lyuba is the sanctuary of my soul. She helps, I don't know how—perhaps by what she took away?

The decision made in Italy to give up literature, to enter service, and to break with people alien in spirit, is not carried out. The hateful literary milieu again "engulfs" the poet: Chulkov, the Merezhkovskys, Meyerhold, poets, actors, feminine admirers appear. Blok writes reviews in the newspaper *Speech* (on Gorodetsky, Krechetov, Prishvin, Timkovsky, and others). In November the first issue of a new literary-artistic journal, *Apollo*, comes out, in which the cycle of Blok's *Italian Poems* appears. The poet complains to his mother of "bustle": "All this arose again because the Italian poems seem to have brought me fame a second time." He is elected to the board of the Society of Zealots of the Artistic Word, which was formed in connection with *Apollo* and consisted of six members: the poet and editor of *Apollo*, S. K. Makovsky; V. Ivanov; the director of the Tsarskoe Selo museum and poet, Innokenty Fyodorovich Annensky; Professor F. F. Zelinsky; Kuzmin; and Blok. In the restaurant Kontan, a splendid celebration in honor of S. K. Makovsky takes place on the occasion of the appearance of the first issue of *Apollo*. At a meeting of the Society of Zealots, V. Ivanov gives a lecture; D. V. Filosofov visits the poet to talk about Italy and gives him Italian photographs. At the end of October Blok's feuilleton, "Gorky about Messina," appears in the newspaper *Speech*—the last of his "Lyrical Articles." Relating the content of Maksim Gorky's and Professor V. Meyer's book, *Earthquake in Calabria and Sicily*, the author asserts that this catastrophe is "an event of worldwide importance," that it "*changed our life*":

> One would have to be simply spiritually blind, uninterested in the life of the cosmos and insensitive to the everyday tremor of chaos to suppose that the formation of the earth proceeds independently and on its own course, in no way influencing the formation of man's soul and of the human way of life.
> [Mochulsky presents the following paragraphs out of sequence in order to make his point.]
> During the earthquake people were seized by panic, by madness, were completely confused and more unfortunate than wild animals. But what miracles of spirit and strength were displayed then!
> With the sudden outburst of subterranean flame the face of humanity appeared for an instant. . . . It was written on that face how pitiful man is and simultaneously how tenacious, strong and noble man is.

Blok, hearing the music of cosmic life and praying to the World Soul, attributed enormous mystical significance to the Sicilian catastrophe. In the *poema Retribution* he places it in the series of ominous portents of the end:

> In the heights the horrible apparition
> Of a terrible and tailed comet,
> The pitiless end of Messina
> (Elemental forces cannot be overcome).

At the end of October the poet falls ill with scurvy. His tonsils, lips and gums swell. For two weeks he stays home with a slight temperature; he plays checkers with his wife and writes "Italian feuilletons." He wanted to publish a book of Italian impressions under the title *Lightnings of Art*, but wasn't able to get it ready for printing. Blok returned to the rough drafts of 1909 in 1912, 1918, and 1920. Of the seven sketches he wrote, only two were printed during his life: "Masks on the Street" in the Journal *Masks* (No. 4, 1913) and "The Phantom of Rome and Monte Luca" in the journal *Dreamers' Notes* (No. 2–3, 1921).

In the "Introduction" to *Lightnings of Art* the author consigns modern machine civilization to damnation:

> The nineteenth century was an iron age.... Year by year, day by day, hour by hour it is clearer and clearer that civilization will fall down on the heads of its creators, will crush them itself.... There were people—for a long time there have been no people, they only call themselves that: slaves, beasts, reptiles. Those who were called people God hasn't protected for a long time; nature doesn't cherish them; art doesn't bring them joy.... Do you know that every nut in the machine, every turn of the screw, every new achievement of technology produces a world rabble? ... The time is already at the door when even art will undergo unheard-of destruction.

These passionate and accusatory words startle with their prophetic pathos. Blok foresees our epoch (of the Second World War), the unprecedented destruction, and the terrible crisis of humanity, to which Berdyaev gives the name "dehumanization" and "bestialization." Civilization really did fall down on the heads of its creators with thousands of tons of bombs, people really were transformed into beasts, and in the most cultured country of Europe the "world rabble" was not long ago still celebrating its victory.

The first sketch, "Masks on the Street," tells of the sudden intrusion into the festive life of Florence of a procession of "Brothers of Mercy" in black cowls, with torches in their hands. On a black cart, in a noiselessly dancing gallop, they are transporting a corpse.

The second sketch, "Mute Witnesses," is devoted to the capital of Umbria, Perugia. In its feudal coat of arms a griffin tears a calf to pieces: its past is bathed in blood. "Italy is tragic in one thing," the author writes, "in the subterranean rustle of history, which has roared past, irrevocable. In this rustle the voice of quiet madness, the muttering of ancient Sybils, is clearly heard." The poet describes in detail the Etruscan grave of the Volumni in the vicinity of Perugia, its sculptures, sarcophagi, and bas-reliefs. These "mute witnesses" will never wake up. Life will never return to the blue valley of Umbria.

The third sketch, "Evening in Siena," is a poetic picture of the medieval town with slender, pointed towers, with the concave oval square, with the resplendent Palazzo Publico. When night falls and the square empties, the tavern Three Maidens blinks the only lantern.

In the fourth sketch, "Glance of an Egyptian Girl," the depiction of an Egyptian girl on an ancient papyrus in the Archeological Museum in Florence is described. Some see in it a portrait of Queen Cleopatra. The eyes of this plain face are striking:

> In them is neither weariness, nor maternity, nor gaiety, nor sadness, nor desire. All that one can see in them is dull, insatiable greed: greed to the death, both in life and beyond the grave—it is all one and the same. . . . The eyes look as terribly, dumbly, and oppressively as the lotus smells. From age to age, from one era to another.

In the fifth sketch, "The Phantom of Rome and Monte Luca," two reminiscences of the Umbrian town of Spoleto are combined. The poet descends into a damp hatchway:

> There, at a depth of about ten feet from the earth's surface, in the weak light of a candle butt, I dreamed or imagined, rather than saw, the clammy block of a stone dome, the beginning of the arch of a bridge. This phantom simply remained in my memory as a phantom of Rome.

Then, outside the city, the author and his companion climb the round Monte Luca. And suddenly he sees himself on a sheer, rocky precipice: an unexpectedly vast expanse opens before him. His heart sinks—the abyss draws him downward. He makes a terrible effort to keep himself on the ledge and not to throw himself down. In the distance gleam the snowy summits of the Appenines.

In the concluding sketch, "Wirballen," the *Notebook* entries about his return to Russia are utilized—about the Russian fields, the stunted bushes, the solitary guard astride the nag, about the depression and deadness of Russian life. *Lightnings of Art* resembles no other "letters of Russian travellers." There are very few "descriptions" and "impressions"; no "experiences" or "raptures" at all. Blok hated modern Italy violently. Its nature seemed to him squalid ("pitiful vegetation," "dusty roads," "misshapen grape vines"). He didn't see ancient and Christian Italy at all; the art of the Renaissance aroused in him merely a cold acknowledgement. He carried away from the "wearisome" trip a few lyrical impressions, which struck his romantic imagination: the funeral procession in Florence; the Etruscan tombs in Perugia; the towers of Siena, "slender to the point of insolence"; the dizziness on Monte Luca; the lifeless absence of people in Ravenna; a red sail in a Venetian lagoon; the Madonna of Giannicola Manni; and the fresco of Filippo Lippi in Spoleto. He rejected all the rest. Italy remained for Blok "the most unlyrical country" in the world. Classical Romance culture was organically alien to his Germanic romantic spirit.

On 19 November the poet receives alarming news about his father: Aleksandr Lvovich was hopelessly ill. He had consumption and heart trouble; he was lying in a hospital in Warsaw, and no one was allowed to see him. Blok writes his mother:

> On Easter Lyuba and I were quite especially pleased with Aleksandr Lvovich, just because death was obviously already in him, and he understood much that the living don't understand. I think that for a long time he has already been at that stage of spiritual development where he is within reach of moving away and bringing death closer. He probably doesn't even particularly want to live really, although outwardly he is "nervous about his health" and is resisting.

Blok delays his departure for Warsaw, fearing that it will be unpleasant for his father or will frighten him. On 30 November he gets a letter from Warsaw from his father's second wife, Maria Timofeevna. She writes that Aleksandr Lvovich is at the point of death. Blok leaves for Warsaw that same evening. At night in the railway coach he notes:

> Father is lying in the Valley of Roses[11] and is terribly delirious; he breathes with difficulty. And I am in the long and hot corridor of the rail coach, and sparks light up the snow. An old man in drawers doesn't trouble me—I am alone. Nothing is needed. I took everything I could from this wretched life; I lacked the strength to take more from heaven. I am deserted on the road to Warsaw, just as in Petersburg. Only She isn't with me, to be bored like a child, to shake her head, to sleep, to play pranks, to laugh.

And in a second entry: "I am approaching Warsaw. As usual I languish without Lyuba—I can't part with her. What about her?"

On 1 December he writes his mother from Warsaw: "Mama, I arrived this evening and didn't find father among the living. He died at five in the afternoon. I like him very much: his face is tranquil, delicate, and pale. He died quietly, only it was difficult physically—from the shortness of breath."

He writes on 4 December:

> Mama, the funeral was today—solemn, as was the requiem. From everything I see here, and thanks to dozens of people with whom I speak incessantly, father's inner countenance is becoming clear to me—to a great extent in a completely new way. Everyone testifies to the nobility and loftiness of his spirit, to a kind of uncommon solitariness and exceptional largeness in his nature.

In Warsaw Blok becomes more closely acquainted with his father's second wife, Maria Timofeevna, a "good, weary, and meek" woman, and with his stepsister Angelina. The poet considers her an "interesting, original, and pure" girl and wants to introduce her to his mother and his wife. On 19 December he returns from Warsaw with mild bronchitis and, on recovering, goes to Revel with his wife on 29 December. The Bloks see in the New Year at his mother's. The joy of meeting is clouded by Aleksandra Andreevna's steadily worsening nervous disorder. From his father Blok received an inheritance of 40,000 rubles, a box of books, an enormous mahogany sofa with cupboards and shelves, and a large walnut desk.

The poems written in 1909 were later distributed among various sections of the third volume. Eight poems entered the section *The Terrible World*, some of which are real masterpieces. The lyrical theme of *The Stranger* is sharpened and intensified in the poem *Out of the crystal fog*. Again there is the intersection of two planes—dream and reality—the union of gypsy melody with angelic song, the restaurant "maiden" with the Magdalene. The contrasts, which tear consciousness apart, are resolved in the madness of passion and death.

The poet in love sings:

Out of the crystal fog,
Out of a mysterious dream
Someone's image, someone's strange image . . .

The mocking double adds parenthetically:

(In the private room of a restaurant
Over a bottle of wine.)

The image of the "maiden" arises in the mirrors—in the screech of the gypsy melody, in the misty howling of the distant violins, in the music of the wind. The world splits: one "half" of life is a "slender goblet and a blizzard beyond the dull glass of the window," the other is a "wind from the desert" and a "land scorched by the sun of the south." But the demon whispers blasphemous and terrible words; he turns the Magdalene into a vulgar whore; he commands that veneration be incinerated in the fire of passion:

So that on the long night's bed
The powers of passion would not suffice!
So that in the deserted howl of the violins
Mortal twilight would extinguish
The frightened eyes.

We descend after the poet into the circles of Hell. The poem *Song of Hell*, written in Dantesque *terzinas*, is accompanied by an authorial note:

The *Song of Hell* is an attempt to portray the "infernalness" (Dostoevsky's term), the "vampirism" of our time. Modernity not only doesn't possess the heavenly companion, the Divine Wisdom, but not even the earthly wisdom of the pagan Vergil, who accompanied Dante in Hell and at the heavenly door handed him to Beatrice.

Along the ledges of the cliffs, in the lilac twilight, the poet descends into Hell: the world where he had wandered during his life. The double comes to meet him "out of the spiderweb of darkness":

A youth comes out. His figure is belted;

The bloom of a wilted rose in his dress coat button hole.
Paler than the lips on a corpse's face;
On his finger—token of a secret marriage—

Shines a ring's pointed amethyst . . .

"With a burned mouth" he tells the poet his story: on the sad earth he "was under the yoke of dismal passion." And here, "out of the depths of an unprecedented dream," the "wonderful wife" shone before him. But the heavenly vision kindled in him only the sensuality of a vampire, and the whirlwind of flame carried him to the underground world. He is eternally doomed to torment his beloved by unquenchable passion, doomed:

Bending over her, in love and sad,

To thrust his ring in the white shoulder!

The "terrible world" of passion, blood, death, the "insane and diabolical ball," the "snowstorm, gloom, and emptiness," the vampirism of sensuality—here is the landscape of the modern Hell, more terrible than Dante's hellish crater. And the poet's companion is not Beatrice, but a woman whose gaze "strikes like a dagger," with a "storm of tangled tresses," with a "bloody charred mouth." The lover-enemies writhe in a torment of sensuality. There is a gap of dull windows, three candles, and a heavy coffin:

Candles, eyes, words are extinguished . . .
"You are dead, finally, dead!
"I know, I drank your blood . . .
"I will lay you in the coffin and sing."
        (*I conquered her, finally!*)

The mortal split in the stricken soul is personified in a meeting with the double (*The Double*). In the October fog, amid wind, rain, and darkness, reeling, an "aging youth" approaches the poet and whispers:

. . . "I am tired of reeling,

> Of breathing the dank fog,
> Of being reflected in someone else's mirrors,
> And of kissing other men's women..."

And, "smiling insolently," the vision disappears. Another double replaces him:

> And a sailor, not taken on board,
> Goes reeling through the snowstorm.
> Everything is lost, everything is drunk up!
> Enough—I can no more...
> *(In late autumn from the harbor)*

Dostoevsky knew that the ultimate limit of all the "demonisms" and "vampirisms" of passion is metaphysical boredom, Svidrigailov's[12] "bathhouse with spiders." In sad and cheerless words Blok tells of the hateful "rite of love":

> Again snow-covered columns,
> Elagin bridge and two lights,
> And the voice of a woman in love,
> And the crunch of sand, and a horse's snort.

He "honors the rite." "With the constancy of a geometrist" he draws diagrams of words, embraces, kisses. Love will pass away like snow; vows of fidelity aren't needed. Everything is merely a continuation of the ball, transition from light to twilight.

The poet includes ten 1909 poems in the section *Retribution*. The wandering through the circles of Hell is finished; the Dantesque visions of sinners, carried away by a whirlwind and writhing in fiery graves, are dispersed. "Life is over." The weary specter wanders on the shores of Lethe; these poems are cloaked in otherworldly quiet. The soul, consumed in earthly passions, glides, incorporeal and transparent, "like an Elysian shadow." The leitmotif of these elegies is *oblivion*:

> Today I don't remember what happened yesterday,
> In the morning I forget my evenings...
> *(Today I don't remember)*

Or:

> Forget that life has been,
> That life will be, forget...
> The night shadows creep from the fields...
>   One thing, one—
>   To fall asleep, to fall asleep...
> But it's all the same—
> Someone will wake me.
> *(The more one wants to rest)*

Aleksandr Blok   This indifference, this reconciling, is death:

> Not hurrying, I impassively collected
> Memories and deeds;
> And it became mercilessly clear:
> Life roared by and departed.

And now, in this posthumous languor, everything that previously seemed like suffering—depression, passion, malice, disease—seems like infinite happiness, enormous wealth:

> When you breathe
> Neither boredom, nor love, nor fear,
> When the dreams are soiled
> By not young and not swift blood—
>
> Then you are robbed and naked.
> *(When, entering the vast world)*

What is there for a dead man to do among the living? How is he to endure "the vanity of desert life?" The "anger of scorn" and "toothless laughter" remain to him. One of Blok's most terrible verses:

> Water, water your creatures
> With a corpse's invisible poison,
> To poison human hearts
> With the angry ripeness of scorn.
> *(Life breathed the grave in my face)*

The cycle of poems ends with the derisive credo of the romantic Don Juan:

> And to me, as to all, the same fate
> Appears in the approaching haze:
> Again—to love Her in heaven
> And to betray her on earth.
> *(The ring of life is tight)*

The poet places the remarkable poem *They don't sleep, nor remember, nor trade* in the section *Iambics*. The triumphant Easter chiming lies over the black city:

> Above the human creation
> Which he drove into the earth,
> Above the stench, death, and suffering,
> They ring till strength is gone . . .
>
> Above the world nonsense.

The cycle of *Italian Poems*, which, in Blok's words, brought him fame for the second time in 1909, opens with a magnificent poem about Ravenna, ringing like the "bronze of solemn Latin." The dying city, forsaken by the far-receding sea, sleeps "in the arms of drowsy eternity":

> Only in the intent and quiet gaze
> Of Ravenna girls, at times,
> Sadness for the irretrievable sea
> Passes in a timid row.

A rapturous hymn is devoted to the *Girl from Spoleto*, in whose features the most pure face of the Virgin Mary shone for the poet. What flight in the verse:

> Past, past everything—the wind drives you—
> Scorched by the sun—Maria! Allow
> The gaze to penetrate the cherubim above you,
> The heart to know the sweetest pain!

Three poems are devoted to Venice:

> Oh, red sail
> In the green distance!
> Black beads
> On the dark shawl!

The poet is stretched out by a "pillar with lions"; on the tower giants strike the midnight hour; Salome passes him, carrying his bloody head on a black tray (*Cold wind on the lagoon*). And at night, when the rumble of the crowd slacks off, the wind sings about the future life. Perhaps in the coming age he is fated to be born of a "Venetian maiden," at the foot of a pillar with lions?

> No! Everything that is, that has been—is alive!
> Dreams, visions, thoughts—away!
> The wave of returning high tide
> Throws them into the velvet night!

The poet curses "Florence-Judas" for its automobiles, its "all-European dust"; but his hatred is full of love. Florence is a delicate iris, for which he pines "with a long, hopeless love":

> I will dream your smoky iris
> Like my early youth.
> (*Florence, you are a delicate iris*)

And again:

> Smoky iris, delicate iris,
> Stream of fragrance . . .
> (*With long, serene passion*)

And finally:

> Smoky irises in flame
> Now seem to fly away.
> Oh, despair of sadness,
> I know you by heart!
> Into the black sky of Italy
> I look with a black soul.
>   (*Scorching stones burn*)

One of the most stinging poems is devoted to Siena. The treacherous, cunning city is a "quiver of pliant arrows"; the spikes of its churches and towers pierce the sky:

> And the icons fill
> The enamored spirit with languor,
> Where perfidious Madonnas
> Squint their long eyes.
>   (*Siena*)

The Annunciation—the most famous of the Italian poems—is inspired by the fresco of Giannicola Manni in the Collegio del Cambio in Perugia. It has: a wind from an angel's noisy wings (a "whirlwind with multicolored wings"), the agitation and confusion of passion, flaming distances, and a dark-faced angel in red clothing. The artist turns the mystery of the incarnation into a mystery of love. He transmits the gold and purple of the fresco in flashing, fiery words.

Another fresco—the *Assumption* of Fra Filippo Lippi in the cathedral of Spoleto—suggests to the poet the tender and reverential lines:

> Her shrouded body
> They laid in the young forest;
> It had grown younger from torments,
> Recovering its former beauty.

Again three kings come to adore; and again the shepherds, already gray, bring their flocks; countless golden nimbi are among the stars:

> And above, along the steep ravines,
> The stream sings, the almond blooms,
> And above the open sarcophagus
> The gravestone angel looks into the distance.

In the *Italian Poems* Blok creates what is for him a new pictorial-plastic style; for the first time the bronze trumpets of "solemn Latin" sound alongside the "harps and violins" in his orchestra.

In the section *Miscellaneous Poems* the author places a free imitation of Pushkin's poem "Whether I wander along noisy streets." His full-weighted powerful stanzas are worthy of the great poet. This verse is perfect:

> In the morning hour, pure and crystalline,
> By the walls of the Moscow Kremlin,
> Will my land return to me
> The original rapture of my soul?
>   (*All this is over, over, over*)

In the section *Harps and Violins* the didactic-philosophical *Meditation* stands out in its solemn aloofness:

> Everything on earth will die—mother and youth.
> Wife will betray and friend forsake.
> But, you, learn to taste a different sweetness,
> Looking into the cold and polar circle.

The concluding verse is:

> And to the quiver of the slow cold
> School your weary soul,
> So that it needs nothing *here*
> When the rays rush *from there*.

The cold reflection, the stern lecture in the spirit of Baratynsky, is a new string in Blok's lyre.

The poetic harvest of 1909 is crowned by the poem *Autumn Day*, one of Blok's most perfect creations[13] and known to every Russian reader:

> I go unhurrying along the stubble
> With you, my unassuming friend,
> And the soul unburdens itself
> As in a dark village church.

On a quiet autumn day, smoke drifts over the barn, and cranes fly:

> They fly, they fly at an oblique angle,
> The leader rings and cries . . .
> What does it ring about, what, what?
> What does the autumn weeping mean? . . .

The concluding verse picks up this weeping—beggared Russia responds to it with a sobbing song:

> Oh, my beggared country,
> What do you mean to the heart?
> Oh, my poor wife,
> What do you weep about so bitterly?

CHAPTER VII
RETRIBUTION
1910–1911

Blok returned from Revel very alarmed about his mother's health. Because of heart disease, Aleksandra Andreevna began to have seizures of an epileptic nature, after which she would fall into depression. Blok inquires into sanatoria, consults with psychiatrists, begs his mother to move to Petersburg. He joins two rooms from a neighboring apartment to his own and enthusiastically sets about arranging a lodging for his mother. In his long letters, full of practical details, advice, and comfort, one senses a deep, concealed tenderness. Aleksandra Andreevna comes to Petersburg at the beginning of February, and in March they take her to a sanatorium in Sokolniky, near Moscow.

His mother's nervous illness manifests itself in a *horror of life*. The poet tries to encourage and calm her, but he is himself living in a "terrible world" and is no less melancholy than she. In January he suddenly brightens up: an unknown comet is approaching the earth, perhaps bringing destruction. He writes his mother:

> Do you know that, besides Halley's comet (harmless, like Natalya Nikolaevna), there is another, unknown, a real stranger? Its tail, consisting of cyanogen (hence the blue gaze), can poison our atmosphere, and we all, reconciled to death, will fall sweetly asleep from the bitter odor of almond in the quiet night, looking at the beautiful comet.

And two days later he writes about the comet again: "I am very animated; the comet, of course, is the main reason. It turns out that one can 'fear' the tail of Halley's comet, but nothing at all is known yet about the *second*, except that it is flying with terrible speed."

But his hopes for the end of the world deceived him, and he is soon disappointed in comets: "I somehow stopped thinking about the comet or think rarely" (letter of 27 January). The poem *The Comet*[1] is devoted to Halley's comet: a star "out of blue eternity" threatens the world "with its final hour," but man doesn't fear destruction—he sends his "steel dragonflies" (his airplanes) to meet the comet. The third verse is very expressive in its growing tension:

> Our world, spreading its peacock tail,
> Like you, is full of the violence of dreams:
> Through Simplon, seas, deserts,
> Through a scarlet whirlwind of heavenly roses,
> Through the night, through the haze, henceforth aim
> Their flight—swarms of steel dragonflies.

And again the detested life of the Petersburg intellectual and man of letters drags on. Blok senses that some denouement must come: "Soon life will turn over, one way or another; it is already time. The nightmares of recent years—one must give them up as a bad job" (letter to his mother on 1 April).

Among these nightmares is a feeling of a mystical tie with the dark shadow of his late father. Blok makes a terrible confession to his mother: "The paternal gloom is still on earth and twines around me. It is necessary to pray away this person." The persistent thought of his father gradually takes possession of his imagination. He will "pray away" his father with the *poema Retribution*.

At the beginning of February, Vera Fyodorovna Kommissarzhevskaya dies suddenly. Blok devotes a note to her in the newspaper *Speech* (12 February). He remembers "her light, swift figure in the semi-darkness of the theater corridors, her sad and laughing eyes, her inquiring, demanding, and fascinating conversations": "Of course we were all in love with Vera Fyodorovna Kommissarzhevskaya without knowing it ourselves, and were in love not only with her, but with what shone behind her restless shoulders, with what her sleepless eyes and always exciting voice called us to." At an evening in memory of the late actress in the city duma, on 7 March 1910, Blok makes a speech:

> V. F. Kommissarzhevskaya has now become a *symbol* for us. She saw further than the naked eye can see: her large blue eyes spoke about something immeasurably larger than herself. Her death was purifying for us. Those who saw how the spring sky opened over her grave when the coffin was lowered into the ground were at that moment blessed and radiant. . . . Vera Kommissarzhevskaya is our faith. The eternal youth of such eyes won't grow dim; the violin of such a voice merges with the world orchestra.

Blok dedicated the poem *She came at midnight*, where strings sing and seraphim weep, to Kommissarzhevskaya:

> What sobbed in her? What struggled?
> What did she expect from us?
> We don't know. The spring voice died,
> The stars of blue eyes went out.

The poet addresses the deceased:

> So sleep, exhausted by fame,
> By love, by life, by slander . . .

Aleksandr Blok

> Now you are with it—with your majestic,
> Your unrealizable dream.

Only after Vera Fyodorovna's death did Blok feel how mysteriously close she was to his soul, how in harmony with his "music" and his depression. He called her a *symbol* of the new art, incarnated passion, and eternal youth:

> A banner unfurled by the wind,
> The promised spring.

And, two months after Kommissarzhevskaya's death, there is a new loss. On 1 April the artist Vrubel dies. Blok writes his mother:

> I saw him for the first time in the coffin. He had a small face all shrunk with suffering, tightly clenched eyes and mouth, under a blond mustache. During the last months he exhausted himself completely because he had decided that, if he would stand for seventeen days, God would give him emerald eyes.

At Vrubel's funeral on 3 April 1910 Blok makes the only speech. He didn't know the great artist personally, and his life seemed to him a fairy tale. The name of the creator of "The Demon" is already enveloped in legend:

> They say that Vrubel repainted the head of the Demon up to forty times; once someone, by chance catching him at work, saw a head of unheard-of beauty. [Vrubel] later destroyed this head and repainted it again—he *spoiled* it, as the legend's language has it.... Vrubel's dreams, his delirium, his conversations, his repentances.... Everything is smashed, broken up for us: those worlds which he saw, we haven't yet seen.

Blok calls the late artist a genius, and asks: "What is a genius?" He answers:

> All the days and all the nights a muted wind swoops down from other worlds, brings scraps of whispers and words in an unfamiliar language. ... A genius, perhaps, is one who through the wind has caught a whole *sentence*, put the words together, and written them down. We don't know many such written sentences and their meaning is roughly the same: "Seek the promised land!" ... He who has caught them cannot disobey. ... He goes on, because the "boring songs of earth" can no longer replace the "sounds of the heavens".... We lost the thread of Vrubel's life not when he went mad, but much earlier, when he was creating the dream of his whole life—the Demon.

Blok's words about genius are mystically profound. They contain the profession of faith of a symbolist artist, the unquenchable longing of all romantic art for the "promised land." Vrubel's famous "Demon," lying with broken arms and outstretched wings on fantastic blue-lilac mountains amid the gold and mother-of-pearl of the sunset, is experienced by Blok as a revelation of his own personal fate. The artist translates the poet's mysterious visions into the language of color. The gold of the sunset, the blue of the night, and the lilac hollows of the mountains are symbols of "world tragedies." "I am vitally linked with Vrubel," Blok writes his mother, "and, it seems, even resemble him in face (yesterday Yaremich brought many of his drawings and self-portraits)."

Articles, speeches, meetings, literary gatherings, all this intellectual bustle so hateful to the poet, brings him to despair. "I torment myself with articles," he complains to his mother, "I am sick of discussions; I want to be an artist, and not a mystical windbag and feuilletonist."

Fits of depression invariably end in trips to the Ravine, to Sestroretsk Station, to Ozerki. The *Notebooks* have a series of entries about "sad raptures":

> (10 January). Sestroretsk Station. After supper, arriving in a smart cab, I drink champagne, kissing the hand of a beauty. Will something happen?
>
> (20 January). The Ravine.... I am already beside myself. I drink cognac after vodka and white wine. I don't know how many glasses of cognac. To spite you, sober one! (Now I can talk with you frankly—do you recognize me? No!!)
>
> (1 March). At Primorsky Station in Ozerki.... And then there was such a whirlwind that here the next day I am all trembling, even after a bath. I remember their oblique glances—questioning and frightened—I even draw them into what is for them unusually sweet and tormenting.... My sins are so grave that the idea of confession came in the morning. When I die all this will stop.
>
> (11 March). In the Ravine for the second time. Oh, how comforting to return to a dear old place—again! (Will something happen?) "How sweet!" I don't know what will happen—the orchestra is playing. I am again in my former "coziest" place in the world—for I'm eating the third dozen of oysters and drinking the third split of Chablis....
>
> I am drunk, of course, completely.... But I want more and more and more. My God, my God, in boredom....
>
> Yes! I am drunk.
>
> (21 March). I am going to Ozerki.... "Will something happen?" It seems to me that I haven't drunk for a long time and I feel young. We will yet overcome. Life is so variedly impressionable, so many plans and thoughts. The spring sunset has died out. What will be? The railway coach sways.
>
> (5 December). An ever-increasing temptation not to be *alone*. What to do and how to live on? I still don't know. I have never yet experienced such abasement, horrible, irreparable, and pitiful.

Astounding entries. This is Blok's alter ego writing, who had already appeared on his path in early youth, in the era of *Verses on the Beautiful Lady*—drunk, dissolute, insane, and terrible. When his voice is heard, the poet abandons everything, sets out to the station of Ozerki or Sestroretsk and plunges into the dark elemental force:

> Shamelessly, endlessly sinning,
> Losing count of nights and days . . .

This is not simply carousing and drunkenness, but a frenzy of sin, a torment of conscience and a challenge to death. It seems that without the *Notebooks* our love for Blok would not be so tormenting and deep.

On 26 March, in the Society of Zealots of the Artistic Word, Vyacheslav Ivanov reads a subtly brilliant paper, "Legacies of Symbolism." In a reply to him, in the same Society, Blok comes forward on 8 April with an essay, "On the Present State of Russian Symbolism." Blok's lyrical prose hasn't yet been assessed; none of the critics have studied it seriously. But Blok is the creator of a completely new genre of artistic prose that has neither predecessors nor followers. In his lyrical articles he sets himself the unusually difficult task of verbally anchoring musical waves, of transmitting in images and sounds the internal rhythms of emotional movement. The article on symbolism is the most significant and most successful of all his attempts at *symbolizing the inexpressible*.

The author recognizes that Russian symbolism has reached the end of an important period of its development, and that the time has come to look back at the path covered. "We find ourselves," Blok says, "as if in a boundless ocean of life and art, already far from the shore, where we mounted the deck of a ship. We still can't make out the other shore, to which our dream, our creative will, draws us."

The poet calls his article a guidebook to an unknown country. It might seem incomprehensible to many, "but," the author adds, "to those for whom my guidebook is obscure, even our countries would remain in fog."

One must remember that the country described by Blok is a *mystical reality*; that its language—symbolic and allegorical—is the mystic's language; that he utilizes the same conventional, leading devices of exposition as the mystical writers of all time, beginning with Dionysius the Areopagite and ending with Theresa of Avila. The unavoidable premise of his personal philosophy is a real knowledge of "other worlds." To those who possess this knowledge, even to the most insignificant degree, Blok's "Baedeker" is comprehensible and useful. To others his descriptions are delirium and madness. The author declares emphatically: "The reality I describe is the only one which for me gives meaning to life, to the world, and to art. Either those worlds exist, or they don't. For those who will say 'they don't,' we will simply remain 'middling decadents,' authors of peculiar sensations." And even more emphatic is the poet's affirmation that *all his creative work* is based on the reality of "other worlds": "I dare to add that I would most humbly ask the respected critics and the public not to waste time on their failure to understand my poems, because my poems are merely a detailed and consistent description of what I am talking about in this article."

These sharp words exactly outline the circle of Russian symbolism. It is not literature at all, not even art; it is a mystical revelation related to the secret knowledge of the saints (Simeon the New Theologian, Francis of Assisi) and of the theosophists (Jakob Boehme, Ekaterina Emmerich, Swedenborg). "The symbolist," Blok says, "is already from the very start a *theurgist*, that is, the possessor of a secret knowledge, behind which stands secret action."

The second premise of symbolism is the contrast of mystical revelation with artistic creativity. Mystical experience reveals other worlds, the Promised Land; art, in Blok's expression, is a "monstrous and glorious Hell." The seer by the spirit, falling from the illuminated heights of Paradise, rushes headlong into the Hell of art. The artist is a fallen angel, Vrubel's beautiful Demon, a prophet who has betrayed his religious calling:

> To be an artist means to withstand the wind from the worlds of art, which don't resemble this world at all, but only influence it terribly. In those worlds are no cause and effect, no time and space, no corporeal and incorporeal, and these worlds are without number. Vrubel saw forty different heads of the Demon, but in reality they are innumerable.

Defining the nature of symbolism as a secret knowledge standing beyond art, Blok prepares us for the acceptance of a strange narrative "about events which have occurred and are occurring in actually existing worlds."

With the help of reminiscences about the visions which visited him in his youth, in the era of *Verses on the Beautiful Lady*, of the mystical poems of his teacher V. Solovyov and of the enigmatic images of the mad genius Vrubel, he speaks of the tragedy of Russian symbolism in the language of images, colors, and sounds.

It is played out in two acts. Blok calls them *thesis* and *antithesis*. The thesis is the appearance of the Radiant Visage. "In the azure of Someone's radiant gaze the theurgist abides; this gaze pierces all worlds like a sword; . . . and through all the worlds it reaches him at first only through the radiance of Someone's serene smile." From these worlds rush plaintive musical sounds, calls, almost words. Gradually the worlds take on color; their predominant color is lilac purple. "The Radiant Visage is *almost* incarnated, i.e., *the Name is almost guessed*." And here—on the dead center of triumph—the break to antithesis begins.

What had happened? And how can this be explained in words? A "change of countenance" ensues, as if someone had cut the golden thread; the blade of the radiant sword grows dim, and the world loses its purple hue. "The blue-lilac world twilight (the best representation of all these colors is in Vrubel) bursts into the rending accompaniment of violins and melodies, like gypsy songs."

In Blok's lyric the collection *Verses on the Beautiful Lady* corresponds to the thesis, the collection *The Earth in Snow* to the antithesis. The author illustrates his idea with a striking comparison. "If I were to paint a picture," he says, "this is how I would depict the experience of this moment: in the lilac twilight of the immense world sways an enormous white catafalque, and on it lies a dead doll with a face vaguely reminiscent of the one seen among the heavenly roses." One who experiences this is not alone; he is full of demon doubles, whom he makes an instrument of his evil creative will. They bring him the best treasures from the lilac worlds—and he throws them into the crucible of his artistic creativity. "Finally, with the help of incantations, [the poet] gets what he sought—to his own surprise and pleasure: what he sought is the doll-beauty." Blok recalls his lyrical dramas, his "cardboard bride" and the Stranger: "The Stranger is not at all simply a woman in a black dress with ostrich feathers on her hat. This is a diabolical fusion of many worlds, primarily blue and lilac. If I possessed Vrubel's means, I would create a Demon, but everyone does what is appointed to him."

A tragic catastrophe had occurred: the magical world was transformed into a puppet show booth, where the poet plays a role together with his amazing dolls. "In other words," the author explains, "I have already made my own life art. . . . And I stand before the creation of my own art and don't know what to do. . . . My creation *lives* beside me, neither alive nor dead, a blue phantom." But how is this tragedy to be understood? Why did the golden sword grow dim, why did the blue-lilac worlds gush out, ravage the soul, and make art out of life? Blok answers in one short sentence: "This is what happened: we were prophets—we wanted to become poets." The generation to which Blok belonged renounced its lofty calling, betrayed the sacred, deceived the fools. "Our 'literary reputation,' " he continues, "(which isn't worth a penny) visited us precisely when we had betrayed the 'Sacred Things of the Muses.' " The thesis of symbolism is an ascent to Paradise, to "other worlds"; the antithesis is a descent into the Hell of art. So it was, but it didn't have to be. The catastrophe was not ordained by fate. The responsibility for the betrayal lies with the symbolists. "Our sin (both personal and collective) is too great. From the position in which we now find ourselves, there are many horrible ways out." And Blok refers to the fate of Lermontov and Gogol, to Vrubel's madness and to Kommissarzhevskaya's death. "The artist is in the black air of Hell, privy to other worlds, and, when the golden sword grows dim . . . in art's dead of night the artist loses his mind and perishes."

But sin and atonement for sin is not the lot of symbolist artists alone: all Russia shares it with them:

> The revolution was accomplished not only in this, but also in other worlds; it too was one of the manifestations of the darkening of the gold and of the triumph of the lilac twilight, that is, of those events whose witnesses we were in our own souls. . . . Russia itself in the rays of the new . . . civic-mindedness turned out to be our own soul.

The thirst for repentance and atonement leads to thoughts of a "return to life," "public service," the church, the "people and the intelligentsia." Blok's publicism of 1909, his mystical populism in *Verses on Russia*, corresponds to this stage.

The tragedy of symbolism broadens to the limits of a Russian tragedy, and only on this plane does it take on all its significance. "We have experienced the madness of other worlds, prematurely demanding a miracle. The same thing took place in the people's soul; it demanded a miracle before its time, and the lilac worlds of revolution reduced it to ashes."

In conclusion Blok says:

> In our first youth a genuine promise was given to us. About the people's soul and about ours, reduced to ashes with it, one must say in a simple and courageous voice: "May they rise again." Perhaps we ourselves will perish too, but the dawn of this *first* love will remain.
>
> Our generation is given the choice between death in submission and a feat of courage. It must choose the feat and begin it with *obedience*. This is my conclusion: the path to the feat, which our service demands, is, first of all, apprenticeship, *self-absorption*, fixedness of gaze, and a spiritual diet....

This article is perhaps the most profound and most exhaustive witness to the new spirituality of the symbolist era. In his conclusions Blok agrees with Andrey Bely and Vyacheslav Ivanov. The three poet-mystics develop a new teaching about the world, life, and art. The tragedy of the symbolists lies in the fact that they couldn't become saints and didn't want to remain artists. But they carried the joyful news of the Radiant Visage and of the "contact with other worlds" (Dostoevsky's expression) through the terrible world in which they languished and perished.

Blok's lecture in the Society of Zealots was a great success. But the author was dissatisfied with it. "I read a paper in the 'Academy,' " he writes his mother, "for which they praised me, and for which Vyacheslav kissed me, but the paper is bad and wordy. I am running like the plague from words, in which I became completely entangled and wrapped myself in lies, to Shakhmatovo" (12 April).

The spring of 1910 passes to Wagner's music. Blok gets a season's ticket to the cycle "The Ring of the Nibelung" and listens avidly to the operas of the German composer. At the same time he reads Nietzsche, and the incantations of these two "demons" are reflected in the plan of the *poema Retribution*. "The influence of music," he writes his mother, "is not without purpose."

At the end of Easter Week, airplane flights began at the Kolomyazhsky hippodrome. Blok speaks of them as of a great event in his own personal life. "We just (evening) returned from the Kolomyazhsky hippodrome, where Latam tried to fly, but didn't. Twice he failed to take off, but the third time he did, described a circle, and landed again" (letter of 21 April). And three days later: "In man's flights, even unsuccessful ones, there is something ancient and predestined to humanity, consequently, lofty." The poem *The Pilot*[2] describes a pilot's flight and crash with great lyrical agitation. The poet questions the dead hero: Why did the screw stop? Why was the singing of the propeller suddenly broken off?

> Or did you learn the destructive
> Rapture of self-oblivion,
> Did you madly crave the crash
> And stop the screws yourself?
>
> Or did the horrible sight of coming wars
> Poison your unhappy brain,
> Night flier in the inclement haze,
> Carrying dynamite to earth?

The poem was sketched in 1910; the last verse is a clairvoyant's prophecy.

Finally, in St. Thomas' Week, Blok succeeds in escaping from Petersburg. For a long time he enthusiastically devotes himself to rebuilding the dilapidated Shakhmatovo home: the manor house is repaired; a second story is erected over the side annex; the owner himself settles into the new upper room which has a view of the fields and forests. Thirty people work—carpenters, painters, stone builders. The poet carries on long conversations with them, "rubs shoulders with the people." He especially likes one young painter, "the image of Filippo Lippi." But the idyll soon changes into a drama: quarrels with the contractor, petty troubles with the workers, delays, begging for vodka, lack of conscientiousness, petty larceny—these exhaust Blok. "House construction," he complains to his mother, "is a very painful nightmare, but the results can make up for all the troubles of tending thirty grown-up children." In July, Lyubov Dmitrievna brought the poet's mother to Shakhmatovo from the sanatorium. Blok decides to stay in the country for the whole winter, but at the end of October the snowstorms began; it became "dreary and terribly empty" in the new house after the departure of his mother and his aunt, Maria Andreevna. The poet is busy compiling a collection of poems, *Night Hours*, for the Musaget publishing house. "October," he writes his mother, "is of a different character than the Peterburgian, brighter; but I prefer the Peterburgian—completely black-yellow." The plan to winter in Shakhmatovo is abandoned. At the end of October Blok gets a telegram from Moscow: "Musaget, Halcyon, Logos[3] greet, love, and wait for Blok." He decides to go to Moscow before returning to Petersburg. On 1 November he is present at Bely's lecture on Dostoevsky in the Moscow Religious-Philosophical Society. A joyful meeting of the friends takes place. Bely recalls: "Blok seemed dried up, thin, but strong, healthy. We shook each other's stretched out, open hands firmly; looked each other straight in the eye." On the day of Bely's lecture the news of Tolstoy's departure from Yasnaya Polyana flew all over Moscow. Blok seemed very upset by this news. Bely describes his friend in the editorial office of Musaget. The poet is sitting on a gray-blue sofa in an oblique-angled room with pale yellow walls. The servant Dmitri brings enormous cups of tea. Blok enters into all the editorial plans of the new publishing house, approves its literary-philosophical program, dreams of publishing a journal-diary of the three symbolist writers (himself, V. Ivanov and Bely), carries on long, friendly conversations with E. K. Medtner. After dinner at Testov's, Bely takes his Petersburg guest to the Turgenevs. Asya,[4] small, with wavy hair and in a goat skin thrown over a loose blue coverall, examines the famous poet with curiosity. Going out onto the street from the Turgenevs, Bely asks Blok: "Well, how did you like Asya?" The latter replies: "Yes, she is such a sharp one, wild and piercing." The next day Blok leaves for Petersburg, finds a new apartment on Malaya Monetnaya Street—four attic rooms on the sixth floor with a view of Kamennoostrovsky Prospect and the lyceum garden. Blok called this apartment "young." The usual Petersburg "restless life" is resumed. The Bloks visit the hospitable home of Professor Evgeny Vasilievich Anichkov, where they meet Sologub, Chulkov, Verkhovsky, Remizov, Knyazhnin, and Pyast. As before, they visit V. Ivanov's tower, are present at evenings of the publisher of *Old Years* (*Starye gody*), Baron N. V. Drizen. Blok has a sharp clash with Merezhkovsky. On 14 September Dmitri Sergeevich's feuilleton, entitled "Religion and the Puppet Show Booth," appears in the newspaper *Russian Word* (*Russkoe Slovo*). Written apropos of Blok's and V. Ivanov's lectures on symbolism in the Society of Zealots, it contains an accusation against the symbolists for betraying the revolution and supporting reaction:

> In the opinion of the decadents, the Russian revolution is a puppet show booth, where the Beautiful Lady—Freedom—turned out to be a "cardboard bride" and a "dead doll," and human blood—"cranberry juice." I won't be surprised if tomorrow V. Ivanov, A. Blok and others turn out to be with the Iliodors and Hermogens.[5] Who today doesn't regard freedom as a "cardboard bride"? Who doesn't spit on the dimmed altar?

Blok was deeply resentful of this "denunciation." On 22 November he writes his mother:

> Mama, I have decided to answer Merezhkovsky's filth. It's better, even though it's late. . . .
> Men of the eighties, not born symbolists, but receiving symbolism from the West by inheritance (Merezhkovsky, Minsky), squandered it, and now kick what they are indebted to for their existence. Moreover, they are petty people, they love words too much, they sacrifice living people to them, they are submerged in the present, mix everything into one heap (religion, art, politics, etc.), and give themselves up to hysterics. I simply had to read Merezhkovsky a reprimand. They no longer, it seems, feel or understand anything.

Merezhkovsky answers Blok's biting letter with a long epistle. The poet informs his mother:

On 26 November I got a long reply from Merezhkovsky. It would have been better if he hadn't written at all; I got thoroughly angry. A Christian, unctuous letter, with assurances of "sincerity" and of "agitation," with explanations essentially dead. To this I wrote him at still greater length and more bitingly (already to Paris; they had left). I won't object in print—it's too late, and Zhenya talked me out of it.

The "open" letter to Merezhkovsky remained unfinished. It was printed only after Blok's death, in the *Russian Contemporary* (*Russky Sovremennik*) in 1924.

The poet responds to Merezhkovsky's insinuations with calm dignity. Why does the assertion "as Russia, so also we" seem so self-assured to the critic? Can a writer really not feel his tie to his native land, be ill with its illnesses, suffer its sufferings? Blok speaks about his native land with a kind of special, piercing tenderness:

One's native land is a vast, dear, breathing being, like a person, only infinitely more agreeable, affectionate, helpless than an individual person. . . .
The native land is fated to be abandoned sometime, like a mother. . . . We always see this doom of abandonment in large, maternal eyes, always sad, even when she is resting and quietly rejoicing.

A lyrical poem grew out of the controversy. It wasn't an answer to Merezhkovsky, but a declaration of love for the "earthly native land, which still gives us to drink and feeds us at the breast."

On 14 December, on the tenth anniversary of V. Solovyov's death, at an evening in the Tenishevsky School, Blok gives a speech, "The Knight-Monk." This is his last public appearance in 1910. The content of this speech we already know.[6] The poet remained dissatisfied with Solovyov's literary memorial evening. He informs his mother:

The Solovyov evening went dully, so that it would have been better if it hadn't even been held. They congregated actresses and then themselves regretted it. I demonstratively left the first row during Musina's reading and heard none of Vedrinskaya's. I began the second section, thought the whole time of drinking tea and wetting my whistle. . . . The only good thing was Poliksena Sergeevna.[7]

The year 1910 is an important stage in Russia's literary life. The autocracy of the symbolist school is coming to an end. A reaction against the symbolist theory of art begins to appear; new trends arise, which at first timidly and then more and more boldly and openly protest against mysticism, "myth-making," a "religious transformation of the world." The provocative and witty "manifesto" of M. A. Kuzmin, a former symbolist but now a "clarist," appears in the new journal *Apollo*. He calls poets to descend from the spaces beyond the stars onto the dear, beautiful earth, to forget about symbols in the name of reality, to abandon foggy mysticism for the sake of "beautiful clarity." He contrasts the French eighteenth century to the Jena romantic school, a real rose to the invented "blue flower." Kuzmin's verses ring with a bold challenge to the symbolists:

> Where will I find the style to describe a walk,
> Chablis on ice, a toasted roll,
> And the agate of sweet ripe cherries?

Briusov writes about this "schism" to P. Pertsov (23 March 1910):

> There is a great schism in our circle of decadents: the struggle of the "clarists" with the "mystics." The "clarists" are *Apollo*—Kuzmin, Makovsky, et al. The mystics are the Moscow Musaget—Bely, V. Ivanov, Solovyov, et al. In essence, the decrepit, the very decrepit, argument about free art and tendentiousness is resumed. The "clarists" defend lucidity of thought, style, images. But this is only a form, and actually they are defending "poetry, whose aim is poetry," as the old man Ivan Sergeevich[8] said. The mystics preach a "renovated symbolism," "myth-making" and the like, but actually they want poetry to serve their Christianity, to be an *ancilla theologiae*. Not long ago in Free Esthetics we had a great battle on this question. The result, it seems, is that Musaget has decisively separated itself from Scorpion with respect to ideology. I, as you guess, am with all my heart with the clarists.

The last phrase is amazingly characteristic of Briusov. He was acknowledged by all as a maître of decadence when the decadents were in fashion; then he became a "grand wizard," the leader of the symbolists in the era of the predominance of this school; now he is "with all his heart with the clarists." He is always "with all his heart" with the new, the strong, the victorious—in this lies the secret of his eternal youth. Briusov's renunciation of symbolism is a symptom of the internal collapse of the school. From 1910 it enters a period of slow dying away and decay; the revolution of 1917 deals it the final, mortal blow. But no "trend" resulted from "clarism." The delicate, young-looking Kuzmin and the lyrical Makovsky weren't suited to be literary leaders. Their ideas were snatched up by the contemporary youth, at whose head was the bold "conquistador and discoverer of new lands," the energetic and gifted Nikolai Stepanovich Gumilyov. Bely tells of his meeting the author of "Pearls" in V. Ivanov's tower. Gumilyov, in a dress coat, a top hat on his knees, with a wooden figure and the triangular nose of a Pierrot, quarrels with a consequential air with the agitated V. Ivanov. Slowly, in a rather hollow voice, in measured tones, he explains to the maître that symbolism is at an end and that a new literary movement is coming to replace it. Ivanov derisively proposes calling this movement "Adamism," hinting at the edenic cultural innocence of its representatives, or "acmeism," from the Greek word *acme*—summit. Gumilyov takes Ivanov's irony seriously: thus "acmeism" or "Adamism," a group headed by Gumilyov and Gorodetsky, still another deserter from the symbolist camp, is born. The tiny journal *Hyperborean* (*Giperborey*) is published, and the Guild of Poets is organized. *Apollo* opens its pages to the new school and Gumilyov preaches "neo-classicism" in "Letters on Russian Poetry." This movement with a purely negative program—the battle with symbolism—would have existed no longer than "clarism" had there not proved to be a few real poets in the group of acmeists: besides the "leaders"—Gumilyov and Gorodetsky—there were Anna Akhmatova and Osip Mandelshtam, the best Russian poets after Blok.[9]

After the wearisome summer of "house building" and the troubled Petersburg autumn, Blok felt a great decline in strength at the beginning of 1911. The doctor found neurasthenia and prescribed treatment with spermine and Swedish massage. Three times a week the poet went to a Swedish masseur and got rapidly stronger. "The massage is proceeding successfully," he informs his mother. "The Swede praises my *prächtige muskulatur*. Around my back and chest something not unlike a musical instrument is forming." But his emotional state was, as before, depressed: the increasing hostility between his mother and his wife made him despondent. Aleksandra Andreevna didn't recover in the sanatorium in Sokolniki. Her nervous illness expressed itself in extreme irritability, sensitivity, and tormenting fastidiousness. The slightest speck led her to despair. After the attacks she would fall into a gloomy dejection, would say: "I am a great sinner, I know the devil well." Several times she attempted suicide. She could barely endure people. Periods of pathological mysticism alternated with periods of passionate God-defiance, and then she would announce that Christianity had had its day, that it is impossible to believe in the divinity of Christ, that worship and prayer are superstition. Adoring her son, she was jealous of his wife, and in the summer of 1910 painful scenes occurred between her and Lyubov Dmitrievna in Shakhmatovo. In January 1911, F. F. Kublitsky got a brigade in Poltava, and Blok's mother wanted to spend the spring in Petersburg before her departure for the provinces. Lyubov Dmitrievna announced that she couldn't meet her. Blok was torn to pieces by this discord. His letters to his mother betray his confusion and depression:

> (3 January). On the thirty-first Lyuba and I talked all day. In the evening Zhenya came and found us in very difficult conversations.
> (14 February). I couldn't fall asleep for a long time and was sad, which hasn't happened for a long time.... In the morning everything had passed, but I suddenly decided to find myself a separate apartment (Lyuba and I have been talking about this for a long time).... I decided to postpone a decision until today.... My whole departure, which didn't take place, is connected with painful thoughts of two nights ago, and everything is connected to the relationship between you and Lyuba, which constantly torments me (we barely speak about this). But leaving won't solve the problem. Sometimes I think that everything will be solved somehow, when the time comes. And what do you think? There is something radiant in Lyuba these days.
> (17 February). I already talked with Zhenya rather a long time ago, a

month ago. He considers that not everything is in Lyuba's hands, and that there are two kinds of truth, which battle in you and Lyuba apart from yourselves. I agree with this.... Actually I think that it is now more than ever necessary to leave all this to *time*, because the way to immediately clear all this up is not in my hands, nor yours, nor Lyuba's. I don't see the possibility at all and I don't know how to influence Lyuba in this respect; I could probably ruin it.... Aunt had dinner with us on the fifteenth; after dinner she talked with Lyuba for a long time about you. Lyuba says that it's fine.

(21 February). Actually, I am relying on *time*: that everything will be settled. And now it is necessary to simply take a recess—for the mutual improvement of relations. This is how it seems to me (and to Lyuba): when you come here I don't know which is better—for you to see Lyuba or not. Lyuba says that she can meet you very well, but that nevertheless there will be falsehood in this. We'll see this later.... I think it will also be useful for me to live without Lyuba.

For the sake of his mother's tranquility Blok decides to part from his wife for a while. This is the plan: Aleksandra Andreevna will settle in Shakhmatovo in the spring, and Lyubov Dmitrievna will go abroad, where Blok will join her in two months. The son writes his mother on 16 March: "As for the fact that we will be in the same house, that is all to the good. All the circumstances have changed, it will be good for you to meet Lyuba." Blok is afraid his mother will guess the sacrifice he is making for her; therefore: "everything will be fine." Finally, the last letter about the "relations" between his wife and his mother (19 March):

> Lyuba hasn't changed at all, essentially. But there is no longer a reason for clashes. She lives an entirely different life. I am sure you can simply meet her, so that there wouldn't be a ridiculous avoidance of one another.
> But it is difficult to write about all this—and painful. One must just treat all this more simply—without "relations."

That is how one writes to a sick child, soothingly, cheerfully, with solicitous tenderness: neither complaints, nor reproaches, but infinite meekness and self-sacrifice. Only at the end does an involuntary admission burst out: "It is difficult to write about this—and painful."

The treatment and the Swedish gymnastics restore the poet's strength. At the end of February he experiences an unexpected renewal of life, both physical and emotional, and he writes his mother a remarkable letter (21 February) about this improvement:

> As a matter of fact I feel much strengthened physically (and, consequently, morally) and therefore have many plans, so far indefinite.... I feel that finally, in my thirty-first year, a very important change has taken shape in me, which is expressed both in the *poema*[10] and in my sense of the world. I think the last shadow of "decadence" has departed. I definitely want to live and I see ahead many simple, good, and fascinating possibilities—moreover, where I didn't see them before. On the one hand I am a

"social animal," I have a real enthusiasm for journalism and a need for contact with people—more and more, actually. On the other hand I have become stronger physically and can take physical culture very seriously, which must proceed on a level with the spiritual. . . . I am able to read with enthusiasm articles on the peasant question and . . . the most banal novels of Breshko-Breshkovsky. . . . By the way of explanation I can say that my *Europeanism* consists of this. Europe should invest in form and flesh that deep and ever-elusive content with which every Russian soul is filled. Hence the constant need for form, my need in particular; form is the flesh of the idea. . . . A real work of art in our time (and in any, probably) can arise only when: (1) a direct (not abstract) relationship to the world supports it; and (2) when my own art is related to others (for me personally—to music, art, architecture and *gymnastics*).

I tell you all this so you won't be frightened by my tendencies, which you didn't expect, and so you would know that I have a need to *broaden* the circle of my life, which until now has been *deepened* (at the expense of the proper breadth). I don't know whether I'll accomplish anything in this direction. In any event, for the time being I will busy myself with massage and gymnastics.

"Accounts with the past are settled." Blok enters a new period of his life—the era of "realism" of the *poema Retribution*. Not only "decadence," but also symbolism, is left far behind; deepening gives way to broadening. Romantic spirituality gives way to the classical rule *mens sana in corpore sano*. In the foreground stands the question of form, of embodiment, of *reality*. The romantic tries to produce a revolution in his own inner world. The *poema Retribution* testifies to its lack of success.

Not long ago the poet still felt himself a prisoner in a "terrible world," and the "sounds of the heavens" prevented him from listening to the "boring songs of earth." Now he wanted to become deaf to the celestial sounds, to settle on earth, and to take on flesh once and for all. How indicative is the striving for "physical culture"—gymnastics, track and field, wrestling. Blok enthusiastically visits the circus and studies the rules of wrestling. He writes his mother:

> Wrestling fascinates me very much, and any strengthening of muscles, and these interests already occupy a definite place in my life; rather unexpectedly for me, . . . artistic creativity is connected with this. . . . In the world orchestra of arts "gymnastics" doesn't occupy the last place; . . . it is an exact copy of the ancient wrestling in Greece and Rome.
>
> I have very many observations (my own) on the art of wrestling, on the quality of individual artists. . . . Only one of those I have seen possesses real genius—the Dutchman Van Ril. He inspires me for the *poema* much more than Vyacheslav Ivanov.

Blok becomes a sportsman: he learns roller skating, goes to Yukki with Pyast for winter sports. "Yesterday I had an amazingly good time with Pyast," he informs his mother. "We went on foot from Levashov to Yukki; on the highway we ate bread and sausage, drank tea in Yukki, and tobagganed down a high hill. There is the so-called 'Russian

Switzerland'—hills, snowy slopes, and dense pine forests." In his memoirs Pyast writes: "Blok so took to tobaggoning from hills that in the summer, in Luna Park, he went down the 'roller coaster' eighty times."

In the spring he sets out on a big excursion to Sestroretsk with Pyast and Yuri Verkhovsky. "This began in the evening at Blok's," Pyast relates, "where other guests besides us were present. . . . The three of us didn't go to bed, talked until six and set out to Primorsky Station for the first train." Pyast later described this trip in an epistle to Verkhovsky:

> I remembered last spring
> And the day of our twenty-four hour, sleepless,
> And innocent outing, when the string
> Of your old-fashioned viol began to sing.
>
> And the bushes overgrown with stunted green
> On the shore of the small, winding stream;
> You again slept there, grave and tired,
> We watched over your sleep.
>
> You slept peacefully, and *I and that poet*
> (Ah, now become unsociable and gloomy!)
> Conducted a council in an undertone
> About everything inexpressible . . .
>
> Then you washed, scooping up water
> With your top hat, as if it were brass . . .
> Ah, will I forget the pastry shells at dinner
> Amid the other food?

Pyast remembers still another outing, with Blok and E. P. Ivanov, to Peterhof on bicycles. Blok loved this sport very much, and with tenderness named his bicycle "Vaska."

But the striving to "take on flesh" was not limited merely to physical culture. The poet also fostered in himself the "social animal." He began to take a lively interest in politics. "I read newspapers with frenzy," he informs his mother. "*Speech* has become very lively and keenly interesting. Milyukov has blossomed and gotten stronger, has become intelligent and broad to the point of unrecognizability. . . . I hate the Russian government—my *poema* is saturated with this." Blok even sets out for Milyukov's lecture, "The Armed Peace and the Limitation of Armaments," and finds it "brilliant and intelligent." Apropos of this lecture he writes prophetic words to his mother: "Perhaps we will still have to see three great wars, our own Napoleons, and a new picture of the world."

The drinking bouts in restaurants outside the city practically cease; meetings with chance "strangers" become rarer and rarer. Now and then reports flash in the letters to his mother: "At night I saw _____ home (across the island)—in a smart cab and against the wind." Or he writes: "Yesterday I drank champagne (a little, a little) and took _____ to Strelka. This embellished the *poema*, even if it wasn't so fine." Finally: "I found a beautiful Jewess, resembling a black pearl in a pink shell.

She had Titian arms and a dazzling figure. But the affair didn't go beyond champagne and red roses, and turned sad."

And all this—the wrestling, and the sport, and the country outings, and the politics, and even driving to the islands with women—is a collection of materials for the *poema*. In 1911 the poet wrote only two poems; he wrote no prose at all. All his creative energy was absorbed by *Retribution*. In its original conception the *poema* did not exceed the dimensions of *The Night Violet*. On 3 January the author informs his mother: "Yesterday I finished writing (almost) the *poema*, which I have been working on for a long time and want to dedicate to Angelina."[11] But by the end of the month the *poema* is growing. "I am writing the *poema*, one small chapter a day. I am satisfied with it" (letter of 30 January). On 24 February a plan for the characterization of the central hero is outlined in the *Notebook*—the first appearance of autobiographical material:

> There were no events in my hero's life. He lived a quiet life with his relatives in the Pobedonostsev period. Since childhood he was silent, and an agitation, restless and indefinite, built up in him more and more strongly. Meanwhile Tsushima drew near, and the bloody dawn of 9 January.[12] He reacted to everything like a poet, he was a mystic; in the surrounding anxiety he saw a portent of the end of the world. The ever-spreading events were for him only images of the developing chaos. Soon his agitation found a channel: he found himself in a society of people from whose lips the words "revolution," "mutiny," "anarchy," "madness," never departed. Here were beautiful women "with perpetually crumpled roses on their breasts," with raised heads and slightly opened lips. Wine flowed in a river. Each one "raved," each one wanted to destroy the family, the home—his own and others'. My hero became engrossed in this mad game, in that indefinitely stormy *Weltanschauung* which laughed at everything, supposing that it understands everything. Once, with a completely empty head, light, carefree, but already with a protest concealed in his soul against his aimless and disastrous existence, he ran up the stairs of his house.
>
> Two letters lay on the table. One—perfumed, ungrammatical and passionate. . . . Then he opened the second. It informed him briefly that his father was near death in a Warsaw hospital.
>
> Abandoning everything, he rushed to Warsaw. Loneliness in the railway coach, "policemen, rails, lanterns." First impressions of Warsaw.

That is how the poet saw his past in 1911; the *poema*'s ironic style was determined by this sketch. The buoyant tone of the letters to his mother, and the re-education according to the rule "a sound mind in a sound body" is the facade of the poet's life. The *Notebook* also sometimes reveals a bit of the underground.

Thus, on 15 March, sitting in the Nikolaevsky Station, he notes: "The most secret thoughts: 'to secretly destroy oneself' (this is just talk). For all that, I am healthy, fresh, strong. Wine. —No, nothing."

Finally, on 17 May, he departs for Shakhmatovo. Blok notes:

We are leaving—Lyuba in the evening for Berlin, I in the afternoon for Shakhmatovo.

People, aviation, Sestroretsk, a sleepless night, a dusty and hot spring, drafts, Pyast's confession, . . . Through it all—sadness and perplexity at parting with Lyuba for the summer. And within, a kind of gnawing apathy and listlessness.

The poet spends six weeks with his mother in Shakhmatovo; he busies himself with managing the estate and correcting the proofs of *Night Hours*. In the *Notebook*: "I am sick of all poems—even my own. More proofs of *Night Hours* came. To detach myself as soon as possible, to finish also the edition of the *Collection*—and not to write any more lyric poems until old age." In May the first volume of Blok's complete *Collection of Poems* comes out in the publishing house Musaget.[13] The poet calls Pyast urgently to Shakhmatovo:

> Could you come here for a few days? Lots of room, a comfortable life, quietness and fragrance. It would be interesting and, I think, necessary for you to see this Russia, 60 versts from Moscow, as if 1000. A fragrant backwoods, in an earthly paradise. Rough, unfortunate and downtrodden people with antediluvian ideas, having forgotten themselves. (24 May)

The theme of the countryside is developed in detail in another letter to Pyast:

> You owe it to yourself to get to know the Russian *countryside*, if only individual spots. First of all, those without which it is impossible to get to know Russia in general (that is, Great Russia); secondly, those places in which your own family lived and was formed. . . .
>
> I think you know this, but you don't conceive clearly enough what a knowledge of the countryside can give, to what a degree it can change the congenital demonism (about which we talked, do you remember?). It can change in two directions: either kill it, that is smash all will, make man Russian in the Chekhovian sense (or Rudinian,[14] perhaps); or increase it tenfold, that is, sharpen the will, tune it, perhaps in the *super*-European manner.
>
> Even not to know the countryside (I speak this way because *it may already be impossible for us to get to know it*, and the division, begun during the reigns of Peter and Catherine, into enemy camps must sometime naturally end in a terrible slaughter), even not to know, but *only* to see with one's own eyes and to love, even if hating.

At the end of June Blok spends a week in Petersburg before going abroad. On 2 June he has a romantic adventure, which so struck him that he describes it three times: in a letter to Pyast, in a letter to his mother, and in the *Notebook*.

This is what he writes to Pyast:

As a matter of fact, Petersburg is a remote province, and the remote province is a "terrible world." Yesterday I took a ticket to Pargolovo and set out on a seven-hour train. Suddenly I saw a poster in Ozerki: a gypsy concert. I felt that this was fate, and . . . stayed in Ozerki. And, really, they sang God knows what; they rent the heart completely. [Variant in the letter to his mother: "And, really, it turned out that the gypsy girl who sang about a great number of worlds then told me unusual things."] But at night in Petersburg, under a pouring rain, that gypsy girl, who was at the root of the matter, let me kiss her hand—dark, with long fingers, all in an armor of prickly rings. Then I reeled along the street, dragged myself, wet, to the Aquarium, where they had gone to sing, looked in the gypsy girl's eyes, and dragged myself home. That's all, but today that all is somehow rather different and a bit terrifying. [Variant in the letter to his mother: "Then, under a pouring rain, in the night twilight on the platform, she flashed her long fingers in an armor of sharp rings, and yesterday turned into a bloody dawn ('a poem!')."]

In the *Notebook* the story of this meeting is accompanied by an entry: "Terrible world. But to be with you is strange and sweet."

This triple entry is actually a "poem" of great charm: a presentiment of a meeting with another gypsy—"Carmen."

On 5 July Blok leaves for Brittany: on the way he sees Paris and, for the first and last time, especially likes this city, "bluish and mysterious." Lyubov Dmitrievna is waiting for him on the small beach, Abervrach, near Brest. They settle down in a seventeenth century house that was once a church. The poet is charmed by "poor and dear Brittany." The large bay with an outlet to the ocean is surrounded by maritime signals; gulls cry during the ebb tide; along the roads, amid thorny bushes, are stone crosses with Christ and the Madonna. "The voice of the ocean is altogether uncommon. . . . At night the ocean sings very distinctly and loudly, but during the day one can only see how the spray scatters on the rocks." The poem *Do you remember?*[15] is devoted to Abervrach; in its light rhythm is the breath of the ocean, and the salt wind, and the fog pierced by the sun:

> Do you remember? In our sleepy bay
> The green water slept,
> When the war ships sailed
> In formation.
>
> Four—gray. And questions
> Agitated us for a whole hour,
> And sunburned sailors
> Walked past us grandly.

And the last verse reads:

> By chance, on a pocket-knife,
> Find a speck of the dust of far-off countries—

> And the world will again appear strange,
> Wrapped in colored fog.

Blok finds something Chekhovian in the local inhabitants: a doctor, a drunken old man with green eyes, runs along the embankment from morning till evening with a thick book about the lives of the Breton saints in his hands; a failed architect sadly relates that he was forced to marry the daughter of a manufacturer; and a "propriétaire" fishes and remembers how he was in Petersburg with Admiral Gervais' squadron. Blok bathes, walks on the hill above the sea, looks at the torpedo boats entering the bay, and is thoroughly bored in this "Hyperborean hamlet." After spending a few days in Quimper, the Bloks arrive in Paris on 27 August. In these hot summer days Paris strikes the poet with its deadness. "Paris is a Sahara," he writes, "yellow boxes, among which, like dead oases, are gray-black bulks of dead churches and castles." The theft of the Giaconda from the Louvre seems to him an event full of secret significance. The culture of Europe is doomed. "One wants to wash one's hands of this puddle formed from human blood, transformed into dirty water. . . . Here all the monstrous absurdity which civilization has reached is clear." Further on he tells his mother about a strike of 250,000 workers in England, about the feverish arming of Germany and France, and adds: "Wilhelm seeks war and apparently *will* fight." He compares Russia with Europe. "Slavdom," he writes, "never entered their civilization and, what is most important, flew past like a kind of alien astral body through the whole Catholic *culture*. This is especially interesting to me." At the beginning of September, Lyubov Dmitrievna returns to Petersburg, and Aleksandr Aleksandrovich goes to Antwerp, Bruges, Rotterdam and Amsterdam. Belgium and Holland disappoint him. He describes Bruges, so celebrated by Rodenbach, with humor:

> A boatman dragged me along the canals for an hour and a half. Actually—canals, swans, old medieval stuff, some thousand-year-old sunflowers and elders along the banks. Turning back: "And now a new view, *n'est-ce pas?*" But there was nothing especially new: another elder grove, another sunflower and another dog barking at the boat from the shore.

In Antwerp Blok enters in the *Notebook*: "From yesterday another fit of depression. In general it is harmful for me abroad: the odor, the sound of voices (especially French), the *fleas* (French ones are the vilest and hardest to get rid of)." He decides to return straight to Petersburg, through Berlin. He spends whole days in Berlin in museums and sends his mother a thick envelope with pictures of animals from the zoo. In the Reinhardt Theater he sees the famous Moissi in the role of Hamlet:

> This is a Berlin Kachalov, only somewhat younger and therefore less developed. . . .
> I sat in the first row and especially felt the cold from the stage when the

curtain rose, and Marcellus began to warm himself by the bonfire in the gray darkness of the winter night, on the background of the dark sky....

Reinhardt, a German Stanislavsky, thought up a very good chirring sound on the appearance of the ghost: not exactly a rooster in the distance, but—who knows what.

On 7 September Blok arrives in Petersburg and learns joyful news: his stepfather, Kublitsky, got a brigade not in Poltava, but in Petersburg. Aleksandra Andreevna settles with her husband on Officers' Street and sees her son often. When his affairs prevent Blok from dropping in on his mother, he mails her short notes of such content: "Mama, you are very sad. But I am thinking about you. Sasha."

In October the fourth collection of his poems, *Night Hours*, comes out. The poems of this book later entered the third volume of his *Collected Poems*.

The Petersburg "yellow-black" autumn envelops the poet in the habitual depression: "It seems it was never so bad for me as now," he writes Pyast on 19 September.

On 17 October 1911 Blok begins to keep a diary and continues it till the end of 1913. His decision is thus motivated:

> We must all write a diary or at least make notes from time to time about the most essential. It is highly probable that our times are great and that namely we are standing in the center of life, that is, in the place where all the spiritual threads come together, where all the sounds are leading.

In the *Diary* we find a chronicle of Petersburg literary life, brief characterizations of writers, reflections on history and culture, and surprising lyrical entries on emotional states: the struggle with the spirit of emptiness, wanderings in the depths of the "terrible world," and dreams, visions, and ecstasies. Blok creates a new form of lyrical confession, free, flexible, keenly expressive. The "people's poet," Nikolai Klyuev, continues to play a big role in his life. After a two-year correspondence Klyuev comes to see him:

> (17 October). I expected a peasant, foulmouthed,[16] P. Karpov—swarthy faced. He enters—without the face, without the voice, not exactly an old man, not exactly middle aged (and he is twenty-three?). But the next time Klyuev is alone, hours—it is boring, I am exhausted. And suddenly infinite rest, his tenderness, his "benediction," his story that they are singing me in the Olonetsk province.... And so clearly and simply for the first time in life—why L. D. Semyonov and even A. M. Dobrolyubov live as they do.
>
> (6 December). I am reading Klyuev's letter. *I know everything that must be done*: to return the money, to repent, to give away my dinner jackets, even books. But I can't, I don't want to. I have finished the short poem: *In the trees' black twigs*.
>
> (9 December). Klyuev's epistle sings in my soul all these days. No—it is still early to leave this beautiful and terrible world.
>
> (17 December). Today I am upset. For the third day—tormenting....

> I wrote to Klyuev: "Much of my life is dark and confused, but I don't lose heart."
>
> (23 December). I was at the Merezhkovskys' from four till eight, saw Zinaida Nikolaevna and Merezhkovsky and Filosofov. . . . I read Klyuev's letter, everyone swore at him like troopers. . . . All this wasn't painful for me, but wordy, not quite right.

Blok's faith in Klyuev's "folk wisdom" and lofty righteousness begins to waver. On 24 December he notes: "We drank evening tea; before bed we thought of lighting the Christmas tree. It is painful for me, both because of the holiday, as always, and because of doubts and weariness, which make me sleepy, humiliated, and unhappy. I have doubts about Merezhkovsky, about Klyuev, about everything."

Klyuev lectured, preached, insisted that Blok abandon everything and "go to the people," as Semyonov and Dobrolyubov did. It is surprising that the poet didn't notice the crude counterfeit of this bast "muzhik," that he took his "*bylina*" bombast seriously. E. Knipovich[17] justifies Blok's error by his terrible emotional isolation:

> Only this can explain his enthusiasm for Klyuev's letters. These letters were preserved in Blok's archive. And now, reading them, it is difficult, almost impossible, to understand how this high-flown twaddle about the "betrothal of the servant of God Aleksandr to the servant of God Russia" could seem like something serious to Blok. . . . It is true, it seemed to Blok that behind Klyuev stood the people, mysterious, with an indefinite yearning for indefinite freedom, for the Kingdom of God on earth.

In the *Diary* representatives of the intelligentsia—V. Ivanov and Merezhkovsky—are contrasted to the representative of the people—Klyuev. Blok writes about V. Ivanov:

> If you want to preserve him—remove yourself from him once and for all. He shaved his beard, and an inexpressibly horrible line was etched on his chin. Inside, Goethe, "classicism," wails (be, be calmer). He bites, chops, hisses, strikes with his tail, teases; great, but less than he *should* be (or could have been). (17 October)

And about Merezhkovsky:

> All these evenings I have been reading Merezhkovsky's *Aleksandr the First*. A writer who never loved anyone in a human way, but who is upsetting. Fastidious, rational, unkind, suspicious even of historical personages; he repeats himself, but he troubles one. Is insanely bored, just like his Aleksandr in his study, but in places an unheard-of beauty. (23 October)

In brief notes on young poets, Blok writes: "Conversation with N. S. Gumilyov and his good verses about how the heart has become a Chinese doll." At a party at V. Ivanov's "Anna Akhmatova read poems, agitating me; poems, one better than the other." "Kuzmin read good poems, sang from *Khovanshchina* with Karatygin. He became somehow good, transparent, crystalline." "Elizaveta Yurievna Kuzmina-Karavaeva read poems, Black Sea coast, her 'Bridge.' "

A diary entry of 30 October speaks of an "important change" in his life, of a return to reality and "humanity":

> I am writing Borya [Bely] and thinking: we abused "psychology" because we had lived through a "spineless" epoch, as V. Ivanov said yesterday in the Academy. The epoch has passed and, consequently, we again need our *whole* soul, everything ordinary, the whole man. It is impossible to love gypsy dreams, one can only be consumed by them. I love life madly, more each day, everything ordinary, simple and complex, both uninspired and gypsy.
> Let's return to psychology. . . .
> Back to the soul, not only to "man," but also to "the whole man" . . . with spirit, soul, and body, with the ordinary—triply so.

The poet wants life, health, clarity, but the dark doubles draw him downward, into the terrible world of gypsy dreams. "Horrors" whirl around him, apparitions surround him with sleepless nights. The *Diary* entries from week to week, from month to month, register the stages of the stubborn struggle of a captive spirit. The history of Blok's soul excites in us horror and sympathy, as in an authentic tragedy. A note of 13 [14] November could be taken as a prologue to it: "The meaning of tragedy is the *hopelessness of the struggle*; but here is no despair, no inertia, no dropping of one's arms. A lofty dedication is demanded." Blok had this dedication: he was given the role in life of the *tragic hero*.

Let us trace through time his life in the "terrible world"—the alternation of ecstasies, falls, passions, and flights.

The lyrical theme of Petersburg sounds in the first entry: "Many more women, wine, Petersburg—the most terrible, inviting, and blood-rejuvenating of all European cities" (17 October). How the light and air of the loved and hated city is retained in his memory: "On the islands—twilight, the rosy smoke of clouds, mire, and in the clay the green leaves mixed with clay. The wind washes the cheeks" (19 October):

> There again the accursed moon shines, and as soon as you open the small window,[18] the wind bursts in. Not yet despair. If only today one could sleep a bit better, and now forget everything, . . . so that it would become quiet. . . . The full moon is horrible, under it the world becomes a naked, deformed corpse. (25 October)

And again about Petersburg: "Gay city, drunken cabby, everything would have ended with the usual ecstasy, if Zhenya hadn't come after dinner" (26 October). Ecstasies are replaced by fears: "In the evening fears came upon me. At night I woke up; I write quietly, thank God, become calmer, pray. Mama says she always prays aloud, and that there is no salvation but prayer" (30 October). Emotional anxiety draws the external world into its movement. "Sky—in the morning downpour and darkness; by three o'clock—broken clouds and red feathers, the wind rises, the stars are visible" (4 November). And again there is wine—drunken nights, ecstasy, and exhaustion. "Again two mad days. On the evening of the fifth, after a horrible conversation with mama, . . . I immediately got drunk in the Tyrol on Officers' Street" (6 November). "In the evening again desperate inspiration, ecstasy bordering on exhaustion. I went to Ozerki. . . . The air these days is like water. Mute sea bottom. The city; something is happening in it. Madness, madness and ecstasy. But today I will calmly go to bed. I will protect . . . " (8 November). There follows a story about a trip in a smart cab with an "acrobat" from the Variety Show. Blok transforms the "adventure" into a lyrical *poema* about the northern night:

> But now there is no end to the nights—November, *our* whole world, is filled with night. . . . In the dead of night, about twelve o'clock, I went out. Restaurant and wine. . . . A smart cab. Variety Show. The acrobat comes out, I beg her to go. We fly, the night yawns. I am completely beside myself. Whether it is the same cab or another, I don't know; . . . they are all voices out of the night. She covers her mouth with her hand—all night. I tear her lace; there is a kind of power and mystery in these coarse hands and sharp heels. . . . I take her back. Something sacred, like a daughter, a child. She steals away in a lane, familiar and unfamiliar; dead of night. . . . Cold, biting, all the branches of the Neva are full, night everywhere, as at six in the evening, so at six in the morning, when I return home.
>
> Today is hopeless, of course. . . . Something hurts in my chest, I want to moan, because this eternal night preserves and increases ten-fold the same feeling. To the point of madness. I almost want to cry.
>
> . . . Again night—streetcar sparks. Evening, morning—these are ends and beginnings. In our November there are no beginnings and endings —all one growing thing, rebellious, piercing like needles with amorousness, with madness, with moans, with ecstasy.
>
> I probably won't see this woman again, and it isn't necessary to see her: . . . she "disembodies" my passions, casts them into the heavens with her Saxon eyes. . . .
>
> It is both terrible and wonderful to live in the world. If one could fall asleep peacefully today.

The plot of the *poema* is a banal adventure with a girl from the Variety Show. But this is semblance: in the poetic reality—the acrobat—the northern, insidious night is mysterious and endless, carrying away, piercing with amorousness, ecstasy, madness, and tears. In this "amorous adventure" sensuality dissolves in the voices of the night, passion is "disembodied" and "cast into the heavens." An entry about a surprising dream of love serves as an epilogue to the *poema*: in it, blood sings like the streams of a river, embraces scorch like a hot wind. All of Blok's lyric poetry springs from this "singing of the blood":

> Resting (from what, one doesn't know), the blood in you sings barely audibly, like the pink streams of a large river before sunrise. I see how the

blood flows measuredly, calmly, and gaily under the skin of your cheeks and in the resilient muscles of your naked arms. And my blood becomes younger in response, so that our fingers stretch toward one another and intertwine, against our will, with inexplicable tenderness. It is still difficult for them to meet, because it seems to me that you are sitting on a tall ladder resting against the white wall of a house, and above you it is already light, and I am below, by the lowest rungs, where it is still foggy and dark. Soon the wind of my arms, burning itself on you, and becoming hot, takes you down from above, and our lips can meet, because you are on a level with me. Then the whistle and tinkling of viols in my ears begins, and my eyes, submerged in your gay, wide-open eyes, already see you below. I become enormous, and you quite small. I surround you easily like a large cloud; you—a bird which has dived into the cloud and calls rapturously.

In the middle of November the poet experienced a puzzling event on the mystical plane, an event which shook him terribly. He can't explain it, but he knows "something had happened to him," "he lost something," "someone dealt him an inward blow." Anxiety grips him on 14 November: "*These* horrors have been whirling around me all week, a terrible snout appears from everywhere, as if it wants to say 'A-a-a, so that's how you are? Why are you tense? You think, do, build—why?' Today a purple-gray dawn." On 15 November: "Yellow, yellow sunset." On 16 November: "The return home at night. Sirius blazes behind my back in every color, like an earthly meteor rapidly flying upward." Then, after a ten-day interruption, on 26 November: "An infinitely troubled day.... I am very tired. What is happening to me? As if someone isn't holding me. Something happened this week. What?" And, finally, on 27 November, a short entry: "Lord, bless me! Lord, bless me! Lord, bless and keep me. I will go wandering." That same day he writes to Pyast:

> Forgive me for calling you up just now. You did very "wisely" in not going to the Variety Show.... And I feel loathsome—even now. *Loathsome* because I *don't know* what happened this week.
> Something held me all this fall and has now stopped holding me. Worst of all is the fact that *I don't know* which element has died.
> I don't know exactly what happened.
> *Therefore* I called you just now.
> I continue to sit in the Primorsky Station, undecided what to do. Right now I am leaving for somewhere. Your Aleksandr Blok.
> Dreams are already beginning. I would give much if it were cleared up tomorrow, WHAT disappeared. A drunken scoundrel is walking past me.

But "tomorrow" was still worse. Blok notes in the *Diary*: "28 November. A terrible day. *No me*—for several days already." In the evening of the same day he listens to Moussorgsky's *Khovanshchina*, with Chaliapin, in the Mariinsky Theater. This powerful impression helps him to recover from the "blow" a little. He writes his mother:

> *Khovanshchina*, it turns out, played a very big role for me. Today I am quite different from yesterday. I hope I will again begin to recover from the blow someone dealt me internally this week. . . . I still don't know the source, but I'm beginning to guess.
>
> *Khovanshchina* is still not of genius (that is, not the breath of the Holy Spirit), as all of Russia is not yet of genius, where the future is only being prepared. But it stands in the very center, just on that narrow strip where the breath of the Spirit sweeps past.

After this enigmatic shock, Blok slowly returns to life. December passes in weariness and torpidity. Entries in the diary follow one after another. On 1 December: "I feel very, very bad, wretched." On 14 December: "After strange, troubled and empty days, when I was too lazy to write." On 22 December: "The recent days were sad and gloomy for me. Cold and thaws." He greets the New Year with a prayer: "Lord, grant it will be better for me!" Here is the last entry of 1911:

> Severe frost. These days we get up early—the moon hasn't yet died out, and under it a rosy sky. . . . The scarlet sun sets in translucent fog. I go to see mama—to see in the New Year. God grant . . . to see in the New Year and live through it . . . in awareness. God grant it.

How to explain the "blow" dealt Blok by "someone" in Moscow? It is easy to shrug it off with references to pathology, to persecution mania, and the like. But this explains nothing. Perhaps this "someone" didn't exist. But the "blow" was a genuine spiritual reality, one of those "struggles" and "temptations" to which the mystics of all epochs bear witness. The November event is new evidence of the mystical gifts of the singer of the Eternal Feminine.

The difficult year, 1911, was creatively barren for Blok. Work on the *poema* progressed agonizingly slowly. The poet abandoned it in disgust and returned to it again. There are traces of doubts and waverings in the *Diary*. On 25 October he notes: "A whirlwind of thoughts, doubts— of everything and of myself, of my strengths, images piling up from the unrealized *poema*. If one could pray about form." On 3 December he writes:

> Mama advised me to finish the *poema* with the "son" being raised onto bayonets on the barricades. The plan of the fourth part is becoming clearer. Part 1: The Demon (not I, but Dostoevsky, so named it, and if he didn't name it, then *é ben trovato*); Part 2: Childhood; Part 3: Father's Death; Part 4: War and Revolution, Death of the Son.

And right here the "tragic idea" of *Retribution* is outlined:

> The world lies in evil. Fate, chance, plays with everything in the world; everything that rose above the world is worthy of the governance of God. In Tyutchev's poems there is a Hellenic, pre-Christian sense of Fate, tragic. There is also another tragedy—the Christian. But, to the extent

that one can talk about everything pre-Christian because it is ours, of this place, now, so one can talk equally about Christ. Even if you know something it is better to be silent (not like Merezhkovsky), so that no "raving" (Moussorgsky) would emerge. We know neither the day nor the hour in which the Son of Man will come to judge the living and the dead.

With this the "theme" of the *poema* takes shape. This is a tragedy of Fate in the ancient, Hellenic sense; in it reigns the law "an eye for an eye"—iron necessity, pitiless retribution. The author consciously builds it outside the Christian teaching on freedom and grace. The idea of finishing the *poema* with the hero's death on the barricades tempts him. On 5 December he writes his mother: "Your observations about the barricades keep me till now in a good mood regarding the *poema*. It seems the plan is ready and I will at once begin to write." Finally, the last note about the *poema* in the *Diary* (27 December):

> I continue that of yesterday. The lamp burns by the icon—my conscience.... My father is an heir of Lermontov, of Griboedov, and of Chaadayev,[19] of course. He expressed this *demonically* in his remarkable "classification of the sciences": there are shining heights (truth, beauty, and goodness), but you, people, are swine.... All this in the unfortunate envelope of A. L. Blok, very sinful, lascivious.

In the foreword to the *poema Retribution* Blok relates in detail the history of the creation of this work. The *poema* was conceived in 1910 and its main features sketched in 1911. The year 1910 was the beginning of a new era in the poet's life. The crisis of symbolism and the appearance of new literary directions, and the deaths of Tolstoy, Vrubel, and Kommissarzhevskaya, signified the end of the "old world." After the mystical hangover came a period of courage, clarity, and realism. The year 1911 is connected in Blok's memory with the "northern, harsh voice of Strindberg," with the flourishing of wrestling in Petersburg circuses, and with the first successes of aviation. This year the newspapers wrote about the approach of war and workers' strikes occurred in London. In the fall Stolypin was killed in Kiev:

> All these facts, apparently so diverse, have one musical meaning for me. I am accustomed to comparing facts from all the areas of life accessible to my sight at a given time, and I am sure that all together they always create a common musical pressure.
>
> I think that *iambic* was the simplest expression of rhythm for this time, when the world, preparing for unprecedented events, was with such strenuous regularity developing its physical, political, and military muscles. Probably for that reason it also drew me, who had long since been driven through the world by the whips of these iambics, to give myself up to its elastic wave for a more protracted time.

At first the *poema*'s content was still unclear to the author. "At that time," he continues, "this was present primarily in a musical and muscular consciousness; I don't speak idly about muscular consciousness, because at that time the *poema*'s whole movement and development was closely connected for me with the development of the muscular system."

The poet experiences, not only in spirit, but also in body, the terrible tension of the world on the eve of the First World War. The "musical pressure" which finds its expression in the rhythm of iambics is born of muscular effort. Blok sensed the inevitability of the impending events, history's tragic destiny. Thus the theme of *Retribution* arose. In the music of iambics the leitmotif of the mazurka sounded for him—it became central to the *poema*:

> The whole *poema* should be accompanied by the definite leitmotif of "retribution"—this leitmotif is the *mazurka*.... In the first chapter, this dance is heard faintly from the window of some Petersburg apartment—the stagnant seventies; in the second chapter, the dance rings out at a ball, mixing with the ringing of officers' spurs, resembling the champagne foam of the famous *fin de siècle veuve Cliquot*, still more stagnant—the gypsy, Apukhtin[20] years; and, finally, in the third chapter, the mazurka broke loose; it rings in the snowy blizzard, sweeping over night-time Warsaw, over the Polish clover fields covered with snow. In it the voice of Retribution is already heard distinctly.

After the father's death, his memory pursued the son tormentingly; he felt a mysterious need to write about the fate of this "sad demon." And if the poet had given himself up directly to his feeling, he would have created a majestically gloomy romantic *poema*. But Blok didn't just want to tell about his father, he also wanted to *explain* the riddle of his death. Seduced by Strindberg's harsh realism and by Zola's naturalism, he devises his own philosophy of history and, with this artificial construction, destroys his own initial plan. The *poema* now presents itself to him "in the semblance of Rougon-Macquarts on a small scale, in a small fragment of a Russian lineage, living in the conditions of Russian life." He sets forth the idea of lineage in the following words:

> The world vortex sucks into its funnel almost the whole man; almost no trace of personality at all remains.... Man was and man is no more; wretched, inert flesh and a decaying soul-let remained. But the seed is sown—and in the next eldest son something new, something more stubborn, grows; and in the last eldest son this new and stubborn thing begins, finally, to act perceptibly on the surrounding milieu. In this way, the lineage, having experienced in itself the *retribution of history*, of the milieu, of the epoch, begins in its turn to take retribution.

Blok, a romantic and an individualist, is ready to bow down before the "wheel of history," which grinds personality "almost without a trace," and to console himself with the hope that the descendants of the fathers, maimed and disfigured by history, will someday in their turn "take retribution," that is, maim other people. This dismal philosophy sets the basis of the *poema*. "By the path of catastrophes and falls," the author continues, "my Rougon-Macquarts gradually liberate themselves from the '*éducation sentimentale*' of the Russian gentry. The coal is transformed into diamond, Russia into a new America."

But the poet's inspiration didn't fit into the philosopher's abstract schema. The *poema* remained unfinished, and the plan of the "last eldest son," beginning to take retribution, simply wasn't realized: it was stillborn. We know about the plan of the *poema* from the foreword: "The *poema* was to have consisted of a prologue, three long chapters and an epilogue. Each chapter is framed by a description of events of world-wide significance: they make up its background." This initial plan was only partly realized: the prologue and first chapter were written entirely, the second chapter was sketched, the third unfinished.

The prologue begins with the solemn lines:

> Life—without beginning and end.
> Chance lies in wait for us all.
> Inevitable twilight above us,
> Or the clarity of God's face.

It is given to the artist to measure everything with a dispassionate measure: his view, firm and clear, must see beneath the accidental features the beautiful face of the world. Then a prophecy of war is made:

> A dragon over all Europe,
> Mouth gaping, parched with thirst . . .
> Who will deal him a blow?
> We don't know: over our camp,
> As of old, the distance is shrouded in fog
> And smells of burning. There—a fire.

The idea of the *poema* is expressed in the terse, tense lines:

> The sons are reflected in the fathers;
> A small fragment of the breed,
> Two or three links—and already the legacy is clear
> Of the dark times of antiquity:
> A new stock matured—
> Coal is transformed into diamond.

Blok invests Pushkinian iambic tetrameter with new rhythmic elasticity. The tone is set immediately—manly and firm. The first chapter begins with the lines:

> The nineteenth century, iron,
> Is in truth a cruel century!
> By you carefree man is thrown
> Into the nighttime, starless darkness.

But in the long list of the sins of the nineteenth century the elevated tone of the epic tale is sharply lowered. The calm contemplation, which had passed "through the heat of the soul, through the cold of the mind," is replaced by malicious irony and cheerless wit. The iambic whip cracks through the air, inflicting no blows. With perplexity we read "satirical" lines like:

> The age of foreheads beating on the wall,
> Of economic doctrines

or:

> The age of shares, securities, and bonds,
> And of inactive minds,
> And of semi-talents
> (More correctly: halved!)

The characterization of the twentieth century is even gloomier:

> (Even blacker and more enormous
> The shadow of Lucifer's wing.)

The poet enumerates the omens of the approach of the end: Halley's comet, the Messina earthquake, the first airplane flights. The theme of death inspires him, and the lines again burn with poetic fire. The following lines are full of lofty inspiration:

> And loathing of life,
> And insane love for it,
> And passion, and hatred for the fatherland,
> And black, earthly blood
> Promises us, swelling the veins,
> Destroying all boundaries,
> Unprecedented changes,
> Unparalleled revolts . . .

After the characterization of the two centuries a picture of Russian daily life in the seventies is given. The author reports in the foreword:

> The first chapter develops in the seventies of the past century on the background of the Russo-Turkish War and the People's Will Movement, in an intellectual liberal family. In this family there appears a certain "demon," the first swallow of "individualism," a man resembling Byron, with some unearthly aspirations and strivings, but deadened by the disease of the century, by the beginning of the *fin de siècle*.

In the fall of 1878, the entry into Petersburg of the victorious troops, of the heroes of Plevna, Shipka and Dubnyak.[21] With epic leisureliness the poet describes the *Pavlovtsy*[22] and the grenadiers, recalls heroic episodes of the war, Skobelev's fearlessness, the valor of the guard, the soldiers' labors and hardships—and ends his narration with a humorous story about the patriotic feelings of the Petersburg crowd:

> And this fleeting surge of feelings,
> Here, in the Petersburg September!
> Look: the head of a respectable family
> Straddles a lantern!

After the "mass scene" there is a conspiratorial meeting of members of the People's Will Movement, who celebrate Sofia Perovskaya's escape from jail. And finally, after these protracted introductions, the story of the gentry family begins:

> In those days, under the Petersburg sky,
> A gentry family lives.

The style becomes more even, the lines simpler and calmer. The poet tells about the life of his grandfather—Professor Beketov—with lyrical tenderness. The dying gentry culture, the "*éducation sentimentale*," the naive liberalism, and the real nobility are sung in lines echoing Pushkin's voice. Blok is not ashamed of his love for the past:

> All this might seem
> Absurd and outdated to us,
> But, really, only a boor can
> Jeer at Russian life.

Three daughters grow "primly" in the Beketov family. The oldest marries a "shaggy idealist," who solves "cursed questions" and argues about socialism and the commune. Marrying, the revolutionary exchanges a Russian blouse for a dickey and enters government service.

The youngest daughter's (the poet's mother's) fate is different; she belongs to the breed of people "with doomed eyes." A "demon with the gloomy flame of sorrow" in his eyes (the poet's father-to-be) enters her life. Blok introduces him to the reader on the background of the brilliant literary-political salon of Olga Vrevskaya (Anna Pavlovna Filosofova):

> At soirees at Olga Vrevskaya's
> The elite flower of society was present.
> The ill and sad Dostoevsky
> Came here in his declining years
> To lighten the burden of a hard life,
> To collect news and strength
> For the *Diary* (at this time he
> Was friendly with Pobedonostsev).
> With outstretched hand, inspiredly,
> Polonsky read poems here.
> Some ex-minister humbly
> Confessed his sins here.

> And the rector of the University,
> The botanist Beketov, came,
> And many professors,
> And servants of the brush and pen,
> And also—servants of tsarist power.

The poet observes the enigmatic image of his father intently and agitatedly. In the mother's reminiscences and in family legends the "young docent" retains an aureole of romantic mystery. This is a Russian Byron with the "rebellious ardor of superhuman aspirations." Aleksandr Lvovich marries the Beketovs' youngest daughter and, after brilliantly defending his dissertation, takes his young wife to Warsaw. Two years pass. Aleksandr II is killed on the embankment of the Ekaterinsky Canal: an ominous cloud hangs over Russia. The Beketovs' house becomes empty:

> Despair! Scant news from the daughter...
> Suddenly she returns...
> What happened to her? How thin her transparent figure,
> Gaunt, exhausted, pale,
> And a child lies in her arms.

The author dramatizes reality: he was not born in Warsaw, but in Petersburg, several months after Aleksandra Andreevna's return to her parents.

Blok writes about the plan of the second chapter in the foreword:

> The second chapter, whose action develops at the end of the nineteenth century and the beginning of the twentieth, never completed, except for the introduction, should be devoted to the son of this "demon," to the heir of his rebellious fits and pathological falls, to the callous son of our age. This is also one link in the long family. Also nothing apparently remains of him except a spark of fire flung into the world, except the seed cast by him in a passionate and sinful night into the womb of a quiet and womanly daughter of another people.

Like the first chapter, the second also begins with a "description of events of worldwide significance." The poet describes the Petersburg of the epoch of Aleksandr III in classically austere and majestic lines. Dostoevsky's terrible dreams are clothed in the solemn sounds of Pushkin's *Bronze Horseman*. Blok introduces new, mysterious features into the portrayal of the "enchanted city." The image of Russia, paralyzed under the owl's wing of the sorcerer Pobedonostsev, and the vision of Peter the Great's spectral fleet, which enters the mouth of the Neva on a white night, belong to the poet's greatest creations.

Here is the funereal leitmotif of this chapter:

> In those distant, stagnant years
> Sleep and haze reigned in hearts:

Aleksandr Blok

> Pobedonostsev over Russia
> Stretched owl's wings,
> And there was neither day nor night,
> But only the shadow of the enormous wings;
> He outlined with a marvelous circle
> Russia, looking into her eyes
> With the glassy gaze of a sorcerer.

In a white night, under a "vast dawn," dead Petersburg has terrible dreams. An alarming sound comes from the sea, and here:

> ... A wonderful fleet,
> Flanks widely extended,
> Suddenly barred the Neva ...
> And the Imperial Founder himself
> Stands on the leading frigate
> As in a terrible dream, but awake:
> A green uniform, towering stature,
> His wide-open eyes are horrible;
> Bloodied by the same dawn
> Both tsar and city and frigate ...
> Tsar! are you again rising from the grave
> To break a new window for us?
> And it is terrible: on a white night, both—
> Corpse and city—are at one.

In Blok Pushkin's Bronze Horseman becomes a corpse in a green uniform, bringing a spectral squadron into the mouth of the Neva. In Pushkin, the question is:

> He is horrible in the surrounding haze ...
> What thought is concealed in him?

Blok provides the answer: the dead tsar, bloodied by the dawn, heralds new and menacing ordeals for Russia:

> Stretched out boundlessly,
> The already bloody dawn,
> Menacing with Port Arthur and Tsushima,
> Menacing with the ninth of January.

According to the author's plan, this solemnly gloomy introduction was to precede the story of the "son's" childhood and youth. Only outlines from it are preserved. The child is brought to Shakhmatovo: to the jangling door of the balcony, the lindens, lilacs, and the blue cupola of the sky.

The outlines break off at the story of the youth's first meeting with the "pink girl" strewn with apple petals—the poet's future wife.

In the foreword Blok writes:

The third chapter describes how the father ended his life, what happened to the former brilliant "demon," what abyss this once striking person fell into. The action of the *poema* is shifted from the Russian capital, where it had developed till then, to Warsaw, which at first seemed Russia's "backyard" and was then apparently called upon to play a certain messianic role connected with the fate of Poland, forgotten by God and mutilated. Here, over the fresh grave of his father, ends the development and life path of the son, who gives way to his own offspring, to the third link in the always soaring and falling breed.

The chapter begins with the lines:

Father lies in the Avenue of Roses,[23]
No longer arguing with fatigue,
And the train rushes the son into the frost
From the shores of his native sea . . .

There is the bespattered train station, the bridge across the Vistula, and the hospital in the Avenue of Roses. Blok runs up the staircase. Someone blocks his way and asks sternly: "You are the professor's son? Come in. He died at five. There. . . ."

And in the room, alien and cramped,
The corpse, laid out for viewing,
Calm, yellow, mute.

The son with difficulty takes a ring from his father's rigid hand, makes the sign of the cross over him, sets his hands right, and leaves, saying: "God be with you!"

Then came the offices for the dead, speeches, the usual bustle of the funeral:

However empty were the hearts,
Everyone knew: this life had burned out . . .
And even the sun looked for a time
Into the father's poor grave.

A woman in mourning sobs "uncontrollably" over the grave:

And I am sorry for the father, immensely sorry;
He *too* from childhood had received
Flaubert's strange legacy,
Education sentimentale.

Having buried his father, the son sets out for the deceased's apartment. There he finds dark, damp rooms, a "wretched lair"; a layer of dust on piles of books. Aleksandr Lvovich, "this modern Harpagon," collected everything and piled it in a heap: scraps of material, sheets of paper, crusts of bread, pens, cigarette boxes, portraits, letters from women and relatives, notices and accounts of the Spiritual-Moral Discussions.

Aleksandr Blok

Thus had his father lived: like a miser forgotten
By people, and by God, and by himself.

But once the spirit of Faust had lived in him; his hands, lying on the piano keys, had awakened "unheard-of sounds."

The "theme of the father" is the main theme of *Retribution*. The fate of the rebellious Byron, transformed into a pitiful Harpagon, is the *fate of the Russian romantic*. It attracted the poet not just by its psychological depth: he saw, with horror, himself in his father; his father posed for him the question of his own existence. In 1910–11 Blok sincerely thought that "the development and life path of the son was ending over the grave of the father"; that he—the second link in the breed—would be "devoured without a trace by the world milieu." It seemed to him that his creativity had dried up and his life ended. In the "theme of the father" he divined his own personal theme: the music, beginning to sound in the life of the one, thundered with new power in the fate of the other. The romantic-father by his fall foretold death for the romantic-son. The theme of *Retribution* is the *tragedy of romanticism*. Blok was the last Russian romantic.

In the beginning of the third chapter the motif of retribution is personified in the image of Pan Moroz, rushing past like a blizzard over night Warsaw:

"Vengeance! Vengeance!" In the cold cast iron
Rings over Warsaw like an echo:
Now Pan Moroz on a vicious steed
Clanks his bloody spurs.

The poet wanders in depression through the streets of the Polish capital, and the wind sings to him of vengeance:

The country under a burden of wrongs,
Under a yoke of naked violence,
Like an Angel, lowers its wings,
Like a woman, loses shame.

And again the Avenger—Pan Moroz—gallops on the vicious steed:

Furiously flies above us
His gray head,
Or his thrown-back sleeves
Will rise swiftly like a storm over the houses . . .
. . . . .
And the cast iron will repeat precisely
The blows of the frozen hoof
Along the deserted roadway . . .

Blok is in the power of the rhythms of the *Bronze Horseman*: he responds to Pushkin's lines:

Retribution

> The heavily ringing gallop
> Along the shaken roadway.

But the howls about retribution, ringing in the blizzardy night over enslaved Warsaw, are an accidental and artistically unjustified embodiment of the poet's personal anxiety. His late father was not a Polish patriot, but a Russian official, and his death in Warsaw was in no way connected with the tragic fate of Poland. The poet artificially unites his sense of death with the "messianic role" of the unfortunate Slavic people. He needs a worldwide resonance to amplify the ringing of his voice. The "Polish theme" gives his verse a lofty tension:

> Already for hours along the bad roads,
> Along the snowy roads he wandered.
> Without sleep, without rest, without aim ...
> . . . . .
> Now there is no one to help!
> Now he is in the very heart of night!
> Oh, your gaze is black, darkness of the night,
> And the stony heart is deaf.

The poet stops by the lattice of the Saxon Garden and leans his head against it. And suddenly:

> A simple girl before him.
> "What is your name?" "Maria."
> "What race are you from?" "From the Carpathians."

There follow a few unpolished sketches in prose and verse:

> "I'm bored with living." "I won't leave you. You will die with me. Are you alone?" "Yes, alone." "I will bury you where no one will find out and I will place a cross, and in the spring clover will bloom over you."

> With a smile she opens
> Her arms to him,
> And all that had been retreats
> And disappears (into oblivion).

And he dies in her arms. All the vague transports, disembodied thoughts, the will to an unaccomplished feat, are dissolved on the breast of this woman.

In 1913 Blok outlines a new plan for the *poema*—not in three but in four chapters:

Chapter 3. Arrival in Warsaw. Father's death. Depression, frost, night. The *second mazurka*. "Her" appearance. A son is conceived. Chapter 4. Return to Petersburg. Red dawns, black nights. His doom (already unlucky!). Barricades. Epilogue. *Third mazurka*. Somewhere, in a *poor room*, in some city, a little boy is growing. Two leitmotifs: one—life marches on hopelessly, like infantry; the other—the mazurka.

The end of the son's life remained unclear to the poet. Now he dies in the arms of a Polish girl, now he is killed on the barricades. Soon the plan of the *poema* in four chapters falls away, and the foreword written in 1919 no longer refers to a fourth chapter. The author sets forth the content of the epilogue in the following words:

> In the epilogue an infant must be portrayed, held and rocked to sleep in her lap by a simple mother, lost somewhere in the broad Polish clover fields, unknown to anyone and herself knowing about nothing. But she rocks her son and feeds him at the breast, and the son grows. He is already beginning to play, he is beginning to repeat by syllables after his mother: "And I will go to meet the soldiers. . . . And I will rush upon their bayonets. . . . And for you, my freedom, I will mount the black scaffold."

The *poema Retribution* reflected the painful crisis Blok experienced in 1910–11. In the years of the decline of symbolism it seemed to him that the lyrical theme of his life and poetry was exhausted. The romantic renounced romanticism, sought a new, sober, and stern life, a new, realistic art. The "senile man" had to die so that the "new" man could rise from the dead. But there was neither death nor resurrection. Instead of a general epos "of worldwide scope" the poet wrote an autobiographical *poema*. The return to the classical forms of Pushkin's verse was not the creation of a new realistic art. Blok dreamed of epic grandeur, of classical architecture, of life's fullness, of harmony and measure, of all the wonderful gifts of Apollo. But he was doomed to another god—to Dionysus—to his music, his holy madness, his erotic frenzy. He was the genius and the victim of romanticism.

CHAPTER VIII

THE DRAMA *THE ROSE AND THE CROSS*

1912–1913

On finishing the first chapter of *Retribution*, Blok reads it to a small circle at V. Ivanov's. Gorodetsky describes his reading:

> The *poema* made a stunning impression. It struck me with its freshness of vision, its wealth of *moeurs*, its concreteness—with all those things forbidden to any symbolist. But our teacher (V. Ivanov) looked like a thundercloud; he stormed. He saw decay, collapse resulting from apostasy, nominalism, as we said a little later, crime, and death in this *poema*. Blok sat depressed: he didn't know how to defend himself. He could only argue musically. And when Vyacheslav went on the attack, unfurling all the banners of symbolism, the neophyte of realism yielded almost without resistance. The *poema* remained lying in a desk till the last years, when Blok made an attempt, if not to finish it, then to put it in order.

The prologue and first part of *Retribution* appear in *Russian Thought* (*Russkaya Mysl*) in 1917. The poet worked on the second and third chapter during the last days of his life (July 1921).

The "neophyte of realism" (Gorodetsky's expression) immediately felt that he hadn't succeeded with the *poema*, and for a long time he lost faith in his creative powers. In the diary he judges his "scribbling" mercilessly. The first entry of 1912 (2 January) begins:

> Lord, bless me!
> When people live in solitude for a long time, for example, they deal *only* with what is inaccessible to the *understanding* of the "crowd," . . . like the "decadents" of the nineties. Then, emerging into life, they . . . prove helpless and *often* fall lower than the "crowd" itself. So it was with many of us. Not to fall low . . . for this one must have great *moral* strength, that is, a certain "cultural discrimination," since moral resources are hereditary. . . . I am writing listlessly and dully, as one only just born. The more I become accustomed to "prettiness," the more awkward come out reflections on the living, on what exists in time and space. Until one finds the *real* connection between the temporal and the eternal, till then one will not become a writer who not only is understood, but who is even needed by anyone and for anything, except overindulgence.

The year 1912 passes for Blok under the sign of the Swedish writer August Strindberg, with whose work Pyast acquainted him. The poet's archive preserves a sketch, "Ibsen and Strindberg"; in it a contrasting characterization of the two northern writers is outlined. Blok placed the article "In Memory of August Strindberg," devoted to the late novelist as a person, in the journal *Contemporary (Sovremennik)*. The author scrutinizes Strindberg's portrait: the large, stubborn forehead, the angry brows, the unyielding look in the stern eyes, the wrinkles of suffering around the mouth; in the whole appearance a calm and open courage. Not the artist, but the man, attracts Blok: great and simple, a creative artist and craftsman. He thinks that the new age will create a new human type, that there will be a "Strindbergian breed." Strindberg seemed to everyone around him a crude, working man, unsociable, stiff, misogynous; but under this stern shell enormous spiritual strength was concealed. "Strindberg," Blok writes, "seems like a beacon indicating what path culture will set out upon at the time of the creation of the new type of man. For our time, he was 'a great man.' " The author believes that the whole literary development of the twentieth century is connected with the predominance of an "experimental type of man," in whom the union of the masculine and feminine principles has not achieved harmony: from this arise all the deformities, and the pathology, and the neurasthenia of our age. The appearance of Strindberg foretells the birth of the new man—a teacher, a brother, a comrade.

Blok's article is a new demonstration of his clairvoyance: he guessed intuitively about the law of alternation of "soft" and "hard" types in Russian culture.[1] Thus the "soft" type—the romantic of the thirties—is replaced by the "hard" type—the nihilist of the sixties; the "soft" populist of the seventies and eighties is displaced by the "hard" Marxist of the nineties. Blok foresees an imminent change: the "soft" type of the symbolist is fated, after 1917, to make way for the "hard" type of the "Bolshevik."[2]

Blok is ill; his disease of the gums recurs—the doctor calls it "gingivitis." He is despondent, he can't work. "I play children's card games with Lyuba. Mortal depression" (27 January). The only occupation which diverts him a bit is cutting out pictures and pasting them in an album. "The pictures save me from depression. First a large sun and a real sunset. Ineffable" (30 January). "Monotony, apathy. I forget that there are people in the world" (4 February).

The January issue of *Russian Thought* comes out with Briusov's review of *Night Hours*. Blok finds it "sad, cold, true, and touching." He reads between its lines: "Boring, friend. You wanted to catch a bird by the tail straightaway? Boring, boring. Does life really just stretch out in reading, writing, polishing, receiving letters and answering them? But isn't it better to 'walk with a bludgeon in a dense forest'?" He has to write an autobiography for Vengerov's *History of Literature in the Twentieth Century*. He intends to say:

There is such a person (myself) who, as Z. N. Gippius says, thought more about truth than about happiness. I sought pleasures, but never hoped for happiness. It came of itself and, coming, as always, immediately became something else. I don't expect it even now; God be with it. It—is not human.

In January Bely comes to Petersburg and writes Blok that he wishes to see him. Blok answers:

> Dear Borya, . . . My letter missed you, which is more than annoying to me. If I were well (I now am not in control of myself), I could see you only quite separately, and especially without V. Ivanov, whom I love, but who is alien to me. . . . In the letter to Moscow I wrote you why it would be terrible for me *to see even you alone*, if I were well. Besides that, I wrote that I am under the sign of Strindberg. . . . The atmosphere of V. Ivanov is unthinkable for me now.

A few days later V. Pyast hands Bely a note from Blok, in which the latter sets a meeting for him in an out-of-the-way restaurant near Tavricheskaya Street. In his *Reminiscences of Blok* Bely describes this strange meeting. Blok seemed to him pinched, pale, and agitated:

> This unassuming restaurant, its yellow painted floor, lit by a yellow light, the gray-brown walls with gray-brown faded blinds, and with an attentive, dejected, and gray waiter (with his right shoulder lowered and his left hunched up)—this gray restaurant suited our conversation. . . . The style of this meeting was the style of the "terrible world." . . . We shook each other's hands, kissed, and embraced.

Bely told him enthusiastically about his new seeking, about theosophy and the paths of initiation:

> A. A. listened with deep attention, his head bent. Hearing me out, he said: "Yes, I understand all this clearly, and for you, perhaps, I accept it. . . . But for myself—no, I don't know. I don't know anything. I don't even know: am I to *wait* or not to wait? I think there is nothing to wait for."

Bely told Blok about Sergey Solovyov's nervous illness, about Ellis' trip to Berlin to see Rudolf Steiner, about Asya's bent for theosophy. Blok listened:

> Then, suddenly settling back and lowering his eyes, he began very slowly to shake the ash from his cigarette, sighed and said: "Yes, here it is—we are wanderers. However different we are, one thing unites us all—we are wanderers. Here I began (at this point he smiled ironically) to roam the taverns, the gypsy concerts. You wandered to Africa, Ellis wanders around 'other worlds.' Yes, yes, wanderers. Such is fate."

They parted on the street, amid the February slush, dirt, patches of lamplight, and pedestrians running past with turned-up collars. "Returning to the 'tower,'" Bely writes, "I kept remembering A. A.'s fate. I sensed that the tragedy, which it was useless to speak about in literary and poetic circles, had already crept up on A. A.; that he is standing on the 'threshold.' "

The outwardly friendly relations between the two poets are renewed, but inwardly they had not been so alien to one another even in the years of open hostility. Blok writes his mother about his meeting with Bely: "In Borya's face there is something reminding one of a completely different life. Therefore today I am especially spiteful and am pursued by some ugly faces in the streetcars. . . .

"Today I got another letter from Borya. We talked yesterday for six hours" (25 February).

And another close friend of Blok's, E. P. Ivanov, unexpectedly exchanges his Christianity for theosophy. The poet informs his mother:

> [Zhenya] has stepped onto the path of theosophy, to speak simply, and, having once understood this, there is no longer any reason to ask why and what for. Theosophy in our time is apparently one of the real paths of knowing the world. . . .
> The other day Borya sent an enormous letter which helped me in part to understand Zhenya's goals. A letter about Steiner, with whom Borya has joined his fate. (6 May)

"Mysticism," which is hateful to him, creeps upon Blok from all sides: his closest friends—Bely and Ivanov—try to drag him into the thickets of theosophy; Aleksandra Andreevna suddenly decides to take up spiritualism; his stepsister Angelina Blok is carried away with the "orthodoxy" of Hermogen and Iliodor. Blok struggles desperately with the approaching specters. Apropos of Hermogen he notes in the *Diary*:

> The last aims of Hermogen . . . to overturn the darkness of the seventeenth century onto the young twentieth century, which is already well begun and exhausted from its first steps.
> Better all the cruelty of civilization, all the "godlessness" of "economic" culture, than the horror of the specters of departed times. The brightest person might fall down dead before an invulnerable specter, but he will endure the monstrosity and horror of *reality*. We need realities; there is nothing in the world more terrible than mysticism. . . . God Himself will help—then to see the clear, *cold*, and crystalline sky and its dawn. In the black soot and red fire this sky and this dawn are not visible. (18 [19] March)

Blok wants to look at the world through Strindberg's eyes: honestly, courageously, and simply. He wants neither heaven nor hell, only solid earth under his feet. "No," he notes, "in my present state (cruelty, awkwardness, maturity, illness) I don't know how and have no right to speak *more* than about the human" (*Diary*, 1 December).

On Easter A. M. Remizov[3] introduces Blok to the art lover, the rich patron Mikhail Ivanovich Tereshchenko. The latter loves Blok's verse and enlists the poet in a large theatrical enterprise he has undertaken. He commissions Blok to write a scenario for a ballet from Provençal life, for which Glazunov is composing the music. After a time the ballet is turned into an opera, and Blok enthusiastically begins to work up the libretto. From this libretto grew the best of his dramas, *The Rose and the Cross*.

The poet becomes friends with Tereshchenko, meets his mother and sisters, and is often in their home on the English Embankment. Apropos of a conversation with Tereshchenko on art, Blok makes a very important entry in the *Diary* about his own "treachery" and "fall":

> 11 October. Tereshchenko says that he was never religious, and he thinks that everything that religion can give, art gives him (two or three moments in his life, chiefly musical). In reply I began to develop my *usual*: that which is in art—*eternity*, we don't know "about what," on the other side of everything, but empty, destructive perhaps—is in religion—the *end*, one knows of what, completeness, salvation. . . . And about art: do I want to repeat or to get back those moments when art opened infinity for me? No, I can't want that, even if I knew how to believe. It is impossible to love what is behind this. (To Love—with a capital letter.)
>
> . . . I argued because I once knew something bigger than art, that is, not infinity, but the End, not worlds, but the World. I didn't argue because I have lost That, probably forever, have *fallen* have *betrayed* it, and now am actually an "artist." I live not by what fills life, but by what makes it black, terrible, by what repulses it. I also didn't argue because I am a "pessimist," "as everyone acknowledges," because where I find despair and horror, others find joy.

This entry develops the ideas of the 1910 article "The Present State of Russian Symbolism." The "prophet," having betrayed his calling and having wished to become a "poet," lives in the black hell of art. All of 1912 passes under the sign of mortal depression and a horror of life. The diary is full of complaints, almost moans:

> I still can't begin my work again—the only personal thing that remained to me in life, since the horrors of life are pursuing me for the fifth day. . . . I will recover—the only hope. In the meantime I fear damned life, I turn my eyes away from it. . . . I fear life. (11 June)
>
> Infinite and degrading depression. (26 September)

It seems to him that everyone around is just as unhappy as he. Not only depression torments him, but also unbearable, infinite pity:

> Sad thoughts; all the people closest to me are on the brink of madness, somehow ill and shattered. There is nothing worse than time. (1 May)
>
> A. M. Remizov is so yellow, tormented. And everyone is the same. Mama is miserable, my aunt is worn out. . . . Everyone is unhappy—both poor and rich. (3 May)

He gets the same impression from a meeting of the Religious-Philosophical Society:

> Today, of the intelligent people sitting at the table, the most positive (Struve) spoke about "the greatest suffering" as about something fitting, so ordinarily and simply. The others didn't even speak—it was written on their faces. (18 October)
> By six o'clock I went to the Merezhkovskys. . . . Things are going badly with them. Zinaida Nikolaevna is quite weak and ill. [28 December]

The nature of the evening walks changes: now he is not attracted by restaurants with gypsies or trips with chance female companions. He selects the most remote and poorest corners of Petersburg. With agonizing intensity he scrutinizes the "terrible world" of human misfortune and poverty. He needs to torment himself with pity so as not to suffocate in solitude:

> Evening walks . . . in gloomy places where hooligans break street lamps; a puppy joins them; dull windows with curtains. A little girl is walking, . . . breathing heavily like a horse: consumption, apparently; she chokes with a hollow cough, bends over after a few steps. . . . A terrible world. (28 February)
> Night on the wide embankment of the Neva near the university. A child, a little boy, barely visible among the stones. The mother ("simple") took him in her arms; he clasped his little arms around her neck, frightened. A terrible, unhappy city, where a child gets lost—the throat clenches with tears. (11 April)
> In utter despair I dragged myself through the quarter. A dampish night. On the Moika, opposite the New Holland, I (together with some young man) pulled out a young sailor who hung on the parapet intending to drown himself. . . . In any case, this helped me a little. (1 October)

In such a mood, slowly and painfully, the drama *The Rose and the Cross* was written. From letters to his mother and entries in the *Diary* one can re-establish the history of its creation. Blok begins to write his "libretto" in May; at the beginning of June the first act is finished in rough draft. On 21 June he informs his mother: "Mama, my work is nevertheless progressing, although slowly. Three acts are written in rough draft, the fourth act remains, the polishing, a few trifles and a few inserted songs." In the *Diary* a note of 13 July [June]: "The work doesn't go. During the day I gad about—intense heat, stench, depression." In late autumn, at Tereshchenko's insistence, the poet again sets to work on the opera; gradually its idea becomes clear to him. He writes in the *Diary*:

> A pivot of images, thoughts, flourishes, to which the whole diversity of things is attached, must exist, and it must be eternal, unchanging under any circumstances. For example, in the opera I put everything I am capable of around one thing: *the fate of the failed man*, at least in the Christian epoch, of which we are contemporaries—this is a constant. (11 October)

But soon, again there are doubts and dissatisfaction with the work.

"Somehow I don't like," Blok notes with painful feeling, "my work on the opera; . . . something is lacking" (17 October). And a few days later: "From early morning, work on the 'opera,' from which I am becoming malicious. Little by little—vicious depression" (22 October). On 25 October Bertran's first monologue is being written, and on the thirtieth, the fourth act is finished. An entry on the thirty-first reads: "This morning, by the deadline set by M. I. Tereshchenko, as it should be, I finished the 'opera.'" The next day he reads it to Tereshchenko. With this the first period of the work ends: the composition of a scenario for an opera. The original draft from this period is preserved in Blok's archive, with brief characterizations of the cast. The author calls the failed knight (Bertran's name is not yet used) the "marrow of the whole idea." He is clumsily built, with a homely face; everyone pursues him with jeers. The "perpetual holiday" of palace life oppresses him, and he dreams of snows, the ocean, an absence of people. Touring singers sing a northern song, which deeply agitates him. "This song," the author writes, "speaks about the only necessity (about Ankou), about the father of suffering, about the fact that the past and the future are equally unknown (emptiness)." In such a vague form the leitmotif of the play, the famous song of Gaetan, is conceived. The knight secretly loves the chatelaine, who, "despising him in the depths of her soul, about once a month deigns to cast him a glance when meeting him on the staircase." The page, in love with the chatelaine (he is not yet called Aliskan)—"handsome, with down on his lip, pushy and a braggart—sighs on the pillows at his lady's feet, always dressed in blue, perpetually languid and voluptuous. The chatelaine's husband—elderly and coarse and ordinary—is a count (or duke), like everyone." The first draft of the character of the future Izora is interesting. She is young and beautiful:

> Two aspirations struggle in her. One is banal, everyday, sensual; with this part of her being she inclines toward the page. But this half of her soul is illuminated by the pink, tender, trembling light of the other half. . . . The expectation and presentiment of something else, special. This presentiment is prompted in her by that same song, which she had heard many times from the lips of the touring singers.

And the draft ends with the sentence: "The rising curtain finds them at this point."

The scenario of the opera coincides on the whole with the plot of the future drama. The main characters are outlined; the dramatic theme—the "northern song"—is stated.

Meanwhile, by autumn Tereshchenko's plans had changed; the idea of the theatrical undertaking was abandoned, and it was decided to found a book-publishing house. The triumphal opening of the publishing house Sirin took place on 16 November 1912. Every Saturday collaborators of Sirin's anthologies, which came out under the editorship of Razumnik Vasilievich Ivanov (Ivanov-Razumnik),[4] gathered here. The publishing house turned out a monumental collection of the works of Briusov, Sologub, and Remizov. The publication of a complete collection of Blok's works was also proposed, but the war of 1914 forced Sirin to discontinue its activity. On Saturdays Blok would meet Ivanov-Razumnik on Pushkinskaya. A friendship was struck up between them which lasted until the poet's death. The opera was no longer needed. Tereshchenko and Blok decide to rework the scenario into a drama. He starts on this all the more willingly, since he had long since sensed the dramatic nature of his "opera." Back in June 1912 he wrote his mother: "At one time it seemed to me that not an opera was emerging, but a drama. . . . One of the characters, who by nature is more dramatic than musical, led me into error. This is the failure, Bertran." Now, on 20 November, he notes in the *Diary*: "To redo the *whole* play, to break up the unity of place, which will make the action more intense and the individual scenes more natural. I have begun the plan. I like the idea, but it's a lot of work." All winter of 1912 he works intensely on the new edition of *The Rose and the Cross*. A 21 November note in the diary reads:

> This morning Lyuba gave me an idea: Bertran ends by building a chapel of the sacred Rose. Considering this proposal tormentedly, I came to the conclusion that I don't have a right to talk about the mystical Rose; this is clear from the simple fact that I don't have enough spiritual strength to look into the symbols of the Rose and the Cross, symbols which are only obscure "for beauty," only artistically. I continue not to know the *end* of Bertran's fate and I am writing to Tereshchenko about this.

He returns to this thought in an entry of 1 December:

> *The Rose and the Cross* is not my theme at all. I am not mastering it. Let it be—the human fate of a failure—and if I am able to "diminish" before art, something more may gleam to someone through my theme. That is, my severity with myself and the greatest possible "modesty" can help the play to become a work of art, and a work of art is a moving being and not a corpse in repose.

By the end of the year the composition of the drama is finally settled. On 26 December he writes: "It seems the whole play has risen up clearly before me." On 27 December: "This morning—two new scenes for *The Rose and the Cross*." By New Year's the play is still not finished. On 4 January 1913 the fourth act is being finished. On 7 January, a note: "A tormenting day—sick. I write almost all day. I quarrel with Lyuba. Everything is written—just a few more 'strokes of the brush' and Izora's monologue with the ghost. Before going to bed I read it to Lyuba; she likes it, and I do too. Calm." On 15 January Blok hears Wagner's *Die Meistersinger von Nürnberg* in the Mariinsky Theater. He doesn't like the execution, but he adds: "nevertheless one swims in Wagner's musical ocean." And a note the next day: "To Wagner's melodies I shifted the last scene into verse." Finally, on 26 January

1913, one underlined note in the *Diary*: "Yesterday *The Rose and the Cross* was completed." That same year it was printed in a Sirin anthology. V. P. [V. N.] Knyazhnin in his memoirs cites an excerpt of a conversation with Blok:

> "I am greatly obligated to Tereshchenko," Blok says. "He forced me to finish *The Rose and the Cross*." "Forced?" A smile (nod of the head). "Forced. I went to him to read each act again and again, till everything came right." Falling silent, naively and modestly: "Otherwise I would not have finished."

Knyazhnin noticed a feature—modesty—which strikes one on reading the notes and entries about *The Rose and the Cross*. Blok, the author of *Verses on the Beautiful Lady*, one of the most spiritually gifted Russian artists, is sure that "he doesn't have the right" to talk about the mystical Rose, that "he doesn't have enough spiritual strength" to look into the symbols of the Rose and the Cross; he doesn't dare to write about the mystical, consciously limits himself "only to the human." And this self-deprecation before art, the humility and modesty after the daring and revelations of the era of the nineties, is a very great victory both for the artist and for the man. For the first time Blok succeeds in creating a perfect and harmonious work of art.

An interesting document, which illuminates the content of *The Rose and the Cross* in a new way, was found in the poet's archive: "Bertran's Notes, Written by Him a Few Hours before His Death." The failed knight tells about his unhappy life dedicated to the service of the beautiful countess Izora, about his wanderings around foggy Brittany and his meeting with the old knight Gaetan. The mystery and illusiveness of the wanderer with the faded cross on his chest is sharply emphasized. Bertran relates:

> The melody about joy and suffering, which he repeated often, especially agitated me. At times his speeches and songs, which had a kind of secret meaning that I couldn't catch at all, horrified me, for it was beginning to seem to me that I didn't face a man, but only a voice calling me into the unknown. Then, to drive away my fright, I had to touch my interlocutor with my hand and, having thus convinced myself that he wasn't a phantom, I carefully put him to bed and fed him bread, like an old infant.

The "Notes" break off with a story about Bertran's last night; Izora commands the wounded knight to stand guard during her meeting with Aliskan. "Now I know I am in God's hands," Bertran concludes, "and, insofar as my strength suffices (for my wounds hurt), I will try to see that no one this night disturbs the peace of the young lovers, remembering, like a good father, that those are not terrible who kill the body, but who cannot kill the soul."

This confession of the drama's principal hero is dated 1913; it proves that the author was not satisfied with the image of Bertran to the very end of his work on it. He seemed to him too vague. To feel him in all his psychological and vital completeness, he composes his detailed autobiography.

In the summer of 1912 the performances of Meyerhold's troupe begin in the summer theater in Terioki. Lyubov Dmitrievna was assigned leading roles. She, as were the other young actors, was under the spell of Meyerhold's "theatrical modernism" and gave herself to the work with passionate enthusiasm. Blok reacted with distrust to the director's ideas. From the time of the staging of *The Puppet Show*, when the poet wrote Meyerhold about how necessary his theater was to him, much had changed. First of all, Blok himself had changed, departing far from "puppetry" and "stylization" toward significant art, which was psychological and realistic. Meyerhold had also changed, having created in these years a whole theory of theatrical performance as *spectacle*. Struggling with the old everyday theater, presented in formal scenes, and with the new "theater of moods" (the Moscow Art Theater), Meyerhold turned to the tradition of the Italian *Commedia dell'Arte*, to Gozzi's comedy-fairy tales, to the romantic fantasy of Hoffmann, to the art of the circus and of the folk puppet theater. First and foremost the question of the technique of the actor's art, of the rhythmic body movements, of the expressiveness of the stage gesture, was posed. The actors no longer "experienced" and "understood," but took up rhythmical gymnastics, choreography, and acrobatics. There was much brilliance, talent, and freshness in Meyerhold's revolution, but a great danger was also concealed: the theater's lack of inner content and the depersonalization of the actor. Blok went to Terioki often, tried to be impartial; he even approved of much. But the spirit of this modernism was deeply inimical to him. On 28 May, after a trip to Terioki, he notes: "There were *speeches* about Shakespeare and about ideas, it was first of all a question of Meyerholdian pantomimes. Kuzmin and Sapunov are wooing the Krommelinkis, etc.—we'll see what it will come to. I don't want to condemn it straight off." On 5 June he goes to the opening of the theater, which was cancelled, sits with the troupe in Meyerhold's dacha. He likes everything, and writes to his mother:

> We sat in their dacha. It is large and smells like an old manor house. . . . Everyone ate together, drank tea, walked around the enormous park. . . . There is no spirit of emptiness: they are all very busy for long hours, really. Everyone is cheerful and serious. . . . Beyond the park of pines, the sea, very majestic. There was a storm, all the bathing huts were smashed. A lighthouse on the horizon.

On 10 June the opening of the performances took place. Blok tells his mother:

> The theater, although it is small, was almost full, and they clapped a lot.
> I didn't like anything. It's impossible for me to judge about Lyuba, especially by yesterday's performance, where it was really impossible for

anyone to display their talent in anything. It's true they played Cervantes' beautiful and variegated farce [*Two Windbags*] animatedly. And Lyuba acted, was at ease on the stage. She had a beautiful costume and makeup, but she sometimes overacted, probably from excitement....

[Mochulsky reverses the order of the following paragraphs to reinforce his point.]

Lyuba is serious, busy all the time; today she will play *The Innkeeper* (I'm not going) and a week later *The Imaginary Invalid* and a Strindberg play—big roles in both.... Two speeches preceded the performance—Kulbin's[5] and Meyerhold's—very involved and dilettantish (fortunately, short). The content (insofar as I was able to catch it) is quite inimical to me (about people as dolls; about art as "happiness")... I didn't want to go drink tea at the dacha, so I just walked a little with Lyuba along the very beautiful and foggy sea, above which a piece of red moon hung—and then I left for the station.

In April Blok became friends with the young artist Sapunov, who painted the scenery for the Terioki troupe. Unusually gifted, joyful and openhearted, he was a favorite of all the actors. Blok went with him to Terioki, invited him to his place. Sapunov intended to paint his portrait. On 11 April the poet notes: "In the evening I went to drink, in depression, but dear Sapunov was sitting in the restaurant. So I talked with him—both he and I were bored.... Such depression—almost to tears..." On the night of 15 June, bathing in the sea at Terioki, Sapunov drowned. This tragic death stunned the poet; he hastens to reassure his mother:

> Mama, don't worry about me when you read in the papers the news that Sapunov drowned in the sea near Terioki. I wasn't there, I didn't go, although six hours earlier he had invited me there by phone, to arrange a carnival.
> We saw each other often in the last days. He was very pure and simple. In a few days he was to have painted my portrait.

Blok sees Calderon's *Veneration of the Cross* in Terioki. Meyerhold's production seems to him unsuccessful, but he fears making a hasty condemnation. "Meyerhold," he writes his mother, "conquered the troupe with his talent, and Lyuba among them. I don't know his ideas well. Lyuba says he has developed a lot and gotten stronger in recent years, when I practically never saw him."

After *The Veneration of the Cross* Blok saw an unsuccessful staging of a Wilde play, in which Lyubov Dmitrievna played the role of a worldly old woman. And finally came the first performance he really liked. Soon after Strindberg's death Meyerhold staged his drama, *Guilty and Not Guilty*,[6] in which the poet's wife played a leading role. Blok describes this production to his mother in detail. How sincerely glad he is that he can praise the young troupe, how proud he is of Lyubov Dmitrievna's success:

> The production was all festive and, despite a few failures in particular,

was genuine. First of all, Pyast read a long speech at a black table in front of the footlights thickly heaped up with ferns. Lyuba didn't leave the stage the whole first act and, finally, really pleased me as an actress: she acted very powerfully.... Lyuba spoke, finally, in her own voice, very powerful both in sound and in expression, which suited Strindberg's language very well. Hearing this language from the stage for the first time, I was stunned: simplicity was carried to frightening dimensions, the life of the soul was translated into the language of mathematical formulas....

The director (Meyerhold) and the set designers,... if they didn't understand, obviously sensed this and, therefore, all eight scenes on a dimly lit stage; the backdrop was a blue-black curtain through which irregular lights shone....

Nothing but blue-black and red. Such are Sophocles and Strindberg.

Strindberg's daughter was in the audience.... In her homeliness and exhaustion she much resembles her father, resembles him in the best way. She said, by the way, that Lyuba acts ... better than the Helsingfors actress. (15 June)

But the Strindberg production was an incidental success of Meyerhold's and didn't shake Blok's opinion of the producer-innovator's theatrical ventures. The theater as splendid and variegated spectacle, as a pantomime in the style of the *Commedia dell'Arte*, was unacceptable to the poet. Meyerhold and his ardent admirer, the doctor-artist Kulbin, try to change the mind of *The Puppet Show*'s author—unsuccessfully. "After the performance," Blok writes his mother, "I argued with Kulbin endlessly and to the point of complete exhaustion" (30 June). Arguments with Lyubov Dmitrievna take place on this same theme: their divergence grows. The poet sadly notes in the *Diary*:

The evening ended in an unpleasant conversation with Lyuba. I constantly raise with her the question of our truth and of the modernists, which she finds extremely burdensome. She doesn't like our language, doesn't like it, and in general doesn't like our conversations. The modernists are separating her from me more and more. The future will show ... About the modernists: I'm afraid they don't have a *pivot*, but only a talented flourish around a vacuum.

A new generation is coming to replace the symbolists; Blok feels old, surrounded by misunderstanding and hostility. The Apollonists, acmeists, Adamists, clarists, futurists—how many of them appeared at the end of the first decade of the twentieth century! And for the poet this is not only a battle of literary schools, but also a personal tragedy. Lyubov Dmitrievna leaves him again: she is heart and soul with "the modernists." From the Beautiful Lady of the era of mystical symbolism she is changed into a Columbine of Meyerholdian pantomime—and changed forever. Blok struggles with importunate thoughts of death. He accepts the "terrible world" only because in it live two beings whom he loves more than himself: his wife and his mother. A tragic note appears in the *Diary* (15 June): "At night (I sleep badly almost all the time) I clearly sensed that, if my wife and mother were not in the world, there would be nothing for me to do here." But Lyubov Dmitrievna has her own life—it is intense, absorbing. She is constantly travelling, rehearsing, or on tour. On 26 June the poet writes:

> Something extremely painful occurs in my life all the time. Lyuba is again deceiving me. Based on my letter, written on the twenty-third, and based on her words, I today could either expect her or a telegram about when she will come. And here it is after two, the day is lost, intense expectation all morning. And that means a bad preparation for a meeting. Maybe she won't come today at all.

And a postscript below: "Bu just arrived."[7] On 16 September, he writes: "Lyuba keeps leaving the house—often." On 28 September: "Lyuba left again till late at night, and dear Zhenichka is with me." On 8 October, a note: "My darling drank tea with me this evening."

In October, Dr. Kulbin and the artist Pronin open the celebrated literary-artistic cabaret, The Stray Dog. Poets, singers, and actors perform there; Olechka Sudeikina, known to all literary Petersburg, dances; the poet Kuzmin sings his "Chimes of Love," accompanying himself on the piano. The Stray Dog—artistic Bohemia's night haunt, a cramped cellar, decorated by Sudeikin, Sapunov, and B. Grigoriev—is described in Kuzmin's novel *The Sailing Travellers* and sung by Anna Akhmatova:

We are all carousers here, debauchees,
How joyless for us together,
Flowers and birds on the walls
Long for the clouds . . .

Lyubov Dmitrievna was there, too, with the other actors of Meyerhold's company. Blok never accompanied her and was tormented when she spent the night there. Kulbin, he notes on 14 December, "tried in vain to restore The Stray Dog in my opinion. I accept some of it, but in general my opinion is unwavering." And, actually, to imagine Blok amid the noisy turmoil of these nocturnal crowds is simply inconceivable. By Christmas the poet's mood has become more cheerful. Lyubov Dmitrievna was to return from a tour. "Somewhat brighter. . . . Weariness. Listlessness. . . . Then I walked. Returning to tea, I find a *letter from my darling*—a weary letter." On 30 December he writes: "Lyuba is coming today." And, finally, a joyful entry on 31 December:

> While I was out walking, Lyuba came, perplexed, from the road. She washes up. . . . At mama's a Christmas tree, champagne, food. It was cozy and quiet. . . . We came home late, along a quiet street.
> Mama was a little better. Lyuba wore a white dress, drank champagne and liqueur, played with Toponka [the dog].
> May God grant brightness for the New Year.

Aleksandr Blok   The tragic is infinitely simple. Often one short sentence is more expressive than a five-act drama. In the *Diary* Blok tells about an "unspeakable dream" he had on the eve of Lyubov Dmitrievna's departure: in it was a "grasping at escaping life." All the entries about his wife are such a "grasping at escaping life." There is hopelessness and love not needed, with humble gratitude for small joys ("in the evening Lyuba drank tea with me").

A few painfully rapturous days emerge from the gloom of 1912. The entry for 29 [24] October reads: "The day was somehow ecstatic—in me.... The sunset was huge, clear, yellow, terrible." And 7 November is another such day. "Both in the afternoon and evening a kind of '*desperate*' ecstasy—indescribable. Wet white snow caresses the face. I roam, I rove." And, finally, on 3 December: "The air is piercing—one feels like shouting."

Lyubov Dmitrievna, busy in the Terioki theater, couldn't go to Shakhmatovo for the summer. Blok goes there infrequently to see his mother and his aunt, and not for long. The Shakhmatovo house, newly rebuilt and furnished with such love, intensifies his depression even more. He spent the whole, unusually hot, summer in the city. He would go to Shuvalovo with Pyast to bathe. He writes his mother:

> The water in the lake is soft and warm. It cheers me up amazingly. It turns out that I like Shuvalovsky Park because it resembles Shakhmatovo; not only the form and age of the trees, but also the era and the flora differ in almost nothing. Even the air is similar. (17 July)

Pyast recalls how in August 1912 he and Blok would go to the Knolls. They went to Lesnoy from the Vyborg Side on a train; there they had a snack in an inn and took a cab to Murino; they bathed in a stream and set out for the Knolls toward evening—"a real oasis in an uninhabited wilderness of marshes and fields." The poet went to Anichkov's dacha on Kamenny Island, listened to the gypsy Raisova in Ozerki, went to horse races with Pyast, and rode on the islands with Tereshchenko and Bakst. The elemental gypsy force took possession of him as before—the poems of 1912 speak of this. "With the gypsies," he writes his mother, "as with the new poets, everything is 'strange.' A year ago Aksyuta Prokhorova sang: 'It is terrible and wild for me without you; my swan song is sung.'" The poet begins a correspondence with an admirer, an enigmatic "stranger." She writes him "fateful letters," calls him into the "starry abysses," talks about the "poetry of death." Blok answers with good-natured humor: "Dear child, why do you call me into astral wilds, into 'starry abysses,' to kiss your perfumed gloves, when you can do much more—not destroy, but create." Another letter, full of pathetic despair, he answers seriously, setting forth his "gypsy philosophy":

> The world is beautiful, even in despair—there is no contradiction in this. One must live and one must talk in such a way that the resultant force

of life is fervently gypsy, a combination of harmony with violence, and of order with disorder. Otherwise one will be lost. My soul imitates the gypsy soul, both its violence and harmony together, and I also sing in some chorus which I won't leave.

The lyric poetry of 1912 is an attempt to master the "violence" and "disorder," to shackle them in forms of classical harmony.

In the autumn Blok finds a new apartment on the corner of Officers' Street and the Pryazhky Embankment. Anna Akhmatova was a guest of the poet "in a tall, gray house by the sea gates of the Neva." A broad view opened from the fourth floor. "Beyond the slips of the Baltic works," Blok writes his mother, "which are expanding to construct new dreadnoughts, the forests around the Sergievsky Monastery are visible. A few churches are visible (a large one on Gutuevsky Island) and masts, although the sea is closed off by houses."

At the end of November, Ariadna Vladimirovna Tyrkova draws Blok into collaboration on the new newspaper *Russian Talk* (*Russkaya Molva*). At an editorial meeting he reads a short report, "Art and the Newspaper"; it appeared in *Russian Talk* on 9 December in reworked form. In it Blok declares that the newspaper is by its very nature hostile to art. Art is:

> majestic. Life can be majestic, death can be majestic, even perdition can be majestic. . . . The order of the relation to art must be slow, significant, not bustling, not publicity-seeking. . . . The newspaper by its very nature is hurried and stormy; the faster the rhythm of life, the more frenziedly shout political and any other commonplaces.
>
> The soul of art, which at all times has the aim, using the language, colors, and forms of our world to recreate "other worlds," and the soul of the newspaper, which has the aim of struggle and of care only for our world, or still more narrowly, of our homeland, or still more narrowly, of our government—what do they have to do with one another? . . .

Literary criticism in a newspaper is "one of the most terrible scourges of our time." " 'Vain talents,' in Merezhkovsky's expression, . . . barren flowers of revolution," and simply "hooligans" writing feuilletons about art, "act on the bad instincts of the crowd" and "lower the general level of culture." The reader draws the conclusion that the newspaper in general shouldn't talk about art, but the author refrains from such a deduction. He suggests making the following experiment: in the newspaper "the people who should speak about art are *qualitatively* different from the people who speak about politics, about the news of the day." "It isn't necessary to speak much, it is necessary to speak *significantly*." Blok's reasoning didn't suit the taste of *Russian Talk*, and the article was printed with extensive cuts. Two clippings from the newspaper and the rough drafts are preserved in the poet's archive. On the folder in which they were placed is a note: "This makes up the core of the article and is what, under a thousand pretexts, the kind editorial office rejected. . . . The essence of the article is excluded; only ornaments remain.... A newspaper needs only ornaments."

D. V. Filosofov's feuilleton, entitled "Solitary Estheticism," appeared in *Speech* on 18 December, in reply to Blok's article. Filosofov sums up the poet's article in the formula "Art must be created by the elect for the elect" and reproaches him for "false aristocratism." "Blok," he writes, "confuses 'vulgarization' with 'democratization.' Fearing vulgarity, he preaches false aristocratism. I say 'false' because genuine aristocratism is necessarily connected with genuine democracy." In a note, "Misunderstanding or Unwillingness to Understand?" Blok defends himself against this accusation and suddenly, somehow in passing, incidentally, makes a very important and very personal admission. His yearning to reconcile art and life had suffered ruin. Now he understands all the unrealizability of the artist's eternal dream. He writes in his reply to Filosofov:

> The more deeply one loves art, the more incommensurable it becomes with life; the more strongly one loves life, the more fathomless becomes the chasm between it and art. When one loves the one and the other with equal force, such love is tragic. Love for two brothers equally alienated from each other, equally in deadly enmity, ready for mortal combat—to the last hour, when the third brother will come and raise their visors, and they will look into each other's faces. But when will the third come? We don't know.

The striking poem *To the Muse*, written in this same year, speaks of this "tragic love."

In November the actor Bravich dies, and Blok in his obituary ("To the Memory of K. V. Bravich") recalls the nineties when he, a first-year student, was carried away with Bravich's acting in Sardou's *Thermidor*:

> And the youth, dreaming of how he will go on the stage and be a tragic actor, dreams: if only I had such a fat chin as Dalmatov has, and such a long nose studded with coarse pockmarks as Bravich has.... Then— other times.... Bravich plays "Someone in Gray" in Andreev's *The Life of a Man*. Darkness in the wings. [Bravich's] eyes—weary, doglike, malicious (he dislikes the role terribly).

In the Kommissarzhevskaya Theater this modest but great actor was the very *soil* of art, "of lands without which the sky can't be seen."

After the poetically barren year of 1911, 1912 is again rich in poems. More than twenty poems of this year are included by the poet in the third volume of the *Collection*. In addition, Blok publishes two small books of selected poems, *The Year Round* and *Fairy Tales* (by the Sytin publishing house).

The year 1912 is marked by the symbolists' attempt to mobilize their forces for a decisive battle with their enemies; these enemies increase with each day, their attacks become bolder and bolder. Blok contemptuously lumps them in one heap under the sobriquet "modernists." But it also becomes clear to him that contempt alone will not get the better of them. He notes in the *Diary* (17 December): "It will be necessary to undertake something apropos of acmeism and Adamism, which is becoming insolent." Such an "undertaking" was the journal *Labors and Days* (*Trudy i Dni*), long ago conceived by the three poets—Blok, Bely, and V. Ivanov. Blok dreamed of a "diary *à trois*," of transforming the long degenerating "symbolic school" into a new, living, *human* art. The first issue of the journal sadly disappointed him: it testified not to "giving life" but to degeneration. In the *Diary* Blok gives an account of the content of his letter to Bely (17 April): "I am finally answering Borya about *Labors and Days*."

> The first issue is at once set up to talk about art and a school of art, and not about man and the artist. For this we are indebted to V. Ivanov. Don't I know the depths of his personal truths? But it is painful for me when he *argues* between the lines with ... Gumilyov, when he exclaims about *catharsis* in the same tone in 1912 as in 1905, and especially when he drags Kuzmin after him, who was not present at *our* feasts.... We come together in *Labors and Days* to be "incarnated," and everything in the first section so far might just as well have been in *Apollo*....
>
> V. Ivanov cooked up the whole kasha. One can turn optimistically and say: V. Ivanov, menacingly attacking someone, shakes a manifesto about the symbolist school—and woe to those who aren't with it.... Vyacheslav has—one must, it seems, understand this—a feminine soul, and his despotism is womanlike. [About personal relations to him—a "romance," and not friendship, not love.]
>
> *Passing considerations* (not from the letter).... It is natural to V. Ivanov to mix art with mirages of superart. The "symbolic school" is *troubled water*. Quasi-real ties lead to still greater atomization. When we (*New Path, Scales*) fought against the dying, banally liberal pseudorealism, it was something real; we were under the sign of the Renaissance. If we fight against the indefinite and perhaps against our (!) Gumilyov, we will find ourselves under the sign of degeneration. To take part in "creating life" ... it is necessary to be incarnated, to show our sad human face, and not the pseudoface of a nonexistent school. We are Russians.

In 1910, the head of the Russian symbolists, Briusov, had solemnly disavowed the symbolist school. In 1912 Blok calls it "nonexistent" and speaks about degeneration. Symbolism's chief theoretician from the time of the discontinuance of *Scales*—Bely—leaves the field of battle and plunges into theosophy. Of the brilliant pleiad of symbolists, only V. Ivanov remains fully armed, and his teaching is not a literary theory, but a religious homily. The symbolist school is disintegrating.

POEMS OF 1910–12

The cycle *The Terrible World* is almost finished in this three-year period. The "demonic" poem *To the Muse*, leading into the circles of the "hell of song," is written in 1912:

> In your concealed melodies there is
> Fateful news of death,
> The curse of sacred legacies,
> The profanation of happiness.

We recall the sentence from the article "On the Present State of Russian Symbolism": "Art is a splendid hell."

Blok's muse is the ambiguous, feminine face of Lucifer; it seduced angels with its beauty; he sees a "soft purple-gray" nimbus above it; for him it is "torment and hell." The poet loves, hating—"all the curse of its beauty":

> And more perfidious than the northern night,
> And more intoxicating than golden Aÿ,
> And briefer than gypsy love,
> Were your terrible caresses.

The artist, rivaling the Creator, makes his magic world, "a meadow with flowers and a sky with stars"; he understands his doom and draws inspiration from it. Pushkin also knew this "fateful comfort":

> Everything, everything that threatens death
> Conceals for the mortal heart
> Inexplicable pleasures . . .

The poem *In the Restaurant* arises from the "delirium of gypsy songs." The vision of the stranger in the "crowded hall" is music suddenly flowering with images: "Somewhere violin bows sang of love"; "And immediately, in reply, the strings burst forth, the bows began to sing frenziedly"; "And the necklace jingled, the gypsy girl danced, and the sunset screeched of love." Out of the whirlwind of frenzied sounds she steps forward, like a dream of love ("It existed or didn't, this evening"). The vision simulates reality: a woman sits with an escort at a little table, receives from the poet a "black rose" in a glass of Aÿ and haughtily whispers: "This one is in love too." But the simulation is exposed by the music: the bows began to sing—and she rushes to him "with the motion of a frightened bird," embraces him with music-love:

> But from the depths of the mirror you threw me glances
> And, throwing, shouted: Catch!

Nietzsche and V. Ivanov taught about the birth of Apollonian dreams from the abyss of Dionysian frenzy. Blok experienced this frenzy in reality.

Meetings in restaurants, trips to the islands, chance encounters, love duels—the poet needs all this nighttime, dissolute, and intoxicated life only to make "the violins sing" in his soul. How many poems are devoted to passion, to sensuality, and how little in these poems of real, physical sensuality. Blok is just as spiritual as Dostoevsky's "sensualists."

He plunges into depravity and continues to be incorporeal. He seeks in it not the quenching of lust, but a shaking of the spirit: passion "bitter as wormwood" swoops down like the wind onto the strings—and they begin to ring. This music is his lyrical life, his inspiration, his breathing. When he doesn't hear the secret inner song, he is dead. But at what a terrible price the gift of song is bought! What humiliation—chance embraces, hateful ceremonies, sham ecstasies! No one after Dostoevsky wrote such terrible words about the metaphysical banality of sensuality as the "debauched" Blok. In the poem *Humiliation* there is a meeting with a woman in a house of prostitution. A note in parentheses in the first verse sets the tone:

> (They lead to the scaffold, to execution,
> The condemned in such a sunset).

Then come the surroundings: "the red damask of the faded sofas," "the dust-covered tassels of the curtains," "a journal's naked drawings," "the dirty call-button." The characters: a merchant woman, a cardsharp, a student, an officer. And suddenly a moan breaks loose:

> Really is this house—a house in fact?
> Really is it *so* judged among people?

Here she is: "white as a kerchief," "lips with dried blood." And again, the poet's shout of horror:

> (Did we really call *this* love?)

A bed sits against the background of an enormous yellow sunset. Her embraces choke like the coils of a replete snake:

> Like a snake, painful, replete, and dusty,
> Your train slinks from the armchairs onto the rug.

The torment of humiliation and loathing ends in an invitation to a shameful execution:

> So thrust, my yesterday's angel,
> Your sharp French heel into the heart!

The heart, pierced by a French heel, is a staggering expression of the meanness, cynicism, and blasphemy of "passion." As in Dostoevsky, banality here borders on the fantastic.

The temptation of passion lies in its mysterious inseparability from death. Here is again a trip with "her" to the islands; again "the sand crunches under melting snow"; she presses herself to him, her veil, fluttering in the wind, strikes him in the face. And again the blood begins to sing, and the wind and sky ring with a musical storm:

Aleksandr Blok

> And it seemed to me, through the horse's snorting—
> The Hungarian dance in the heavenly mob
> Rings and weeps, teasing me.

The love meeting is a dream and a deception. The music "rings and weeps"—not about love. She first hears this voice:

> And suddenly—you, distant, alien,
> Said with lightning in your eyes:
> *That is a soul, stepping onto the final path,*
> *Madly weeping over past dreams.*

The concluding lines—prolonged and heavy—end the love verses with the mourning sounds of a requiem.

In the poem *Hours and days and years pass*, the illusiveness of images of love and their submersion in the dark bosom of music are expressed by a play of shadows and by snatches of reminiscences. "I want to shake off a kind of dream." Something had happened: it was night, mournful cold, moon, and sea:

> Words? —There were none. —What happened?
> Neither dream nor waking. In the distance, in the distance
> It rang, died out, departed,
> And separated itself from the earth . . .

This "something" (neuter gender) is primary, premature; it is vague agitation, from which lyrical images are born. Pushkin spoke about this condition:

> The soul is clenched with lyrical agitation,
> It trembles and rings . . .

The poet dreams: the sword fell from his hand; the wound is dressed in silk; disarmed and obedient, he serves her. But love's deep sleep is finally interrupted. He understands that that which "rang, died out, departed," sang not of love, but of death:

> But the hour came. In retrospect
> I remembered: *no, I am not a servant.*
> So fall, colored sling!
> Gush, blood, and crimson the snows!

Blok said (in articles and letters) that art is bought at the price of life, that it is "damnation and death," that the face of the artist, like Dante's face, is scorched with hellish flame. This "philosophy of art" is expressed with classical perfection in the famous poem:

> How painful to walk among people
> And to pretend to be alive,

And to tell those not yet living
About the tragic game of passions.

And, scrutinizing one's nightmare,
To find order in the disordered whirlwind of feeling,
To recognize the destructive fire of life
In the pale glow of art!

The poetic theme of "the dead among the living" inspires Blok to a cycle of poems, *Dances of Death*. These *danses macabres* open with a description of the earthly life of a corpse rising from the grave. The poet intensifies the contrast of life and death with an original device: death is depicted as "real", and life as a meaningless and hideous delirium:

Already evening. Light rain splashes with dirt
The passers-by and the houses and other nonsense . . .

In the daytime the corpse works on a report in the senate; in the evening a taxi takes him *"to another deformity"*—to a society ball. N. N. is in love with the corpse:

In her face, girlishly beautiful,
The senseless rapture of living love . . .

Thus—in malicious and intentionally coarse words—life is destroyed. At the ball the corpse meets a dead friend:

Behind their conventional polite speeches
You hear real words.

Everything is deception and a lie, only the dead have real words:

"Weary friend, this hall is strange to me.
"Weary friend, the grave is cold."

Not for long can the ball music—the music of life and passion— muffle the "rattle of bones." Through the enamored speeches of her admirer N. N. hears:

In her ears—an unearthly, strange ringing:
 Bones rattling on bones.

This is one of Blok's most malicious "nihilistic" poems—his naked, frenzied negation, his scorched, empty soul. Still more terrible in its lifeless lapidary quality, in its wooden rhythm, is the poem:

Night, street, lantern, drugstore,
Senseless and dim light.

Aleksandr Blok

Live another quarter of a century—
Everything will be the same. No way out.

You will die—you will begin all over again.
And everything will repeat itself, as of old:
Night, the icy ripple of the canal,
The drugstore, the street, the lantern.

The last line repeats the first, the circle of the eternal return is closed. The two verses—life and death—reflect one another endlessly, like two mirrors. The exactness of the reflection is underlined by internal rhyme. What was on the right in the first mirror is on the left in the second: "Street, lantern, drugstore"—"drugstore, street, lantern." And these three most ordinary words are filled with mystical horror, as with poison:

Everything will be the same. No way out.

The third poem is a Germanic engraving of the sixteenth century: "a skeleton muffled to his eyes in a cloak" gets a vial from a cupboard in a drugstore with the inscription "Venena" and

Thrusts it from under his cloak to two noseless women
On the street under the whitish lamp.

The theme of "living death" culminates in an ecstasy of liberation: the corpse no longer needs an artificial paradise, the music of passions; losing his soul, he grows deaf to sounds. This is the second and final death. The dead man stops pretending to be in love. He tells the truth: passion is a "surf of unutterable boredom":

—I concede, knowing
That your snake's paradise is a bottomless hell of boredom.

This is that metaphysical boredom of nonbeing which Dostoevsky's "sensualist" Svidrigailov speaks about with an ironical smile. The spirit, imprisoned by the flesh, deceived by the "snake's paradise" of sensuality, smashes his prison with furious contempt. In the poem:

I came to know the power of contempt
Over God's best creation.
I struck it with a stick.

is the ecstasy and triumph of liberation. He is alone, he is free, he again hears the singing of the violins:

They sing wild songs
Of how I became free!
Of how for a better fate
I exchanged base passion!

In Blok's nature there is a monastic, ascetic basis, a frenzied chastity in an eternal struggle with the witchcraft of sensuality. The flesh is for him contemptible, passion is downfall, woman is a demon. Some terrible fate dooms the poet to pass through a hell of passions: he drags himself like one condemned to execution, with horror, loathing, shuddering. "Terrible embraces," "protracted torments," "ordeal," "a terrible abyss," "trampling on cherished sacred things"—he finds no other words.

The inspiration of the "love poems" is an acute sense of sin, a torment of repentance, a thirst for atonement. Minutes of oblivion and of demonic ecstasy are bought by years of mortal depression. One must interpret Blok's poetry as a *tragedy of the Christian conscience*. Happiness? He knows no such word. In the poem *Worlds fly. Years fly*, the poet asks:

> What is happiness? Evening coolness
> In the darkening garden, in the remote forest?
> Or the gloomy, depraved pleasures
> Of wine, of passions, of the soul's ruin?

Happiness is "depraved pleasure" and "the soul's ruin." Thus did the Thebaid hermits of the first centuries of Christianity speak; thus did the medieval ascetics teach *de contemptu mundi*. In this same poem a religious "nonacceptance of the world" is expressed sharply: the "brilliant cover" is thrown off the universe; all its splendor is merely a variegated exchange of "invented causes, expanses, times" (Blok is a Kantian!); its movement is "insane, unknown flight":

> Neglected somewhere, helter-skelter,
> A top flies, hums, hurries!

Insanity, senselessness, chance, semblance—such is Blok's nihilistic cosmology. And a poem written in the melancholic-reasoning style of Lermontov's "meditations" ends with the cry: "How long?"

> When is the end? To the importunate sound
> There is no strength to listen without rest . . .
> How terrible everything is! How savage—Give me your hand,
> Comrade, friend! We will seek oblivion again.

All the disconnected features of the "terrible world" are collected here, like focused rays. Life is hell, the universe is an importunately humming top, death is deliverance.

A poem of 1910–12, *Steps of the Commander*—the highest peak of Blok's entire lyric—is included in the *Retribution* section of the third volume. The themes of this brilliant "word symphony" are prepared for by two short poems of 1910, which entered the section *The Terrible World*. In the first of them the motif of life's "emptiness" is already connected with the sound of a car flying by:

Aleksandr Blok

Life is deserted, homeless, fathomless,
Yes, I have believed this since the time
There sang to me, like a siren in love,
That car flying through the night.
(*Accounts with peaceful happiness are closed*)

In *Steps of the Commander* he writes:

Life is empty, insane, and fathomless!
   Come out to battle, old fate!
And in reply—triumphantly and lovingly
   In the snowy haze a small horn sings . . .
    . . . . .
A black car, quiet as an owl,
   Flies past, spattering lights in the night.

In the second poem an automobile horn mysteriously reminds the poet of his faithlessness:

An automobile sang in the distance
With a triumphant horn.

Look through the pale window,
Pressed close to the glass . . .
Look. You were unfaithful long ago,
   Irrevocably.

The motif of life's emptiness and of the irreparability of unfaithfulness, sounding in the car's horn, grows into the tragedy of Don Juan, who was unfaithful to the Maiden of Light—Donna Anna. The Beautiful Lady, descending to the poet in the sun's azure in the days of his youth, "sleeps, her arms folded on her heart." The betrayer is doomed to fate ("Come out to battle, old fate"). And at his call the Fate-Commander enters the house "with quiet, heavy steps." The impression of the funereal splendor of Don Juan's last night is created with magical art. The funereal luxuriance of the bedroom is portrayed in hollow, stony words, like the "hoarse striking of a night clock." Repetitions intensify the deadly torpidity of waiting:

Cold and empty in the luxurious bedroom,
   The servants sleep, and the night is still.

In the luxurious bedroom it is terrible in the hour of dawn,
   The servants sleep, and the night is pale.

In the hour of dawn it is cold and strange,
   In the hour of dawn, the night is turbid.

And here fate draws near. In the "snowy haze, the horn" of the car flying past "sings," the steps of the Commander clatter. From the fairy tale distance of legend ring the words:

"You invited me to supper.
"I came. And are you ready?"

Don Juan is mute. The quiet. The clock strikes for the last time:

Donna Anna will rise in your death hour,
  Anna will rise in the death hour.

Blok sees the legend of Don Juan as a tragedy of conscience. Having been unfaithful to the Maiden of Light, the hero falls into the power of dark forces. The last hours of his life are—*night*: the "night window," "the night is still," the "snowy haze," "spattering lights in the night," "the striking of the night clocks," "the night is pale," "the night is turbid." And only at the moment of death comes dawn. "In the hour of dawn" is repeated three times, preparing the final victory of light:

Anna will rise in the death hour.

The struggle in the soul of the unfaithful one is embodied in images—of the Fate-Commander and the Maiden of Light, Donna Anna. It determines the illumination of the *poema*, the sinking of the world into night, the struggle of darkness with light, and in death the promise of resurrection (the dawn). But the flashing of images and shadows is only surface: the foundation of the *poema* is the sound and rhythmic fabric, the real musical magic. We will limit ourselves to a few elementary observations. In the very sound of the name Don Juan the poem's phonetic plan was given to Blok: the low, hollow O and the broad, open A (Don Žuan). The O becomes the leitmotif of the "darkness-Commander"; A the leitmotif of "light," of Donna Anna. In the first two lines both motifs are already joined, as in a musical introduction:

Tjažkij, plotnyj zanaves u vxoda,
  Za nočnym oknom—tuman.

The heavy, solid curtain by the entrance,
  Beyond the night window—fog.

O is night, cold, death; to it are joined the still more hollow and resonant overtones of U and Y:

Xolodno i pusto v pyšnoj spal'ne,
  Slugi spjat, i noč' gluxa.[8]

Č'i čerty žestokie zastyli?

Cold and empty in the luxurious bedroom,
  The servants sleep and the night is still.

Whose cruel features congealed with cold?

Aleksandr Blok In this kingdom of darkness the doomed hero hurls his last challenge to fate: into the deep basses bursts a sharp high note—the sound I:

Vyxod*i* na b*i*tvu, staryj rok!

Come out to battle, old fate!

This sound, like a breaking string, is drowned by the stone step of the Commander:

Čërnyj, t*i*xij, kak sova, mot*o*r.
T*i*ximi, tjažëlymi šagami
   V d*o*m vstupaet Komand*o*r.

   A black car, quiet as an owl.
   With quiet, heavy steps
      The Commander enters the house.

The voice of fate—the O triumphs (5 O's for 2 I's). Whole lines are orchestrated on O:

Sl*o*vno xriplyj b*o*j nočnyx čas*o*v:
   . . . . .
"Ja prišël. A ty got*o*v?"

Like the hoarse striking of the night clock,
   . . . . .
"I came. And are you ready?"

The motif of light, A sounds distant and muted, suppressed by the motif of darkness. But its development is already predicted in the first verse:

Strax poznavšij Don Žuan

Don Juan, having learned fear

It enters with the theme of Donna Anna, at first combined with the piercing high I, then with the muffled, deathly Y:

D*o*nna *A*nna sp*i*t, skrest*i*v na serdce ruki,
   D*o*nna *A*nna v*i*dit sn*y*.

Donna Anna sleeps, arms folded on her heart,
   Donna Anna dreams.

And further there is:

*A*nna, *A*nna, sl*a*dko l' sp*a*t' v mogile?
   Sl*a*dko l' v*i*det' nezemn*y*e sn*y*?

Anna, Anna, is it sweet to sleep in the grave?
   Is it sweet to see unearthly dreams?

The Commander stands before Don Juan. Dying, the betrayer calls Anna, Anna, is it sweet to sleep in the his beloved:

D*e*va Sv*e*ta! Gd*e* ty, Donna Anna?
   Anna! Anna! —Tišina.

Maiden of Light! Where are you, Donna Anna?
   Anna! Anna! —Silence.

The A already predominates—the sounds of night (O, U, Y) have disappeared. But why is this triumphant A combined with E (three E's in the first line)? Blok has no "meaningless" sounds. And, rereading the poem, we notice that the E had already sounded before the appearance of the Commander, like a harbinger of resurrection, like a hope of salvation:

Iz strany blaž*e*nnoj, n*e*znakomoj, dal'n*e*j
   Slyšno p*e*n'*e* petuxa.

From a blessed, unknown, distant country
   The song of the rooster is heard.

The sound E mystically colors the song of the rooster from a blessed country. This is why, in the finale, conquering all the rumblings and echoes of the night, the triumphal trumpets of A also include the melody of E:

Donna Anna v smertnyj čas tvoj vstanet,
   Anna vstanet v smertnyj čas.

Donna Anna will rise in your death hour,
   Anna will rise in the death hour.

The Steps of the Commander is a masterpiece not only of sound, but also of rhythm.

Its perfection does not lie in the fact that the stony step of the Commander is actually heard in it—at first at a distance, like the hollow blows of a grave shovel, then nearer and nearer, more and more menacing:

Tiximi, tjažëlymi šagami
   V dom vstupaet Komandor.

With quiet, heavy steps
   The Commander enters the house.

Such sound imitation is not essential to the poet. The *poema*'s particularity lies in something else. Blok succeeded in changing the very nature of Russian trochaics; from a light, winged, "dancing" melody he transformed it into a deadly heavy meter barely crawling along the earth. In textbooks of versification we are taught that the Russian language has no long vowels. Blok by various devices—by consonant clustering, by word arrangement, by pauses, by logical accents—creates *vowel length*. In such lines as:

> Anna, Anna, sladko l' spat' v mogile?

or:

> Anna, Anna! —Tišina.

or:

> *Anna vstanet v smertnyj čas*

the accented A's are perceived by the ear and pronounced by the voice as long. This is authentic trochee in the old sense, that is, a combination of a long and a short sound: *Anna, sladko, vstanet* (– ᴗ). We have already indicated the special sounding of A in Blok's lyric poetry. In *The Steps of the Commander* it is revealed in all its emotional force. The deceleration and heaviness of the rhythm is achieved not only by vowel length, but also by the accumulation of tonic accents. In such lines as:

> Boj časov. "Ty zval menja na užin."
>
> The clock strikes. "You invited me to supper."

or:

> V pyšnoj spal'ne strašno v čas rassveta
>
> In the luxurious bedroom it is terrible in the hour of dawn

all the words (except the pronoun "*ty*") are so selected and arranged that each of them carries both a logical and a tonic accent: five stresses fall with the dull, merciless regularity of a clock, cutting off equal time units, drops which measuredly wear away a stone; inhuman, iron necessity is the *rhythm of fate*.

The stanzas *A Dream* (*To My Mother*) are included in the section *Miscellaneous Poems*—one of the rare works of Blok imbued with Christian faith in the resurrection of the dead. The poet dreams that he and his wife and mother are buried in an ancient crypt. The trumpet of Resurrection sounds:

> And He comes out of the smoky distance;
> And angels with swords are with Him:

> Such as we read in the books,
> Bored and not believing them.

The mother asks her son to push the stone away from the grave. The son answers:

> "No, mother. I suffocated in the grave,
> And my former strength is gone.
> Both of you pray and ask
> The angel to push away the stone."

This humility, prayer, and faith are so unexpected after the poems of *The Terrible World* and *Retribution*. The "fallen angel" didn't forget the sounds of the heavens. The poem *And again the impulses of young years* was written that same year, 1912, as was the poem, familiar to us, *Worlds fly. Years fly*, on the same theme of happiness. But they are opposite in emotional tone and lyrical melody. *Worlds fly. Years fly* is the embittered negation of the world-top flying in a void; in the poem *And again the impulses of young years* there is a benediction of life more wonderful and deeper than the childish dream of happiness. Creative rapture demolishes the prison of solitude and unites the poet with the world. A moment of completeness and harmony, a rare guest, visits the poet. This light in the country of "death's canopy" is blinding:

> That the cup
> Of creative rapture overflowed,
> And everything is no longer mine, but ours,
> And a bond with the world was forged,
>
> And only with a tender smile
> You will at times remember
> That childish, vacillating dream,
> That we got used to calling happiness!

In another poem the former, long forgotten "angel songs," carried through the "night, gloom, and void," ring again with benediction and joy:

> I bless everything that happened,
> I didn't seek a better fate.
> Oh, heart, how you loved!
> Oh, mind, how you blazed!
>
> Let both happiness and torment
> Put down their bitter trace,
> But in a passionate storm, in protracted boredom—
> I didn't lose the former light.

A magic circle of harmony is traced around the poet. And however he tried to break it—with curses, cynicism, blasphemy, irony, irreverence—all the dissonances are changed into order, everything chaotic into a cosmos. Like King Midas, the artist turns everything he touches into the gold of art. From torment, horror, death, a song emerges. *The poet is irreparably doomed to harmony.* He can rebel, can summon hordes of demons, can imagine himself a Lucifer—his fate is immutable. Destroying, negating, cursing, he is always *pure affirmation*, a triumphant yes to the Creator and to creation. Blok, the "pessimist" and "nihilist," knew this. In 1914 he spoke of himself words blinding in their beauty and wisdom:

> *Let us remit gloominess—is this really*
> *His secret motive force?*
> *He is all—a child of goodness and light,*
> *He is all—the triumph of freedom!*

In the three-year period 1910–12 the section of the third volume, *Harps and Violins*, was enriched by ten poems. This title conveys exactly the musical nature of the lines:

> Already the clarity of vision had waned
> And the violin lay down under the bow,
> And the conductor's evil will
> Carried the wind along the harps.

And again, as in the poem *In the Restaurant*, her "passionate outline" floats along the waves of music when:

> The tenor sang hymns on the stage
> To the mad violins and to spring.

We already know this "law" of Blok's lyrics and we can predict that the emotional sound, "exploding, will stir up the springs"[9] in the poet's soul and will waft on him the cold of death:

> When suddenly a sigh, not far off,
> Rushing up, froze the blood,
> And someone pale and sad
> Put their hand on my heart.

This triad—music, love, death—is repeated with invariable consistency. In the poem *Where echoes in the long halls* the violins again sing:

> And the violins, fading away and weakening,
> Surrender to the frenzied bows.

She emerges from the round dance and throws a flower to the "appointed friend." And again comes the music of death:

> Don't pick up the flower: it has the sweetness
> Of forgetting all the past days,
> And all the furious joy
> Of your approaching death! . . .

The "furious joy" of the gypsy dance, the forgetting, the intoxication and depression, the usual circle of raptures and torments—the tambourine in the gypsy girl's hands rings of it. She "dances his life" (the poem *Once proud and haughty*):

> And the horrible dance lasts a long time,
> And life passes before me
> Like a mad, sleepy, and beautiful
> And repulsive dream.

All of Blok's "gypsyness" is under the sign of "repulsive beauty"; he brings contradictions together, plays on dissonances, combines the sacred and the vile, introduces the sad Angel into the furious gypsy dance:

> From the irrevocable distance
> The sad Angel is seen . . .

In the poem *Voices of the Violins*:

> A wave of turbulent music
> Splashed in the glowing sea.

The poet knows that music is the soul of the world, that the "harmony of the spheres" sings with its voice, and asks sadly:

> Why, in the clear hour of triumphs,
> Are you angry, my shrill bow,
> Bursting into the world orchestra
> With a private, hurried song?

This poem is completely Tyutchevian in theme and in form. Another skilfully varies Baratynsky's stylistic devices:

> Wordless thought, nameless agitation,
>   What sign do you send me?

Life is a phantom, but the soul dimly remembers something distant: it prefers "unrealizable reality" to the dreams of existence. And the last verse speaks in the language of Baratynsky:

> In order, through dreams of everyday rushing,
>   Losing its way,
> With knowledge of ineffable outlines,
>   To pass as with a torch.

The poet seeks this knowledge, this heavenly harmony, in the wild and discordant sound of the gypsy songs: in their spontaneity, their wild passion, he catches the trembling of "nameless agitation," the echo of the "world orchestra." And the moment comes when, through the screech and racket, in the whirlwind of the dance and the mutter of the tambourine, the song of the "otherworldly violins" is heard:

> I napev zaglušënnyj i junyj
> V zataënnoj zatronet tiši
> Usyplënnye žizniju struny
> Naprjažënnoj, kak arfa, duši.

> And the muffled and young melody
> Will touch in the hidden quietness
> The strings, lulled to sleep by life,
> Of the soul taut as a harp.

This very delicate melody is created by the fourfold repetition of the participles in -ënnyj (*zaglušënnyj, zataënnoj, usyplënnye, naprjažënnoj*). Other words also resound on long, liquid N's: *napev, junyj, struny*. The N sets the *tone* of the verse—velvety soft, dully ringing. On it the sibilants Š and Ž glide with a light rustle: *zaglušënnyj, tiši, žizniju, naprjažënnoj*. The voiceless Š in the word *zaglušënnoj* corresponds to the Š in the word *tiši*; the voiced Ž in *naprjažënnoj* to the voiced Ž in the word *žizniju*. Parallel to the sibilants Ž and Š, the corresponding hissing sounds Z and S pass through the stanza:

> V zataënnoj zatronet tiši
> Usyplënnye žizniju struny.

> Will touch in the hidden quietness
> The strings lulled to sleep by life.

Here the sound texture extends to whole sound complexes: *zat-ë-n* (*zataënnoj*) and *zat-o-n* (*zatronet*);[10] *usy-n* (*usyplënnye*) and *s-u-n-y* (*struny*). In the last line the sound A (*kak arfa*) appears for the first time. A delicate harmony with the word *arfa* is already made in the word preceding it, *naprjažënnoj* (*a-p-rja : a-r-fa*).

One of the poet's best-known poems is included in the section *Harps and Violins*: the story of first love, the appearance of the ghost of the dead paramour:

> Everything memory tries to keep for me
> Vanishes in the mad years,
> But with a burning zigzag this story
> Soars in the night skies.

> Life is long ago burnt up and narrated,
> Only first love is dreamed of,

As a priceless coffer is tied
Crosswise with a ribbon red as blood.

The stanzas are striking in the depth of their lyrical breath, in the breadth of rhythm. The dactyllic rhymes of the odd lines (*staraetsja : vzvivaetsja, rasskazana : perevjazana*) cast the lines upward with a powerful sweep; the two unaccented syllables after the accented one seem to hang in the air. And after each upward flight there is a sharp fall: the masculine rhymes of the even lines (*godax : nebesax, lyubov' : krov'*).

Another remarkable poem, *Along the marshy, deserted meadow*, is a variant of *The Stranger*. To the line "breathing perfume and fogs" answer here the lines "And the bitter and sad odor of fogs and perfume"; to the line "And a slender hand in rings" corresponds "And rings through a thin glove." But in the later poem not only the everyday, but even the earthly, disappears. Only flight "over the ringing wilderness," only the soul's lofty aspiration, remain:

Everything speaks of the *boundless*.
Everything wants to help us,
Like this world, to fly aimlessly
Into the shining night!

Blok is a genius of metaphor. Out of similarity he creates identity. Here is the first verse:

Along the marshy, deserted meadow
    We fly. Alone.
Over there, like cards, in a semicircle
    Lights fan out.

The distant lights of the city remind the poet of cards spread out in a semicircle. The comparison "lights, like cards"

Tell fortunes, child, by the cards of night,
    Where your beacon . . .

And here is the second stanza: the lights are no longer "like cards," but are real cards, by which one can tell fortunes. The simile has become a metaphor, "the cards of night," and is filled with new content. "Inevitable gloom" surrounds the lovers; but the night spreads its mysterious cards before them. They read their fate in them ("Where your beacon . . .").

The last poem, *In the damp night fog*, written in December 1912, calls to mind folk incantations, witchcraft charms, the sorcery of dark forces. The strange, half-mad mutter of the rhymes: *tumane : bur'jane, tumani : gerani, gerani : tumane, bur'jane : gerani*. At night, a forest, a mysterious light: "hut, window, geranium." He approaches on a horse. A voice says to him:

Aleksandr Blok

> Oh, friend, you won't be safe here,
> Quickly, away from here!
> You will arrive—you'll forget everything,
> You'll forget—you will vanish into the night!
> In the fog and in the tall weeds,
> Look—you will sell Christ
> For greedy geraniums,
> For crimson lips!

The unexpected line, for which we are completely unprepared—"Look—you will sell Christ"—completes the impression of inexplicable horror. This "bad dream" vaguely calls to mind the "black magic" of the *poema Night Violet*.

Finally, in the section *Native Land*, we find six poems written in 1910–12. Blok made the following note on one of them, *On the Railroad*: "Unconscious imitation of an episode from Tolstoy's *Resurrection*. At a small station Katyusha Maslova sees in a coach window Neklyudov in the velvet armchair of a brightly lit first-class sleeping compartment." Here is the first stanza:

> Under the embankment, in an unmown ditch,
> A young and beautiful girl
> In a flowered kerchief thrown over her hair
> Lies and looks, as if alive.

In a sensitively plaintive tone he tells about the "wasted youth" of a girl who killed herself, about "empty dreams," about "travel depression." On the platform of a small station she meets and sees off a train. The best stanza of the poem is about the coaches:

> The coaches moved in the usual line,
> They trembled and screeched
> The yellow and blue ones were quiet;
> In the green ones they wept and sang.

And here is the reminiscence of Tolstoy's *Resurrection*:

> Only once the hussar, leaning
> A casual arm on the crimson velvet,
> Glanced at her fleetingly with a tender smile . . .
> Glanced—and the train whirled off into the distance.

The sentimentally humane story about the young suicide is steeped in the style of Nekrasov. The Nekrasovian manner even seems exaggerated in the last stanza:

> Don't approach her with questions,
> It's all the same to you, and she's had enough.

> Whether she is crushed by love,
> By dirt, or by the wheels—it's all painful.

This poem belongs among Blok's "stylistic exercises." After V. Solovyov, Fet, Lermontov, Tyutchev and Baratynsky, he draws near to Nekrasov's "humane" lyric.

Three poems are devoted to the dreams of childhood and youth. He is again a child: the green ray of an icon-lamp over his bed; his nurse tells him a fairy tale about bogatyrs, about a tsarevna beyond the seas.

> Sweetly dozes on a cot.
> "Are you dozing?" "I am listening . . . I am sleeping."
> Green ray, ray of the icon-lamp,
> I love you!

These are light, simple, pensive lines—like a children's book with colored pictures.

The second dream is a vision of youth (*The sound draws near. And obedient to the plaintive sound*):

> Dreams—I am again a little boy and again a lover,
>   And the ravine, and the tall weeds,
> And in the tall weeds—prickly sweetbrier,
>   And evening fog.

Through the flowers, an old house with its rosy window looks at him, and

> Though in a dream, I press to my lips
>   Your once-dear hand.

Everything in this beautiful poem recalls Fet: the gentleness and the tenderness, and the clear, even light.

The third dream is a deathbed dream (*The Visitation*). Two voices call to one another in a snowstorm. The first says:

> Here I again bent
> Over your bed; I breathe, I recognize . . .
> I through the nights, through the long nights,
> Through the dark nights—in a crown.
> Here they are—still blue eyes
> On my face grown old!

Another voice answers: the soul had grown blind to visions, his house is snowbound by the blizzard:

> I don't dare look into your eyes,
> Everything that happened—is far away.
> The heart is full of the terrible memory
> Of the long years of never-ending night.

This is the poet's last meeting with the Eternal Friend. What sadness in this snow, in this night, in this "hearth grown cold." And how the heart transfixes her eyes, still blue in the face grown old.

In 1910 the pathetic poem *My Rus, my life, are we to suffer together?*, which ends the cycle *On the Field of Kulikovo*, was written—it is a fortissimo of enormous sonority. Sinister Asiatic Rus, black shadows and red glow, numb face and fiery Tatar eyes—his native land stands before the poet as a terrible, fateful enigma. Who will solve it? Who will answer the agitated, avid questions?

> My Rus, my life, are we to suffer together?
> Tsar and Siberia and Ermak and prison!
> Oh, isn't it time to part, to repent . . .
> For what is your darkness to the free heart?
>
> Did you know something? Or did you believe in God?
> What will you hear there from your songs?

And there is no answer: the sleepy mirage looms, the black haze flows from the steppe. The next stanza takes up the word "black" as a basic theme:

> Beyond the Black Sea, beyond the White Sea,
> In black nights and white days,
> The numb face looks wildly,
> Tatar eyes cast fires . . .

The furious steppe melody, wild, like the wailing of a shaman, pierced the heart of Russia "with the arrow of ancient Tatar ferocity." And in 1918, when Blok wrote his *Scythians*, he again saw Russia in the red glow of the Tatar camp:

> Yes, we are Scythians! Yes, we are Asiatics,
> With slanted and avid eyes!

The Rose and the Cross is the culmination of Blok's romantic theater. Like the "lyrical dramas," it is constructed on the intersection of two planes of consciousness, "dream" and "reality." The two-planed composition is carried skillfully through the whole action of the play. The "reality" is sunny Languedoc, the castle of Archimbaut, a historical and genre picture of France at the beginning of the eighteenth century; the "dream" is misty Brittany, its legends and songs. In the play there is no struggle of passions, no clash of people, no real dramatic conflict. The contrast between the bright reality, saturated with movement and color, and the poetic Breton fairy tale has to replace them. The drama's artistic expressiveness depends on the tension of this contrast; Blok, the romantic, moves with ease among the mists of legend, but his self-assurance leaves him when he touches the soil of "reality." Therefore, depicting the life of the castle in Languedoc, he has recourse to historical materials, to literary sources, to scholarly research; he strives for "everyday realism."

The action of the drama is set on a "historical background." In the first act Count Archimbaut speaks about the uprising of the "weavers," about Raymond VI, the Toulouse count who came over to the side of the Albigensians, and about the campaign of Simon de Montfort against the heretics. In notes to the play the author, with the seriousness of a scholarly historian, gives short biographies of Simon de Montfort and Raymond of Toulouse, and declares: "The crusade against the Albigensians began in 1208, to which the action of *The Rose and the Cross* must also be dated." In order to recreate the "spirit of the epoch," Blok studies the sources diligently. Archimbaut sends Bertran to meet the troops of Montfort; he turns from the "Toulouse road" to the north and goes to Brittany. This detail, not essential to the course of the action, is justified "documentarily" in the notes: "Bertran went north, on the count's commission, having first come out onto the Toulouse road (la via Tolosana), the usual route of pilgrims to Santiago from the north. This route is indicated in a 'guidebook of the pilgrims' (*Codex Campostellanus*, twelfth century)."

Historical realism triumphs. The customs and daily life of the French Middle Ages are depicted with no less thoroughness in the play. From the Provençal novel of the twelfth century, *Flamenca*, Blok borrows concrete features, images, and expressions:

> Many places in the dialogue of Izora and Alisa, especially the place where Alisa plays the role of a clerk, I borrowed from the twelfth century Provençal novel *Flamenca*. It suggested to me the character of the count. From it the name of Count Archambaut (Archimbaut in E. V. Anichkov's transcription) is taken, the names of Alisa (the chatelaine of Flamenca has two "damoiselles"—Alisa and Margarita), Otton, and Clara. Finally, from that same novel I took a few of the play's isolated images and expressions, for example: the count's hair "like the devil's in the picture"; "when he smiles, he bares his teeth like a dog"; "the ferocity of any dragon can be softened by gentleness," et al.

Blok also reads another courtly novel about Lancelot du Lac; from it he borrowed the legend about the fairy Vivian.

In the first act Izora and Alisa play chess. The author makes a "scholarly note": "In the novel of the Round Table, *Lancelot*, the fairy Vivian plays chess with Lancelot. Both Walter Scott in his *Essais sur la Chevalerie* and the popular histories of literature and customs testify that chess was widespread in the castles of the feudal lords." Alarmed by Izora's incomprehensible depression, the count summons a doctor, who makes a diagnosis:

> Your Grace, your wife is subject to melancholy, which is cold, dry, and bitter. The reign of melancholy lasts from August to the ides of February.... Soon the blood will begin to increase. And when too much blood

accumulates, we will release it through the nose, as the ancient sages Galen and Hippocrates teach.

Blok could also have found a satire on the physicians' art in the theater of Moliere and in any Italian *Commedia dell'Arte*, but he wasn't content with this: he needed "historical authenticity." He writes this in a note: "I borrowed the doctor's diagnosis from a medieval medical book, part of a thirteenth- to fourteenth-century manuscript in the municipal library in Cambrai."

The striving for "historical truth" also extends to the drama's lyrical elements. In the fourth act, a folk festival takes place on a flowering meadow. The girls sing around a May tree, minstrels delight the ear of the knights and beautiful ladies with their songs, jugglers run out and entertain the assemblage with jests and tricks:

> The first juggler: Knights, barons and beautiful ladies. I will tell you about the renowned King Arthur.
> The second juggler: Don't listen to him, noble knights. I play the zither and walk on my head.
> . . . . .
> The first juggler: I will sing about true lovers: about Hero and Leander, about Helen and Paris.
> The second juggler: And I dance on a rope, leap through a hoop, play with knives.

Blok takes both the songs of the minstrels and the buffoonery of the jugglers from "sources." In the notes he explains:

> I took the song of the young girls ("Here is is, May, bright May") from various May songs (*tremouzettes*). Its beginning: "*C'est le mai, le joli mai!*" (Compare E. V. Anichkov: *Spring Ritual Song*, part I, chapter 3, p. 168 ff.). The May tree—a post decorated with flowers and ribbons—was carried by young girls in crowns, with songs, or transported on a cart harnessed with oxen.

The first minstrel's song, "I love the breath of beautiful spring," is a free translation of a sirventes by Bertram de Born. The author retained all of the famous troubador's alternations of rhyme and all the characteristic features of his "martial style." The song of the second minstrel, "Through the dense forest, in the spring time," is a free adaptation of a thirteenth-century song of a Picardie trouvère. Both these songs belong to Blok's best translations. The song of the third minstrel—Gaetan —was composed by the author himself, but even in it "certain motifs are evoked by Breton poetry." As for the jugglers' jests, the note to them reads: "The same jugglers who could sing could often do acrobatic tricks. The words of my jugglers are borrowed."

The "historicity" of the drama is not exhausted by these "borrowings" and "adaptations." The author attempts to stylize his characters' speech. Alisa frees herself from the embraces of the sensual chaplain;

running away, the latter exclaims: "Saint James!" The count, alarmed by the uprising of the villeins, shouts: "I swear by Saint James-Compostela." Blok considers it his duty to explain in a note that the apostle James the Elder, "Saint James-Compostela," was one of the saints most revered in the thirteenth century, that his remains were transported to Compostela in the ninth century, etc.

Blok strives to create a drama full of intense action from concrete historical material. He devises a complicated, intricate plot. The wife of the lord of the castle of Archimbaut, Izora, hears the strange song of an itinerant juggler and falls ill with melancholy. The chaplain chases after her chatelaine, Alisa, but she is in love with the handsome page, Aliskan, and rejects the attentions of the sensual monk. Aliskan sighs languidly for Izora and is indifferent to the chatelaine. The chaplain takes revenge on Alisa, arousing in the jealous count suspicion of his wife's infidelity. The latter shuts up Izora and her confidante in the "Tower of the Inconsolable Widow." In the castle lives the old, humiliated Knight of Misfortune, Bertran. He secretly and selflessly loves his beautiful lady, who takes his worship with contemptuous pity. On her commission he sets out to Brittany and brings back from there the author of the song about "Joy-Suffering"—the poor knight Gaetan. Aliskan, worn out by Izora's indifference, sends Alisa a love note in a pie; Izora thinks that the letter is addressed to her. At the May holiday Gaetan sings his sad song in the presence of the ladies, barons, and knights. Seeing his gray locks, Izora recovers from her "painful dreams" and notices at her feet the enamored young Aliskan. Earthly love conquers foggy dream, and the beautiful lady grants the page a rendezvous in her room. The festival is broken up by a sudden attack on the castle by the troops of Count Raymond. In single combat, Bertran vanquishes the knight with the dolphin on his shield, and the enemies retreat. At Izora's request the Knight of Misfortune, gravely wounded in the combat, stands on guard at night under his lady's window, protecting the lovers' peace. Offended by Aliskan's unfaithfulness, Alisa receives with favor the love of the fat chaplain. Bertran dies at dawn, dropping his sword ringingly on the flagstones of the castle yard.

The drama *The Rose and the Cross* has an involved love intrigue; a motley crowd of extras (knights, vassals, guests, chatelaines, kitchen boys and other servants, peasant girls, minstrels, and jugglers); frequent changes of scenery ("Castle Yard," "Passage in the Castle," "Izora's Room," "The Count's Room," "Castle Kitchen," "Tower of the Inconsolable Widow," "Rose Thicket," "Flowering Meadow," and in the second act, "Shore of the Ocean," "Castle of Troménec"); showy theatrical spectacles (songs and dances by the May tree, the knighting ceremony, the appearance of the ghost in the dungeon, the enemies' attack on the castle). The author utilizes the most varied stage devices to fill his drama with motion and colors.

In the division of acts into short, expressive scenes, in the mixture of the amusing and the sad, the lofty and the trivial, in the alternation of lyrical monologues and prose dialogues, in the combination of poetic invention with everyday realism, Blok is following Shakespeare's dramatic technique. Much knowledge, stage experience, formal ability is put into the play. And despite all these efforts, the "artistic realism" didn't come off for the author. The drama has bustling movement, but no action; incidents, but no events; masks, but no people. Count Archimbaut, a deceived, jealous husband; the chaplain, an intriguer and sensualist; the doctor with his jester's pedantry; the coquettish and sly confidante Alisa; the enamored and dark page Aliskan—all these are masks, well known to us from the comedies of Moliere. The involved plot works against its plausibility. The emotional shifts of the characters are far from any kind of psychology. (Izora "suddenly" falls in love with Aliskan. Aliskan loves Izora, but "unexpectedly" agrees to love Alisa, too. Alisa is in love with Aliskan, but out of vexation "suddenly" arranges a rendezvous with the chaplain.) Living people and human passions in the spirit of Shakespeare don't come off for Blok. Against his will the play of masks—the style of the *Commedia dell'Arte*—triumphed. But in this crowd of actors stands one human being, one living character is visible—Bertran. His position in the drama is special; in him two worlds are united—reality and dream, the "real" Languedoc and the legendary Brittany.

The Rose and the Cross was conceived by the author as an artistic diptych. Half of it is a historical drama with realistically copied details; the other half is a lyrical *poema*. From gay and sultry Languedoc we are transported to sad and mysterious Brittany, from the castle of Archimbaut to the uninhabited shore of the ocean. Bertran (on horseback) says: "Where have I ridden to? The snow blinds my eyes, the wind whistles in my ears." And as soon as the noise of the ocean and the whistle of the snowstorm is heard, the tone of the play changes sharply: the lyrical theme is born, grows, and submerges the artificial constructions of historical and everyday realism. We again hear the poet's personal voice. His "foggy Brittany" is created out of memories of the summer of 1911, spent in the small town of Abervrach on the shore of the ocean. In the notes the locality where the second act of the drama takes place is described in detail:

> Abervrach lies on the very shore of the bay, at the mouth of the stream from which it got its name, and directly opposite it is an outlet to the ocean, fortified in the fifties of the past century by a small fort, which is now abandoned. . . . Near this fort are rocks and stones of fantastic shapes. Landeda and the ruins of Troménec lie on the heights above Abervrach, in sight of the ocean. From this whole shore the deserted island of the Virgin (île de la Vierge), lying in the sea, is visible, on which the greatest of French lighthouses is erected, marking the entrance to La Manche.

This harsh and mysterious land struck the poet's imagination. He became acquainted with its past from the book of the sixteenth-century Dominican monk, Albert le Grand, called *Les vies des Saints de la*

Bretagne—Armorique. From it he learned that, on the hill above Abervrach, there existed a monastery, Notre Dame des Anges, and not far from it, "on a beautiful and pleasant grassplot near a beautiful spring," was located "a chapel of the Mother of God which belonged to the noble house of Troménec."

The image of the poet-knight Gaetan, the owner of the castle Troménec, arose from personal reminiscences and ancient legends. In the second act Gaetan explains to a fisherman how to find the road to the castle:

> "Past the monastery garden to the well—from the well to the hill, to the first houses of Landeda. Turn left before you reach the church, along the field; Troménec will soon be there."
>
> . . . . .
>
> The fisherman: So this is Troménec? And a queer duck the seignior there must be.
> Gaetan: Why do you think so?
> The fisherman: Not only I, everyone says so. They say he grazes his flock himself, and he has a flock of three roosters in all. He lives poorly, must be a miser. Other knights feast and fight at tournaments, but this one just wanders and tells fairy tales.

Thus Brittany's barren nature and the ruins of the poor castle overgrown with ivy and enveloped in legend give birth to the image of the poor knight, the eccentric and storyteller.

In the bay of Abervrach, Blok saw "rocks and stones of fantastic shapes": they were connected in his imagination with the legend of the underwater city of Keris, the Breton Kitezh.[11] He became acquainted with this poetic legend from Villemarque's book, *Chants populaires de la Bretagne.* Its content is set forth in the notes:

> History has preserved the vague memory of some city of the fifth century, which was named ville d'Is, or Keris. The legend tells that Keris was the capital of Armorica. The pious king Graalon ruled it, who was friendly with the holy Gwenole, the first abbot of the first monastery built in Armorica. The city Keris stood on the seashore and was separated from it by an immense pond, which saved it from flooding during the rising tides. There was a secret door in the dyke separating the pond from the city, and its key was kept by the king. . . . Once the old king fell asleep after a banquet. He slept in a purple mantle, with a golden chain on his neck. His hair, as white as snow, streamed on his shoulders. At this time Graalon's perfidious daughter, the beautiful Dagyu (Dahut), stole into his bedroom, knelt, took the chain from his neck and the key with the chain. She opened the secret door to admit her lover, whose speech flowed into her ears as quietly as water. The ocean gushed in and inundated the city. Only a woodman then heard how Graalon's wild horse, fast as flame, galloped into the dark night. He saw a water sprite combing her golden hair on the shore in the midday sun. She sang, and her songs were sad, like the lapping of the waves. The holy Gwenole turned the perfidious Dahut into a siren. Even to this day fishermen see the remains of the walls

and towers jutting out of the water at ebb tide, and in a storm they hear the ringing of bells on the sea bottom.

The song about Keris, written in the Cornwall dialect, begins with the words: "Don't believe love!"

> Don't believe madness!
> Behind joy—suffering.

Out of this Breton legend Blok built a musical accompaniment to the image of the "wanderer" Gaetan, and the words of the song, "Behind joy—suffering," were transformed into the leitmotif of the drama:

> Law immutable to the heart:
> Joy and suffering are one.

In the second act the song of the fisherman prepares for the appearance of Gaetan:

> Do not sleep, king, do not sleep, Graalon,
> Your city is submerged in water!
> Keris lies at the bottom of the seas,
> A curse on your daughter!

After Bertran's duel, Gaetan takes him to his own place, to the castle Troménec, and tells him about the underwater city:

> And the old king fell asleep.
> Then the perfidious daughter,
> Quietly stealing the keys,
> Opened the door to her lover. . .
> But the door was in a dyke,
> The ocean gushed into it. . .
> Thus Keris sank,
> And the old king perished.

Bertran takes the wanderer to Izora. They pass on horseback along the shore of the ocean. For Gaetan the fairy tale is more real than reality: he sees the world with the eyes of a poet. His dialogue with Bertran is one of the best passages in the drama:

> *Gaetan:*
> Now the underwater city is not far away.
> Do you hear the bells ringing?
> *Bertran:*
> I hear
> How the noisy sea sings.
> *Gaetan:*
> And do you see,
> Gwenole's dark chasuble floats
> Above the sea?

> *Bertran:*
> I see how the gray fog
> Is lifting.
> *Gaetan:*
> Now do you see
> How the roses play on the waves?
> *Bertran:*
> Yes, it's the sun rising behind the fog.

Bertran take the wanderer to the castle of Archimbaut and hides him in the rose thicket. Again the motif of Keris sounds:

> *Gaetan:*
> That means tomorrow
> I will sing at the king's?
> *Bertran:*
> At the count's,
> You mean to say?
> *Gaetan:*
> So she is not the daughter
> Of old Graalon!
> . . . . .
> I understand!
> I must free the golden-haired
> From captivity!
> *Bertran:*
> She is swarthy. And her hair
> Is blacker than night.
> *Gaetan:*
> But all the same,
> Her name is Morgana? Isn't it?

The legend of Keris, like a musical wave, bears the image of the knight-wanderer. Gaetan is a poetic vision, the singing of the waves, the distant sound of the ocean. The author entrusts to him the main lyrical theme of the drama: "Joy and suffering are one." Gaetan is not only an eccentric, pasturing three roosters on Mount Troménec and telling unintelligible fairy tales to the fisherman; he is a wise child brought up by a fairy and bringing mysterious glad tidings to the world. He recalls his past in the conversation with Bertran:

Near the blue lake my young mother
Late in the evening, in the fog,
Walked away from my cradle...
The fairy carried me, an infant,
Into her lake palace
And raised me in foggy captivity...
And with a crown of pink roses
Decorated my curls.

Before turning the child loose in the world, the fairy pressed him in her arms for a long time and wept. On farewell she said to him:

> The world's boundless rapture
> I put in your heart!
> Listen to the songs of the ocean!
> Look into the crimson dawns!
> You will be a pointless summons to people.
> . . . . .
> You will be a wanderer in the world!
> In this is your purpose,
> Joy-Suffering is yours.

In this scene of fairy tale beauty, together with the reinforcement of the solemn, triumphal melody, the figure of Gaetan develops. The pitiful, the poor, the ludicrous fall from him like decrepit scales; on the shore of the blue lake, in a crown of pink roses, the Poet stands before us with his boundless rapture and pointless summons, with his Joy-Suffering. Thus the lofty, pathetic tone of the song at the May festival is prepared for. And when, in the fourth act, the gray-haired singer appears before the barons and beautiful ladies, we with new agitation listen attentively to the magical, already vaguely familiar sounds:

> Yield to the impossible dream,
> What is fated will come to pass.
> Law immutable to the heart:
> Joy and Suffering are one.
>
> Your future path is wandering,
> The noisy ocean sings.
> Joy, oh Joy-Suffering,
> The pain of unknown wounds!
>
> Everywhere—misfortune and losses,
> What lies before you?
> Set your shaggy sail,
> Mark the breast of your strong armor
> With the sign of the cross!
>
>> The hurricane roars,
>> The ocean sings,
>> The snow whirls,
>
> The fleeting age rushes,
> The blessed shore is dreamed!

Gaetan's song is the height of Russian romantic poetry. On the border of two worlds—sunny Languedoc and foggy Brittany—the major hero, the Knight of Misfortune, Bertran, stands. In articles and notes about his drama Blok repeats constantly: "*The Rose and the Cross* is the story of the failure Bertran." He is put in the center of the action, in the double illumination of "reality" and "dream." In him all the dramatic power of the play is concentrated; the remaining characters *act*, he alone *lives*. The drama begins with his "muted song." Bertran, standing guard in the castle yard, repeats Gaetan's enigmatic song. He, "shaken by the February storm like the trunk of an old apple tree," is a freak, ridiculed by all:

> With what, old man, will you answer spring?
> Only with the agitation of hopeless love.

Alisa drives him away from the window: the guard's singing disturbs the lady. In the fourth scene the count showers the unfortunate knight with insults:

> Be silent! You are very likely of that same stripe
> As all you failures and cowards,
> Who are knocked out of the saddle
> In the very first tournament.

In the fifth scene Izora forces Bertran to confess to her his secret love. He bows his knee; she says to Alisa:

> Oh, how strong and beautiful love is!
> Even to this breed,
> Low, ridiculous, and insignificant,
> It gives knightly fidelity.

The reason for Bertran's debased position in the castle of Archimbaut is explained in the second act. The Knight of Misfortune tells Gaetan of his life. He is the son of a simple weaver from Toulouse; the count girded him with a sword for his long service in the castle. Once at a tournament a knight with a dolphin on his coat of arms unseated him with a foul blow. Izora waved her kerchief and the victor spared his life:

> Since that time no one makes way for me,
> Everyone laughs in my face...
> And she laughs, I know,
> In her high window...
> But a greeting, or the shadow of a greeting,
> I saw from her alone...
> Like grass from the rose, I am far from her.

The Knight of Misfortune knows how hopeless his love is, but nonetheless this pitiful, relentless dream lives in his heart. Recognizing in the old man Gaetan the author of the song about Joy-Suffering, he weeps from happiness. But his tears are not only from joy at meeting the one he had sought so long:

> Second joy—forgive me for it—
> I see you are not a youth.
> Better for Izora to hear the song

Unconfused by base masculine beauty,
Listening piously to your song.

The poor knight's shy jealousy prepares the tragic denouement of the last scene: of his renunciation and death. In the third act Bertran asks Gaetan what his song means, how suffering can become joy:

The idea glimmers to me, but a simple, dark mind
Can't attain all the bright depth.

In the fourth act the Knight of Misfortune wakes Gaetan, who is sleeping in the rose thicket. On his chest he sees a black rose, thrown out of the window by Izora. The singer willingly gives up the flower to him. From the duel with the knight who once knocked him from the saddle, Bertran emerges the victor. He saves the castle from pillaging, defends his lady. The last scene is full of lofty and pure tragedy. Bertran is mortally wounded:

Oh, how the wound sears the heart!
Straight into the rose on his chest
That sword-blow fell.

Izora appears at the top of the staircase. The painful dreams have passed; the appearance of the gray-haired singer shattered the magical spell of his song. Now she sees: spring in the world; at her feet the handsome enamored page, Aliskan:

Izora
... Disappeared,
Those terrible visions ...
Is it true it was only a dream?
Bertran
Only a dream. Your daydream.
Izora
Only a dream ... My daydream ...
What are you clutching in your fingers
On your breast, Bertran?
Bertran
The rose of my fidelity.
Izora
The rose of fidelity ... oh, yes!
Your fidelity has saved us all!
Bertran
I only did my duty.

Izora asks the knight to stand guard by her window during her rendezvous with Aliskan; as reward she extends her hand to him.

Bertran
My lady! holy

> To me is your will.
> I am unworthy to touch
> Your pink hand.

Aliskan appears; to climb up to his love's window he stands on Bertran's shoulders. The poor knight's last monologue is interrupted by Izora's speeches of love, as she embraces the young page through the window. Bertran speaks, gasping, in semidelirium:

> Bloom, oh rose,
> In the secret garden,
> Be fragrant, while over the world
> Holy spring sails.
>   . . . . .
> I hear, I hear,
> The waves rage,
> The ocean roars,
> The cross burns over the blizzard,
> Calls you into the snowy night!
>   . . . . .
> Damned wounds,
> Don't sear my heart! . . .
>   . . . .
> Oh, what torment!
> And sweetness—after the torment!

The black rose of love, watered by the blood of the mortal wound, lay on the cross of life. Bertran did everything his Lord commanded him. His honor is restored; his duty of service is fulfilled; his vow of fidelity is kept; everything is given up: strength, love, life. And at the moment of death, renouncing everything and sacrificing everything, in the depths of abasement and impoverishment, streaming blood and exhausted under the burden of the cross, the poor knight finally discovers the meaning of the song about Joy-Suffering.

His last words burn with joy:

> How beautiful the night!
> Hark, into the solemn trumpets' voice
> Bursts a rustling . . .
> No, again silence . . .
> Nothing disturbs the peace any longer.
> God, Your thunderous silence
> Your poor slave
> Hears clearly.
> The wound opened,
> My strength weakens . . .
> Burn, rose!
> Death, you make the heart wiser . . .
> I understood, understood, Izora:
> "Law immutable to the heart—
> Joy and Suffering are one . . .

Joy, oh Joy-Suffering,
The pain of unprecedented wounds! . . ."

Falling dead, Bertran drops the sword on the flagstones. He promised Izora to forewarn her of danger by ringing the sword. And even in death he remained true to his word, true to his love.

Constraining his lyrical genius, Blok strove to create a "realistic drama"—and suffered defeat. But the defeat was transformed into victory. A lofty *romantic* drama arose by its own artistic law. The clash of two worlds—dream and reality—became the tragic fate of the knight of the Beautiful Lady; the torment of unshared and disdained love was revealed as the "law immutable to the heart," and the hero's death was crowned by the mystical sign of the Rose and the Cross.

The poet put his own suffering and joy into the Knight of Misfortune. In his wretched and humble image he saw the mystery of self-crucifying love. "Joy and suffering are one," as the Rose and the Cross are one.

The drama *The Rose and the Cross* was completed on 19 January 1913. Blok reads it to a small circle. Meyerhold, who is present at the reading, is enraptured with the balance of structure and the polish of the craftsmanship. He tells the author: "You have never done such work before." Then Blok reads his drama to Tereshchenko and his two sisters; two days later to A. M. Remizov in the presence of Zonov, the director of Our Theater. "By the reaction," the poet notes in the *Diary*, "expressed on their faces when the observations touch merely upon trifles, I see that I have finally written something real." And on 11 February he makes an even more decisive statement: "A significant day. The further I go, the more firmly I 'become established' 'as an artist.' There is an instrument in me, a good piano, the strings are taut." But this doesn't prevent the poet from noting a few days later: "I don't like my own—I looked through *The Rose and the Cross*—clumsy style." At the end he adds: "Art is linked to morality. This is the 'phrase' penetrating a work (*The Rose and the Cross*, as I sometimes think)."

At the beginning of April a "society of poets" is formed on the initiative of the young poet and brilliant investigator of rhythm, N. V. Nedobrovo. In it poems were read and analyzed, reports were discussed. Those who took part were: the "poet of the people," A. D. Skaldin; Pyast; A. A. Kondratiev; V. R. Khovin; the poetess Moravskaya; B. Sadovskoy; Yu. Verkhovsky; the assistant professor A. A. Smirnov; O. Mandelshtam; the beginning poet Ryurik Ivnev; and the venerable maître himself, V. Ivanov. At the first meeting on 4 April, Blok read *The Rose and the Cross*; after him N. V. Nedobrovo read "On the Connection between Certain Phenomena of Russian Poetic Rhythm and Breathing." Blok remained dissatisfied with the new society and didn't go again. On 30 April he wrote to V. N. Knyazhnin: "I feel rather sour. I disliked the society of poets very much the first time, and therefore I don't go."

In the spring depression again swept over him. We read in the *Diary*:

30 March. Days of inexpressible depression and terrible twilights—from drifting ice, but not only from drifting ice.

9 April. Bottomless depression. Thoughts of departure. Dinner at the Finland Station, sad sunset in Shuvalovo.

12 April. I dined at Beloostrov, then sat over the darkening sea in the Sestroretsk resort. The world began to seem new; the thought of death became more real, more vivid ("subversive thought")—from the sea, the pines, the sunset.

20 April. Thus my incomprehensible life drags on, drags on.

In the spring the Art Theater comes to Petersburg as usual. Blok is dreaming that Stanislavsky will stage *The Rose and the Cross*. He notes in the *Diary*: "If *his* [Stanislavsky's] *genius touches the play*, I'll be calm about *all* the rest. Stanislavsky's mistakes are as enormous as his positive acts. *If he doesn't want to* himself, I will again depart into 'my hold.' I need no one else." On 26 April the author reads the play to Stanislavsky. Blok gives a curious description of that reading:

> It was especially difficult for me to read the play, and I read it especially badly, feeling that Konstantin Sergeevich was listening intently, but not taking it in. . . . He took all the action as monotonous, gray; he lost the thread. . . . Here's how the conversation went. At first I began telling him that Bertran is "a human being" and Gaetan a "genius," what Izora is (why "a seamstress"). . . . He, constantly apologizing for the coarseness of his imagination ("our art is coarse"), began to amplify and to let his imagination run away with him. And this is what came out between us. Bertran lives—*a humiliated man*. To show this immediately by having Alisa order him to empty the slops, almost a chamber-pot. The *knight* puts down his sword and shield and carries the bucket. "Here, give this to me as to an actor," Stanislavsky would constantly repeat in such cases. . . . Apparently nothing will come of it with the Art Theater either, and I'll have to just publish *The Rose and the Cross*.

Two days later he writes another entry:

> *Today*. Nonetheless all this is sad. I wrote for a year, lived the play, it is honest. . . . A sensitive man came, in whom I believe, who created something great (Chekhov in the Art Theater), and he *understood nothing*, "*accepted" and felt nothing*. Again it means writing "in oblivion."

And, finally, he notes on 4 May: "The dear and wonderful K. S. Stanislavsky nonetheless told me a lot of horrible stupidities. They say he listens only to Efros. . . . I want to live, if there were something to live by, if I knew how."

After the failure with staging *Song of Fate* came the failure with *The Rose and the Cross*. Between Blok's romantic art and the deeply concealed, but ineradicable "positivism" of the Art Theater lay an insurmountable barrier. It is terrible to think that the "brilliant" Stanislavsky "didn't understand, didn't accept, didn't feel" the tragic poetry of *The Rose and the Cross*, that he preferred the ungifted hack-work play of

Surguchev, *Autumn Violins*, to Blok's drama. But two years later he changed his opinion, and *The Rose and the Cross* was accepted for staging. The revolution prevented its realization.

In 1913 the enemies of the "symbolist school" loudly celebrated their victory. The "pioneer" of acmeism, the free-and-easy, spirited Gorodetsky, buries the symbolists in an article, "Certain Trends in Contemporary Russian Poetry" (*Apollo*, 1913). Here are the most provocative passages from this literary obituary:

> The symbolists themselves turned out to be heretics: heresy began at the center. No one else's vassals entered into such endless combinations of quarrels and peace in the realm of theory as the vassals of the symbol. And isn't it surprising that the symbolists overlooked one of their noblest figures: Innokenty Annensky was not crowned by them. The heroic activity of V. Briusov can be defined as an experiment at combining the principles of the French Parnassus with the dreams of Russian symbolism. This is a typical drama of freedom and environment, of personality and the moment. . . . F. Sologub never concealed the irreconcilable contradiction between the ideology of the symbolists, which he half professed, and his own solipsistic ideology. . . . The catastrophe of symbolism occurred in silence, although with the curtain raised. The blinding "crowns of sonnets"[12] smothered the stage. One after another dreams of a mystery play, of a tragedy, of a great epos, of lyric poetry great in its simplicity, ended in suicide.

The end of symbolism seems to Gorodetsky something like the denouement of a Shakespearian tragedy: the whole stage is filled with the bodies of "suicides." And here come new, bold, and energetic people; they remove the corpses and quickly create a new art. He continues:

> The struggle between acmeism and symbolism, if it is a struggle and not the occupation of an abandoned fort, is first of all a struggle for *this world*, resounding, colorful, having form, weight, and time—for our planet Earth. Symbolism, in the final analysis, having filled the world with "correspondences," turned it into a phantom, important only insofar as it lets through and is translucent with other worlds and diminished the world's lofty self-worth.

This reproach is not relevant to a single *real* symbolist poet: neither to Briusov, nor to V. Ivanov, nor to Sologub, and least of all to Blok. Poetry that turns the world into a phantom is simply bad poetry; symbolism and acmeism have nothing to do with it. But the controversy is about something else. Gorodetsky, on behalf of the acmeists, is not fighting symbolist art, but art in general, with its eternal religious foundation, with the sole meaning of its existence: "touching other worlds." The new generation simply doesn't understand the language of the older generation. Dreams of a mystery play, of a national tragedy, of a great epos, seem to him eccentricity. "Mysticism" becomes an abusive word, "romanticism" is ridiculed. The "modernists" of the

1910s are sceptics and positivists. They pave the way for the appearance of the "imagists," "ego-futurists," and simple "futurists." The flowering of Russian poetry of the beginning of the twentieth century is coming to an end.

Blok senses this end; on 22 March he writes in the *Diary*:

> On the whole literary front a clearing of the atmosphere is proceeding. This is gratifying, but it is also painful. People are ceasing to pretend that they "understand symbolism" and that they love it. Soon they will stop pretending a love for art. Art and religion are dying in the world; we are entering the catacombs, we are held in utter contempt. The cruellest type of persecution is complete indifference. . . .
>
> [March 25.] The futurists as a whole are probably a more important phenomenon than acmeism. The latter are sickly. "Taste" weighs Gumilyov down; his baggage is heavy (from Shakespeare to . . . Théophile Gautier), and they retain Gorodetsky as the well-known pioneer. I think that Gumilyov is frequently embarrassed and scandalized by him.

To replace the symbolists' tragic attitude—their depression, despair, premonition of destruction—comes the new buoyancy, optimism, and "gay craft" of the acmeists and futurists. This "major key" and official "cheerfulness" of the youth depress Blok:

> 11 March. . . . Everything, it seems, is noble and cheerful, and it will soon be necessary to pine mortally for the prerevolutionary "depravity" of the epoch of *World of Art*. Five more years will pass and "morality" and "cheerfulness" will pave the way for a new revolution (from them it will perhaps be more unbearable to live than from any kind of despair, any kind of anguish).
>
> People are not doing all this, it is done to them; despair and cheerfulness, pessimism and "acmeism," "deadening" and "reviving," reaction and revolution. . . . What the "healthiest" of us call "life" is nothing more than *gossip about life*.

Blok surmises the law of alternation in Russian life of "major-" and "minor-key" epochs. Actually, the regularity of such alternations in the nineteenth and twentieth centuries is striking: the "major-key" epoch of the Fatherland War is replaced by the "minor" romanticism of the thirties and forties; the "major" construction of the sixties gives way to the "minor" Chekhovianism of the eighties; the "major" renaissance of the beginning of the new epoch ends with the "minor" "degeneration" at the end of the first decade, and the acmeists' and futurists' "major key" rings out again. Blok, the pessimist, interprets this regularity as historical fate: "people don't do this, it is done to them."

The poet rejoices at the "clearing of the atmosphere," but what a wilderness surrounds him! Neither like-minded persons nor friends. He is alone. In the *Diary* a review of the "dispersed army" is made:

> (Filosofov grumbles, plays the liberal; Merezhkovsky gives talks about "Saint Leo," compromising both Tolstoy and the saints equally. Gippius

scribbles untalented religious-political novels. A. Bely—life separated us too much.) M. I. Tereshchenko departs into his own affairs. . . . The rest simply don't exist for me—those who "did exist" (V. Ivanov, Chulkov). (29 April)

Sometimes, in rare moments of emotional cheerfulness, the poet accepts his isolation as a fortunate gift. On 10 February, on a frosty, sunny day he writes:

> It is time to untie my hands. I am no longer a schoolboy. There are no longer any symbolisms. I alone answer for myself, I *alone* can still be younger than the young "middle-aged" poets, burdened with posterity and with acmeism.
> All day in Shuvalovo—snow and sun—a marvel!

This is not the only attack on Gumilyov. In another place in the *Diary* Blok notes: "Hatred for acmeism." A note on 20 April reads: "In acmeism there is apparently a 'new attitude,' Gorodetsky mutters in the telephone. I say—why do you want to 'give yourself a name,' you are in no way different from us. . . . I say the main thing is—write your own things."

But these fits of martial mood are very rare. Blok doesn't want a fight, he departs into his own "hold," he fears life. The new epoch seems to him personified in the figure of the famous organizer of exhibitions and ballets, S. P. Diaghilev, who inspires mystical horror in him:

> Diaghilev's cynicism and his power. There is something terrible in him, he doesn't *walk alone*. Art, in his words, arouses sensuality; there are two geniuses—Nijinsky and Stravinsky. . . . A very gloomy impression, a terrible epoch, reality, for example, has far outstripped Dostoevsky's imagination. Svidrigailov is a kind of innocent child. Everything in Diaghilev is terrible and meaningful. (11 [12] March)

The "terrible" in Diaghilev didn't escape Blok's clairvoyance. The biographer-panegyrists must take the poet's insight into account.

The correspondence with Bely continues, but it becomes a burden to Blok:

> I don't like our relationship and correspondence. Always the same thing in his letters, he somehow doesn't reach manhood, childish exaltation, the same crooked handwriting, nothing about life, nothing drawn from life—from anything you like, except life. Including our eternal "Thou" (with a capital letter).

And in another place he writes: "In Borya the very worst was intensified to the highest degree (like: 'I don't know who I am' . . . 'I, I, I . . . and there the birch tree fell'). . . .

"Jesus for Steiner is that one who was 'possessed by Christ' " (20 January).

Bely's new novel *Petersburg*, not accepted by *Russian Thought*, is published, at Blok's insistence, in the Sirin anthology. Apropos of this, the poet notes:

> I consider it essential to print everything connected with A. Bely. I always repeat: misty confusion, a feeling of some personal affront, striking coincidences (places in my *poema*), aversion for his seeing horrible muck, a *malicious* work, the approach of despair (if the world is really such).... And with all this, A. Bely is immeasurable; behind two words something else suddenly lurks, everything becomes *different*.

In May, Bely and Asya Turgeneva come to Petersburg. Blok notes briefly in the *Diary*: "Three meetings with A. Bely and his wife. The second was terribly painful. After it—Inferno.... Such apathy that I don't want to do anything.... The diary is losing its meaning, I won't write any more." It is a pity that Bely's *Reminiscences of Blok* are not brought up to 1913. We simply don't find out why the conversations with Bely depressed Blok. He carried out his decision: the *Diary* breaks off until 1917.

At the end of the winter a former actor of the Kommissarzhevskaya Theater, Zonov, opens a popular theater on the Obvodny Canal under the name Our Theater. Lyubov Dmitrievna takes part in his troupe. Blok sometimes visits the performances. Zonov suggests that he put on *The Rose and the Cross*, but he declines this offer.

On 12 June Blok and his wife go abroad and settle on the Biscay seacoast, in Guéthary. He writes his mother:

> The ocean is directly in front of me, not obstructed by anything. Far away under the windows—a terrace of tamarind and a beach. Behind us—the chain of the Pyrenees.... So far I like all this, especially the ocean and the sky. Now everything is black; only the lights of Biarritz, some distant lights in the ocean, and a clear space in the sky. My whole room is saturated with the sea.

Blok takes a fancy to bathing, "spends a lot of time with crabs," communicates the latest news: "Yesterday we found a starfish, octopi, and large crabs among the stones in the sea. This is the most interesting thing here." The poet and his wife are often in Biarritz, take carriage trips to St. Jean de Luz, to the Spanish village Vera, and ride horseback to the mouth of the Adour. At the beginning of August they move to Paris. Blok writes his mother: "I was very sorry to leave Biarritz. The last days I went bathing twice a day (thirty-two times in all).... All this Spanish-French seacoast is a beautiful country." As before, he doesn't like Paris, but he understands its "uniqueness." In a letter to Pyast he writes: "Paris is nevertheless unique in the world. It seems that nowhere else are beings more victimized and baited: from this all people seem better and one can live as one pleases, simply and luxuriously, banally and not banally—no one will pay attention anyway." Most of all French classicism alienates the romantic Blok. After a trip to Versailles he tells his mother: "Everything, starting with the proportions, is repulsive to me in the eighteenth century and therefore Versailles seemed to me even more ugly than Tsarskoe Selo." Returning to Russia, the poet lives with his mother and aunt in Shakhmatovo till the middle of September. M. A. Beketova tells how he enthusiastically occupied himself with clearing the garden and, "with no apparent need," cutting down a whole plot of old lilacs. After his bathing in the ocean, Blok had become stronger and more cheerful; for days at a time he made up charade stories, "forced in meaning, unwieldy in form, and extremely funny." When at the end of August Lyubov Dmitrievna came to Shakhmatovo, "he composed in her presence a very long charade in the spirit of a thirties novel, which he told all day from morning till evening, constantly inventing new details of style."

In all of 1913 Blok wrote one article, "The Flame," (apropos of Pimen Karpov's book *The Flame: From the Life and Faith of the Grain Farmers*, St. Petersburg, 1913). It appeared in a Sunday supplement of the newspaper *Day* (*Den*) on 28 October. The author agrees with the critics that Karpov's book is outside literature, that it is "delirium," but he asks that this delirium be listened to. "Karpov sees nothing in Russian life but rivers of blood and seas of fire; passion, violence, murders, executions, all sorts of mental and physical torments—this is the 'background' of the story." On it is depicted the flagellant Krutogorov, coming through the darkness to a bright city. Blok ends his article with the terrible and prophetic words:

> From *The Flame* we will have to, whether we like it or not, keep in mind something about Russia. Let this be added to the "knowledge of Russia." Once again we are afraid, remembering that our mutiny, just as it has been, can again be "senseless and merciless" (Pushkin); that there were "blood, axe, and fire" in Russia, and now "the book" began, and then again there will be "blood, axe, and fire."

In October 1913, just four years before the October revolution, its face was already revealed to Blok. "It isn't possible to foretell and foresee everything," he writes. "Blood and fire can speak when no one expects them. There is a Russia which, having escaped one revolution, avidly looks into the eyes of another, perhaps more terrible."

Besides this single article and twenty-five lyrical poems entering the third volume of the *Collected Poems*, Blok outlined two short plans for dramas which he never carried out (*Diary*). Here is the first:

> A new idea is fermenting: to write about a man *with power*—the antithesis of Bertran. Somewhere here, of course, Venice and Colleone and Byron. When the crowd guessed that he held it in his fist and wanted to tear him to pieces, it was too late, for he had perished.... Sun, morning, a dogaressa is feeding pigeons, a blue lagoon. A *distant* column with a lion.... When they rushed to tear him to pieces, he had perished, but "Venice is saved"—through monstrous risk bordering on deceit, through "provocation," while the "worthy" (but "powerless") fell victim. Some

kind of conspiracy, some kind of democratic woman of ineffable beauty, a candle (if eighteenth century; then without the dogaressa).

The plot à la Byron remains unclear. Here is the second plan:

> A *"ridiculous man,"* the first act, two pictures (broken into scenes?). The first—apple trees, May, our forests and meadows. Long and lofty love, a fence; he jumps over; a female tramp; a proposal. She for all of life.
> The second—city, night, tavern, gypsies; he goes, a scuffle, singing. . . .
> Constant dropping of hands—everything is boring and nothing is worthwhile. Then suddenly, the reverse—seething activity. Reading a dictionary(!), he discovers coal, digs, and—lucky man—finds a stratum, knowing nothing ("Knowledge of Russia"). Again women.
> He dies by accident—and just as easily as he lived. "Incidentally," he helped many—both spiritually and materially. Everyone says: ridiculous, I don't understand. Fantasies, decadence, they say he's a debauchee. Endless gossip apparently separates him from his wife. And everything is falsehood, everything is much simpler, but what is *alive* is rich, and easy and difficult—and one doesn't understand where difficulty ends and easiness begins. Like life itself. The gypsyness in him.
> When he dies, everyone curses him, laughs. Only one woman sobs unrestrainedly, and she herself doesn't know why.

Such is the plan of a new autobiographical drama. It didn't inspire the poet, even despite the fantastic episode of the "discovery of coal." Perhaps the memory of the failure of *Song of Fate* deterred him.

In 1913 Blok made very few entries in his *Notebook*. One of them is significant:

> In any work of art (even in a short poem) there is more *nonart* than art.
> Art is radium (very small quantities). It is capable of making everything radioactive—the most difficult, the crudest, the most natural: ideas, tendencies, "experiences," feelings, daily life. . . . Contemporary naturalism is harmless because it is *outside of art*. . . . Modernism is poisonous because it is *part of art*.

Blok summarizes his "philosophy of life" in a concise note in the *Diary* of 11 February: "The world's morality is unfathomable and bears no resemblance to that which is so called. The world is moved by music, passion, prejudice, power."

This is the exact formula of the "romantic sense of life," of its own kind of Russian Nietzscheanism.

The diary of 1913 breaks off with unexpected tragic exclamations: "How the conscience torments! Lord, give me strength, help me!"

CHAPTER IX
YEARS OF THE WORLD WAR
1914–1917

In the Theater of Musical Drama Blok sees the actress Lyubov Aleksandrovna Delmas in the role of Carmen; in March he meets her. The indomitable, wild gypsy conquers him with her elemental passionateness. He is "in the rapacious power of beautiful arms." M. A. Beketova writes about Delmas:

> Yes, this woman's attractive power is great. The lines of her tall, lithe figure are beautiful, the golden fleece of her red hair luxuriant, the irregular, changeable face fascinating, the alluring coquetry irresistable. And at the same time talent, a fiery artistic temperament, and a voice so deeply ringing on the low notes. There is nothing gloomy or heavy in this captivating appearance. On the contrary—it is all sunny, light, festive. It breathes emotional and physical health and endless vitality.

In love—and again come the sounds of the "world orchestra," the stormy flood of inspiration. At the end of March, within a few days, the cycle *Carmen* is written. In the poem *The angry gaze of pale eyes* the poet recalls the first meeting:

> In the stalls—night. Impossible to breathe.
> The black vest is near, near . . .
> And a pale face . . . and a lock
> Of hair, falling down . . .
> . . . . .
> In the movements of the proud head
> Direct signs of annoyance . . .
> . . . . .
> And the song of Your tender shoulders
> Already familiar to the point of horror,
> And the heart is fated to preserve,
> Like the memory of another homeland,
> Your image, dear forever. . . .

Short entries about the "music" of this new love appear in the *Notebook*:

9 March. Cold wind. All these days were very intense and rapturous—got a little tired, calmed down.

16 March. Rain, haze, I am bored. . . . March feels like a nightmare.

29 March. Everything is singing.

1 April. Cold, gray wind from the sea, I am at home, tired. Demonic "frame of mind."

14 May. Passionate abyss and above it scud fragments of thoughts about the future—the Spirit of God.

P. E. Meyerhold and the litterateur and director, V. N. Solovyov, publish a journal devoted to the theater, named for the well-known comedy of Carlo Gozzi, *Love for Three Oranges*. It preached a return to the tradition of the *Commedia dell'Arte*, of the country-fair theater of the epoch of Molière, of the fantastic fairy tales of Gozzi and Hoffmann. Blok is not sympathetic to Meyerhold's ideas, but out of friendship for him agrees to run the poetry section. In August his cycle of poems *Carmen* appears in the new journal. Meyerhold tests his theories in practice in the theater of pantomime and improvisation. Lyubov Dmitrievna visits his studio assiduously. At Easter, in the auditorium of the Tenishevsky School, Meyerhold puts on *The Puppet Show* and *The Stranger*. The auditorium is decorated with varicolored lanterns. In view of the audience, splendidly dressed servants arrange the scenery. In the intermissions oranges fly from the stage into the audience. Lyubov Dmitrievna sews costumes and plays the lady-proprietress in the third vision of *The Stranger*. The performances aren't very successful. In the summer the poet's wife joins Zonov's troupe and acts in Kuokkala.

Meyerhold insists on staging *The Rose and the Cross*. Blok informs his mother (17 May): "Here is a description of these days: Meyerhold comes to me, he is giving *The Rose and the Cross* to the censor (Drizen) for the summer. He thanked me for the *Carmen* cycle of poems, which will appear in *Oranges* in August."

The business with the censorship dragged on for almost a year. The ecclesiastical censorship was even more dreadful than the secular; one could fear that the very title of the play, *The Rose and the Cross*, would seem reprehensible to it. "You ask about Meyerhold," Blok writes his mother (22 May): "It seems to me he is not an enemy and sincerely loves me. I talked quietly with him about Lermontov, about *The Green Ring*,[1] about censorship of *The Rose and the Cross*." Leonid Andreev comes forward unexpectedly as an intercessor for Blok's drama. In the fall of 1913 he writes to Stanislavsky: "I read Blok's *The Rose and the Cross* the other day, and it seemed to me that the play could work in the Art Theater: there is soul in it." In May 1914 he returns to this idea:

> I again remind you of Blok's tragedy *The Rose and the Cross*, which I wrote about back in the fall, and with all my heart I adjure you to put it on instead of Surguchev's mediocre drama. . . . Blok's tragedy is a truly remarkable thing, which I can say with especially calm assurance, not being friendly or related to that symbolist. And if it was possible up to now, although with some stretching, to pass over Sologub and Blok and

> the others, then now, when such a work is at hand, the stubbornness of the theater passes into one-sidedness and unfairness.... Staging it, the theater won't depart at all from the legacy of truth and simplicity: only in new and beautiful forms will it present this truth and simplicity.

Andreev's noble intercession for Blok's drama forces Stanislavsky to read it more attentively. He begins to like it. In December he decides to stage it and the first talks with the actors about *The Rose and the Cross* take place in the theater.

The spring of 1914 passes for the poet under the sign of "Carmen"— L. A. Delmas. She is the "echo of a forgotten hymn" in his fate; she sings in it:

> Everything is music and light; no happiness, no faithlessness . . .
> Sadness and joy ring with one melody . . .
> But I love you: I myself am such, *Carmen.*

The music of love separates him from friends, from the world. He writes his mother (27 May): "These days I see no one except Lyubov Aleksandrovna [Delmas]."

On 8 June they separate. Blok leaves for Shakhmatovo. Bored, he idly translates Flaubert's novella, *St. Julien l'Hospitalier* for *Sweetbrier* (*Shipovnik*). The translation doesn't go well; he drops it. Aleksandra Andreevna, under her son's editorship, translates Flaubert's letters. Only the first volume appears in print. Blok enters in the *Notebook*: "15 June. Depression and boredom. Is my song really sung?" On 23 June he writes: "The days drag on. Flaubert and reminiscences of Fet, and food, and nature. Both boredom and fascination."

The poet greeted the declaration of war as a fulfillment of all his premonitions. He was gripped by profound mystical agitation. "Russia's terrible years" were beginning; the world had entered the "incinerating years." Blok saw before him a chaotic confusion of light and darkness, he had a foreboding of his own death. On 8 September 1914 the celebrated, prophetic poem was written:

> Those born in the stagnant years
> Don't remember their own path.
> We are the children of Russia's terrible years—
> Unable to forget anything.
>
> Incinerating years!
> Is there madness in you, the news of hope?
> From the days of war, from the days of freedom—
> A bloody reflection on the faces.
>
> Muteness—the noise of the alarm
> Forced us to block our mouths.
> In hearts once enraptured
> A fateful emptiness.
>
> And over our death-bed let

> The carrion crows fly up with a screech—
> Those who are more worthy, God, God,
> May they see Your Kingdom!

The generation which lived through the years of revolution and two world wars hear the voice of their own fate in these lines. How terribly familiar to them the "bloody reflection on the faces"! How they remember the fire of the "incinerating" years! The poet's stepfather, F. F. Kublitsky, was called to Petersburg: mobilization had found him in the Crimea. He set out for his brigade, stationed in Peterhof. Aleksandra Andreevna accompanied him. Lyubov Dmitrievna enrolled in nursing courses and at the end of August left for the front with a detachment of the Kaufman commune. She worked energetically and courageously in the hospital in Lvov. After the enthusiasm of the first days of the war, Blok enters a period of hopeless gloom. He wants to work. He writes in the *Notebook*: "Nothing is needed except unskilled labor." But even work doesn't save him. On 21 August he makes a tragic entry: "When will I at last be free to lay hands on myself?" The tone of his letters alarms his mother, and he has to reassure her: "Mama, it's very painful for me to make you worry about my bad mood, but I hope it will soon pass, and that I'll begin to occupy myself with literature. Judging by today's newspaper, the war will end soon. The Lord be with you" (letter of 31 August). In the autumn in Petersburg he gradually gets control of himself. He begins preliminary work on an edition of Apollon Grigoriev's poems: collects biographical materials, comments on the poems, goes regularly to the library of the Academy of Sciences, and to the Public Library. "Every day," he writes his mother, "I work for hours in the Academy of Sciences and sometimes more at home and therefore I feel much steadier."

In 1915 Blok continues to work in the libraries and writes a long article about Apollon Grigoriev. The collection of Grigoriev's poems, under Blok's editorship, with his introductory article and notes, comes out in November. The resurrection of this remarkable, heretofore unnoticed and long forgotten poet is Blok's great literary service. The same year he finishes the *poema Nightingale Garden*, begun back in the autumn of 1914. By spring a cheerful mood returns to him; Lyubov Dmitrievna comes from Lvov; in the summer she again acts in Zonov's troupe in Kuokkala. In addition, he learns that the composer Bazilevsky, having written music to *The Rose and the Cross*, is getting ready to perform it at a concert in Moscow. He tells his mother:

> I wrote about *The Rose and the Cross* for Bazilevsky. Today I'm going to see Baron Drizen. Bazilevsky writes that the Free Theater is thinking about putting on *The Rose and the Cross*. A. A. [A. N.] Chebotarevskaya informed me that Nemirovich-Danchenko is also considering it and told someone about it.

But the question of staging the play in the Art Theater nevertheless doesn't move from dead center. From a letter to his mother of 4 July: "Vengerov called me just now and gave me a difficult assignment. First, to amplify the autobiography printed in Fidler's book (for the *History of Literature of the Twentieth Century*). Secondly, to write an article about Poliksena Sergeevna [Solovyova] for that same *History of Literature*." On 22 June he informs her that the autobiography is already finished. All spring Blok feels depressed: he hates the war but feels that he should participate in some way in the general misfortune. "I still don't know what to do," he admits to his mother. "At one time there was terrible depression, now it's better" (letter of 7 June). "I feel terribly unstable —one day good, and the next depressed" (letter of 22 June). He wanders in the outskirts of Petersburg, rides a steamship up the Neva, writes to his mother (13 June): "The outlying districts are very grand and *Russian*—both in the grandeur and in the absurdity connected with it. Beyond Smolny begin vast grain depots, elevators, freight cars for goods, green shores, bulky temples, and tugboats with the names Prophet, Freedom, cut the large waves." N. [V.] Zorgenfrei recalls his meetings with Blok:

> Dropping in at Filippov's cafe on the corner of Bolshoy Prospect and Ropshinskaya Street in the evenings, I would not infrequently meet Aleksandr Aleksandrovich at a table there.... "I know each of the waitresses by name and can tell you many details about each one," he once said to me.... I remember a quiet summer evening, the long avenue on Petrovsky Island, a car noiselessly rushing past.... "From such a car, once sweeping past, *The Steps of the Commander* emerged," said Aleksandr Aleksandrovich.... And he added, after being silent for a time: "Only the word car is bad—it's not correct to speak that way."

Sadly, in inertia and weariness, the spring passes. Pyast, called up for military service, writes to Blok that the dark period will end with the war and the "next period" will begin—a completely new life will come. The latter answers melancholically:

> So much of the old guard (Grigoriev, Flaubert, and I myself) that for the time being it is difficult for the new to break through. Besides, damned *weariness* grinds and builds its nest, weariness not of body or soul, but somewhere between body and soul; now I am glad about it all, and then suddenly *taedium*. I want the "next period" as strongly as you do; that is, apparently, not strongly enough, because we are both weary.

Only work helps him to bear "life's depression." In another letter to Pyast he says: "For the hundredth time I have to confess with sorrow that I must have recourse to work in order to bring back rhythm, and for the time being there is no other way."

At the beginning of June, departure for Shakhmatovo. Blok fells trees and works in the garden. At the end of the summer L. A. Delmas arrives for a short time; she sings from *Carmen*, from *Khovanshchina*, and from gypsy romances. In the evenings she and Blok light bonfires behind the Shakhmatovo garden. Aleksandra Andreevna is convinced that only the red-haired "Carmen" can soothe and revitalize "Sasha." Between the women there is a kind of secret compact, about which Blok, however, at once guesses. He writes to his mother (1 June): "Lyubov Aleksandrovna said it's 'still early' for her to write to you. You must have arranged something with her—how to 'handle' me. Oh, oh, it's boring. I know everything." Returning to Petersburg in the fall, the poet throws himself into new work: Gorky is organizing the publication of collections of literature of all the peoples of Russia. Blok enthusiastically begins to translate Armenian, Lettish, and Finnish poets; men of letters of these nationalities visit him, read their poems in their own languages. Blok keeps in mind the rhythm of lines, and at times whole verses, incomprehensible to him. His translations of the poems of the Armenian poet Isahakian are especially successful.

In November 1915 two entries are made in the *Notebook*: one is about the future, the other about the present. The first contains a striking prediction of the *great renaissance* awaiting Russia; the second speaks about the collapse of the old world. Here is the first (5 November):

> And what a great *renaissance*, that is, an *advancement in all our powers*, is in prospect for us, and to what a degree technology and artistic creativity are inconceivable without one another (*techné* in Greek is "art")—we will soon see, because, if only we straighten ourselves out after this deluge, we have the prospect of being carried as if on wings into an epoch of *great renaissance* taking place under the sign of *courage and will*.

The second note (10 November) reads:

> *Going wild*—that is the word; and bookish, timid Merezhkovsky found it. Why did he find it? Because he alone *was working*. . . . And so—going wild.
>
> Black, impenetrable mire in the streets. Lamps on every other street. . . . Youth is complacent, "apolitical," boorish and vulgar. Verbitskaya, Igor Severyanin et al. have replaced culture for it. No language. No love. They don't want victory, or peace either. When and from where will the answer come?

Destruction of the old world and a great rebirth in the future—thus Blok experienced the war of 1914. P. Sukhotin,[2] telling of his meeting with the poet "in a night hangout," confirms this conclusion:

> In a night hangout, we sat at a crooked table. . . . And before us a teapot with prohibited vodka. . . . And beside us a drunken country lad sobbed violently. . . . We parted. But at this same meeting Blok told me: "This terrible disorder will end—and will end in something good."

Aleksandr Blok   POEMS OF 1913-1915

In 1914 Blok finishes the cycle *Dances of Death*. The last poem, *Again the rich man is malicious and glad*, is written in the rhythm of a factory song set to an accordion: the pale moon looks from the roof of stone bulks; don't search for the tsar in the palace—he isn't there:

> He—from distant wastelands,
> In the light of sparse lanterns—
>   Appears.
> Neck bound in a kerchief,
> Under a cap peak full of holes—
>   He smiles.

This phantom comes to life in the *poema The Twelve*, transformed into the soldier Vanka:

> He in a soldier's overcoat,
> With a foolish physiognomy,
> Twirls, twirls his black mustache,
>   And twists it,
>   And cracks jokes.

In the rhythm of the factory song Blok already hears the "revolutionary pace" of *The Twelve*.

The next cycle of poems is entitled *The Life of My Friend*. It concerns the terrible wasteland of life, unbelief, and sorrow in a black soul; the useless day will pass, night will come, and

> The senselessness of all things, the joylessness of comfort
>   Will come to your mind.

Despair will clench the throat and drive you out onto the "deserted streets":

> Wherever you turn, night looks into empty eyes
>   And accompanies you . . .

And then everything—sadness, languor, petty labors, and trifling cares—will seem so insignificant:

> And, finally, the desired weariness will come,
>   And it won't matter . . .
> What? Conscience? Truth? Life? What a trifle this is!
>   Well, really, isn't it absurd?

The theme of the "loss of the soul," "living death," returns with the persistence of an idée fixe: here is the reckless daring of a losing gambler, and the gloomy buffoonery of a drunkard, and the indifferent cynicism of a "hopeless case." He lived in a daze, sought consolation in the *torment of hell*:

> He woke up: thirty years,
> Suddenly, but no heart.
>
> The heart is a painted corpse.
> And when the end came,
> He found highly banal
> The death of his sad soul.

The Germans call this "gallows humor." The poet plays on the lowering of a lofty romantic theme ("the death of the soul"), submerging it in the banality of Philistine life:

> When by chance on Sunday
> He lost his soul,
> He didn't go to the criminal division,
> He didn't seek witnesses.

But there were witnesses: an old woman by the gate, a yardman, a house puppy, and a bedraggled cat. This is a device of Gogolian grotesque: thus, too, Major Kovalyov[3] "accidentally" lost his nose.

In the next poem, written in free verse, there is an ironic report of the poet's day:

> The day passed, as always,
> In quiet madness.

All around they speak of diseases, doctors, service, newspapers, Christ. Poets send their little books, ladies in love—roses, a girl student—a manuscript with epigraphs from Nadson[4] and the symbolists; the critic inveighs against futurism and eulogizes realism; and in the evening, in a movie theater, a baron kisses "a young lady of humble station" under a palm tree. And only at night do dreams from another world agitate:

> No, you will come to at times,
> Agitated, alarmed
> By a vague memory,
> By a secret premonition ...

This is the sterile fever of inspiration, unneeded dreams; isn't it better that the new day also pass "as always, in quiet madness."

The last two poems of the cycle are entitled *The Devils Speak* and *Death Speaks*. The devils advise writing sinful poems, drinking wine, and kissing women—all the same "the insane hour" will come when the poet will curse them in "frenzied repentance":

> And you will begin to fall. But in a crowd
> We all, like pure angels,
> Will pick you up, so that you would not dash
> Your foot against a stone.

It is terrible when the secret life of the soul lies before our eyes, like the mechanism of a dismantled clock; when one knows that sin will inevitably be replaced by repentance, and repentance by new sin. This dead regularity in the living, this necessity in freedom, is terrible. For Blok this is also a demonic "temptation in the wilderness"; that explains the gospel words:

> . . . so that you would not dash
> Your foot against a stone.

The poem *How alarm grows at night!* borders on the cycle *The Life of My Friend*.

Let everything around be cold and dark, let the conscience lie heavy:

> Ah, isn't it all the same to me!
> Again I'll make friends with the tavern violin,
> Monotonous and singing,
> Again I'll drink wine.

Why pretend to be alive?

> Anyway, I lack the strength
> To drag myself to the end
> With a sober, false smile,
> Concealing fear of the grave,
> The uneasiness of a corpse.

When the war of 1914 came, Blok wrote the prophetic words: "In hearts once rapturous, there is a fateful void."

Then the terrible wasteland lying on his soul in these "incinerating years" was revealed to him; it wasn't his personal fate, this was Russia's fate. Not only his heart was a "painted corpse": the whole old world was writhing in torments of agony. The terrible verdict of history was coming; the voices heard by the poet-prophet were calling to repentance. There were approaching

> Unprecedented changes,
> Unparalleled revolts.

In the poem *Well, so what? The weak hands are wrung wearily*, written a few months before the war, the poet speaks about his prophetic gift with calm certainty:

The sun, describing the prescribed circle, has set.
Open my books: there everything that will occur is told.
Yes, I was a prophet, while this heart prayed.

And Blok is right. His verses predict everything: war and revolution and the future *great renaissance* of Russia.

In 1914 the cycle *Black Blood* is finished. The poems, addressed to a woman "whose very name is contemptible to me," again speak of the evil power of passion. This painful witchcraft is not human love. This is a demonic fusion of contempt, hatred, cruelty, horror, and sensuality. The will is powerless, struggle is futile: "No, in vain I lowered my eyes; It breathes, it pursues—the storm is close."

She looks at him sidewise; a quiver runs along the trembling hand. And he knows:

No! Will not subdue this black blood
Even a meeting, even—love!
    (*You rose to me in a half-turn*)

She draws near: "the avid breast heaves." Stormy silence. He shouts incantations:

No! Avert the eyes and don't dare, don't dare
To look into this terrible abyss!
    (*I look at you*)

The next poem has the same feeling of elemental force, of inevitability:

I hear: the foaming torrent howls,
The storm approaches from the wasteland.

An ancient, fateful legacy awakes in the subconscious: an animal attraction for torture and murder:

The eye, golden and brown, is silent,
The slender fingers seek the throat. . .
Approach. Creep up. I will strike—
And, like a cat, you bare your teeth.
    (*Your very name is contemptible to me*)

Both terrible embraces and the horror of possession:

And in horror she whispers incoherently. . .
    And, hiding her face,
Winds more strongly the singing ring
    Of her frightened arms. . .
            (*Gripped, drawn by fear*)

Aleksandr Blok   There is no more startling revelation of the "possession" by passion in Russian poetry.

The cycle *The Terrible World* ends with the poem *A Voice from the Chorus*—an epilogue-prophecy of the "darkness of coming days." The poet introduces rhythmical interruptions, unexpected and breathtaking, into the system of iambic tetrameter. These pauses and syncopes suddenly obstruct the measured flow of the line. It seems that the heart stopped for a moment, then pounded more rapidly and again stopped:

> Kak často plačem—vy i ja—
> Nad žalkoj žizniju svoej!
> O, esli by znali vy, druz'ja,
> Xolod i mrak grjaduščix dnej!

> How often we weep—you and I—
> Over our pitiful life!
> Oh, if you knew, friends,
> The cold and darkness of coming days!

The first foot of the fourth line, changed from iambic to trochaic (*"xolod"*), is like a quiver of the heart. The word *"xolod"* gets special force. Still more terrible is the rhythm of the third verse:

> Lži i kovarstvu mery net,
> A smert'—daleka.
> Vsë budet černee strašnyj svet,
> I vsë bezumnej vixr' planet.
>   Eščë veka, veka!

> No measure to lies and deceit,
> And death is far away.
> The terrible world will be ever blacker,
> And the whirlwind of the planets madder and madder,
>   For ages, ages yet!

Tonic measures predominate. The word *lži* in unstressed position is intensified, the pause after *"a smert'"* gives broad resonance to the word *smert'*. The last line cuts short the sad melody of the two preceding lines.

The fifth verse has no equal in Blok's lyric: the four-stressed odd lines alternate with the two-stressed even lines. The even lines rise, exclaim, call for help; the odd lines cast them down, press them to the ground, crush them like a heavy stone. In the rhymes *obmanet, vstanet, kanet* there is dull heaviness, colorlessness, the hollow rumble of a fall:

> Child, you will wait for spring—
>   Spring will deceive you.
> You will call the sun to the sky—
>   The sun will not rise.

> And the shout, when you begin to shout,
> Will fall like a stone.

This is the voice of hopelessness. It prepares the return of the leitmotif of the first verse:

> Oh, if you knew, children,
> The cold and darkness of coming days!

Blok was fated to know it. He suffocated in the "cold and darkness" in 1921.

In 1913 the poet finishes the section *Retribution*. He places a short lyrical *poema, How was it done, how did it happen?*, as an epilogue, which develops the theme of his long *poema Retribution*. The poet was "poor, weak, and small," but the "secret of certain Grandeurs" was revealed to him. An unworthy guard, he didn't protect the treasures entrusted to him (compare "A *treasure* lies in my soul" in *The Stranger)*. Crowds of monsters attack him, and he sets out for the enemy camp:

> A fallen angel, I was met
> In their camp like a young god.

Thus is noted the moment of the angel's fall into "blue-lilac worlds": the prophet is transformed into a poet. The "splendid hell" of art and the "terrible world" of passions is revealed:

> There was long languor.
> I thought: day won't come.
> Mad delirium, passionate babble,
> Vows, songs, assurances
> Didn't reach me.

"Dazzling eyes" draw him into the "tsarina's palace." And here retribution comes: "But my menacing avenger didn't sleep." The poet stands before people in the halo of his own death:

> I don't hide from you.
> Look at me:
> I stand amid charred ruins
> Scorched by tongues
> Of hellish flame.

The tragic face visible in the poems, articles, letters, and the diary is now revealed completely. This is the face of a fallen angel scorched by the fire of hell.

The section *Iambics,* dedicated to the memory of his late sister, Angelina Aleksandrovna Blok, is finished in 1914. The poet recalls

Aleksandr Blok meeting his sister in December 1909 in Warsaw, at their father's funeral:

> When I met you
> I was ill, my soul rusted.
> A sister ordained by fate,
> The whole world seemed to me Warsaw.

Black nights over the Vistula, Warsaw, "a den of depression and boredom," cold and delirium—in those terrible days by his father's coffin Angelina saved him from despair:

> Only you, sister, repeated to me,
> With your disturbing anxiety,
> About the world as God's dwelling
> About cold and about fire.

In the poem *So. The storm of these years has passed* the poet indignantly rejects the temptation of calm and reconciliation. His anxiety was justified, his premonitions didn't deceive him. In vain the voice of the tempter whispers:

> *Forget, forget about the terrible world,*
> *Flap your wing, fly there...*
> No, I wasn't alone at the banquet!
> No, I will never forget!

To shout about death, to meet the cold head-on, to disturb the sleepers, to preserve "an unrequited love for people in the absence of people," is the prophet's curse. But it is impossible to renounce:

> Let them call: *forget, poet!*
> *Return to the beautiful refuges!*
> No! Better to vanish in the fierce cold!
> There is no refuge! There is no rest!
> *(The earthly heart grows cold again)*

The concluding poem *In the fire and cold of alarms* is the last affirmation of the "holy alarm." The poet's despair doesn't reflect personal failures, nor personal choice. He doesn't weep for himself: the soul of the world trembles and breaks in his mad song. He sees:

> To everyone—the holy sword of war
> Flashes in unavoidable storm clouds.

He senses how a great and fateful event is ripening in the depths. Blok ends with a classical verse:

> Exactly so—black diamond
> Sleeps a mysterious and strange sleep,

> In a lifeless spell,
> Among the depths—until
> The pick begins to sing in the mountains.

Begun in 1910, the poem was finished in 1914, when the world's lifeless sleep was destroyed by the first seismic shock of war.

The section *Miscellaneous Poems* for the three-year period 1913–15 was enriched by eight poems. Among them the poem *The Artist*, devoted to the mystery of creativity and inspiration, bears comparison with Pushkin's *The Poet* and *The Poet and the Mob*.

For Pushkin, the classicist, harmony is the aim of art. For Blok, the romantic, harmony is only an echo of "other worlds"; it contains both a blessing and a curse. The romantic believes in the wonder-working power of the word and expects from it a transformation of the world. For him the harmony of poetry is not enough; he needs the harmony of the cosmos. The limitedness of art seems to him a prison, and its beauty a false likeness.

Pushkin wrote:

> Until Apollo demands of the poet
> Holy sacrifice,
> In the cares of the vain world
> He is cravenly immersed.

So too Blok's "artist," awaiting inspiration, lives "in mortal boredom." In Pushkin:

> But once the divine word
> Touches the sensitive ear . . .

In Blok the "light, hitherto inaudible ringing" reaches the poet's hearing.

This "music" is the primary, mysterious sounding from which lyric poetry is born. Where is it from? What is it? What does it speak about?

> A whirlwind from the sea? Or heavenly sirens
> Singing in the leaves? Or is time standing still?
> Or did the May apple trees strew
> Their snowy blooms? Or is an angel flying?

We recall in Pushkin:

> And I listened to the shudder of heaven
> And the celestial flight of angels.

Blok describes the state of inspiration in the following verse:

> Hours stretch, carrying the universe.

> Sounds, movement, and light broaden.
> The past looks passionately into the future.

In mystical literature this state is called "ecstasy," "going forth," "rapture." Blok depicts it in symbols close to St. Theresa of Avila and St. John of the Cross. Time stops; the soul, expanding, contains the whole world. The universe is flooded with immaterial light. And suddenly the upward movement breaks off; ascent is replaced by descent; inspiration by creativity. The poet-romantic experiences this moment as a "fall":

> The curse, as with thunder, smites the soul:
> Creative mind overpowered—murdered—it.

The celestial vision is incommunicable: its embodiment in meager human words is impoverishment, limitation, coarsening. "A thought expressed is a lie,"[5] and in this sense everything the poet *says* is a lie in comparison to what he *sees*. For the poet-romantic this is a profound tragedy. In ecstasy the transformed world, victory over death, universal salvation are revealed to him. And instead of theurgical action there is an esthetic work, instead of a mystery play—a poem. Blok depicts the "failure" of art in these words:

> And I lock in a cold cage
> The light, good, free bird,
> The bird who wanted to take away death,
> The bird who flew to save the soul.

The creative burst is exhausted. One more beautiful *poema* came into being, one inspired symphony. That's all. The world is *not* transformed. Everything is as before: "death and time reign on earth" (V. Solovyov):

> The wings are clipped, the song is learnt by heart.
> Do you love to stand under a window?
> Do you like the songs? I, exhausted,
> Wait for something new—and I'm bored again.

The mystery play ends as a diversion for empty idlers who love to hear a song!

Blok isn't talking about the banal "psychology of creative work"—he is revealing the metaphysical depths of *romantic art*. The most celebrated victories of romanticism are its "brilliant defeats."

Eighteen poems of 1913 and 1914 are included in the section *Harps and Violins*. The verses of 1913 are devoted to "gypsy love"; in one of them the gypsy girl Ksyusha is named. In 1912 the poet, carried away with gypsy singing, in a letter to his mother mentions, in passing,

Aksyusha Prokhorova, who was singing the love song, *But it is sweet and strange to be with you*. One can surmise that she was also the heroine of this wild but fleeting romance. The cycle begins with the poem *Gray Morning*, with an epigraph from Turgenev: "Foggy morning, gray morning." After a night spent with the gypsies, the guests depart on a rainy and foggy morning. The gypsy coldly lets him kiss her hand, which is covered with silver rings. How unlike her "morning and boring voice" is to the voice which sang on the stage at night to a guitar:

> No, life and happiness till morning
> I found not in this glance!

The poet squeezes her fingers till they hurt—they won't meet again. On farewell he gives her a ring:

> "Farewell, take another ring.
> Clothe your little hand
> And your swarthy heart
> In silver scales."

Sober morning killed the night love. One remembers the lines from the poem *To the Muse*:

> And briefer than gypsy love
> Were your terrible caresses.

And again the lyrical theme of the "madness of love" sounds. And the same "elemental symbols": dawn in blood, storm cloud. The stanzas sing rapturously and tenderly, like a gypsy guitar:

> Like a frightened and wild bird
> You fly, but the dawn is in blood . . .
> With despair, with passion, with fever,
> Comes the madness of love . . .
>
> Half a heart—storm cloud;
> Under it—all is wilderness, all is muteness,
> And she—the former, simple—
> Is already different, no longer the same . . .
> (*There are times, there are days*)

It seems as though her voice, "low and throaty," sounds in the sobbing of the violins, that she responds to his first love.

In a country of "eternal snow and the blizzard's howling" she is a beautiful dream, a "southern radiance"; her figure recalls the figure of a gazelle; the light ringing of the waltz surrounds her. Not for nothing is this poem placed in the section *Harps and Violins*; the verses ring with the limpid and delicate melody of a harp:

> I ja bojus' tebja nazvat'

Aleksandr Blok

Po imeni. Začem mne imja?
Daj mne trevožno sozercat'
Očami žadnymi moimi.

Tvoj nežnyj blesk, zabytyj mnoj,
Napominajuščij naprasno
Den' uletevšij, den' prekrasnyj
Ubityj noč'ju snegovoj.
      (*Ty govoriš', čto ja dremlju*)

And I am afraid to call you
By name. What is your name to me?
Let me uneasily contemplate
With my avid eyes.

Your delicate radiance, forgotten by me,
In vain reminding
Of the day flown away, the beautiful day,
Killed by the snowy night.
      (*You say I'm dozing*)

The melody of these lines is created by the combination of the sibilants Č, Ž, ŠČ (*začem, trevožno, žadnymi, nežnyj, napominajuščij, noč'ju*) with the drawn-out liquids M and N (*imeni, mne, imja, očami, žadnymi moimi, mne nežnyj, mnoj, napominajuščij, naprasno, noč'ju, snegovoj*). Blok's elegy is melodically close to Pushkin's brilliant lines:

Ne poj, krasavica, pri mne
. . . . .
Napominajut mne one.

And alongside the charm of the romantic song is a gypsy chorus sung to a guitar, violent and free as happiness. The transmission of this melody in the sounds and rhythms of verse is the height of technical mastery:

The guitar strings stretched,
   The heart waits.
Only touch it with your young voice,
   It will break into song!
And the old man before the chorus
   Already stamped his foot.
Burn me with your voice, your look,
   Ksyusha, sing!

And the guttural sounds
   Rushed along
Like the swarthy hands in silver
   Entwined . . .

The delirium of madness and passion,
   The delirium of love . . .
Impossible happiness!
   Here! Catch!

The acceleration of the tempo, the increase in tension, the breathlessness of the rhythm, the song changing to a shout—"the delirium of madness and passion"—such is Blok's "gypsyness."

But the swarthy Ksyusha with her hands in silver rings only blazed up "with southern radiance" and flashed past like a passionate dream. Another gypsy, a Spanish gitana with the dazzling aureole of Mérimée's romantic poetry and Bizet's romantic music, came to replace her. The poems of 1914 in *Harps and Violins* and the cycle of poems *Carmen* are dedicated to the red-haired Carmen, L. A. Delmas.

Bright like the day, but incomprehensible is the first impression of Carmen. *And after her is always spring* is the beginning of love. The poet listens attentively "to her broken speech," looks intently into the "radiance of her eyes," gets drunk on the odor of her perfume. She has "snow-white arms" and "fine red hair." She bursts into his life with the singing of violins, with "sobbing sounds." She is like a "May thunderstorm." The poet dedicates one of his most lyrical reminiscences to her:

> Byla ty vsex jarče, vernej i prelestnej,
>   Ne kljani že menja, ne kljani!
> Moj poezd letit, kak cyganskaja pesnja,
>   Kak te nevozvratnye dni . . .
>
> Čto bylo ljubimo—vsë mimo, mimo,
>   Vperedi—neizvestnost' puti . . .
> Blagoslovenno, neizgladimo,
>   Nevozvratimo—prosti!
>
> You were brighter, truer, lovelier than all,
>   Don't curse me, don't curse!
> My train flies like a gypsy song,
>   Like those irretrievable days . . .
>
> What was loved—all is past, past;
>   Ahead—an uncertain path . . .
> Blessedly, indelibly,
>   Irrevocably—forgive!

The assonances on "-imo" (*ljubimo, mimo, neizgladimo, nevozvratimo*) are like assurances of faithfulness and constancy; the short ones (*puti : prosti*) speak of an end. The first verse prepares the tonality of the high I (*Ne kljani že menja, ne kljani*). In the second verse I predominates (*ljubimo, mimo, mimo, vperedi, puti, neizgladimo, nevozvratimo, prosti*). They are truly "sobbing sounds."

Months pass; separated from Carmen, in an empty and cold house, the poet recalls with grateful tenderness his fleeting happiness:

> And the snow fell,
> And it is not for me to dispel
> The winter's witchcraft . . .
> And it's strange to remember
> That there was fire.
>   (*That life has passed*)

She excites him in dreams: she is all light and exultation:

> Oh, these distant arms!
> Into this dreary life
> You carry, even in separation,
> Your charm!
>   (*Let me too live, not loving*)

Now she "blooms under other skies." But when spring comes he is again "in the whirlwind of her flame, in the radiance of her eyes":

> I recognize you in sad dreams,
> And with my hands I press
> Your enchantress' hand,
> Repeating the distant name.
>   (*Beyond the mountains and forests*)

The 1914 cycle of poems *Carmen*, dedicated to LAD, opens with an operatic overture, triumphal and joyful, like Bizet's music:

> As the ocean changes color,
> When in a heaped-up cloud
> A blinking light blazes suddenly—
> So the heart in a melodious thunderstorm
> Changes order, afraid to breathe,
> And the blood rushes to the cheeks,
> And tears of happiness choke the breast
> Before the appearance of the Carmenists.

The image of a real woman, L. A. Delmas, and the image created by art; romantic Spain, of which Mérimée dreamed; sunny Seville, the tavern of Lillas Pastia, the cigar factory, the camp of the smugglers, the bullfight, the soldiers, the gitanas, the toreadors; daggers and roses; Bizet's music, seguidillas and fandangos, songs and dances, castanets and tambourines—everything merged for Blok into

> *There*—a wild fusion of worlds, where part of the universal soul
> Sobs, arising with the harmony of the heavenly bodies.

The appearance of the Spanish gitana was prepared for him by Russian gypsyness. Carmen is a brilliant culmination of gypsy nights, of "the dark fog of gypsy songs." Into the delirium and frenzy of "unleashed passions" she introduces the romantic charm of Latin grace. In the midst of chaos, there is personified harmony; in the midst of the violins' wailing, "the echo of a forgotten hymn." How unlike the swarthy savage Ksyusha is this "tsarina of blissful times"!

> And you pass by in thoughts and dreams,
> Like a tsarina of blissful times,
> With your head buried in roses,

Sunk in fairy tale sleep.
(You, like the echo of a forgotten hymn)

No more muttering and shrieking of guttural melodies. The poet dresses his Carmen in "spring, trembling and babbling and rustling," in sweet melody about a distant, blissful homeland. He sings about her with nightingale trills, strews her with magical moon luster. What languorous, exhausting music is in these stanzas:

You see the endless and burning day
And your beloved, native land,
Blue, blue, melodious, melodious,
Immovably blissful, like paradise.

In that land quiet is breathless,
Only in a crown of intertwined branches,
Your wonderful voice, low and strange.
Glorifies the storm of gypsy passions.

He calls her a demon of the morning. Smoky-bright, golden-haired and happy, he conceals in himself the "rumble of forgotten storms."

In the night tavern of Lillas Pastia, among Carmen's admirers, he alone doesn't expect and doesn't demand love:

He remembers the days of spring,
He amid raging harmonies
Looks at her melodious figure
And dreams creative dreams.
(Amid Carmen's admirers)

He knows—her love will bring him death:

And the voice sang: "With the price of life
You will pay me for love!"
(Snowy spring rages)

Thus superstitious horror is admixed to the ecstasy of love. As to Don José, she throws him a rose, and like Don José he knows: his fate is to be strangled "in the predatory power of beautiful arms":

Roses—the color of these roses is terrible to me.
Is this the red night of your tresses?
Is this the music of secret unfaithfulness?
Is this the heart in captivity to Carmen?
(Pussy-willows—a pledge of spring)

The cycle *Carmen* is crowned with an exultant declaration of love (*Oh, yes, love is free as a bird*). In the rhythm of this poem rings the derisively passionate melody of Carmen's aria "*L'Amour est un oiseau de Bohême.*"

Aleksandr Blok   The verses don't speak, they sing—and no reading can destroy this persistent melody:

> *O, yes, love is free as a bird,*
> Yes, all the same—I am yours!
> Yes, all the same I will dream
> Of your figure, your fiery figure!

The fourth stanza picks up the melody:

> You will rise like a stormy wave
> In the river of my poems,
> And I won't wash from my hand,
> Carmen, your perfume . . .

The last stanza, slowed down by a fifth line, ends the poem with a skillful ritardando:

> After the storm of life, after the alarm,
>   After the sorrow of all unfaithfulness—
> Let this thought appear, stern,
>   Simple, and white, like a road,
>   Like a distant path, Carmen!

After the creative bounty of 1913 and 1914, 1915 is striking for its poverty. Blok practically doesn't hear the music, inspiration leaves him. He writes a few poems—cold, forced. The best thing he creates in this unfruitful year is a small *poema, Nightingale Garden.* M. A. Beketova reports: "In this *poema* there are echoes of the last trip abroad. In Guethary there was a villa from whose fence hung climbing roses. The Bloks often passed it and saw a worker with a pick and a donkey on the rocky shore." The poet rather unsuccessfully selects this worker as the hero of the *poema.* He "breaks the schitose rocks at ebb tide on the silt-covered bottom," and the donkey drags them to the railway roadbed. Every day he passes the fence of the cool garden:

> Along the high and long fence
> The blooms of superfluous roses hang down to us.
> The nightingale song doesn't cease,
> The streams and leaves whisper something.

In the blue twilight behind the lattice a white dress gleams—she beckons him, twirls, sings. There is another, magical world. The poet doesn't describe it, he dissolves it in music: roses and nightingales and sunset mist and the white dress sing in the lines:

> And she, light, beckons me
> And calls me with her whirling and singing.

> And in the inviting whirling and singing
> I catch something forgotten,
> And I begin to love languor,
> I love the inaccessibility of the fence.

The hero approaches the fence—she opens it for him. The nightingale song rings out, the streams make noise, her bracelets, falling, jingle. The melodiousness of the verse is delightful:

> Vdol' proxladnoj dorogi, mež lilij,
> Odnozvučno zapeli ruč'i,
> Sladkoj pesn'ju menja oglušili,
> Vzjali dušu moju solov'i.
>
> Along the cool road, among the lilies,
> The streams sing monotonously,
> The nightingales took my soul,
> Deafened me with a sweet song.

The melodic *i* (*lilij, ruč'i, oglušili, solov'i*) with the trills '*ju, oju, 'i* (*ruč'i, pesn'ju, moju, solov'i*), with the internal assonances (*oglušili : dušu, vzjali : solov'i*) are reminiscent of the luxurious pleasure of the sound of Pushkin's *Fountain of Bakhchisarai*.

But neither streams, nor lilies, nor nightingales can muffle the distant roar of the sea:

> Otdalënnago šuma priliva
> Už ne možet ne slyšat' duša.
>
> The soul cannot help hearing
> The distant noise of the rising tide.

And the muted music of the ocean (*šu, už, že, ša, ša*) conquers the nightingale's song of love. The worker leaves the enchanted garden: his heavy crowbar grew rusty under the rock—neither the donkey nor the hut remain on the hill:

> And from the path I wore,
> Where the hut used to be,
> The worker with the pick began to descend,
> Urging on someone else's donkey.

The folklore plot about a blissful country where years seem like minutes is transformed by Blok into a fairy tale about a *Nightingale Garden*—into a canvas woven of the most delicate melodic patterns.

Three poems devoted to the war of 1914 are placed in the section *Native Land*: *The Petrograd sky grew dull with rain*, *I didn't betray the white banner*, and the poem *Those born in the stagnant years*, which is already familiar to us. The first describes the departure of a troop train for the front. The soldiers, platoon after platoon, fill the coaches, shout "Hurrah," quietly cross themselves:

> In this train, in thousands of lives, flowered
>   The pain of separation, the anxieties of love,
> Strength, youth, hope. . . . In the sunset dust
>   Were smoky clouds in blood.

The poet forces himself not to grieve and not to pity:

> This pity—the fire deadens it,
>   The thunder of guns and the clatter of horses,
> Sadness—the poisoned steam
>   From the bloody Gallician fields covers it. . . .

Blok recognizes the "beginning of lofty and turbulent days." Neither sadness nor pity clench his heart, but a prophetic anxiety on the threshold of a new world. In the poem *I didn't betray the white banner*, over Russia's death-sleep the star of Bethlehem burns, the torments of Russia are the labors of a land giving birth to Christ:

> The cross and embankment of the brotherly grave,
> You are there now, quietness!
> Only from a distance rushes the wave
> Of the plaintive soldier song.
>
> And near by—everything is empty and mute
> In mortal sleep—enemies and friends.
> And the star of Bethlehem burns
> As brightly as my love.

The outbreak of the world war sharpens in Blok the sense of Russia's mystical calling. In her past is the burning faith of the schismatics, the illuminated glory of the monastery crosses. In the dense forests, on the precipices, in rusty-colored marshes, the wood-fellings of the Old Believers once blazed:

> The steep slopes impenetrable with forest:
> Once there on the summit,
> The grandfathers felled a tree for burning
> And sang about their Christ.

Now the deep quiet of the marshes is there, but the past doesn't die:

> And the rusty-colored forest drops,
> Born in the backwoods and darkness,
> Carry to frightened Russia
> News of the burning Christ.

But the Russian people knew not only the "burning Christ"; the radiant and grace-giving Christ lives in the person of the schema monks, hermits, saints, surrounded by the people's love. Blok speaks of the radiant quiet of the monastery in a poem dedicated to his mother:

> The wind quieted, and sunset's glory
>   Vested the ponds over there.
> There a schema monk. Closing the book,
>   He humbly awaits the star.

The poet, repeating stubbornly that he doesn't know Christ, is drawn to him in spirit. In the terrible year of 1914 he yearns for the monastic life:

> From a distance the monastery cross
>   Appears golden with the sunset's glory.
> Shouldn't I turn to eternal peace?
>   And what is life without a cowl?

This is the only time this sigh escapes from him, and with what light does it illuminate his whole life! On the eve of the Russo-Turkish War of 1854, the Slavophile Khomyakov, dreaming of erecting a cross on St. Sophia in Constantinople, called his native land to repentance. In angry, accusatory lines he enumerated her sins and vices. At the beginning of the world war of 1914–17 Blok, believing in the star of Bethlehem over Russia, hurls a fiery indictment at her. In the power of its indignation, pain, passion, it surpasses Khomyakov's indictment. These lines are etched in every Russian soul:

> Shamelessly, endlessly sinning,
> Losing count of days and nights,
> And, head hurting from drunkenness,
> Going by a side-path into God's temple.
>
> Bowing down three times,
> Making seven signs of the cross,
> Touching with a burning forehead,
> Secretly, the spit-upon floor.

Returning home, to hold one's neighbor not worth a penny, to drink tea under an icon, to count coupons, spitting on one's fingers, and to fall onto downy feather beds—this is the bestial face of dark Russia. And there is an unexpected ending:

> Yes! And such, my Russia,
> You are dearer to me than all countries!

This is that love which knows no evil, forgives everything, rejoices at everything; this is the love Christ taught.

Aleksandr Blok

The lyrical poem *Last Parting Words* serves as an epilogue to the poems *Native Land*. Perhaps it is inspired by Turgenev's beautiful elegy, which ends with the lines:

> Dear friend, when I will
> Die, here is my command . . .
> . . . . .
> I will pass into another world,
> Lulled by the light ringing
> Of light earthly music.

Blok has a similar verse:

> That the sounds, barely disturbing,
> With the light music of earth,
> Would ring, would weary,
> Over the bed's last peace,
> And would carry away into another . . .

Death-bed visions visit the dying poet: here she appears—"a light image of paradise"—and touches his heart "like a tender violin." Floating past are people, buildings, cities—perfidy, fame, gold, flattery, irreparable and majestic and unending human stupidity. "Is this the end?" the dying one asks:

> No . . . still forests, clearings,
> Both country roads and highways,
> Our Russian road,
> Our Russian fogs,
> Our rustling in the oats . . .
>
> And when everything passes by,
> With which the earth alarmed,
> The one whom you loved much,
> Will lead you with a beloved hand
> Into the Elysian fields.

This is no longer a voice, but an incorporeal breeze; the words are translucent with unearthly light; they take flight with a quiet sweep of wings. The Eternal Friend and the Homeland—"those whom he loved much," two feminine shadows, bend over his bed. The Russian country roads and Russian highways lead the liberated soul into the Elysian fields of death.

The last small section of the third volume is called *What the Wind Sings About*. In it six poems written in October 1913 stand out. If in this year the author were not only thirty-three years old, we would have called this cycle "Senilia," so agedly calm and wise are these verses. Everything is in the past. Everything is over. Life had roared past:

> We are forgotten, alone on earth,
> We sit quietly in the warmth.

The poet and his friend while away the joyless days "in a warm corner":

> Behind the window, as then, lights.
> Dear friend, you and I are old.

To expect nothing, not to grumble, not to grieve for what has passed—that is the cheerless wisdom of old age. But the wind sings and walks near the house. And a hollow voice says:

> There is no return
> For passions and thoughts . . .
> Look, look:
> With a midnight noise
> The wind comes to us from sunset . . .
> The last light
> Has faded. Die.
> The last light of sunset has faded.

The weary heart beats with short strokes (two-foot iambics). Toward the end the beat accelerates (four-foot iambics: "The last light of sunset has faded"), and the heart stops. But neither the warm corner, nor the walls, nor the books will defend from alarm: behind the window "voices sing, the blizzard calls, someone's eyes watch":

> Behind your quiet shoulders
>   I hear the quiver of wings . . .
> There beats into me with shining eyes
>   The angel of the storm—Azrael!

The poem *From nothing—in a blue fountain* is the most perfect in this cycle. The sudden brilliance of a rocket flying into the sky, the rainbow of sparkling colors, is not described, but shown in magical words and sounds:

> From nothing—in a blue fountain—
>   Light suddenly splashed.
> We tilt our heads upward—
>   It's already gone.
> It spilled over the black distance
>   In a golden bundle,
> And here, again—another, like a spiral,
>   A ball, a top,
> Green, yellow, blue, red—
>   All the night in rays . . .
> And, startling it for nothing,
>   Withered.

The regular alternation of four- and two-foot iambics breaks off with the stress of the last line (one-foot iambic: "začax"). The whole poem prepares for this effective finale. The last poem begins with the lines:

> That happened in the dark Carpathians,
> Happened in distant Bohemia . . .

The fairy tale breaks off. This wind sang him "an accidental fragment—from another life." And, addressing an old friend, he calls him to what the romantic Zhukovsky called "resignation":

> Wait, old friend, endure, endure,
>   Not long to endure, sleep more soundly,
>   Anyway, everything will pass.
> Anyway, no one will understand,
>   Will understand neither you nor me,
>   Nor what the wind sings
>   To us, ringing . . .

With this epilogue the third volume of Blok's poems ends.

In March 1916 Nemirovich-Danchenko informs Blok of his decision to stage *The Rose and the Cross* in the Art Theater and calls him to Moscow. The poet spends a week there. He writes to his mother:

> Everyday at half-past one I go to rehearsals; we break up after five. For the time being mainly I speak; I read the play and explain. Stanislavsky, Nemirovich, and Luzhsky also speak; the others make observations and ask questions. The roles have been changed somewhat: Kachalov wants to play Bertran, and an actor whom I saw as Mephistopheles in Goethe's *Faust* (at Nezlobin's)—a good actor—will play Gaetan. . . . I have little fear for Kachalov, he makes very subtle observations. Stanislavsky has some complicated plans for staging, which he will try. . . . The question of Gzovskaya and Germanova, apparently already decided, agitates me. Gzovskaya listens very well, wants to act. But she is in love with Igor Severyanin and is afraid to make herself swarthy, so as to preserve the fluttering of her eyelashes. Besides that, I can't at all fall in love with her. Yesterday I saw Germanova in Merezhkovsky's play and already began to fall in love with her, as is my custom. During the intermission I ran into her near the dressing room. She regretted that she isn't playing Izora. She said: "They say I've grown old." After that, of course, I fell in love with her even more. Anyway, her voice is impossible for Izora (I like it, however). On the other hand, her appearance and movements are amazing.

On 4 April he writes:

> I am working every day, I talk for hours, I explain, as if with my own. . . . The other day I spent the night at Kachalov's with gypsies and a cup; this was delightful. Bertran, Gaetan and Aliskan have been hired by me. I spent whole hours with Izora; today, finally, I will go to her

place—to talk again. Gzovskaya is intelligent and talented and subtle, but terribly alien.

For the actors of the Art Theater, Blok writes explanatory notes to the play: "Sketches," "*The Rose and the Cross* (For the Production in the Art Theater)," and "Introduction, For the Production." In them he sets forth in detail the content, gives characterizations of the cast of characters, and explains the "main idea":

> [*The Rose and the Cross*] is first of all the drama of a *man*—Bertran. He isn't the hero, but the mind and heart of the drama; the poor mind sought a reconciliation of the Rose of never-experienced Joy with the Cross of habitual Suffering. The heart, covering the long path of ordeals and love, found this reconciliation only at the moment of death, so that the poor knight's *whole* life path is presented in the drama. . . . *The Rose and the Cross* is, secondly, the drama of Izora. . . . Izora is still too young to appreciate devoted, *merely human* love, which protects inconspicuously and calls nowhere. . . . But Izora's fate has not yet been realized, as her tears over Bertran's corpse testify. Perhaps they are incidental, and she will soon forget about them. Perhaps she too had approached an understanding of Joy-Suffering. Finally, perhaps her fate is completely unlike the fate of the man who loved her with a *Christian* love and died for her like a *Christian*, having, by his death, opened new paths for her.

This invaluable authorial testimony allows us to understand the conception of the play, which was never fully brought to realization. *The Rose and the Cross* is a tragedy of "human" love standing on a narrow peak between two precipices: "angelic love" and "animal love." As in a medieval mystery play the hero, Bertran, appears with two companions: Gaetan on his right, Aliskan on his left. The first is a mystical call, an unearthly song; the second is youth and animal beauty. There are three images of love in the three allegorical figures; and all of Blok's life is contained in this trio. In the notes, "Introduction, For the Production" the author speaks about Gaetan:

> Gaetan is first of all a certain force acting apart from his own will. This is a call, a voice, a song. This is an artist. Behind his human appearance something else continually shines through; he is, so to speak, transparent, and even his outward appearance is a little transparent. He is all gray-blue, shaken by the wind.

Such was Blok in the epoch of "mystical love" and the Beautiful Lady.

Aliskan personifies the period of *The Snow Mask* and *The Earth in Snow*—a time of "passions and insanities." And, lastly, Bertran is the ideal of the "manly man"; he has a "weather-beaten, coarsened face"; he is "implacably honest"; "he loves his native land"; "he is a servant"; "service and duty entered deep into his life"; "he has a square exterior, but not a square soul." In 1911 Blok dreamed of the appearance of such a new "Strindbergian" human breed, when he was developing in himself healthy manliness and vital force. At that time he wanted to be a Bertran. The poet gives his hero "a tender heart, loving everything which no one else loves or can love as he does."

For Blok-Bertran, mystical love and sensual love are paths long since traversed. Now he knows one love—real, *human* love, demanding nothing and sacrificing everything. He comprehended the meaning of the song about Joy-Suffering and understood that the one he has loved from his youthful years is not the mystical Eternal Friend and not a "cardboard bride," but a "person whose fate has not yet been realized," and who can yet approach an understanding of "Joy-Suffering." Izora is not merely a part of Bertran's fate; *The Rose and the Cross* is not only Bertran's drama but also Izora's. She is "predatory, greedy, capricious"; "a woman to the marrow of her bones"; she has a "hawklike vigilance" and a "feline softness." She is too young and passionate to appreciate the selfless love of the poor knight. She prefers the handsome, banal Aliskan to Bertran, but she is also "a delicate and noble instrument, made of such irreproachably pure and receptive metal that the most distant call echoes in her." Her love for the page is not the final word in her fate: "her tears over Bertran's corpse testify to this." At the time of his writing the drama, Blok, seeing himself in the image of the awkward and homely failed knight, gave traits of his wife to Izora. Bertran's drama ends with his radiant death in "Joy-Suffering"; Izora's drama is only beginning. The author believes that she is a "delicate and noble instrument" which *perhaps* will *someday* resound in answer to his love.

After the pagan tragedy of fate (the *poema Retribution*) Blok creates a Christian tragedy of love (*The Rose and the Cross*). Real "human" love is Christian love. "Bertran," he writes, "loved her with a *Christian* love, and died for her like a *Christian*." The poet often spoke about his alienation from Christianity, even considered himself an atheist. But Christianity, in Dostoevsky's words, is deeper than any atheisms. Blok's soul was, "by nature, Christian."

The work on staging the drama advanced slowly. On 23 May Blok informs his mother:

> Luzhsky wrote that I probably won't have to come before fall. They will show what they have done only to their chiefs. They rejected Bazilevsky's music (opera and moderne, Gzovskaya wrote). Yanovsky will soon do the staging, but first of all will be Vasilenko. Dobuzhinsky and the theater artists will probably partly do the scenery. . . . Gzovskaya writes that it is very difficult for her, but she has done a little.

Seeing Gzovskaya on the cinema screen, Blok wrote his mother: "I am convinced that Stanislavsky is profoundly right; she is a so-called 'character' actress, and can do very much in this direction. Therefore I hope to give Izora 'features of the common people,' which I want very much, on the stage of the Art Theater."

The recognition of the Christian basis of *The Rose and the Cross* prompts the poet to compare his mystical experience with the experience of Christian ascetics and monks. He immerses himself in reading the *Philokalia*—a collection of ascetic works of the Eastern Church fathers and hermits. In the works of the monk Evagrius (sixth century), he finds "things of genius" and is convinced that his personal spiritual experience coincides completely with the experience of the Christian mystics. Evagrius' chapter on the struggle with devils especially strikes him. He writes his mother: "Very simple and useful observations, often known, to be sure, to artists too—of the type to which I also belong. . . . For me personally it is amusing that Evagrius' attitude toward demons is exactly the same as mine toward doubles, for example, in the article about symbolism." This checking of his individual theosophy against the experience of the Church is extraordinarily significant. Blok continues to spurn "frenzied New Testament metaphysics," but Christian mystical asceticism attracts him. In the perhaps subconscious depth of his spirit he was an ascetic and a mystic.

After a long interruption the poet again sets to work on the *poema Retribution* and by the beginning of June finally finishes the prologue and the first chapter; he informs his mother that together they make up 1,019 lines: "If I succeed in writing in addition the second and third chapters and the epilogue, which the plan demands, the *poema* could grow to the dimensions of *Onegin*. Whatever its quality, in the quantity of work I have in these days surpassed even some industrious poets!"

In the spring of 1916 the second edition of the three-volume collection of poems and the small volume *Theater* came out in the Musaget publishing house. Blok's books were sold out in a few hours; in two weeks the 2,000 copies of *Theater* were sold out. Republishing his poems, the poet enters in the *Notebook*: "The other day I thought how I shouldn't write poems, because I am too able to do this. It is still necessary to change (or something around me has to change) to again get the chance to master the material."

And he writes in another note:

> Despite the fact (or precisely thanks to the fact) that I "understood" myself to be an *artist*, I not often and rather stupidly am in a flood of tears over a creative idea and revel in harmony. The freshness is no longer the same as initially. . . . The *Verses on the Beautiful Lady* remain the *best*. Time shouldn't touch them, however weak I am as an artist.

On 7 June Blok was called to military service, and that same day, through the intercession of V. A. Zorgenfrei, he was entered in the Union of Zemstvos as a "timekeeper of the Thirteenth Engineering-Construction Division." On 25 May he set out for his place of service—in the Pinsk marshes. Until March 1917 he was there occupied with the supervision of manual laborers building fortifications; he lived on a prince's estate, rode horseback, wrote in the office. He informs his mother: "We are constructing a very long position—several versts in length. Simultaneously we are digging new entrenchments, repairing old ones, nailing up stakes, stretching wire, clearing a firing zone, opening up lines of communication—in the field, in the forest, on the marsh, in clearings, around the villages."

In October he got a leave and went to Petersburg. Z. N. Gippius remembers his visit:

> I clearly remember Blok in high boots, in an elegantly belted tunic, unusually rapidly, agitatedly pacing my rug. And I remember his words, he kept repeating the same ones: "How to serve it . . . the Russian people . . . better now." His face was not joyful: at times lost and perplexed.

Returning to staff headquarters in the Pinsk marshes, he writes his mother on 21 November:

> Headquarters life continues to be absurd. . . . I got a very long letter from Nemirovich, in which he describes all the work. He writes that they won't need me for at least a month.
> Lilina is playing Alisa. He fears for Gaetan, Aliskan, and several others. He is quite carried away. The music will hardly be Rachmaninoff's (he is busy). It seems they have also not yet persuaded Medtner.

At the end of October the poet complains: "Very lonely and crowded. I am just a bit tired. One has to swear a lot. Nature is amazing. Just now a soft and rather deep snow and a moon. Snow on the trees and bushes. This helps me every day. The rest is all—cinema."

His letters to his mother from the front are courageous and cheerful; but this is a tone adopted entirely to calm a sick person. Beneath it is alarm for Russia, a premonition of military catastrophe, almost despair. An entry in the *Notebook*: "When one thinks about everything that is happening to everyone and to me, one could lose one's mind." And another:

> *Bo suggested an idea*: There once lived a husband and wife. It was bad for both of them. Finally the wife says to the husband: "It's unbearable to live this way. You're stronger than I am. If you wish me well, go out into the street, find a string, pull it, and overturn the whole world."

In 1916 Blok wrote only four poems; the last ones entering the third volume of the *Collected Works*. One of them, ending the section *Miscellaneous Poems*, begins with the verse:

> You keep repeating that I'm cold, reserved, and dry,
> Yes, I will be so with you:
> I didn't forge my spirit for tender words,
> I didn't struggle with fate for friendships.

The world had entered the "dark night," had "gone wild" in the darkness. There was a time when the poet believed and hoped; when he approached people "with an open and childlike soul." Not so now; his soul had grown weak from love-hate, had burned to ashes:

> Don't knock in vain at the solid doors,
> Don't torment yourself with futile moaning;
> You won't meet sympathy from poor beasts,
> Who once called themselves people . . .

Blok followed the slow "falling-apart" of the war, saw its terrible bestial face and the "coarseness without beginning or end" begotten by it. He places the remarkable poem *The Kite* as an epilogue to the section *Native Land*—his last "lament" over his unfortunate native land:

> Tracing smooth circle after circle,
> The kite circles above the sleepy meadow
> And looks at the deserted meadow.
> In a hut a mother grieves over her son:
> "Take the bread, here! Suck the breast!
> "Grow, obey, wear a cross."
>
> Ages pass, war bellows,
> Rebellion rises, villages burn,
> But you are always the same, my country,
> In tear-stained and ancient beauty.
> How long must the mother grieve?
> How long must the kite circle?

These concise and simple words contain a miracle of verbal expressiveness. Every trace of lyrical "prettiness" is destroyed. There are two image-symbols: the kite and the mother. And the fate of Russia is contained in them. The two concluding questions have tragic power:

> How long must the mother grieve?
> How long must the kite circle?

The poem *The Demon*, included in the section *The Terrible World*, is a brilliant variation on the theme of Lermontov's *poema*. Blok adopts Lermontov's melody, reproduces the lines of his rhythm, for example:

> I will carry you above the abyss,
> Teasing you with its depth.
> Your useless horror will be
> Only an inspiration to me.

or:

> Yes, I will take you with me
> And will lift you there,
> Where the earth seems like a star,
> A star seems like the earth.

But the poet unites Lermontov's romantic Demon with Vrubel's mystical Demon. His fallen angel is more seductive and more terrible. He lifts Tamara into "new worlds," shows her "inconceivable visions, creations of his playing," burns her "divinely beautiful body," and with a tender smile hurls her into the abyss:

> And beneath the divine smile,
> Destroyed in flight,
> You will fly like an unsteady stone
> Into the shining void . . .

This last verse sparkles with a "divine," Luciferian brilliance. Blok's and Lermontov's genius are akin.

At the beginning of 1917 the nervous illness of Blok's mother assumed such an acute form that, on the advice of psychiatrists, it was again necessary to place her in a sanitorium. In February, F. F. Kublitsky moved her to the Chekhov sanitorium near the Kryukovo station of the Nikolaevsky railroad line. Blok's letters are filled with alarm, advice, consolation. He is bored in his marsh:

> Despite the fact that this marsh is forgotten not only by the Germans, but even by God, there is astonishing air here, constant wind shifts, deep snow, lights at night in the village windows—all this is, as always, real. Tonight, for example, we heard that frequent firing had begun on the front, searchlights and rockets went to work, the horizon was lit by flashes of shells. We mounted horses and rode on the hills toward the front. . . . A dark night, the path in snow. Oncoming trees and bushes one takes for sleighs; they seem to be moving, skeletons of windmills with broken arms, a strong wind.

Blok greets the February revolution with joyful excitement:

> All that has occurred gladdens me. No one can yet evaluate what has occurred, because history hasn't yet known such a scale. It had to happen; it could occur only in Russia.
> The minutes are of course very dangerous, but the danger, if it is in prospect, is *illuminated*, which hasn't happened for a very long time in our life, perhaps never. All the countless dangers which arose before us were lost in demonic darkness.

On 19 March the poet comes to Petersburg on a month's leave. He writes his mother:

> I wandered along the streets, looked at the spectacle unique in the world and in history, at gay people who had become kinder, swarming on the uncleaned streets, without surveillance. The unusual consciousness that everything is possible, threatening, capturing the spirit, and terribly gay. . . . Everything is overcome by the consciousness that a miracle has occurred and that, consequently, there will be other miracles. Never

could any of us have thought he would be a witness of such simple miracles taking place every day.
Nothing is terrible, here only cooks are afraid.... Yesterday I dropped in on the Merezhkovskys.... They told me a lot, so that the picture of the upheaval is more or less clear to me: something supernatural, delightful.

On 30 March he relates that he had received a telegram from Nemirovich-Danchenko, calling him to Moscow in the middle of St. Thomas' Week; but a few days later Nemirovich himself comes to Petersburg:

Day before yesterday Nemirovich-Danchenko invited Dobuzhinsky and me to dine at Donon's, but he himself had to leave unexpectedly... so that Dobuzhinsky and I found ourselves at Donon's together. A. Benois and Grabar dropped in there by chance, ... and we dined very nicely as a foursome.... A bright spring day today. By me stands a basket of small red roses from Lyubov Aleksandrovna [Delmas].

At the beginning of April the poet is called to Moscow:

Mama, on the thirteenth [of April] I heard the entire first act and two scenes from the second in the theater. Everything, except details, is completely right, and everyone is excited (a good sign).... Kachalov is superb, Luzhsky is on the right track, Gzovskaya cut only a pale figure, Alisa also makes one want something better.... They confer in the theater all the time. Nemirovich might leave, and almost certainly Gzovskaya.
I have no confidence that the play will be staged next year.

At the end of the letter there is a postscript: "Nevertheless I can't deny a certain insight that I have a sense of the present. What is happening is happening within the spirit of *my* alarm." The next letter from Moscow is dated 17 April:

Gzovskaya is almost certainly leaving. What will happen to the play, and when, I don't know.... In the theater, of course, everyone is also distracted by the extraordinary circumstances and is occupied with "politics." If history continues its extraordinary games, then perhaps all people will separate themselves from work, and culture will perish once and for all, which will be a perhaps just retribution for the "humanism" of the past age.... Actually, essentially only Stanislavsky is a *very great artist*, he really loves art. By the way, *The Rose and the Cross* is completely incomprehensible and useless to him; in my opinion he is pretending (fooling himself) in praising the play. He would only torment himself with it.

The "schism" in the Art Theater ended with Gzovskaya's departure. Koreneva or Time were to get the role of Izora. Nemirovich and Luzhsky removed themselves as directors. The staging of *The Rose and the Cross* passed to Stanislavsky. The production was being done all over again. It simply remained unfinished.

Blok understands that his arrival in Moscow "proved to be essentially useless," and a feeling of hopelessness grips him. He writes his mother:

> I hung around the dressing rooms and corridors, spoke with various theater people. It is painful for everyone. Let, let Europe still howl for a time, an unhappy, played out courtesan: all the world's wisdom will flow through her fingers soiled by war and politics—and others will come and lead her "where she doesn't want to go." Yellow, perhaps?

On 27 April he gets a telegram from the aide to the commander of the detachment: "Telegraph express the time of your arrival in the division or your wish to be reassigned." He answers immediately: "Deadline 15 May. I ask to be reassigned, if that's too late."

V. Zorgenfrei recalls his meeting with Blok: "In a military uniform with the narrow shoulder straps of the Zemsoyuz,[6] fresh, simple, and elegant, as always, Blok sat at my table in the spring of 1917; he had returned to Petersburg at the first opportunity, openly numbering himself with the deserters."

Idelson offers the poet a position as editor of stenographic material for the Extraordinary Investigating Commission. He meets the chairman of the commission, Muravyov, goes often to the Winter Palace, and on 8 May takes up his job. In an entry in the *Notebook* he writes: "I won't give up my 'desertion.' For seven months I played the fool. If they ask me what I did during the great war, I will, however, be able to answer that I did my duty: I edited A. Grigoriev and was staging *The Rose and the Cross* and writing *Retribution*" (5 May). Another entry: "Everything will be fine, Russia will be great. But how long to wait, and how difficult to wait till the end" (22 April). And finally: "In the evening I wandered, wandered. A white night, women. It is cozy for me in this gloomy and lonely abyss whose name is Petersburg, 1917, Russia, 1917. Life, where are you rushing? From the day, from the white night—stimulation, as from wine" (15 May).

Blok goes with Muravyov to the Peter-Paul Fortress, where he is present during the interrogation of the director of the department of police, Beletsky. "This," he writes, "is all a gigantic laboratory of autocracy, tubs of slops, dirtiness, all kinds of filth, a colossal rubbish pile." Then in the Winter Palace he hears the depositions of Goremykin, visits the prisoners in the fortress: Voyeikov, Prince Andronikov, Vyrubov, Makarov, Kafafov, Klimovich, Protopopov. He notes: "The heart melts in tears of pity for everything, everything. And remember that it's impossible to judge anyone. Remember also—more, more, cry more, the soul will be purified" (21 May). He writes his mother:

> "I am crucified with everyone," as someone at A. Bely's said. Actually, it is very, very painful. Yesterday the Tsarskoe Selo commandant related in detail everything that the tsar's family is doing now. This too is painful. In general everyone is right: the Cadets are right, and Gorky "with two souls" is right, and there is a terrible truth in bolshevism. I don't see

anything ahead, although I don't always lose optimism. They all, all, the "old" and the "new" are in us, at least in me. I am hanging in the air: now there is neither earth nor sky. With all that, Petersburg is again unusually beautiful. (26 May)

And in the *Notebook* he writes: "Somehow my nerves are deadened from the things seen and heard.... This Rasputin within me.... They all, all—the living and dead children of my era—are within me. How many, how many of them! It rained on the street" (27 [22] May).

From the "nightmare" of the Winter Palace and the Peter-Paul Fortress the poet escapes for a few hours to Lesnoy. "After dinner," he notes, "the charm of Lesnoy Park, of the road where, under a lilac winter sky prophesying rebellions and blood, I once walked with Lyuba, already engaged."

The chairman of the commission, Muravyov, assigns the poet the task of putting the stenographic reports in order. On 25 May Blok enters in the *Notebook*: "God, God, what depression. It came this afternoon and presses me tighter and tighter; by evening it suffocates me in its embrace. I sit and think in vain about the plan for the report." On 3 June Blok again begins to keep the *Diary*, broken off in 1913; he keeps it till the last days of his life. He writes little about the "external" —politics, literature, society. His attention is turned to the "inner," to the life of the soul. "This is all for 'introspection,' " he declares, half-joking, half-serious. The entries of 1917, the year of war and revolution, are particularly significant. The poet is caught up in the whirlwind of events, is shaken, lost, tormented. But the former despondent inertia is gone; he lives in a terrible tension, full of an invincible will to live. One principal "lyrical theme" runs through all the *Diary* entries— his love for his wife. It gets stronger with each year and is purified of the temporary and the accidental. Toward the end of his life Blok recalls the years of his youth, and begins a commentary on *Verses on the Beautiful Lady* in the style of Dante's *Vita Nuova*. After all the unfaithfulness and falls, there remains in his heart eternal love for "the only one in the world." The *Diary* begins and ends with Lyubov Dmitrievna's name. On 3 June 1917 the first entry: "Bu came in the morning; she is sleeping on my sofa. Her arrival startled me so, 'it unsettled me.' "

On 4 June he writes:

> Conversation with Lyuba about *New Life*. A whirlwind of ideas and feelings—to the point of tears—and this constant pain in my back.... During the intermissions I was with my darling, who never left me. In the evening I took Lyuba to the station, settled her in a coach; I won't forget even the details. How good.
> At night on the street the pale Delmas gave me three roses which she took from the concert.

This summer Lyubov Dmitrievna was acting in Pskov and came to Petersburg only for short visits. Blok lived alone and dreamed of going to Pskov, but work on the Investigating Commission took up all his time. He complains of weariness and of an incessant pain in his back—the first symptom of the disease which ended his life. Trying to understand, he notes down his strange "mystical" states:

> 8 June. Over everything—white nights. Lyuba. Lyuba! What will happen?
> 9 June. After ten pages of Beletsky,[7] at two o'clock on a hot day—suddenly my own. No me—till night. It seemed I had lost a cross, searched for it for two hours, looking through the slender blades of grass and the ringing tubes of reed, a whole anthill under a dried-up, rough alder tree. And in the distance large sails, the noise of a hydroplane, the charm of the sunset. And *as always*. I return; the cross is lying at home, I had forgotten to put it on. And I already, praying to God, praying to Lyuba, thought that misfortune threatens me and it stirred again—it's time to finish.

Daylight, empirical consciousness disappears ("No me, till night"), and night consciousness awakens: the poet finds himself on the shore of a sea, looks for a cross, sees sails and the sunset. "And *as always*"—by this formula Blok is accustomed to denoting the state of ecstasy he had never tried to describe. The emotional coloration of this enigmatic experience is alarm, a premonition of misfortune, and thoughts about his wife. On 11 June he writes: "And again since morning a stitch and ache in my back. Sweet old age is near."

The "strange state" comes again at the end of June. A note on 24 June:

> Suddenly, for a few minutes, almost insanity (a kind of conscience, an attack, as happened at the end of 1913, but sharper), almost unbearable. Then the reverse and until night—no me. All this is for "introspection" (Lord, Lord, when will the government finally release me?). . . . To business, to business.

And two days later:

> Broken, and weary, and inspired, I want—working and drunk on the sunset—everything together.
> What strange states sometimes occur. Sometimes it seems to me that I might nevertheless lose my mind. That is when clouds of thoughts flow, some special rays, lighting up these clouds by a kind of special revelation, begin to break through them. And, together with that, a depressed and weary body, without losing its weariness, somehow becomes younger and begins to bear, takes wing. This is described a bit literarily, but what I want to describe happens after great labors, restless nights, when ceaseless dreams torment for several nights in a row.
> Often in dreams, as also in life: someone attacks, pursues, I defend myself, I am terrified. What kind of fear is this? Sometimes I think I'm cowardly, but it seems, no, I am not a coward. This fear came long ago from two sources, a negative and a positive: from where I have corrupted myself, and from what I discovered in myself.

Again we meet the same formula, "until night—no me," and again the shift of consciousness, which happens so suddenly that the mystic fears "losing his mind." Aglaya in *The Idiot* talks about the "small" and the "large" mind. The "large" mind, revealing itself in the ecstatic state (Prince Myshkin has a "moment of harmony" before an epileptic seizure), carries a "special revelation": it is connected with images (clouds, "some special rays"), and is reflected in the physical state (the body grows younger, takes wing). In Blok, with his acute sense of sin (a "revelation" was given to him—and he was unfaithful to it), ecstasies are colored with a sensation of fear ("I have corrupted myself").

In the days of the July uprising the poet notes briefly:

> What a suffocating night; soon one o'clock and many sleepless people on the street. Hubbub, loud laughter, leaden clouds.... They are shooting (machine-guns, it seems).... The city isn't sleeping. How tired and weak I am.... I am too tired. But there was *a letter from Lyuba*.... Dawn is breaking a little. Two o'clock at night.

He emphasizes "a letter from Lyuba." This name rings in all the July entries:

> 5 July. A little sparrow flew into my room while I was working and I immediately felt the sadness of the moment, the government dirt in which for some reason I am sitting up to my ears. I began to remember Lyuba.
> 6 July. Oh, sinful day. All Petersburg sinned and worked much, and I—worked much and sinned.
> Lyuba, Lyuba, Lyuba.
> 8 July. The charm of the sunset sky, many airplanes aloft, the "foreigners" at Karpovka, the sadness of memories in the Botanical Garden and near the barracks, our windows with Lyuba.

He longs for "real" work. "Really," he writes, "will it be long, or will I never return to art?" On 13 July he writes:

> The ineffable in nature, but life, as is always the case, is boring and incomprehensible. Incomprehensible especially: it is quiet, military, the nasty newspaper news.... I want to whisper, but sometimes to shout: leave me in peace, it isn't my affair how reaction sets in after the revolution.
> Night, like a nimble mouse, gray, cold, smells of smoke and some kind of sea casks, my eyes like a cat's, Grishka [Rasputin] is within me, and I love living, and I don't know how—and when old age comes, and much, much will have happened. And behind everything—Lyuba.
> 16 July. Sun toward evening, and it is brighter and I am warmer, a poor beast. Note to Lyuba.
> 19 July. In the morning Manya came with a long letter from Lyuba and with trunks. All this disturbed me very much, much rose from the bottom of my soul—both good and bad. To work today so much that everything within would come into order.

The interrogations, the shorthand reports, and the endless meetings in the commission bring him to despair. A 28 July letter to his mother reads:

> Again I am thinking about "serious business," such as art and the degenerating and overgrown with weeds "personal life" connected with it, sacrificed to it, invariably seems to me.... "Long ago, cunning slave, I planned my escape to the quiet abode of labors and peaceful bliss,"[8] if this will ever be feasible.

On 29 July he notes in the *Diary*:

> My weariness has reached such a limit, I am broken. Lazy work with shorthand reports. I am annoyed with Lyuba, why does she stay there and not come, when it is already late?
> 30 July. My taste for the *mists* of bolshevism and anarchy (elemental force, "destruction," to hasten the "faces of the roses under the black lumps").[9]
> 31 July. I am waiting for my Lyuba.
> 1 August. *Lyuba arrived in the morning.* Intense heat and wind, park and bathing. All evening—conversation with Lyuba.
> 2 August. How Lyuba has changed. I still can't figure out in what way.

And, finally, a tragic note of 3 August is impossible to read without wracking emotion:

> Stifling, smell of burning. Something disturbing in the newspapers. I can no longer entertain Lyuba. She wants to be with me, but it's difficult for her with me; it's difficult to listen to my conversations. I myself feel the burden and tiresomeness of the wheels turning in my brain and on my tongue. "The old bachelor."
> Lyuba said today that in Pskov she had thought about joint suicide (also!). "It's too difficult. All the same we won't get clear." But we'll wait a while longer—she thinks so too.
> Everything is full of Lyuba. Both the burden and the responsibility of life are more severe and behind it—the faint possibility of a rosy smile, the only path to the rosy, an almost inconceivable path, impossible. . . . Depression. But nevertheless I don't end the day with this word, but with the opposite—"Lyuba.". . . But with what wormwood, painful to the point of sweetness, all this lies on our souls tormented by the war! It compels with the dust of weariness, with this stifling smell of burning; the head hurts, bends.
> Lyuba!

What humility ("I can't entertain Lyuba"), what sadness, what shy tenderness and love!

On 4 August, Blok writes his mother: "Russia has again entered her tragic (with an eternal vaudevillian tinge) time, everyone drags an 'onerous yoke.' In other words, it's so sickening one doesn't even want to speak. Only work saves me. . . . Lyuba and work. Now I no longer see anything." And the same day he notes in the *Diary*: "Again—Lyuba's housekeeping and coziness in the morning."

Lyubov Dmitrievna is with him again. He needs nothing more.

On 17 August the poet notes: "Fourteenth anniversary." Since the day he climbed the "jagged" Boblovo hill on horseback and saw a young girl in a pink dress beyond the park fence, he understood that all his life was in her. For him she was a real incarnation of the Eternal Feminine, the Beautiful Lady, his only love, his Muse. Looking at her, music began to ring in his soul for the first time—and all his lyric poetry was about her and for her. She made him a poet and opened to him the secret of "Joy-Suffering." And now, approaching "sweet old age" (his expression), he tries to understand the tragedy of his love. On 15 August he notes in the *Diary*:

> Barely had my fiancée become my wife, when the lilac worlds of the first revolution seized us and drew us into a whirlpool. I was the first, so long secretly wishing death, to be drawn into the gray purple, the silvery stars, the mother-of-pearl and the amethyst of the blizzard. My wife followed me, for whom this transition (from the difficult to the easy, from the unpermitted to the permitted) was tormenting, more difficult than for me. When the blizzard passed, the iron void of the day was revealed, which, however, continued to threaten with a new blizzard, to conceal in itself the blizzard's promises. Such were the years between the revolutions, wearying and wracking soul and body. Now another squall swooping down (I still can't determine the color and odor). . . . The company of the Kommissarzhevskaya Theater, Zinaida Nikolaevna (closeness to Kerensky), Sologubism, the Terioki company, the war ministry of the new regime, *The Puppet Show* (a work which came from the womb of the police department of my own soul), Rasputin (alongside—boredom), Vyacheslav Ivanov, Ableukhov,[10] Remizov, and SR-dom—here is all that *whirlwind of atoms* of the cosmic revolution: when, where and as what will we emerge from it, will Lyuba and I emerge?

Blok takes on himself the whole responsibility for the transition from the golden azure of *Verses on the Beautiful Lady* to the lilac worlds of *The Snow Mask* and *The Earth in Snow*. He secretly wishes for death and draws his wife along after him. For him "there was a fateful delight in trampling on cherished holy things," because in his soul was his own "police department," from which the blasphemous *Puppet Show* emerged. He drew his wife into a world of snowstorms and passions, since within him was a Grishka Rasputin.

This entry is a feat of love: the poet indicts himself in order to acquit Lyubov Dmitrievna.

The last note in the *Diary* of 1917 is dated 30 August—Blok's name day. "Name day. Food. L. A. Delmas sent me flowers and a letter. . . . Lyuba dressed up, entertained, chattered, bought me shaggy pink asters (children's). . . . I am exhausted, as I haven't been for a long time. It seems to me that I won't succeed in anything."

Two months before the October revolution Blok is already vibrating from the "musical waves" of revolution striking him. He *already knows everything*. In this hot summer in the environs of Petersburg peat burns and there comes a stifling smell of burning. As in a medium's trance the poet senses the odor, noise, and light of the spreading fire. The smoke of enmity spreads in millions of souls, the flame of bolshevism already stalks around Russia. This prophetic dream is noted in the *Diary* on 6 August:

> Between two dreams: "Save, save!" "Save what?" "Russia," the "Homeland," the "Fatherland"—I don't know what and how to call it, so that it wouldn't be painful and bitter and shameful before the poor, the indignant, the ignorant, the oppressed! . . .
> But—save! The yellow-brown puffs of smoke are already approaching the villages, the bushes and grasses are catching fire in broad stretches, but God doesn't send rain and there is no grain, and what there is will burn up.
> The same yellow-brown puffs, behind which are decay and burning (as near Pargolovo and Shuvalovo, from which at night the whole city is always enveloped in the smell of burning), spread in millions of souls. The flame of enmity, savagery, Tatarism, malice, abasement, oppression, mistrust, vengeance blazes up now here, now there: Russian bolshevism is stalking, and there is no rain, and God doesn't send it.

On waking, Blok interrupts his vision: this "violent freedom" is just; the fire can become purifying; it is necessary to "fan it to the sky," so that the old Rasputin Rus would be consumed. The lyrical theme of *The Twelve* is given in the prophetic dream: "We to the grief of all bourgeois will fan the worldwide conflagration" already sounds. Already the "purifying bonfire" of revolution is rising to the sky.

On 7 August he writes:

> Having woken up: and here is *the task of Russian culture*—to direct this fire toward what must be burnt down; to transform the violence of Stenka and Emelka[11] into a spontaneous musical wave; to place on destruction such limits as will not weaken the fire's pressure, but organize this pressure; to organize the violent freedom; to direct the lazy decay, in which the possibility of violence is also concealed, into the Rasputin corners of the soul and there to fan it into a sky-high bonfire, so that cunning, lazy, servile carnality would be consumed.

Such is Blok's "bolshevism": the passion for destruction of the anarchist Bakunin, Tolstoy's thirst for purification, Nietzsche's "elemental music" are united in him. The poet seems not even to suspect the existence of Marx and Lenin.

The "musical pressure" from which *The Twelve* was born grows with each day. At first it blends with the vague rumble of the city—then separates from it. "But the glimmering flashes," Blok writes on 12 August, "yellow and sometimes pale, sometimes gripping a large band of the sky, continue, and it is beginning to seem to me that beyond the city rumble I hear another kind of rumble."

In August 1917 the poet put in order the materials of the Investigating Commission and began to put together a compilative essay based on them, "The Last Days of Imperial Power." This work was finished in April 1918 and published under the title "The Last Days of the Old Regime" in the journal *The Past* (*Byloe*) in 1919. A separate edition, prepared for the press by the author himself, came out after his death (Alkonost publishing house, 1921). This historical sketch, put together on the basis of depositions of the last representatives of the old regime, is written in an official, businesslike tone; the author refrains from personal evaluations.

After the abolition of the Investigating Commission, Blok was left without work and almost without income. He therefore had to accept the offer of the director of state theaters, F. D. Batyushkov, to enter the Literary Commission, which replaced the Theater-Literary Committee of the Aleksandrinsky Theater. In the poet's manuscripts are preserved eight detailed reviews of various plays (by Pimen Karpov, A. Lukyanov, A. Fyodorov, S. Naidenov, I. Potapenko, and others). In Petersburg, in the autumn of 1917, the newspaper of the Left SR Party, *The Banner of Labor* (*Znamya Truda*) appeared. The literary section was headed by Ivanov-Razumnik. Blok began to collaborate on it. The enthusiasm of the publicist and "public-spirited person" awoke in him again.

M. A. Beketova relates in her book on Blok:

> Aleksandr Aleksandrovich greeted the upheaval of 25 October joyfully, with new faith in the purifying power of the revolution.... He went around young, gay, cheerful, with shining eyes, and listened to that "music of the revolution," to that noise from the fall of the old world, which, according to his own testimony, resounded ceaselessly in his ears.

V. Zorgenfrei writes in his memoirs: "I remember a cold winter morning when, coming to see him, I heard that he 'felt totally' and that 'one had to accept' everything that had happened."

A. N. Gippius tells about her telephone conversation with Blok: she invites him to join Savinkov's anti-Bolshevik newspaper. He refuses, and adds: "Yes, if you like, I am rather with the Bolsheviks.... Yes, even I.... Perhaps I am also a 'lost child.'"

CHAPTER X
THE TWELVE. LAST YEARS
1918–1921

In the terrible winter of 1918 Petersburg is covered with snow drifts, is without streetcars, without streetlights. People sit in fur coats in icy apartments. Instead of bread, they eat pieces of black clay, rotten dried fish, and biscuits made from potato peels. Blok was starving, tormented at not being able to help his family, at having almost no income, at having become unaccustomed to literary work. In the *Notebook* he writes:

> Aleksandrinsky Theater. "Poverty is not a vice.". . . Going on foot—slippery, cold, dark, far (I am old). No streetcars. (4 January)
>
> All day and evening I am sad, bad-tempered; I hide. Somewhere, it seems, they were shooting, but I don't know. And it's not interesting. (5 January)

He wants to write; he conceives a drama about Christ. "Thoughts, thoughts and plans—so many that they prevent me from starting anything solid. If I could write *my own* (Jesus)." But hungry and dark Petersburg presses, it won't let him go. In despair he exclaims: "To the devil with everything, to the devil! To forget, *to remember something else*" (5 January).

This agitation is a premonition of the "whirlwind of inspiration" which is already rushing upon him from the abyss of the revolution. The poet is as taut as a stretched string; he is waiting. K. Chukovsky relates in his memoirs:

> One day at the beginning of January 1918 Blok was at acquaintances' and in a noisy argument was defending the revolution of the October days. His friends had never seen him so excited. Formerly he argued calmly, earnestly, but now he was gesticulating and even shouting. Soon he said in passing: "And I see angel wings on the shoulders of each Red Guardsman."

These words contain the conception of the artistic idea of *The Twelve*: "So they march with sovereign tread. . . . Ahead—Jesus Christ."

Finally the calm before the storm comes to an end. Far away, barely audibly, the music begins to sound; with each day it grows stronger. At first this is a hollow rumble; the poet still doesn't know where it is from and what it is speaking about. In the *Notebook* (9 January) there is the entry: "Drunkenness. The other day, lying in the dark with open eyes, I heard a rumble, a rumble; I thought an earthquake had begun." Important evidence: the rumble from which the "music of the revolution" took shape was not imagined, but completely real; the poet at first took it for the noise of an earthquake. Two days later he begins to distinguish musical order in this rumble. He hears: this is music, but unfamiliar, unlike that which rushed upon him early in the sobbing of the violins and gypsy songs; music not yet comprehensible. On 11 January he notes: "Different music (if . . . yellow?)." This is the first attempt to *understand*. The first possible explanation is sought out: V. Solovyov's idea about the "yellow peril," about panmongolism, is close to Blok. Suddenly and blindingly the conception of the *poema The Scythians* blazes up. That same day he notes in the *Diary*: "We looked at you with the eyes of Aryans while you represented something to us. And we will look at your snouts with our squinting, cunning, swift glance; we will reveal ourselves as *Asiatics*, and the East will spill over you. Your hides will go to make Chinese tambourines."

We are discovering: "Yes—we are Scythians! Yes—we are Asiatics! With slanting and avid eyes!" And further: "We will turn our Asiatic snouts toward you."

Finally the solution is found: not the rumble of an earthquake, not a physical noise, but a mysterious "world music"—"a noise from the collapse of the old world." The sound theme of *The Twelve* is grasped and given meaning. At the time of writing the *poema* the rumble keeps growing: "A terrible noise," Blok writes, "growing *in and around me.* Gogol heard this noise (to muffle it he called up family and Orthodox order)" (29 January).

Two years after finishing *The Twelve* (1 April 1920) the poet indignantly answered the critics who saw "political verse" in his *poema*:

> In January 1918 I for the last time gave myself up to the elemental force no less blindly than in January 1907[1] or in March 1914.[2] I therefore also don't disavow what was written then, that it was written in harmony with the elemental force; for example, at the time of and after finishing *The Twelve*, for several days I felt physically, with my hearing, a great noise of the wind—a continuous noise (probably the noise from the collapse of the old world). Therefore those who see political verse in *The Twelve* are either very blind to art, or are sitting up to their ears in political dirt, or are possessed by great rancor—be they enemies or friends of my *poema*.

The "collapse of the old world" is not only the theme of the *poema The Twelve*—it is the theme of the poet's whole life. Eschatological forebodings had agitated him from early youth, blending at first with the apocalypticism of his teacher, V. Solovyov, then with the decadent *fin de siècle*, with Bely's mysticism and Vyacheslav Ivanov's theurgy. Tidings of destruction rang in the irony of *The Puppet Show* and *The Stranger*, raised the blizzards of *The Snow Mask*, overflowed in the "sobbing sounds" of *The Terrible World* and *Retribution*. *The Twelve* is the culmination both of his creative work and of his life: it is justified alarm, fulfilled prophecy. In the October revolution Blok saw the last triumphal uprising of the elemental force, "the final destruction," "worldwide conflagration," and the end of "new history." An elemental inspiration, dictating *The Twelve* and *The Scythians* to him in a few days, was fed by an *ecstasy of destruction*. Rapture "on the brink of a terrible abyss," a breathtaking flight "above the gap, into eternity," gave birth to the choking, convulsively broken rhythm of the *poema*. Blok believed that the old world was done for, with all its decrepit bag and baggage—religion, culture, art; that everything is aflame—Russia, Europe, honor, morality, law. His response to Z. N. Gippius' accusatory letter is:

> Don't you really know that "Russia will not be," just as Rome was no more, not in the fifth century after the birth of Christ, but in the first year of the first century? Nor will England, Germany, France be. That the world is already changed? That the "old world" has already melted down? (31 May)

Bakunin's passion for destruction is connected in Blok with a distinctive "religion of music." The old world is perishing for its betrayal of music, for its fateful *anti-musicality*. One must give oneself up blindly to the elemental force of music, for only music saves. This idea is developed in the *Diary*:

> Something is happening. Be prepared. Nothing but music will save.
> Europe has obviously been *committing outrages* for nearly four years (has sinned against the spirit of music). . . . It is clear that the outrage cannot pass at no cost. It is clear that restoring its trampled sovereign rights to music was possible only by *betraying* what has died. . . . But music will still not be reconciled with morality. There is needed a long *antimoral* series (that the "Bolsheviks betrayed us"); the fatherland, honor, morality, law, patriotism, and other corpses must be *really* buried, so that *music would agree to be reconciled with the world.*

In the fiery days of popular disturbance, in Blok's soul there rose up headlong the ancient, primordial Russian elemental force: the rebellion of Razin and Pugachov, schism, flagellantism; the nihilism of Tolstoy, the anarchism of Bakunin, the maximalism of Nechaev; the Russian ecstasy of self-immolation. It raves and behaves like a madman, negating *everything*. A 20 February *Diary* note reads:

> Patriotism is dirt (Alsace-Lorraine is the belly of France, the coal).
> Religion is dirt (priests, etc.). . . .
> Romanticism is dirt. Everything that has accumulated in dogmas, fine dust, the *fantastic*—has become dirt. Only *élan* has remained.

> Only flight and outbursts; fly and burst, otherwise there is doom on all the paths.
> ... All dogmas have been shattered, they cannot exist. Movement is contagious.
> Only one who has loved as much as I has the right to hate. And it is for me to be a catacomb.
> A catacomb is a star speeding in the empty blue ether, shining.

And two weeks later he makes an entry in the *Notebook*: "Solitude. But something painful is happening. Nothing but music will save." Such is his "religion of music": all the stable forms of the world must be melted down, everything motionless thrown into movement; only *élan*, flight, and outbursts, the eternal striving of the spirit will remain. The romantic elemental force has never been exposed in such nakedness in world literature. Blok affirms the irrational freedom of the human spirit with the fearlessness of a genius or a madman.

But it is only possible to speak about the philosophy of "a star speeding in the empty ether" in the catacombs; it is impossible to approach people with such a "revelation"—they wouldn't accept it. The poet understands that a passion for destruction must be justified morally and socially. And he does this in the article "The Intelligentsia and the Revolution."[3] Returning to the journalistic themes of 1907 and 1908, he shows that the October revolution displayed the genuine face of Russia:

> Before me is Russia, that Russia which our great writers saw in frightening and prophetic dreams; that Petersburg which Dostoevsky saw, that Russia which Gogol called a speeding troika.
> Russia is a storm.... Russia is fated to experience torments, humiliation, division, but she will emerge from these humiliations new and, in a new way, great.

This is the first attempt at justifying destruction; it is masked by the Slavophile and messianic ideas close to Blok (*Verses on Russia*). The second attempt at justification is the Tolstoyan preaching of the untruth of the old world, the exposure of its moral and social evil: the last black years of tsarist power—Witte, Durnovo, Stolypin, "the sleepless, ghost-filled night." "Rasputin is everything, Rasputin is everywhere; Azevs,[4] exposed and unexposed; and, finally, the years of European carnage." Blok concentrates the impressions of seven months of military service in the Pinsk marshes into one ominous picture. "What is war?" he asks, and answers:

> Marshes, marshes, marshes; overgrown with grass or covered with snow. In the west a despondent German searchlight rummages from night to night; on a sunny day a German Fokker appears. It flies stubbornly along one and the same path, as if it is possible to beat and pollute a path in the sky itself.... A bomb will fall—sometimes on a cemetery, sometimes on a herd of cattle, sometimes on a herd of people, but more

often, of course, into the marsh. Thousands of the people's rubles in the marsh.... It is difficult to say what is more sickening: that bloodshed, or that *idleness*, that *boredom*, that *banality*. The name of both—"the great war," "the fatherland war," "the war for the liberation of oppressed peoples," or what else?

The intelligentsia curses the Bolsheviks, is horrified by the destruction. It doesn't understand that this is retribution. The author poses the questions: "Why 'Constituent Assembly?'" "Why 'down with the court?'" "Why are they blowing up the ancient cathedral?" "Why do they befoul the gentry estates dear to the heart?" "Why do they fell centuries-old parks?" And he answers with an enumeration of the sins of the past. Everything is just: "We are answering for the past. We are links in a single chain. Or do the sins of the fathers not lie on us?" With fierce irony he sets forth the moral code of the bourgeoisie (family, lower school, middle school, upper school, state service) and draws a conclusion: "The soil under the bourgeois' feet is determined as is manure for a pig: the family, capital, position in the service, medal, rank, God on an icon, the tsar on the throne. Pull this out—and everything will fly topsy-turvy."

The satirical sketches of *The Twelve*, with their childlike mischief, are already prepared: the old woman, the writer, the priest, the lady in the astrakhan, the prostitute:

> And the bourgeois on the crossroads
> Hid his nose in his collar.

Blok hews down the "old world" with one fell swoop, helter-skelter, clearing space for the "elemental force," just as he loved to fell bushes and trees in the Shakhmatovo garden. Having finished with the "moral evil" and "social injustice," the author turns finally to his real theme, to music. And here he reaches high lyrical eloquence:

> A stream, departing into the earth, flowing silently in depth and darkness—here it again makes noise, and its noise contains a new music. We loved these dissonances, this roaring, this ringing, these unexpected transitions... in the orchestra. But if we *really loved* them... we should listen to and love those same sounds now, when they fly from the world orchestra; and, listening, should understand that it is about the same thing, always about the same thing.... The job of an artist, the *obligation* of an artist is to see *what* has been conceived, to listen to that music with which "the air torn asunder by the wind" thunders.[5]

Before our eyes a miraculous transformation is occurring: the rumble, the "collapse of the old world," the flight, the outburst, the aimless striving become a "great creative force"; pure destruction turns into creation. The poet interprets his mystical experience (a star in the empty ether) as the coming of the Kingdom of God to earth. He believes that the music of the revolution sings "about the great," believes that it bears "peace and the brotherhood of peoples." He addresses the intelligentsia:

> You loved little, but much is asked of you, more than of anyone else. The crystal ringing, this music of love, was not in you. . . . Love creates miracles, music charms beasts. But you (all of us) lived without music and without love. Better to be silent now, if there is no music, better not to hear music. Because everything except music, everything that is without music, . . . will now only rouse and anger the beast.

In these intense, persistent repetitions of the word "music" is a Dionysian possession. A fiery faith in the wonder-working power of music ("only music will save") forces the poet to equate music and revolution. Let there be in revolution blood, mob law, and fire; let palaces fall to ruin and kremlins be wiped from the face of the earth; let its turbid stream carry chips, debris, and dirt; let there be boorishness and brutality, brigands, murderers, and provocateurs—none of this "changes the general direction of the stream or that menacing and deafening rumble which the stream issues. This rumble is nevertheless always about the great." Never before was Blok's soul so scorched, so melted, as in these fateful and great days. His words about the world mission of the revolution contain the height of his prophetic frenzy:

> Such is the sweep of the Russian revolution, which wants to seize the whole world: it cherishes the hope of raising a worldwide cyclone which will carry warm wind and the delicate odor of orange groves to snow-bound countries; it will wet the sun-scorched steppes of the south with a cool northern rain. "Peace and the brotherhood of peoples"—this is the sign under which the Russian revolution is passing. This is what its stream roars about. This is the music which he who has ears should hear.

The article ends with a "Hymn to Joy." The great Russian artists—Pushkin, Gogol, Dostoevsky, Tolstoy—lived in darkness. "But they knew that, sooner or later, *everything will be new*, because *life is beautiful*." And the author concludes:

> It is worth living only to make boundless demands of life, everything or nothing; to expect the unexpected; to believe not in "what is not in the world"[6] but in what should be in the world even though this doesn't exist now and won't for a long time. But life *will give this back* to us, because it is *beautiful*.

In the finale come the solemn and important words: "The spirit is music. The demon once ordered Socrates to obey the spirit of music. With all your body, all your heart, all your consciousness—listen to the revolution."[7] In such air—of Dionysian intoxication, ecstasy, and inspiration—the *poema The Twelve* was created. In it are the dark night of the revolution, the twelve robbers, the bloody reprisal, the plundering and murders, "the rumble of the collapse of the old world." And nevertheless it is a "hymn to joy"; the sounds of the *poema*'s rhythms are drunk on the hops of freedom, are unbridled and unrestrained, like the rebelling elemental force. This is why, above the raging ocean of the revolution, there is the dawn of a new "beautiful life":

> In a white crown of roses—
> Ahead—Jesus Christ.

After Simeon Polotsky's and Kantemir's unsuccessful attempts to introduce Polish syllabic verse into Russian poetry, Tredyakovsky and Lomonosov create Russian syllabo-tonic metrics on German models. It is based on three elements of rhythm: the number of syllables, the number of accents, and the rhyme. Thus, for example, four-foot trochaic—*Mčatsja tuči, v'jutsja tuči*—consists of eight syllables, four accents, and the rhyme *tuči : letučij*; four-foot iambic—*S bol'nym sidet' i den' i noč*—consists of the same elements (the rhyme here is *noč':proč'*). The meters are distinguished from one another only by the system of alternation of stresses. Thus in trochaic the stress falls on uneven syllables (first, third, fifth, and seventh) and in iambic on even syllables (second, fourth, sixth, eighth). In trinary meters (dactyllic, anapest, and amphibrach) the stressed syllables are separated by two unstressed syllables. This classical system chains rhythm in an armor of strict regularity.

For the poet the only possibility of varying rhythm is the introduction of paeons. Thus in iambic tetrameter one or even two accents can be omitted: *Kogda ne v šutku zanemog* (three stresses); *Poluživogo zabavljat'* (two stresses). All the rhythmical possibilities of classical metrics are exhausted by the omission of stresses.

Russian folk poetry knows no such regularity; its rhythm is purely tonic. The line carries a definite number of stresses, but there can be a different number of unstressed syllables between them. In the course of the nineteenth century, constant experiments were made in Russian poetry by Pushkin, Lermontov, Delvig, Fet, and Tyutchev to bring artificial metrics closer to the free rhythm of the folk song. But only the symbolists brought the revolution in versification to a victorious conclusion. Among them the historic role of the canonization of tonic verse belongs to Blok. After the successes of free rhythm in *Verses on the Beautiful Lady, Unexpected Joy,* and especially *The Snow Mask,* tonic earns a place in Russian lyric poetry equal in dignity to syllabo-tonic verse. The further development of poetic technique brilliantly justified the reform made by Blok. In the creative work of the acmeists (Gumilyov, Akhmatova, Mandelshtam), the futurists (Mayakovsky) and the contemporary Soviet poets, tonic verse predominates.

The *poema The Twelve* is a triumph of the new rhythmical element. The wealth, variety, and expressiveness of its rhythms are unprecedented in Russian poetry.

Free folk melodies collide with strict classical meters: the musical counterpoint of the *poema* is built on dissonances, syncopes, contrasts, and breaks. The "music of revolution" absorbs the "urban themes" of all of Blok's poetry. In the black night of the uprising we hear only the voice of the city; peasant, rural Russia is silent in Blok; the urban poor, workers, factory people, the agitated dregs of the capital sing. *The Twelve* is not Russia, but Petersburg: its wind, its snowstormy night, its mischievous song. The poet raises the vulgar philistine dialect to the pinnacle of art:

> Or don't you remember, you plague,
> Or is the memory not fresh.

or:

> Hold your head up!
> Get a grip on yourself!

or:

> Lock the house doors,
> There will be looting today.

He overheard his rhythms in taverns and slums, in a drunken song to a guitar, in a dance with an accordion, in a gypsy love song, in the "sentimental" singing of a hurdy-gurdy, in the factory *chastushka*.[8] Dostoevsky loved dirty taverns with an organ grinding out an aria from *Lucia*; he loved banality bordering on the fantastic. Blok transformed this "philistine music" into the voice of the elemental force, orchestrating it with the rhythms of the snowstorm, destruction, and freedom.

The *poema* begins with tonic lines:

> Čërnyj večer,
> Belyj sneg,
> Veter, veter,
> Na nogax ne stoit čelovek.
> Veter, veter,
> Na vsëm Bož'em svete.

> Black night,
> White snow,
> Wind, wind,
> A man can't keep his feet.
> Wind, wind,
> In all God's world.

The alternation of two-stressed lines with three-stressed prepares for the "sovereign tread" of the twelve. The theme is given: *wind*—revolution, elemental force, wind. Both the rhythms and the sounds are windy: the world whirled, flew, everything broke loose from its place—only "flight," only "outburst," only movement gone mad. The theme of wind pierces the *poema* with a sharp whistle:

Aleksandr Blok

> The wind curls
> The white snow.
> . . . . .
> The biting wind!
> The frost doesn't lag behind.
> . . . . .
> The gay wind
> Is malicious and glad,
> Whirls the skirts,
> Mows down the passers-by,
> Tears, crumples, and carries away
> The large placard.

Two rhythmical blows are more and more hurried, more and more violent—with interruptions, accelerations (three blows: *rvët, mnët i nosit*). And finally:

> A tramp
> Stoops,
> And the wind whistles.

The second chapter is a sharp change in rhythm, the sounds of a gay march:

> The wind carouses, the snow flutters,
> Twelve men are marching.
> . . . . .
> Keep the revolutionary pace!
> The relentless foe won't sleep—

and right after a rollicking dance tune:

> Freedom, freedom!
> Ah, ah, without a cross!
> Katka is busy with Vanka—
> Busy with what, with what?
> Tra-ta-ta!

In the tenth chapter the theme of the wind returns with new force. The snow no longer "flutters," but curls in a column, the blizzard howls, the snowstorm raises dust:

> The blizzard raged on,
>   What a blizzard, what a blizzard!
> One can't see each other at all
>   At four paces!
>
> The snow twisted in a funnel,
> The snow rose in a column.

In the last, the twelfth, chapter the theme of the blizzard is linked symbolically with the theme of the revolution:

> The wind with the red flag
> Frolicked ahead.

Everything disappears in the snowy blizzard; the shots die away, the red flags grow pale. The blizzard triumphs; it answers the killers and the killed with side-splitting laughter:

> Trakh-takh-takh!—But only the echo
> Responds in the houses . . .
> Only the blizzard splits its seams,
> Laughing in the snow. . . .

The "snowstorm" rhythms of *The Twelve* are the culmination of Blok's "elemental" lyrics. In 1918, as in 1907, he "blindly gave himself up to the elemental force" ("Note on *The Twelve*"). At that time it had dictated to him *The Snow Mask* and *The Earth in Snow*. In this is the inner law of his creativity: the musical pressure of the elemental force explodes in his verses in a whirlwind of wind and blizzard. But in *The Twelve* this original perception is revealed on two planes. Two visions glimmer dimly through the "funnel" and "column" of the snowstorm: the specter of the "old world" and the "twelve Red Army men." The first vision is schematized in the image of the "bourgeois at the crossroads" and the "hungry dog." The poet speaks about the old world in a classical, ironically solemn meter: four-foot "Pushkinian" iambic. Its unexpected intrusion into the dissipated elemental force of tonic rhythms intensifies the effect of contrast:

> The bourgeois stands at the crossroads
> And hid his nose in his collar,
> And alongside, its coarse wool pressed close,
> A mangy dog with tucked-in tail.
>
> The bourgeois stands, like a hungry dog,
> Stands silent as a question mark.
> And the old world, like an orphaned dog,
> Stands behind him, tail between its legs.

In 1918 the poet concentrated all his hatred of the old world on this Russian bourgeois he had invented (not at all characteristic of the Russian old order). In the *Diary* we find a curious note of 1 March: "Depart from me, Satan, depart from me, bourgeois; only not to touch, see, hear; whether I am better than he, or even worse, I don't know; but it is vile to me, nauseous to me; depart, Satan." The second vision is: "Twelve men are marching." Who are these "our children," who went "to serve in the Red Guard?" Their outlines are spectral, their social face indeterminable. Are they workers?, the poor?, robbers? Isn't it all the same? They are faceless, like the elemental force which gave them birth. Allegorical figures of rebellion pulled on Red Guard uniforms in a slapdash manner:

> In their teeth—cigars; caps rumpled,
> On their backs should be convicts' stripes!

One would have to be blind from birth to take these new Stenkas and Emelkas as a faction of the Social Democratic Party! Blok has not a "proletarian revolution," but a "Russian revolt, senseless and merciless" (Pushkin). And like every Russian revolt it is first of all God-defying:

> Freedom, freedom,
> Eh, eh, without a cross!
>   Tra-ta-ta.
>   . . . . .
> Comrade, grip your rifle, don't be afraid!
> We will shoot bullets at holy Rus—
>   At unrefined,
>   At wretched-hovelled,
>   At fat-assed Rus!
> Eh, eh, without a cross!

Looting ("there will be looting today"), murder ("I will slash, slash with my knife"), and robbery—and above it all is a red flag and a slogan:

> Forward, forward
> Working men!

Just this—black night, white snow, red flag, red blood on the snow, and a blizzard—Blok sees in the dark mirror of music. He doesn't believe the "writer-orators" speaking in undertones: "Traitors! . . . Russia has perished." He believes music and only music. A "world conflagration" ignites in the blood:

> We, to the grief of all bourgeois,
> Will fan a world conflagration,
> A world conflagration in blood—
>   Lord, bless us!

This "Lord, bless us" on the lips of the robbers "without a cross" is not accidental. The music doesn't deceive: it speaks of purifying sacrifice, of the dawn of a new day.

At the center of the *poema* is a "love drama": "Vanka with Katka in a tavern," "Vanka and Katka fly in a smart cab." Katka is unfaithful and Vanka kills her.[9]

> What, Katka, are you glad? Lost your tongue.
> Lie, carrion, on the snow.

A typical "philistine drama" maintained in the style of love songs to a street organ, like "Marusya poisoned herself." The stanzas about Katka with dance refrains are indeed masterly:

The Twelve.
Last Years

Went around in lace underwear—
   Go ahead, go ahead!
Played the whore with officers.
   Whore on, whore on,
     Eh, eh, whore on!
       The heart missed a beat in the breast.
    . . . . .

You wore gray gaiters,
Gorged on Mignon chocolate,
Went on sprees with a junker,
Now you've gone with plain soldiers?
   Eh, eh, sin on,
     It will be easier for the soul!

The leaping, stamping trochaics yelp and twitch like the sounds of an accordion.

In the last verse one line belongs to the poet's wife. On 17 February Blok observes in the *Notebook*: "*The Twelve*—I trimmed; gaps. . . . Lyuba composed the line 'Gorged on Mignon chocolate,' instead of the line she destroyed: 'Swept the street with her skirt.' "

Why a philistine drama, which could have happened any place and any time, in the foreground of a revolutionary *poema*? Why was it necessary for the poet to surround it with the black frame of 1917 Petersburg? In "A Note on *The Twelve*" Blok states that he had "blindly given himself up to the elemental force" three times in his life: in January 1907, in March 1914, and in January 1918. The first and second times the elemental force was revealed to him through the agitation of passion (for N. N. Volokhova in 1907, for L. A. Delmas in 1914). The mystical contact with other worlds, the music of the "world orchestra," is experienced by Blok *erotically*: in Nietzsche's terminology, this is a state of Dionysian frenzy (ecstasy). Therefore even the "music of the revolution" rings for the poet with the melody of passion: from its bosom springs the story of love and death. Revolutionary Petersburg gives birth to a Petersburg philistine drama; the rhythm of *chastushkas*, accordion, and street organ of itself predetermines the "criminal romance" of Vanka and Katka.

The *poema* about night and blood ends with the singing of angelic harps:

Vperedi—s krovavym flagom
   I za v'jugoj nevidim,
   I ot puli nevredim,
Nežnoj postup'ju nadv'južnoj,
Snežnoj rossyp'ju žemčužnoj,
   V belom venčike iz roz—
   Vperedi—Isus Xristos.

Ahead—with a bloody flag,
   And unseen behind the blizzard,
   And unharmed by bullet,

Aleksandr Blok

> With a tender step above the storm,
> In a pearly, snowy field,
> In a white crown of roses—
> Ahead—Jesus Christ.

The repeated assonances (*nevidim-nevredim, nežnoj-snežnoj, nadv'južnoj-žemčužnoj*); the pleasant trills (*v'jugoj, postup'ju, rossyp'ju*); the velvety V (*v'jugoj, nevidim, nevredim, nadv'južnoj, venčike, vperedi*); and the rustling Ž, Č, S (*nežnoj, postup'ju, nadv'južnoj, snežnoj, rossyp'ju, žemčužnoj, venčike iz roz*) arrange themselves in a radiant nimbus around the name of Christ. The harmonic waves of the seven-line period, building up slowly, suddenly break at His feet: "Ahead—Jesus Christ."

The Dionysian agitation carried the holy name from its depths out onto the shore, perhaps unexpectedly for the poet himself. Finishing the *poema*, Blok observes in the *Notebook*: "That Christ goes before them is unquestionable." This image is artistically truthful: it is born of music, and Blok believes that music doesn't deceive. But how does one explain His appearance rationally? After all, the music spoke of the destruction of *everything*: of fatherland, morality, religion. And here is Christ with the "destroyers." The *Diary* reflects the poet's confusion and perplexity. On 20 February he notes: "The terrible thought of these days: it's not a matter of the Red Guardsmen being 'unworthy' of Jesus, who now walks with them, but of the fact that precisely He goes with them. But 'Another' should have gone with them." The capitalized "Another" is the Antichrist. This is really a terrible thought and a diabolical temptation: to give the new Russia being born in torment into the power of the Antichrist! Blok overcomes this temptation: he no longer doubts that *Christ is with them*. His "large mind" is an indisputable witness to this; but the "small mind" rebels against Christianity, struggles against the "feminine phantom." The tragic split of consciousness between mystical faith and rational unbelief is stamped on a remarkable diary entry of 10 March:

> The Marxists are the most intelligent critics, and the Bolsheviks are right to fear *The Twelve*. But the "tragedy" of the artist remains a tragedy. Besides, *if* there had existed in Russia a real clergy, and not just a class of morally obtuse people of ecclesiastical rank, it would long ago "have taught" the fact that "Christ is with the Red Guardsmen." It is scarcely possible to call into question this truth which is simple for people who have read the Gospel and thought about it. In Russia, instead of that, they are "excommunicated from the church.". . .
>
> The "Red Guard" is water on the mill[10] for the Christian church (as is sectarianism, etc., zealously persecuted). . . .
>
> In this is horror (if it were understood). In this is the weakness of the Red Guard; children in an iron age; a lonely village church amid a drunken and bawdy marketplace.
>
> Did I really "eulogize"? . . . I merely stated a fact: if one looks into the columns of the snowstorm *on this path*, one sees Jesus Christ. But I myself sometimes deeply hate this feminine phantom.

Here two people are speaking: to one it is given from above to "state the fact" (what prophetic confidence!) that Christ is "on this path"; the other fears this fact, experiences a surge of hatred for the "phantom." The first is a clairvoyant, the second a nihilist and destroyer.

On 29 January, the day he finished *The Twelve*, Blok enters in his *Notebook*: "*Today I am a genius.*"

The *poema* appeared in the newspaper *The Banner of Labor*, then in the journal *Our Path* (*Nash put*), and, finally, came out that same year as a separate booklet with Ivanov-Razumnik's article. A literary storm arose; a rare artistic work was subjected to such absurd interpretations, and called forth so much hatred, malice, rapture, and lack of understanding. The poet was declared an ideologue of Bolshevism, was reviled, boycotted; recent friends refused to shake hands. The poet Vsevolod Rozhdestvensky[11] tells of a dramatic episode occurring at a literary morning of the Arzamas circle in the auditorium of the Tenishevsky School on 13 May 1918. Lyubov Dmitrievna was reading the *poema The Twelve*. In a small room backstage passionate arguments started among the participants of the morning:

> And suddenly everyone fell silent. Blok had entered the room. He felt this unexpected and painful silence. They made way for him silently and with hostility. Someone ostentatiously turned his back. A bearded man in a narrow uniform frock coat drew back the hand he was on the point of extending. . . . Blok stopped in the middle of the room, as if deciding not to go further. "Look," a professor whispered to his neighbor, "what a guilty back he has." This rather distinct whisper couldn't have failed to reach Blok's ears. He turned sharply and looked almost point-blank at the speaker. And I saw his face close up for the first time. It was infinitely weary and, as it seemed to me then, was covered by a spiderweb of contemptuous indifference. Unhurriedly, coldly, and somewhat insolently, Blok looked round at those present. Everyone was silent, their eyes lowered. And he was silent, obviously expecting something, prepared for anything. The corners of his grave, sorrowful mouth twitched bitterly.

Z. N. Gippius' story about meeting Blok on a streetcar (17 September 1918) is very characteristic of the attitude of the "intelligentsia" toward the "traitor":

> A face under some kind of cap (it *was* a cap, not a hat)—long, dry, yellow, dark. "Will you give me your hand?" Slow words, pronounced with such effort, so grave. I stretch out my hand to him and say: "Personally—yes. Only personally. Not socially." He kisses my hand. And, after a silence: "Thank you." Falling silent again, then: "They say you're leaving?" "Why not? . . . Here one must die or leave. If, of course, one is not in your position." He was silent for a long time, then said especially gloomily and distinctly: "One may die in any situation." Suddenly he added: "I love you very much." "Do you know that I love you too?"

What a tragic meeting! It's impossible to read about it without pain—and shame.

Aleksandr Blok

The Scythians was created at the same time as *The Twelve*, in the same surge of inspiration. The first *poema* was finished on 29 January, the second was written in one day—30 January. In his autobiography Blok relates that his early youth was spent in a milieu of people who understood poetry in the spirit of old-fashioned *éloquence*. The *poema The Scythians* is a perfect, brilliant example of "poetic eloquence." The poet returns to the first literary impressions of his youth, to the lofty rhetoric of the beginning of the nineteenth century, to the tradition of the solemn odes of Lomonosov and Derzhavin. His closest inspirations are Pushkin and Lermontov. The passion of Pushkin's address *To the Slanderers of Russia* ("What's all the noise about, folk orators? Why do you threaten Russia with anathema?") and the fiery words of Lermontov's accusation *On Pushkin's Death* ("And you, haughty descendants—with the notorious baseness of your illustrious fathers") come to life in the bronze ringing of Blok's stanzas:

> For you—ages; for us—one hour.
>   We, like obedient slaves,
> Held a shield between two hostile races—
>   The Mongols and Europe!

Blok takes two lines from Vladimir Solovyov as an epigraph to his *poema*: "Panmongolism. Although the name is wild, / It caresses my ear." He collects the Mongolian, Tatar, and Asiatic features of Russia scattered in the lines of *Homeland*. Long ago this specter with "slanted and avid eyes" had already alarmed him. He wrote: "Our path pierced our breast with the arrow of ancient Tatar ferocity." He saw: "The dumb face looks wildly, the Tatar eyes fling fires."

And now in answer to the new "slanderers of Russia," Europe, indignant at the "Russian treachery"—the peace of Brest-Litovsk—he flings a "Mongolian threat" in its face:

> We through dense thickets and forests
>   Let comely Europe
> Through! We will turn to you
>   Our Asiatic snout!

Russia will stop defending the Western world with her breast: let Europe itself measure its strength against the "wild Mongolian horde," let it also bear the burden of the "Tatar yoke":

> We won't budge when the fierce Hun
>   Rummages in the pockets of the corpses,
> Burns cities, and drives horse herds into church,
>   And roasts the meat of the white brothers!

With contempt and hatred you call us Asiatics, you accuse us of treachery. You are right:

> Yes—we are Scythians. Yes—we are Asiatics.
>   With slanted and avid eyes.

We will answer hatred with hatred, contempt with vengeance. But behind the "Asiatic snout" is concealed another face of Russia, which the arrogant "comely" Europe stubbornly wishes not to see, the face of an unquenchable, insatiable love:

> Russia is a Sphinx. Rejoicing and grieving,
>   And steeped in black blood,
> She looks, looks, looks at you
>   Both with hatred and with love.

Suddenly, in a lyrical whirlwind, five inspired stanzas about love burst into the political, accusatory rhetoric:

> Yes, to love as our blood loves,
>   None of you has loved for a long time!
> You have forgotten there is a love in the world,
>   Which both burns and destroys.

Love is revealed as Russia's universal *panhumanity*. Blok expresses this faith of Dostoevsky in an enumeration of all the world's treasures. Russia loves everything: the "heat of cold numbers," and "divine visions," and the "sharp Gallic sense," and the "gloomy Germanic genius." Russia remembers everything: the hell of Parisian streets, and the coolness of Venice, and the aroma of lemon groves, and the smoky bulks of Cologne. And this Russia, turned to Europe with a sorrowful and passionate face, doesn't threaten, doesn't curse—it calls for the "brotherhood of peoples":

> Come to us! From the horrors of war
>   Come to peaceful embraces!
> Before it's too late—the old sword sheathed.
>   Comrades! We will become—brothers!

The pathetic call resounds with new, staggering power in the finale:

> For the last time—come to your senses, old world!
>   To the brotherly feast of work and peace,
> For the last time to the bright brotherly feast
>   The barbarian lyre calls.

But the West didn't hear the call of the "barbarian lyre." Twenty-three years later Germany, having enslaved all of Europe, answered the invitation "to the brotherly feast of work and peace" with fire and iron. With what prophecy about Germany Blok's verse rings:

> You have looked at the East for hundreds of years,
>   Storing up and melting your pearls,

Aleksandr Blok

> And you, scoffing, only calculated
> When to aim the cannon muzzles!

Russia was fated, "steeped in black blood," to pass through the fire of the Second World War.

In the Socialist Revolutionary (SR) magazine *The Banner of Labor*, Blok republishes six of his 1907–9 articles devoted to the question of the people and the intelligentsia. In November 1918, adding a seventh article, "The Intelligentsia and the Revolution," he publishes them as a separate book under the general title *Russia and the Intelligentsia*. In the preface the author forewarns: "I never approached the question from the political side. My theme, if I may so express myself, is *musical*. . . . A new gust of the world wind . . . impels me again to address these same questions to the reader."

Blok recalls his collaboration on SR organs and the persecution to which he is subjected for this in 1920 ("Note on *The Twelve*"):

> From the beginning of 1918 roughly to the end of the October revolution (3–7 months?) freedom of the press existed in Petersburg and Moscow. That is, besides the government agitational leaflets, there were newspapers of various directions, and certain journals were living out their age. Besides that there was a special phenomenon in cultural life, which in general was perceptibly on the wane. One of the political parties which enjoyed the backing of the government during the revolution gave space to culture also: quite a lot of space in a large newspaper[12] and almost an entire monthly journal.[13] The newspaper came out for about six months; the second issue of the journal was held back and then prohibited. A small group of writers taking part in this newspaper and this journal was revolutionarily disposed. The majority of the other organs of the press reacted hostilely to this group, even considering it a collection of government toadies. I myself participated in this group, and the persecution which was raised against us is very memorable to me. There was the petty and vile, but there was also the acute.

The newspaper persecution, the spiritual isolation, and the anxiety for his starving mother and aunt abruptly cut short the poet's joyful intensity in the period of *The Twelve*. Maria Andreevna Beketova is living in the same building as her nephew, and in the middle of winter she falls ill from exhaustion, with an acute psychic disorder. It is necessary to place her in a clinic for the mentally ill. In the summer she leaves for the country home of her sister, Sofia Andreevna, and quickly recovers. The poet's mother's nervous illness intensifies from the semistarvation existence. In March 1918 his stepsister Angelina Aleksandrovna dies: she was serving as a nurse in a military hospital in Novgorod and became infected with encephalomyelitis. Blok dedicates his *Iambics* to her memory. Entries in the *Diary* and *Notebook* are full of hopeless gloom. "If I have done so much that is horrible in life, it is necessary at least to die honestly and worthily" (*Diary*, 21 February).

"The main thing is not to lose wings (the presence of the spirit). The revolution—this is I; not I alone, but we. Reaction is isolation, lack of talent, kneading clay" (1 March). But calls to cheerfulness don't help much. On 14 May the poet observes in the *Notebook*:

> The swine behind the wall has become perceptibly insolent—plays exercises from morning to evening, turning my room into a torture chamber. Everyone who doesn't possess vital capacity is losing his mind; everything spidery, carnal, dirty is inhabited by vampirism (as behind the wall).

On 19 August: "Some disease is gnawing. If it were only a cold. Again listlessness, bitterness, silence. A cold autumn." On 21 August: "How hopeless everything is. To abandon, to sell, everything, to go far away—to the sun—and to live completely differently."

For income Blok has to write a lot for the Moscow newspaper *Life* (*Zhizn*) and for the Petersburg *Life of Art* (*Zhizn Iskusstva*). In the article "Art and Revolution" (apropos of Richard Wagner's work),[14] Blok emphasizes a contradiction in Wagner's book *Art and Revolution*. This contradiction is also Blok's. In one place Wagner speaks about Christ with hatred and in another proposes erecting an altar to Him. Blok calls *The Twelve* to mind, and asks:

> How can one hate and at the same time erect an altar? How in general can one simultaneously hate and love? . . . If such an attitude becomes general, if they begin to relate to everything in the world that way? To "native land," to "parents," to "wives," etc.? This would be unbearable, because it would be unsettling.

There is alarm in this irony. For Blok, his relationship to Christ is a tormenting enigma; what he calls "hating love." On 19 May the poet gives a lecture, "Catiline (A Page from the History of World Revolution)"[15] in the recently opened School of Journalism. The lively and fascinating story about Catiline's conspiracy in 60 B.C. is spoiled by a tendency to see the "first bolshevik" in the dissolute and ambitious representative of the Roman "golden youth," and a "tragedy of Roman bolshevism" in his attempt to burn Rome and disrupt the Senate. Henrich Ibsen, who had written an unsuccessful rhetorical drama about the revolutionary Catiline, drew the author into this half-comic misunderstanding. Blok accepted the youthful fantasies of the Norwegian playwright on faith and prepared "a page out of Roman history" in the modern taste. He wrote two feuilletons, "Fellow Citizens" and "Russian Dandies,"[16] in a completely different spirit. Blok tries his strength in a new genre, unusual for him: a sketch of everyday life. In "Fellow Citizens" he tells how the chairman of a house committee "in a blue shirt with old suspenders" whispers in his ear: "The Germans said: 'tomorrow, we'll come and, if we don't make it, then on Saturday' "; how "all the citizens living in the house . . . sit in the yardman's lodge every night armed with Nagan revolvers and by turns hail everyone who knocks at the gate." There is much humor and lively keenness of observation in the sketch. "Russian Dandies" begins with a description of a charity evening: "Before the evening the doorbell rang. Unfamiliar young people came in and took me to engage in a dishonest affair: to read old poems which I had long ago outlived at a charitable evening for the benefit of some very useful and good undertaking." About Petersburg in 1918 he writes: "hilly snowdrifts" on the streets; shots were heard from various directions—somewhere they were looting wine cellars. In the "green room" a "famous baritone," a "not very famous tenor;" an indifferent accompanist is eating pieces of black bread with red caviar; a "small pink bundle"—a charming dancer—flies in from the stage. On the way back a young poet—a "dandy"—accompanies Blok. He says:

> We are a minority, but for the time being we are running things among the youth: we ridicule those who are interested in socialism, work, revolution. We live only on poetry; in the last five years I haven't missed a single collection. We know everything by heart—Sologub, Balmont, Igor Severyanin, Mayakovsky. But all this is already stale; all this is finished; now, it seems, the fashion will be for Ehrenburg. . . . Nothing interests us but poetry. We are empty, completely empty.

And the author exclaims sadly: "So here it is—Russian dandyism of the twentieth century!"

The revolution swept away this generation of pale youths with tulips in their buttonholes. Its fragments were cast out into the emigration.

In the spring of 1918 Blok begins an autobiographical story, "Confession of a Pagan (My Confession)." In it he tells of his school years, of his love for his fellow gymnasium student Dmitri, and of a trip on horseback from Shakhmatovo to Boblovo with him. The story breaks off at the first meeting with Lyubov Dmitrievna:

> Suddenly an unexpected wind swept past and showered apple and cherry blossoms. Behind the blizzard of white petals flying onto the road I saw a stately girl in a pink dress, with heavy golden tresses, sitting on a bench. Apparently the unexpectedly resounding horse's tread had frightened her, because she got up quickly, and color flooded her cheeks. She ran deep into the garden, leaving me to watch how her pink dress flashed behind the blizzard of petals.

This vision of the pink young girl in a blizzard of apple petals shone for the poet with steady radiance all his life.

But the story is conceived as a confession and is called "Confession of a Pagan." In the introduction the author speaks of the decline of the Russian church:

> The church died, the temple became an extension of the street. . . . Opposite, across the street, a coffee house. . . . The profiteers in the

church anathematize the Bolsheviks, but the profiteers in the coffee house sell cancelled loans. Both the one and the other exchange winks across the street: they understand each other.

This is not said with the indifference of an atheist, but with the anger of a Christian offended in his faith. In the lines following this the true face of the alleged "pagan" is revealed. This really is a confession:

> But I am a Russian, and Russians always think about the Church. There are few who are completely indifferent to it. Some hate it very much, and others love it—the one and the other with pain.
> And I too once went to church. True, I selected a time when the church was empty.... In an empty church I sometimes succeeded in finding what I sought in vain in the world.
> Now even the empty churches are no more.
> I haven't gone to confession for a very long time, and I need to make a confession. One of the advantages of the revolution consists in its awakening the whole man to life; if he goes to meet it, it strains all his powers and reveals those abysses of consciousness which were tightly closed.

This is a striking admission. The atheistic revolution, having declared religion the "opium of the people," opened to Blok those "abysses of consciousness" which had hitherto been closed to him. The struggle between the negating and destroying mind and the soul immersed in mystical visions ended with the victory of the religious element. Now, when the church is no more, he remembers that he had found in it what "he had sought in vain in the world"; he understands that he loves it—with pain. And the most surprising thing: having lived almost his whole life without confession, he now, in the era of official atheism, dares to declare publicly: "I need to make a confession." This testimony of the poet is indisputable. We repeat: Blok's soul was by nature Christian. But the poet didn't know the inner life of the church. A Russian intellectual, having grown up in the Pobedonostsev era, a contemporary of the Iliodors and the Hermogens, could only go to an "empty church." And this was not his personal tragedy, but the tragedy of all the Russian intelligentsia. This is why Blok—a Christian, an ascetic and a mystic—calls himself a "pagan."

At the beginning of 1918 the poet was selected chairman of the repertory section of the Theatrical Division. He looked over countless dramas which had for long years accumulated in the library of the Aleksandrinsky Theater, put together lists of plays for the popular theaters, conscientiously read manuscripts of the theatrical works of new and in most cases untalented writers, visited drama theaters, and continuously "sat" in conferences. He gave himself up to this exhausting work with enthusiasm, wrote long articles, made speeches, gave lectures, and published proclamations. He believed that the Theatrical Division (TEO) would produce a real theatrical revolution in Russia, that the new government would support his far-reaching plans. In his

"Report to the Executive Board of the Theatrical Division," Blok declared decisively: "We must throw into the marketplace millions of copies of books. Consequently, we should strive to equip our vast typography, whatever the price; we should turn out trainloads of paper, whatever this costs. The business necessarily involves immense risk, but this is a State risk." The poet planned the formation of cadres of instructors for village theaters, the creation of an enormous new repertoire. All these plans remained on paper—TEO had neither the means nor the professionals. The chairman's selfless, intense work went to waste. Finally surmising that the "labors of the section" were empty and fruitless schemes, Blok leaves TEO in February 1919.[17]

E. Zamyatin (from "Reminiscences of Blok," *Russian Contemporary*, 1924) recalls one of the first conferences in the majestic office of the Theatrical Division:

> Blok read his scenario for a historical play. I don't know whether this scenario has been preserved, but I know that the play remained unwritten. There were Blok's favorite Middle Ages, knights and ladies, pages, minstrels. And I remember a slight shrugging of the shoulders of the theatrical authorities when this was read. And Blok hid the scenario somewhere.[18]

Lyubov Dmitrievna's new undertaking ended just as sadly. She wanted to create a theater of a "noble type" for workers, formed a troupe, and in May opened the dramatic season in Luna Park. But the workers didn't come to the theater, the resources soon dried up, and the plays were discontinued.

In April 1918 Maksim Gorky founds the large publishing house World Literature, which prints old and new translations of foreign writers and a special "library for the people." Blok was commissioned to edit the works of Heine. In addition, at Gorky's insistence, he wrote introductory articles for the issues of the people's library. The editorship of World Literature, which was on Nevsky Prospect, met twice a week. N. S. Gumilyov edited translations of French poets, and an interminable argument about poetry went on between him and Blok. V. Rozhdestvensky recalls:

> They obviously had no particular liking for one another, but didn't express their hostility in any way. On the contrary, their every conversation represented a subtle duel of reciprocal politeness and courtesy. Gumilyov was profuse in subtly ironic compliments. Blok listened sternly and with a particularly cold lucidity added somewhat more often than necessary to each sentence: "Esteemed Nikolai Stepanovich," distinctly, completely articulating each letter of the first name and patronymic. Gumilyov presented Blok with his recently published book of poetry, with a few words of deferential dedication. The next day Blok brought Gumilyov his collection *Gray Morning* with the inscription: "To deeply esteemed and nice Nikolai Stepanovich Gumilyov, whose poems I always read in daylight."

The Twelve. Last Years

From World Literature, Blok invariably walked home across the whole city. V. Rozhdestvensky often accompanied him. Usually they walked in silence, exchanging infrequent remarks, but once after the recurrent argument with Gumilyov, Blok began to speak agitatedly:

"Here, you know Gumilyov better than I do. Does he really actually think that it's possible to weigh, dismember, chemically analyze a poem?"

"He is convinced of it."

"Amazing! How convenient and simple to live with such a consciousness. And I can never see after the first two lines what will come next. That is, of course, this is not completely so," he added here with unusual haste. "I first of all hear some kind of sound. Intonation before meaning. Someone speaks in me—passionately, with conviction. As if in a dream. And the words come later. And it is only necessary to watch that they are in this intonation, that they contradict nothing. Here then is truth. Every poem is a ringing point, dispersing in concentric circles. No, it isn't even a point, but rather an astronomical nebula. From it worlds are born."

The musical, intonational nature of Blok's poetry could not possibly be defined more exactly. In Blok's argument with Gumilyov two poetic worlds collided: the romantic's "inspiration of genius" and the classicist's "sober craftsmanship."

That same year one more publishing house, Alkonost, came into existence. Its founder, S. M. Alyansky, a great admirer of the poet, continually had recourse to his advice. Thus the whole day passed in conferences, reports, reviews; no time remained for artistic work. On 26 March Blok writes his last poem[19]—a tired and pale one:

Soul! When will you tire of believing?
Spring, spring! It is languid,
Like the secret of a partly opened door
Into the pagan chapel of a golden dream . . .

And the last verse reads:

But shrouded by the spring haze
Is everything that seethed here in the breast . . .
Don't sing, don't demand, Margarita,
Don't look into my heart . . .

After this he still composed facetious poems, epistles, occasional poems, but it was no longer lyric poetry. The muse of poetry deserted him in the spring of 1918.

On 21 February the poet notes in the *Diary*: "Lyuba calls the Stray Dog (Comedians' Stopping-Place) and offers to perform *The Twelve* there." In the artistic cabaret Comedians' Stopping-Place, which had replaced the Stray Dog, Lyubov Dmitrievna reads *The Twelve* every evening for a meager remuneration. Blok bears even this humiliation: even without that he has to sell books and things and go to dine in the cafeteria of Musical Drama. In the autumn Aleksandra Andreevna and her husband find an apartment in the same building where the Bloks live. Maria Andreevna Beketova rents a room on another staircase. The whole family lives together until the poet's death. In the winter Blok enthusiastically prepares materials for the edition of Heine. "All day I read Heine to Lyuba in German and became younger" (*Notebook*, 8 December). The last *Notebook* entries of 1918:

> On the brink of despair. (10 December)
> Night dreams are such that I am on the brink of despair and insanity. How many people have lost their minds in our days. To add to everything —a severe frost. (12 [11] December)
> Why did I so dissolve in tears tonight in dreams about Shakhmatovo? (31 [12] December)
> Frost. Passers-by are carrying some kind of sacks. Almost pitch-dark. Some old man shouts, dying of hunger. One clear and large star is shining. [31 December]

We remember the prophetic lines of 1910:

> Oh, if you knew, children,
> The cold and darkness of coming days!

Having with great difficulty liberated himself from TEO, Blok ties himself down to another "theatrical department" two months later. On 26 April 1919, at the insistence of Gorky's wife, M. F. Andreeva, he takes on the duties of chairman in the production board of the Bolshoi Theater. The director, A. N. Lavrentiev, the theater manager, Grishin, the talented actors Yu. M. Yuriev, N. F. Monakhov and V. V. Maksimov, and the set-designers, A. N. Benois and Shchuko, work with inspiration. They surround the poet with love and attention, and at first he devotes himself enthusiastically to his new activity: he conducts conferences, reads plays, writes articles, and composes speeches. In the article "The Bolshoi Dramatic Theater in the Coming Season,"[20] Blok speaks about the "great treasure-house of old classical and romantic art," asserts that the Bolshoi Theater should be a theater of "high drama: high tragedy, and high comedy," warns against "modernistic" experiments and searchings, and in conclusion writes: "We must be rhythmical and faithful to music, because the great task of today is to soak and permeate life with music, to make it rhythmical, well-knit, sharp." The author of *The Puppet Show* and *The Stranger* steps onto the path of strict classicism. In "A Speech to Actors" he talks about the repertoire for the next season, which is to have seven new productions: Shakespeare's *Othello*, Schiller's *The Robbers*, V. Hugo's *Hernani*, Dumanoir's and Doneri's *A Mother's Blessing*, Sem-Benelli's *The Torn Cloak*, M. Levberg's *Danton*, and Merezhkovsky's *Tsarevich Aleksei*. In this "harmonious plan" will be presented: tragedy, drama, a dramatic *poema*, and a melodrama. The "enormous world of art" is bigger than any of us:

It is bigger than both Schiller and Shakespeare, it is elemental force. And to return a fraction of this world to the blind elemental force—to that crowd which once brought it into the world—this is the greatest task, this is the most responsible and noblest business of the stage expert.

Blok's basic theme permeates all his theatrical articles: music and the elemental force. In the long article "On Romanticism" he gives a very personal and original definition of this complex and multi-meaninged phenomenon:

> Genuine romanticism is not merely a literary trend. It aspires to become and for the moment has become a new form of sensation, a new means of experiencing life . . . The soul became younger, looked at the world in a new way, was shaken by union with it, was filled with trembling, alarm, secret ardor, with a feeling of unknown distance, was lashed by rapture from closeness to the World Soul.

This characterization is an exact description of the poetics of Russian symbolism and of the work of Blok himself. Russian symbolism is a brilliant culmination of world romanticism; this conditions its historical role in the tradition of European culture. The poet draws important conclusions from his definition of romanticism:

> Romanticism is not a renunciation of life; . . . on the contrary, it is a new means of living with tenfold power. . . . Romanticism is a conventional designation of a sixth sense. . . . It is nothing but a means of arranging or organizing man, the bearer of culture, in a new connection with the elemental force.

And Blok again comes to his favorite juxtaposition of culture and elemental force:

> Romanticism is culture which is in ceaseless struggle with the elemental force. In this tireless struggle it keeps repeating to its enemy: "I hate you, because I love you too much. I fight with you because I long for you, as you long for me, and I want to save you, and you, beloved, will be mine."

The poet's whole lyric is musical variations on the theme of this conversation of the poet with the World Soul.

Before each new production Blok assembled the actors and explained its meaning to them. His speeches have been preserved: "For Staging the Play *The Torn Cloak*"; "The Hidden Meaning of the Tragedy *Othello*." In addition he composed "Speeches for Reading to Red Army Men before Performances" (on Schiller's *The Robbers* and *Don Carlos*, on Shakespeare's *Much Ado About Nothing*, on Levberg's *Danton*, and on the plays of others). The director Lavrentiev read them at Red Army performances. The poet's work in the Bolshoi Theater paid a modest salary: cheese, butter, and flour.

Ivanov-Razumnik consulted with Blok about establishing a "Free Philosophical Association," but this plan was interrupted by the arrest of the founders: Ivanov-Razumnik himself, Remizov, Petrov-Vodkin, and Shteinberg. On 15 February Blok was also arrested. He was accused of belonging to the party of the Left SRs. M. A. Beketova relates:

> Blok went for a stroll in the evening, as was his custom. In his absence a commissar appeared, whom Lyubov Dmitrievna received. As soon as Aleksandr Aleksandrovich returned from his walk he was arrested. They released him on the morning of the third day. He came home at about eleven in the morning, having first dropped in on his mother.

Nevertheless, the opening of the "Free Philosophical Association" (*Volfil*) took place in April 1919.

That same spring, Blok worked in the Union of Workers of Artistic Literature for two months; he read manuscripts of the poems of new poets and determined the degree of their suitableness for publication.[21]

World Literature took up much of his time. He wrote reviews for the editorial board, made endless comments on plays and on critical articles, and read a report on Russian translations of Heine's poems.

At first Blok's collaboration with M. Gorky proceeded quite satisfactorily. On 30 March at a jubilee celebration in Gorky's honor at World Literature, the poet gives him a friendly salutatory. He calls him an intermediary between two camps—the people and the intelligentsia—and expresses the wish that the "stern, angry, elemental, but gracious spirit of music would not leave him." Blok ends his brief speech: "For, I repeat Gogol's words, if music also abandons us, what will then happen to our world? Only music is capable of stopping the bloodshed which becomes a sad banality when it stops being a holy madness."

According to M. A. Beketova, this award of the "spirit of music" was a complete surprise to Gorky.

In the spring of 1919 a rather extravagant idea occurred to the founder of World Literature: educating the masses with the help of a "series of pictures from the world history of humanity." Endless conversations, reports, and discussions begin. At Gorky's insistence Blok draws up a "General Plan of Historical Scenes," whose aim is an "attempt to instill education into life, to catch the savage unawares, and to cast into the lazy and idle hours of his spare time a spark of Promethean fire." The poet proposes composing these scenes on a single principle: "To illustrate the struggle of two bases—culture and the elemental force—in every possible direction." Nothing comes of this plan. Blok alone, the most trustful and conscientious of all the collaborators, writes the historical scene "Rameses."[22] This is one of the poet's weakest works, something completely Egyptian, with Pharoahs, pyramids, chariots, priests, and slaves, and even "social protest." E. Zamyatin recalls:

Blok said that he had already done some drafts for "Tristan," and suddenly, unexpectedly, from Egyptian life. "Rameses" is almost the last thing he wrote. . . . They read it, made some remarks about "Rameses." Blok made a joke of it: "But I only reset Maspero. I have nothing to do with it."

But from this time his divergence from Gorky begins. The artist couldn't forgive the "chief" the violence done to his creative freedom. He finally understood that in the company of Gorky and Gumilyov he was alien, and he began to find his "service" in the publishing house difficult. The work in the Bolshoi Theater depressed the poet still more. M. F. Andreeva's meddling in all the details of production, her despotic manner and caprices, poisoned life for him. The entries in the *Notebook* stop suddenly in June 1919. The last entries read:

> 22 April. Someday I will go mad in my sleep. What horrors I dreamed at night. Impossible to describe. I shouted. Such a horror that it is no longer frightening, but I feel that my mind is sweetly confused.
> 4 [3] May. What destroyed the revolution (the spirit of music)?—The war.
> 23 June. It's no longer worth noting anything down, except business.

In the fall the Bloks' life became even harder. With difficulty they succeeded in avoiding eviction from the apartment and in freeing themselves from an exorbitant tax imposed on the poet. Aleksandra Andreevna discharged her maid, sold things, stood in lines. Maria Andreevna again fell ill with a nervous disorder and left for Luga. Lyubov Dmitrievna worked in the Hermitage Theater and didn't have time for housekeeping. There was no electricity; Blok had to work by candlelight; the telephone didn't work; the house committee assigned the poet to night duty at the gates of the house.

Ivanov-Razumnik writes in his reminiscences of Blok:

> He experienced the winter of 1918–19 as "terrible days" (he thus inscribed one of his books presented to me in 1918). . . . He was on the point of blazing up for the last time at the news of a new wave of revolution in Germany, but soon died out. The "terrible days" beset him. He saw them in the past, he foresaw them in the future.

K. Chukovsky also remembers these "terrible days":

> Blok related that, having written *The Twelve*, for several days in a row he heard an incessant noise or rumble, but that afterward even this fell silent. It would seem that the noisiest, most clamorous and loudest epoch he suddenly felt as silence. . . . We walked past the palace square and listened to the guns rumbling. "For me, even this is silence," he said. "I get drowsy in this din. . . . In general, in the last years I am drowsy." Of course his life was difficult; he didn't even have a separate room for working; there was no servant in the apartment; often due to the absence of light he didn't

touch a pen for weeks. And it scarcely helped for him to walk such a terrible distance almost every day on foot—from the very end of Officers' Street to Mokhovaya, to World Literature. But this wasn't what oppressed him. . . . He wouldn't even have noticed this if it weren't for the silence he suddenly felt. When I asked him why he didn't write poems he always gave one and the same answer: "All the sounds have stopped. Really, don't you hear that there are no sounds?"

Blok lived on the elemental force of music, on the sound of the "world orchestra," and when the music abandoned him, he lost the will to live.

In the "terrible days" of 1919 Blok writes a long article, "The Collapse of Humanism," which occupies the same central place in his creative work after October as the report "On the Present State of Symbolism" occupies among his prerevolutionary writings.

For four centuries—from the middle of the fourteenth to the middle of the eighteenth—Europe developed under the sign of *humanism*, "whose slogan was *man*, the free human personality." But at the moment when personality stopped being the chief motive force of European culture, when a new motive force—the masses—appeared in the arena of history, a crisis of humanism came. It was prepared by the Reformation and burst out in the epoch of the great French Revolution. Schiller and Goethe are the last great humanists of Europe, "the last of the flock of those faithful to the spirit of music." With Schiller even the style of humanism—Baroque—dies. The nineteenth century loses wholeness and unity of *culture*. The spirit of music flies away from it; mechanical civilization develops with monstrous speed. "The balance between man and nature," Blok writes, "was lost, between life and art, between science and music, between civilization and culture—that balance by which the great movement of humanism lived and breathed." Civilization is the degeneration of culture, a separation from the spirit of music. Culture is rhythmical wholeness, musical unity. Civilization lives in historical, calendar time; culture is "incalculable, musical" time. "Balance is indispensable for us," Blok continues, "in order to be close to the musical essence of the world—to nature, to the elemental. For this we need, first of all, a healthy body and a healthy spirit, since one hears world music with one's whole body and whole spirit together." This balance was lost by the "civilized" nineteenth century—by the century of the construction of the tower of Babel. European artists, the last bearers of the spirit of music, sensed the "elemental and stormy character of the century." Ibsen, Strindberg, and Wagner accumulated in their creative work "terrible and explosive material"; art menaced dead civilization with the voices of the elemental force, with explosions of the world orchestra. "Civilization" took revenge on artists for their betrayal of "humanism," raised persecutions against them, tortured them with the most refined tortures, understanding that the "spirit of music" is its mortal enemy. Blok sums up his main thought:

> Every movement is born out of the spirit of music; it acts, imbued with it; but, at the expiration of a certain period of time, this movement degenerates; it is deprived of that musical moisture of which it was born, and thereby is itself doomed to destruction. It stops being culture and is transformed into civilization. So it happened with the ancient world, so it also occurred with us.

The author moves to his second position. Music abandoned "civilized" humanity and returned to that elemental force from which it arose: to the people, to the barbarian masses:

> It would therefore not be paradoxical to say that the barbarian masses turn out to be the preservers of culture, possessing nothing except the spirit of music.... To the civilized ear this music is a wild chorus, discordant howling. For many of us it is almost unbearable.... It is destructive to civilization's achievements; ... it is antithetical to the melodies about "truth, goodness, and beauty," to which we are accustomed. [The music of the "barbarian masses" is already inundating the old world; the outcome of the battle is decided: humane civilization is already vanquished by the new powerful movement.] The bell of antihumanism is ringing throughout the whole world ... man is getting closer to the elemental force, and man is therefore becoming more musical.

Blok sees a new man coming into the world:

> Man is an animal, man is a plant, a flower. Features of extreme cruelty, as if not human, but animal, shine through in him; features of primordial tenderness—also as if not human, but vegetable.... A new selection is being produced, a new man is being formed: man—the humane animal, the social animal, the moral animal—is being reconstructed into an *actor* speaking Wagner's language.... [Only man the actor] will be capable of *avidly living and acting* in the developing epoch of whirlwinds and storms into which humanity has irrepressibly rushed.

"The Collapse of Humanism" is a paradoxical, fantastic article and—let us say boldly—a work of genius. The coincidence of Blok's ideas with the conceptions of Spengler is striking. Blok couldn't have known the famous book *The Decline of the West*, but nevertheless his juxtaposition of "culture" and "civilization," his view of Baroque as the style of the "aging culture," and of the eighteenth century as the moment of the replacement of "culture" by "civilization" repeat the basic theses of the German scholar.[23]

The characterization of the civilization of the nineteenth century is striking in its keen expressiveness; the foreboding of the onset of the new antihumanistic epoch and the destruction of "humane, social, and moral" man borders on clairvoyance. This new being—"man-animal" and "man-plant," endowed with "inhuman cruelty" and striving "to live and to act avidly"—has really appeared in our days. But Blok saw as a prophet what he couldn't understand as a philosopher. Seduced by the Nietzschean religion of music, he equated the concepts: culture—

music—elemental force—folk masses. From this comes his paradoxical assertion: "the barbarian masses are the bearers of culture"; from this his idealization of the new, antihumane, and antimoral man, deaf to melodies about "truth, goodness, and beauty." The author believed that "man-animal" would be the Nietzschean "superman," the Wagnerian "actor." He didn't know that this "new breed" would show the world the animal snout of the German fascist.

Hatred for bourgeois civilization with its "enlightenment" and positivism blinds Blok. Saving himself from it, he rushes head down into the "elemental force," seduced by the "music" of antihumanism—of Nietzsche and Wagner.[24]

Preparing the article "The Collapse of Humanism" for publication, the poet notes down his ideas about art in the *Diary*. The artist, "visiting the world in its fateful moments," doesn't have the right to lock himself in the tower of "pure art": "Every culture, whether it be scientific or artistic, is demonic. Exactly what makes it more scientific, more artistic, makes it more demonic. . . . But demonism is power. And power—that is to conquer weakness, to *offend the weak*" (6 January). Estheticism is a "void, a rope on the neck." Another entry reads:

> Christmas. Tereshchenko and I in our time hypnotized each other with art. If it had gone on that way, we would have departed into this bottomless well. It—Art—would have carried us there, would have forced the rejection not only of all of me, but of everything. And there would have remained: three strokes of a Michelangelo picture, a line of Aeschylus, and that's all. All around a void, a rope on the neck. (7 January)

And a third entry reads: " 'To be outside of politics' (Levinson)? Why should this be? . . . No, we can't be 'outside of politics' because thereby we will betray music. . . . To be outside of politics is that same humanism inside out."

In 1919 Blok experiences a painful crisis. In the article "The Collapse of Humanism" he bids farewell to the "spirit of music" by which his lyric had lived. He no longer writes poems, no longer feels himself an artist. He completely loses hope of finishing the *poema Retribution*. In July 1919 he sketches a foreword to *Retribution*: "Since I will hardly succeed in finishing this *poema*, I want to preface to it the story of how it was born."[25]

At the end of January 1920 Blok's stepfather, Franz Feliksovich Kublitsky, passed away. Blok laid him in the coffin himself and alone accompanied the wretched hearse to the cemetery. To avoid eviction and to use less firewood for heating, the Bloks move to Aleksandra Andreevna's apartment. The room where the poet works serves as a bedroom and common dining room. In the daytime he wanders around his "establishments," and at night, when the household is asleep, he is busy editing the works of Heine; this year he prepares the first two volumes for publication and writes a long preface to Heine's *Travel Pictures* (the first and second parts), *Memoirs*, and *English Fragments*.

Discussions concerning Professor V. Zhirmunsky's article "Heine and Romanticism" arose in the literary board of World Literature. During the argument Blok accused Heine of a betrayal of Judaism. His remark called forth a passionate and brilliant lecture by A. L. Volynsky. In the article "On Heine's Judaism" the poet argues with Volynsky, pointing out the incompleteness of his analysis of Christianity. Volynsky distinguishes four elements in Christian teaching: Judaic, Canaan-Babylonian, Hellenistic, and Evangelic-Prophetic. Blok, a true disciple of V. Solovyov, turns the lecturer's attention to a fifth element, "which lay at the cornerstone of the Jena romantics . . . and also of the Russian symbolists at the turn of the twentieth century, and which one can call Platonic or gnostic." Volynsky, the author writes, "doesn't sense . . . the gigantic and purely Aryan basis of Christianity: the Vedanta, Plato, the gnostics, the Platonic tradition in the Italian Renaissance, . . . the Jena romanticism of 1787–1901, and . . . Russian symbolism at the turn of the twentieth century." In this argument apropos of Heine, two antithetical conceptions of Christianity collided: the Judaic—rationalistic—and the Hellenic—Platonic. The late philosopher Lev Shestov constantly pointed out this eternal struggle of Jerusalem with Athens in his works. It is significant that Blok includes in the Hellenistic-Platonic tradition not only his own creative work, but also that of the whole *Russian* symbolist school.

Parallel with his work on Heine, Blok prepares a new edition of Lermontov (*M. Yu. Lermontov 1814–1841. Selected Works in One Volume*. Ed., with an introductory article and notes, by Aleksandr Blok [Berlin-Petersburg: Grzhebin, 1920]) for publication. Many valuable observations are scattered among the poet's commentaries to the poems.

In 1920 two collections of Blok's poems appear: *Beyond the Border of Past Days* (Grzhebin publishing house) and *Gray Morning* (Alkonost publishing house). In the first are placed selected poems of 1898–1903; in the second, sixty poems of the period 1907–16; to the poems reprinted from the third volume the poet adds five unpublished poems. Among them is the lovely poem of 1914 about L. A. Delmas:

> I remember the tenderness of your shoulders—
> They are shy and sensitive—
> And speech interrupted by a caress,
> Suddenly, after chatter and jokes.
>
> The pure ore of hair
> And the throaty sounds of the voice.
> The five-pointed star
> Of dark lilacs in the hour of parting.
>
> And what is bigger and stranger:
> From the whirlwind of music and light—
> The look, full of long greeting,
> And the mystery of thy *faithfulness*.

The five-pointed star of lilacs, the unexpected transition to "thee" ("thy faithfulness")—and these pale lines suddenly come to life. Another 1914 poem is written in a Russian style:

> Fluffed up, swung to and fro,
>   Under the window the willow.
> The Mother of God smiled
>   From the icon corner.

A young married woman leaves her flax. Her red sarafan flashes above the river, the ends of her kerchief shine like two scarlet flowers:

> And who went along the road
>   From the distant village,
> Began to ask God for spring.
>   And spring came.

The poem is full of spring wind and light:

> The fog began to breathe
>   With happiness, daring, depression.

The work in World Literature burdened the poet more and more. K. Chukovsky recalls a conference of the editorial board at which Blok read his introductory article to the edition of Lermontov. They explained to him at length that one cannot refer to the poet's prophetic dreams, and that, in general, one should write in a more "culturally instructive" tone. Chukovsky continues: "The more they proved to Blok that it is necessary to write differently, the sadder, haughtier, more reserved his face became. From that time too began his alienation from those with whom he was forced to sit in conference. This alienation grew with each week."

In the poet's rough drafts, a sketch of a lecture dated 5 April was found, in which he decisively asserts that the revolution in Russia ended two years ago: "Having assembled now, we, even involuntarily, are differently disposed: besides the word 'art' there is present in our consciousness, of course, the word 'revolution,' whether we want this or not. There is nowhere to escape from this word, because the revolution in Russia ended two years ago."

In his "Note on *The Twelve*" the departure from "politics" is stamped in even sharper lines:

> It would be a falsehood to deny any relationship of *The Twelve* to politics. The truth is that the *poema* was written in that exceptional and always short time when the revolutionary cyclone sweeping past calls up a storm in all the seas of nature, life, and art; in the sea of human life there is also a small backwater like the Marquis Pond, which is called politics. And a storm also occurred then in this glass of water.... The seas of nature, life, and art ran high, spray rose in a rainbow over us. I was looking at the rainbow when I wrote *The Twelve*. From that a drop of politics remained

in the *poema*. . . . We will see what time will do with this. Perhaps any politics is so dirty that one drop of it will trouble and corrupt all the rest; perhaps it won't kill the idea of the *poema*.

For Blok in 1920 the revolution had ended a long time ago. Music was replaced by sepulchral silence, the "world conflagration" by a gravelike darkness, the "brotherly feast of labor and peace" by a "dirty pool of politics."

In May the organizer of concerts, Dolidze, and the wife of Professor P. S. Cohen, N. L. Nolle, set up Blok's trip to Moscow. There he reads his poems on five evenings. The Muscovites greet him rapturously as the first poet of Russia. Returning to Petersburg, he enthusiastically takes up a new project: organizing the Petersburg Union of Poets. The young poetess N. A. Pavlovich brings all the necessary mandates from Moscow. Blok is elected chairman. At the first meeting on 4 July 1920 he says:

> In my opinion it would be simplest of all to define the aim of our meeting thus: each of us wants and should try to cast off from himself any particle of that boring and hideous material preoccupation with each day which prevents the writer from being a writer, which fetters his art and transforms him into an average man, equal to all the other preoccupied average men.

On 4 August the Union of Poets sets up its first evening, at which the poets Sergei Gorodetsky and Larisa Reisner perform. In Blok's introductory speech he points out the "wild and unnatural word combination 'Union of Poets,'" emphasizes the difficulty for poets of uniting and "going out into the world," but ends with words of hope:

> Some of us nevertheless think about a new aspiration, which can transform the words "Union of Poets" into a certain reality. . . . Perhaps without force we can form a kind of nucleus which will unite poetry with life at least a bit more closely than they have been united up to now.

On 29 September the Union celebrated M. A. Kuzmin's jubilee. Blok addressed a welcoming speech to him and began it thus:

> Dear Mikhail Alekseevich. Today I must greet you in the name of the institution which bears the dismal bureaucratic name "the professional union of poets." Permit me to tell you that this union . . . has one justification before you: it, like all institutions similar to it, is established to find a means of protecting you, the poet Kuzmin, and such as you, from the various accidents with which life is full and which could be painful for you. . . . It is very easy to lose a poet, but very difficult to acquire a poet, and poets like you are now very few in the world.

The speaker said that much which is seemingly stable will pass; that the legacy of poets is no less necessary to people than bread; that those same people "who today importunately demand utility from 'marble,' will understand tomorrow that marble is God." V. Rozhdestvensky recalls one meeting of the Union of Poets in an uncomfortable arched room near the Chernyshev Bridge:

> The session ended by their taking turns reading poems. Blok read no more than five or six poems. Everyone fell silent under the spell of his voice. And when no one expected him to continue, Aleksandr Aleksandrovich began the last: *A Voice from the Chorus*. His face, hitherto calm, was distorted by a tormented crease near his mouth; his voice rang hollowly, as if cracked. He hunched forward a little in his armchair, heavy lids fell over his eyes, half closing them. He pronounced the last lines almost in a whisper, with agonizing strain, as if forcing himself.
>
> And a kind of depressed feeling gripped us all. No one wanted to recite more. But Blok was the first to smile and said in his normal voice:
>
> "Very unpleasant lines. I don't know why I wrote them. It would have been better to leave these words unspoken. But I had to say them. One must overcome what is difficult. And afterward there will be a clear day.... And you know, let's read something from Pushkin. Nikolai Stepanovich, now it's your turn." Gumilyov was not at all surprised by this suggestion and after a moment's pause began:
>
> Skirmish behind the hills;
> Their camp and ours looks:
> On the hill in front of the Cossacks
> The red cap waves.
>
> Pushkin's bright name discharged the general tension.

Blok's hopes for a "new aspiration" of poets was not justified. Dissatisfaction, squabbles, intrigues began—and the chairman finally announced his decision to divest himself of his duties. N. Pavlovich writes in her memoirs:

> The work of the Union of Poets was slowly normalized.... Our chairman was unusually conscientious.... He didn't miss a single session—entered into every trifle. After his announcing his intention to leave, the entire membership of the Union appeared at his apartment to ask him to stay. They stood on the staircase, in the yard. And he stayed, but kept aloof from business, and in January at new elections Gumilyov was elected chairman of the Union.... I have a book of Blok's; written in it is: "In the days of new hopes. August 1920."

His departure from the Union of Poets made Blok's life somewhat easier. K. Chukovsky tells of its "load":

> At one and the same location, on Mokhovaya, we sat in conference, sometimes all through the day: first as directors of the Union of Writers, then as the board of World Literature, then as sections of the historical scenes. Most often of all Blok spoke with Gumilyov. An unending argument about poetry went on between the two poets.

Blok notes in the *Diary* (22 October) about Gumilyov:

> *Evening in the poets' club on Liteinaya on 21 October*—the first after they expelled Pavlovich, Shkapskaya, Otsup, Syunnerberg, and Rozhdestvensky and asked me to stay. . . . Gumilyov runs the show rather interestingly and skillfully. The acmeists, one senses, are in a certain conspiracy, they treat each other in a special way. All are under Gumilyov.
> The hit of the evening, O. Mandelshtam, who came having spent time in Vrangel's prison. He has developed a lot. . . . Gumilyov and Gorky. . . . Neither knows about *tragedy*—and about the two truths.

The poet more and more spurns the rationalism and formalism of Gumilyov and his school, senses more and more deeply the irrational, mystical basis of art. Among Blok's manuscripts there remained the sketch of an article obviously directed against the theory of the founder of acmeism:

> The more they try to approach art with attempts to explain its devices scientifically, the more enigmatic and inexplicable these devices seem. It seems the whole Studio crowd of all these years has as its final aim affirming the simple fact that art is not analyzable by scientific methods. . . . The theoreticians are losing (or they aren't losing, but will lose) the hope of bridling art, of shoving the bit of science into the artist's clenched teeth.

In the summer life becomes a little easier for Blok. Every day he bathes in the Pryazhka and sometimes, putting on his cap and taking some bread and suet with him, he "bolts" the sessions for whole days at Strelna. There he wanders in the forest, bathes, basks in the sun, and returns sunburnt and cheerful. S. Gorodetsky recalls:

> The first thing that Blok said to me, when we embraced in the summer after a long separation, was that he was splitting and carrying firewood and bathes every day in the Pryazhka. He was sunburnt, red, looked like a Finn. His eyes were stubbornly gay; those eyes which made a tragic grimace, linked to the wrinkles of suffering in the last portrait.

The work in the Bolshoi Theater continues in the summer. Blok gives a review "On Five Plays of 1920," selected in a competition of the Moscow Theatrical Section, makes a "Speech on the Jubilee of the Bolshoi Dramatic Theater," writes a note "On Merezhkovsky" on the occasion of the staging of *Tsarevich Aleksei*, and at the end of the 1919–20 season addresses the actors with a speech in which he thanks them for their selfless work and congratulates them on their "indubitable achievements"—the staging of *Don Carlos*, *Othello*, and *Tsarevich Aleksei*. A dramatic and psychological analysis of Shakespeare's *King Lear*, drawn up in the form of a speech to the actors, is written with great inspiration. In another speech, "On Maeterlinck's *Blue Bird*," there are keen observations on the poetic rhythm of this "neo-romantic fairy tale."

E. Zamyatin writes in his memoirs:

Aleksandr Blok

In the summer of 1920 I had to work with Blok on the text and staging of Lear in the Bolshoi Dramatic Theater. "Aleksandr Aleksandrovich is our conscience," the director Lavrentiev, it seems, once said to me. And I heard this phrase as a proven formula many times after that from people in the theater. The last stage and dress rehearsals ended at about two or three in the morning. Blok always stayed till the end and it seems the later it was the more he came to life, the more he talked—a night bird. "Doesn't this tire you?" I asked. The answer: "No, the theater, backstage, such a dark auditorium—I love it. I am a very theatrical person."

The poet writes in the *Diary* about his love for the "old, dirty theater" (13 December):

> The large old theater in which I work is full of dirt, intrigues, tawdriness, boredom, and luster. A collection of people who know how to gorge, drink, kick up a row, and act on the stage. This place hasn't died, it hasn't stopped being a school of life, while all around they are trying to kill life. ... When *life* takes the upper hand, only then will this fat, malicious, gay, and not very healthy nest, whose name is the old theater, stop attracting.

On 15 August a gala session dedicated to V. Solovyov took place in Volfil (on the occasion of the twentieth anniversary of his death). Blok delivered a speech, "Vladimir Solovyov and Our Day." It was published subsequently in the journal *Dreamers' Notes (Zapiski Mechtateley)* (Nos. 2–3, 1921). That same summer he read his *poema Retribution* in Volfil. The meeting was crowded and the *poema* was a great success. The poetess Anna Radlova wrote in a newspaper that our time will someday be called "Blokian."

In October Lyubov Dmitrievna joined the company of the dramatic theater People's Comedy, at the invitation of the young director S. V. Radlov. For whole days she was busy with rehearsals and performances. His wife's continual absence tormented Blok very much. M. A. Beketova tells of his emotional state in the winter of 1920:

> One must say that as time went on, the more he needed constant contact with his wife. The reason for this was not only his very tender and deep love for her, but also her health, vitality, childlike carefreeness, and ability to distract him from sad thoughts with an original joke and with her unfailing bright gaiety. ... In former years too Aleksandr Aleksandrovich didn't like it when she would leave or often absent herself from the house, but he endured all this comparatively easily. Now, without her, he grieved, his spirits fell, he didn't want to start eating until she returned.

The year 1921 begins with a tragic entry in the *Notebook* [*Diary*] about the destruction of the Shakhmatovo country estate:

> In a small package saved from the Shakhmatovo house by Andrey and brought by Ferol[26] in the autumn: sheets of Lyuba's notebooks (very numerous). *Not a trace* of her diary. Sheets from the notebooks, parts of my

lost manuscripts, parts of my father's archive, notices, university abstracts (juridical and philological), some rough drafts of poems, pictures which were on the wall of the annex. On some—dirt and traces of human hooves (with horseshoes). And that's all. (3 January)

A feeling of infinite weariness takes possession of Blok; with his last strength he goes on foot to Mokhovaya, to World Literature, and sits in conference in the Bolshoi Theater. On 22 January, at a jubilee celebration for the actor N. F. Monakhov, he addresses a brief speech to him and ends it with the words: "We fervently wish you, actor and master, many, many more times to paint before the footlights your always clear-cut images, your delicate patterns; to ignite hearts and thereby soften their bitterness; to help contemporary people not to renounce their difficult paths."[27]

The work in World Literature dragged on cheerlessly. The poet submits the third volume of Heine's works to the press, and continues to edit poems. "The *historical scenes*," he notes, "(Gorky's undertaking, galvanized by Gumilyov and Tikhonov) are slowly dying."

The repellent work and the wretched existence lead him to despair. A 17 January note in the *Diary* reads: "Biting morning thoughts, to the point of horror, amid depths of despair and doom: to learn to read *The Twelve*, to become a poet-singer of topical songs. One could always have money and decorations."

On 25 May Blok summarizes the story of his life in the first five months of 1921 in brief words (*Diary*): "Our poor and gloomy life in the first five months; relations between Lyuba and mama. Lyuba's theater. . . . My disease progressed, weariness and depression were tearing me to pieces, in our apartment I was only silent. . . . In February they drove me out of the Union of Poets and elected Gumilyov chairman."

The sick poet was deeply insulted by the ingratitude of the young poets and by Gumilyov's stubborn hostility. Out of pride he never admitted this to anyone. But the battle with the acmeists forces him to turn to the past again and to evaluate the significance of the symbolist epoch. In a note "On the Alkonost Publishing House" he declares decisively:

> The fact that a group of writers siding with symbolism were united around Alkonost is explained, in our conviction, only by just these writers turning out to be for the most part bearers of the spirit of the time. The group of writers united in Alkonost was full of alarm at the unfolding world events, whose approach it sensed and predicted.

Blok, the last Russian romantic, courageously defends the fortress of symbolism, beseiged on all sides.

During the winter the poet didn't complain of illness. He continued to drag enormous bundles of wood from the cellar and to work at night. Only once did he feel a sharp pain in the region of his heart, but he didn't see a doctor. He explained his depressed mood by overtiredness and "nerves." He was silent for whole days, but at times he became animated, acted out a political meeting, drew caricatures and distributed homemade decorations with the names "Rev-mama," "Rev-Lyuba."[28]

On 10 February, on the eighty-fourth anniversary of Pushkin's death, the House of Writers organized a gala meeting. Blok read a speech "On the Poet's Calling"—his poetic testament. The lyrical fire which was burning down flared up for the last time. Blok spoke about harmony, about the cosmos, about sound waves, with his former inspiration. In places the speech itself became music:

> In the bottomless depths of the spirit, where man stops being man, in the depths, created by civilization, inaccessible to the state and society, sound waves roll like waves of the ether surrounding the universe. There comes rhythmical vibrations like the processes which form mountains, winds, sea currents, the vegetable and animal world.

"A gay name—Pushkin; a light name—Pushkin." But the poet's fate is always tragic. "What is a poet?" Blok asks, and answers:

> The poet is a son of harmony; a role is given to him in world culture. Three tasks are entrusted to him: first, to liberate sounds from the native eternal element in which they dwell; second, to bring these sounds into harmony, to give them form; third, to bring this harmony into the external world.

The poet should throw off the "cares of the vain world." Wild, stern, full of confusion, he runs "To the shores of deserted waves / To the noisy oak groves."

The disclosure of spiritual depths is just as difficult as the act of birth; the poet joins the "native chaos," the elemental force driving the sound waves. The first "task" is ended: the sound is taken into the soul. The second "task" begins: the sounds and words are embodied in harmony. This is the realm of craftsmanship. And, finally, the third "task" comes: the sounds taken into the soul and led into harmony are to be brought into the world. Here the poet's clash with the mob takes place.

The mob is not the "common people" and not the nation; it is officials, sharp operators, and the vulgar; it is those spiritually blind men who demand that the poet "sweep the litter from the streets," "enlighten the hearts of their fellows." The bureaucrats of Pushkin's day are in no way distinguishable from the officials of today.

Pushkin needed "secret freedom" more than personal freedom or political freedom. Without this freedom the poet can't live. The conclusion of the speech is Blok's personal confession, full of serene and lofty tragedy. Blok's fate is mysteriously pre-inscribed in Pushkin's fate: he knows this and accepts death:

> D'Anthes' bullet didn't kill Pushkin at all. The absence of air killed him. His culture was dying with him: "It's time, my friend, it's time! The heart asks for peace."

Peace and *freedom*. They are indispensable to the poet for the liberation of harmony. But peace and freedom are also taken away. Not outward, but creative, peace. Not childish freedom, not the freedom to play the liberal, but creative freedom, secret freedom. And the poet dies because he no longer has anything to breathe: life has lost its meaning.... Let those officials who intend to direct poetry along some channel of their own, encroaching on its secret freedom and hindering it from fulfilling its mysterious purpose, beware of worse nicknames [than the "mob"].

Six months later Blok died.

E. Gollerbakh[29] discusses the poet's speech:

The gala celebration of Pushkin's memory in the House of Writers on 10 February 1921 is especially memorable to me. I remember Blok's erect, stately figure standing on the rostrum, reading his speech "On the Poet's Calling" from a notebook. In his every word, in each sound of the cold, impassive voice, there was boundless weariness, wretchedness, waning.... Blok had barely finished his last sentence; stormy applause resounded, an approving rumble of voices. Blok folded up the notebook from which he had read and sat down at the green table beside the other members of the presidium. His face was somewhat agitated. But always the same weariness, always the same indifference to his surroundings was in his gaze, gliding apathetically along the heads of the audience. Sometimes his bright blue eyes took on an unpleasant expression of alienation. The ovation didn't subside. Blok got up, his snowy sweater white above the green cloth of the table, his head thrown back slightly, as always. He got up, stood for half a minute. The applause became even more deafening. Everyone clapped. Blok looked somewhere into the depths of the auditorium, intently, coldly, not bowing, in no way responding to the noisy signs of approval. Then he sat down.

He gave the speech "On the Poet's Calling" twice more: in the same House of Writers and at Petersburg University. It was published in the journal *Herald of Literature (Vestnik Literatury)* (No. 3, 1921).

Blok's last poem, written just before his death, is connected with Pushkin's "light name": *To the Pushkin House*. Written in the rhythm and meter of the poem *Above the Neva the varicolored ships' flags wave playfully*, it is devoted to "Pushkinian Petersburg": to an ice floe on the "triumphant river," to the sphinx on the embankment, Falconetti's Bronze Horseman, to the white nights "over the mysterious Neva." In the seventh verse the author addresses the poet:

Pushkin! *Secret freedom*
   We sang after you.
Give us your hand in the bad weather,
   Help us in the mute struggle.

And it ends:

Aleksandr Blok

> This is why such a familiar
>   Sound, dear to the heart,
> The name of the Pushkin House
> In the Academy of Sciences.
>
> This is why, in the hours of sunset,
>   Departing into the night darkness,
> From the white Senate Square
>   I quietly bow to him.

In March 1921, looking through his old manuscripts, Blok finds prose drafts relating to 1907, 1908, and 1909. He reworks them, bringing them together; he rearranges them in a different order. He intends to create an autobiographical story, "Neither Sleeping nor Waking," out of this material. The story remained unfinished. It begins with the story of how the mowers sang in the neighborhood of Shakhmatovo. This reminiscence goes back to 1901 (in the 1921 manuscript this chapter is called "Of How the Peasants Sang Twenty Years Ago"). It begins:

> The whole household sat under the lindens and drank tea in the sunset. Behind the lilacs fog was already rising from the ravine.... The neighboring peasants came out to mow the merchant's meadow.... The scythes began to scrape on the grass, one could hear—twenty of them. ... Suddenly one of them struck up a song. A powerful silvery tenor poured out effortlessly and at once filled the ravine and the grove and the garden.... The peasants caught up the song. And we were all terribly moved.... I don't know, I can't make out the words, but the song keeps growing.... It's awkward for me to sit, there's a tickle in my throat, I want to weep. I jumped up and ran off into a distant corner of the garden.

From this song everything "bleared," "everything went to rack and ruin": the merchant became an inveterate drunkard and set fire to the hay sheds on his estate; a "political" appeared who kept "getting lost" on the roads on a bicycle; the peasants' huts fell to pieces and were not repaired. The author himself, gripped by a thirst for destruction, started cutting down a century-old lilac: "The clusters of flowers are thin and bluish, and the trunk is such that the axe barely takes it. I cut it all down, and behind it was a birch grove. I also cut down the grove." Another "dream" is given:

> Behind the forest ... a vast crowd of peasants.... And bogatyrs remained outside the village on the hills: the radiance of chain armor, nothing more to be made out. One rode ahead, the horse set his feet firmly to the earth, the rider stretched out his arm, pointing far away beyond the forest. Suddenly the crowd moved in the direction indicated by the bogatyr's arm. Pitchforks waved on their shoulders; others had strange old-fashioned swords.

In these misty visions the "elemental folk force," mysterious and fairytale-like, knocks at the poet's consciousness with dull blows. He hears that under the ground, in the unknown depths, "chaos is stirring."

The last vision is reminiscent of Anna Karenina's death dream about the peasant puttering at the rails. In the evening the author walks around the Shakhmatovo garden. By the back fence he sees:

> Someone is digging in the ground, kneeling, with his back to me. Having dug, he puts his hands together into a megaphone and speaks into the open hole in a hollow voice: "Eh, you! hurry!" I don't look or listen further—it is so unbearably terrifying that I run without a backward glance, stopping up my ears. "But that's the gardener." Once they even answered him, many voices from the hole said: "We will always be on time." Then he got up, without hurrying and without turning to me, and crept away into the bushes.

These are "terrible dreams" amid the dead silence of the beginning of the century: a premonition of an approaching storm. Twenty years later the Shakhmatovo estate was destroyed by the peasants.

At the beginning of April K. Chukovsky arranged an evening dedicated to Blok in the Bolshoi Theater. After Chukovsky's introductory speech, the poet read poems of various periods. The hall was overflowing, they presented flowers to Blok, gave him ovations. E. Zamyatin recalls this evening:

> His last sad triumph was in Petersburg on a white April night (in the Bolshoi Theater).... Lit from below, by footlights, Blok with a pale, tired face ... hesitates for a moment, searches with his eyes where to stand—and stands somewhere beside a small table. And in the silence—poems about Russia. A kind of hollow voice, as if from somewhere far away—on one note. And only toward the end, after the ovations, for one moment higher and firmer—the last upward flight.

A. M. Remizov recalls with tenderness his last meetings with the poet:

> You remember the Chukovsky evenings in the House of Arts, the celebration in honor of M. A. Kuzmin, and our last evening in the House of Writers. I read *The Sidewalk Gang*, and you read poems about the "French heel." We went home together—Serafima Pavlovna, Lyubov Aleksandrovna,[30] you, and I—along deserted Liteinaya. The moon shone fiercely.... The February memorial banquet to Pushkin—this is your apotheosis.

And there is one more touching reminiscence. "Poor Aleksandr Aleksandrovich," Remizov writes, "you gave me a cigarette, a real one! Your fingers were bandaged. And you said then that you can't write: 'In such a yoke it's impossible to write.'"

Blok's last critical article was directed against the acmeists and their "leader," Gumilyov. It is called "Without Divinity, Without Inspiration (Guild of Acmeists)" and is written in an irritated, sharp tone unusual for the critic. This tone is explained not so much by Blok's personal hostility to the author of *Pearls* as by the sense of responsibility for the fate of Russian literature. Blok understood that the Russian renaissance of the beginning of the century was over; that the level of culture fell catastrophically after the revolution; that he is the last warrior and that his cause is lost beforehand. And nonetheless, with Don Quixotean faithfulness, the poet considered it his duty to defend the "deserted temple" of symbolism. Having set forth briefly the history of the new "currents"—acmeism, Adamism, futurism, and ego-futurism—the author ends the article with a stern accusation:

> The acmeists . . . are drowning themselves in the cold swamp of soulless theories and all kinds of formalism. . . . They don't have and don't want to have the shadow of an idea of Russian life and of the life of the world in general. In their poetry (and consequently in themselves) they ignore the main thing, the only valuable thing—the *soul*. . . . They want to be distinguished shop and guild foreigners. In any case one can only speak seriously to each and about each of them when they leave their "guilds," renounce formalism, curse all "eidologies," and become themselves.[31]

M. A. Beketova writes:

> The first symptoms of illness began in the middle of April. Aleksandr Aleksandrovich felt a general weakness and a sharp pain in his arms and legs, but didn't undergo treatment. His mood at this time was horrible, and any unpleasant impression intensified the pain. When his mother and wife began an argument in his presence he would experience an intensification of physical suffering and would ask them to be silent.

Beketova adds: "This discord between the two beings closest to him tormented Aleksandr Aleksandrovich cruelly. This tormenting ulcer on his soul was also among the complicated bundle of causes affecting the development of his illness." On 18 April, he writes a gloomy note in the *Diary*:

> Again conversations about the fact that it is necessary to live apart, that is, for mama to live separately. . . . And in the weather, and on the street, and in E. F. Knipovich, . . . and in Europe—everything is the same. Life has changed (it was changing, but not new, not *nuova*), the louse has conquered the whole world, this has already taken place, and everything will now change only in *another* direction and not in that by which we lived, which we loved.

K. Chukovsky also talks about Blok's emotional gloom:

> In May 1921 I got a terrible letter from him about the fact that *it* had conquered. "Now I have neither soul nor body, I am ill as I have never been before: the fever doesn't stop and everything always hurts. Thus it's

impossible to say we are healthy even till now. Vile, snuffling, dear Mother Russia gobbled me up after all, like a pig her piglet."

Quite ill, he goes to Moscow on 1 May. Leaning on a cane, he gets off with difficulty, brows knitted from pain, gets into a cab. K. Chukovsky accompanies him. "In the coach," he writes, "on the way there, he was gay, talkative, read his own and others' poems, treated us to Easter cakes, and only sometimes got up from his seat, straightened his aching leg and said smilingly: 'It hurts.' (He thought he had gout.)" The six poetic evenings in Moscow, the triumphs and celebrations (in his honor) so wearied the sick man that he returned to Petersburg before the set time. Chukovsky recalls:

> Once, in Moscow in May 1921, I was sitting backstage with Blok at the House of Print and listened to how some "orator" on the stage was gaily proving to the crowd that Blok had already died as a poet: "I ask you, comrades, where is the dynamism here? These poems are carrion, and a corpse wrote them." Blok leaned toward me and said: "That's the truth." And although I didn't see him, my whole back felt that he was smiling. "He is speaking the truth. I have died."

In another terrible reminiscence, Chukovsky continues:

> We were sitting at a tea table and chatting. I said something, not looking at him, and suddenly, inadvertently raising my eyes, I almost screamed: before me sat not Blok, but a different man, completely different, not even remotely resembling Blok. Rigid, emaciated, with empty eyes, as if covered by a cobweb. Even his hair, even his ears, had become different. And the main thing: he was obviously cut off from everyone, blind and deaf to everything human.

No less tragic is the testimony of E. Gollerbakh:

> In Moscow Blok's mood was especially gloomy. The will to death showed clearer and clearer in him, the will to life became weaker and weaker. Once he asked Chulkov: "Georgy Ivanovich, do you want to die?" Chulkov answered not exactly "no," not exactly "I don't know." Blok said: "But I want to very much." This "I want to" was so strong in him that people who closely observed the poet in the last months of his life assert that Blok died because he wanted to die.

Blok died not from illness, but from the fact that music had abandoned him, that he had nothing to breathe, that he wanted to die. His death was *mystical*, as was his whole life.

One of the last *Diary* entries reads:

> Moscow is worse than last year, but there are many people, there are beautiful people who are gone, the street is noisy, automobiles speed, it is warm (not for me), everything is blooming at once (apple trees, lilacs,

dandelions, cowslips), thunderstorms and downpours. I sometimes dozed in the sun near the Smolensky Market on Novinsky Boulevard.

Lyuba met me at the station with Bilitsky's horse;[32] I wanted to weep—one of the few living feelings in this time (for a long time, the shadow of feeling).

Soon after his return from Moscow Blok had his first heart attack. Doctor A. G. Pekelis diagnosed heart disease and psychosthenia. They forced the patient to stay in bed, but this depressed him. After two weeks the doctor allowed him to get up; he would wander slowly through the rooms, sit silently in an armchair. Visits so tired him that even close friends like E. P. Ivanov and L. A. Delmas couldn't see him. He rapidly lost weight, gasped for breath, complained of heart pains. Lyubov Dmitrievna, with the help of the poet's numerous friends and admirers, succeeded in obtaining medicine and foodstuffs. She gave up her work in the theater and didn't leave her husband. They sent Aleksandra Andreevna to Luga; her nervous illness and ever-anxious mood could only worsen the patient's condition. At the end of May a slight improvement in Blok's health came: he cheered up, began to sort out his archive, burnt unneeded manuscripts and letters, finished the list of his works, and put the catalogue in order. The last entry written in his hand is: "The card catalogue of my Russian books is finished. Entry of 25 May." In the intervals between attacks he would sketch plans and passages for the second and third parts of *Retribution*. On 4 June he writes to his mother in Luga:

> It's unbearably boring to write about illness, but there's nothing else to write about. I can't do anything, because my temperature is rarely normal, everything hurts, it is difficult to breathe, etc. They don't know what's wrong. If my nerves improve a bit it will be possible to find out whether this heart disease is real, or only neurosis. My temperature must be lowered. I am taking a vaudevillian quantity of medicines.
>
> I eat well; I can't say that I like the food or anything in general. Lyuba is almost always at home. . . . It seems that's all. Sasha.
>
> Thank you for the bread and eggs. The bread is real, Russian, almost without admixture; I haven't eaten such for a very long time.

In the middle of June the patient's condition took a sharp turn for the worse. A note by Dr. Pekelis has been preserved: "On my initiative a consultation was called with the participation of Professor P. V. Troitsky and Dr. E. L. Gize, who identified in the patient the presence of acute endocarditis and also psychosthenia." It was decided to take Blok to a sanatorium in Finland. Gorky undertook to intercede for permission for the poet and his wife to go abroad. The permission came after Blok's death. During the last weeks of his life the patient suffered unbearably. Lying down, he gasped for breath, and a sitting position was tormenting because of the pain in his whole body. K. Chukovsky writes:

He died in agony. His heart constantly caused horrible suffering, he constantly gasped for breath. By the beginning of August he was already unconscious most of the time. At night he was delirious and shouted a terrible shout, which I won't forget in my whole life. . . . The sick leave (to the Finland sanatorium) was signed, but on 5 August it turned out that some Moscow section had lost the forms and it had therefore been impossible to write out the passports.

M. A. Beketova reports: "A month before his death the patient's mind began to be clouded. This expressed itself in extreme irritability, a despondent, apathetic state, and in an incomplete awareness of reality. There were moments of lucidity, after which the former again ensued. Medicines no longer helped. . . . Weakness reached extreme limits."

Four days before his death the poet's mother was called from Luga.

On Sunday, 7 August, at ten in the morning, Blok passed away.

"Death greatly changed his features," E. Gollerbakh writes. "The general appearance remained the same—noble, sad, concentrated. The hair was cropped short, the muscles of the nose, which seemed enormous, were sharply prominent. Blok had become very emaciated and pinched during his illness."

They buried Blok on the tenth of August. Men of letters carried his open coffin, strewn with flowers, to the Smolensky cemetery. Among them was the poet's friend and spiritual brother—Andrey Bely. An immense crowd walked behind the coffin. No one made speeches at the grave. They placed a simple, unadorned cross and laid wreaths. E. Zamyatin writes about Blok's funeral:

> A blue, hot day, the tenth of August. Blue incense smoke in the crowded room. An alien face, long, with prickly mustaches, with a pointed beard—resembling the face of Don Quixote. . . . The full church of the Smolensky cemetery. A slanting ray above in the cupola, slowly descending lower and lower. An unknown girl makes her way through the crowd to the coffin, kisses the yellow hand, leaves.

V. Rozhdestvensky relates:

> Ten years later, on the same summer evening, I dropped in at the Smolensky cemetery. I wanted to find Blok's grave. I succeeded in finding it, not without difficulty. It was all overgrown with thick and lush grass. Near it hung the withered stems of flowers brought by someone not long ago. On one of the arms of the cross some lines of poetry, half washed away by rain, showed black. . . . I went closer to the lopsided cross and, by the last rays, with difficulty made out two lines in pencil:
> He is all—a child of goodness and light,
> He is all—the triumph of freedom.

Finished on 7 August 1945—the date of Blok's death. [K. M.]

NOTES

Notes from Mochulsky's text are not marked; those supplied by the translator are indicated by an appended [Tr.].

CHAPTER I

1. E. Spektorsky, "Aleksandr Lvovich Blok, Political Scientist and Philosopher," *Warsaw University News,* III (1912).
2. There is no English equivalent for the Russian word *poema,* a narrative or epic poem of some length; it may have lyrical content as well. The word is discussed in the Introduction. [Tr.]
3. The Bestuzhev courses, at a university level, were open to women before institutions of higher education would formally admit them. [Tr.]
4. Aleksandr Ostrovsky was a leading nineteenth-century playwright, whose dramas often dealt with the merchant class. [Tr.]
5. A. N. Maikov was a poet of the second half of the nineteenth century. [Tr.]
6. A. A. Grigoriev was a nineteenth-century Slavophile poet, critic, editor, and prose writer. [Tr.]
7. M. A. Beketova, *Aleksandr Blok* (Leningrad, 1930) and *Al. Blok and His Mother* (Leningrad-Moscow, 1925).
8. Pechorin is the main character in Lermontov's novel *A Hero of Our Time.* [Tr.]
9. V. A. Zhukovsky was a poet-translator of the early nineteenth century and a precursor of Russian romanticism. [Tr.]
10. Ya. P. Polonsky was a romantic poet of the late nineteenth century who also wrote civic poetry. [Tr.]
11. *Rus* is a word used to designate Old Russia, with overtones of cultural nostalgia. [Tr.]
12. *Kotya* is a diminutive of the Russian word for cat. [Tr.]
13. Kozma Prutkov was the joint pseudonym of three nineteenth-century Russian authors who wrote satirical and nonsense verse, plays, aphorisms, etc. [Tr.]
14. Melodeclamation is recitation of poetry accompanied by music. [Tr.]
15. Blok stayed in the second course for a second year.
16. N. I. Gnedich was an early nineteenth-century poet, best known for his translation of Homer's *Iliad.* [Tr.]
17. Russian has two words for "you": the familiar *ty* and the formal *vy*. In referring to the Beautiful Lady, Blok usually uses the familiar form. I have translated it as "you" except in those places where a distinction is indicated: in such cases *ty* is translated as "thee" and *vy* as "you." [Tr.]

CHAPTER II

1. A. Bely, *Arabesques* (Moscow: Musaget, 1911).
2. The "untouchable" (*nedotykomka*), a demon who keeps appearing to Peredonov in Sologub's *The Petty Demon*, is both a reflection of Peredonov's paranoia and a symbol of the various nastinesses in the novel. [Tr.]
3. Streets on Vasilievsky Island in St. Petersburg were called "lines." [Tr.]
4. K. D. Balmont, one of the so-called decadent poets of the late nineteenth and early twentieth centuries, did many translations, especially of Shelly and Poe. [Tr.]
5. Andrey Bely.
6. It was printed in the January issue of *New Path*, 1903, under the signature "A Science Student."
7. Kitezh is a legendary city supposed to have sunk into a lake, thereby escaping destruction by the Tatars. [Tr.]
8. L. D. M.—Lyubov Dmitrievna Mendeleeva.
9. About suicide.
10. Heinrich Blok was a Petersburg banking firm.
11. At Russian weddings both the bride and groom had male attendants. "Best man" is the closest approximation in English. [Tr.]
12. *The Hippolytus*, Euripides' tragedy, translated by Merezhkovsky.
13. *New Path*.
14. Moscow Anthology.
15. V. P. Burenin, critic and translator, systematically badgered the "decadents" in his feuilletons in *New Time*. He persistently called Blok "Blokh." [*Blokha* is the Russian word for "flea"; Tr.]
16. Selected poems from this period were later included in the first volume of the *Collected Poems*, in the section *Crossroads*. Others were included in the collection *Beyond the Border of Past Days* in 1920. The rest were printed in the 1932 edition, *Blok's Collected Works*.

CHAPTER III

1. A. Bely, *Reminiscences of Blok* (Berlin, 1922).
2. Repetilov, a character in Griboedov's play *Woe from Wit*, a windbag and exaggeratedly self-deprecating liar, is also a parody on liberalism. [Tr.]
3. A. Bely, *Reminiscences of Blok* and *The Beginning of the Century*.
4. Pavel Pestel was a leader of the Decembrist conspiracy. [Tr.]
5. M. A. Voloshin was a minor poet of the early twentieth century. [Tr.]
6. Schema monks are monks of very strict observance. [Tr.]
7. It appeared in *Scales* in 1905.
8. Contributors to the Griffin publishing house.
9. The statue of Peter the Great outside St. Isaac's Cathedral. [Tr.]
10. Bely describes this tragic period of his life in two books: *Reminiscences of Blok* (Berlin, 1922) and *Between Two Revolutions* (Leningrad). In the first he passes over his relations with L. D. Blok in silence. In the second, beside her, he portrays a certain Mme. Shch. Both camouflage devices completely distort the perspective of events and relationships. It is very difficult not to get lost in the forest of ambiguities, reservations, conscious distortions, and deceptions piled up by the author.

CHAPTER IV

1. The pun here is untranslatable. *Kosa* means both a "braid" and a "scythe." [Tr.]
2. *The Puppet Show* was printed in the first anthology of *Torches* in April 1906.
3. Printed in *The Pass* (No. 4, February 1907).
4. This letter is used to designate Lyubov Dmitrievna in *Reminiscences of Blok*.
5. Nikolai Karamzin, the major literary figure of the Russian sentimentalist school, introduced important changes in the poetic lexicon. [Tr.]
6. Hilarion was an eleventh-century Metropolitan of Kiev, whose sermons were in a very ornate rhetorical style. [Tr.]
7. In 1906 he wrote nine reviews for *The Word*, two for *Golden Fleece*, one for *Scales*, and one for *The Pass*.
8. Lev Shestov's name for V. Ivanov.
9. G. Chulkov, *Years of Wandering* (Moscow, 1936).
10. In *Reminiscences of Blok* Bely depicts this scene as a meeting of the three (himself, Blok, and Lyubov Dmitrievna). The version in *Between Two Revolutions* seems to us psychologically more plausible.
11. The pun is untranslatable. *Povod* in Russian can mean either "reason, cause" or "reins." [Tr.]
12. V. F. Khodasevich, *Necropolis. Reminiscences* (Petropolis, 1939).
13. See note 1, Chapter IV.
14. *The King on the Square* was published in the journal *Golden Fleece* (No. 4, 1907).
15. It appeared in the first volume of the edition: *People's Literature* (Moscow: The World Publishing House, 1908).
16. The *byliny* are a genre of Russian epic folk poetry often dealing, though without accuracy, with historical events. They were originally sung or recited. [Tr.]
17. A character in Dostoevsky's *The Idiot*. [Tr.]
18. On the cover it is marked 1907.
19. Death (*smert'*) is feminine in Russian. [Tr.]

CHAPTER V

1. Maeterlinck's play, *Sister Beatrice,* was running that season in the Kommissarzhevskaya Theater.
2. *On Aleksandr Blok. Collection of Articles* (St. Petersburg: Kartonnyj Domik, 1931).
3. From Wagner's *Rhinegold*.
4. Evgeny Pavlovich Ivanov.
5. Znanie was a publishing house founded by Gorky; a group of writers, mostly of a revolutionary bent, was formed around it. [Tr.]
6. Of Blok's other 1901 articles we note: "Fyodor Sologub's Art" (*The Pass*, No. 10, August); "On Contemporary Criticism" (the newspaper *The Hour*, No. 61, December); "V. Briusov: 'Earth's Axis' " (*Golden Fleece*, No. 1); "D. Merezhkovsky: 'Eternal Companions' " (*Chrysoprase, A Literary Collection*. [Moscow: Samocvet, 1907]).
7. In Ibsen's drama, *The Master Builder*.
8. Isadora Duncan, the famous dancer.
9. Dante's words, addressed to Vergil, in *The Divine Comedy*.
10. "Man of the soil" (*pochvennik*) was a member of the "rooted in the soil" (*pochvennost'*) movement, a movement of conservative Russian nationalist bent, emphasizing the importance of the peasantry. [Tr.]

11. D. Blagoy, "A. Blok and Apollon Grigoriev," *On Blok. Collection of the Literary Research Association* (Moscow: Nikitinskie Subbotniki, 1929).
12. See note 10, Chapter V.
13. A quotation from Nekrasov's poem "The Peddler." [Tr.]
14. Pushkin's *poema*. [Tr.]
15. Blok quotes excerpts from Klyuev's letter in "Literary Review for 1907."

CHAPTER VI

1. *Raznochintsy* means, literally, "people of various ranks." Their appearance marked the end of the dominance of the gentry and nobility in Russian literature and culture. In practice the word means "not of gentry origin." [Tr.]
2. Merezhkovsky's doctrine.
3. Minsky's theory.
4. Z. N. Gippius' poem.
5. In *The Stranger*: "And drunks with rabbit eyes shout: '*In vino veritas.*' "
6. Blok's paper was printed twice: the first time under the title "Russia and the Intelligentsia," *Golden Fleece* (No. 1, 1909); the second time under the title "The People and the Intelligentsia" in the newspaper *Banner of Labor* (19 February 1918).
7. Vasily Rozanov is best known for books consisting of fragmentary essays and aphorisms, for his critical work on Dostoevsky, and for his philosophical writings on Christianity and sex. [Tr.]
8. "Elemental Force and Culture" was printed three times: in *Our Newspaper* (6 January 1909); in the anthology *Italy* (Sweetbrier, 1909); and in the newspaper *Banner of Labor* (1918).
9. First published in the newspaper *Speech* (No. 77, 20 March); secondly in the newspaper *Banner of Labor* (No. 151, 8 March 1918).
10. In Italy Blok reread *War and Peace,* and this reading revived in him the memory of Mitya's death.
11. The Avenue of Roses is the Warsaw location of the hospital in which A. L. Blok died.
12. A character in *Crime and Punishment*. [Tr.]
13. It was placed in the section *Native Land*.

CHAPTER VII

1. It entered the *Miscellaneous Poems* section of the third volume.
2. Included in the *Terrible World* section of the third volume.
3. Three new Moscow publishing houses.
4. A. Bely's fiancée.
5. Iliodor, a monk, and Hermogen, a bishop, at first supported Rasputin, then turned against him. Iliodor, who was unfrocked, was apparently later involved in attempts on Rasputin's life. [Tr.]
6. See Chapter VI.
7. P. S. Solovyova—Allegro—was V. Solovyov's sister.
8. Turgenev.
9. In 1910 two of Blok's critical articles appeared in the newspaper *Speech*. In the first of them, "Contradictions," the author analyzes A. M. Remizov's latest book of short stories. In the second article, "Literary Conversation," Blok bemoans the decline of the new literature and exclaims: "Insane Russian literature. When will it finally become what only literature can be—service?"

10. *Retribution.*
11. Angelina Aleksandrovna, Blok's stepsister.
12. The day 9 January 1905 was "Bloody Sunday," when a peaceful demonstration was fired upon by tsarist troops. This action initiated an epidemic of strikes, which resulted in some reforms. [Tr.]
13. The second volume appeared in December 1911; the third in March 1912.
14. Rudin, the protagonist in Turgenev's novel of the same name, is a person of some gifts and eloquence, but one incapable of action. [Tr.]
15. Included in the *Miscellaneous Poems* section of the third volume.
16. The Russian word is *materovshchina*, a lexicon of Russian swear words based on various things that can be done to one's (or, rather, to someone else's) mother. [Tr.]
17. Evgeniya Knipovich, *A. Blok in His Diaries* (Press and Revolution, 1929).
18. A *fortochka* is a small opening in a large window, permitting ventilation during the winter months. [Tr.]
19. Chaadayev, P. Ya. One of the more extreme Westernizers. He thought that Russian development must depend on union with European civilization in general, and with the Catholic Church in particular. [Tr.]
20. Aleksey Apukhtin was a minor poet, some of whose lyrics became popular as songs. [Tr.]
21. Campaigns during the Russo-Turkish war. [Tr.]
22. The *Pavlovtsy* were a grenadier regiment. [Tr.]
23. A street in Warsaw.

CHAPTER VIII

1. N. A. Berdyaev's terminology.
2. Blok's third article, "From Ibsen to Strindberg," placed in the journal *Labors and Days* (1912), is a simple reworking of his 1908 paper, "Henrich Ibsen." In it Strindberg's name is barely mentioned.
3. Aleksey Remizov, a twentieth-century author who wrote about the common Russian, was especially noted as a stylist, combining contemporary Russian with many archaisms and dialectical expressions. He emigrated in 1921. [Tr.]
4. Ivanov-Razumnik (the pseudonym of R. V. Ivanov), leader of the so-called Scythian group of writers and intellectuals, was a literary critic, sociologist, and historian who influenced Blok to some extent. [Tr.]
5. Dr. N. I. Kulbin, the theater's managing director, a futurist artist.
6. This is the title suggested by Strindberg for the French translation of his play, usually translated into English as *There Are Crimes and Crimes* or *Crime and Crime*. [Tr.]
7. "Bu" and "Bo" were among Blok's pet names for his wife, Lyubov. [Tr.]
8. We deal only with *accented* vowels, which determine the sound tone of the poem.
9. Tyutchev's words.
10. O and Ë are phonetically the same sound.
11. See Chapter II, note 6.
12. An allusion to V. Ivanov's *Crowns of Sonnets*.

CHAPTER IX

1. Z. N. Gippius' play.
2. P. Sukhotin, "Recollections of Blok," *Krasnaya Niva*, 1924.
3. Major Kovalyov is the protagonist in Gogol's story "The Nose." [Tr.]

4. S. Ya. Nadson was both a "civic" poet and, to a very minor extent, a precursor of the decadents. [Tr.]
5. Tyutchev.
6. Zemsoyuz is an abbreviation for Union of Zemstvos. The engineering division in which Blok served was under its jurisdiction. [Tr.]
7. Blok edited the depositions of the director of the department of police, Beletsky.
8. Pushkin: "It's time, my friend, it's time."
9. V. Solovyov's lines.
10. Ableukhov was the hero of A. Bely's novel *Petersburg,* and was a figure symbolic of the old regime.
11. Stenka Razin and Emelian Pugachov were leaders of popular uprisings in tsarist Russia. [Tr.]

CHAPTER X

1. In January 1907—the "elemental force" of his love for N. N. Volokhova and the creation of *The Snow Mask.*
2. In March 1914—the "elemental force" of his love for L. A. Delmas and the creation of the cycle *Carmen.*
3. Published in the newspaper *Banner of Labor* (19 January 1918); for the second time in the journal *Our Path* (April 1919).
4. Azev was one of the leaders of the Socialist-Revolutionary party and a secret collaborator of the police. [Tr.]
5. Gogol's words. [The quotation from *Dead Souls* is not exact; Tr.]
6. Z. N. Gippius' words.
7. On 1 January 1918 Blok answers a "questionnaire on the monopolization of the classics." He doesn't object to the abolition of the right to literary property. The sense of property, he declares, must naturally grow weaker in the artist, "who is absorbed in finding forms capable of bearing the pressure of increasing creative energy, and not at all with the laying up of capital."

   On 14 January he writes an answer to another questionnaire: "How to emerge from the blind alley? Is reconciliation of the intelligentsia with the Bolsheviks possible?" The author is so carried away "with the music of the revolution" that he is prepared to renounce his cherished idea of the gulf between culture and the elemental force, between the intelligentsia and the people. He contends that the intelligentsia "can, is obligated to" work with the Bolsheviks, that they will achieve "musical agreement." "Beyond the dependence on personality," he writes, "that same music rings to the intelligentsia as to the Bolsheviks. . . . The decrees of the Bolsheviks are the symbols of the intelligentsia. . . . The animosity of the intelligentsia toward the Bolsheviks is superficial. It seems to be already passing. Man thinks differently than he expresses himself. Reconciliation, musical reconciliation, is coming."
8. A *chastushka* is a relatively modern type of folk song, usually of two or four lines, often humorous and topical. One variety, the factory *chastushka,* is the type referred to here. [Tr.]
9. In *The Twelve* it is Petka who actually kills Katka. [Tr.]
10. "Water on the mill" is an expression denoting something which is of help, which advances a cause, etc. [Tr.]
11. Vsevolod Rozhdestvensky, "Aleksandr Blok," *The Story of My Life* (Star, No. 3, 1945).
12. *Banner of Labor.*
13. *Our Path.*

14. It appeared in the newspaper *Life of Art,* 23–24 August.
15. The article on Catiline was published as a separate brochure in the publishing house Alkonost, Petersburg, 1919.
16. The first appeared in the newspaper *Life,* 13 June 1918; the second in the same newspaper, 21 June 1918.
17. Blok's work in the repertory section takes up more than seventy pages in the ninth volume of the *Collected Works:* "Letter on the Theater," "On the Repertoire of Communal and State Theaters," "Reflections on the Poverty of Our Repertoire," "Proclamation," "Report to the Executive Board," "Work of the Repertory Section," and seventeen detailed reviews of plays.
18. It was placed in the ninth volume of the *Collected Works* under the title "Plan for a Performance."
19. It entered the *Harps and Violins* section of the third volume.
20. *Life of Art,* 7 May 1919.
21. In Blok's manuscripts there were preserved reviews on collections of the poems of Dmitri Tsenzor, Georgy Ivanov, M. Dolinov, A. Meisner, V. Svyatlovsky, and V. Polyansky under the unwieldy title: "Reviews for the Editorial College of the Publishing House of the Comrades' Cooperative of the Trade Union of Workers of Artistic Literature."
22. It came out as a separate booklet in the Alkonost publishing house in 1921.
23. D. S. Mirsky, in the article "On the Prose of Aleksandr Blok," *Collected Works,* Vol. 8, points out this coincidence.
24. Blok gave his lecture, "The Collapse of Humanism," twice: on 9 April 1919 at a meeting of the co-workers of World Literature; and on 16 November 1919 at the opening of the Free Philosophical Association. It was published in the journal *Banner,* January–March, 1921.
25. Blok compiles lists of Russian writers of the eighteenth to twentieth centuries, and plans editions of their works for the editorial board of Z. I. Grzhebin's publishing house. As a foreword he prefaces an article, "On a List of Russian Authors." Even in this businesslike program note, a lyrical theme sounds—a farewell to life. "Just now," he writes, "the whole path covered by our ancestors is remembered clearly; we don't deny that especially this memory can occur at the point of death: before death the memory of what has been lived through suddenly flares up vividly, so as to die out quickly after this."

    In a short note, "To the Memory of Leonid Andreev," the poet recalls with tenderness the man with whom he was linked "by a mysterious closeness," out of which, however, "nothing came." The author speaks about the spiritual isolation of writers of the symbolist era. "The history of those years, which Russian artists spent between two revolutions, is in essence the history of lonely rapturous states; this is the best that was and that brought real fruit.... I remember the shock I experienced on reading *The Life of Vasily Fiveisky* on our country estate on a rainy autumn night. Now nothing remains of those dear places where I spent the best times of my life; perhaps only the old lindens make noise, if they haven't also stripped the bark from them. And what is bad there, what is bad everywhere, is that the catastrophe is near, that horror is at the doors. I have known this for a very long time, I knew it even before the first revolution, and *The Life of Vasily Fiveisky* at once echoed my knowledge. L. Andreev carried chaos within him.... We would meet and shout to one another independent of personal acquaintanceship—most often in 'chaos,' more rarely in 'lonely, rapturous states.' "
26. Andrey and Ferol Kublitsky, Blok's cousins.
27. Blok's last theatrical reviews relate to 1921: "Among the Judges of the Competition of Revolutionary Plays of the Petersburg Theatrical Section" and "*Goreslavich.* Dramatic Activity of A. Chapygin."

28. "Rev" here means "revolutionary." [Tr.]
29. "Image of Blok," *Rebirth* (Moscow, 1923).
30. Serafima Pavlovna Remizova-Dovgiello, the wife of A. M. Remizov; Lyubov Aleksandrovna Delmas.
31. The article "Without Divinity, Without Inspiration" was published with gross errors in the collection *Contemporary Literature* (Leningrad, 1925), after Blok's death.
32. A prominent Communist who had lent his carriage to Lyubov Dmitrievna.

INDEX OF WORKS BY BLOK

Note: where K. M. quotes from untitled poems in the text, the poem is indexed by first line, though the line itself may not be quoted.

POEMS

About courage, about feats, about glory, 233–34
Above the Lake, 207
Accordion, accordion!, 203–4
Accounts with peaceful happiness are closed, 315–16
Again I walk above this deserted plain, 86
Again the rich man is malicious and glad, 354
Again with age-old despair, 236
Alarm, 199–200
All being and essence are one, 50
All day like any other, full of small labors, 354
All this is over, over, over, 254–55
Along the marshy, deserted meadow, 325–26
Along the shore trudged a sick man, 90
Already the clarity of vision had waned, 322
Always the same smooth surface of the lake, 32
Always to wish you joy, 229–30
Amid Carmen's admirers, 367
And Again Snows, 200
And again the impulses of young years, 321
And I loved. And I came to know, 228
And I spent a mad year, 201–2
Angry gaze of pale eyes, The, 348
Annunciation, The, 254
Artist, The, 361–62
As the ocean changes color, 366
Assumption, 254
At night when Mamai lay in hiding with the horde, 214, 235–36
At the Call of the Blizzard, 198
Autumn Dances, 160
Autumn Day, 255
Autumn Freedom, 165–66
Away!, 200

Behind Masks, 186–87
Beyond the mountains and forests, 366
Blue-eyed one, so God created you, 31
Born in the dead of night, 37
Bright like the day, but incomprehensible, 365
But I am afraid: you will change your countenance, 58
By the unfading radiance of past days, 35

Caught by a Blizzard, 172–73, 198, 201
Clock hand approaches midnight, The, 228
Cold Day, 168
Cold wind on the lagoon, 253
Come down, faded curtain, 228–29
Comet, The, 256–57
Conceived at night, I am born at night, 161–62
Confusion, 198–99

Day passed, as always, The, 355
Day's twilight brings sadness, 71
Day will come—and the great will be accomplished, The, 75
Dead of night places a slow cover, 88–89
Dear brother! Night is falling, 126
Dear friend, even in this quiet house, 373
Death Speaks, 355
Deception, 168, 170
Delirium, 162
Demon, The, 379–80
Devils Speak, The, 355–56
Ditty, The, 170
Do not lure me, freedom, 165
Do you remember? In our sleepy bay, 274–75
Do you remember the disturbing city, 31
Doomed, 198

Index of Works by Blok

Door creaked. The hand began to tremble, The, 71
Double, The, 250–51
Dream, A (To My Mother), 320–21
Dreams, 327
Dreams of unprecedented thoughts, 74
Drowsiness lay down on the gray stones, 170

Earthly heart grows cold again, The, 360
Empty street. One light in the window, 314
Everything happened according to scripture, 355
Everything memory tries to keep for me, 32
Everything on earth will die—mother and youth, 255, 324–25

Factory, The, 90, 97
Faina's Song, 202–3, 212
Fall day descends in slow succession, The, 40
Florence, you are a delicate iris, 253
Fluffed up, swung to and fro, 420
From nothing—in a blue fountain, 373–74
From the Newspapers, 90

Girl from Spoleto, The, 253
Gray Morning, 363
Gray sky is still beautiful, The, 114
Gray twilights lay, 316
Grieving and crying and laughing, 231–32
Gripped, drawn by fear, 357–58
Guitar strings stretched, The, 364–65

Heady breath of March was in the lunar sphere, The, 312
He appeared at the stately ball, 77
Here He is—Christ in chains and roses, 167
Here she appeared. Overshadowed, 203
Her Songs, 172, 200–201
Horizon of the heavens—the star Omega, 39
Hours and days and years pass, 312
How alarm grows at night!, 356
How painful for a corpse among people, 313
How painful to walk among people, 312–13
Humiliation, 311

I am a sword honed on both edges, 88
I am a trembling creature, 75
I am nailed to the tavern bar, 230
I and the world—snows, streams, 74
I aspire to luxurious freedom, 39
I believe in the Sun of the Testament, 73
I bless everything that happened, 321

I conquered her, finally!, 250
I didn't betray the white banner, 369–70
I didn't call you, 231
I enter dark temples, 74
I, exhausted and wise, 87
I guarded them in John's temple, 86
I keep telling your fortune, 76
I look at you. Every demon in me, 357
I love to visit lofty cathedrals, humbling my soul, 76–77
I move from torture to torture, 202
Importunate one stands on the road, The, 54–55
In late autumn from the harbor, 251
In October, 139
In the damp night fog, 325–26
In the Dunes, 205–6, 207
In the fields outside the city, the air breathes spring, 74
In the fire and cold of alarms, 360
In the Garret, 139
In the Northern Sea, 207
In the Restaurant, 310, 322
In the taverns, in the lanes, in the windings, 169
Invisible One, The, 169
I preserved among young harmonies, 53–54
I remember the hour of the late sleepless night, 77
I remember the tenderness of your shoulders, 419
I seek salvation, 37–38
I sense your coming. The years pass, 42, 58, 75
I stand in power, lonely at heart, 87
I tried to rest at heart, 77
It sings, it sings, 373
I waited a long time—you came out late, 54, 75–76
I walked in the dark of a rainy night, 40
I walk, I roam downcast, 139
I was confused and gay, 174–75
I went to sea with her, 253
I won't go out to meet people, 88

Kite, The, 379

Last Day, The, 168
Last Parting Words, 372
Leave me in my far-off place, 163–64, 244
Legend, The, 170
Let me too live, not loving, 366
Life breathed the grave in my face, 252
Lifeless old age wanders around, 162
Little Marsh Devils, 110, 159
Little Swamp Priest, The, 159–60

Index of Works by Blok

Meeting, The, 114
Meri, 230
Monk, The, 211–12
Moon floated in the pale azure, The, 168–69
More one wants to rest, The, 251
My enchanted evening is long, 88
My Rus, my life, are we to suffer together?, 328

Night, 162
Night is already falling over the sea, 231
Night like any other night, and the street's deserted, A, 233
Night, street, lantern, drug store, 312–13
No End, 176
No, never mine, nor anyone's, 350, 366

Oh, I want to live mindlessly, 322
Oh, no! I don't want us to fall, 314
Oh spring without end and without limit, 205
Oh what to me the sunset glow, 203, 204
Oh yes, love is free as a bird, 367–68
Old Woman and the Devils, The, 159
On a wild and gloomy night, 77
On Death, 206
On Grandfather's Death, 60
On the Death of an Infant, 239
On the Death of Kommissarzhevskaya, 257–58
On the Islands, 251
On the Railroad, 326–27
Once proud and haughty, 323
Out of the crystal fog, 249
Over God's best creation, 314
Over this autumn—in everything, 87

Pale Legends, 187
Persistent din of life weakens, The, 253
Peter, 170
Petrograd sky grew dull with rain, The, 369–70
Pilot, The, 263–64
Poet, The, 164
Poet in exile and doubt, The, 36
Poets, 228
Puppet Show, The, 118–19
Purple west oppresses, The, 101
Pussy-willows—a pledge of spring, 367

Ravenna, 253
Ring of life is tight, The, 252
River spread. It flows, mourns lazily, The, 214, 235
Rus, 146–47, 166–67
Russia, 237

Scorching stones burn, 254
Seaside, 163
Second Christening, 176, 215–16
Shamelessly, endlessly sinning, 259–60, 371
She, as before, wanted, 232–33
She left. But the hyacinths waited, 203
She was fifteen, 88
Siena, 254
Snow Maiden, The, 212
Snow storm sweeps along the streets, The, 204
Snow Wine, 171
Snowy spring rages, 367
So inspiredly, so melodiously, 165
Son and Mother, 164–65
Song of Hell, 249–50
So. The storm of these years has passed, 360
Soul! When will you tire of believing?, 411
Sound draws near. And obedient to the plaintive sound, The, 327
Spring Creatures, 159
Spring day passed idly, The, 252
Steep slopes impenetrable with forest, The, 370
Steps of the Commander, 316–20, 352
Steps reddened and go out, The, 86
Stranger, The, 107, 131–32, 150, 325

That happened in the dark Carpathians, 374
That life has passed, 365
There are moments when does not alarm, 324
There are quiet moments, 32
There are times, there are days, 363
There in the night's howling cold, 148
There in the street stood some house, 71
There women show off fashions, 147–48
They don't sleep, nor remember, nor trade, 252
Those born in the stagnant years, 350–51, 369
Today I don't remember, 251
To My Friends, 227
To N. N. Volokhova, 194
To the Muse, 308, 309–10, 363
To the Pushkin House, 427–28
Train, sprayed with stars, The, 148
Transparent, mysterious shadows, 73
Tsarina looked at the pictures, The, 87

Unostentatious white nights will come, The, 162

Visitation, The, 327–28
Voice from the Chorus, A, 358–59, 422
Voices of the Violins, 323–24

We are forgotten, alone on earth, 372–73

Index of Works by Blok

Weariness, 161
We halted above the steppe at midnight, 214, 235
Well, so what? The weak hands are wrung wearily, 356–57
When by chance on Sunday, 355
When despair and malice die down, 232
When, entering the vast world, 252
When I met you, 360
Where echoes in the long halls, 322, 323
White horse's weary legs barely tread, The, 160–61
Windows Overlooking the Yard, 139, 168
Wind quieted, and sunset's glory, The, 371
Wings, 198
Winter will pass—you will see, 70
With its bitter tears, 205
With long, serene passion, 253
Wordless thought, nameless agitation, 323
Worlds fly. Years fly, 315, 321

You are as radiant as virgin snow, 232–33
You are leaving the earthly vale, 53
You keep repeating that I'm cold, reserved, and dry, 378–79
You left forever into the fields, 158–59
You, like the echo of a forgotten hymn, 366–67
You look in the eyes of clear dawns, 168
Young girl sang in the church choir, The, 163
Your face is paler than it was, 149, 170
You rose to me in a half turn, 357
Your very name is contemptible to me, 357
You say I'm dozing, 363–64
You were the most vivid, most faithful, most charming of all, 365
You will dress me in silver, 161–62
You won't deceive me, pale phantom, 31

POEMAS

Her Coming, 141–42, 162
How was it done, how did it happen?, 359–60
Lyrical Poema, 173
Night Violet, 133–34, 157, 161
Nightingale Garden, 351, 368–69
Retribution, 19, 21–23, 24–25, 28, 33, 103, 246, 272, 281–92, 293, 359, 377, 418
Scythians, The, 391, 392, 404–6
Twelve, The, 115, 354, 388–89, 390–403, 407, 415–16, 420–21

CYCLES

Black Blood, 357–58
Carmen, 348, 365–68
City, The, 157–58, 167–70
Crossroads, 85–90
Dances of Death, 313–15, 354
Earth's Bubbles, 157–61
Faina, 174–75, 196, 201–5
Free Thoughts, 177, 196, 205–7
From the Dedications, 79
Harps and Violins, 255, 322–26, 362–66
Iambics, 252, 322, 359–61
Invocation by Fire and Darkness, 202–5
Italian Poems, 245, 252–54
Life of My Friend, The, 354–56
Miscellaneous Poems, 157–58, 161–67, 254–55, 320–21, 361–62
Native Land, 326–28, 369–72, 379
On the Field of Kulikovo, 214, 234–37
Retribution, 251–52, 315–20, 359
Snow Mask, 171–75, 191–92, 194, 196–201
Terrible World, 239, 242, 249–51, 309–13, 315–20, 358–59, 379
Twelve Years Later, 31–32
What the Wind Sings About, 372–74

BOOKS

Ante Lucem, 38–40
Beyond the Border of Past Days, 67, 88–89, 419
Earth in Snow, The, 191–92, 194–95, 196–97, 211
Fairy Tales, 308
Gray Morning, 419
Iambics, 252
Night Hours, 241, 294
Russia and the Intelligentsia, 406
Unexpected Joy, 90, 108, 113, 133–34, 141, 147–49, 156, 157–70, 173, 196
Verses on Russia, 165, 237, 393
Verses on the Beautiful Lady, 66, 67–68, 79, 85–90, 104–5, 123, 164, 179, 196, 377, 383
Year Round, The, 308

DRAMA

Ancestress, The (Die Ahnfrau), 217, 240
Dionysus the Hyperborean, 154, 171
King on the Square, The, 141–45
"On Love, Poetry, and State Service. A Dialogue," 145–46
Puppet Show, The, 111, 118–25, 127–28, 135–36, 154–56, 349, 387
Rameses, 414–15
Rose and the Cross, The, 296, 298–302, 328–42, 349–50, 351–52, 374–77
Song of Fate, 187, 209–17, 234
Stranger, The, 147, 149–53, 349

Index of Works by Blok

PROSE

"Art and Revolution," 407
"Art and the Newspaper," 307–8
"Balmont," 241
"Bolotov and Novikov," 104, 108
"Bolshoi Dramatic Theater in the Coming Season, The," 412–13
"Catiline," 407
"Child of Gogol," 240
"Collapse of Humanism, The," 416–18
"Confession of a Pagan," 26–28, 408–9
"Elemental Force and Culture," 222, 223–24, 227
"Evening in Siena," 247
"Evenings of Art," 220
"Fellow Citizens," 407–8
"Flame, The," 346
"Glance of an Egyptian Girl," 247
"Gorky about Messina," 245
"In Memory of August Strindberg," 294
"Instead of a Preface," 194
"Intelligentsia and the Revolution, The," 393–95, 406
"Irony," 220–21, 227
"Knight-Monk, The," 45–46, 266
"Last Days of Imperial Power, The," 389
"Letters on Poetry," 219
Lightnings of Art, 246
"Literary Review of 1907," 207–8
"Maiden of the Pink Gate and the Ant Tsar," 193
"Masks on the Street," 246
"Merezhkovsky," 241
"Misunderstanding or Unwillingness to Understand?", 308
"Mute Witnesses," 246–47
"Neither Sleeping Nor Waking," 238, 428–29
"On Drama," 187–88
"On Heine's Judaism," 419
"On Lyric Poetry," 178–79
"On Romanticism," 413
"On the Poet's Calling," 426–27
"On the Present State of Russian Symbolism," 260–63, 297
"On the Realists," 177–78
"On the Theater," 217–18
"People and the Intelligentsia, The," 222–23, 227, 438 n.6 to ch. VI
"Phantom of Rome and Monte Luca, The," 246, 247
"Poetry of Spells and Incantations," 146–47
"Poet's Soul, The," 240–41
"Questions, Questions, Questions," 219
"Russia and the Intelligentsia." *See* "The People and the Intelligentsia"
"Russian Dandies," 407–8
"Speech to Actors, A," 412–13
"Three Questions," 218–19
"To the Memory of K. V. Bravich," 308
"Troubled Times," 156–57
"Vladimir Solovyov and Our Day," 46, 424
"Wirballen," 247
"Without Divinity, Without Inspiration," 429–30

JUVENILIA

Around America, 29
"Fate," 29
Herald, 29
"In Summer. Adventures of Beetles," 29
"Vengeance for Vengeance," 29

INDEX OF NAMES

Abervrach, 274–75, 332–33
Akhmatova, Anna, 268, 277
Aleksandr II, 287
Alkonost, 411
Andreev, L. N., 178, 187, 349–50, 441 n.25
Andreeva, M. F., 412, 415
Anthony (bishop), 96
Apollo, 292
Apollo, 245, 267, 268
Argonauts, 96–97
Azev, E. F., 393, 440 n.4 to ch. x

Bad Nauheim, 193, 243
Balmont, K. D., 97, 98, 436 n.4 to ch. ii
Baltrushaitis, Yu. K., 97
Banner of Labor, 389
Baratynsky, E. A., 323
Beautiful Lady, 73–75, 76; and apocalypticism, 73; and Blok's inner doubles, 68, 74–76; Blok's ironic treatment of, 164; Blok's meeting with, 68; Blok's mystical hopes concerning, 236; Blok's return to, 245; and Blok's wife, 56; disappearance of, 102; inaccessibility of, 72; loss of, 232–33; and native land, 25; related to Dante's Beatrice, 67–69; related to Solovyov's philosophy, 46, 68, 73
Beketov, A. N., 19, 25, 32, 59–60
Beketova, A. A. *See* Kublitsky-Piottukh, Aleksandra Andreevna
Beketova, E. A. *See* Krasnova, E. A.
Beketova, Maria Andreevna, 20, 100–101, 406, 415
Beketova, S. A. *See* Kublitsky-Piottukh, S. A.

Beletsky, S. P., 382, 440 n.7 to ch. ix
Bely, Andrey: attack on Blok of, 177; beginning of correspondence with Blok, 78–79; Blok's attitude toward, 219–20; Blok's impatience with mysticism of, 103; Blok's reaction to work of, 186; Blok's sympathy with, 98; breakup of the "brotherhood," 110–11; "brotherhood" with Blok and Solovyov, 95–96; cooling of relationship with Blok, 344–45; cult of Blok's wife, 95–96; end of affair with Blok's wife, 189–90; first acquaintance with Blok's poetry, 51–52; first meeting with Blok, 92–94; his fiancée, 265; love for Blok's wife, 116–17, 124, 126–30, 137–38, 139–40; meeting at lecture with Blok, 264; polemic with Blok, reconciliation, 179–85; reaction to Blok's poetry, 58; relation to the Merezhkovskys and Blok, 107–8; renewal of friendship with Blok, 295–96; second trip to Shakhmatova, 110–11; similarity with Blok in philosophy, 263; and the Solovyov family, 46–47; and Solovyov's poetry, 44–45; spiritual affinity with Blok, 58, 66–67; as symbolist, 40–43; trip with Blok to Kiev, 188–89; visit to Shakhmatova, 102–3
Benois, A. N., 217
Bestuzhev courses, 19, 435 n.3
Blok, Aleksandr Lvovich (father), 17–19, 282; death of, 248–49, 288–90; evaluation of son's poems, 104–5; first marriage, 20–23, 287; scholarly career, 17; and son's education, 52; son's psychological resemblance to, 18–19, 21, 28, 257, 290

Index of Names

Blok, Aleksandra Andreevna. *See* Kublitsky-Piottukh, Aleksandra Andreevna
Blok, Angelina Aleksandrovna (stepsister), 21, 249, 296, 359–60, 406
Blok, Dmitry ("Mitya") (wife's son), 226–27, 237–39
Blok, Johann, 17
Blok, Lyubov Dmitrievna (née Mendeleeva) (wife), 33–34; absences from Blok, 224–25, 424; acting career, 176, 302, 302–4, 349, 410, 424; Bely's love for, 116–17, 124, 126–30; birth of son, 226–27, 238; Blok's despair over, 63–64; Blok's love for, 62–63, 383, 385–87; Blok's proposal, 65–66; Blok's reminiscences of, 387, 408; break with Bely, 137, 139–40, 185, 189–90; and Chulkov, 177; discord with Blok's mother, 110, 268–69, 430; during Blok's last days, 432; as earthly embodiment of Sophia the Divine Wisdom, 94, 95–96, 103–4; estrangement from Blok, 225–27, 304–5, 305–6; and the Eternal Feminine, 56, 63–64; first days of married life, 82; first meeting with Blok, 33–35, 49; indifference to Blok, 53–54, 56–57; war service as nurse, 351; wedding of, 81–82
Blok, Maria Timofeevna (née Belaeva) (step-mother), 21, 249
Boblovo, 33
Bolshevism, 387–88, 389, 402–3, 440 n.7 to ch. x
Bolshoi Dramatic Theater, 423–24, 429
Bravich, K. V., 308
Brittany, 274, 328, 332
Briusov, V. Ya., 50, 83–84, 90, 97, 99, 105–7, 167, 267, 342
Bruges, 275
Bugaev, B. N. *See* Bely, Andrey

Calabria, 224
Carmen, 365, 366–67
Catiline, 407
Chekhov, A. P., 241
Christ, 104, 116, 370–71, 402–3, 407
Chulkov, G. I., 125, 131, 136–37, 176–77, 186, 223

Dante Alighieri, 68–69
Delmas, L. A., 348–49, 350, 352–53, 365, 366
Diaghilev, S. P., 344
Dionysus, 27–28, 153–54, 292
Dobrolyubov, A. M., 50, 208

Dostoevsky, F. M., 20, 22, 113, 157, 251, 286, 397

Ellis, 138, 295
Ern, V. F., 98
Eternal Feminine, 43, 47, 47–48, 56, 64, 73, 126, 236
Eternal Friend, 42–43, 45, 327–28
Europe, 404–6, 416
Evagrius, 377

Fate, 196–97, 281–82
Fet. *See* Shenshin, A. A.
Filosofov, D. V., 308
Florence, 241–42, 253–54
Florensky, P. A., 99
Free Philosophical Association, 414

Gippius, T. N., 100
Gippius, Z. N., 55, 56, 58–59, 61, 64–65, 82–83, 105, 128, 403
Gogol, N. V., 157, 240
Golden Fleece, 177
Gorky, Maksim, 177–78, 245, 353, 410, 414–15, 432
Gorodetsky, S. I., 115, 180, 342
Grigoriev, A. A., 194–96, 351, 435 n.6
Grillparzer, Franz, 217
Guéthary, 345
Gumilyov, N. S., 267–68, 309, 343, 344, 410–11, 415, 422–23, 425, 429–30
Gzovskaya, O. V., 374, 376, 381

Halley's comet, 256–57
Heine, Heinrich, 241, 418–19
Herald, 29
Hermogen, 296, 438 n.5 to ch. VII
Horae, 177

Ibsen, Henrich, 221–22, 407, 416
Iliodor, 296, 438 n.5 to ch. VII
Italy, 246–48
Ivanov, E. P., 99–100, 104, 180, 296
Ivanov, V. I., attitude toward acmeism, 267; Blok's attitude toward, 110, 183, 186, 277, 295, 309; and Dionysian religion, 153–54; influence on Blok, 153–54; and mystical anarchism, 136; reaction to *Retribution* of, 293; "religious" rites of, 109–10; repudiation of mystical anarchism of, 186; and symbolism, 260, 263, 309

Index of Names

Ivanov-Razumnik, 299, 414, 439 n.4

Kachalov, V. I., 374
Kantemir, Antioch, 396
Karelin, G. S., 20
Karelina, E. G., 20
Karpov, P. I., 346
Keris, 333–34, 335
Khomyakov, A. S., 371
Khrustaleva, Katya, 34
Kitezh, 60, 333, 436 n.7 to ch. 11
Klyuev, N. A., 207–8, 276–77
Kobylinsky, L. L. *See* Ellis
Kommissarzhevskaya, V. F., 154, 224, 257–58
Konevskoy, Ivan, 50
Krasnova, E. A., 20
Kublitsky-Piottukh, A. A. ("Andryusha") (cousin), 26, 52
Kublitsky-Piottukh, Aleksandra Andreevna (née Beketova) (mother), 20; discord with Blok's wife, 110, 268–69; during Blok's last days, 432, 433; first marriage, 20–21; health, 30, 79, 244, 249, 256, 268, 380, 406; relations with Blok, 187, 276; relations with Blok and his wife, 304–5, 430; relations with Delmas, 352–53; second marriage, 26
Kublitsky-Piottukh, F. A. ("Ferol") (cousin), 26, 52
Kublitsky-Piottukh, F. F., (stepfather), 26, 276, 351, 418
Kublitsky-Piottukh, S. A. (née Beketova) (aunt), 20, 26
Kulbin, N. I., 304, 439 n.5
Kuzmin, M. A., 155, 266–67, 305, 421

Labors and Days, 309
Languedoc, 328–39
Lenin, V. I., 388
Lermontov, M. Yu., 379–80, 404, 419
Lomonosov, M. V., 396
Love for Three Oranges, 349
Luzhsky (real name V. V. Kaluzhsky), 381

Mandelshtam, O. E., 268, 423
Markonet, V. F., 91
Marx, Karl, 388
Marxism, 402
Mendeleev, D. I., 33, 175
Mendeleeva, L. D. *See* Blok, Lyubov Dmitrievna
Merezhkovsky, D. S., 58, 59, 64–65, 79–80, 105, 177, 220, 265–66, 277, 343, 353

Merezhkovsky, Z. N. *See* Gippius, Z. N.
Merezhkovskys, the, 100, 105, 107, 108–9, 128, 298
Messina, 224, 245–46
Meyerhold, V. E., 154–56, 216, 224, 302–3, 303–4, 340, 349
Minsky, N. M., 109–10
Moissi, 275–76
Monakhov, N. F., 425
Moscow, 99, 431–32
Moscow Art Theater, 302, 341–42, 374
Muravyov, N. K., 382, 383

Nedobrovo, N. V., 340
Nekrasov, N. A., 199, 216, 327
Nemirovich-Danchenko, V. I., 210, 351, 374, 378, 381
New Path, 64–65, 79, 80, 82
Nietzsche, Friedrich, 263, 417–18
Nijinsky, V. F., 344
Nikolsky, B. V., 65, 85

Oreus. *See* Konevskoy, Ivan
Ostrogorsky, V. P., 38
Our Theater, 345

Paris, 275, 345
Perugia, 246–47
Pekelis, A. G., 432
Pertsov, P. P., 66–67, 132
Peshkov. *See* Gorky, Maksim
Pestovsky. *See* Pyast, V.
Petersburg, 26, 71, 113, 130, 167–70, 195, 278, 298, 390
Peter the Great, 287–88
Petrovsky, A. S., 102
Philokalia, 377
Plato, 36–37
Pobedonostsev, Konstantin, 287–88
Poland, 291
Polotsky, Simeon, 396
Polyakov, S. A., 97
Prokhorova, Aksyuta ("Ksyusha"), 306, 362–63, 365
Pushkin, A. S., 83, 170, 194, 254, 288, 290–91, 292, 310, 361, 404, 426–27, 427–28
Pyast, V., 115–16

Questions of Life, 108

Rachinsky, G. A., 96
Radlov, S. V., 424

Radlova, Anna, 424
Rasputin, G. E., 393
Ravenna, 241, 252
Religious Philosophical Society, 190, 222, 297–98
Rozhdestvensky, V. A., 411, 433
Rozvadovsky (count), 81, 82
Rus, 26, 147, 165–66, 177, 328, 435 n.11
Russia, 165–67, 193, 234–35, 237, 240, 350–51, 356–57, 370–71, 393, 404–6
Rutebeuf, 193
Ryabushinsky, N. P., 177

Sadovskaya, K. M., 30–32, 34–35
Sapunov, N. N., 303
Scales, 97, 177, 185–86
Schmidt, Anna Nikolaevna, 48, 100
Shakespeare, William, 331–32
Shakhmatova, 24–25, 70–71, 100, 109, 264, 424–25, 429
Shenshin, A. A., 39–40
Shestov, Lev, 419
Shlyapkin, I. A., 82, 108
Siena, 247, 254
Social Democrats, 114, 115
Society of Free Esthetics, 190
Society of Zealots of the Artistic Word, 245
Sologub, Fyodor, 178, 342
Solovyov, M. S., 36–37, 46, 47, 48, 78
Solovyov, S. M.: attitude toward Blok, 34; "brotherhood" with Blok and Bely, 51, 81, 94–95, 103, 110–12, 121; cult of Blok's wife, 103–4, 121; death of parents, 78; duality, 94–95; first meeting with Blok, 29; friendship with Rozvadovsky, 82; influence of V. S. Solovyov on, 47; plan for theocratic organization of Russia, 94; visits to Shakhmatova, 100, 103–4, 110–12
Solovyov, V. S.: attitude toward sex, 61; Blok's reaction to Chulkov's article on, 112; Blok's speeches on, 266, 424; Chulkov's article on, 112; duality, 47–49; influence on Bely, 44–47; influence on Blok, 44–47, 49–50; "The Meaning of Love" of, 61; and panmongolism, 404; as philosopher, 42–45, 72; relations with Anna Schmidt, 48; Sergey Solovyov's inferences from philosophy of, 94; and Sophia the Divine Wisdom, 42–44; spiritual connection between Solovyov and Blok, 68
Solovyova, O. M., 58, 75, 78
Somov, K. A., 176

Sophia the Divine Wisdom, 42–44, 47–48, 51, 58, 78–79, 94, 126
Spektorsky, E. V., 18
Spengler, Oswald, 417
Spoleto, 247, 253
Stanislavsky, K. S., 210–11, 341–42, 349–50, 381
Steiner, Rudolf, 296, 344–45
Stray Dog, The, 305
Strindberg, August, 282, 294, 296, 303–4
Struve, P. B., 222–23
Sventsitsky, V. P., 98–99

Tarakanovo, 81
Tereshchenko, M. I., 296–97, 298–301 *passim*, 418
Theatrical Division, 409–10
Tolstoy, L. N., 29, 264, 326, 343
Torches, 135
Tredyakovsky, V. K., 396
Turgenev, I. S., 363, 372
Turgeneva, Asya, 265
Tyutchev, F. I., 281

Union of Poets, 421–23, 425
Union of Workers of Artistic Literature, 414
Unknown Terror, 183, 184
Untouchable, 48, 178, 220–21, 436 n.2 to ch. II

Vengerov, S. A., 114
Venice, 241, 253
Verhaeren, Emile, 133, 167
Verkhovsky, Yu. N., 271
Verne, Jules, 29
Villemarque, 333
Volokhova, N. N., 124, 156, 171–72, 173–75, 176, 191, 401
Volynsky, A. L., 419
Vrubel, M. A., 258–59, 261
Vvedensky, A. I., 36

Wagner, Richard, 243, 263, 300, 407, 418
World Literature, 410, 414, 420
World Soul, 44, 45, 49, 58, 78

Zhukovsky, V. A., 26, 29, 39
Zonov, A. P., 345

Doris Johnson teaches in the Department of Slavic and Eastern Languages and Literatures at Wayne State University in Detroit. She holds the Ph.D. degree from the University of Michigan. She has taught at Purdue University and has published articles on Russian literature and translated the work *Russian Science Fiction*.

The book was designed by Mary Primeau. The typeface for the text is Mergenthaler VIP Baskerville, based on an eighteenth-century design by John Baskerville. The typefaces for the display are Baskerville and Windsor Elongated. The text is printed on 60-lb. International Paper Company's Bookmark text paper. The book is bound in Holliston Mills' Payko cloth over binder's boards.

Manufactured in the United States of America.

UNIVERSITY LIBRARY
this book as soon as you
with it. In order to avoid a
returned by the latest date